# TO THE GREATER GLORY —

## A PSYCHOLOGICAL STUDY OF IGNATIAN SPIRITUALITY

W. W. Meissner, S.J., M.D.

Training and Supervising Analyst
Boston Psychoanalytic Institute

University Professor of Psychoanalysis
Boston College

MARQUETTE UNIVERSITY PRESS
1999

MARQUETTE STUDIES IN THEOLOGY No. 16
Andrew Tallon, Series Editor

**Library of Congress Cataloguing in Publication Data**

Meissner, W. W. (William W.), 1931-
To the greater glory : a psychological study of Ignatian spirituality / W. W. Meissner.
p. cm. -- (Marquette studies in theology ; no 16)
Includes bibliographical references and index.
ISBN 0-87462-640-4
1. Ignatius, of Loyola, Saint, 1491-1556 — Psychology. 2. Spiritual exercises — Psychology. 3. Psychoanalysis and religion. I. Title. II. Series: Marquette studies in theology ; #16.
BL4700.L7 M553 1998
248'.01'9--ddc21

98-25328
CIP



Member, THE ASSOCIATION OF AMERICAN UNIVERSITY PRESSES

MARQUETTE UNIVERSITY PRESS
MILWAUKEE

The Association of Jesuit University Presses

MARQUETTE UNIVERSITY PRESS
MILWAUKEE WISCONSIN USA
1999

## TABLE OF CONTENTS

## Section V

## Asceticism and Mysticism

# PREFACE

To adequately introduce my reader to this work, I want to make some preliminary clarifications so that neither the interested reader nor I will entertain any illusions about what lies ahead. Lest anyone misconstrue my intention and purpose in undertaking this study, let me be clear that this is not a religious book — more to the point it is not a spiritual book. It is fundamentally a psychoanalytic study of a profoundly meaningful spiritual subject matter, but its intention is to seek a deeper understanding of Ignatian spirituality in psychoanalytic perspectives. Therefore, if anyone were to look herein for the development of religious insights, for a spiritually uplifting or inspiring illumination, or for material for pious and meditative reflection, he will be sorely disappointed. This is no more than a psychoanalytic study that means only to enter into dialogue with the spiritual teaching of one of the greatest contributors to spiritual lore in Western Christendom with the goal of seeking greater understanding of the nature of his spiritual adventure, and by extension to achieve some fuller, if not more psychologically meaningful, apprehension of the relation between the spiritual dimension of human experience and the realm of psychic actualization through which it is realized and achieved.

Such an enterprize is not without its risks and problems. One of the first we encounter is the culturally embedded difficulty of a dialogue taking place across historical barriers of centuries and across the cultural barriers separating a medieval religious mentality from a more modern or even postmodern understanding of religious experience. Part of the problem is whether bringing the questions and concerns of our own age to bear on texts from nearly half a millennium ago introduces certain preconceptions that alter the subject matter as we examine it. As Buckley (1984) comments, ". . . any such inquiry is a "fusion of horizons" by which the past is continually made present and constituted a partner of a new or ongoing discussion. But it is in continual dialogue with succeeding questions that any tradition and the documents in which it is objectified lives, and the issues of conceptual structures of our age can perhaps draw from these classical works virtualities whose inherent powers other centuries with other problems may have passed over" (p. 66). There is a hermeneutic of dialogue with the text (Gadamer 1989) that has particular value in interpreting texts so intimately linked to experience as those of Ignatius. It is not so much an effort to discover the mind of Ignatius, but more of allowing the questions and concerns of our own perspective to engage the Ignatian corpus and illumine their depth, their excess of meaning that may never have dawned on the consciousness of their author. My approach here is to enter a dialogue with the Ignatian material and find the interdigitating ground of meaning that can illumine both Ignatian spirituality and psychoanalytic perspectives.

If we can envision this undertaking as an effort in dialogue between the psychoanalytic perspective and the spiritual doctrine of Ignatius, we might say that this primary storyline involves several related subplots. The first subplot is the connection of Ignatius' spirituality with his own personal spiritual pilgrimage and the range of personal experiences that involved. Ignatius' spiritual teaching is profoundly rooted in his own experience, especially of his conversion, and the shattering, psychically wrenching struggles he experienced at Manresa, and finally the almost unrelieved flooding with spiritual illuminations and ecstatic enhancements that characterized his spiritual odyssey from its very beginning. As we shall see, these experiences were distilled first into the text of his *Spiritual Exercises*[1] and found further elaboration in the magisterial texts of the *Constitution*[2] and in the torrent of spiritually inspiring letters and instructions found in his massive correspondence from his years as first General of the Society of Jesus. At every step of his spiritual heritage, his own powerful spiritual and psychic history looms in the background, qualifying and lending perspective to everything he wrote and said. It is against this backdrop that our inquiry proceeds, but in such a way that the origins of his spiritual perspective in his own psychology and personality are never far from consideration. For this reason, I have chosen to begin my investigation with a condensed reconstruction of his life, with particular attention to the conversion experience and the purgative trials at Manresa.

With this perspective in mind, it is fair to say that the present study is in effect an extension of my previous attempt to discern the lineaments of Ignatius' personality and the psychodynamic dimensions of his life history and mind (Meissner 1992b). The intent of

[1] References to the text of the Exercises will be written in italics — e.g. *Exercises* or *Spiritual Exercises*; references to the actual exercises as practiced or performed will be written normally.

[2] As with the *Exercises*, references to the text of the Constitutions will be in italics.

that study was to bring into focus in terms of a psychoanalytic model what might be learned about the man Ignatius rather than anything about his teaching. My emphasis fell on the combination of psychic determinants and processes that undergirded his remarkable life experience and career, including not only the impressive accomplishments of his tenure as general of the newly founded Society, but his remarkable standing as one of the greatest mystics in the history of the Church. That study stands as the foundation for the present one, but the direction of the inquiry in this work takes an almost diametrically opposite tack to its predecessor. Here we presume the psychology of the man and seek to understand what role it might have played in the development and form of his profoundly influential spiritual heritage — a heritage that is preserved not only in his own spiritual writings, but in the history of the Society he founded whose efforts over the centuries have carried the tradition based on his spiritual vision throughout the Christian world.

A second subplot in this absorbing drama reaches beyond a focus on Ignatius and the psychological determinants of his doctrine to a more contemporary dialogue between some of the specifics of the Ignatian perspective and the understanding of human psychodynamics in the psychoanalytic perspective. It is inevitable that these perspectives should come into conflict, even taking into consideration the remarkable degree to which these respective approaches to the human phenomenon find themselves in substantial agreement and congruence. Both aspects, the degree of congruence and the points of difference, are worthy of comment and exploration.

Here again cultural and historical disparities play a role, so that part of this discussion is a matter of bringing attitudes and approaches of an older tradition into greater approximation to contemporary viewpoints. But there are also fundamental differences related to basic understandings of the human mind and how it works. The role of the unconscious assumes a central position in this respect. The understanding of superego dynamics and their role in various aspects of ascetical and spiritual praxis will also come into question. But more of this later — my point here is that the dialogue has both its areas of positive and mutually reinforcing congruence along with areas of divergence and difference of apprehension and significance.

In a somewhat broader perspective, another significant subplot pertains to the interface between psychoanalysis and religious experience. The Ignatian prototype provides an exemplar and a kind of test case, in which the dynamic interdigitation of psychic processes involving meanings and motives, with spiritual processes and dynamics can be studied in more concrete and specific terms. By and large, the psychoanalytic study of religious phenomena has taken place in more or less general terms, without much detailed attention to the kind of specific case material that psychoanalysis knows best. Exceptions to this generalization can be noted,[3] and increasingly the exceptions may well be on the way to becoming more of a rule. But the more specific and detailed study of the intersection of human psychic experience with the spiritual realm of human potentiality is called for and remains one of the fruitful frontiers of exploration in the dialogue of psychoanalysis and religion.

And there is one final subplot I can suggest. Although it remains more or less a background consideration in this book, it is a matter consistently indicated by Ignatius himself and a factor constantly at issue in all aspects of the discussion. I refer to the question of the interaction between the influence of divine grace and human motivation. I have made previous efforts to suggest a possible approach to a psychology of grace (Meissner 1987), but that argument remains tentative and open to further modification or even refutation. Moreover, it did not make any effort to develop a theory of the action of grace in specifically Ignatian terms. There is resident in Ignatius' formulations and understanding the components of such a psychology, but it remains implicit and assumed in his thinking. I have made some suggestions regarding this issue *pari passu* without attempting a more encompassing formulation — an effort that would require an extension of these reflections beyond the scope of the present work. But the issue should not be ignored, since it is a constant and oft repeated *leitmotif* whose echoes are heard throughout. My assumption throughout is that, to the extent that grace operates in human nature and has effects in and on that nature, its influence does not do violence to man's psychic capabilities, but works in and through those potentialities to effect whatever psychic changes might be in question. Grace does not work its effects exclusively from or in contradiction to the inherent potentialities of the human mind and heart. The pervasive question, then, concerns how Ignatius envisions these effects and what psychological perspectives can we draw on to illumine that understanding of the interplay of grace and nature that lies at the heart of his method.

I hope these comments will help the interested reader to find his way through this exploration. The plan of attack leads along a path

[3] One of the salutary features of Rizzuto's (1979) study is the concentration on individual case material.

that moves from phase to phase of Ignatius' spiritual journey, leading finally to his scaling of the mystical mountain. The story begins with a brief resume of his life (Section I), and then turns to the *Spiritual Exercises* which contain the essence of his spiritual inspiration, derived primarily from his trials at Manresa (Section II). The *Exercises* would become the foundation for everything that was to follow. The spiritual inspiration of the *Exercises* was extended and amplified in the *Constitutions* where Ignatius translated the lapidary formulae of the *Exercises* into explicit norms and directives for a life of holiness and apostolic effectiveness for his followers (Section III). In this context, the question of obedience, both in the sense of the vow of obedience members of the Society would take as part of their commitment to a life of religious obedience, and in terms of the virtue of obedience that was essential to the spiritual development of any believer, became increasingly important in Ignatius' thinking, such that it was to become one of the primary pillars of his more mature spiritual vision (Section IV). This aspect of Ignatian spirituality calls for a more extended effort to understand and reformulate his thinking in terms more resonant with modern sensitivities and orientations (Section V). And finally, as the transcendent summit toward which all the preceding directs itself, Ignatian mysticism, exemplified most directly and profoundly in his own mystical transports, but also as an aspect of Ignatian spirituality toward which everyone who chooses to follow his path is invited, is approached and explored (Section VI). My emphasis in that part of the undertaking is to underline that the furthest reaches of Ignatian mystical experience are founded in and never remove themselves from the rudimentary and essential foundations of the *Exercises*, as is the case for all Ignatian spirituality. Further, the understanding of mystical phenomena does not provide a separate or different realm of analysis than the understanding of the spiritual underpinnings that lead to and sustain it. Nonetheless, whatever can be grasped of the mystical experience and formulated in psychoanalytic terms, the experience itself remains transcendental and extends to the furthest reaches of human capacity, and as such may offer a greater challenge to the psychoanalytic mind to expand or modify its categories and convictions than vice versa. In short, readers and all those who take these questions seriously would do best to proceed with an open mind, for you will find that the questions far outweigh the answers.

My hope is that this exploration of Ignatian spirituality in psychoanalytic terms will not only serve to advance the discussion of the interface between psychoanalysis and religion on one hand, but also on the other that it may offer some thoughtful perceptions and understandings of aspects of Ignatian thinking that will serve the purposes and endeavors of spiritual directors and retreat masters, if not those who seek further personal spiritual development, to better understand the human material with which they deal and to help souls to find their individual way to God — a hope and desire that was at the root of Ignatius own intents and purposes on his path to God.

W. W. Meissner, S.J., M.D.

Saint Mary's Hall,
Boston College

# SECTION I

# THE LIFE

# CHAPTER I

# ORIGINS

## The Spiritual and the Personal

A study of the spiritual heritage of any of the great saints can not find any authentic meaning without understanding its origin in the mind and heart of its originator. As de Guibert (1964) commented, "In order to understand a school of spirituality with depth, we must first of all study the supernatural experience which is its basis and point of departure" (p. 21). But this truism is uniquely applicable to Ignatius of Loyola. Ignatian spirituality bears the marks of his personality in unique and distinguishing ways. If our aim was simply to gain a deeper understanding of Ignatius' spiritual doctrine, we would certainly want to situate it in the context of Ignatius' personal spiritual experience. But since our objective in the present work is to bring the resources of a psychoanalytic reflection to the understanding of that spirituality, the reverberations of the spiritual with Ignatius' own psychology becomes even more relevant and pressing.

But the exploration of the relevant aspects of Ignatius' psychology has already been done. In a previous study (Meissner 1992b), I subjected Ignatius' personality and his inner psychic life to a detailed scrutiny — to the extent that available sources and the limits of the psychoanalytic perspective would allow. The result is a partial, limited, and highly conjectural reconstruction of the dynamic forces and conflicts that pervaded his inner life and provided the driving forces of his spiritual ascent to the heights of the mystical mountain. My purpose in this present study is to carry the inquiry a step further — to bring the results of that previous investigation to bear on understanding Ignatius' spiritual teaching — one of the major currents of spiritual interest and influence in Western Christianity.

The focus of our exploration, however, is not limited to understanding the impact of Ignatius' own psychic life on his spiritual heritage, but simultaneously embraces a psychoanalytically rooted reflection on the specifics of that doctrine in themselves. One legitimate subject of inquiry is the manner in which aspects of any spiritual doctrine reverberate with what we can understand of the basic psychological forces and processes that it calls into play in the service of spiritual development and enrichment. Consequently, the derivation of aspects of Ignatian spirituality from Ignatius' own experience provides only part of the story; there is more to be learned from a psychoanalytic scrutiny of the doctrine on its own terms.

Such a reflection opens the door to a further and deeper probing of the action of divine grace as it works within the human soul. If it is true, as I would propose in the course of this study, that spirituality cannot be adequately understood in isolation from the psychological mechanisms through which it exercises its effects, it is equally true that such a spirituality would have little meaning to Christian understanding without a pervasive and effective influence of grace. The challenge to the Christian psychologist and psychoanalyst is to find the grounds for beginning to understand the interplay and intersection of these conceptually disparate realms of discourse — the theological and spiritual on one side, and the psychological-psychoanalytic on the other. The one thing we can assert with certainty from the beginning of our investigation is that they do work synonymously and synergistically in the heart and mind of the spiritual subject, as they did for Ignatius and for those who follow in his path.

## FAMILY BACKGROUND

The psychoanalytic study of any subject cannot take place in isolation from its cultural and historical setting.[1] The history of the times and culture into which Iñigo de Loyola was born in 1491 placed their mark on him and profoundly shaped the lineaments of his personality. They carry with them the matrix of tradition, legend, family history, family values and family mythology that shaped the emerging personality of the youngest Loyola as he grew to adolescence and young adulthood. The echoes of these mythic elements can be heard through the entire course of his life journey.

The Loyolas were one of the leading families of Guipuzcoa, major figures in the dynastic and frontier struggles of that Basque country. For a period covering several centuries, the Loyolas and their related clans were prominent protagonists in the campaigns against the Moors and in the wars that gradually established the hegemony of the kings of Castile. Their loyal service to the cause of the kings of Castile earned them royal honors and favors. They stamped them-

[1] These details will be presented in summary fashion here, but can be found in greater length and detail in Meissner (1992b).

selves as fierce and heroic fighters — from the victory of Juan Perez de Loyola and his seven sons (known to history and legend as "the band of brothers") at the battle of Beotibar in 1391, roundly defeating the forces of the French and Navarrese, down to the ferocious exploits of Beltran de Loyola, Iñigo's father.

The exploits of an earlier Beltran against the Moors had won royal favor and allowed him to build his fortress-castle in the valley between two medieval towns — Azpeitia and Azcoitia. From this stronghold he set about establishing his hegemony over the surrounding countryside. The fierce temper of the Loyolas won them a none-too-favorable regard as a ruthless and contentious lot; and they became one of the most powerful families in the territory. The Lord of Loyola was one of the *parientes mayores* contending for power and position. In Guipuzcoa the contending parties were the Onacinos and the Gamboinos, and their factional rivalries bathed the countryside in blood. The Loyolas were the leading family of the Onacinos. The family history reflects the up-and-down fortunes of this transgenerational crusade. Iñigo's grandfather, the testy and rambunctious Don Juan Perez, tried to seize the towns bordering his castle lands in 1456, but he was overmatched, had his castle razed down to the second story, and found himself banished to fight in the king's service against the Moors in Andalusia. He returned in 1461 to rebuild the castle in the more graceful Mudejar style — much as it remains today.

If the Loyolas were a proud and aggressive lot, known for their quickness and prowess with sword and buckler, there were few who outdid them in sexual proclivities. Beltran had fathered thirteen children in all, at least three of them out of wedlock. Such sexual exploits were not uncommon among the nobility of the time; Iñigo's oldest brother, Martin Garcia, had three illegitimate daughters, and another brother, Pero Lopez, an ordained priest and pastor of the church of San Sebastian in Azpeitia, had four illegitimate children. Thus the family into which Iñigo Loyola was born was prosperous and powerful, well connected to the sources of royal power, and privileged.

The impact of these influences was channeled through the family and the castle environment into which little Iñigo was born. The family legends and traditions embody a kind of family mythology that becomes a vital part of the family culture and impresses itself, positively or negatively, for good or ill, on its offspring. I have described this family mythology previously (Meissner 1992b):

> Military prowess and adventurous daring were highly valued, and that courage was part of the fiber of a man — a real man would

> never back away from a fight even when the odds were against him. Young Iñigo was instilled with the pride of the Loyolas, which called them to be leaders, heroes, extraordinary men. It must also be remembered this heritage included a profound, almost instinctive, religious faith. For Beltran was a man of deep faith, and Catholicism was ingrained in the family tradition. Yet it was that peculiar brand of faith that could willingly shed blood in defense of religion and celebrate the victory with a night of unbridled lechery. (p. 16)

## EARLY YEARS

Iñigo was born in 1491. The psychoanalyst takes note of the circumstances of that event. Shortly after his birth, Iñigo's mother, Marina de Licona, daughter of a noble family of Azcoitia, died. The timing is uncertain — we do not know whether she died in childbirth or soon after. We do know that Iñigo was still young enough to require nursing. He was put out of the castle to live with the family of the blacksmith. Maria de Garin, the blacksmith's wife, became his nursemaid and second mother.[2] Iñigo lived with the Garins for the first seven years of his life. His return to the fold of the Loyolas was precipitated by the marriage of his brother Martin Garcia in 1498 to Magdalena de Aroaz, a lady of noble birth, a maid of honor to Queen Isabella, and one of her favorites. As a wedding gift, the queen presented a painting of the Annunciation that Magdalena brought with her to Loyola and had installed in a special chapel constructed for the purpose.

There was now a woman in the castle of Loyola who could look after a young boy, so Iñigo was brought back into the bosom of his family. This move may have precipitated a second traumatic loss and separation — this time from his second mother Maria de Garin. Giving full credit to the exigencies of the situation and to the culture and common practice of the nobility of the time, the impact of these events cannot be ignored from the point of view of their potential psychological impact. The literature on early childhood deprivation, especially maternal deprivation, does not provide us with firm con-

[2] The custom of wetnursing was quite common in even late medieval times, especially among the aristocracy. More often than not, the wetnurse took the baby to her own home and raised the child, often for several years. The extended separation in Iñigo's case might have been due to conditions in the castle, where there seems to have been no woman of the house until the arrival of Magdalena de Araoz in 1498. In many such cases, alienation was unavoidable. In a sermon, one Fra Bernardino told his parishioners: "You give your child to be suckled by a sow where he picks up the habits of his nurse. . . . And when he comes home you cry, 'I know not whom you are like; this is no son of ours!' " (Gies and Gies, 1987, p. 285).

clusions, especially since so much depends on other supportive and compensating contingencies beside the mere fact of deprivation itself. Despite the conjectural and somewhat controversial nature of the findings, a list of possible effects that may have relevance for Iñigo's later spiritual journey might include ". . . a pervasive sense of loss and an underlying depression[3] and unsatisfied yearning for attachment and reunion with the lost mother that would affect future relationships with women, idealization and aggrandizement of the repressed image of the lost mother, a powerful identification with the lost mother, a yearning for reunion with the mother in death and an attachment to and idealization of the state of death itself" (Meissner 1992b, p. 12).[4]

The other salient factor was Iñigo's relationship with Dona Magdalena, who now became — for all practical purposes — his third mother. Magdalena was evidently an extraordinary woman, of great intelligence and piety, who would have had a powerful influence on the young Iñigo. She raised him for about the next decade, and when he was borne back to the castle of Loyola after the disaster of Pamplona, she nursed him back to health; and it was her pious books that fed his conversion. The picture of the Annunciation that

[3] One form of depression in maternally deprived children is an anaclitic depression resembling the clinical expression of adult depression; it is seen in children who have been deprived of their mothers after having developed a relatively normal relationship with her during the first six months of life. Hospitalism is a form of anaclitic depression, involving both somatic and psychic features, seen in infants under eighteen months of age who are subjected to prolonged stays in a hospital or similar institution and are thus deprived of maternal care for that period. The condition can develop into marasmus, a condition of extreme emaciation in young children, usually not due to any obvious or specific physical cause.

[4] The most noteworthy sequela of early parental deprivation is the tendency to depression that can afflict the individual throughout life, especially when it evolves into a factor in the individual's character structure. The unresolved mourning for the lost mother can also influence relationships with women and make forming mutually satisfying love relationships problematic. There may be long-term narcissistic difficulties involving issues of self-esteem regulation and the prolongation of infantile narcissistic grandiosity. The combination of identification with the lost mother and the wish for reunion may contribute to the unconscious motivation underlying suicidal impulses.

The effects of early parental loss may depend on the age and level of development of the child as well as the availability of proper support for facilitating the mourning process (Furman 1964, 1968; Furman and Furman 1974). Some findings suggest that a critical factor in determining whether childhood parental loss contributes to the later development of adult depression is the lack of care, defined more in terms of neglect than hostility and more often found after the death of the mother than after the death of the father (Harris et al. 1986).

hung in the chapel of Loyola became an object of special devotion of our future saint.

We can draw some tentative conclusions from this sketchy picture of Iñigo's early years that will contribute to our further efforts to understand the psychological makeup of the future saint and spiritual guide. He was raised to be a gentleman, a noble, and a man of arms. The mark of a man in those troubled times was his skill in the use of arms — the sword at his side had to be ready to leap to his hand at the slightest provocation. The next qualification of masculine prowess was his sexual potency — and there seems little question that the dominating figure of Beltran de Loyola provided a striking model for both attributes. His influence on his youngest son would be powerful and determining.

The psychoanalytic perspective focuses on the identification with the father — the idealized model of mature masculinity. But the pattern of identifications defining the residues of early development reflects the influence not only of the father, but of the mother as well. On this maternal side, the pattern of influences is more complex, compounded of the residues of early maternal deprivation, of the series of possibly traumatic losses of sequential mother-figures, and finally the attachment to the last of this procession of mothers — Magdalena. If the paternal pattern was cast in terms of power, forcefulness of character, aggressive prowess in battle and sex, fearless courage and heroic self-sacrifice in the service of his lord and leader, the maternal influence would have carried with it elements of piety, devotion, humility, and love. I will argue that these contending identifications would set the stage for Iñigo's lifelong inner conflicts that played themselves out in varying patterns and vicissitudes throughout the course of his journey down to his final days in Rome and found poignant expression in his spiritual teaching.

## AREVALO

The succeeding stages of Iñigo's career were rooted in the paternal identification almost exclusively. Beltran died sometime during the years 1504-7, when Iñigo would have been 13-16 years old. The customary practice was for one of the sons of noble families to be taken into the service of the royal court to be trained in the skills and graces of a noble courtier and man of arms. Beltran had made arrangements with Juan Velasquez de Cuellar, the majordomo of Queen Isabella and treasurer-general of Castile, to take Iñigo into his household. The conjunction of Beltran's death and the move to Arevalo signalled the end of Iñigo's childhood and his attachment to the castle of Loyola. He moved from a world of nobility and substance into one of royal magnificence, wealth, and power. Velasquez was a nobleman in the finest traditions of old Spain, a kind and virtuous gentleman who welcomed the young hidalgo as though he were his own son.

Under Velasquez' tutelage and the training of the court, Iñigo developed into a distinguished courtier. He learned to appreciate music, to write with a good hand; his manners became polished, even elegant as befitted a page in the royal court. He learned the fine points of the use of sword and dagger, to fence, ride, and fight as was expected of a future man of arms.[5] He learned other courtly arts as well — dancing, gambling, courtly intrigues, and the lure of libidinal attractions and sexual exploits. The evidence is skimpy, but what we have suggests that young Iñigo held his own with the best of them on all counts. He was a Loyola of the Loyolas — strong, forceful, daring, ready for any encounter, aggressive or libidinal, never backing away from a fight or neglecting the opportunity for an amorous adventure.

Iñigo became enamored of the romantic literature of the Spanish Renaissance, especially the tales of amorous intrigue, chivalrous ideals, and courtly love. His favorite was the story of Amadis of Gaul (Vita 17)[6] which he absorbed wholeheartedly for better or worse. Amadis was the perfect knight, courteous and courageous, the model of the loyal vassal or the constant lover. His virtues greatly outweighed his shortcomings. He was devout, honest, brave, never boastful, always courageous and considerate, faithful in love and in the service of his lord (Brodrick 1956). Amadis and his lady Oriana were devout and pious, Catholic to the core, but beyond this their passion was constant and noble. The *Amadis*, then was a compendium of all the virtues of romantic chivalry — the central place of love and passion, the exaltation of the feminine, a degree of moral laxity, and the cult of chivalry, embracing ideals of prowess in the use of arms and the arts of war, loyalty, generosity, courtesy, fierce pride, indominable courage, and the pursuit of glory (Wickham 1954). The ideals of

[5] Nadal remarks in his dialogues that Iñigo "though educated with distinction as a noble at his home, he did not devote himself to studies, but moved by a generous ardor, dedicated himself, in conformity with the traditions of the nobility of Spain, to win the favor of the King and of the grandees, and to signalize himself in military glory" (Leturia 1949).

[6] References to the *Autobiography* (Loyola 1956) will be designated henceforth as Vita.

romantic amorous exploits and of deeds of bravery and courage were largely congruent with the ideals and traditions of the Loyola family mythology that Iñigo carried with him on the journey from Loyola to Arevalo. Iñigo's immersion in the ambitions and ideals of romantic chivalry only added to and deepened his commitment to these values.[7]

The picture of the emerging young hidalgo is overburdened by the elements of his identification with the forceful figure of Beltran — his character and personality at this time seems almost a carbon copy of the once powerful lord of Loyola. Perhaps a more salient factor in this development for Iñigo's future career was the fact that he was schooled in the arts of dealing with the rich and powerful of the world and church, and his endowments of tact and diplomacy grew apace. These qualities would serve him well in the years in Rome when dealings with kings, popes, cardinals, and royalty of all kinds became essential to insure the fate of his struggling and growing Society.

Even though the lineaments are dimly sketched, the psychoanalytic observer can venture some tentative impressions of this emerging hidalgo. As I have argued previously (Meissner 1992b), Iñigo's character structure bears many of the marks of a phallic narcissistic personality. Phallic narcissism stems from the phallic period of development in which the penis in males prototypically becomes invested with narcissistic libido and thus becomes highly valued and prized, the so-called phallic or oedipal stage of development, usually occurring around the third to fifth year. Along with this investment in the penis or its symbolic equivalents comes the threat of its loss in the form of castration anxiety. Phallic narcissistic qualities can be found in females as well as males but take different forms. Qualities associated with this narcissistic configuration are pride in phallic prowess and performance, the search for admiration especially of skill or mastery, a sense of daring, counterphobic behaviors, unwillingness to accept defeat, omnipotence in the face of seemingly impossible obstacles, exhibitionism, assertiveness, and self-aggrandizement. The underlying themes are the wish for admiration of the phallic accomplishment and the need to defend against anxiety from castration fears and vulnerability. Individuals with these character traits tend to be self-centered, independent, difficult to intimidate, often fearless, ready to spring into action — strong personalities that step readily and willingly into positions of leadership (Freud 1931). Reich (1949) described them as "self-confident, often arrogant, elastic, vigorous and often impressive. . . . The outspoken types tend to achieve lead-

[7] The *Amadis* also was an important influence on Cervantes and found its echoes in *Don Quixote* (see Part II, Book III, ch.1 and passim).

ing positions in life and resent subordination" (p. 201). To this Kernberg (1979) adds, ". . . because narcissistic personalities are often driven by intense needs for power and prestige to assume positions of authority and leadership, individuals with such characteristics are found rather frequently in top leadership positions" (p. 33). The narcissistic need in such a personality compels him to take risks and undertake arduous tasks for the sake of winning a narcissistic prize and gaining a position of power and grandiose satisfaction. Moreover, the capacity to maintain self-esteem and integral psychic functioning depends on gaining the required narcissistic gratifications.

Such personalities usually demonstrate a constellation of characteristics including exhibitionism, pride in prowess, counterphobic competitiveness, and a willingness to undertake risks or court danger for the purpose of self-display and gaining admiration from others. They are frequently self-centered and have an intense need for approval and admiration from others, along with a certain arrogance and contempt for others based defensively on underlying feelings of inferiority and inadequacy. While such personalities evidence certain strengths and a capacity for daring that often brings them into positions of leadership or power, the character pathology has built into it certain lines of cleavage that under the right conditions of stress or narcissistic injury will bring about symptomatic reactions or regressive crisis.

I should immediately note that to a certain extent this phallic narcissistic profile was culturally endorsed and sustained. This alignment of psychological factors would have been based primarily on the identification with the phallic narcissistic figure of Beltran, but the character structure was embedded in the culture of the times and reinforced by Iñigo's family history and tradition. Given the historical position of Spain of the sixteenth century and the turmoil of the period, there may have been selection factors at work making the phallic narcissistic resolution a preferred pattern for making one's way in the world — the world of the hidalgo and the conquistador. But the psychoanalytic lens does not allow us to see the strengths and potential adaptability of this profile without seeing its flaws and weaknesses at the same time.

## Pamplona

Iñigo remained in the household of Velasquez for nearly a decade. His tenure there came to a sudden and tragic close. Early in 1516 King Ferdinand died — Velasquez was at his side. From that point on, Velasquez' fortunes took a turn for the worse. Ferdinand's grandson, the Flemish-born Charles, succeeded to the throne of

Castile. Charles' insensitive rearrangement of Queen Germaine's pension effectively dismembered the royal patrimony and violated the rights of towns in Velasquez' charge. The threat of armed rebellion ended with Velasquez' discharge; deprived of resources and influence, he retired to Madrid in debt and died there on 12 August 1517. Iñigo remained loyal to his liege, but after Velasquez' death, he found a place in the retinue of the Duke of Najera. As he left Arevalo, he mounted his steed and rode forth as an equipped young man of arms, a trained and skilled knight in the best courtly tradition, carrying with him a proud name and the confidence of his own strength and courage.

The Duke of Najera welcomed the young hidalgo into his service, especially since the Duke was then caught up in the dynastic struggles between the Spanish Hapsburgs and the French. Iñigo established himself as a valued figure in the Duke's retinue, a man who could meet any challenge, fight with the best of them, and capable of command of an armed force. He also demonstrated his considerable diplomatic skills on several occasions. In the face of general unrest and the threat of border incursions from the French, Iñigo's services were increasingly utilized. The critical event for our story, however, came in the form of the uprising of some old Castilian towns against the "foreign" influence of Charles' government, ostensibly setting the interests of the empire ahead of the kingdom. The heaping of honors on his Flemish cohorts and the undermining of traditional rights and privileges of the towns angered some of the nobility, resulting in the uprising of the *Comuneros*. Francis I of France lost little time in taking advantage of the revolt, and quickly invaded Navarre. The Duke of Najera was called on to intercept the French.

Iñigo played a prominent role in these events, at times leading the charge to take a rebellious town, or negotiating delicate agreements that averted an armed showdown. The confrontation with the French led him to Pamplona, where he commanded a contingent of the forces of the Duke. The situation at Pamplona was desperate. The townspeople, faced with the overwhelming superiority of the French army surrounding their town and the imminent likelihood of devastating destruction from the French cannon — easily the best in Europe — rebelled against the use of armed resistance. The troops had to retreat to the citadel, where any hope of survival was bleak and any effort at resistance seemed suicidal. The commander Herrera opted for surrender in the face of overwhelming odds. But, our intrepid hidalgo could not accept defeat and surrender. He assumed command of the forces in the citadel and roused the troops to a spirited resistance. Under the merciless hammering of the French cannon, the garrison gave a good account of itself, inflicting severe losses on the French. Finally, the walls were breached and Iñigo, sword in hand, was at the point of attack leading his embattled troops. Suddenly he was struck down by a French cannonball that severely fractured one of his legs and injured the other. When he fell, the citadel fell with him. In this moment of high drama, the phallic narcissistic dynamic in Iñigo's personality reached its climactic crescendo — and, with the impact of the well-aimed cannonball, came crashing down into ignominious defeat.

The wounded man was treated respectfully by his captors. His wounds were treated by the French surgeon as well as he could. In appreciation, the wounded hidalgo gave what he could to his benefactors — his shield to one, his dagger to another, and so on. Within a few days, he was placed in a litter and set out on the long, painful journey to Loyola. After several weeks of torturous journey, he arrived at Loyola, much weakened and in danger of his life. Thus the career of the noble hidalgo and man of arms came to an inglorious end.

# CHAPTER II

# CONVERSION

## Personality

Iñigo's formative years led through the trials of early childhood, the shaping influences of early adolescence and the crisis of identity formation, into the consolidation of that identity in its adult realization. The boy gave way to the dashing and daring young hidalgo, and the young hidalgo became the skillful and courageous soldier and promising statesman. As we approach this period of religious crisis, we need to assess the inner balance of strengths and weaknesses of his personality to provide the foundation for a further inquiry of his evolution from the rough and ready soldier into the saint. There is no question that there is a direct line of continuity, and that the polarities of this evolution enable us to better understand the depth and meaning of the process that led from one to the other and provided the dynamic underpinnings of his emerging spirituality.

Since Iñigo was a product of his culture and his time, the features that stand out in his personality are those that were characteristically valued highly by the code of chivalry (Wickham 1954) and the culture of sixteenth century Spain — prowess in self-defense and in the arts of war; loyalty, generosity, courtesy, and the pursuit of glory; fierce pride and unquestionable courage. While these values permeated Iñigo's culture and the romantic literature he absorbed, they only partially explain these aspects of his personality. Any culture, carries a multiplicity of values from which the individual selects a certain subset to internalize. Yet chivalric values, with their peculiar appeal and intensity for Iñigo, were not only ideals that defined his behavior tendencies, but wishes which dominated his inner life of fantasy and desire. He admits to us that, during the enforced idleness of his convalescence, his fantasies were taken up with matters of romantic chivalry and heroic deeds (Vita 6). In this fantasy world, Iñigo must have seen himself in the image of Amadís of Gaul, the hero of Montalvo's popular book, which he had so eagerly devoured. The libidinal current in these romantic fantasies was marked and reflected a predominantly genital drive organization, with highly sexualized fantasies and behavior.

But there were other matters that loomed large in this intrepid hidalgo. In his summation of the first three decades of his life, Ignatius mentioned the exercise of arms and the desire to win glory as defining characteristics (Vita 1). Prowess in the use of dagger, sword, buckler, and crossbow, good horsemanship, and related skills were essential components of the young Loyola's sense of identity. Of course, there was already an image born of chivalrous ideals and early identifications and nourished by youthful fantasy. Later prowess in arms served both to activate such fantasies and to progressively define an emergent identity. It is woven not only out of self-awareness but also out of perceptions of the self projected by others in the course of social interactions; in Erikson's phrase, identity is compounded out of "self-realization coupled with a mutual recognition" (Erikson 1959, p. 114). Further, identity formation involves the fashioning of a role and function within the community. The development of such a competence and its reciprocal recognition by the community are significant parts of the process by which identity evolves.

If we look at the adolescent Iñigo in the court of Velasquez, we can presume an antecedent desire to translate his fantasies into reality. After all, the young pages at the court were more or less playing games in their jousts and bouts. But at the same time, these boyish enterprises were not idle. In Renaissance Spain a young gallant's life might easily hang on his skill with the sword. Even in these training exercises, we can see the first interplay between prowess and recognition of prowess, between self-recognition and mutual recognition, which contributed to a growing structure that defined the emerging Loyola as a man of arms. In a sense, Iñigo was cut out to be a soldier, but his view of himself as a man of arms had to be fashioned out of countless events in which success in combat both gratified his existing wishes and shaped his concept of himself as a man possessing these skills. Along with this inner self-definition, he would have established his reputation among his fellows as a skillful swordsman, and this would have bolstered his perception of himself.

## THE EGO IDEAL

In Ignatius' recollection of his "great and vain desire of winning glory" (Vita 1), the glory was spelled out in terms of the chivalric ideal: military glory won in the service of his king in great victories and valorous deeds. But beyond this, it expresses an ambition, a consuming wish that mirrored Iñigo's fantasy about himself, an idealized self-image cast in the mold of chivalrous heroics that was Iñigo's ego ideal or ideal self. The chivalric code included fidelity — devotion to a lord to whom one had sworn fidelity was a primary quality of the soldier and nobleman (Wickham 1954). In a sense, Iñigo's loyalty was as much to his own ego ideal as it was to the persons and causes to which he pledged himself; that ideal would not allow him to abandon any cause to which he had pledged himself. By the same token, we cannot conceive of young Iñigo pledging himself to any enterprise that did not satisfy the requirements of his ideal. The fierce intensity with which he clung to his ideal gives us some sense of its importance both for the maintenance of his own narcissistic integrity and equilibrium and for reinforcement of his sense of self. We can also be impressed by Iñigo's gallant generosity. His bestowal of all his worldly possessions, meager as they were, on his captors in return for their kindness to him was a chivalrous gesture. Such liberality bespeaks a certain freedom from attachment to objects. The chivalric code demanded generosity not only in giving one's possessions but also in denying oneself profit at the expense of others.

Iñigo's ego ideal serves as a point of conjunction for much of the psychology of his development. It ties together the early primary libidinal relations and identifications with his parents, especially with the virile figure of his father, the imaginative impact of the romantic literature that gave concrete shape to his fantasies, and the formative impact of cultural expectations and norms. We have by no means exhausted the elements represented in these fantasies, for the ideal image they project conveys a major portion of the complex psychology of Iñigo de Loyola. Yet, in some sense, this whole inquiry is an exploration of elements of this same ideal. The desire to win glory, a major theme in this ideal, is a motif forms one of the lines of continuity between the swashbuckling Iñigo and the saintly Ignatius. They will likewise underlie fundamental themes in the later spirituality of the saint.

## PSYCHOPATHOLOGY

Along with these chivalric values that contributed to the strength of Iñigo's character, his ideal was also permeated with strains of pathological narcissism. If the heroic events of the siege of Pamplona demonstrate Iñigo's unusual strengths of character, they also tell us much about his potential weakness. His refusal to capitulate, even in the face of overwhelming odds, seems foolhardy, if not suicidal. Death held no terrors for him. The impossible situation brought no rational acceptance of defeat, no compromise, but only stirred him to greater efforts. Such behavior can only be spurred by fantasies of invincibility that reflect underlying elements of grandiosity and omnipotence.

Coloring this complex identity was the impact of his noble family tradition on Iñigo's psychology, undoubtedly mediated by his strong identification with his father, himself the embodiment of this heritage. The family's refusal to have its rights or honor brought into question was unmistakable. These values were distilled into that precipitate of parental identifications within the ego, the ego ideal. Pride and vanity are the trappings of and accompany pathological narcissism, and Iñigo de Loyola, the strutting peacock with his gay colors and jaunty plume, presented a picture of all three: proud, vain, and narcissistic. Yet pride can exist on a continuum and, in fact, a moderate degree of displacement of libido is required for self-esteem and ultimately a positive sense of identity. But the very notion of pride carries with it the possibility of excess. The ego ideal can be too highly valued. A surfeit of pride places the self and its ideal above all other considerations, regardless of the rights and needs of others. It takes the form of egoism which erects a façade of self-sufficiency and pseudo-strength, so radically opposed to real ego-strength and identity. Such excessive "ego-interests" are usually preconscious and are often difficult to bring to consciousness because of their closeness to underlying wishes and instinctually motivated desires (Hartmann 1964).

In the developing personality, psychic potential is normally channeled into the synthetic construction of an identity. If these forces are diverted into the elaboration of an egoistic and hypertrophied ego ideal, the evolution of identity suffers. Pride becomes then a mechanism to compensate for an inadequate sense of identity; it becomes, then, a "lasting and characterologically significant aspect of a personality" (Hartmann and Loewenstein 1962). The pride of the Loyolas, often bridging into vanity, was an almost necessary complement and consequence of the ego ideal forming a central part of Iñigo's personality. In this lay both his strength and his weakness.

All this reached a thunderous climax in the dramatic siege of Pamplona. The dazzling light that was Iñigo de Loyola was snuffed out, and the light was not to be rekindled. As the litter bore the wounded soldier on the painful miles to the Castle of Loyola, Iñigo was carried into a new and decisive phase of his life. Perhaps it is better to say that he was carried into a new life. It was somehow fitting that the very house that first gave him life, should be the place to give him the new life that lay before him.

## The Conversion Story

The conversion experience that Iñigo de Loyola underwent at the castle of Loyola in 1521 was a pivotal event. The circumstances of this profound spiritual experience set the stage for the transformation of the fearless and flamboyant hidalgo and soldier into the humble pilgrim, the man of God, and finally the saint. In recasting these crucial events, the first task is to tell the story, and then reconstruct the elements entering into a psychoanalytic understanding of these events. First the story.

The dramatic events that brought the wounded Iñigo to Loyola set in motion a process that was to prove decisive for the life course of this broken hero. The bones of one leg had been severely fractured and the other leg injured as well. The defeated warrior was carried over the painful miles to Loyola, the broken bones having been hurriedly set by the French surgeon. Finally at Loyola, the agonizing recuperation began. The rigors of the journey had done his broken leg no good. The surgeons decided that the leg should be reoperated and the bones reset. Thirty years later, he recalled this surgery as a "butchery", so severe must have been the pain: "Again he went through this butchery, in which as in all the others that he had suffered he uttered no word, nor gave any sign of pain other than clenching his fists" (Vita 2). This brutal and painful surgery was carried out several centuries before the introduction of surgical anesthesia and antiseptic technique.

His reaction to the surgical insult was not good. His condition grew worse, he lost appetite. He was told that if he showed no improvement, he could expect to die. He made his confession and received the last sacraments. But the hardy Basque was not finished yet. His condition improved on the feast of Saints Peter and Paul, and within a few days he was judged to be out of danger of death.

But the ordeal had not yet ended. The healing of this second fracture was not very satisfactory. He recalled:

> When the bones knit, one below the knee remained astride another which caused a shortening of the leg. The bones so raised caused a protuberance that was not pleasant to the sight. The sick man was not able to put up with this because he had made up his mind to seek his fortune in the world. He thought the protuberance was going to be unsightly and asked the surgeons whether it could not be cut away. They told him that it could be cut away, but that the pain would be greater than all he had already suffered, because it was now healed and it would take some time to

> cut it off. He determined, nevertheless, to undergo this martyrdom to gratify his own inclinations. (Vita 4)

We can imagine that the weeks of pain and immobility took their toll. But his health was otherwise good, and he looked for some means of diverting himself during the enforced idleness of his recuperation. He asked for some of the romances he loved to read, but none could be found. Instead Magdalena could only offer him the four volumes of the *Life of Jesus Christ* by the Carthusian Ludolph of Saxony and a volume of the lives of the saints, commonly called the *Flos Sanctorum*.

What follows is a crucial phase in the transformation that was to be wrought in Iñigo de Loyola. We can best follow his own account:

> By the frequent reading of these books he conceived some affection for what he found there narrated. Pausing in his reading, he gave himself up to thinking over what he had read. At other times he dwelt on the things of the world which formerly had occupied his thoughts. . . . Nevertheless, our Lord came to his assistance, for He saw to it that these thoughts were succeeded by others which sprang from the things he was reading. In reading the Life of our Lord and the Lives of the Saints, he paused to think and reason with himself. "Suppose that I should do what St. Francis did, what St. Dominic did?" He thus let his thoughts run over many things that seemed good to him, always putting before himself things that were difficult and important which seemed to him easy to accomplish when he proposed them. But all his thought was to tell himself "St. Dominic did this, therefore, I must do it. St. Francis did this, therefore, I must do it". These thoughts also lasted a good while. And then other things taking their place, the worldly thoughts above mentioned came upon him and remained a long time with him. This succession of diverse thoughts was of long duration, and they were either of worldly achievements which he desired to accomplish, or those of God which took hold of his imagination to such an extent, that worn out with the struggle, he turned them all aside and gave his attention to other things. . . . He acquired no little light from this reading and began to think more seriously of his past life and the great need he had of doing penance for it. It was during this reading that these desires of imitating the saints came to him, but with no further thought of circumstances than of promising to do with God's grace what they had done. . . . (Vita 6-9)

At this juncture, the critical experience occurred that seems to have been the central event in Iñigo's conversion experience, namely a vision of our Lady holding the Christ Child.

> One night, as he lay awake, he saw clearly the likeness of our Lady with the Holy Child Jesus, at the sight of which he received most abundant consolation for a considerable interval of time. He felt so great a disgust with his past life, especially with its offenses of the flesh, that he thought all such images which had formerly occupied his mind were wiped out. And from that hour until August of 1553, when this is being written, he never again consented to the least suggestion of the flesh. (Vita 10)

This vision had a powerful psychic and emotional impact, and lead to the dramatic elimination of all temptations of the flesh. These experiences cry out for psychological understanding.

This brief autobiographical account is substantially all that is known about the series of events that resulted in the transformation of Iñigo de Loyola from the proud and gallant hidalgo into a man filled with the desire of serving God. His heart was inflamed with the desire to imitate the saintly warriors of God whose heroic deeds he had been reading about. He experienced intense desires to retreat to the desert and live on herbs like the holy hermits, to turn his back on the world and its pleasures and devote himself to fasting, flagellations and penances like God's heroes. He first thought of devoting himself to a life of solitude, silence and prayer among the monks of Cuevas; but this was soon replaced by the urge to wander as a poor pilgrim through the world, begging for his bread and bearing the contempt of men after the model of St. Francis and St. Dominic. He had a strong desire to enter the Carthusian charterhouse at Seville, fired no doubt by reading Ludolph's *Life*, and even dispatched a servant to Burgos to inquire about the Charterhouse of Miraflores (Clancy 1976).[1]

[1] For further Carthusian influences, see Iparraguirre (1965) and Buckley (1979). Later on the Paris Charterhouse was a frequent place where Ignatius and his companions gathered, and the Carthusians became the only exception to the rule in the *Constitutions* [CS99] (Ganss 1970) forbidding transfer of a Jesuit in final vows to any other religious order.

Opinions regarding the nature of the ego ideal and its relation to narcissism are still somewhat diverse and unsettled in psychoanalytic circles. See the discussion in Milrod (1990). One view of the relation between ego ideal and superego regards the ego ideal as narcissistic in origin and leading to the dynamics of narcissistic vulnerability and shame, while the superego derives from the oedipal situation and leads to the complex of drive-superego-castration anxiety-guilt. See Grunberger (1989). Chasseguet-Smirgel (1973), following Grunberger's lead, writes: ". . . there exists a fundamental difference between the ego ideal, heir to primary narcissism, and the superego, heir to the Oedipus complex. The first represents — at the outset at least — an attempt at recovering lost omnipotence. The second, in a Freudian perspective, is a production of the castration complex. The first tends to

## BACKGROUND FACTORS

The religious conversion experienced by Iñigo de Loyola on his bed of convalescence did not take place in a vacuum. A series of determinants played their part in influencing the course of that experience and its consequences. I will try to put in place some of the elements that lend themselves to a psychoanalytic hypothesis regarding his conversion. The points I will focus on are his family background and the family myth it conveyed, the issues surrounding his early maternal deprivation, and the narcissistic quality of his personality structure.

Iñigo de Loyola's family traditions were rich with legends of valor, heroism, courage, ambition, power and strength. This constituted a kind of family mythology embodying a constellation of beliefs, values and expectations to which the young Loyola was exposed from the beginning and became part of the very fabric of his existence and sense of himself. This family myth provided the core elements of his preconversion ego-ideal.[2]

The next salient fact is the death of his mother soon after his birth. This unfortunate event and its consequences may have cast a long shadow over the subsequent events in Iñigo's life story (Meissner 1992b), and may have contributed important determinants to his religious conversion and his subsequent road to sanctity (Wolfenstein 1966, 1969; Rochlin 1965; Fleming and Altschul 1963; Deutsch 1937). Wolfenstein (1969) described a pattern of overt or uncon-

reinstate illusion, the second to promote reality. The superego comes between the child and the mother, the ego ideal . . . pushes him towards fusion" (p. 76). If one does not distinquish them as separate structural formations, as Chasseguet-Smirgel seems to, the can be distinguished in terms of separable functions.

[2] Opinions regarding the nature of the ego ideal and its relation to narcissism are still somewhat diverse and unsettled in psychoanalytic circles. See the discussion in Milrod (1990). One view of the relation between ego ideal and superego regards the ego ideal as narcissistic in origin and leading to the dynamics of narcissistic vulnerability and shame, while the superego derives from the oedipal situation and leads to the complex of drive-superego-castration anxiety-guilt. See Grunberger (1989). Chasseguet-Smirgel (1973), following Grunberger's lead, writes: ". . . there exists a fundamental difference between the ego ideal, heir to primary narcissism, and the superego, heir to the Oedipus complex. The first represents — at the outset at least — an attempt at recovering lost omnipotence. The second, in a Freudian perspective, is a production of the castration complex. The first tends to reinstate Illusion, the second to promote reality. The superego comes between the child and the mother, the ego ideal . . . pushes him towards fusion" (p. 76). If one does not distinquish them as separate structural formations, as Chasseguet-Smirgel seems to, the can be distinguished in terms of separable functions.

scious denial of the finality of the loss, allowing the hopeful fantasies of reunion and restitution to persist unabated. Such patients tend to develop elaborate fantasies in which the lost parent is idealized and glorified — this is one of the major outcomes of early parental loss. But the parental image is no longer that of the parent as he was known in life, but the glorified parent of early childhood who is now perpetuated in fantasy, most often unconscious fantasy (Miller 1971).

There are also long-term sequelae of this syndrome of loss-and-restitution (Rochlin 1965; Birtchnell et al. 1973).[3] Such patients are often caught up in a life-long effort to maintain the denial and rewrite the tragedy with a happier ending, acting out symbolic repetitions of the loss of the parent again and again in the unsuccessful attempt to master the trauma of loss (Wolfenstein 1969). This can involve the powerful motif of identification with the dead parent. As Birtchnell (1969) wrote in his review of the effects of early parental death: "Identification with the lost object.[4] is a feature of adult grief, but in children it is commoner and usually takes a more dramatic form. . . . Identification occurs irrespective of the sex of the parent lost. Such a reaction is probably an attempt to deny the loss" (pp. 7-8). The identification may also take the form of an identification with the state of death itself, reflecting an unconscious wish to achieve reunion with the lost parent in death.

These dynamic elements continue to play themselves out throughout the course of the individual's adult life. Loss becomes inextricably bound with damage to self-esteem (Rochlin 1965). The need for restitution may become a dominating force in the patient's unconscious and may take the form of various unconsciously dictated enactments and may impair the development of child's capacity for object relationships. In many cases there are also significant anniversary reactions that may take the form of the exacerbation of emotional or psychosomatic symptoms on the anniversary of significant childhood losses (Pollock 1970, 1989; Mintz 1971). Psychiatric research in this area tends to confirm the association of early maternal deprivation through death, divorce or separation with relatively severe forms of lifelong psychopathology (Gregory 1985; Earle and Earle 1961; Bradley (1979), although there are some indications that

[3] The psychoanalytic view of the dynamics and consequences of loss have been detailed by Rochlin in terms of the "loss complex" and by Pollock in terms of the "mourning-liberation process." See Rochlin (1965) and Pollock (1989).

[4] "Object" here is used in the psychoanalytic sense of other persons toward whom libido can be directed and attached. Object-libido is thus distinguished from libido directed to the self or narcissistic libido.

in addition to the loss of the mother the quality of subsequent home life and childrearing may also play a critical role in determining whether psychopathology will develop in adult life (Breier et al. 1988; Krueger 1983). The effects of early parental loss may depend on the age and level of development of the child as well as the availability of proper support for facilitating the mourning process (Furman 1964, 1968; Furman and Furman 1974).

The implications of these possible reactions, particularly activation of his identification with the image of the lost mother, become all the more salient in the face of the castrative trauma of his wound and the destruction of his dreams for glory and honor in military exploits dictated by his phallic narcissistic propensities and identification with his phallic father. The possible implications of early maternal deprivation for Iñigo's conversion experience would include an unconscious but pervasive sense of loss and an underlying core depression, an unsatisfied yearning for attachment and reunion with the lost mother, an idealization and aggrandizement of the repressed image of his lost mother, and perhaps more significantly a powerful identification with her. The yearning for reunion with the mother would also imply the idea of reunion in death and a further attachment to and idealization of the state of death itself.

## Developmental Influences

I will argue that these developmental vicissitudes provided the psychic substratum that fed into Iñigo's conversion experience. But there are considerable pitfalls in any attempt to reconstruct the infant iñigo's developmental career. The early loss of his mother, for example, is rife with problems. We do not know how old Iñigo was at the time; we do not know the circumstances surrounding the event. How salient, then, were the elements of loss and abandonment? What were the conditions of his living in the peasant hut of the Garins? All these factors would qualify the impact of this early traumatic loss on his infantile development. Particularly, we would like to know how his mother's death affected the process of separation and individuation that would lay the foundations for the ensuing process of development on which the structure of his evolving personality would build. The age at which this separation occurred makes a considerable difference in how the trauma is integrated or defended against and what long term sequelae it might induce.

My hypothesis is that these events had a pathogenic impact, leading to continued reworking and efforts to master the effects of loss, in Ignatius' more mature years as well as in childhood. The loss of his mother would have left him with a deep-seated unconscious wish for reunion with her, specifically through death. Correlative with this wish, we could infer unconscious fantasies, formed at an infantile level in his mind, of rejoining his mother in the heavenly kingdom, where mother and son could be reunited in eternal bliss. This dynamic would contribute an essentially depressive core to his personality organization, rooted in his sense of abandonment, intolerable and inexpressible rage at the abandoning mother, and a devalued sense of himself as a child who was not worthy of his mother's love and fidelity.

The other side of this psychic coin is an idealization of the lost mother, whose image would embrace the highest and purest virtue. The perfection of this unconscious image would be proportional to the imperfection and lack of worth of his own self-image — a sense of inferiority and worthlessness that could be redeemed only by the longed-for reunion with the idealized mother. These dynamic processes would have been synthesized into an identification with the mother, particularly with the image of her as patient, long-suffering, deeply religious and faithful, and the paragon of feminine virtues. These elements of his maternal identification would determine a variety of important patterns and experiences that would shape and direct his later life.

The other important developmental influence in Ignatius' life was the powerful identification with the image of his father as strong, masculine, phallic, aggressive — the image of the dominant, authoritarian warrior and leader, characterized by effectiveness of action and will and by sexual potency and prowess. This identification with the phallic narcissistic father-image was culturally reinforced, particularly the male-dominated culture of late fifteenth- and early sixteenth-century Spain, manifested in patterns of physical and sexual aggressiveness (Gilmore and Gilmore 1979). This brand of machismo can be seen not as an assertion of secure masculine identity, but as a defensively motivated attempt to resolve deeper conflicts between masculine and feminine identities.

Part of the issue here is the lifelong struggle in the male to establish and maintain a masculine identity in the face of passive and dependent yearnings that exert an often powerful psychic pull toward the feminine. The male begins life in a state of dependence and attachment to the mother; the regressive pull toward that early and idealized infantile dependence is the force he must struggle against to preserve his sense of masculinity. Rochlin (1980) puts the argument in the following terms:

> It is the human condition to evolve inner defenses against our private, often ill-defined, emotional conflicts, and men, even as boys, are prone to particular defenses in regard to their masculinity. The most persistent, disturbing, and anxiety-provoking are those associated with the never-ending need to prove one's masculinity in the face of doubts as to its degree. Thus, we find at all stages of manhood — young boys, whose defenses of masculinity are developing; youths, whose masculinity is being tested in reality; and men, whose masculinity needs a constant reaffirmation — alarming fears that return in varying forms in even more distressing wishes. Principal among these are the fears and wishes to be feminine or to engage in what once may have been associated with notions of femininity. Such reverses of the "normal" conscious imperative of masculine striving, set off by the eruption of unconscious rooted desires, call out vigorous defenses: most commonly striving to be and to seem more "masculine." (p. 4)

These unconscious fears and wishes, along with their associated defenses, are the common lot of all normal males but would have been subject to special conditions for Iñigo. The loss of his mother provided an additional unconscious pull toward the feminine — a wish that would have been repugnant to his culture and the world he lived in. The unconscious theme of return to the feminine and reunion with the lost mother would have played itself out in this context of his struggle to achieve adult masculinity. The model for this process was, of course, the powerful phallic and narcissistic figure of his father, Beltrán.[5]

These conflicting identifications, with the phallic, narcissistic, and aggressive figure of his father, on the one hand, and the passive, self-sacrificing, pious, virtuous, humble, and self-effacing image of his mother, elevated to the status of an idealized and sublime object through death on the other, were to contend for the intrapsychic

[5] Behaviors or mental phenomena are thought to be drive-determined to the extent that they reflect the influence of basic motivations, usually limited to libidinal, narcissistic, and aggressive motives. Defense mechanisms are usually brought into play to limit, channel, regulate, modify, or otherwise modulate motivatioal influences. Identifications can be defensive — defending, for example, against the pain of loss of a loved one — or motivationally determined — as, for example, identifications that involve narcissistic determinants. Iñigo's identification with his mother would have been based on the need to defend against the loss; his identification with his father would have involved the defensive integration of phallic narcissism.

hegemony of his inner world throughout Iñigo's life. This deep-seated conflict would never be fully resolved.

But further events also played their part. The years Iñigo spent in the service of Juan Velasquez steeped him in courtly graces and developed his skill in the use of arms, but it also shaped his internalization of the ideals of courtly romance and knightly chivalry. These provided the substance of his preconversion ego-ideal. As he told us himself, "Up to his twenty-sixth year he was a man given over to the vanities of the world, and took a special delight in the exercise of arms, with a great and vain desire of winning glory" (Vita 1). The elements of this narcissistic personality configuration would include high ideals, the need for great and significant achievements, a sense of omnipotence and invulnerability, a willingness to take the greatest risks in the service of heroic ideals and the overcoming of seemingly impossible odds. Such phallic narcissistic personalities do best in times of war and great danger, since their omnipotence and invincibility allows them to take risks and face dangers from which others would beat a prudential retreat. Iñigo's heroics at Pamplona bear the stamp of such counterphobic daring and reveal his sense of invincibility and even grandiosity. We can focus these dynamic elements in terms of his ego-ideal in which the residues of archaic grandiosity and infantile narcissism are preserved. The ego-ideal of Iñigo de Loyola was cast in heroic terms that would accept no defeat, would yield to no odds no matter how overwhelming, and was dedicated to deeds of the highest valor and glory.

## The Conversion Process

If we return to Iñigo's conversion experience, it seems clear that the impact of the cannon ball at Pamplona set in motion a series of events that were to have immense consequences. The first effect of the French cannonball was to shatter not only his leg, but his romanticized and chivalric ego-ideal as well — that ideal based on his identification with phallic narcissistic model provided by his father. The convalescence consequently required not only physical repair of his wounds, but reconstitution of his shattered ego-ideal and the sense of self formed around it. In the castle of Loyola, Iñigo experienced the first movements of conversion which characteristically had the quality of sudden illumination or revelation. But these were only the first in a long series of events that would lead him, step by difficult step, away from the home of his ancestors and the tradition and loyalties of the house of Loyola to the cave of Manresa and its bitter spiritual and psychic struggle.

As William James (1902) and others have observed, the more or less acute and climactic experience of religious conversion is frequently accompanied by a long, arduous process that brings about a gradual restructuring of the individual's personality. He described the symptoms — "a sense of incompleteness and imperfections; brooding, depression, morbid introspection, and sense of sin; anxiety about the hereafter; distress over doubts, and the like." And he goes on to add: "And the result is the same — a happy relief and objectivity, as the confidence in self gets greater through the adjustment of the faculties to the wider outlook. In spontaneous religious awakening . . . we may also meet with mystical experiences, astonishing subjects by their suddenness, just as in revivalistic conversion" (p. 167). We can hear the echoes of these sentiments clearly in Iñigo's shattered sense of self. The second element is the positive ideal for which the individual yearns and toward which he struggles. This element too emerges clearly in Iñigo's imaginative stirrings and fantasies of doing great and heroic deeds in imitation of the great saints. In the ordinary run of cases, the sense of sinfulness dominates the picture, almost becoming an obsession. The process of conversion is thus at first dominated by the need to escape from sinfulness rather than to strive towards an ideal.

The conversion experience is also associated with certain more or less regressive phenomena — a loosening or relaxation of the synthetic capacity of the ego, resulting in a degree of internal dissociation and fragmentation connected with a sense of estrangement. The onset of the subjective experience of estrangement heralds the initial disintegration of the ego and is often associated with a sense of confusion regarding the self and its identity (Conn 1986). The fragmented aspects of the self-organization, dissociated from their integration with the individual's sense of self, are usually dealt with defensively, more often than not, by projection. We can conjecture that in some degree Iñigo must have experienced something like this state of internal self-disintegration.

Prior to the actual conversion experience, there is a period during which the individual is caught up in a struggle with both conscious and unconscious conflict. At its peak intensity, when the conflict threatens the ego with disintegration, there is a tendency for the individual to stop trying to actively and consciously resolve the conflict. The giving-up phenomenon tends to occur immediately before or concurrently with the sense of divine presence. The sense of divine presence may be regarded as a projective phenomenon, but an important aspect is that it may inspire guilt feelings if its assumed dictates are not followed. The guilt may be atoned by acts of expiation or submission. Inevitably, the sense of psychic presence was related to the individual's concept of God. Christensen (1963) felt that the projection involved in the experience of divine presence was related to the defensive projection of the mental representation of the mother. Thus, the surrender and submitting to the will of God has as one of its psychic equivalents the giving up to the demands of the mother on the part of the child. With the feeling of submission and the sense of acceptance and conformity to the divine will, there is a sense of sudden understanding accompanied by a feeling of elation, a feeling of change within the sense of self, or in relation to other important persons (Conn 1986).

The regressive crisis in the conversion experience can be resolved in several ways. In one, conflicts on both an unconscious and conscious level are sufficiently resolved so that they can be meaningfully integrated with the functioning ego. The resulting synthesis is compatible with current reality experience and adaptively integrated to provide a sense of completeness or totality, and of deep understanding. Energies previously bound up in conflict may then become available for more creative, productive and adaptive use by the ego. With such individuals, the conversion experience represents a process of growth toward greater personal and spiritual maturity.

More often the strength of the ego seems to be insufficient to synthesize and integrate the underlying conflicts, as though suppression of more conscious conflicts allows them to gain strength from association with unconscious conflicts, thus becoming a source of psychic threat. The ego may respond with a variety of defense mechanisms, often resulting in a kind of symbolic representation in religious terms of a mystical nature. While this solution does not resolve the conflict, it does allow for some alleviation of anxiety, creating a sense of relief and some understanding. The sense of completeness and integration cannot be felt internally, but more in relation to an object outside the self, specifically God. To the degree that the ego remains embroiled in continuing repression and defense, it is relatively less free for more adaptive resolution. The religious belief system in such cases serves the function of maintaining repressive barriers and of supporting the somewhat fragile ego, so that any challenge to the belief system will be perceived as a threat and must be defended against. The conversion experience of Loyola seems to reflect elements of both these resolutions.

## A PSYCHOANALYTIC PERSPECTIVE

If we return to the sickbed at Loyola, we can retrace some of the elements of Iñigo's conversion. To begin with, the strains of narcissistic grandiosity and omnipotence so prominently displayed in his character were shattered at Pamplona. That singularly aimed cannonball shattered not only the bones of his leg, but also his ideals, ambitions, and dreams of glory. There followed weeks of pain and passivity, a situation of considerable psychic strain and regressive potential. After all, in this sword-swinging and heroic hidalgo, phallic activity and a sense of counterphobic invincibility and omnipotence had been major defensive modalities forming a considerable part of the basis of his character structure. The almost total immersion in pain, passivity and dependence on Magdalena for all his natural needs, required by his convalescence would inevitably have activated and mobilized those basic anxieties against which such defenses had so effectively operated. Basic to this underlying core of anxiety had to be the threat of castration which the trauma of physical injury and broken bones must have severely intensified.

His response to the ordeal of the various operations on his shattered and deformed leg was quite remarkable, suggesting the resources Iñigo could bring to the service of his ego-ideal. That ideal carried with it a bodily component. The unsightly deformity would not fit the image of a handsome soldier, when the fashion of the day, especially the tight-fitted cavalier's boots, would reveal such a deformity so readily. The intense narcissistic cathexis of his body image had suffered a severe insult in the traumatic deformity of his leg. How could he maintain the image of the handsome, dashing, heroic hidalgo with a leg that was misshapen and a gait that was deformed by an obvious limp? The motifs of castration and defectiveness here blend with the narcissistic strains of diminished self-worth and the countering of exhibitionistic wishes and impulses in the sense of shame. The power of this need for the psychic well-being of the handsome soldier of fortune is manifest in his willingness to undergo further surgery — however painful — in the interest of overcoming this unsightly impediment.

His willingness to undergo the torment of surgery is a measure of the extent the ego-ideal dominated his life and behavior. But beyond the ego-ideal, we get a glimpse of the fundamental strength of Iñigo. He was full of courage, unflinching determination, and possessed a superb capacity to endure unbelievable hardship and suffering to attain a goal he had set himself. He was the same Iñigo, whether he was facing the overwhelming odds of the battlefield or the torment of the surgeon's knife. The convalescence was long and painful, and since he was unable to stand on the leg, he was forced to remain in bed. Little wonder then, as he lay on his bed of pain, Iñigo's mind would have been searching for substitutes for the shattered ideals, ambitions and values that had been so central to his sense of himself and his well-being.

It is clear that in the early phases of this period of convalescence, the ego ideal which had served as a major focus of the psychological life of Iñigo was still intact and quite functional. His insistence on cosmetic surgery at exquisite cost seems utterly unintelligible without an appeal to some such powerfully determining normative image. He assures us that his intention in not only undergoing, but undertaking, this torment was to pursue his life in the world. It seems obvious that physical appearance would play a very considerable role in this projected career as chivalrous nobleman and heroic man-at-arms. But the impact on his body image would have had even more severe consequences. The body image is intimately associated with self-awareness and self-perception. The deformation must have formed a focus for the mobilization of deep-seated anxieties stemming from the insult to Iñigo's basic self-concept.

In this state of mind his imagination was captured by the heroic tales of the saints and the life of Christ. He tells us in his autobiography how he became fascinated by these tales of saintly heroism, and how be alternated back and forth between the residues of his former narcissism, the vanities and worldly deeds of glory, particularly those gallant heroics he might have performed in the service of his royal lady, and the new forms of more spiritual heroics that he found in his readings of the lives of the saints. The residues of shattered narcissism were beginning to be shaped to a new form and a new meaning.

In this process, the elements of a typical conversion experience began to assert themselves. As he read the accounts of the lives of the saints, he began to think more seriously of his own past life and his sinfulness, and the need for doing penance for it. He began to think of the penances he might do, the ways in which he might imitate the lives of the saints, of doing various penances and fasts, even of making a pilgrimage to Jerusalem.[6]

In this context there came the profoundly meaningful vision of the Blessed Mother and the Child Jesus. The vision provides consid-

[6] Iñigo's obsession with Jerusalem may have been triggered by the introduction in Ludolph's life of Christ, in which the joy and devotion gained from visiting the Holy Land are highly praised. See Tylenda (1985, p. 15).

erable food for thought in psychoanalytic terms. During the period of his convalescence, Iñigo's brother Martin, the master of Loyola, had been away still carrying on the campaign against the French. During this time, Martin's wife, Doña Magdalena, cared for the sick man. This was the same Magdalena of whom Ignatius years later was to speak, when he confessed to one of his novices that a picture of Our Lady in his prayerbook reminded him so much of her beauty that he had to cover the picture in order that his intense affection and passion for her might not be aroused. It does not strain credibility then that in his weakened, regressed and tormented condition Iñigo might well have been erotically stimulated by the tender and intimate ministrations of the beautiful Magdalena.

Is it at all possible that, just as the saint of later years in his devotions had replaced the picture of the Blessed Mother with the face of Magdalena, that here in this central conversion experience the bedridden soldier had substituted the vision of Our Lady for the loved and desired Magdalena? If so, the vision would represent a form of sublimation of powerful libidinal drives that called for equally powerful defense. After all, the Blessed Mother was in a unique way the dominant idealized image of chaste feminine perfection in Iñigo's culture.[7] In the present context, it seems safe to say that Doña Magdalena was a most significant participant in the drama that unfolded around the fallen warrior. When she came to the castle of Loyola as Martin's bride, she became, for all practical purposes, his mother through the years of his latency development and on into adolescence.

We have already commented on the powerful identification of the young Iñigo with his powerful, phallic and narcissistic father. This phallic narcissistic identification was a major line of defense against the underlying castration anxiety that had to be aroused in his relationship with the powerful figure of his father. This identification with the powerful, aggressive, phallic and narcissistic father was undermined and destroyed by the symbolic castration of Iñigo's wound and his convalescence. As the identification with the phallic,

[7] The place of the Virgin Mary, the Blessed Mother, as a cultural symbol of these ideals, particularly in southern European cultures, has been traced by Saunders (1981). These dynamics, which I infer were active in Ignatius' time, have remained part of these cultures and in a way determine the character of masculine and feminine gender roles and sustain an ambivalent view of the nature of women, as madonna and whore. As Saunders argues, the son's erotic tie to the mother results in an idealization that implicitly connects her with the madonna, so that any woman who will have sex with him is automatically associated with the whore.

narcissistic father was undermined, the identification with the maternal elements began to assert themselves through the conversion experience. Might not Iñigo's loss of his mother soon after his birth have cast its shadow over these conversion experiences? We can recall some of the possible consequences of early maternal deprivation: there would be a pervasive sense of loss and an underlying depression; there would be an unconscious and unsatisfied yearning for attachment and reunion with the lost mother; there would be an idealization and aggrandizement of the repressed image of his lost mother; there would be a powerful identification with the lost mother; there would be a yearning for reunion with the mother in death and an attachment to and idealization of the state of death itself. In this sense, the idealized aspects of Iñigo's lost mother would have been projected onto the lovely Doña Magdalena, whose pious influence led him increasingly toward an identification with the saints.

The saintly heroes thus embodied maternal qualities of suffering, resignation, penance, self-denial, and ascetic resignation. These qualities were set over against the phallic striving, aggressiveness, and ambitious search for glory that were tied into Iñigo's identification with his father. However, the wish to imitate the saints was contaminated by aspects of the earlier configuration, particularly with regard to the competitive wish to outdo the saints in their heroic deeds. The themes of phallic conquest are reflected in his ambitions for penance and ascetical heroics, in his plans for a pilgrimage to Jerusalem, and in the themes of spiritual ambition, even grandiosity, that seem to characterize his thinking.

We can return at this juncture to the vision of Our Lady with the Child Jesus. We can conjecture that the vision of Our Lady was the embodiment of the idealized mother, the reflection of his idealized image of his own mother who had died so early, as well as the reflection of the lovely Magdalena toward whom unconscious libidinal impulses had been stirred. We might conjecture as well that in his fantasy Iñigo saw himself as the baby Jesus who could be cared for, loved and could in turn possess his idealized mother. The wishful regression to a preoedipal state would avoid any of the destructive consequences of the potential oedipal conflict. The regression to a state of blissful union with the idealized mother would thus serve to undercut and deny any incestuous longings that might carry the stamp of a more mature and differentiated sexuality.

The regressive wishful fantasy is followed by the imposition of a powerful repressive barrier, outlawing all sexual (incestuous) wishes. Such a powerful repressive barrier can be taken here as a sign of the institution of a new and powerfully narcissistically invested ego ideal. When Freud (1914) first began to discuss narcissism, he connected it with the mechanism of repression. He observed that an individual would repress instinctual impulses and wishes only if they were in conflict with his own ethical ideas and ideals. Such ideals in fact seem to be a necessary prerequisite for repression. Repression would defend against threatening impulses that give rise to anxiety insofar as they violate an ideal which the individual has set up in himself and by which he measures himself. Any content that would not be consistent with and acceptable to the ideal thus becomes repressed. While Ignatius presents this repressive reaction in total and absolute terms, the wise psychologist will find room to ponder whether in fact the repression was as absolute as Ignatius seems to have thought, and whether or not there was room for the return of the repressed.

Our first interest is in trying to understand what kind of psychological transformation was taking place in Iñigo. The first thing we notice in Iñigo's case is that the values inherent in the lives of the saints were first assimilated to the ego-ideal. He saw the heroic deeds of the saints as projections of heroic chivalry to the level of the service of God rather than to the service of a human lord. He bears testimony to this assimilation when he tells that later, after his departure from Loyola, "He continued his way to Montserrat, thinking as usual of the great deeds he was going to do for the love of God. As his mind was filled with the adventures of Amadis of Gaul and such books, thoughts corresponding to these adventures came to his mind" (Vita 17).

Plainly, then, the initial mechanism involved an ego-orientation and perception of an order of values, followed by an assimilation of these perceived values to a pre-existent internalized value-system. However, the impulses he felt stirring within him were still cast in the frame of the phallically narcissistic structure of his preconversion ego-ideal. It is immediately apparent that these fundamental sets of values are so radically different that they could not coexist in the same coherent value-system. The conflict had to come to light sooner or later, and the intensity of the conflict would be determined by the extent to which the respective values had been effectively internalized.

The significant point, then, is that the transformation that was taking place in Iñigo at this time did not consist in the substitution of one value system for another. The value system that had sustained Iñigo over the years and that had stirred him to noble and heroic deeds was too solidly established to collapse without a struggle. Iñigo hints at the beginnings of this conflict when he observes that he began to feel dry and dissatisfied with fantasies of worldly glory, but when he thought of the heroics of the saints he felt cheerful and satisfied. When he speaks of the difference between the two spirits moving him, we can see the conflict developing between the two value-systems. At first Iñigo sought to reconcile these divergent value-systems by assimilating the newly perceived spiritual ones to the older and more familiar system. But as his understanding of the dimensions of the new value-system deepened, he was gradually compelled to face the impossibility of reconciliation. But this realization and understanding did not come in a moment. It took time, and during that time the only partially grasped values inherent in the spiritual orientation were more or less adherent to the older structure of values. With time, they would precipitate the crisis of Manresa and only in the resolution of that crisis would they achieve a degree of autonomy.

So it was that Iñigo de Loyola, as he lay on his bed of convalescence, began to experience the transformation of his own inner values. He found himself shifting from a narrower, narcissistic and even juvenile ideal and set of values, to a broader, higher, nobler and more spiritual orientation. The shift somehow implied that the order of spiritual realities, which his religion had always taught him, gradually entered into a new relation in which there was born in on him the actuality of its existence and the pertinence of its existence to himself. This realization and the process by which it became operative in him required the accepting and internalizing of this segment of reality. This implied a new awareness and a deepened understanding. It implied also an initial and possibly hesitant commitment of himself to the values that slowly became apparent to him.

## CONFLICT OF IDENTIFICATIONS

Taking all these components into account, I would offer the more general hypothesis that in his conversion experience Iñigo abandoned the identification with his phallic, powerful, narcissistic, authoritarian and domineering father and turned to an equally powerful identification with his passive, vulnerable, pious, religious, and idealized mother. I have already argued that the pattern of phallic narcissistic masculine identification was in some degree motivated by the need to counter and deny the unconscious, but decidedly threatening feminine identification. The tension between these internalized configurations in his internal psychic world had been maintained in large part by a powerful narcissistic cathexis. When this structure was shaken by the severe narcissistic trauma of his defeat and injury, the masculine pattern of identification could no longer be maintained adequately; some effective substitute had to be found. No surprise that the narcissistic resolution was purchased at the cost of a feminine identification and the substitution of a masochistically tinged submission to the power and will of God. The reward would have taken the form of divine benevolence and caretaking, replacing the lost phallic narcissistic power with the grandiosity of divine allegiance and favor. As Steiner (1990) comments:

> Turning to omnipotence is a mechanism resorted to only in extreme situations when something has gone radically wrong in the individual's relationship with primary objects. If these objects are destroyed, and the guilt becomes unbearable, self-mutilating attacks on the perceiving ego may be resorted to. The resulting damage, to both the object and the ego, leaves a disability which can only be patched over by means of omnipotence since ordinary human figures are too weak to be of help. The individual is then possessed by monstrous forces which serve as suitable receptacles into which omnipotent parts of the self are projected. . . . When they take on a paranoid grandiosity . . . they seem to function primarily as a defence against disintegration and fragmentation. (p. 234)

We should also remind ourselves that the conversion experience was extended and reworked during the more prolonged crisis in the cave of Manresa, so that these same elements also contributed to his emotional, psychological, and spiritual struggles and conflicts during that period.

## NATURE AND GRACE

These reflections would seem to lead us on to further considerations for our understanding of Ignatian spirituality. The above analysis poses questions about our basic understanding of such deeply significant religious experiences and their implications for the interaction of grace and nature that presumably played such a pervasive role in the spiritual career of Ignatius and is embedded in his spiritual teaching, especially in the *Spiritual Exercises*. We can do little more than remind ourselves that these issues pervade the context of our reflection — their understanding lies beyond our grasp, even though the issues related to the role of grace in Ignatian spirituality cannot be ignored. The psychoanalyst has no interest in the role of divine grace as it might enter into religious experience, and in fact he has nothing to say about it. The relevance of grace and the understanding of its place in the causality underlying such experiences is matter for theological reflection (Meissner 1986).

The psychoanalyst or any psychologist who studies religious experience is bound by the limitations of his methodology. Within those limits he can reach little more than tentative hypotheses that, if they can entertain a measure of validity, can offer some meaningful basis for an emerging dialogue with a more specifically theological frame of reference. If we can accept the above analysis and interpretation as one possible and valid assessment of the motivational structure of Iñigo de Loyola's conversion experience, we are left to ponder what questions it might raise for the further exploration of the relationship and interaction between grace and the workings of intrapsychic dynamics and processes? Can we think of God's efficacious grace as working its effects of psychic transformation unilaterally, independently and regardless of the natural psychic substratum? Or does it make more sense to think in terms of the interplay of the initiatives of grace with extant levels of psychic structure and motivation, both conscious and unconscious?

The case of Iñigo de Loyola as framed here would seem to argue to the latter conclusion. If so it would seem to open the door to a whole realm of theological reflection that demands integration of psychic realities and dynamic processes as integral to its understanding of the relationship between God and man.

# CHAPTER III

# THE PILGRIM AND STUDENT YEARS

## Introduction

Tracking Iñigo along the stages of his journey would involve us in a myriad of details with their own burden of interest and implication. But in the interest of keeping the focus on Iñigo's psychology and its relevance for the understanding of his spirituality, economy and selection are the order of the day.[1]

## The Pilgrim

After leaving Loyola, Iñigo found his way to the cave at Manresa where he spent the next ten months and underwent a series of profound spiritual experiences that extended the work of his conversion. We will return to that part of the story later.[2] He finally bade farewell to Manresa and the cave in mid-February 1523, and made his way to Barcelona and the home of Inez Pascual, who had befriended him in Manresa. He traveled on foot with none but the barest necessities — he carried no money or food, but in the spirit of the true pilgrim begged his way, constantly praying, performing penances, and visiting churches. He was obsessed with the idea that he should go to Jerusalem and there follow in the footsteps of Jesus, preaching and ministering to the poor and unfortunate. He sought to find passage to Italy and from there hoped to find a way to get to the Holy Land. The Pascuals did what they could to help him, but he refused to take any alms with him.

[1] I will follow the order of events I have previously traced in my study of Ignatius' psychology (Meissner 1992b). Readers who are interested in greater detail or depth are encouraged to look there — needless to say many of the specifics are obtainable in any of the excellent available biographies. The most representative biographies in English are Dudon (1949), Brodrick (1956), and Dalmases (1985). Unfortunately none of these studies, despite their respective merits, has much to say about Ignatius' personality or psychology.

[2] See chapter VI below.

He finally made his way to Rome, and gained permission from Adrian VI, the reigning pontiff, to travel to Jerusalem, despite the risks from the Turkish menace. The Holy Land was at that time in the hands of the Turks, and the risks of capture or worse were considerable. Apostolic blessing in hand, he made his way to Venice on foot, where he received the approval of the Doge and an order for free passage for his journey. He shipped out on the *Negrona*, a merchant vessel, with a group of other pilgrims, on 14 July 1523. After a perilous and storm tossed voyage, they finally landed at Jaffa on 25 August. Throughout the voyage, Iñigo continued to experience visions of Our Lord who consoled and strengthened him, along with other mystical experiences.

Once landed, he moved on to Jerusalem, lodging with the Franciscans charged with care of the holy places. Iñigo made the rounds of the places of Christ's life and passion with the greatest devotion and ecstatic transport. But he soon ran into difficulties. Tensions were increased by the presence of a contingent of Turkish cavalry, so that keeping tourists off the streets was advisable. Iñigo did not react well to the confinement. His purpose was not simply to visit the holy shrines, but to live and work there permanently in the service of souls. The Franciscan superior would not listen to his objections. From the Guardian's perspective, Iñigo's request was impractical and dangerous. The matter was referred to the Provincial, who tried to dissuade Iñigo. But the intransigent Basque would not take No for an answer. Only when the Provincial informed him that he had authority directly from the Holy See and refusal carried the penalty of excommunication, did Iñigo accept the verdict.

Despite the prohibitions, Iñigo could not restrain his desire to visit for a final time certain holy spots, especially the Garden of Olives. He contrived to sneak out and visit the garden, bribing the guards to let him in. When his absence was detected, the Franciscans were greatly upset and searched out the miscreant, dragging him back to the monastery by force. To Iñigo, nothing mattered — he was in an ecstasy, seeing the figure of Christ before him until they reached the monastery.

The episode tells us something about the character of this devoted pilgrim. The intensity of his devotion and the degree of determination with which he pursued his aims are striking. His fanaticism would brook no obstacle and would hardly count the cost to achieve his aims — even the threat of prison and death could not deter him. His obstinacy in the face of the Provincial's orders is also impressive. He would not yield until faced with a definitive and ultimate authority. We shall recognize the same quality in other confrontations with authority in the course of his pilgrim's way.

The journey back to Italy was long and perilous. The pilgrims were imprisoned for a time, then embarked on a storm-tossed voyage in which they were driven off course, battered by high winds and waves and nearly capsized in one of the most severe winters on the Mediterrenean in memory. When the little ship made port at Parenzo on 12 January 1524, they had been on the water for three-and-a-half months.

## BARCELONA, ALCALA, AND SALAMANCA

Upon returning to Barcelona, Iñigo determined that his lack of education and especially his ignorance of theology was a hindrance to his ability to work effectively for the good of souls. The first step in obtaining an education was to begin the study of Latin. His good friend and benefactor, Isabel Roser, arranged for him to study privately with Jeronimo Ardevol, a master of the University of Barcelona. It was a courageous step for a man of thirty-three to undertake the studies of a schoolboy, but Iñigo plunged in with his usual determination.

In the meanwhile, he continued his usual routine of prayer and penance, fasting, begging his food in the streets, catechizing children, and tending the needs of the poor and sick. It was not long before the well-to-do ladies of Barcelona came to know this noble beggar and assisted him with alms and donations of food and clothing which he distributed to the needy. He seemed tireless in his zeal to do good, and his mortifications were continual and unrelenting. Continuing such activities created difficulties in his efforts to study, since severe penances, fasting, and sleepless nights do not provide the best circumstances for studious application. But he kept on.

He remained in Barcelona for two years — praying, fasting, doing penances, begging, doing good works, and studying his grammar. Finally, Ardevol advised him that it was time to move on to the next level, so he made his way to Alcala where the great university founded by Cardinal Ximenes de Cisneros in 1508 was flourishing. In Alcala, Iñigo's efforts to pursue his studies were less than successful. He enrolled in courses in a haphazard and unsystematic fashion, without any direction or organization. He was eager to learn as much as he could in as short a time as possible, as though simply attending lectures was sufficient to gain the knowledge he sought for his mission.

He also continued his apostolic efforts together with the three companions who had accompanied him from Barcelona. They taught catechism and preached, and adopted a common rough wool garb, gradually becoming known as "the Graycoats." But as their notoriety grew, they fell increasingly under suspicion by the inquisitors in Toledo. Some of what they were teaching was probably based on Iñigo's notes on the *Spiritual Exercises* he had begun to formulate at Manresa. In any case, two inquisitors came from Toledo to subject his teaching to scrutiny. The inquisitors were suspicious that his doctrine was connected with an heretical sect known as the *Alumbrados* or *Illuminati*, whose heretical propositions had been condemned in September 1526. Attacks were launched by certain Spanish theologians, especially Melchior Cano and Tomas Pedroche, who found the *Exercises* too mystical, contemplative and affective, insufficiently ascetical and rational, too much attuned to subjective experience and divine illumination — echoes of the doctrine of the heretical Free Spirit movement and the Alumbrados. The judges found nothing to condemn in the teaching of the Graycoats, but ordered them to stop wearing their characteristic garb, since they were not religious (Vita 58). This was Iñigo's first brush with the Inquisition and would not be his last. He accepted the decision of the judges, but characteristically argued his case to good effect (Vita 59). Further suspicions arose regarding "secret meetings" with women, presumably in connection with the Spiritual Exercises, but further investigation in March 1527 came to naught.

But that was not the end of it. In April he was again summoned by the Inquisition, and this time put in prison where he remained for forty-two days. At the end of it, he was forbidden to teach or to speak on matters of faith under pain of excommunication. His work in Alcala was finished. The suspicions that he was connected with the *Alumbrados* was not ill founded. Later investigations (Longhurst 1957; de Vries 1971) indicate that a number of Iñigo's contacts in Alcala were known to have affiliations with them, suggesting that some of the *Illuminati* might have found some appeal in Iñigo's teaching.  Hysterical fainting spells and ecstasies among some of his female adherents may also have stirred suspicions. In addition Iñigo's lack of education and the fact that he based his teaching on his own experience rather than from books would have raised questions, since the *illuminati* appealed to the voice of the Spirit within them rather than to scripture or theology (de Vries 1971).

Since the decree of the court was limited to the jurisdiction of the Toledo archdiocese, Iñigo moved on to Salamanca, where the

University of Salamanca was at the height of its reputation as one of the leading centers of learning in Europe. Iñigo arrived there in July 1527, and his timing could not have been worse. The city was engulfed by controversy over the teachings of Erasmus and northern humanism. Within a matter of weeks, Iñigo was again interrogated and imprisoned (Vita 64-70). Again the shadow of the *alumbrados* had fallen across his path, and once again he met the same verdict — that no fault was found in his teaching, but he was forbidden to teach or conduct the Spiritual Exercises. Further training in theology had become mandatory — but where? The best school of theology in Europe was at the University of Paris. After consultation with his friends in Barcelona, he decided that to Paris he would go. Despite warnings about the difficulties, particularly the hostile tensions between the French and the Spanish, Iñigo set out for Paris and arrived there on 2 February 1528 (Vita 71-4).

## PARIS[3]

Iñigo first matriculated at the notorious College de Montaigue, where he remained about a year studying grammar. He lived in the hospital of St. James and tried to beg alms to support himself. His lack of success led him to seek support among the wealthy Spanish merchants in Bruges, and after several visits gained enough generous assistance to allow him to pursue his studies without undue anxiety about money. He transferred to the College de Sainte Barbe in October 1529 where he continued his studies with great diligence and spartan discipline. The curriculum included the study of Aristotle and scholastic philosophy. He moved into crowded quarters with three others — Juan de Pena was a professor in the college and Iñigo's tutor, Peter Faber was a Savoyard, and Francis Xavier, from Navarre, had obtained his doctor's biretta and was a Regent of Philosophy in the College de Beauvais. Faber and Xavier fell under Iñigo's spell — he persuaded Faber to undergo the Spiritual Exercises early in 1534, and the month of prayer, penance, and spiritual reflection turned the gentle Savoyard into a saint. Xavier was tougher stuff. He was cut from the same cloth as Iñigo himself — proud and vain, the ambitious son of a noble family of Navarre, his head filled with dreams of worldly glory, not a little grandiose. But he was in the end no match for the relentless Basque. He too soon made the Spiritual Exercises with much the same result. In 1533, they were joined by Diego Laynez and Alfonso Salmeron, recent graduates of Alcala, and soon after Nicho-

[3] A good brief account of Ignatius' Paris years can be found in Ravier (1992).

las Bobadilla and then Simon Rodriguez. They all made the Spiritual Exercises and joined the little group forming around Iñigo at St. Barbe.

Iñigo took his bachelor's examination and passed it in January 1532. His name appears for the first time on the university records as "Ignatius of Loyola." On 13 March 1533, he received the licentiate in philosophy and finally the degree of Master of Philosophy in March 1535. During this time he continued penances, mortifications and fasting to the detriment of his health. Severe attacks of abdominal pain incapacitated him for days at a time and all remedies proved fruitless (Vita 84). He had continued his efforts to study theology with the Dominican fathers at the Rue Saint-Jacques, reputed for the training of future teachers of theology. But his health was an increasing concern.

Under his inspiration, the group of companions had formed a common resolve — to consecrate themselves to the service of God and to labor for the salvation of souls, particularly to work in Palestine for the conversion of the infidel. They decided to live a common life together and to vow themselves to evangelical poverty and chastity. They gathered in the chapel of St. Denis on Montmartre on the feast of the Assumption 1534. Faber, the only priest, offered the mass and together the six companions pronounced their vows.

The doctors had urged Ignatius to return to his native land for the sake of his health. So, in April 1535, Ignatius decided to return to Spain. The companions agreed that they would leave Paris in January 1537 and rejoin Ignatius in Venice, and from there embark for Jerusalem. Ignatius' time in Paris was at an end. He turned his face toward the Basque country where his pilgrimage had begun.

His Paris sojourn had not been without profit. He had completed his bachelor and master's degrees, and enough theology to qualify for ordination. One of the doctors of theology, after undergoing the Exercises, remarked that he had never heard anyone speak of theological matters with such mastery and reverence (H. Rahner 1968).[4]

## Azpeitia

Ignatius covered the 450 miles from Paris to Azpeitia in about a month, arriving on 30 April 1535. He took up residence in little

[4] Out of about 100 candidates for the master's degree in 1533, Ignatius ranked 30th. In 1530, Faber had ranked 24th and Xavier 22nd. Laynez would later comment: "Although he had more difficulty in study than the others, nevertheless he was so diligent that he made as much progress, *ceteris paribus*, as his companions attaining to an honest average of knowledge" (FN I, 100-1; cited in Clancy (1976), p. 39).

Hospital of the Magdalena outside the town. He was unquestionably a center of local curiosity — a son of the Loyolas now returned as a Master of the University of Paris, but carrying on like a poor beggar and holy man. It did not take long for curiosity to turn to wonder and amazement. The time Ignatius spent in his home town was a saga of apostolic accomplishment and conversion. He turned quickly to the work of converting sinners and expunging evil practices. His teaching and preaching drew large crowds, so that the numbers could not be contained in the little church. As was his custom, he begged for food and alms at the doors of relatives and neighbors — to the great consternation of his brother. But Martin Garcia's complaints fell on deaf ears. The pilgrim could not be deterred from his care of the sick and needy (Vita 88-9).

The pilgrim also turned his attention to obvious abuses that cried out for reform. He used his influence to set up regulations controlling gambling; he attacked the practice of concubines by the local clergy, persuading the governor to pass a law instituting public punishment for the practice; he saw to it that regular provisions were made for the care of the poor; and he even arranged to have the church bells rung three times daily for the angelus. His zeal for reform even affected his family. He persuaded his brother to bring an end to the scandalous controversy over the rights of the Loyolas over the convent church, so that before he left he could affix his signature to the official document that put an end to this bitter quarrel that had lasted for over thirty years.

The list of reforms was extensive, but the pilgrim had other matters on his mind. He finally left the land of his ancestors, never to return — but he left behind him a legend of good works and the reputation of great sanctity. But destiny called him on — toward Venice and the mission to Jerusalem.

## VENICE

When Ignatius finally arrived in Venice it was toward the end of 1535. He spent the ensuing year alone, devoting himself to theological study, prayer, penances, and his usual apostolic efforts. This consisted primarily in giving the Spiritual Exercises, in the process of which his influence began to reach influential persons. His friends and benefactors provided for him generously, especially the ever faithful Isabel Roser and others like Jaime Cazador, a future bishop of Barcelona. Spiritually his prayer was filled with great consolations and graces, lifting his soul to the heights of mystical ecstasy and rapture. If this was a time of good works and the fullness of grace, it was also not without difficulties and trials. The usual suspicions and charges that dogged his teaching arose again, accusations of heresy, again unsubstantiated (Vita 93).

This was also the time of a major miscalculation that would return to haunt him in his years in Rome. He wrote to Gian Pietro Carafa, the founder of the Theatines, criticizing their mode of life and apostolic activities. The details are complicated and the issues not altogether clear, but the upshot was that Ignatius earned the enmity of the powerful cardinal who was to become Pope Paul IV (Meissner 1992b). Carafa's hostility and opposition did not make matters easier for the fledgling Society when he ascended the papal throne.

Finally, on 8 January 1537, the companions arrived from Paris after a long and difficult journey. In the interim Claude LeJay, Paschase Broet and Jean Codure had joined the group. Ignatius was able to present Diego de Hocez and the Eguia brothers as new recruits. Their goal was Jerusalem, so they decided to prepare themselves and wait for the opportunity to undertake the journey. While they waited, they carried on a variety of apostolic works in hospitals. But the prospects for a pilgrimage to Jerusalem were far from bright, and grew dimmer with each passing day. The Turkish menace made any such venture perilous in the extreme.

During Lent, they decided to seek the blessing of the Holy Father for their mission and gain his approval for holy orders. Because of the cloud of suspicion over Ignatius' head and possibly also because of the opposition of Carafa, the companions went to Rome without him. Their mission was eminently successful; Paul III had granted all their requests and they returned to Venice with good tidings for Ignatius. But the uncertainty of the Jerusalem mission persisted. They dispersed to various towns to carry on their charitable efforts. Ignatius, together with Faber and Laynez, went to Vincenza, where he would later recall "many supernatural visions and much ordinary consolation" (Vita 95)

## ROME

Finally in November 1537, Ignatius and his companions made their way toward Rome. A few miles outside the city, at the little chapel of La Storta, Ignatius experienced one of the most powerful and influential mystical illuminations of his life. In his vision, the Father and Christ, carrying his cross, appeared to him. The Father said to Christ, "I wish that thou take him for thy servant," to which Christ replied to Ignatius, "I wish that you be my servant." The Father then added, "And I will be propitious to you at Rome." We will return to this event later in our discussion of Ignatius' mystical experience, but the message could hardly have been more encouraging and supportive to Ignatius as he faced the uncertainties and anxieties that lie ahead of him — he even confessed to Laynez he feared crucifixion in Rome, like the apostle Peter before him.

They gained an audience with His Holiness Paul III, who told them that Rome would have to be their Jerusalem. He assigned the companions to various apostolic works. Ignatius began giving the Spiritual Exercises to influential individuals. Dr. Ortiz, whom he had known in Paris, the Spanish ambassador, made the Exercises and became a powerful friend and protector. Their favorable reception made it possible for the Iniguists, as they were known, to assemble in a little house put at their disposal at the end of Lent 1538. But their path was hardly smooth. Accusations and controversy over Ignatius' teaching again surfaced. With his familiar determination and decisiveness, Ignatius launched a counterattack — presenting the governor with evidence refuting his accusers, demanding an official hearing and judgment, then calling for letters of approbation and support from all dioceses where he and his companions had worked. He even confronted Paul and demanded an official declaration refuting the false charges.

## Founding a Society

The failure of the Jerusalem mission left the companions in a quandry. When they gathered at Easter 1539, they were uncertain what course to follow. They had not thought of forming a religious congregation, but were dedicated to the service of God. During their deliberations of the Lent, the idea emerged of forming themselves into a religious order and to seek papal approval. They concluded:

> God in his mercy graciously willed to assemble and to unite us, although we were weak and strangers to each other by virtue of nationality and mind. It is not up to us to break up that which God has united, but we must rather affirm and stabilize this unity by drawing closer into a single body, each having responsibility and understanding of the other; for courage itself when it is concentrated has more vigor and strength to accomplish all sorts of good but difficult deeds than when it is divided. (Cited in Ravier 1987, p. 84)

The difficult question was whether to bind themselves by a vow of obedience to a religious superior. After lengthy deliberations, they decided on 3 May 1539 to undertake vows of obedience to the Pope and to place themselves under a religious superior. Their decisions were included in a slender document, probably drawn up by Ignatius, setting forth the details of the projected order that would be presented to the Pope. This document has become known to history as the *Deliberatio primorum patrum*; it would provide the basis of the "Formula of the Institute" on which the *Constitutions of the Society of Jesus* are based. The document was handed to Cardinal Contarini for presentation to His Holiness. After months of close examination and intrigues of curial maneuvering, Paul III finally fixed his signature to the bull, *Regimini militantis ecclesiae*, in the Palace of St. Mark on 27 September 1540. The Society of Jesus thus became a reality.

## ELECTION OF A GENERAL

The next critical question was whom to elect as the Superior General of the new order. Ignatius had been the central figure of the group of companions from the beginning and was the obvious choice. Deliberations for setting up rules to govern the new order began in March 1541 — forty-nine points were approved by all. When the vote for the General was taken, to no one's surprise the unanimous choice was Ignatius. But the matter was not that easy. Ignatius demurred and rejected the decision. He sought another extended discussion and another vote — the result was the same. He sought further delay and the advice of his confessor. After three more days and a general confession, the good Franciscan told him that to refuse would be resisting the grace of the Holy Spirit. Still unconvinced, Ignatius asked the confessor to pray over the matter for three more days and then put his decision in writing. Only then he did he yield to the verdict.

Ignatius' maneuvering in this regard peaks the curiosity of the psychoanalyst and may suggest something further about Ignatius' psychology. Whatever tentative conclusions we might draw can only be offered with the caution that the questions it poses are not to be taken as answers — the gap between hypothesis and fact looms large here. Nonetheless, as we watch Ignatius back off, delay, and maneuver to escape the apparent sentence passed on him by his brothers, are we witnessing an exercise in saintly humility, seeking every possible means to escape preferment, any recognition by his fellow men? Possibly. But might we also be seeing an exercise in conflict, ambivalence, or the struggle with narcissistic residues in the form of conflicts over ambition and omnipotence? In the vacuum of certainty, it falls to the theologian to emphasize the aspects of saintliness and humility permeated by grace. It falls to the psychoanalyst to play devil's advocate and propose the venal yet psychologically meaningful aspects of the human drama of this peculiar behavior of our hero.

Might Ignatius have been ambivalent about assuming the role of general? There can be little doubt that the responsibility was potentially awesome, especially if the Society were to grow in numbers and influence. The general would inevitably become a powerful and important figure. Ignatius had surrendered his youthful ambitions of power and glory — or had he? As a young man, he had dreamed of conquest, military glory, fame, success. When those hopes were shattered at Pamplona, he had found other dreams to replace them — this time dreams of saintly heroics, of self-conquest, self-denial, and the glory of saintly sacrifice. The office of General to which he had been elected was a position of power and command. Was Ignatius torn between his denied and repressed wishes for power and influence on one side and the desire for saintly self-denial and humble service on the other?

And what of the narcissism that seems to surface again and again in the character of Ignatius? He has told us too many times that he continues to struggle with sinful and worldly desires. Perhaps the narcissistic wishes were too pervasive, too insistent. On the road to Rome, in an ecstasy of wish-fulfillment, God the Father and Christ the Son appeared to him in his hour of doubt and anxious fear, to reassure him that they would support and sustain him in Rome. What greater testimony to the fulfillment of his spiritual ego ideal? What better sign of divine favor and selection, the nearly unalloyed gratification of narcissistic impulses and desires, than to receive such divine favor? The narcissistic elements here are overpowering — sublimated, spiritualized, even transcendental — but narcissistic nonetheless. Could it be that the wish to be to be chosen as a spiritual hero, the vessel of divine grace and blessing, still occupied a corner of his soul?

The long journey from his bed of pain and his conversion experience at Loyola to Rome and the burdens of establishing and nurturing a new religious order had led Ignatius through many difficulties and trials. But throughout we are confronted with the mettle of the man. Again and again we can see his determination, his courage, his unwillingness to let any obstacle stand in his way, his fervor, the intensity of his devotion and dedication — the relentless pursuit of perfection. He had set his mind and heart on becoming one of God's heroes, of scaling the mountain of Christian perfection and doing great deeds in the name of his Lord and Master, Jesus Christ.

To keep the psychoanalytic perspective in place, I would suggest that there is continuity and coherence in terms of underlying unconscious layers of motivation that remain operative and determinative at every step along the way. The narcissistic ego ideal that drove him to the death-defying exploits on the ramparts of Pamplona was not altogether destroyed by the trauma inflicted by the French cannonball. That same ideal found a way to survive — transformed, sublimated, translated from the language of worldly exploits and the quest for glory into the language of self-denial, self-sacrifice, saintly virtue and mortification befitting a holy man of God — one of the saints in the image of Francis, Dominic and the other heroes of God who became his models and guides to virtue. But these narcissistic themes carried with them their burden of conflict and the depressive undercurrent that was such a marked aspect of Ignatius' personality structure. These conflicts could not be left behind, forgotten, or ignored. They remained with him and dogged his steps at every point along the journey from Loyola to Rome. He had constantly to struggle against them, constantly to mortify his desires and wage an unremitting struggle against them. The turmoil created by his election as General may have reflected this unconsciously rooted fixation. One salient point is that to a large extent we can surmise that these desires were cast in narcissistic terms, and that this preoccupation of Ignatius' inner world had a great deal to do with determining the style of his spirituality and the content of his spiritual doctrine.

# CHAPTER IV

# GENERAL OF THE SOCIETY OF JESUS

## The Scene

Hardly had the ink on the papal documents approving the new Society of Jesus dried and the crucial election of the general been accomplished when Ignatius and his companions moved into a dilapidated house near the church of Santa Maria della Strada. The house was small but large enough to begin their apostolic work. The chapel and some neighboring houses were soon added, so that gradually it evolved into the center of the Society of Jesus in Rome. It included the little room Ignatius lived in for the next fifteen years, where he organized and directed the work of the Society, where he wrote the *Constitutions*, and where he was to die. "In fact," as Ravier (1987) puts it, Ignatius " would scarcely ever leave this place during the fifteen years of his generalship, but from the heart of his little room, he would follow the flight of his sons on the roads of the world, he would inspire them in their missionary zeal, sustain them in their battles. There, success and failure, sorrows and joys, good news and bad would blend; hundreds of companions would pass through there to be trained or to work" (p. 11).

Ignatius became director of an apostolic and intellectual venture global in scope that involved him in details of the work of the Society too numerous to count. The mission of the Society was to go to any corner of the world where the Vicar of Christ might send them. The house of La Strada became the headquarters for all the Society's endeavors, including the training of novices under the supervision of Ignatius.

## Governing

As the years passed, the work of the Society grew by leaps and bounds. Missionary beachheads and colleges were established in all parts of the globe, and the dealings with the papal court, with kings, bishops, and nobility of all ranks, and with Christians of all walks of life and all levels of society reflected the scope and complexity of the mission (Bertrand 1985). Ignatius became daily more and more absorbed in the details of governing this unwieldy organization. The training and spiritual direction of the novices demanded much of his attention. Increasingly his efforts were taken up by the essential task of writing the *Constitutions*, which were to provide the guiding norms for governance of the Society and would form his legacy for generations to come. Writing the *Constitutions* became a major purpose and burden of his generalate. He once told Nadal that "I have asked God to grant me three graces before I die; in the first place the confirmation of the Society of Jesus by the Holy See, secondly a similar approval of the *Spiritual Exercises*, and thirdly that I might be able to write down the Constitutions" (FN I, 351; cited in Clancy 1976, p. 62).

It became clear, not only to Ignatius but to others, that the weight of the general's office was excessively burdensome and the task too complex for one man. Ignatius' health had not been robust for many years, and under the burdens of his office it grew worse. Something had to be done. In March 1547, Juan de Polanco was appointed Secretary of the Society. Ignatius could not have made a better choice. Polanco turned out to be a superb administrator and organizer, and as Secretary, he remained unobtrusive but extremely effective. He was gifted with intelligence and sensitivity, a capacity for work, and a remarkable ability to understand the mind and heart of Ignatius, and to make his efforts complement those of Ignatius in an extraordinarily effective manner. They would work closely together until Ignatius' death.

Polanco immediately set about reorganizing the vast correspondence that Ignatius carried on with companions throughout the world. The task took years to complete. Polanco also began to classify the material required for the writing of the *Constitutions* (de Aldama 1973). He also devoted his efforts to organizing archives for the Society, and, on the basis of this material, wrote his own *Chronicon*, an invaluable account of the early years of the Society under Ignatius.

If Polanco's efforts succeeded in lifting much of the burden from Ignatius' shoulders, the weight that remained was considerable. Ignatius had thoughts of resigning — he may have hinted as much in a letter to Laynez. His health would have been reason enough. In fact, in 1551, he made a formal attempt to resign. On 30 January, he presented a gathering of the professed, who had met to discuss the recently finished *Constitutions*, with a letter of resignation. I have speculated on the extent to which this attempt to resign might have reflected underlying conflicts over his role as superior and authority figure (Meissner 1992b), but even granting this possibility, the move was far from capricious. Toward the end of 1550 Ignatius' health had deteriorated to the point that there was fear for his survival. Prudence dictated that a younger, healthier, and less moribund specimen assume such a responsible position. But the fathers declared that no one else should hold the office of General as long as Ignatius was still breathing. The layers of determination are no doubt multiple, but Ignatius' reluctant manner calls to mind his response to his original election. As I have suggested, underlying conflicts over the having and exercising of power and authority, which may have further implications in our consideration of his views on obedience, doubtless played a part. In any case, Ignatius accepted the decision without complaint, and the next day immersed himself once again in the arduous tasks of his office — a labor not to be interrupted until his death five years later.

## FATHER GENERAL

The more we come to know of the details of Ignatius' work as general, the more remarkable is the picture we gain of his personality and character. He was beyond question charismatic — he attracted men to his cause and edified and inspired them. His character was Basque to the core — headstrong, obstinate, passionate, stern, taciturn, but even so at times charming and playful. He was a man of great gifts and obvious limitations. He could be stern and demanding at one moment and kind and gracious at the next — and the transition was often abrupt, leaving his listeners confused and puzzled. As the Society grew, he was confronted by relationships with figures in political and ecclesiastical authority, by matters of finances, diplomacy, difficult negotiations that called the skills of the old courtier into play in many ways. The whole was pervaded by his spiritual presence — his devotion, his singlemindedness to do God's work, his unfailing charity, and his almost total self-abnegation.

Ignatius was revered as a saint by those around him, but his manner was simple and unpretentious. He exercised special — almost maternal — concern for those who were ill or depressed. He seems to have been supportive and reassuring to his novices. To one young novice troubled by feelings of guilt and unworthiness, he recounted the sins of his youth, weeping all the while. He tailored the regimen to the individual needs of his subjects. One novice from a noble family found manual work in public humiliating, so Ignatius put him to work inside the house. Ribadeneyra, later to be his first biographer, impishly imitated the limp behind his back. Ignatius found out and told the miscreant to choose his own penance. The young wag suggested a day off for everyone in the house, and so it was. There was kindness and consideration along with obdurate severity.

His companions, to a man, remarked on his magnanimity, his spiritual goodness, and his persistence in important causes. Nadal particularly remarked on his "*excelente grandeza de alma y una vehemente apetencia del honor y de la gloria*," excellent greatness of soul and a vehement desire for honor and glory (FN II, 62; my translation). It seems that his companions were not blind to the narcissistic aspects of Ignatius' character, but they were also deeply impressed by his self-possession and the prudent reflection, seemingly regulating all his actions by the criteria of spiritual discernment (of which he had become a master) and the service of God (Nicolau 1957). Ganss (1970) summarized some of his style:

> By character and temperament he was a born leader. He loved people and was ever eager to converse with them, assuredly in the hope of drawing spiritual fruit. He won the affection of the followers whom he inspired and whose opinions he constantly sought before he issued commands. Thus he made them feel that they were persons as well as a part of an organization in which their opinions were valued. He made much of discussion between a superior and subjects, whom he expected to be respectfully but completely frank and open. But when the consultation was done, the superior was to be the one to make the decision. Sometimes he has been pictured as a stern martinet pointing ever to rules. However, if that had been his character, or if he had not been spontaneous and animated in conversation, it is hard to see how he could have inspired the affection which his followers so manifestly had for him. Father Jerome Nadal, who knew him so intimately, said that those who were in his room were always cheerful and laughing. (pp. 26-27)

His unwavering determination, once he had decided on a course of action, was legendary. His fortitude and persistence in the face of adversity were accompanied by an indomitable energy (Nicolau 1957). On one occasion he sat in the waiting room of one of the cardinals for fourteen hours, until finally the cardinal received him (FN IV, 899; cited in Becher 1977). His disposition seems to have been generally amiable and courteous, but he could also be harsh and uncompromising. Many of those who worked most closely with him felt the sting of his lash — Laynez, Nadal, Polanco, even da Camara. Polanco complained that in the nine years he served as Ignatius' secretary he scarcely heard a good word. Nadal was often so harshly rebuked that he could hardly keep from crying; Laynez was to moan to Ribadeneyra, "What have I done against the Society that this saint treats me this way?" (FN III, 690).

His desire to win souls for God was a consuming passion. He wrote to Jacqueline de Croy that God, "to whom all things, even our inmost hearts, are known, knows what desires of the salvation and progress of souls he has given to me" (Epistolae II, 303; cited in Rahner 1960, p. 160). His zeal for souls was a consuming passion — were he to be stopped as he led one of the courtesans of Rome to the House of St. Martha he had set up for their protection, and someone suggest that the conversion was not lasting and hardly worth the effort, he would have replied: "And if with all my trouble and care I could persuade only one single person to refrain from sin for one night for the sake of my Lord Jesus Christ, then I would stop at nothing that for this time at least she might not offend God — even if I knew that she would afterwards fall back into her old vice" (Scripta I, 355-356; cited in Wulf 1977).

Ignatius seemed to flourish in the penumbra of respectability. In his characteristic style, he would carry on determinedly in the face of disapproval, criticism, and against the wishes of powerful figures. His ministry to the prostitutes of Rome was considered scandalous by many and was publicly condemned. This and other of Ignatius' activities did not sit well with the conservative cardinals and certainly did not conform to Paul IV's view of what was proper for religious. Carafa's eighty-year-old sister, Beatrice, threw one of the Jesuits out of her house for fear he might ruin her reputation. But despite financial hardships and political difficulties, the apostolic work of the Society prospered; La Strada, the Roman College, and the German College, continued to flourish. Young candidates eagerly filled places in the novitiate as soon as they became available (Ravier 1987).

## The General at Work

One of the most striking aspects of Ignatius' career as general was his immense correspondence. The letters and instructions from 1524 to 1556 number nearly seven thousand documents. Ribadeneyra described the painstaking care Ignatius exercised on this correspondence, especially in the many letters to important personages about matters of significance. Every letter was written, corrected, and rewritten, pored over with great care and thought, every word examined. He would often cross out and correct sections, even making several copies. As far as he was concerned, the time and effort expended in this work was well worth it (FN II, 494). In the letters he constantly bent every effort to instruct, organize, and consolidate the work of the Society in the far corners of the globe. He seemed indefatigable, despite his chronic illness and the long hours of mystical absorption. He was anxious, even obsessed, with passing on to his sons the spirit of prayer and sacrifice that he himself had won through the grace of God with such pain and fortitude in a lifetime of prayer and penance. In his letters he exhorted, encouraged, inspired, directed, scolded, and punished.

The record is impressive, if not brilliant. Beyond the external achievements, there was also a measure of charisma. The psychic world in which Ignatius lived and worked was never far removed from the cave of Manresa and the spirit of the *Exercises*, which permeated every aspect of his life and thought. We will have the opportunity later to judge the extent to which this spirit was distilled onto the pages of the *Constitutions*.[1] There was a spirit of vitality and mission — the sense that the hand of God was guiding Ignatius and the Society, using them as an instrument to restore the spirit of the primitive church to the world. As Ravier puts it: "The arm of God — the Dextera Excelsi, or the *Verbi Dei energia* to use the language of Polanco — was perceptible to the whole generation of companions. They had a very strong feeling of disproportion between acts and effects, especially the spiritual effects of their acts: between what they did and the results of what they did, the power of God intervened. A very apostolic, very Pauline feeling: it was in weakness that the force of the spirit was revealed" (1987, p. 322). It was as though the charisma — the *energia* — of Ignatius had been communicated to his companions, so that the rich rewards of their labors became for them a sign of divine favor. Ignatius, in his prudent discernment, often found it necessary to curb the understandable spiritual pride and enthusiasm of some of his sons.

These last fifteen years of Ignatius' life were spent mostly within the confines of the modest house of La Strada. At the same time, the Society he founded and governed was growing by leaps and bounds and had become a vital force in Christendom, both in Europe and in the far-flung missionary lands of the globe. At the the center of this vast organization sat Ignatius, guiding, directing, exhorting, counseling, and above all praying. Ravier (1987) describes the scene: "It is a simple man who lives here; there is a tiny room where he works and sleeps; he takes his meals in a neighboring room, very often he has as

[1] See chapters XVIII, XIX and XX below.

guests a few companions from whom he likes to get advice on current concerns, or, more rarely, "people from outside"; whoever the guests may be, the meal is frugal; a third room serves him as a chapel: here he celebrates Mass or merely attends, according to the physician's orders; in the fourth room sleeps the Brother who is at his service. A modest life, poor without outward glamor, without pretense, and monotonous" (p. 377).

His most noteworthy characteristic, above all others, was his life of prayer. It was prayer of intense devotion, of mystical intensity — prayer for the work of the Society, for the missions he and his companions were undertaking for the glory of God, prayer for strength and courage for his sons to persevere in the difficult paths they had chosen, prayer that his decisions and choices would be governed by God's will and the good of God's children. He took upon himself the onerous task of shaping the Society according to the spirit that had prevailed among the first companions before 1539. His mode of governing, his method of instructing and training the novices, the tasks and apostolic missions he undertook, the endless stream of letters and instructions — all were directed to keeping this spirit alive as the Society grew and became more diverse and complex.

## Shortcomings

Yet the record is not unblemished; Ignatius had failures and disappointments along with successes. His financial management was an aspect of Ignatius' administration that was not only disconcerting to his supporters but skirted disaster. He was chronically up to his ears in debt; he had to learn the bitter lesson that the poverty that frees the spirit in individual terms, can become a burden and an impediment for a community and an institution. Many of the houses of the Society had no stable revenue but were dependent on the good will of individual cardinals, bishops, or princes. The financial stability of La Strada itself depended on the generosity of Pietro Codacio; his death in December 1549 was a near disaster for the house. The Roman College opened its doors in January 1551 with the financial support of Francis Borgia, then Duke of Gandia. This generous support continued as long as Francis had control of his resources, but when he renounced them to enter the Society, the promised revenues were no longer forthcoming, and this heavy debt had to be assumed by La Strada. The German College was founded in 1552 with the promise of support from the King of the Romans Ferdinand I and some cardinals, but they soon found it convenient to ignore their promises. Julius III had promised assistance but the arrangements could not be completed before his death; prospects for continuing papal support were complicated by Ignatius' difficulties with Paul IV — whatever good intentions Carafa might have had were frustrated by the drain on the papal treasury from the war with Spain. From 1551 to 1556 the Roman houses were constantly in debt, and Ignatius had to exploit the Society's every resource to beg money for their support.

This was undoubtedly another dimension of the increasing tension Ignatius experienced between the religious ideals of the pilgrim and the practical functions and obligations of the Superior General. He had struggled arduously in his own mind and heart to overcome all attachments to money and creature comforts. But he could not expect his men to carry on their work, especially the younger scholastics to persevere in pursuit of the advanced degrees and higher learning so essential to the work of the Society, without sufficient and stable financial support. More to the point, he had to provide for a growing number of communities and for the many novices who were flocking to the Society. That all required funds — and not just a pittance. Despite his devotion to evangelical poverty, Ignatius had come to see that money and financial resources were essential means for achieving apostolic goals — the touchstone of reality (Bertrand 1985). We can also suggest that this same tension found its way into his *Constitutions*, in which the highest ideals of spiritual abnegation and discipline are often juxtaposed with practical directives and decisions that both moderate the norms and leave the door open to future adaptation and modification to the demands of the effectiveness of the work of the Society in the world.

## Charismatic Leadership

These details raise the question of the charisma of Ignatius as a religious leader, and correspondingly the extent to which he was successful in transposing this charismatic influence into the institutionalized structure of the Society he founded. There seems little doubt that Ignatius was surrounded by intense positive and idealizing transference reactions in his followers, but this realization only leads to the further question of what it was about Ignatius' personality that made it possible for him to elicit such powerful responses. The issue reaches beyond Ignatius' personal charismatic qualities to the leader-follower interaction. In Max Weber's (1947) pioneering definition of charismatic authority, the emphasis fell on the compelling forcefulness of the leader's personality — "a certain quality of an individual personality by virtue of which he is set apart from ordinary men and treated as endowed with with supernatural, superhuman, or at least specifically exceptional powers or qualities. These are such as are not accessible to the ordinary person, but are regarded as of divine origin or as exemplary, and on the basis of them, the individual concerned is treated as a leader" (pp. 358-359).

Charismatic leaders have been found to possess both paternal and maternal characteristics that enable them to inspire love and awe, offer hope for salvation and deliverance from distress, and deal with subordinates with both tenderness and harshness. These characteristics can be found amply displayed in Ignatius, reflecting the basic organization of his personality around the paternal and maternal identifications.[2]

More recent work on charismatic leadership has broadened the focus to include the leader-follower interaction (Abse and Ulman 1977; Wilner 1984; Post 1986). Wilner (1984), for example, defines charismatic leadership as a relationship in which the followers' perception of the leader sees the leader as in some fashion superhuman, leading to their blind acceptance of the leader's statements, their unconditional compliance with his directives, and their unqualified emotional support of his cause. This view of Ignatius charismatic leadership would strike a resonant chord with many of the statements about obedience, particularly obedience of will and judgment and blind obedience.[3]

One view emphasizes the basically narcissistic basis of the interaction (Post 1986; Kets de Vries and Miller 1985). Deficits in narcissistic development can result in either ideal-hungry personalities, who constantly seek an idealized object to which they seek to attach themselves to salvage their damaged narcissism, or mirror-hungry personalities who look for a constant flow of admiration and acceptance in order to satisfy narcissistic needs. On these terms, charismatic leadership is based on a charismatic marriage in which the mirror-hungry leader satisfies his followers' narcissistic need for an ideal to follow, and the ideal-hungry followers contribute their nurturing and sustaining admiration and compliance to maintaining the narcissistic balance in the leader (Post 1986).

Individuals with such narcissistic dispositions and the need for power and prestige are often drawn into leadership positions (Kohut 1971; Kernberg 1979). We can recognize that, in the preconversion

[2] See chapter II above.

[3] See further discussion of this points in chapters XVIII, XXI, XXII and XXIII below.

Iñigo, the young hidalgo's narcissism was salted with the mirror-hunger — we need only recall his vanity and his lust for worldly honor and glory. He was stamped as a hero, a leader, and he seemed willing to suffer any pain, undergo any risk, even the threat of death, to serve that ideal. But we might ask, what had become of these traits in the mature, postconversion, spiritual leader? In his role as general, the narcissistic strains were more muted and ambivalent. There is no doubt that he exercised a powerful charismatic attraction on his followers, especially the band of brothers who founded the Society under his leadership. And in the house of La Strada, he was regarded as the saint, the father; his word was law, his every utterance regarded as if divine in origin, or nearly so. To what extent did this adulation and reverential awe, which come through so impressively even over the centuries, reflect the ideal-hungry narcissistic need of his followers?

Certain aspects of Ignatius leadership reflect narcissistic issues. In more constructive terms, he combined a capacity for transformative and inspirational leadership with an ability to interact with his followers in transactional terms that was remarkable (Kets de Vries and Miller 1985). But in other respects, his relation to his followers encouraged them to establish a pattern of idealization that allows them to share in the grandiosity of the leader (Volkan 1988). Part of Ignatius' inspiration was his vision of the Society as carrying out the mission of Christ to defend and extend His kingdom throughout the world. His followers were caught up in this powerful vision and idealized crusade.

But reactive traits cannot be ignored. It is not always clear that he was attuned to the needs and best interests of his subordinates — the mission of the Society and the will of God took precedence. He was at times rigid and uncompromising, opaque to any objections or reactions in others, but at other times he could be exquisitely sensitive and responsive to the needs of his followers. If he at times took counsel from others before making a decision, he tended to close the door once the decision was made. At times the door may have been closed prematurely. The occasions when he entertained no compromise in his harsh treatment of some candidates to the Society or in his attitudes toward obedience may offer some testimony to the underlying grandiosity that supported his religious vision and convictions.

We should not overlook the fact that Ignatius was able, in quite a remarkable and successful way, to institutionalize his religious inspiration. His highly personal and individualized vision, which he himself experienced as divine in origin, and his sense of connection with a transcendent or immanent divine source, is typical of charismatic religious leaders (Barnes 1978). The translation of this inner vision into a common inspiration and program of action was the major achievement of his years as general. He accomplished this task by placing the *Exercises* at the center of his spiritual teaching, and by further extending this program into the writing of the *Constitutions*, which gave a stable and explicit form to his vision for the Society. This was accompanied by his unflagging effort to organize, direct, and promote the work of the Society throughout the world, to articulate the vision and the mission to his followers, so that through them and through the Society the apparatus would be set in place to continue for centuries the work he had begun. Ignatius saw his leadership as intended by God for the centuries, for the future accomplishment of God's purposes and the glory of His kingdom on earth.

## ASSESSMENT

What conclusions can we draw from this portrait of Ignatius in his role as Superior General of the Society of Jesus? Certainly we can say that the picture is a far cry from the fanatic intensity and impracticality of the pilgrim years. Establishing a religious order and integrating it within the structure and mission of the Church meant that Ignatius had to abandon his rebellion against and rejection of the norms and conventions of the world in order to achieve the apostolic goals of the Society. As administrator of a newly formed and burgeoning organization, his decisions and directions were crucial for setting his sons on a path that would guarantee the continued existence of the Society — hardly secure in many places where it became established — and in the process facilitate God's work. Ignatius constantly sought divine guidance through prayer and discernment, but in human terms the burden rested largely on his shoulders. There were no rules, no guidelines, no precedents. He had to rely on his own prudence and worldly wisdom to guide him — bolstered by his unwavering conviction that his work was God's will and that he was guided by a divinely appointed destiny. He clung, desperately, stubbornly, to his religious ideals — to poverty even though the service of God required large sums of money and resources to educate students, support houses and communities, and fund various missionary and apostolic enterprises, etc. He valued education and urged his followers to absorb the most advanced thinking of the times, yet even the most learned were bound to the task of teaching catechism to little children. His Society gained favor, privileges, power among the most powerful lords and churchmen, yet he insisted on humility and obedience as the hallmark of his sons in imitation of the ideal of the humble Christ who suffered and was humiliated. Whatever success and privilege came their way, the members of the Society were always and everywhere to regard themselves as the *instrumentum Dei*.

Ravier (1987) poses the crucial question regarding the continuity or discontinuity between the image of the pilgrim and that of the general:

> Was it really the same man who here roamed at random, asking on the "Way" the thrill of long prayers, the joy of providential encounters, and then immobilized himself into a punctilious administrator — the same man who asserted himself on every occasion, enamored of total Christian freedom and then legislated, created rules and even minutely detailed regulations, and distributed penances — also the same man who formerly quarreled openly with money, its property, its litigation, its security, and then changed into a man of business, filled his correspondence with requests, questions of inheritance, of "stable revenues" to assure the colleges? One could multiply the contrasts, if not the contradictions. (p. 393)

There is no question that his demeanor was saintly and cast an aura of holiness and charisma that impressed those who knew him. But the picture is far from consistent. The man who turned his back on worldly power and glory to choose a path of abject humility and self-effacement found himself in a position of great power and influence, not only within the Society but vis-à-vis the outside world as well. One would guess that the internal conflicts had by no means found resolution. One can catch only a fleeting glimpse of his uneven and conflicted superego, shifting unpredictably and precipitously from rigidity to tolerance, from harshness and severity to gentleness and kindness, from humble tolerance to authoritarian peremptoriness — often with a rapidity that confused and confounded his contemporaries. One might conclude that the possession and exercise of power was a conflictual issue that he never adequately resolved, to the end of his life, and that the failure to resolve these deeper conflicts found their way into his religious and spiritual teaching.

# SECTION II

# THE *SPIRITUAL EXERCISES*

# CHAPTER V

# PROLEGOMENA

Before engaging with the *Spiritual Exercises,* it may be useful to consider several interlocking themes pervading this core component of Ignatian spirituality and recurring quite persistently throughout the text. Rather than reconsidering these issues repetitively as they occur, I have opted to treat them in a more focused and consolidated manner here, so that when they come to our attention subsequently, we will have a context for more specific comments and not have to continually reinvent the wheel. The themes I have in mind are the relation between the theological perspective and the psychoanalytic perspective, the question of freedom, the issue of transvaluation, the interrelationship between grace and nature, and the existence and nature of the spirit world to which Ignatius continually appeals.

## Theological and Psychoanalytic Perspectives

To avoid unnecessary confusion or misunderstanding, some qualifying remarks are in order. First of all, comments offered here are intended as specifically psychological. The rich spiritual treasury of the *Exercises* is being considered from only one aspect — an important aspect, but not necessarily the most important or meaningful for purposes of retreat masters or students of Ignatian spirituality. One should not look here for more than has been attempted. The limited psychological focus introduces other limitations. It would be possible to approach such an analysis from a number of more or less meaningful psychological orientations, each emphasizing different dimensions of the complex psychological reality. My central concern, however, is the problem of accurately reinterpreting Ignatius' insights into a consistent psychological schema with an eye toward articulating a reasonable theory of the intermeshing of grace and nature.

At the same time, we cannot ignore the fact that the spiritual approach Ignatius developed was a direct expression of his inner psychological life. In my previous study of the psychology of Ignatius

(Meissner 1992b), I advanced the hypothesis that the *Spiritual Exercises* could be read as an expression of the inner life of the struggling pilgrim, grappling with the turmoil and torment of the psychic forces within him and torn by the aftershocks created by his profoundly transforming conversion experience. My examination of the *Spiritual Exercises* focused on trying to discover what this document, so central and essential to Ignatian spirituality, might reveal about Ignatius himself — about his motives, feelings, attitudes toward the world and himself, about his vision of reality and his place in it. The purpose here is quite different — to read the *Exercises* through a psychoanalytic lens, to translate Ignatius' instrument for spiritual change into psychoanalytic terms as far as possible, or to define more clearly those points at which his views go beyond or are no longer reconcilable with psychoanalytic understanding. My assumption is that Ignatius, always an astute psychological observer, demonstrated profound insight into human psychodynamics, but his insights were cast in terms of his own spiritual vision. By refocusing his vision through a psychoanalytic lens, we might learn something more about the *Exercises* themselves and possibly something useful about the bridges between human psychology and human spiritual life. The psychology and spirituality of the *Exercises* do not stand in opposition, but complement each other (Rahner 1964).

This does not mean that tensions between respective points of view do not exist, or that those divergences can be eliminated or resolved. They may be radically exclusive orientations that will inexorably retain their specificity and points of view, however we might seek to interpret them. Nonetheless, we have every reason to seek to find a meeting ground that — if it is not common — may at least provide an intermediate space for meaningful dialogue and mutual understanding. The dimensions of these divergences in perspective between a religious and the psychoanalytic orientation can be sketched in terms of several polarities: (1) conscious vs. unconscious aspects, (2) relative emphasis on freedom vs. determinism, (3) the view of behavior as teleological vs. causal, (4) understanding human experience in epigenetic vs. reductionistic terms, (5) emphasis on moral aspects of human action vs. motivation, and (6) understanding human experience as supernatural vs. natural. These topics are obviously a rich terrain for extended reflection and discussion,[1] but I will limit my consideration here to merely indicating their relevance for the present study.

[1] See the expanded discussion of these aspects in Meissner (1984).

*Conscious vs. unconscious.* The theological approach to religious experience is cast exclusively in terms of conscious experience. Religious reflection centers on manifest content and subjective awareness as its subject matter. Ignatius' understanding of spiritual experience was cast entirely in conscious terms — his time and culture had no awareness of unconscious phenomena, although they were obviously as much under its influence as we are. The psychoanalytic hermeneutic deals in latent content that is not at all or only inferentially available to consciousness, and functions according to different laws and processes than are familiar to conscious thought — for example, primary process or the influence of unconscious fantasy material, defense mechanisms, and so on. The traditional freudian perspective was cast in terms of unconscious instinctual drives, libidinal, aggressive and narcissistic, but subsequent developments in ego psychology, a more elaborated conception of superego functioning, and recent developments in the psychology of object relations and the self have drawn the scope of psychoanalytic understanding considerably closer to more traditional religious concerns and perspectives. Even the basic understanding of basic drives has been subject to significant revision.

*Freedom vs. determinism.* I will discuss this issue later in this chapter, but I would note here that the form of strict causal determinism associated with Freud's early metapsychological views has had to be qualified in ways that seem to bypass the stark opposition that once pervaded any discussion of these topics. It can no longer be maintained that the determinism found in psychic systems excludes the possibility of human self-determination and responsible choice. Both concepts have undergone revision in a direction that allows both to claim acceptibility and legitimacy. The challenge in the present discussion will be to understand how spiritual freedom, so central to the Ignatian perspective, especially in the *Exercises,* can persist along with unconscious determinants reflecting the influence of psychological motivations and developmental residues.[2]

*Teleology vs. causality.* The theological view of human nature is cast in terms of purposes, goals, and intentionality as opposed to a psychoanalytic view of man as driven by powerful motivational forces. The rather mechanistic and deterministic view has largely been abandoned by thoughtful analysts and replaced by a more authentically motivational perspective emphasizing teleology over causality in some sense — these issues have not found consensus among analytic theo-

[2] See the further discussion below.

rists and the degree to which these factors are brought into balance differs considerably. Proponents of a noncausal, intentional, semantic, and hermeneutically based approach to psychoanalysis have taken a radical stance in opposition to the causal, mechanistic, and even substantive explanatory concepts as the basis for psychoanalytic understanding and explanation. The point at issue and the problem for the psychoanalytic interpreter is that, in addressing the range of human religious experience, the analyst is confronted with the necessity of bring his interpretive resources to bear on religious and spiritual phenomena in such a way as to address the inherent meaningfulness of those phenomena without reducing them to unrecognizable and falsifying categories or distorting their authentic value and significance. The analytic perspective must in this sense come to meet the religious in order to contribute anything meaningful to the dialogue.

*Epigenesis vs. reductionism.* Earlier psychoanalytic approaches to religious phenomena, including Freud, can be faulted for their efforts to reduce religious experience to analytic categories, especially to some form of drive derivative. The capacity of analysts to recognize this fallacy, not only in areas of applied psychoanalysis but also in everyday clinical practice, has contributed greatly to the more sophisticated and fruitful engagement of analytic perspectives with other humanistic disciplines (Meissner 1985). An important distinction here is between reductive and reductionistic explanation. Reductive understanding allows for an account of higher order phenomena that provides some understanding of the integration of lower order phenomena in their organization and functioning. Thus religious phenomena may involve a substratum of unconscious motivation and meaning, but their full intelligibility is not limited to that level of understanding nor is it completely exhausted by it. The complexity and density of the phenomena require other accounts and other perspectives to begin to approach adequate understanding. In contrast, reductionist thinking interprets the higher order phenomena as an expression of lower order processes and forces, and holds that this account is complete or all that is necessary for a comprehensive understanding of the phenomena in question. Psychoanalysis has moved historically from a mind set that was predominantly reductionistic to one that is more appropriately reductive. It is in this spirit that the approach to the interpretation of spiritual phenomena in this study is undertaken and intended. An epigenetic approach recognising levels of explanation and the possibility of emergent properties in the movement from lower levels of intelligibility to higher is reductive without being reductionistic.

*Morality vs. motivation.* One of the recurrent stumbling blocks in the dialogue between psychoanalysis and spiritual thought patterns is the divergence between the religious preoccupation with morality and sin on one hand and the relative lack of it in psychoanalysis; and conversely, the concern of analysis with issues of motive and the relative de-emphasis of motivational concerns in religious thought. Religious consciousness focuses on responsibility, either positively in seeking merit and grace, or negatively in accepting blame and guilt for sinful behavior. This disposition to moral effects sets the stage for playing out superego dynamics, a process that psychoanalysis finds all too often at the root of neurotic dispositions and behavior. However, despite its best efforts to divorce itself from moral considerations (Hartmann 1960), value orientations and issues of value-systems and value-integration have become increasingly pressing in psychoanalytic praxis in relation to aspects of therapeutic alliance and countertransference (Lichtenberg 1983; Meissner 1981, 1995).

*Supernatural vs. natural.* This last point of difference may be the most decidedly recalcitrant to modification or compromise. The spiritual orientation is rooted in the realm of spiritual realities and a belief system that encompasses a concept of the supernatural, and more to the point, espouses belief in a loving and saving God. None of this has any place in psychoanalysis; this is an irreconcilable point of difference about which psychoanalysis has nothing to say. One either accepts the religious belief system through faith, or one does not. The proper grounds for either accepting or rejecting it do not exist for psychoanalysis. Ricoeur (1970) has commented on this inherent precision of psychoanalysis:

> It is difficult to pinpoint what is properly psychoanalytic in Freud's interpretation of religion. However, it is essential to put into sharp focus those elements of his interpretation that merit the consideration of both believers and unbelievers. There is a danger that believers may sidestep his radical questioning of religion, under the pretext that Freud is merely expressing the unbelief of scientism and his own agnosticism; but there is also the danger that unbelievers may confuse psychoanalysis with the unbelief and agnosticism. . . . Psychoanalysis is necessarily iconoclastic, regardless of the faith or nonfaith of the psychoanalyst, and this "destruction" of religion can be the counterpart of a faith purified of all idolatry. Psychoanalysis as such cannot go beyond the necessity of iconoclasm. This necessity is open to a double possibility, that of faith and that of nonfaith, but the decision about these two possibilities does not rest with psychoanalysis. (p. 230)

## FREEDOM

One of the most profound messages contained in the *Exercises* is that human freedom and growth in human freedom is intimately connected to spiritual growth and ultimately to freedom of God (Fessard 1956/1966; Divarkar 1991). In considering the interrelation of psychological and spiritual factors in relation to the concept of freedom, we need to keep in focus certain differentiating aspects of freedom in the theological sense from freedom in a psychological sense.[3] Theologically, freedom is essential to a theological view of man and for his participation in the life of grace and the supernatural order. Freedom, as the capacity to choose between limited goods, is therefore presumed as a given of human nature. The human agent retains the unique capacity to determine lines of future activity as long as different possibilities of reaction and contingency remain open. Liberty, as an existential given, reaches beyond the bounds of contingency to embrace self-determination and an affirmation that man comprehends the limits of possibility and can exercise choice in controlling its actualization. This form of freedom implies self-affirmation, that lends meaning, structure, and inherent intelligibility to one's sense of self within a cultural and religious context. The Christian and theological notion of freedom, therefore, is not an expression of unconditioned autonomy, but an acceptance of an existential and divinely revealed order of things.

In this perspective, freedom is given to man not so that he do good or evil, but so that he can do good in a meaningful and rational way. To the extent that this freedom is limited or compromised, reflecting the flawed nature of historical man, the potentiality for evil persists. Thus, man's capacity for authentic freedom must rely on an influence beyond and outside himself by which he is enabled to achieve the fullness of his freedom, and without which he remains mired in his flawed state of concupiscence, unable to reach the level of self-affirmation he is called to by grace. The Augustinian view of freedom, then, implicitly asserts that man's self-affirmation is ultimately and synonymously an affirmation of God in the self. It is this notion of freedom that pervades the considerations of freedom in the *Exercises* advanced by Fessard (1956/1966), Rahner (1964), Egan (1976) and others.

Yet, while it is God who is the source and giver of human freedom, he is also the primary condition for the existence and exercise of that freedom. As Ramsey (1962) observed:

[3] See my discussion of these issues in Meissner (1984).

> Still there is another primary meaning of God in human experience: He is one who, on account of the dynamic upthrust of human freedom, alone can put a limit upon man and set boundaries that may not be removed. Both the atheist Nietzsche and the theist Kierkegaard knew this; and as the former exclaimed, "If there were a god, I could not endure not being he," so the latter wrote, "Without God, man is [not too weak, but] too strong for himself. (pp. 23-24)

And further: "Absolute humanism wills its own freedom; it must subordinate everything else to this absolute freedom; and the last thing which must be subordinated if one is to have no God is one's own being. To live atheism means subordinating one's own existence to one's own absolute independence" (p. 27).

The man who clings to perfect and absolute freedom, to a concept of total self-determination and direction, is drawn inexorably into a state of internal contradiction and into a condition of unbridled and potentially malignant narcissism. Ramsey (1962) proposed this internal contradiction in the following terms:

> For now he has become the one who gives himself being and each moment continues to give himself being. He lives from freedom and not from any necessity. He is his own creator and sustainer and bows to no one and no thing. Freedom will then have encompassed within its grasp, if only in thought, what formerly came from beyond himself. Each moment he passes from death in life, from non-being into being, by his own choice and by the power of personal freedom. . . . The contrast is complete: a religious man who says in his heart there is a God receives his life daily by divine appointment as a gift and a task set before him. The man who says in his heart there is no God, if he is free and not just a pawn, receives his life daily by self-appointment. Thus it is impossible to live by and live out the thought that there is no God except by exalting one's self beyond all measure. "The human being who denies his nature as a created being," Marcel writes, "ends up by claiming for himself attributes which are a sort of caricature of those who belong to the Uncreated" (Marcel 1952). (p. 28-29)

Even in the theological framework, human freedom dictates that human nature cannot be reckoned as a fixed or static essence. Freedom means that man's nature is more rooted in becoming rather than being — a view that finds its echoes in psychological terms (Allport 1955). Freedom enables man to transcend the fixity of nature, reason and history to explore the limits of possibility and meaning. As Ramsey (1962) put it, "Man stands before possibilities for action which are not to be calculated in terms of the potentialities of a fixed essential nature of any sort. His freedom means that his self-understanding affects what he is or what he is to become; and he grasps after possibilities only envisaged when, from the heights of self-transcending consciousness of himself and the present historical actuality, he seeks to reshape both himself and his social environment" (p. 144).

The perspective articulated by Ramsey (1962) in this regard, basing his view on the thinking of Reinhold Niebuhr (1941), seems aptly resonant with the Ignatian spirit. He wrote:

> "While egotism is `natural' in the sense that it is universal, it is not natural in the sense that *it does not conform to man's nature*, who transcends himself indeterminately and can only have God rather than self for his end" (Niebuhr 1953). . . . Therefore, "the law of love is the final law for man in his condition of finiteness and freedom because man in his freedom is unable to make himself in his finiteness his own end. The self is too great to be contained within itself in its smallness" (Niebuhr 1949). . . . *Agape* is "the final law of human existence because every realization of the self which is motivated by concern for the self inevitably results in a narrower and more self-contained self than the freedom of the self requires (Niebuhr 1949)." (p. 145)

This view of freedom and the self draws the theological perspective another degree closer to a more psychologically or psychoanalytically meaningful perspective on freedom. Yet tensions remain.

If the primacy of freedom is fundamental in the theological image of man, it is neither a given nor fundamental for the psychoanalytic perspective. Rather it remains open to question, always precarious, and calling for confirmation or proof. Where the theologian presumes freedom, the analyst questions it. This tension in the analytic perspective is reflected in the polarity between deteminism and freedom and the understanding of ways in which they are opposed and in which they are compatible. Freedom in the analytic sense is correlative to the degree of autonomy the individual enjoys — autonomy not merely from external constraint or coercion, but from internal constraint or coercion. Internal limits on freedom and its exercise come from psychic conflicts, defenses, compromises, needs, desires, and attachments. Ignatius covers a good bit of this ground when he addresses inordinate attachments, detachment from which results in the increase of psychological freedom. That freedom is more or less propaedeutic to the further increase of freedom to which he calls the exercitant in the course of the Exercises. But that freedom of choice inherent in Ignatian indifference is not necessarily impelled by grace, although in some degree it may be. But his intention is not merely to open the potentiality for unencumbered choice to the exercitant — he seeks to go further to the more definitive exercise of freedom in the choice for God and God's will, namely to lead the exercitant into the terrain of theological freedom and the affirmation of self that is simultaneously an affirmation both of God and of God in the self.

The concept of freedom in the *Exercises* carries a twofold connotation: as an act of self-positing. and as a passage from non-being to being. In this latter sense, freedom finds expression in the passage of becoming, from the immersion in the inherent nonbeing of sinfulness through spiritual liberation and growth to a greater fullness of being in an enhanced sharing in the freedom of God. Fessard (1956) postulated a dialectical movement within the *Exercises*, from before the liberating moment of the election to after. This movement can be schematized as follows:

A. Before the act of freedom:
- I. First Week: positing of nonbeing
- II. Second Week: negation of this positing

B. After the act of freedom centered in the election:
- III. Third Week: exclusion of nonbeing
- IV. Fourth Week: positing of being (Pousset 1971)

The process takes place through the individual's increasing freedom — "becoming oneself by oneself" (Fessard 1956). As Pousset (1971) put it, "Of itself the creature is nothing, but God entrusts the creature to itself by enabling it to become and to be by itself.[4] As for the act constituting human freedom, it can only be the "yes" or the "no" by which this freedom becomes itself in the world and ultimately posits itself in relation to the Creator, whether or not its affiliation with God is recognized" (pp. 20-21). Or in Rahner's (1967) terms, "God is the One Who constitutes me in mysterious freedom, deals

[4] An important point, but one that is more presumed than central to my argument here, is that freedom and psychic determinism are not contradictory. For a clarifying discussion of the various meanings of "psychic determinism" and their reconciliation with the concept of freedom in Freud, see Wallwork (1992). Also see my (1984) discussion of related issues. This misunderstanding may play a role in the opposition some theologians pose between unconscious causation and human liberty — for example, Egan (1976) argues that unconscious causality cannot be admitted in CSCP because that response "springs from the deepest depths of liberty" (p. 25). A fuller understanding of psychic determinism would admit unconscious causality without impinging on human freedom in the slightest.

with me, and disposes over me in such a way that through the divine absoluteness my autonomy and self-direction are not diminished, but rather firmly established" (p. 16).

The freedom of the *Exercises* is the freedom of choice — "It is necessary to make ourselves indifferent to all created things in all that is llowed to the choice of our free will and is not prohibited to it" [SE23].[5] This is the freedom that unites with desire and serves as the basis for self-determination and decisions by which we determine our individual destiny. It is an ambivalent potentiality, an openness to possibility, even to contradictory meaning and ambiguity. This is not the liberty of Locke or Hume based on the absence of external constraint. Nor is it Augustine's *libertas* as distinct from *liberum arbitrium*. The latter was free choice, the capacity for self-determination; the former was realized in perfect and utter fulfillment. As Buckley (1984) expresses it:

> Freedom in the *Spiritual Exercises* is neither the liberation from external compulsions and internal hindrances nor the liberty of completion. It is a reflexive potency with a double object: the things chosen, which could be all created things, and the personal self, which is constituted through this choice as one makes himself indifferent and appropriates these thoughts as his own. In offering his freedom, he offers his entire person and all that he has. Freedom for Ignatius is the person as potential, as question — the question before one's world, before the self, and thus the question before God. The fulfilment of its human ambiguity, its completion, is not freedom but liberality; that is, giving of oneself to another. The fulfilment of freedom is not freedom itself;it is interpersonal liberality. (p. 70)

And again: "Freedom is not the end of the Exercises; it is its prerequisite and its increasingly heightened reality as one faces choice; it is the question out of which the Exercises issue. Freedom is not for itself; it is for something else — liberality. Why? Liberality is the embodiment of that interchange which concretizes and constitutes mutual love" (p. 72).

The consideration of the times of election[6] in a sense encompasses the whole psychology of the action of grace. In each instance, grace is operating in and through the self and its proper functions. But the measure of ego responsiveness is the degree of ego-autonomy and its concomitant diminution of resistances to ego-functioning.

[5] References to the text of the *Spiritual Exercises* will henceforth be designated by the official paragraph numbers, e.g. SE#.

[6] See chapter XIII below.

Thus, as the positive growth to spiritual identity takes place, there is an increasing capacity of the self to respond to the action of grace. As an increasing degree of control and freedom from obstructive conflicts between ego and id and between ego and superego evolves, there is a corresponding development of the exercitant's capacity for utilizing the empowering effects of grace. And to this, we can add the comment from Modell (1993):

> . . . that meaning *in* life (as distinct from the meaning *of* life) rests upon the emergence of self-created values, interests, and imaginative acts. For those who retain a belief in God, there is a ready-made sense of one's place in the universe — a sense that contributes to the coherence of the self. Conversely, in the absence of such beliefs there is a greater strain placed upon the self in order to maintain this sense of coherence. (pp. 202-203)

The development of personal autonomy, therefore, parallels the development to spiritual identity. The gradual working through of the impediments to autonomy, both from the side of the id and from the side of the superego, and the progressive establishment of ego control involves an increasing capacity of the self for independent and autonomous action. It is this autonomy that Ignatius strives for in the ideal of indifference. The spiritual development of the self is wrought at the expense of the effort of the ego itself. At each step there is required a decisive commitment, an acceptance of values inherent in that level of development and consequent reconstruction and resynthesis within the self itself. The self's capacity to accomplish this is a function of the degree of its autonomy. Implicitly in such development, then, there is a continual process of free self-determination on the part of the ego. Such self-determination is equivalently a realization of self, an actualization of the potentialities of the self, a maturation of personality and projection of self into a new synthesis. Thus, the innermost synthetic efforts of the self are dependent on and reflective of the inherent freedom of the self — a freedom that discovers itself in gaining responsible and autonomous commitment of self to the divinely ordained plan for salvation and for each individual's personal self-realization and destiny.

Pousset (1971) envisioned free choice as erupting, somewhat unpredictably, into established patterns of life and provoking a creative disruption in the individual's perspective and self-understanding. He commented:

> This irruption of freedom is so violent that it breaks duration or time in two, the breach preventing the before from passing into

> the after, and there ensues an action that is somewhat coherent, a beginning of history. At least we have here an Instant. But how can this absolute Instant become inscribed in duration? How can it become history, which develops patiently, day after day? . . . . How does a decisive Instant, the Instant of a Yes rather than a No — and that obviously changes everything — become history? The Instant is categorical, even absolute, and yet it is capable of becoming embodied in a duration where, in a sense, there is nothing except what is relative; but without the relative, the Instant itself would be nothing. (p. 9)

Pousset's concept of "irruption" does not connect with the ordinary experience of the exercise of human freedom. Psychologically speaking, man is free to the extent that he is capable of autonomous choice and action. Far from an irruption, this is part and parcel of everyday mature and adaptive functioning. Irruptions of a mystical order are a different matter.

The problem confronts that dimension in human experience that allows man to become author of his own personal history — a history that is decisive, rooted in his autonomy and freedom. A decision made in a moment of time perdures in virtue of fidelity — a "virtue" Erikson (1964) defined as "the ability to sustain loyalties freely pledged in spite of the inevitable contradictions of value systems" (p. 125). The choice involves risk and uncertain consequences, opens the way to both regressive and progressive dynamic influences, but, as Pousset (1971) put it, "All of this means creating one's life through the renewed and ever fruitful irruption of freedom, the instant which innovates not by arbitrary impulses, but through acts of lavish generosity" (p. 11). Ignatius seeks a form of responsible freedom in which one is reborn to a history that never loses its creative power, or as Fessard (1956) put it, a freedom that "passes from non-being to being by becoming itself."

At higher levels of spiritual growth, the self becomes capable of increasingly more complete and effective reorganizations and coordinations, so that responses rooted in liberty can become more and more spontaneous. And thus, by a normal law of development, the self can pass from more labored commitments of the third time of election to more fluent and spontaneous responsiveness of the second and first times. This is not to say that every response to grace of the self possessing a mature spiritual identity must follow this pattern, since it remains profoundly true that spiritual growth, as all growth, remains differential, and consequently there is a sense in which no one ever passes decisively out of the purgative process of the first week. But growth in spiritual identity does imply a sensitivity and an internalized acceptance of God's will, the response to which becomes generally more facile and spontaneous. We can be sure that the marvelous illuminations of Ignatius' later mystical experience were a reflection of this evolution to greater responsiveness and spontaneity.[7]

At each stage of spiritual growth, the self is confronted with a decisive crisis. In Ignatius' reconstruction, the decisive crisis of the first week evolves around the acceptance of man's basic finality and the perversion of that finality through sin. In the second week, the crisis evolves around the determination to perfection in following Christ. These are not the only crises, but they serve as examples. Each crisis must be faced and worked through, and only insofar as each is successfully resolved, can the self move on to the next crisis. At each step, there is required a decisive commitment, an acceptance of the values inherent in that level of development, and the consequent reconstruction within the self. If we regard the free act as a "position du soi par soi" (Fessard 1956), or as the act by which man determines himself to be what he is in the existential order, human freedom implies on the psychological level the progressive actualization of self and the gradual realization of the potentiality of the self. The resolution of each stage in the growth of spiritual identity is achieved at the cost of a projection of itself within the self to a new phase of being. The progression within the self from nonbeing to being signifies the more complete actualization of the self by itself— the "position du soi par soi." Thus, the process we have been describing in psychological terms of internalization and synthesis is from another point of view a process of self-determination through the free response to the promptings of grace. Consequently, the progressive synthesis of the self is equivalently a continual "position du soi," a prolongation and extension of the process of election. But growth in spiritual identity does imply a sensitivity and an internalized acceptance of God's will, the response to which becomes generally more facile and spontaneous. We sometimes marvel at the ease with which the great saints accomplish the most difficult things.

This very sensitivity, this responsiveness to grace, implies an ever increasing facility in the exercise of freedom — a growth in freedom itself. This would seem to be a concomitant and resultant of the increasing security and autonomy of the self. Thus, by slow degrees, the self comes to participate in "the glorious freedom of the sons of God" (Rom. 8: 21) reaching its fuller perfection in perfect submis-

[7] See section VI on Ignatius' mystical experience below.

sion and responsiveness to the impulses of divine guidance and inspiration. This is the liberty St. Augustine defended so well, and which has been well described as "liberté sans option."

## TRANSVALUATION OF IDENTITY

The conversion experience, as we saw in Iñigo's case,[8] means that, on both unconscious and conscious levels, underlying conflicts can be sufficiently resolved to allow for meaningful integration with the subject's functional and reality-adapted ego. The synthesis and resolution of conflicts, then, are not only compatible with the current sense of reality but also give rise to a sense of completeness and a deepened understanding or illumination, which can have an enhancing, elevating, and even expansive effect within the convert's self-awareness. In such individuals, the conversion process represents a reshaping of the self-organization and its core elements, giving rise to a newly integrated identity cast in a religious or spiritual framework.

Religious conversion experiences, however, may leave the underlying conflicts less than fully synthesized and integrated (Christensen 1963). Residual conflicts may be repressed to some degree and dealt with by a variety of defense mechanisms. One result may be transformation of psychic experience into symbolic representations in the form of mystical experiences. For the pilgrim of Manresa, the psychic crisis he endured brought about a regressive state, marked by severe suicidal depression, loss of ego boundaries undermining differentiation of self and object, and acute identity diffusion. As the conversion process continued, the emerging resolution allowed for shaping of a new identity, now cast specifically in religious and spiritual terms. The spiritual experiences at Manresa were undoubtedly expressions of the transforming process which found expression in symbolic representational terms that acquired spiritually illuminating and mystical force.

From a psychoanalytic perspective, however, we would have to conclude that the resolution may well have been only partial and can readily be summarized under the rubric of a deepening and broadening of his value orientation. That value system was highly cathected with libidinal and aggressive elements, permeated with a sublimated set of romanticized masculine sexual ideals, and shot through with highly narcissistic elements. At Loyola, under the psychic pressures of his traumatic regressive crisis, Iñigo became aware of another di-

[8] See chapter II above and Meissner (1992b).

mension of reality, the spiritual dimension, which emerged with renewed vitality and meaning during his convalescence. Iñigo gave the values implicit in his new spiritual awareness a tentative acceptance, which grew quickly into an internalized and operative value system.

Yet the new system of values cast his previous identity into a state of crisis; the pilgrim had to experience a transvaluation of identity, a transformation of the value system and ideals that formed the core of his sense of identity. That transvaluation required, in a sense, an internal reorganization and resynthesis of the structure of the pilgrim's psyche.[9] The primary agency of that reconstruction was centered in the pilgrim's ego. The primary target was the superego, along with those narcissistic elements constituting the ego ideal. Under the force of this onslaught, the superego and the old ego ideal began to fragment, inducing a kind of superego regression, attended by the unleashing of hostile, destructive and punitive impulses against the self. The fragmentation of superego likewise relaxed the grip of the ego's repression on unconscious libidinal forces. The ego was consequently under severe attack from two directions, from both the superego and the id. The pilgrim was wrestling with an angel of God.

The transvaluation of the identity of Iñigo de Loyola involved an almost total transformation. If the moratorium at Manresa produced a new personality, the lines of continuity between Iñigo the courageous man of arms and the emerging personality of the pilgrim were all too clear. If the superego had been reconstructed, it nonetheless retained some of its old characteristics, now assimilated into a totally new system of spiritual values. They were purged of some of the old narcissistic involvements, at least the pathological phallic narcissism of the proud and noble hidalgo, and transformed — indeed, transvaluated. In some profound sense, the transvaluation of identity that transformed Iñigo de Loyola into Ignatius was a process of evolution that was less elimination of an old identity and its replacement with a new one and more one of transformation, a reflection of the extension and mobilization of ego resources. The ego of Iñigo de Loyola matured to a new level of functioning and effectiveness. Rather than an exchange of identities, there was an enrichment of the ego which achieved a fuller realization of its own potentiality and a higher level of internal organization and synthesis. In a sense, then, the transforming experience of Iñigo made him more fully, more authentically himself.

[9] Details of this tormented period of transformation are found in chapter VI below; see also Meissner (1992b).

## SPIRITUAL VALUES AND TRANSVALUATION

The value-system dominating Ignatius' spiritual vision was centered 'the will of God' or more specifically *ad majorem Dei gloriam*. But there remains a line of continuity between the values of the courtier and soldier and the saint. We can trace in Ignatius the saint a transformation in some fashion of the idealism, courage, chivalry, and vanity of the bold courtier and warrior. Part of the ideal that formed such an important aspect of Iñigo's character involved a system of values, whose significance should not be overlooked. Values are internalized normative standards according to which the individual determines the course of optional behavior. Values are important constituents of psychic organization in that they are operative elements in accordance with which the ego directs, evaluates, judges and organizes behavior. Values are thus action and goal-oriented aspects of the self (Meissner 1986). When the self is functioning maturely and stably in its own right, that is, when it is functioning in virtue of well-integrated and structured psychic systems rather than in virtue of instinctual forces of libido or aggression, values are maximal components of its activity. This is not to say that the value-system can not serve an integrative function for instinctual forces. I would argue that integration of basic instinctual drive capacities, narcissistic, aggressive and libidinal, is essential to effective and adaptive functioning of the self, and particularly that integration of narcissistic drive components is an integral part of the organization and functioning of the value-system.

A central component of the conversion and post-conversion changes was redistribution of the narcissistic investment that gave Iñigo's ideal its force and vitality. Adherence to the values of that ideal carried with it narcissistic gratification and a degree of ego- and self-enhancement. The value-system, then, can be regarded as significant in the integration of narcissistic libido and ego- and superego-functioning in a coherent and well-functioning self-structure. Narcissistic cathexis of the ego-ideal and its inherent values strengthens the value-system and reinforces it. The same investment increases the measure of ego-enhancement and self-esteem so essential for mature and integral ego-functioning. The value-system thereby serves an integrative function within the ego. That the value-system attendant on the chivalric ideal was a source of strength and ego-enhancement for Iñigo is more than likely. The motivations that drove him to superlatives of action at Pamplona included love of country and devotion to a cause, but, in a deeper and more interior sense, the narcissistic need to serve an ego-ideal and observe its inherent values. To have acted otherwise would have meant the depreciation of self-esteem and the depressive anxiety of guilt and/or shame.

The constructive and synthetic process through which the pilgrim had to pass consisted in the re-organization of an ego-ideal, in which narcissistic dynamisms could be meaningfully invested in a new and internally realized system of values. This re-organization of the ego-ideal was an essential step toward reconstituting the balance of psychic forces which had been so badly disturbed. In terms of a reconstituted ego-ideal, it became possible once again for aggressive impulses to be integrated with libidinal energies. The resultant neutralization of these energies provided an additional source of energy for reinforcement of ego-functioning. The necessary leverage for this reorganization came through the internalized value-system which the pilgrim came to embrace and finally to endorse as a vital part of his existence. The value-system, as a schema of Christian and spiritual standards, in a sense pre-existed and were culturally determined. In this cultural sense, they had to be assimilated and internalized. But in a deeper sense, the process cannot be limited to the mere acceptance of a prior set of values. To internalize such standards and norms means to personalize them, to make them a functioning part of one's own inner psychic reality. In the process of internalization, therefore, such values are modified, changed, given a uniqueness and specificity within the personality of which they are a part. They must become an integral and functional part of the person. They are, therefore, uniquely his, sharing a community of generalized meaning with fellow men of his culture or society, but with meaning unique to himself.

The conversion process in Iñigo de Loyola brought with it the undermining and destruction of this ego-ideal and its inherent values. While this destructive process was taking place, there was also a constructive process at work. Had it not been for this constructive dynamism, the struggle at Manresa would have ended in disaster. This constructive process is the central concern of this analysis, for it was the extension and prolongation of this process which supplied the psychological dimension of the future course of the pilgrim. There was a metamorphosis in values which mark the *terminus a quo* and its transition to the *terminus ad quem*. The constructive intrapsychic developments can probably best be traced in terms of the display of these value-transformations. More importantly, for our present reflection, the residues of these complex experiences provided the substance of the spiritual processes and movements that were distilled into the compressed and at times formulaic prescriptions of the *Spiritual*

*Exercises* and became the guiding principles of Ignatius lifelong ascent of the spiritual mountain and the spiritual legacy he left in his wake.

The correlate of this growth in Ignatius as in the participant in the Spiritual Exercises is an enrichment of the self and deepening of the sense of identity. Identity is linked to the internalization of a value-system. What the pilgrim experienced, then, *pari passu*, was a growth in his own sense of identity — more fully realized as he grew in internal realization of a fuller, more comprehensive, more realistic and more spiritual system of values. What we have been describing in metapsychological terms we have chosen to call "transvaluation." The role of the self as a supraordinate structural integration is a paradigm that is only beginning to emerge in psychoanalysis (Meissner 1986b). It can be thought of as a hierarchical organization of levels of functional integrations involving preprogrammed biologically rooted organismic needs and functions, wishes, macro- and microstructural subsystems of id, ego and superego, and symbolic capacities, not the least of which has to do with value systems. All these elements are organized and integrated in terms of the personality structure and its correlative personal identity. Transformation of this personality system can take place through acquisition of new values which can organize the individual's psychic life and provide new motivational resources for transformed goals and ambitions.

My reason for dwelling on this subject at such length is that it was such a process that the pilgrim experienced in intensely affecting ways in the cave of Manresa, and that it was his grasp of this process that he distilled into the pages of his *Spiritual Exercises*. The *Exercises* not only reflect Iñigo's own spiritual conflicts and struggles, but they offer a generalization of his spiritual travails as a model for spiritual development applicable to all souls open to their influence and to the influence of divine grace. The ensuing analysis of the psychological dimensions of the *Exercises* is based on this hypothesis. The *Exercises* are the personal spiritual testament of Ignatius and thus form the core of his spirituality.

## Grace and Nature

The transformation between Iñigo the hidalgo and Ignatius the saint was wrought through such transvaluation. While this transvaluation can be analyzed metapsychologically in terms of redistribution of narcissistic libido and related processes, we have reason to extend the range of our consideration to suggest the possibility that part of this process, spiritually conceived, was due the energizing action of grace. Transvaluation in the case of Iñigo de Loyola was an effect of grace.

My basic supposition in dealing with the interaction of grace and nature has been that grace has an effect on man's psychic processes (Meissner 1987). A psychological analysis must work with a phenomenological base of evidence, precisely because it is a scientific undertaking. It can only deal with the reality of grace insofar as the effects of grace manifest themselves in and through psychic phenomena. Consequently, a psychological analysis has nothing to say about the elevating or supernatural effects of grace, but must limit its consideration to the sanating effects of grace. From this point of view, it is my presumption that grace always exercises a sanating effect, whether or not it has a properly elevating effect.

The problem from the point of view of a psychological theory, of course, is where to locate the sanating effect of grace. In the following analysis, I have chosen to regard the operation of grace as both an energizing influence within the self, whether conscious or unconscious, particularly enabling the ego to mobilize its intrapsychic resources and functions, and as an expression of interpersonal dynamics articulated in terms of an object relations paradigm expressing the personal communication of divine influence as personal presence through grace.[10] In these terms, the sanating effects of grace can be spelled out in relation to specific psychic functions so that the self remains free and more or less autonomous in response to grace. From the interpersonal perspective, grace reflects the more personal impact of the presence of God in the soul. From this psychological point of view, the operation of grace depends upon the free responsivity of the ego — any other conception would imply an opposition or contradictory influence within grace itself. It also embraces a more comprehensive theory of self-integration and of the self-system as the locus of personal responsiveness and experience.

Ignatius does not address the subject of grace in the *Exercises*, but it is implicit in his understanding of the action of the Exercises throughout. The entire organization is directed to opening the soul more fully to the action of grace, based almost exclusively on his own experience of the action of grace in his own life — particularly in the conversion and at Manresa. The Exercises depend uniquely on the action of grace — they are meant to provide a place for the encoun-

[10] The effort to ascribe the action of grace to a third level of psychic functioning, along with affective and intellectual levels (Divarkar 1991), seems constraining and not consistent with Ignatius' usage, but it does offer access to a concept of the action of grace as at least in some part unconscious.

ter and communication between God and his creature [SE15-16].[11] The exercitant's effort is directed to seek those dispositions needed "to receive graces and gifts from His Divine and Sovereign Goodness" [SE20]. The petitions throughout are expressions of the increasing desire and receptivity to grace. While grace is the free and unencumbered gift of a loving God, Ignatius seems convinced that the spiritual gifts and fruits he anticipates for the exercitant will be given, if only the exercitant develops sufficient generosity and responsiveness to God's action in his soul.[12] The necessity for him to properly dispose himself became essential, even urgent, for anything to be effected in the Exercises. Ignatius seeks to place the exercitant before God and to ask "What do you want from me according to the sovereignty of Your divine will?" (Rahner 1967, p. 12). Throughout he is guided by the conviction that God will guide each person to his or her own point of election through grace, that God will (God willing!) tell each well disposed soul what it is that he wants from them.[13] The presumption and reliance on grace in the mind of Ignatius remained a persistent aspect of his thinking throughout his postconversion career. Not only does the theme of grace permeate the *Exercises*, but frequent references in the *Constitutions* and throughout his numerous letters come back again and again to the need for grace and for the additional grace to be open and receptive to the divine call (Kolvenbach 1992).

It is noteworthy the extent to which Ignatius leans on affective experience in determining the movement of spirits. If we assume

[11] On the action of grace in the Exercises, see also Boyer (1956), Lawlor (1943), Orlandis (1936), and Steger (1948).

[12] The same persuasion is expressed over and over in much the same terms in his Autobiography and again in letters of spiritual direction. See Lofy (1963).

[13] What little evaluation we have of the psychological effectiveness of the Exercises is not encouraging. Imoda's (1991, 1992) report on religious who had undergone four years of formation, including the Exercises for thirty days, concludes that over 90% showed no improvement of maturity as evaluated by structural and existential criteria. Moreover, the improvement in professed "self-transcendent ideals," taken as a measure of spiritual progress, although higher in more mature subjects post-retreat, tended to deteriorate during the two years of novitiate following the Exercises, more in immature subjects than in mature. Sacks (1979) study of "integration of the self-system" following a thirty day retreat found change from a level between "conformist" and "conscientious," following Loevinger's (1966) stages of maturity, to a level of practically conscientious. Despite the limits of such studies, they underline the fact that whatever changes result from undergoing the Exercises do not necessarily express themselves in psychologically measurable terms, nor are the Exercises intended to produce such effects. Again we face the issue of whether grace and spiritual effects have any relation or resonance with psychological functioning or maturity.

that the movements of the good spirit are by implication effects of grace, we may be skating on thin ice. None of these affective currents can be identified as exclusively grace effects; none of the experiences of consolation and desolation described by Ignatius are beyond the capacity of psychological determinants to produce. There is a constant temptation to interpret positive and spiritually uplifting affects as related to the action of grace, but such an interpretation may prove to be illusory and misleading. This leaves open the further question as to how best to understand Ignatius' rules in the context of more modern psychological understanding.

## SPIRITUAL IDENTITY

The second purpose of the *Exercises*, seeking and finding the will of God concerning the ordering of one's life, represents in psychological terms what I shall call development of spiritual identity. In theological terms, just as the natural level of existence is ordered to the more excellent perfection of the supernatural and provides the substructure for its erection, just as the powers of nature are required as operative potencies, in and through which grace exercises its effects, so psychological identity can be regarded as the foundation on which grace builds and which is perfected and complemented in the growth of spiritual identity. The one is a work of nature; the other a work of grace.

In the course of development of psychological identity, man achieves a conscious sense of his own individual and unique identity, as well as the continuity of his personality and the satisfactory integration of structural subsystems composing his body and mind. There is also a sense of solidarity with a set of realistic values as embodied in a certain social and cultural context. The governing influences, in terms of which integration is achieved and maintained, flow from the ultimate source of unity in the personality, the cohesive self-organization. Integration is a product of the synthetic and executive functions of the ego acting in concert with other psychic capacities and functions. The entire self-system operating in terms of a basic ego-orientation is reality-oriented, that is to say, the response of the individual, who is secure in the possession of his own identity, to his life situation and the complex of stimulus factors deriving from both external and internal sources, is appropriate and proportioned to the intensity and quality of the stimulus as well as to the total context of realized values in terms of which he must adjust. For the Christian, the total framework of response includes not only the reality of sensible existents, not only the reality of interpersonal relations and consequent social obligations, not only the value systems inherent in and dependent on the ontological structure of the created order, but also the reality of divine influence and providence and the divinely revealed means for finding God's will and the consequent process leading to ultimate salvation.

Spiritual identity is a matter of growth through grace. Consequently, the *Spiritual Exercises* are primarily directed to disposing the soul to accept and respond to the influence of divine grace. Spiritual identity, however, is best effected where it builds upon the firm foundation of mature psychological identity. But the arm of the Lord is not shortened. There is no reason to limit the effects of His grace and of His divine influence to the strictly supernatural. The impact of grace on the soul is not only to nourish growth of spiritual identity, but may also bring about profound growth in psychological identity as well. God touches the soul in all its parts, even to its innermost depths. He influences not only man's rational conscious self, but also the inner recesses of his unconscious.

In a sense, the self at the end of the first week is envisioned as not so very different from a more or less well-adjusted psychological identity. But if the self's activity is much the same as that in psychological identity, there are important differences. Ideally it has achieved not only control of inordinate attachments, but it has found a sense of true contrition and a vigorous purpose of amendment. It has also oriented itself in the realm of spiritual realities which it has begun to internalize and make the norm of decision and judgment for its functioning. The presumption of the second week is that the movement through repentance of the first week has found some degree of resolution in a motivated conversion leading to the desire to learn more about and follow Christ. Implicit in this is an orientation to a value-system which is likewise internalized. This internalization is accompanied by a preliminary synthesis within the self itself, representing on a psychological plane the initial disposition of the self on the level of spiritual identity. It is this initial self-synthesis which represents the seed which is to grow in the succeeding weeks.

As the exercitant moves into the second week, he enters upon a phase of more positive growth in spiritual identity. He is no longer focused on the struggle to establish the primacy of regulatory systems over the uncontrolled emotional forces of the psyche, over id and superego; as these forces begin to yield to more and more effective control, the ego can begin to divert more and more of its efforts to more positive self-enhancing goals. The pressing concern over instinctual control is left behind, but it remains a concern, if no longer a pressing concern. In its stead, Ignatius calls on powerful psychological mechanisms to shape and fashion this internal reorganization. What is ultimately in question is a process akin to identity formation, not so much in Erikson's (1959) now classic sense, as in the sense of a transvaluation of identity as we have already had occasion to discuss it. But here the steps of the process are detailed in such a way as to bring into clearer focus the kind of effort the pilgrim must have experienced in his harsh engagement in the cave of Manresa.

The self, therefore, can begin to work toward an ever more fully and completely effected spiritual self-realization. In the perspective of this study, the individual's progressive realization of a spiritual identity is continuous with and to some extent influenced by his already attained psychological identity. But in reference to the work of the second week, we shall ignore this relationship for the moment and concentrate on the aspect of growth in spiritual identity. The process of identity formation at this level is effected by a gradual approximation to the exemplar of spiritual identity contained in the person of Christ. Ignatius expresses this objective in a number of ways: ". . . to imitate Thee (Christ) in bearing all insults and reproaches," ". . . to follow and imitate better Our Lord," ". . . and for grace to imitate Him," ". . . in bearing reproaches and insults, the better to imitate Him (Christ) in these." To which, the *Directory* adds: "For He (Christ) is the model set before mankind by the Father. By imitation of Him, we are to mend and order our corrupt ways and to guide our footsteps unto the way of peace. Wherefore, since Christ's life is most perfect, is, in fact, the very ideal of virtue and holiness, it follows that the closer our life approximates to His, by imitation, the more perfect too does it become" (Dir. XVIII, 2). The basic mechanism, therefore, which Ignatius calls on to implement spiritual growth, is identification with the person of Christ. The person of Christ is proposed as a kind of ideal to which the self is drawn by increasing admiration and love — this "christomorphic theme" (Egan 1976) is central to the *Exercises* and plays a dominant role in the second week.

This same dimension of the Christian experience was noted tangentially by Freud (1921), who observed:

> Every Christian loves Christ as his ideal and feels himself united with all other Christians by the tie of identification. But the Church requires more of him. He has also to identify himself with Christ and love all other Christians as Christ loved them. At both points, therefore, the Church requires that the position of the libido which is given by group formation should be supplemented. Identifica-

> tion has to be added where object-choice has taken place, and object-love where there is identification. (p. 134)

In Ignatius' formulation, the identification of the exercitant with Christ involves a concomitant theme of service to others. Just as the theology of the Incarnation makes a strong appeal to the ancient biblical theme of the "suffering servant" in the elaboration of the mission of the Son, so the Christian identifying with Christ internalizes that value system which Christ himself embodied and expressed. The identification, therefore, is equivalently a process of internalization of the value system which is summed up and concentrated in the person and mission of Christ — a transforming of the ego-ideal to embrace a new value-orientation and a corresponding shift in identity (Divarkar 1991).

This process of identification is central to the evolution of spiritual identity. Ignatius tells the exercitant that he must "put on the Lord Jesus" in Paul's phrase (Romans 13: 14). The ideal must take shape through long meditation on the mysteries of Christ's life, particularly on the internal dispositions and attitudes and values which are expressed in his words and actions. The internalization of these spiritual values calls forth an effort of reconstruction within the self. Identification itself, as a mechanism, is not sufficient to explain the synthetic aspects of the self's activity in this process. The active intervention of the ego is required to transform the incipient identification into a sense of identity that transcends the identification and cannot be reduced to it. The Christian personality evolves not as a passive mirror of the personality of Christ, but its formation involves an active process within the self issuing in a unique formation of an identity which has achieved a synthesis of spiritual values into a personal ego-ideal. The interposition of the ego. therefore, puts the stamp of the individual's personality on the process and on the spiritual identity which emerges from it. Thus, becoming more Christ-like implies an assimilation and internalization of the value system implicit in Christ's person and mission and an internal synthesis of this value system into an integral and unique sense of self and identity.

The exercitant thus progresses from an imaginative recreation of the actual person and actions of Christ to an empathic understanding of our Lord's interior reactions, motivations, attitudes, and values to an internalization of these values and attitudes, to a progressively approximating identification with the person of our Lord, becoming always more Christ-like, and finally to a progressively more vital and spiritual synthesis of these elements into a totally unique and increasingly effective spiritual identity. Such a process requires a high degree of ego-activity and strong sources of motivation. At the very beginning of the second week, Ignatius tells the exercitant to seek "for interior knowledge of the Lord, Who for me has become man, that I may more love and follow Him" [SE104]. The motivational strength, as Ignatius perceives the process, stems from the action of grace and from the intimate knowledge and love of Christ. And as Rahner (1967) noted, "Only when we really carry on His life in our own way, and not by trying to produce a poor literal copy, is the following of Christ worth living" (p. 119).

Just as in identity formation of psychological identity, there is an active synthetic process effected by the self which cannot be understood in terms of identification alone, as a mechanism (Erikson 1959). There is an independent and active ego-function which transforms the additive combination of significant identifications into an identity transcending them and only inadequately reducible to them. Consequently, "formation" in the phrase "identity formation," must be regarded as an active and synthetic function. The ego interposes itself, imposes itself, on the essence of particular identifications putting on each the stamp of its own personality. It is, moreover, through this synthetic process that the organization and unity of the personality is maintained. For Ignatius, the motivation springs from grace and from the knowledge and love of Christ. What is in question, then, is no purely objective and mechanical process; it is rather an intense and deeply felt personal relationship, based on love, and progressively deepened and intensified throughout this second week.

Identification is possible, in psychological terms, because in it the individual desires and seeks to establish and maintain a satisfying and self-defining relationship to another person. A deep attraction to the person of Our Lord and a strong desire to unite oneself with Him, to share the same burdens and to live the same life — in other words a profound love of the person of Jesus Christ is essential to the process of growth in spiritual identity. The Directory remarks in this regard that fervor and the desire to amend one's life (Dir. XVIII, 4), together with a leaning toward that which is more perfect (Dir. XIX, 2), are the necessary and essential dispositions for successful engagement in the exercises of the second week.

## THE SPIRIT WORLD — THE ENEMY

Another important note sounded in the *Exercises* is that union with Christ serves to defend against the power of the "malignant enemy." The theme of combat against this spiritual enemy is a dominant leitmotif that pervades the consciousness of this hidalgo turned saint. This ever-present and menacing force is referred to as "the enemy of human nature," [SE 7, 10, 135, 136], "the enemy," [SE 8, 12, 140, 217, 314] "enemies," [SE 96, 196] and "the evil spirit" [SE 315]. The most vivid portrait of the enemy comes in this meditation on the Two Standards [SE 136-148], contrasting the standard of the evil one with the standard of Christ. Keeping in mind that the portrait of the devil is painted by a man of the sixteenth century, we can regard these references as a personalized and culturally derived projection, reflecting inner conflicts between spiritual ideals and the destructive wishes that continued to torment him. Ignatius had to struggle against these desires and their consequences all through his life, but they caused a particularly wrenching agony in the cave of Manresa. The enemy was never far from his conscious experience.

The question of the meaning of this personification is fraught with difficulty and ambiguity. Theologically, the belief in the existence and activity of the devil is well established and has long served to the religious mind as a focus of concern and anxiety. To modern ears, however, such belief sounds naive or primitive, and smacks of the delusional or near delusional. Modern attempts to demythologize belief in good or bad spirits run afoul of the question of whether the existence of such beings is part of divine revelation — if not in the personified form of traditional belief, in what form? The theological insistence on good and evil influences, however they are named, remains intact. As Toner (1982) notes: "The influence on human life and salvation to which we refer is not that of visions or diabolical possession or obsession or miraculous events or anything of that sort. It is principally their influence on the interior movements of human minds and hearts in hidden ways, and through these on the events of human history on a bigger scale, where good and evil are written large, in splendid or hideous ways" (p. 261).

If a clear position can be taken psychologically about the existence of the devil, the same cannot be said theologically. Theological opinions about the existence of spiritual beings, good and bad, as revealed truth and therefore believed, range from the absolutely certain to the not-so-certain and skeptical. No serious theologian has gone so far as to maintain that the existence of angels is certainly not revealed or a matter of faith. As eminent a theologian as Karl Rahner (1968a) took the position that rejection of angels would be unreasonable, especially when mythological accretions had been expunged. The pivotal text in his estimation was the profession of faith in the Fourth Lateran Council of 1215 which speaks of a "spiritual or angelic world." Specifically regarding the devil, he wrote that he "is not to be regarded as a mere mythological personification of evil in the world; the existence of the devil cannot be denied" (1968b, II, p. 73). However, the Council declaration can be read more narrowly as simply rejecting the Albigensian heresy embracing a gnostic sounding belief in the Devil as creator of the corporeal world. But Quay (1981), reviewing the council's statements on the matter, concluded that any doubts about the existence of angels or devils have no serious grounding. Needless to say, an unqualified belief in the existence of the Devil has been challenged by others — the existence of the Devil has been regarded as improbable and not an issue for unqualified faithful assent (Kelly 1968).

And so, the theological argument continues to run the full gamut of opinion. As far as a meaningful psychological understanding of Ignatius goes, the influences of the good or evil spirits he describes are cast almost exclusively in terms of influences on the interior life of man — on his thoughts and feelings. The question whether Ignatius actually believed in the existence and activity of such spiritual beings — as he undoubtedly did as a devout Christian of the sixteenth century — becomes secondary. Whether he did or didn't, the effective implications for his spiritual teaching comes out to be the same — what counted to his mind was the movements of the psyche that led the soul closer to or farther away from God. In his teaching regarding the discernment of spirits, as we shall see, these movements are specifically psychological. Consequently, if we regard the metaphorical Ignatian language as referring exclusively to psychological dimensions of human experience, and the references to the Devil as expressing a projective personification whose point of reference was the disordered and evil inclinations of the human heart and mind, we shall not miss the mark by much.[14]

These projective elements were written into the *Exercises*. The identity of the enemy is clearly the devil and his minions on their mission of destruction. The exact psychological mechanisms are difficult to pinpoint in this context, because Iñigo's allusions were common among the spiritual writers of his day reflecting a long-standing Christian usage. That tradition tends to personify the devil as an

[14] As Toner (1982) makes explicit, one can dispense with the spirit language of the *Exercises*, interpreting these expressions in terms of tendencies to good or evil, without detriment to the understanding of Ignatius' teaching. This leaves the theological issue moot. I will frequently use Ignatius' manner of speaking about spirits, but it should be understood that I am taking these expressions metaphorically as representing identifiable psychological phenomena.

actual spiritual force, going about like a roaring lion seeking to devour men's souls and to lead them into temptation, then into a variety of sins, and finally to damnation.[15]

Despite this traditional rhetoric, I would argue that projective mechanisms are also at work in this depiction of the spiritual struggle. What is in question is not merely a culturally endorsed style of spiritual discourse, but a personalized realization of determinate projective mechanisms. The impulses that were so central in the psychology of the preconversion sinner are now internally denied, then externalized and attributed to the evil one, the prince of darkness. The enemy becomes the embodiment of the repentant sinner's deepest desires and impulses. This inner conflict, the burden of guilt attached both consciously and unconsciously to the sinner's own wishes for riches and worldly power, for the honor and esteem of men, is deprived of its internal power and is attributed to the hated and feared enemy.

The projective resolution is all the more effective in that it is supported by the traditions of Catholic spirituality in Spain and the theological doctrine, carried down through the centuries, regarding the devil and his wiles. Projections that find such a culturally adaptive niche can often be cognitively sustained, and may even serve important adaptive ends, whereas the delusional projections of the psychotic, which tend to be idiosyncratic and culturally deviant, do not.

[15] The extent to which these beliefs were extant in the minds of mature and competent men of the sixteenth century, even in the highly educated and cultured Peter Fabre, one of Ignatius' closest first companions, is striking. See O'Leary (1979).

# CHAPTER VI

# THE MANRESA EXPERIENCE

## Introduction

We have good reason to think that the spiritual doctrine Ignatius incorporated in his *Spiritual Exercises* originated in his experiences in the cave of Manresa. Consequently, our understanding of his spirituality would be incomplete without a meaningful perspective on that critical period in his development. In a profoundly meaningful sense, the Manresa experience was a continuation and extension of the powerful psychological and spiritual transformation set in motion by the tragic and fateful meeting with the French cannonball on the ramparts of Pamplona. The months the pilgrim spent at Manresa proved to be decisive for his remarkable conversion. Through the dim mists of history, we can only catch occasional glimpses of what must have transpired. The pilgrim himself gives us only a bare smattering of hints, and even his autobiography, dictated to the faithful Gonsalves da Camara many years later, does more to pique our curiosity than to satisfy it. But let us return then with the pilgrim to Manresa.

The pilgrim left the chapel of Our Lady of Montserrat[1] after his night of vigil, and, clad in rough pilgrim garb, made his way to the nearby town of Manresa. He found a room in the little hospital of Santa Lucía, earned his bed by working in the hospital and begged his food in the town. He planned to move on to Barcelona, and from

[1] The dark visage of Mary at Montserrat was redolent with ancient associations and unconscious meanings. The cult of the Blessed Mother reaches back to the female deities of ancient times, to the worship of Isis and Diana. See Festugiere (1949). Johnson (1989), commenting on the iconography of Our Lady, writes: "Artistic symbols of the goddess [Diana] accrued to Mary: her dark blue cloak, turreted crown, link with the moon and the stars, with water and wind. The iconography of Mary seated on a royal throne presenting her child to the world was patterned on the pose of Isis with Horus. Similarly, the still-venerated statues of the Black Madonna at Le Puy, Montserrat, and elsewhere derived from ancient black stones connected with the fertility power of maternal deities, black being the beneficent color of subterranean and uterine fecundity" (p. 506). See also the reconstruction of the history and cultus of the Black Virgin in Begg (1985).

there embark for Jerusalem, but as it turned out he remained in Manresa from March 1522 until February 1523. These were to be the most important months in the entire life of Iñigo de Loyola.

## THE CAVE

Manresa was a small town nestled on the banks of the Cardoner. Iñigo occupied a small cell in the Dominican priory (Dudon 1949; Dalmases 1985) and continued his prayers and penances in a little cave overlooking the valley of the Cardoner. His penances were severe and intensive. He ate no meat and drank no wine, except on Sundays when he interrupted his fast. His penitential fervor came to bear on other aspects of his preconversion attachments. Because he had been fastidious about caring for his hair, of which he was quite proud, he made up his mind to neglect it and let it grow wild, without combing or cutting it or covering it either day or night. For the same reason, he allowed his fingernails and toenails to grow (Vita 19).

There was method in the pilgrim's madness. In launching this ascetical onslaught against every aspect of his person and behavior that had once been a source of vain satisfaction to him, he was following the principle of *agere contra*. He described it later in the *Exercises*: "Hence, that the Creator and Lord may work with greater certainty in His creature, if the soul chance to be inordinately attached or inclined to anything, it is very proper that it rouse itself by the exertion of all its powers to desire the opposite of that to which it is wrongly attached" [SE16].

The psychoanalyst might be tempted to regard this neglect of personal appearance as reflecting some breakdown in self-esteem regulation and a disruption of socially acceptable norms of behavior. But in the pilgrim's case, this strange conduct was less regressive than expressive of his engagement in a conflictual struggle with powerful inner drives and conflicts, and in this sense more adaptive to spiritual values than regressive. The behavior can be seen as part of his effort to destroy the old ego ideal and its associated values by attacking the image at any point where the old narcissistic investments found expression, specifically his love of elegance and worldly honors and his boundless desire for glory. His inclinations to charm and attract the fair sex would also have a place on this list (Wilkens 1978). Psychodynamically, this process would involve mobilization of his psychic resources to gain control over these libidinal, aggressive, or narcissistic investments that, in terms of his spiritual ideal, he judged to be inordinate. Because he once took pride in his fine hair, for example, this slice of narcissism had to be brought under control and into conformity with the spiritual value system that he was assimilating.

The pilgrim's effort was proportional to the strength of these narcissistic and libidinal attachments, compounded by his naive understanding of spiritual principles. But we have already seen that our spiritual hidalgo was capable of heroic efforts. He seemed driven on by a consuming passion, a desire that would yield to no obstacle that opposed his quest for spiritual perfection.[2] In his penances, he came to grips with himself in a profound sense, reconciling ingrained patterns with new beliefs, drawing on tremendous resources of energy and strength. The goal was nothing short of complete control and direction of all his energy toward his spiritual goal. He continued without remission to exercise himself in his severe routine of prayer and penance. He begged his food in the streets of the town and spent sleepless nights in his prayer vigils. He became known among the townsfolk as the "Holy Man" who had become Christ's fool. His fasts and penances were so severe that his health began to suffer. On several occasions he became deathly ill, and began to suffer symptoms of the painful biliary colic that troubled him the rest of his life.

## Regressive Crisis

This rigorous penitential regimen had its psychic side effects. The assault on defensive and other psychic structures had the effect of inducing a regressive activation of conflictual drives that found their way into symptomatic expression and filled the pilgrim's way with painful inner torment. One such striking manifestation was a recurrent vision[3] of a beautiful serpent:

> It often happened to him in broad daylight to see something in the air close to him, which gave him great consolation because it was very beautiful. He could not make out very clearly what the thing was, but somehow it appeared to have the form of a serpent. It was bright with objects that shone like eyes, although they were not eyes. He found great delight and consolation in looking at this thing, and the more he saw it the greater grew his consolation. When it disappeared, it left him displeased. (Vita 19)

[2] This compulsion has been given a theological spin as "spiritual desire" — a form of grace-impelled motivation urging the soul to seek God and promoting spiritual growth (Cusson 1988). The theologized view does not override psychological motivation.

[3] Ignatius recalled a variety of visions and other mystical experiences during his Manresa sojourn. I will postpone consideration of these experiences to the discussion of his mysticism in section VI below.

The vision of the serpent was followed by a period of severe regressive turmoil. He recalled:

> Up to this time he had continued in the same interior state of great and undisturbed joy, without any knowledge of the inner things of the soul. Throughout the days when this vision [the serpent] lasted, or a little before it began, for it went on for many days, there occurred to him a rather disturbing thought which troubled him by representing to him the difficulty of the life he was leading, as though he heard a voice within him saying: "How can you stand a life like this for the seventy years you have yet to live?" But this he answered also interiorly with great strength, feeling that it was the voice of the enemy: "You poor creature! Can you promise me even one hour of life?" In this way he overcame the temptation and remained at peace. This is the first temptation that came to him after what has been said above. It happened while he was entering the church in which he heard high mass daily and in which he found great spiritual comfort. As a rule he read the passion during the Mass, always preserving his serenity of soul. But soon after the temptation just now related, he began to experience great changes in his soul. Sometimes his distaste was so great that he found no relish in any of the prayers he recited, or in hearing Mass, or in any kind of prayer he made. At other times, everything was just the contrary, and so suddenly, that he seemed to have got rid of the sadness and desolation pretty much as one removes a cloak from the shoulders of another. Here he began to marvel at these changes which he had never before experienced, saying to himself: "What new kind of life is this that we are now beginning?" At this time he still spoke occasionally with a few spiritual persons who had some regard for him and liked to talk with him. For although he had no knowledge of spiritual things, he showed much fervor in his talk and a great desire to go forward in the service of God. (Vita 20, 21)

From July through October of 1522, he suffered a severe desolation,[4] which he described in the *Exercises* as "darkness of soul, turmoil of spirit, inclination to what is low and earthly, restlessness rising from many disturbances and temptations which led to want of faith, want of hope, want of love. The soul is wholly slothful, tepid, sad, and separated, as it were, from its Creator and Lord" [SE317]. I would understand this description as directly pertaining to Iñigo's experience in the cave.

[4] I will leave open here the question of whether and in what sense desolation can be distinguished from depression — the former being a spiritual, the latter a clinical term. See my further discussion in chapter XV below.

Hartmann (1964) remarked that healthy psychological adaptation requires a capacity to suffer and be depressed. Depression may actually serve a constructive and adaptive function. The rapid alternation of depression or, as the pilgrim would say, "desolation," and consolation must have reflected the pilgrim's continuing effort to reconcile discharge of intrapsychic impulses he was experiencing with the system of spiritual and moral values he had embraced. The struggle in which the pilgrim was caught up had to do with the infiltration of instinctual derivatives into his superego. In Freud's (1917) classic analysis of depression, he described the essential mechanism as turning of sadistic impulses of the superego against the ego.

Conflicts with libidinal impulses constitute only one aspect of the ego's struggle to establish control over and integrate these psychic forces. The superego enjoys a certain autonomy, but where its harsh and severe code is transgressed, it can direct its rage against the ego, usually experienced in the form of guilt or need for punishment. The pilgrim's ego was caught up in just such an onslaught, very likely triggered by the pilgrim's attempts to subdue deeply entrenched narcissistic investments. It was as though all the hostile and sadistic elements in the personality were focused in the superego and turned against the ego (Freud 1923) in a masochistic onslaught.

The onslaught of the superego also contributed to the development of obsessive symptoms. The pilgrim goes on to tell us:

> But at this time he had much to suffer from scruples.[5] Although the general confession he had made at Montserrat had been entirely written out and made carefully enough, there still remained some things which from time to time he thought he had not confessed. This caused him a good deal of worry, for even though he had confessed it, his mind was never at rest. He began, therefore, to look for some spiritual man who would cure him of his scruples, but without success. Finally, a doctor of the Cathedral Church, a very spiritual man who preached there, told him one day in confession to write out all he could remember. He did so. But after confessing it his scruples returned, each time becoming more minute, so that he became quite upset, and although he knew that these scruples were doing him much harm and that it would be good to be rid of them, he could not shake them off. Sometimes

[5] Scruples are a form of obsessional self-doubt and self-criticism that condemn the subject to an unremitting feeling of having done wrong, of having sinned, even when there is no objective data to support that judgment. They are an effect of a harsh superego persistently criticizing the subject and subjecting him to constant self-doubt and guilt. Ignatius suffered mightily from scruples and left a set of rules in the Exercises [SE345-351] for dealing with them. See chapter XVII below.

> he thought the cure would be for the confessor to tell him in the name of Jesus Christ never to mention anything of the past, and he wished that his confessor would so direct him, but he did not dare tell the confessor so. But without his having said a word to him, his confessor told him not to confess anything of his past life unless it was something absolutely clear. As he thought that everything was quite clear, this direction was of no use to him and he remained always with his trouble. At this time he was in a small room which the Dominicans had given him in their monastery, where he continued with his seven hours of prayer on his knees, rising faithfully every midnight, and performing all the other exercises already mentioned. But none of them provided him with a cure for his scruples, although it was now some months that they had been afflicting him. (Vita 22, 23)

These obsessive symptoms represent the ego-dystonic demands of the superego. The punitive demands and anticipated punishments implicit in such scrupulous obsessions result from a "superego regression" to more drive-determined levels of functioning, specifically primitive destructive impulses deflected from the unconscious. The ego, of course, must defend itself from this punitive attack. For the pilgrim, destructive and punitive inroads of the superego constituted a major battlefield.

The intensity of these destructive impulses is suggested by the continuation of the pilgrim's account:

> While these thoughts were tormenting him, he was frequently seized with the temptation to throw himself into an excavation close to his room and adjacent to the place where he did his praying. But, knowing that it was a sin to do away with himself, he cried again: "Lord, I will do nothing to offend you," frequently repeating these words . . . . Here he recalled the story of a saint who, to obtain from God something he much desired, went many days without eating until he got what he wanted. Giving a good deal of thought to this fact, he finally made up his mind to do the same thing, telling himself that he would neither eat nor drink until God did something for him, or he saw that death was approaching. For, if he saw himself reduced to the extremity of having to die if he did not eat, in that case he would ask for bread and food (as though in that extremity, he could either ask for it or even eat it).
>
> He resorted to this one Sunday after having received communion, and went through the whole week without putting a morsel of food into his mouth. He omitted none of his ordinary exercises, even going to the divine office and praying on his knees from midnight on and so forth. But on the following Sunday,

> which was his confession day, as he was accustomed to be very detailed with his confessor, he told him also that he had eaten nothing that week. The confessor bade him give up this abstinence, and although he was still strong, he obeyed his confessor and that day and the next found himself delivered from his scruples. But on the third day, which was Tuesday, while he was praying, he began to recall his sins, and so went on thinking of his past sins, one after the other, as though one grew out of another, until he felt that it was his bounden duty to confess them once again. As a sequel to these thoughts, he was seized with a disgust of the life he was leading and a desire to be done with it. It was our Lord's way of awakening him, as it were, from sleep. As he now had some experience of the different spirits from the lessons he had received from God, he began to look about for the way in which that spirit had been able to take possession of him. He therefore made up his mind, which had become very clear on the matter, never to confess his past sins again, and from that day on he remained free of those scruples, holding it a certainty that our Lord in His mercy had liberated him. (Vita 24, 25)

The destructive forces of his superego had driven the pilgrim to the brink of suicide. The destructive impulses unleashed in this process were derived from hostile elements previously effectively sublimated by Iñigo's chivalric ego ideal and accordingly directed against external objects in various forms of aggressive action. We cannot forget that this son of the Loyolas was well-endowed with the temperament of the Loyolas — including a generous complement of destructive hostility. The heroics of the man of arms and the drive to fight to the death at Pamplona, for example, carried a powerful complement of aggression in a form entirely consonant with the demands of his ego ideal. As that ideal was gradually replaced and transformed by another set of values, destructive impulses were no longer permitted expression along the customary channels of external action. Instead of being directed externally, this destructive force was directed internally against the himself. Freud (1923) observed: "It is remarkable that the more a man checks his aggressiveness towards the exterior, the more severe — that is, aggressive — he becomes in his ego ideal. . . . the more a man controls his aggressiveness, the more intense becomes his ideal's inclination to aggressiveness against his ego" (p. 54).

Iñigo was, of course, still a babe in these woods. It was in the hot fire of these torments that he would fashion the greater spiritual maturity reflected in his rules for discernment. But that degree of spiritual discernment could not be achieved in any other way than by this agonizing passage through the dark pits of despair, suicidal obsessions, scrupulous self-torment and doubt, and depression. He would cry out: "Help me, O Lord, for I find no remedy among men nor in any creature; yet if I thought I could find it, no labor would be too great for me. Show me, O Lord, where I may find it; even though I should have to follow a little dog so he could help me, I would do it" (Vita 23). He was filled with "disgust at the life he was living" (Vita 25) and deep discouragement. In his despair, he finally put his trust in God: "In this way the Lord wished to awaken him as if from a dream . . . . he remained free of those scruples and held it for certain that Our Lord through his mercy had wished to deliver him" (Vita 25).

The psychological and spiritual crisis through which Iñigo de Loyola passed in Manresa was an extension of the conversion process begun on his sickbed at the castle of Loyola. The hypothesis we have been following here is that the strong, courageous, and fearless identity the young Iñigo had shaped, in the image of the chivalrous knight who feared no danger and sought glory and conquest on all sides, whether libidinal or aggressive, was formed around a phallic narcissistic core that left him vulnerable to certain kinds of regressive stress. The core element in the pathological narcissistic organization of his personality lay in the ego ideal, in which residues of archaic, narcissistic grandiosity and omnipotence were firmly embedded. The residues of earlier archaic narcissistic structures left him with a certain narcissistic vulnerability that carried with it the potentiality for regressive crisis. The ascetical drive of his Spiritual Exercises were directed against these pathological narcissistic investments.

The physical trauma at Pamplona and the subsequent convalescence, enforced helplessness, and painful dependence, as well as the intolerable resulting deformity, severely undermined his narcissism with far-reaching consequences (Meissner 1992b). In the cave at Manresa, these narcissistic vulnerabilities and their inherent regressive potential came to full realization. He struggled to overcome his depression by obsessive ruminations and by mobilizing hypomanic defenses. At times the depression would suddenly lift, and he would find his taste for spiritual things renewed — perhaps a form of manic defense.

We might infer that the intense and prolonged periods of meditation and seclusion to which the pilgrim subjected himself produced a corresponding reduction of environmental stimulation and a narrowing of the field of consciousness. The degree of sensory and other deprivations accompanying his ascetical practices would have had the effect of increasing his vulnerability to internal, drive-related influences and may have induced altered states of consciousness. The shift in levels of autonomous functioning of the ego is reflected in modification of certain ego functions such as reality perception. For example, we can understand the pilgrim's experience of visual illusions as reflecting a diminished degree of autonomous visual functioning resulting in intensified and less organized sensory experience. The diminution of autonomous structure of normal perception could have allowed the phenomenon of "sensory translation" (Deikman 1966), by which psychic actions, such as conflict, repression, and problem-solving, are perceived in relatively unstructured experiences of light, color, movement, sound, and so on.

In his bouts of desolation, scruples, and suicidal impulses, the pilgrim's ego felt the wrath of the superego. But more significant for our present interests is the manner in which he overcame these symptoms. As far as we can make out from these sketchy accounts, the pilgrim's method took the form of mobilizing the resources of his ego to bring his appetites under control. Whatever the physiological effects of these ascetical practices, however they may have contributed to the weakening of his functional ego autonomy in the short run, in the long run the resilient strengths of his embattled ego seem to have won out. The effort of self-mastery brought his life and patterns of behavior closer to the spiritual values he had espoused.

## THE ROLE OF THE CONFESSOR

Iñigo was not unaided in this titanic struggle with the contending forces within him. Undoubtedly, the father-confessor to whom the pilgrim turned in his hour of torment played a crucial and highly influential role. This Dominican priest (for he must have been one of the members of the Dominican community in the monastery where the pilgrim stayed) remains nameless and faceless to the eyes of history, but he undoubtedly served his function well in his efforts to aid the tormented pilgrim. Confronted by the pilgrim's depressive torments, suicidal impulses, and seemingly endless obsessional ruminations, the good father would undoubtedly have been severely challenged even had he possessed all the skills and knowledge of an experienced psychoanalyst.

As the case turned out, he managed to do well enough under the circumstances. He offered advice and directions to his troubled penitent, probably serving in many ways as an auxiliary ego, assisting the pilgrim to discern more carefully, to integrate and master his overwhelming anxiety. In the midst of the pilgrim's scrupulous torment and depression, the confessor served as a wise teacher who helped the pilgrim to discern what was real from what was fantastic, helped him understand that there was a difference between impulses and graces from God and temptations and delusions arising from the influence of the devil. By his advice, and even use of his confessional authority, he also served the important function of softening the severity of the pilgrim's superego. And finally, he must have served as a sort of idealized object whom the troubled pilgrim could trust and whose authority he would accept as leading him closer to God. In short, the confessor seems to have provided an effective object relationship, including the function of a possible transference object, which served to sustain the troubled pilgrim in his spiritual agony and also served as a firm, accepting, supporting, and spiritually uplifting model for identification. Without the advantages of modern psychological insight, he was able to do a creditable bit of psychotherapeutic work with the pilgrim.

If we think of this significant relationship, coming at such a crucial point in the development of the pilgrim's spirituality, as a kind of religious transference, we can assume that in the course of the conversion process Iñigo must have experienced a revival of rather infantile impulses originally directed toward his parents. These impulses were then projected into a religious context, and the confessor became, in effect, the good father to whom the infantile yearnings in the depths of Iñigo's heart responded with a sense of attachment, devotion, and humble submission. Ignatius himself tells us that "he obeyed his confessor, and that day and the next found himself delivered from his scruples" (Vita 25). This turn of events carried all the marks of the well-known transference cure. But in any case, it seems that the desperate inner conflict was being won by the ego. Unconscious elements have been successfully assimilated to the conscious sphere of ego-activity, enriching and reinforcing the ego and its functioning. We might suggest that experiences of this sort might have had a considerable influence on Ignatius' own experience of spiritual direction, especially in the course of giving the Exercises, and consequently on his understanding of the role of the director in the Exercises.

# CHAPTER VII

# THE SOURCES OF THE *SPIRITUAL EXERCISES*

## Traditional View

The traditional theologizing view of the origin of the *Exercises* is that they were the fruit of divine enlightenment — along the model suggested by the inspiration of scripture. Polanco wrote: "Thus he was taught by God himself, so much so that even if he had never studied Scripture or the Doctors, he would have known enough to be able to instruct others" (Chronicon I, 23; cited in Cusson 1988, p. 3), and again: "At Manresa he began to communicate to many others these Spiritual Exercises which he himself had received, having been instructed by God himself" (Chronicon I, 25; cited in Cusson 1988, p. 4). Further testimony from Polanco occurs in the *Fontes Narrativi*: "Among other things which he "who teaches men knowledge" (Ps 93: 10) taught him in that year were the meditations that we call the Spiritual Exercises and their method" (FN I, 163-4; cited in Cusson 1988, p. 4). And the preface of the Vulgate edition (1548) states that Ignatius "composed these *Exercises* after having learned more from the unction of the Holy Spirit, his own personal experience, and the practice of spiritual direction than from books" (in Cusson 1988, p. 4).

Nor were these isolated sentiments — they were supported by testimonies from Laynez, Nadal, Ribadeneyra, and the depositions for the canonization process. Such views are a little surprising, given the accusations of illuminist influences and association with the *Alumbrados*.[1] Their endorsement by so many of the first followers and presumably by Ignatius himself indicates the intensity and con-

[1] Hardly had the *Exercises* come to light when they were vigorously attacked, particularly by Melchior Cano and Tomas Pedroche, two Spanish theologians. They found the *Exercises* excessively affective and mystical in tone and leaning too much on subjective experience and the illumination of the Holy Spirit rather than on sound and objective doctrine. Particular targets manifesting this illuminist tone were certain annotations and the rules for discernment of spirits where the role of

viction of their sense of divine mission. Certainly there is abundant evidence for this in Ignatius, for whom the wish to join with Christ would have been reason enough to desire his inspiration to be the work of the divine majesty. This sentiment was well expressed by Nadal: "Our Lord communicated the *Exercises* to him, and guided him in such a way that he devoted himself entirely to God's service and to the salvation of souls. The Lord showed this to him especially in two exercises, those on the Kingdom and the Two Standards. Ignatius understood that this was his goal, that he should devote himself to it completely, and keep it as his aim in all his works" (FN I, 306-7; in Cusson 1988, p. 6).

With due consideration for the pious rhetoric of the day, in more sober perspective these phrases may have meant little more than that the *Exercises* were recognized as the fruit of Ignatius' experience and the belief that that experience was in some degree under the influence of grace. From the perspective of a later age, we have no reason to challenge that view, but we would be able to add that a significant set of determinants would have to include Ignatius' inner psychic life, both conscious and unconscious, and a complex of historical and literary sources. These latter would have come increasingly into play as Ignatius grew in learning and sophistication in his own understanding of his Manresa experiences, and as he became more aware of the spiritual tradition on which he was building.

## PERSONAL NOTES

While it seems certain that Iñigo based his formulations in the *Exercises* largely on his own experiences, we have very little idea of where and when these observations were set down. Yet we know that from the earliest days of his conversion Iñigo kept notebooks, one of which he used to record citations from the lives of Christ and the saints, but another that carried more personal observations on his experiences.[2] It seems that this notebook was with him at Manresa, and we have evidence to suggest that those notes served as the basis for what we now know as Ignatius' *Spiritual Exercises*. The locale of these jottings may have been the cave, the hospital, the Dominican priory, Villadordis, or anywhere else in the area of Manresa.

the spirit becomes essential to the Ignatian method, opening intuitively toward the mystical. These elements would have raised suspicions of an illuminist influence, an association that would have been at least possible. See Meissner (1994).

[2] Iñigo may have copied as many as 300 pages of notes in his own hand from his reading at Loyola, all of which he would have carried to Manresa (Cusson 1988).

## IMMEDIATE SOURCES

We have limited knowledge of the sources for Iñigo's notes. A major contribution would have come from Ludolph of Saxony's *Vita Jesu Christi*, one of the staples of Iñigo's conversion reading at Loyola. The impact can be seen in the structure of the *Exercises*, in the content and style of the methods of prayer, particularly on the contemplations and the technique of "application of the senses." Ludolph himself drew on the earlier *Meditationes Vitae Christi*, composed in the late thirteenth or early fourteenth century and attributed to St. Bonaventure. In any case, it reflects the strong current of Franciscan piety on Ignatian spirituality (O'Malley 1993). The introduction of Ludolph's work may have been especially influential, since many of its exhortative features find their echo in the *Exercises*. It must have provided much material for meditation in the long hours at Loyola. The emphasis on Christ as the foundation of salvation and the call to imitation of Christ would have been particularly salient. The stages of initial seeking for forgiveness followed by imitation of Christ would have set the pattern for the first two weeks of the *Exercises*. The meditations on evil and man's sinfulness in the second chapter may have influenced Ignatius treatment of these subjects in his own text. The method of meditating on the mysteries of Christ's life were also incorporated into the Ignatian approach. Even the Ignatian colloquies have their anticipations in Ludolph (Cusson 1988). In contrast to Ludolph's life the *Flos Sanctorum* found little direct representation in the *Exercises*, but had its influence more directly on Iñigo himself, shaping the emerging spiritual ideal and providing him with idealized images of the great heroes of God — Francis, Dominic, and perhaps more intimately Onuphrius.

His confessor at Montserrat, the kindly monk Dom Chanon had given him a copy of Cisneros' *Ejercitatorio de la vida espiritual* (in Latin *Exercitatorium Spirituale*), a manual of spiritual practice printed in Castilian and Latin in 1500. Iñigo would have carried this volume with him to Manresa. Thus Cisneros' work may have served as an important basis for the *Exercises* (Leturia, 1941, 1949), even though no single passage can be found repeated in the text of the *Exercises*. Cisneros himself was heavily dependent on Gerhard, Mombaer, and Groote, among other northern writers (Clancy 1976). The overall framework, the division into "weeks," the organization of some subjects of meditation on the basis of the life and death of Christ, and certain of the annotations are probably derived from the earlier work. Both Ignatius and Cisneros were influenced by the Brothers of the

Common Life, a Dutch order founded by Gerard Groote to promote the *devotio moderna*, which Ignatius would have encountered in Paris (after 1528) if not before (Buonaiuti 1968). The influence of the *devotio moderna* was reflected especially in Ignatius' devotion to the *Imitatio Christi* (Leturia 1941; O'Malley 1982; Boyle 1983). O'Malley (1993) also calls attention to the influence of Alonso de Madrid's *Arte para servir a Dios* of 1521 on the "Principle and Foundation" and Gerson's *Monotessaron* on the Kingdom meditation. Iñigo probably did not have this small library with him in the cave, as some have imagined — his own notes and the *Imitation* are certain. Other candidates, however, have been suggested — Gerhard of Zutphen's *Spiritual Ascensions* and Jan Mombaer's *Rosetum* (Clancy 1976).

## The *Imitation of Christ*

The spirituality of the *devotio moderna* has characteristics that are profoundly resonant with that of the *Exercises*. Some aspects that may find familiar echoes in the Ignatian text are the christocentric emphasis with its focus on the humanity of Christ and imitation of his virtues, an emphasis on affectivity that tended to be more rational than emotional, an intense devotion to the eucharist and passion of Christ, the introduction of method in meditative exercises, seeking the basis for perfection in self-knowledge and practice of virtue, insistence on self-abnegation and will power, a tendency to eschew speculation, a higher valuation of interiority and subjective experience and intentionality than of external works and ritual, retirement from the world so that God could be sought in silence and solitude, devotional meditation on the scriptures, and an antihumanistic drift separating it from humanistic movements of the time (Clancy 1976). All of these tendencies have their parallels in Ignatius' text, even though in his later life the direction of his apostolate would have led him along somewhat different paths.

The single greatest literary testament of the *devotio moderna* was the *Imitation of Christ*. It probably originated from the practice of *rapiaria* among the Brethern — little notebooks recording visitations and consolations from God — these were eventually distilled into the text of the *Imitation*. The practice may have influenced Iñigo to keep his own notes, beginning at Manresa and persisting later, even on his pilgrimage to Jerusalem. The influence of the *Imitation* on Ignatius' thinking was marked. Besides the New Testament and the life of Christ, the *Imitation* was the only reading recommended during the Exercises. Ignatius probably came across the work at Manresa and became quite attached to it. Its commendation of monastic values and the solitary consolation of the monk's cell and its bias against scholastic philosophy and theology and learning in general make it seem antithetical to Jesuit practice — quite different than the view of Jesuit vocation in the *Constitutions*: "Our vocation is to travel through the world and to live in any part of it whatsoever where there is hope of the greater service of God and the good of souls" [CS304].[3] Further, its concept of grace was heavily Augustinian — grace and nature are somehow opposed, moving in contrary directions, echoes of the corruption of human nature by the sin of Adam. The inclination of Ignatius and the early Jesuits was to follow the guidance of Aquinas and Trent, understanding the relation of nature and grace in a more positive light. Nonetheless, Ignatius and his followers found it appealing for its intense spirituality, especially in the encouragement of frequent confession and communion, daily examination of conscience, and its emphasis on inner dispositions and the theme of spiritual consolation so central to Ignatian discernment. Even the meditations on the Kingdom and the Two Standards were anticipated by references to Christ as commander and king for whom one must be prepared to die in battle (O'Malley 1993).

## Stages of Composition

Expert opinion on the stages of writing of the *Exercises*, of course, differs considerably. Some argue that the *Exercises* were essentially completed from beginning to end before Iñigo left Manresa, except for some sections such as the "Rules for Thinking with the Church" (Codina 1926). Codina (1938) argued convincingly that the *Exercises* were the fruit of the Manresa experience and were not written prior to that time. Others hold that the experiences reflected in the teachings of the *Exercises* must extend over more than the few months of Iñigo's conversion. Certainly, the book as we now know it was complete by 1541. On Ignatius's own testimony, the origins of the book derived from the Manresa experience in 1522. Consequently, we can assume that the essential parts of the *Exercises* were written in the context of the Manresa experience, but that other elements may have been added during the following years between 1522 and 1541 (de Guibert 1964; Dudon 1949; Leturia 1941; Pinard de la Boullaye 1950).

[3] References to paragraph numbers in the *Constitutions* will be designated by [CS#].

In the course of writing the autobiography in 1555, Gonsalves de Camara asked Ignatius about composition of the *Exercises*:

> After this recital, about October 20th, I asked the pilgrim about the Exercises, the Constitutions, wishing to learn how he drew them up. He answered that the Exercises were not composed all at one time, but things that he had observed in his own soul and found useful and which he thought would be useful to others, he put into writing — the examination of conscience, for example, with the idea of lines of different lengths, etc. The forms of election in particular, he told me, came from that variety of movement of spirits and thoughts which he experienced at Loyola, while he was still convalescing from his shattered leg. (Vita 99)

Further testimony comes from a letter from Laynez to Polanco in June 1547, recounting that at Manresa Ignatius made a general confession of his whole life and began those meditations which were included in the *Exercises*. He added that Ignatius received so many illuminations regarding the Trinity that "although a simple man, and not knowing how to read and write except in Spanish, he began nevertheless to write a book on the subject" (FN I, 82; cited in de Guibert (1964) p. 114). Polanco himself tells us in his life of the saint that Ignatius had begun to formulate his ideas about the Exercises from the beginning of his conversion experience and during the course of his first experiment at Manresa, but that subsequently his own practice and experience helped him to perfect this first effort. Nadal, arguing in 1553 against the charge that the *Exercises* had been composed by an uneducated man, wrote:

> When for the first time Ignatius wrote a good part of the *Exercises*, he had not yet begun to study for when, after his departure from the country . . . he prepared to wipe out his sins by contrition and general confession, he wrote down in a notebook the meditations which helped him the most for this. Then, when he was meditating on the life of Jesus Christ he did the same, but in such a manner that he showed his confessor . . . not only what he wrote then, but all the thoughts which seemed to be (inspirations from) the spirit. Once he had finished his studies, he gathered together these first sketches of the *Exercises*, added many things, put them all into order, and gave them to the Apostolic See to be examined and judged. (Mon Nad IV, 826)

The consensus view is that Ignatius revised his notes for the *Spiritual Exercises* in the light of his Paris experience, probably around 1535. Larrañaga (1956) argues from the testimony of the first companions and from internal evidence that further revisions may have been made during the Roman period, from 1538-1541, prior to the issuance of the *Versio Prima.*

It seems, therefore, that the essentials of the *Exercises* were already written down at Manresa. Moreover, at the trials at Alcala in 1526-27, the pilgrim was able to provide his examiners with at least the substance of the first week, and later at Salamanca he gave Bachelor Frías a copy of the *Exercises* (Vita 67). The same was true in Paris in 1535, when a copy of the *Exercises* was handed over to the Inquisitor Valentin Lievan, who examined them carefully and praised them highly, asking to have a copy for himself. This copy has been lost, but two other Latin texts dependent on the *Versio Prima* are extant. One was left by Peter Faber with the Carthusians of Cologne in 1543, the other was preserved by the English humanist, John Helyar, in a book of notes in the Vatican Library (de Guibert 1964), probably obtained from Ignatius himself at Venice in 1536 or 1537. But the uncertainty of these versions tells us little about the state of the text before 1541.

The depositions from the trial in Alcala provides some information about the spiritual direction given to the group of women around Ignatius. De Guibert (1964) recounts some of this material:

> Ignatius "showed them the service of God" . . . . He explained to them "the three faculties, the five senses, the commandments of God, venial sin, and mortal sin; and he had them make the examen of conscience twice a day, and confess and communicate every week." This was, in resume, the matter which constitutes the first week of the *Spiritual Exercises*, along with the first of the Three Methods of Prayer in them. He taught them also not to be surprised or discouraged at desolations which alternated with consolations — a bit of advice which anticipates the future Rules for the Discernment of Spirits for the first week of the *Exercises.* (pp. 75-76)

At the same time, Ignatius required those undergoing the Exercises to do so for a whole month continuously. The advice about discernment of spirits can be traced back to Manresa, and even further to the conversion experience at Loyola. The careful notes the new convert took even then on the mysteries of the life of Christ would have provided the first material for the contemplations in the *Exercises.*

Other testimonies suggest other aspects of the *Exercises* that may have been extant at Manresa. Manareo reported that at Manresa Ignatius "applied himself chiefly to two exercises, namely those of the Two Standards and of the King, thus preparing himself for the war against the infernal enemy and the world" (cited in de Guibert

(1964) p. 118). Again, Nadal, in an exhortation of 1544, claimed that at Manresa "Our Lord communicated the Exercises to him, guiding him in this manner to employ himself solely in His service and the salvation of souls. He showed his devotion especially in two exercises, that of the King and that of the Standards" (cited in De Guibert, p. 118). And de Guibert adds: "For the contemplation of the Kingdom, these texts only confirm what we have already seen as the clear result of the role played by the *Flos Sanctorum* in the conversion of Ignatius. This is especially true if, as is more probable, he read this book in the edition with the Preface by Gauberto Vagad. In this contemplation Ignatius merely alters into a general formula the thoughts which were most important in his conversion" (p. 118). As for the Two Standards, the similarity to a homily of Werner, the Benedictine abbot of St. Blaise in the twelfth century, suggests a degree of dependence. De Guibert (1964) suggests that Ignatius could have come across the abbot's homily during his studies at Paris, but that the essential idea was already in the rough drafts from Manresa.

De Guibert (1964) also regards the Foundation [SE23] and the Comtemplation for Obtaining Love of God [SE230-237] as doubtfully part of the Manresa version. He argues that the first point of the Contemplation were pious commonplaces that could have easily found their way into Iñigo's reflections, but the later points elaborating ideas of God's presence, power, and essence, and the more scholastic considerations of God's immensity, concurrence and exemplarity, would not have been possible until after the Paris experience. The Principle and Foundation [SE23] are not mentioned in any source from the Manresa or Alcala periods, and the Helyar notes places it among the annotations, suggesting that Ignatius might have detached it from the annotations and put it down as the starting point for the whole *Exercises* on the basis of further experience — a view supported by the fragment of the Directory dictated by Ignatius to Juan de Victoria in 1555. As De Guibert (1964) comments:

> Besides, although the idea of the service of God — outstanding service — rules the whole interior life of Ignatius from its beginning, nevertheless in the development of his thought the more abstract and reasoned concepts of ends and means, of the proportion of means to the end, and of the need of indifference in the presence of these means — all these concepts seem to have taken only little by little the place and importance which they have at the beginning of the *Exercises*. As study familiarized him with the more speculative considerations, experience and the action of God in his soul developed in him, along with the generous yearning for

> service which never left him, habits of strict reasoning, of deliberate and prudent weighing of values. These habits too form one of the characteristic traits of his life and government. (pp.120-121)

Other parts of the *Exercises* seem to have been added at various times. The Rules for Thinking with the Church [SE352-370] were added after the Paris period, probably suggested by the anti-Lutheran propositions circulating at the time or possibly the Decrees of the Council of Paris of 1528. There was a certain fluidity in the organization. We have little idea, for example, when certain central exercises, e.g. the meditation on the Three Classes of Men [SE149-157] or the consideration of the Three Kinds of Humility [SE165-168], were introduced. The argument, as de Guibert notes, that the substantial parts of the *Exercises* date from the Manresa period is troublesome, since it is not clear what is to be included as substantial. His conclusion sums up the situation succinctly:

> We must, then, be content with facts that are well attested, and they are these: that the book of the *Spiritual Exercises* had its first and principal origin in the experiences at Manresa; that from then on there existed a corpus of written documents which Ignatius made use of in his apostolic work; that these documents comprised at least the matter of the first week, the thought pertaining to the Kingdom of Christ and the Two Standards, the contemplations on the mysteries of the life of Jesus, the notes on the election of a state of life, the methods of prayer, and the principles for the discernment of spirits. It does not seem possible to go further with certainty, although it remains quite probable that other parts, we do not know which, already existed at least in outline. (p. 122)

## VERSIONS

The original version was written in Spanish, Iñigo's native tongue, and is preserved in the so-called autograph, which is actually a transcription by a copyist with corrections of a number of errors in Iñigo's own handwriting. There are three principal Latin translations of this text. The oldest, the *Versio Prima*, is contained in a manuscript of 1541 and may well date to Ignatius' sojourn in Paris (1528-1535); it is not impossible that he himself could have translated it. Whoever wrote the translation knew little Latin and provided a quite literal translation of the original Spanish. In 1546-47 the *Versio Vulgata* was made under Ignatius' direction by André des Freux, an accomplished Latinist. At the time, it was thought expedient to provide a more polished text before offering the slim volume to the Holy See for approval. The Vulgate version is certainly more elegant, but also less literal. Both Latin versions were handed over to the censors appointed by Paul III and were approved in the papal brief of 31 July 1548. The Vulgate version of des Freux became the official text. The first printing in September 1548 was issued by Antonio Blado in Rome and financed by Francis Borga, then Duke of Gandia, and utilized the Des Freux version, making it the official version. Prior to that only a few manuscript copies in Spanish were available containing many transcription errors. It was not until 1919 that the *Versio Prima* was also printed in the critical Madrid edition of the *Monumenta Historica Societatis Jesu* (MHSJ). All the myriad documents from the life of Ignatius have been collected and meticulously edited into this massive many-volumed collection.[4]

Because of the liberties in the Vulgate version as compared with the rough but often more expressive text of the original Spanish version and the *Versio Prima*, in 1835 the General of the Society of Jesus, John Roothaan, had a new Latin translation published, and continued to revise it until his death in 1853. This third version has consequently largely replaced the Vulgate in practical use, since it preserves some of the nuances of the original Spanish (de Guibert 1964). But the older versions retain their prestige in that they have been solemnly approved by the Church, and during the last eight years of his life Ignatius himself used the Vulgate version in giving the Exercises.

[4] This monumental series, consisting of nearly a hundred volumes, was begun in 1894 and continues to the present. The project was moved from Madrid to Rome in 1929 where it is published under the auspices of the Institutum Historicum Societatis Jesu. Most of the material in these volumes is based on manuscripts kept in the Archives of the Society of Jesus in Rome. The material in the MHSJ pertaining to Ignatius' life and work is contained in the series of volumes designated as the *Monumenta Ignatiana* (MI). The *Spiritual Exercises* are found in MI, Series II, Vol. I. Madrid, 1919.

# CHAPTER VIII

# THE *ANNOTATIONS*

## Introduction

The *Spiritual Exercises* became a guide for spiritual renewal in the Roman church during the Counter-Reformation and has been a primary influence in the spiritual life of the church ever since, particularly through the efforts of Ignatius' followers in the Society of Jesus. The unique quality of this small volume is evident from the very first. It is not a book *on* spirituality; it is a book *of* spirituality. It contains a series of practical directives — methods of examining one's conscience, engaging in prayer of various kinds, deliberating or making life choices, and meditating. This program of spiritual development, if you will, is interspersed with outlines and directives for various meditations and contemplations.[1] It proposes no spiritual doctrine, but rather offers a pragmatic program of prayerful spiritual exercises, a systematic outline and methodology of Christian spirituality. It is in no sense a book simply to be read; rather, it is a book to be put into practice (de Guibert 1964). Rather than answers or directives, it offers the exercitant a method for answering the call of grace to deeper faith and greater freedom.

The movement of these exercises can be envisioned in objective and subjective terms — objectively in terms of God's communication of the mysteries of salvation history and the meaning and purpose of human life; subjectively in terms of the inner experience of the exercitant interacting with the impulses of divine grace. The subjective aspect is immersed in Ignatius' own experience of God, the fruits of which have been distilled into the *Exercises*. Through his reflection on these intensely personal experiences, Ignatius tried to express the nature and quality of human activity that can lead the exercitant toward greater openness to God and greater cooperation with the liberating dynamisms of divine grace.

We encounter here the Ignatian paradox — that the effectiveness of the Exercises depends wholly on personal effort and wholly on divine grace. The familiar Ignatian formula says "Pray as though everything depended on God, and work as though everything depended on you."[1] As Veale (1996) points out, his syntax often reveal his way of thinking, especially the "although . . .nevertheless" formula: in writing about forming the scholastics and the kind of flexibility and adaptability they needed to learn, he said:

> Although all this can be taught only by the uncotion of the Holy Spirit and by the prudence which God our Lord communicates to those who trust in His Divine Majesty, nevertheless the way can at least be opened by some suggestions which aid and dispose one for the effect which must be produced by divine grace. (CS414)

This paradox reflects Ignatius' own *modus operandi*. In his life of Ignatius, Ribadeneyra wrote: "When he undertook something, most frequently he seemed not to count on any human means, but to rely only on divine providence; but in carrying it out and bringing it to completion, he tried all means to achieve success" (FN IV, 882; cited in Cusson (1988) p. 71, n. 75).[2] It is for this reason that an understanding of Ignatius' personal psychology assumes such significance for understanding the basic psychology of the *Exercises*. Further, this paradox is but a modification of the deeper paradox of human freedom — that man becomes more free in the degree to which he submits to the freedom of God.[3]

## PRENOTES

When one opens Ignatius' *Spiritual Exercises*, one sets foot into a world of spiritual combat, in which forces of goodness and truth labor to establish the kingdom of God, and forces of evil and falsehood struggle against them to destroy that kingdom. Images of the battlefield are never far from the mind of Iñigo de Loyola. For him, it is on the basis of self-denial that the kingdom of God can be estab-

[1] Ignatian "contemplations," particularly as utilized in the Second Week, was a current prayerful practice in his time and an aspect of fransciscan spirituality that found its way into Ludolph's *Life of Christ* that played such a critical role in Iñigo's conversion.

[2] Similar expressions are found in FN III, 631 and IV, 846. See also CS813-814.

[3] It may be advisable to lay the axe to the root of an old bug-a-boo here. The freudian insistence on determinism as the guarantee of scientific rationality does not eliminate or stand in opposition to the notion of human freedom. The case for freedom in human action and as a necessary element in psychoanalytic therapy has been amply and effectively argued elsewhere. See Holt (1965), Wallace (1985), Meissner (1971b, 1984), and Wallwork (1992). Psychoanalysis and the psychology of the *Exercises* share a common goal — the enhancement of freedom and the capacity for free choice.

lished, and it is man's deep-seated unwillingness to overcome his unruly desires that is his greatest tragedy. Without victory over self, there can be no rationality, no belief, no salvation. If man does not rule his passions, he is inevitably ruled by them — a position congruent with the analytic perspective. A Christian who shrinks from the task of self-denial at the same time denies the example and teaching of Christ and refuses to follow in his footsteps. The lesson of the saints is also a lesson of self-denial. In their lives and in their preaching they teach victory over self-indulgence and rejection of worldly honors and passions; their lives are a war without truce against pride, honors, and riches which destroy the soul by drawing it away from Christ and God.

***Spiritual program.*** The second important qualification has more to do with the mechanics of the *Exercises* themselves. The interpretation used in this study views the *Exercises* as a long-term program of asceticism and spirituality. Although the *Exercises* as composed by Ignatius were intended as a relatively intense endeavor extending over a rather brief period of time — usually thirty days — his presumption included several other important factors: one retreatant, one director, complete solitude, excellent dispositions in the exercitant, and so forth. The psychological analysis offered here primarily has this ideal situation in mind, but at the same time it seems valid to project the Ignatian schema as a further reaching program of Christian spirituality. This is, in fact, Ignatius' practice in his own spiritual life and it represents the development in the tradition of an Ignatian spirituality (de Guibert 1964).

From a psychological perspective, each new engagement in the *Exercises* finds the exercitant at one or other stage of progression toward spiritual perfection outlined in the *Exercises.* No matter where he is in the process of spiritual development, his re-engagement in the *Exercises* should tighten his hold on ground already won and enable him to move forward another step on the long hard road to Christian perfection. In any case, Ignatius became increasingly concerned over proper preparation and selection of anyone considering the Exercises. Such individuals required a degree of maturity, sufficient intellectual capacity to allow for deeper spiritual understanding, and a desire to seek God's will and service. This probably arose from his own increasing experience of giving the Exercises and from his failures. The practice of the Exercises became more intensive, based on complete seclusion, continual prayer, and personal direction throughout. He became more aware that often a lengthy preparation was indicated to insure that the retreatant would approach the Exercises with positive dispositions.

***Director.*** The title "director" does not appear in the *Exercises*, but is usually referred to as "one giving the Exercises," a phrase with less of an authoritarian ring. Ignatius viewed the process as conversational, so that the work of the Exercises was left in the hands of the exercitant. The director was to be a helper or facilitator only. Ignatius frequently warned of harm spiritual guides could bring to others by insisting on following a certain path or using their own experience as a norm for others. The director is warned against excessive zeal or efforts to rouse the exercitant to greater fervor. His role is to be modest, sober, and respectful of the exercitant's needs and capacities. He too, along with the exercitant must submit himself and be open to the movements of grace, and interact with the exercitant in a way that is respectful and supportive of the inner movements in the exercitant's soul. The director is to present material for reflection, and then let the inner workings of the exercitant's soul and his relation to God take effect (Iparraguirre 1959). The Exercises are not an exercise in psychological manipulation or therapeutic intervention — they are meant to be a process by which the soul seeking God can be helped to better dispose himself to receive God's grace. Any effort to convert them into a psychological or therapeutic program would run counter to their spiritual intentionality and purpose. The cautions are directed against possible countertransferences[4] that may come into play in the director, either as expressions of his own psychology or as elicited by transferences of the exercitant. The question of transferences and their role in the dynamics of the Exercises is of central significance and cannot be ignored.

In Rome, Ignatius took an active interest in supervising and guiding others in learning this art — all the more difficult and delicate when the exercitant was making a retreat of election (O'Malley 1993). The importance of the role of the director was a stimulus for the emergence of the series of Directories anticipating the final official version in 1599. The two major contributions were from Polanco and Diego Miro. Polanco emphasized the need for individual accommodation and the role of affectivity; Miro insisted on a literal adherence to the text as an ideal of spiritual proficiency. Efforts at

[4] Countertransference includes those reactions and attitudes experienced by the analyst insofar as they are rooted in his own unconscious — whether they are elicited by the patient's transference or derive in some of other way from the analyst's inner world.

collaboration broke down, but the final version of 1599 was a compromise (O'Malley 1993).

## THE *Spiritual Exercises*[5]

### Anima Christi

Soul of Christ, sanctify me.
Body of Christ, save me.
Blood of Christ, inebriate me.
Water from the side of Christ, wash me.
Passion of Christ, strengthen me.
O good Jesus, hear me;
Within thy wounds hide me;
Suffer me not to be separated from thee;
From the malignant enemy defend me;
In the hour of my death call me,
And bid me come to thee,
That with thy saints I may praise thee
Forever and ever. Amen.

This beautiful prayer has traditionally been placed at the very beginning of the *Spiritual Exercises* since the end of the sixteenth century.[6] The prayer dates from about two centuries before the time of Ignatius and was one of his favorites. The prayer itself is not found in the Spanish autograph nor in the two early Latin versions, but is mentioned in the triple colloquy of the meditation on the Two Standards [SE147] and in the Second Method of Prayer [SE253]. The motifs of union with Christ, self-immolation and absorption into the body of Christ as the vehicle for achieving eternal salvation, are articulated from the very beginning. The sense of utter devotion is unavoidable. Union with Christ, service to the divine Master, and total dedication and commitment of self, are keys to spiritual growth

[5] The text of the *Spiritual Exercises* of St. Ignatius used here is from the translation provided in Fleming (1978). The literal translation of the Exercises in this edition by Elder Mullan, S.J. is based on the autograph version of the *Exercises*, was done in 1909, and published in 1914. Paragraph references to the official Latin text are indicated in brackets [SE#]. References to the *Directory* are to Iparraguirre (1955). They indicate a series of suggestions and recommendations to those giving the *Exercises* that were compiled at various times after the death of Ignatius; they provide a more-or-less official commentary or interpretation of parts of the text of the *Exercises*.

[6] Leturia (1948) discusses the origins and variations of this traditional prayer, as well as the Minor Hours or Office of the Blessed Virgin Mary, and their numerous influences on the *Spiritual Exercises*.

and salvation. The prayer, although addressed to Christ, Lord, Master, and Savior, nonetheless has a maternal quality.[7]

## ANNOTATIONS

> [1] Annotation I:
> The first Annotation is that by this name of Spiritual Exercises is meant every way of examining one's conscience, of meditating, of contemplating, of praying vocally and mentally, and of performing other spiritual actions, as will be said later. For as strolling, walking and running are bodily exercises, so every way of preparing and disposing the soul to rid itself of all the disordered tendencies, and after it is rid, to seek and find the Divine Will as to the management of one's life for the salvation of the soul, is called a Spiritual Exercise.

The *Spiritual Exercises* have a twofold purpose: (1) preparing and disposing the soul to free itself from all inordinate affections, and (2) seeking and finding the will of God concerning the ordering of life for the salvation of one's soul. The second depends on the first. The first represents the establishment of reasonable control over emotionality and *ipso facto* a degree of self-integration to allow a secure and cohesive sense of self and psychological identity. The supposition is that the personality achieving a mature psychological identity has presumably resolved conflicts characteristic of the infantile stages of psychosexual and psychosocial development. These "disordered tendencies" or "inordinate attachments" reflect conflictual desires and wishes that remain unintegrated and unregulated sources of distraction and impediment to the attaining of spiritual values and graces (Iparraquirre 1959).

[7] In my previous interpretation of this prayer (Meissner 1992b) I advanced the hypothesis that the imagery of protection and being enfolded within the sacred wounds, recalls associations to a fantasy of reunion with the lost mother — damaged in the delivery of her last child, perhaps even to the point of death. Might we not hear in this prayer echoes from the depths of Ignatius' heart — the long repressed longing to rejoin the mother, who was torn away from him by death, perhaps even death brought about by giving him life? Can we presume to interpret the water as amniotic, or the wounds as the bloody consequence of a delivery that threatened, if it did not terminate, his mother's life? Can we discern the unconscious fantasy that Iñigo himself was the murderer who by his birth brought death to his mother? See the extensive contextual considerations for this suggestion in Meissner (1992b), as well as the relevance of the maternal influences in Iñigo's conversion experience in chapter II above. The implications for this unconscious fantasy on the sense of unconscious guilt and possibly the need for punishment on Ignatius' ascetic disposition and on his spiritual doctrine, especially in the *Exercises*, will be discussed later.

The *Exercises* set to work on the presumption that the contemporary situation of the personality in terms of its level of development and its degree of effective functioning is neither fixed nor static. The contemporaneous identity of the self is a terminal product of an ongoing process which constantly modifies the status of the self in such a way that the residues of prior stages of development, whether successfully or unsuccessfully resolved, are effectively integrated as functioning components of the personality. Unsatisfactory resolutions of infantile conflicts may thus leave a subtle influence on the functioning of the contemporary psyche, but the defect is presumed not to be totally irreparable. From the Ignatian point of view, some part of the lost ground can be recovered by the self-modifying effort of the contemporaneous psyche.[8] The potentiality of spiritual growth can take place in spite of the fact that rectification of basic defects in psychosexual or psychosocial development is difficult to achieve in any degree and may defy any definitive solution. The *Exercises* share this supposition with clinical psychoanalysis.

The general rubric, under which Ignatius develops the notion of securing psychological identity, is that of freedom from inordinate affections. Psychologically speaking, an inordinate affection is an emotional attachment, an emotional responsiveness (Iparraquirre 1959) that has escaped effective control of psychic regulatory systems. To the extent to which such control has failed, effective functioning of the ego is impeded. A large component of such areas of uncontrolled emotionality can be unconscious in origin; the more deeply imbedded such factors are, the more difficult it will be to establish control over particular disordered affections related to it. The *Exercises* are not directly concerned with conditions of emotional dysfunction that would be considered psychiatrically as pathological. Consequently, the proper framework for considering psychological aspects of the *Exercises* is not psychiatric. Nonetheless, the same psychological dynamisms are operative in normally developed personalities, and it is with these dynamisms that we have to deal. Insofar as inordinate affections, from which the exercitant seeks to free himself,

[8] This dynamic has been addressed by various students of the *Exercises* as a form of "transformation of the ego" (Alemany and Garcia-Monge 1991; Divarkar 1991), a theoretical perspective I had originally proposed (Meissner 1964). Attribution to the ego of these complex transformations seems somewhat antiquated, reflecting a limited ego psychological frame of reference. I would prefer a broader and more updated frame of reference locating the agency of change in the self-system, within which the ego can be regarded as a functional subsystem. See Meissner (1986, 1993).

are motivated by unconscious dynamisms, such dynamisms cannot be excluded from the work of the *Exercises*. The psychoanalyst would tend to speak of unconscious conflicts and the need for their resolution, rather than inordinate attachments; the difference between the psychiatric and spiritual language may be more rhetorical than actual.

> [2] Annotation II:
> The second is that the person who gives another the way and order in which to meditate or contemplate, ought to relate faithfully the events of such Contemplation or Meditation, going over the Points with only a short or summary development. For, if the person who is making the Contemplation, takes the true groundwork of the narrative, and, discussing and considering for himself, finds something which makes the events a little clearer or brings them a little more home to him — whether this comes through this own reasoning, or because his intellect is enlightened by the Divine power — he will get more spiritual relish and fruit, than if he who is giving the Exercises had much explained and amplified the meaning of the events. For it is not knowing much, but realising and relishing things interiorly, that contents and satisfies the soul.

Ignatius stresses the fact that insight obtained by the exercitant through his own active participation is considerably more effective in fostering growth of spiritual identity than passive acceptance of points provided by the director. Activity of the ego is a paramount requirement for development. This annotation touches on the Ignatian psychology of spiritual development. This psychology is central to the entire structure of the *Exercises* since it provides the basis upon which many practical suggestions are founded. The basic principle would seem to be that the exercitant actively progresses through stages of development by exercise of his own creative and synthetic capacities, particularly through the combined application of functions of understanding, incorporation and identification. The accent falls on intellectual understanding, since in the Ignatian perspective it is through enlightening the mind that spiritual growth is experienced and the influence of grace implemented. But Ignatius never works through intellect alone without emphasizing accompanying affective currents — here it is not merely knowing what is in question, but "relishing things interiorly."[9]

By engaging his own powers in an intrapersonal dialectic, by coming to grips with fundamental truths and realities of the spiritual

[9] Similar emphases are found, for example, in the first week [SE76] and in his appeal to consolation and desolation. See chapters XV and XVI below.

life and by moving from the level of observant understanding to that of participant understanding, the self begins to mature in spiritual identity. By a progressively deepened understanding, the ego is able to embrace realities forming the substance of the spiritual life and gradually and more effectively bring to bear its own executive functions to achieve greater stability of affective functioning. As Ignatius puts it so well, "It is to understand and savour the matter interiorly, that fills and satisfies the soul." The operation of grace at this level is found in the assistance and support it provides the self by enlightenment of the understanding and by the support of the executive and synthetic functions by which the ego integrates various elements into an harmoniously developing identity and regulates affective dispositions which can interfere with the effectiveness of these operations.

The necessity for mobilization of the resources of the ego is underlined by recommendations of the *Directory* that "it is a lesson of experience that all men are more delighted and more moved by what they find out for themselves. Hence it will suffice just to point, as with the finger, to the vein in the mine, and let each one dig for himself" (Dir. VIII, 1). These are wise words for any form of psychotherapy, and a familiar counsel for practicing psychoanalysts. To the degree that the patient can be enlisted in active participation in the analytic process in terms of the therapeutic alliance (Meissner 1992a, 1995), analytic effectiveness is enhanced and options for meaningful and constructive internalizations increased.

The *Directory* adds some clarifying notes (Dir. VIII, 3). The exercitant, who is presumed to be a novice in the spiritual life, is to avoid excessive tension and the exhaustion of excessive effort. Rather than forcing himself, he is to be taught the means and principles of thinking calmly on things divine. The psychic resources called into play are exercised best in moderation and tranquillity avoiding emotional extremes. Reasons presented are: (1) excessive effort cannot last and therefore the continuous application and activity required in meditation cannot be maintained; (2) solid fruit is found in knowledge of those truths and in movement of the will, both of which proceed from inward light. The inward light is essentially a profound insight and realization of spiritual truths. The insight is the foundation upon which change can be effected, but mere insight alone is not enough. The insight must be "worked through," that is, the realization of its impact upon the exercitant's life must be grasped to the fullest possible extent. By gradually realizing in what way each truth has meaning and significance for all the facets of his life and activity, the exercitant grows in participant understanding. At each phase of the working through, incorporation and integration are advanced by the ego's effective acceptance of each new partial and personalized insight. The comparison to issues of developing insight and working-through in the psychoanalytic process is apt. (3) The final reason stresses the necessary role of grace upon which growth in spiritual identity must ultimately depend. It is of greater importance for the ego to dispose itself in tranquillity and humbly to receive the movement of God within it, than by trusting in its own autonomous functioning to achieve the desired result.

> [3] Annotation III:
> The third: As in all the following Spiritual Exercises, we use acts of the intellect in reasoning, and acts of the will in movements of the feelings: let us remark that, in the acts of the will, when we are speaking vocally or mentally with God our Lord, or with His Saints, greater reverence is required on our part than when we are using the intellect in understanding.

> [4] Annotation IV:[10]
> . . . . For, as it happens that in the First Week some are slower to find what they seek — namely, contrition, sorrow and tears for their sins — and in the same way some are more diligent than others, and more acted on or tried by different spirits; it is necessary sometimes to shorten the Week, and at other times to lengthen it. The same is true of all the other subsequent Weeks, seeking out the things according to the subject matter. However, the *Exercises* will be finished in thirty days, a little more or less.

The principle of personal adaptation requires that certain modifications be made in the manner of presenting the *Exercises*. The course should be followed that leads to the greatest growth in the exercitant. Ideally the *Exercises* are given to only one exercitant at a time, so that the director is able to adapt the program for the needs of this particular person. This requires that the director possess a thorough and intimate knowledge of the workings of the exercitant's personality (Dir. V, 6), certainly enough to attune himself to the individual rhythm and degree of responsiveness and sensitivity of each exercitant — adapting the pacing and selection of the material for meditation to the needs of the individual. In ideal circumstances, the director would want to spend a considerable amount of time gaining such an inti-

[10] Text omitted. The fourth Annotation describes the content of the four weeks — the first week on sins, the second on the life of Christ up to Palm Sunday, the third on the passion and death, and the fourth on the resurrection and ascension. These "weeks" are not understood as lasting seven or eight days, but as stages of spiritual progression.

mate knowledge of the exercitant, even before beginning the *Exercises* themselves. The travails of modern psychology and particularly psychotherapy bear eloquent testimony to the complexities and difficulties involved. But analogously, the effectiveness of the Exercises would seem to hinge on the degree of accurate knowledge of the exercitant's personality possessed by the director, and also on the degree of rapprochement between them. The analogous factor in the analytic situation is the therapeutic alliance — an essential ingredient in the effectiveness of the process. We could speak here of an alliance between the exercitant and the director. The many factors in the practical order, mitigating these aspects of the process, can only water down the effectiveness of the *Spiritual Exercises*. Even so, grace is still capable of extraordinary effects.

It is interesting in this respect to consider Ignatius' recommendations for deciding to whom the Exercises could be given and on what terms. In the *Constitutions*, he recommended giving the Exercises to doubtful candidates to the Society as a way of testing their vocation [CS196]. He recommended that those learning how to give the Exercises should adapt them so as to give satisfaction to those taking them and to encourage their desire to make the Exercises. He comments that as a rule only the first week should be given, and the whole of the Exercises only to outstanding persons or to those desiring to decide their state of life [SE409].

The affects sought for here — "contrition, sorrow and tears for their sins" — and the guilt and shame connected with a deep recognition of one's sinfulness put the exercitant's ego-ideal under pressure and begin the process of transformation of the sinful self (Tornos 1991). The narcissistic investment of the ideal has in part the function of preserving the self from any sense of its fallibility, weakness, vulnerability, and limit. The narcissistically invested ego-ideal traffics more in a sense of superiority, omnipotence, and invulnerability — not unlike the ego-ideal of the preconversion Iñigo (Meissner 1992b). Realized shame and a sense of guilt for one's failures and limitations runs counter to any such narcissistic self-investment.

[5] Annotation V:
The fifth: It is very helpful to him who is receiving the Exercises to enter into them with great courage and generosity towards his Creator and Lord, offering Him all his will and liberty, that His Divine Majesty may make use of his person and of all he has according to His most Holy Will.

The question of motivation is basic in undertaking the Exercises. The exercitant must enter them motivated to follow them fully and generously and thereby dispose himself to God's will. The Exercises, however, do not rest content with this initial motivation, but progress to arousal of further considerations and realizations whereby additional sources of motivation are brought to bear. However, it remains true that, just as in therapy there can be no effective change in the subject without motivation to change, so here effectiveness of the undertaking depends upon the generosity and purposefulness with which the exercitant follows the prescribed exercises. The *Directory* suggests therefore that he "resolve to behave manfully, to remove all obstacles to grace, and to bend all the powers of his soul to cooperation with grace; and let him dispose himself, as best as he can, to receive it" (Dir. II, 1).

Ignatius presupposes here that the individual is in possession of his freedom and that his disposition of mind be open to offering that freedom to God as he enters and leaves the Exercises.[11] Freedom is thus "a presupposition of the Exercises, the condition for their possibility, more than their product" (Buckley 1984, p. 67). This annotation, then, is foundational insofar as it embodies the dynamic of the whole Exercises. Desire and freedom, attributes the exercitant brings to the Exercises, are given primary place; they are not to be destroyed, but given over to God with liberality and magnanimity — *con grande animo*.[12] The dispositions are specified in some detail. The objective is to bring the capacities of the psyche to bear with greatest efficacy possible. The exercitant is asked to organize and direct his energies toward positive engagement in the work he is undertaking (Dir. II, 3). Through hope, he is encouraged to adopt a prospective attitude which readies ego-functions to respond with some expectancy of fulfillment. Hope consequently implies preliminary mobilization of ego-resources as well as an already realized reality-orientation (Meissner 1973, 1987). It is a preliminary disposition preparatory to the execution of the working-through of the retreat process.

The purpose set before the exercitant is "not so much to taste spiritual delight, as to understand God's will concerning himself" (Dir. II, 4). This is accomplished by countercathectic control over emotional attachments, but more centrally and more positively, a resignation to place oneself in God's hands in all matters where the person is still free to determine the course of his life.

[11] See the final *Suscipe* prayer at the end of the fourth week [SE234].

[12] Buckley (1984) notes that no other spirituality encourages one to deal with God with such magnanimity.

The annotation speaks of "liberality and a large heart" in describing the disposition on entering the *Exercises*, which the *Directory* expands in terms of generosity. It is required that the person dispose himself to be ready to respond without restriction or limitation to impulses of grace. This is possible, of course, only in the measure to which instinctual (libidinal, aggressive, and narcissistic) impulses and attachments have been sufficiently subjected to the regulatory functions of the ego and effectively integrated in the self. Since this is in part the work of the retreat, the initial disposition of generosity can be expected to grow through various stages of the retreat in the measure to which inordinate attachments have been successfully eliminated. The *Directory* remarks: "Rather should he dilate his heart, and crave, with all his might, to unite himself with God, and receive of those heavenly treasures, to his utmost capacity, rich and bountiful largess. These are the exercitant's duties towards God" (Dir. II, 5). The psychoanalyst might address similar issues in terms of the therapeutic alliance. But it is also important to note that the *Exercises* presume the availability of suitable and spiritually oriented motivations; they provide no device for overcoming resistances or instilling such motivation, as might concern the psychoanalyst in the work of analysis.

This emphasis reminds us that all the dynamic issues familiar from study of the psychoanalytic situation are also to be discovered in the relationship between retreatant and director. There is first of all a real relationship of two human beings mutually engaged in a process of seeking and finding God's will and spiritual growth. There is an alliance, akin to the therapeutic alliance, by which each of the participants accepts an obligation to engage in the work of the Exercises with appropriate motivation, good will, sincerity, honesty, and industry so as to gain the sought for benefits from the process. In this vein, the exercitant is encouraged to entrust himself completely to the director, in whom he is to see God's instrument to guide him along the path of God's will (Dir. II, 6). He is, therefore, to conceal nothing from the director, but is to open his heart to him in all sincerity (Dir. II, 7). We are reminded here of the suspension of censoring activities required in psychoanalytic free-association. The situation is analogous, but not identical. What is in question is a more controlled association in which the progress of the meditation, lights, consolations, desolations, desires, etc. are to be reported to the director without the interference of the superego's censorship function — whether in the form of guilt, shame, or repulsion.

But along with these more or less positive dispositions, there are unavoidably elements of transference. Transferences of various kinds, positive and negative, oedipal and preoedipal, infantile and mature, will find their way into the relationship with the director, and inevitably into the exercitant's relation to God. Ignatius was not unaware of these predominantly emotional contaminants, but any notion of transference was far from his mind. He deals with them under the rubrics of resistances, temptations of the devil, and especially in affective terms in the form of consolations and desolations (Newman 1985). I shall return to this theme in due course.

What is basically required, then, of the exercitant is basic trust, one of the basic components of the healthy personality (Erikson 1959, 1963). It implies, therefore, the capacity to open oneself receptively to the influence of another and to dispose oneself in a kind of trusting dependence on that other. Defensiveness and lack of security in the sense of one's own trustworthiness would constitute a severe block to progress in the growth of spiritual identity.

> [6] Annotation VI:
> The sixth: When he who is giving the Exercises sees that no spiritual movements, such as consolations or desolations, come to the soul of him who is exercising himself, and that he is not moved by different spirits, he ought to inquire carefully of him about the Exercises, whether he does them at their appointed times, and how. So too of the Additions, whether he observes them with diligence. Let him ask in detail about each of these things.

The recommendation of this annotation has deep psychological significance. As the individual enters upon the Exercises, he or she engages upon a powerful effort of reconstruction and synthesis, calling for often strenuous efforts to redirect one's psychic energies and motivational investments,[13] to effectively reorganize and direct resources available to the ego, and above all, to diminish and redirect appropriately investments absorbed in narcissistic tendencies. Every psychotherapist knows how difficult such reconstructions are and what tremendous resistances are often put in the way. The ego is pitted, in a sense, against id and superego, and even against itself. Where reconstruction succeeds, consolation should follow; where it fails or proves excessively difficult, some form of desolation might be

[13] Ignatius refers to pre-existent psychic investments as "inordinate attachments." In psychoanalytic usage, this can refer to attachment to other persons, but it can also have the more general connotation of investment in nonhuman objects or their equivalents. The pilgrim's crusade of self-denial was directed to rooting out such inordinate attachments and narcissistic investments.

expected. Consolation and desolation are not to be conceived merely in terms of pleasure and pain, but rather in terms of integration with the reality principle governing ego-functions of reality-orientation, organization and synthesis.

The director is to keep a close watch on all of this. He is to visit the exercitant daily and inquire into his progress (Dir. VII, 1). The exercitant is expected to inform the director of details without concealing anything. If he is experiencing consolation, he is to be encouraged, but also taught how to use this consolation to greater effect. As the *Directory* observes, if no action were to follow upon the feeling (which does not last very long), there would be little profit from the exercise (Dir. VII, 2). It is necessary, then, that the self progress from the stage of understanding and incipient reorganization to a more effective stage of execution and synthesis. The danger is that temporary gains may be lost, particularly when forces involved in the interplay of ego, id and superego never lose their power. If it is a question of desolation, the director is to inquire into the method of meditation and particularly keeping of the Additions (Dir. vii, 4).

Insofar as the work of the Exercises is concerned, the presumption is that, in these circumstances, the exercitant is not following the program properly. The failure may be merely a matter of method, or it may indicate lack of generosity, on which the initial mobilization of ego-resources depends even in natural terms. Or it may reflect a more serious personality disorder stemming from defective ego-strength, unresolved unconscious conflicts, or even character pathology of various sorts. The director, especially when symptoms seem severe, should not press the retreatant on details of method, since this may only intensify the problem by undermining self-esteem or increasing guilt dynamics. This would be especially true of obsessive types. This difficulty is minimized where the Exercises are given in diluted form, but there is still danger that inexperienced or naive directors might mistake compulsivity for generosity. In such cases, the director can afford to be supportive and encouraging; there is little he can do if motivation is lacking, and ultimately grace cannot be forced. Difficulties in the analytic situation in dealing with certain forms of intractable resistance are not dissimilar. It should be remembered, however, that the Exercises are intended for normal personalities and there are no provisions in them for dealing with the pathological.

> [7] Annotation VII:
> The seventh: If he who is giving the Exercises sees that he who is receiving them is in desolation and tempted, let him not be hard

> or dissatisfied with him, but gentle and indulgent, giving him courage and strength for the future, and laying bare to him the wiles of the enemy of human nature, and getting him to prepare and dispose himself for the consolation coming.

It is especially important in early stages of the Exercises that desolation from the subject's failure to achieve his objective be properly handled. The situation is somewhat similar to the patient in psychotherapy suffering from depression. Insofar as desolation represents resistance of libidinal or narcissistic attachments to efforts of the exercitant to gain control, the director should ally himself with the ego in this struggle (Dir. VII, 6). The strategy is familiar to analysts in terms of the therapeutic alliance (Meissner 1992a). He is to support, encourage, reinforce the desires and good intentions of the exercitant, explaining the nature of the affects he is experiencing. The more the director can support the exercitant's basic generosity and encourage his trust and hope, the better.

The *Directory* observes that the best means of obtaining devotion is that of self-humiliation together with subjection and resignation to God's will. "Indeed, this displeasure and bitterness proceeds often enough not so much from fervour, as from a certain latent pride, whereby reliance is placed on one's own industry, whether because this too is a point of excellence to which one would aspire, or because of self-love which hankers after consolation" (Dir. VIII, 7). This is the central problem of narcissism which lies at the root not only of the neurotic process, but also of sin. Narcissism interferes with the capacity of the self to establish proper reality-oriented object relations. The primary object-relation in the spiritual order is man's relation to God. Acceptance of this basic element in the spiritual reality of our existence undercuts such narcissistic tendencies, insofar as they impede spiritual progress, and provides the substance of the first crisis of spiritual development, the successful resolution of which enables the ego to advance along the path of the development of spiritual identity. The analytic rubric here, as we shall see, is not the elimination of narcissistic investments, but rather their transformation (Kohut 1966).

> [8] Annotation VIII:
> The eighth: If he who is giving the Exercises sees that he who is receiving them is in need of instruction about the desolations and wiles of the enemy — and the same of consolations — he may explain to him, as far as he needs them, the Rules of the First and Second Weeks for recognising different spirits.

The interpretative norms contained in the rules of discernment of spirits can be given to the exercitant insofar as they offer a resource to the understanding for more effectively dealing with and recognizing the psychological reaction he is passing through.[14] The importance of these rules should not be underestimated, since they "are most useful and hold up a light, so to speak, on the whole of this spiritual pilgrimage" (Dir. VIII, 4). They are also in a unique sense an immediate distillation of Ignatius' own spiritual experience and personality.

> [9] Annotation IX:
> The ninth is to notice, when he who is exercising himself is in the Exercises of the First Week, if he is a person who has not been versed in spiritual things, and is tempted grossly and openly — having, for example, suggested to him obstacles to going on in the service of God our Lord, such as labors, shame and fear for the honor of the world — let him who is giving the Exercises not explain to him the Rules of the Second Week for the discernment of spirits. Because, as much as those of the First Week will be helpful, those of the Second will be harmful to him, as being matter too subtle and too high for him to understand.

A certain discretion is called for in proposing the rules for discerning spirits. Persons who are not capable of refined discernment should not be given the rules of the second week since they would be more confusing than helpful. The limitation may be due to lack of understanding or limited introspective capacity. In any case, the exercitant is helped by principles he or she can grasp clearly and utilize. Here again an intimate knowledge of the exercitant's capacities by the director is essential. Moreover, there is operative here a principle of progressive growth in spiritual identity: only insofar as the ego has successfully passed through and resolved certain critical phases of growth, do the rules of the second week become pertinent. The ego must grow in familiarity with the spiritual life and must exercise its functions of introspective discernment in progressively more sensitive and refined reality-testing. The testing has to do with responsivity to influences of grace which constitute the framework of orientation and the reality structure within which spiritual identity is to develop. The interpretive principle involved is not unlike that in analysis — interpretations must be tailored to the understanding of the analysand in order for them to bear any fruit.

[14] See chapters XV and XVI below on Rules for Discernment. See my discussion of his ascetical practices in chapter XXXII below.

Here again we might catch a glimpse of the conflicted Iñigo behind the description of the beginner in spiritual combat as "a person who has not been versed in spiritual things, and is tempted grossly and openly — having, for example, suggested to him obstacles to going on in the service of God our Lord, such as labors, shame and fear for the honor of the world . . ." [SE9]. The description, I would submit, passes for a portrait of the ambivalent Iñigo struggling to find his spiritual footing. In his autobiography, he describes himself in similar terms: "Up to this time he had continued in the same interior state of great and undisturbed joy, without any knowledge of the inner things of the soul. . . . there occurred to him a rather disturbing thought which troubled him by representing to him the difficulty of the life he was leading, as though he heard a voice within him saying: "How can you stand a life like this for the seventy years you have yet to live?" (Vita 20). The mention of "shame and fear for the honor of the world" speaks to the narcissism so close to the heart of his personality organization.

> [10] Annotation X:
> The tenth: When he who is giving the Exercises perceives that he who is receiving them is assaulted and tempted under the appearance of good, then it is proper to instruct him about the Rules of the Second Week already mentioned. For, ordinarily, the enemy of human nature tempts under the appearance of good rather when the person is exercising himself in the Illuminative Life, which corresponds to the Exercises of the Second Week, and not so much in the Purgative Life, which corresponds to those of the First.

The essential elements in the work of the Exercises are disengagement of libidinal and/or narcissistic attachments that might influence the exercitant's efforts to follow the will of God. From a structural point of view, whether objects of such investments involve morally good or evil elements is not of much importance, since what is in question in either case is some form of instinctual gratification. When such gratifications escape ego-regulation, they impede growth in both psychological and spiritual identity. However, from the point of view of ego-dynamics, attachment to a morally good object is a much more subtle matter in that such channeling of libido, even though it escapes the regulating function of the ego, is in conformity with the value-orientation of the self — at least in the early stages of growth in spiritual identity. Thus, the rules of the second week provide a set of norms by which the individual can recognize such attractions to the good as not in conformity with the value-orientation of a more mature level of spiritual functioning. The rules provide a set of norms for ego-functioning and at the same time introduce the exercitant into the value orientation of a more advanced stage of spiritual development.

Ignatius asserts a correspondence between the first week and the purgative way and between the second week and the illuminative way. The correspondence is traditional and has been supported by the Directories; the fourth week in this schema would correspond to the unitive way (Dir. XI, 3; XVIII, 3). There has always been difficulty, however, in placing the third week in this scheme; some have placed it in the illuminative, some in the unitive way (Fessard 1956). The question will have pertinence in trying to bring to focus the obvious progression of the Exercises on the psychological level. It is well to recognize here that there is a developmental principle at work.

> [11] Annotation XI:
> The eleventh: It is helpful to him who is receiving the Exercises in the First Week, not to know anything of what he is to do in the Second, but so to labor in the First to attain the object he is seeking as if he did not hope to find in the Second any good.

The force of the developmental principle is felt here with special intensity. Concentration on work of the moment is sought for, but there would seem to be more at stake. Since we are dealing with a process of psychospiritual growth, success in succeeding stages of development will depend on the degree to which the work of preceding stages has been effectively carried out. The entire process is subject to a law of organic growth. That is not to say that what is achieved or not achieved at each given stage is irrevocably lost, or that developmental recapitulation in later stages is not possible. Even where psychological laws are operating, grace is not bound by them.

> [12] Annotation XII:
> The twelfth: As he who is receiving the Exercises is to give an hour to each of the five Exercises or Contemplations which will be made every day, he who is giving the Exercises has to warn him carefully to always see that his soul remains content in the consciousness of having been a full hour in the Exercise, and rather more than less. For the enemy is not a little used to try and make one cut short the hour of such contemplation, meditation or prayer.

The locus of work in the Exercises is in meditation, for it is here that resources of the self are brought to bear. A most likely form of resistance will take the form of abbreviating periods of meditation, or of diluting the intensity of effort by other means. The personal activity of the exercitant is at stake, without which nothing is to be accomplished.

> [13] Annotation XIII:
> The thirteenth: It is likewise to be remarked that, as, in the time of consolation, it is easy and not irksome to be in contemplation the full hour, so it is very hard in the time of desolation to fill it out. For this reason, the person who is exercising himself, in order to act against the desolation and conquer the temptations, ought always to stay somewhere more than the full hour; so as to accustom himself not only to resist the adversary, but even to overthrow him.

A refinement of the previous annotation. Where resistances are strong enough to bring on desolation or depression, the danger of the ego's capitulation to libidinal forces is all the greater. The principle is the basic Ignatian "agere contra." His persuasion is that the most effective means to establish ego-control over a particular form of instinctual attachment is to direct effort to the opposite — if one is tempted to shorten the time of meditation, the opposite tack is to extend it. Ignatius does not leave matters at the intrapsychic level of opposing the desire to shorten the time, but launches his attack on the level of concrete externalized action bringing executive functions of the ego into play. The emphasis on action is a recurrent theme in the *Exercises*. Psychoanalytic interest here is directed more to the motivational substratum than behavioral directives.

> [14] Annotation XIV:
> The fourteenth: If he who is giving the Exercises sees that he who is receiving them is going on in consolation and with much fervor, he ought to warn him not to make any inconsiderate and hasty promise or vow: and the more light of character he knows him to be, the more he ought to warn and admonish him. For, though one may justly influence another to embrace the religious life, in which he is understood to make vows of obedience, poverty and chastity, and, although a good work done under vow is more meritorious than one done without it, one should carefully consider the circumstances and personal qualities of the individual and how much help or hindrance he is likely to find in fulfilling the thing he would want to promise.

Wise advice, and one that operates equally in the analytic sphere. In analysis, the patient is advised to make no important decisions without adequate exploration and analytic understanding. Ignatius shows us here his sensitivity to the vulnerability of fervent souls when operating on the basis of emotional enthusiasm or zealous inspiration. His preference is for thoughtful and prudent decision-making. He also takes a stand against any form of suggestion or exploitation or undue influencing of the exercitant.

> [15] Annotation XV:
> The fifteenth: He who is giving the Exercises ought not to influence him who is receiving them more to poverty or to a promise, than to their opposites, nor more to one state or way of life than to another. For though, outside the Exercises, we can lawfully and with merit influence every one who is probably fit to choose continence, virginity, the religious life and all manner of evangelical perfection, still in the Spiritual Exercises, when seeking the Divine Will, it is more fitting and much better, that the Creator and Lord Himself should communicate Himself to His devout soul, inflaming it with His love and praise, and disposing it for the way in which it will be better able to serve Him in future.[15] So, he who is giving the Exercises should not turn or incline to one side or the other, but standing in the centre like a balance, leave the Creator to act immediately with the creature, and the creature with its Creator and Lord.

The fundamental principle on which the efficacy of the Exercises is based is the direct action of God on the soul. Particularly, the director should not get in the way between God and his creature. The exercitant should not be distracted by much reading, but should make use of a few well-chosen books — the gospels, the *Imitation of Christ,* and perhaps some lives of the saints — but not even these until after the first week (O'Malley 1993). The model behind these directives is, of course, Ignatius and his Manresa experience. This fundamental principle of divine influence was one of the tenets brought under attack as reflecting the influence of the heretical *alumbrados* — an accusation that bought Ignatius to grief on several occasions at the hands of the Inquisition. In 1553, the Domincan theologian Tomas de Pedroche, abetted by Siliceo the archbishop of Toledo, connected these annotations with the second method of making an election [SE176, 184-8] by following the movements of consolation and desolation as evidence of the teaching of the *alumbrados*. As O'Malley (1993) points out, the objections focused on excessive or exclusive reliance on inner inspiration and refusal to

[15] This aspect of annotation XV was targeted by Pedroche, the Spanisn inquisitor, as evidence of Ignatius' illuminism, along with aspects of his doctrine on spiritual consolation (see chapters XV and XVI). Ignatius was not entirely innocent of associations with the *alumbrados,* but these aspects are more congruent with his mysticism than illuminism (see below, chaperts XXXIV and XXXV).

urge the life of religious vows (poverty, chastity, and obedience) as superior choices. Ignatian indifference did not satisfy them, even though Ignatius was not slow to endorse a life of poverty, since that was the way chosen by his Lord, as in the meditations on the Kingdom [SE91-99] and the Two Standards [SE136-148]. The taint of illuminism lingered on, such that the Directories and later commentators — e.g. Suarez — led to attempts to stress Ignatius' orthodoxy and to underplay the radically new elements in the Ignatian synthesis (Egan 1976).

> [16] Annotation XVI:
> The sixteenth: For this — namely, that the Creator and Lord may work more surely in His creature — it is very expedient, if it happens that the soul is attached or inclined to a thing inordinately, that one should move himself, putting forth all his strength, to come to the contrary of what he is wrongly drawn to. Thus if he inclines to seeking and possessing an office or benefice, not for the honor and glory of God our Lord, nor for the spiritual well-being of souls, but for his own temporal advantage and interests, he ought to excite his feelings to the contrary, being instant in prayers and other spiritual exercises, and asking God our Lord for the contrary, namely, not to want such office or benefice, or any other thing, unless His Divine Majesty, putting his desires in order, change his first inclination for him, so that the motive for desiring or having one thing or another be only the service, honor, and glory of His Divine Majesty.

*Agere contra* is spelled out here in greater detail. The objective here as always is to strengthen the position of the exercitant by helping him gain greater control of the psychic forces at work in his soul. Understanding and insight are essential to effective ego-functioning, but they do not constitute the total realm of effective ego-function. Sources of motivation must be brought into play, if gains achieved through insight are to be consolidated and made effective. Two things are in question here: (1) effective mobilization of spiritually attuned motives, and (2) progressive insight and reality-orientation in terms of the value-system governing authentically spiritual growth, namely, "the service, honor, and glory of His Divine Majesty."

In classical analytic theory, countercathexis implied conflict between forces of the ego and those of the id. The restraining function of countercathexis could only hold instinctual forces in check at the cost of exhausting energy resources of the ego. The conflict could be successfully resolved, however, by sublimation of instinctual energies channeling them to a more acceptable substitute object. The resolution of intrapsychic conflict, envisioned in the Ignatian "agere contra," is more a question of progressive establishment of ego-control, but such internal regulation and resolution of drive-defense complexes does not take place without integration of other structural subsystems. Moreover, ego-control implies neither repression of drive impulses nor resolution through sublimation, but rather continued operation of drive energies with a direction and intensity determined by the reality-orientation of the ego operating in conjunction with other psychic systems. There is a radical difference between repression of the sex drive, for example, and adequate regulation, sublimation and direction of the sex drive in chastity. Likewise, there is a radical difference between religious behavior as simply a sublimation of sexual impulses and religious behavior as a response of an autonomous ego to a spiritual reality and value-system. Consequently, the term "counter-cathexis" is used in these notes in a more flexible sense as referring to regulatory activity of the ego operating as a subsystem within the self (Meissner 1986, 1993).

Speaking more generally, the psychoanalytic perspective would have a different slant from the Ignatian in this regard. A fuller understanding of defenses and forms of resistance, including character resistance, would lead the analyst to be less sanguine about the potential for overcoming defects of persistent attachment or character by *agere contra.* Unconsciously determined fixations and attachments may be driven underground, only to resurface in some disguised or displaced fashion and thus elude well-meaning intentions of the subject for reform and self-correction. Freud (1930) commented in this regard, "When saints call themselves sinners, they are not so wrong, considering the temptations to instinctual satisfaction to which they are exposed in a specially high degree — since, as is well known, temptations are merely increased by constant frustration, whereas an occasional satisfaction of them causes them to diminish, at least for the time being" (p. 126) Temptations that are so denied or repressed thus tend to break through either with greater strength or in some displacement. This, I have argued (Meissner 1992b), may well have been the case in Ignatius' massive repression of sexuality during his own conversion. Conclusion — *agere contra* has a limited scope and carries with it a variety of complications and difficulties. However, it was quite consistent with Ignatius' character and seems to have been more or less effective for him. In any case, it plays a significant role in his *Spiritual Exercises* and in his own spiritual experience.[16]

[16] See my discussion of his ascetical practices in chapter XXXII below.

[17] Annotation XVII:
The seventeenth: It is very helpful that he who is giving the Exercises, without wanting to ask or know from him who is receiving them his personal thoughts or sins, should be faithfully informed of the various movements and thoughts which the different spirits put in him. For, according as is more or less useful for him, he can give him some spiritual Exercises suited and adapted to the need of such a soul so acted upon.

This annotation emphasizes the necessity of intimate knowledge of the exercitant by the director, and consequently complete suspension of censorship in the exercitant.[17] The analogous role of the basic analytic rule of free association is clear.

[18] Annotation XVIII:
The eighteenth: The Spiritual Exercises have to be adapted to the dispositions of the persons who wish to receive them, that is, to their age, education or ability, in order not to give to one who is uneducated or of little intelligence what he cannot easily bear and profit by.

Again, that should be given to each one by which, according to his wish to dispose himself, he may be better able to help himself and to profit.

So, to him who wants help to be instructed and to come to a certain degree of contentment of soul, can be given the Particular Examen [SE24], and then the General Examen [SE32]; also, for a half hour in the morning, the Method of Prayer on the Commandments, the Deadly Sins, etc. [SE238]. Let him be recommended, also to confess his sins every eight days, and, if he can, to receive the Blessed Sacrament every fifteen days, and better, if he be so moved, every eight. This way is more proper for illiterate or less educated persons. Let each of the Commandments be explained to them; and so of the Deadly Sins, Precepts of the Church, Five Senses, and Works of Mercy.

So, too, should he who is giving the Exercises observe that he who is receiving them has little ability or little natural capacity, from whom not much fruit is to be hoped, it is more expedient to give him some of these easy Exercises, until he confesses his sins. Then let him be given some Examens of Conscience and some method for going to Confession oftener than was his custom, in order to preserve what he has gained, but let him not go on into the matter of the Election, or into any other Exercises that are outside the First Week, especially when more progress can be made in other persons and there is not time for every thing.

[17] See above, Annotation IV and V.

Principle of personal adaptation. Ignatius is careful to note that not all subjects have the capacity to advance to higher levels of spiritual development. Besides the assistance of grace, there is necessary a certain degree of capacity and maturity of psychological identity in those who can profitably enter upon exercises directed toward growth in spiritual identity. While all can profit to some extent from consideration of the first week, discretion is called for in going beyond.

These accommodations, emphasizing the examination of conscience and methods of prayer of the First Week, was probably the basic format followed by Ignatius from the time he left Manresa until he reached Paris. They were presumably the vehicle for more intense conversations leading to deeper religious sensibility and renewed commitment, closer to the true goal of the Exercises. They also probably set the tone of early Jesuit catechesis and other ministries of the Word of God (O'Malley 1993).

> [19] Annotation XIX:
> The nineteenth: A person of education or ability who is taken up with public affairs or suitable business, may take an hour and a half daily to exercise himself.
>
> Let the end for which man is created be explained to him, and he can also be given for the space of a half-hour the Particular Examen and then the General and the way to confess and to receive the Blessed Sacrament. . . [18]
>
> [20] Annotation XX:
> The twentieth: To him who is more disengaged, and who desires to get all the profit he can, let all the Spiritual Exercises be given in the order in which they follow.
>
> In these he will, ordinarily, more benefit himself, the more he separates himself from all friends and acquaintances and from all earthly care, as by changing from the house where he was dwelling, and taking another house or room to live in, in as much privacy as he can, so that it be in his power to go each day to Mass and to Vespers, without fear that his acquaintances will put obstacles in his way.
>
> From this isolation three chief benefits, among many others, follow.
>
> The first is that a man, by separating himself from many friends and acquaintances, and likewise from many not well-ordered affairs, to serve and praise God our Lord, merits no little in the sight of His Divine Majesty.
>
> The second is, that being thus isolated, and not having his understanding divided on many things, but concentrating his care

[18] The rest of this annotation deals with scheduling of meditations on sin.

> on one only, namely, on serving his Creator and benefitting his own soul, he uses with greater freedom his natural powers, in seeking with diligence what he so much desires.
>
> The third: the more our soul finds itself alone and isolated, the more apt it makes itself to approach and to reach its Creator and Lord, and the more it so approaches Him, the more it disposes itself to receive graces and gifts from His Divine and Sovereign Goodness.

It should be obvious that the Exercises call for a rigorous introspective effort on the part of the exercitant. He is called, on even purely natural terms, to summon up his best resources of self-control, understanding and execution, and to engage in an effort of self-analysis, reorganization and synthesis. For the full program of the Exercises optimal motivation is required — as was described in the fifth annotation [SE5] above. Such an effort requires serious and concentrated effort demanding that the exercitant's best effort be brought to bear. Distractions, therefore, and continuing preoccupation with other affairs would hinder effectiveness of these efforts. Attuning oneself to movements of the spirit — "listening to God" — requires certain dispositions: inner quietude, tolerance for separation and solitude ("verbum Dei qui loquitur in silentio"), and humility. But perhaps more significantly, growth in spiritual identity depends upon responsiveness to grace. Additional effort must be thrown into prayerful petitioning for God's grace. On both counts, silence and solitude are advisable. The director should remember, however, that this degree of effective psychic work consumes energy and that it may often promote the effectiveness of the retreat to allow periods of relaxation (Dir. VI, 3). Ignatius also sounds here, for the first time, the note of freedom so central to the principles of the Exercises — he seeks a deeper understanding that a deepening of the life of faith is also a deepening of the life of freedom, "our freedom and God's Freedom, completely united" (Pousset 1971, p. xvi).

# CHAPTER IX

# THE FIRST WEEK — SIN

## First Week [SE23-90]

### The Foundation

> [23] First Principle and Foundation:
> Man is created to praise, reverence, and serve God our Lord, and by this means to save his soul.
>
> And the other things on the face of the earth are created for man and that they may help him in prosecuting the end for which he is created.
>
> From this it follows that man is to use them as much as they help him on to his end, and ought to rid himself of them so far as they hinder him as to it.
>
> For this it is necessary to make ourselves indifferent to all created things in all that is allowed to the choice of our free will and is not prohibited to it; so that, on our part, we want not health rather than sickness, riches rather than poverty, honor rather than dishonor, long rather than short life, and so in all the rest; desiring and choosing only what is most conducive for us to the end for which we are created.

This great statement of the Ignatian credo comes at the beginning of the First Week — an enunciation of the "Principle and Foundation" that is to govern all that follows. The purpose is twofold — to turn the exercitant toward the cosmic perspective of the divine plan of creation and salvation history, and to set before him the task of situating himself within this grand design (Cusson 1988). The Foundation was probably added at some later time to provide a statement of the basic framework of ideas on which subsequent meditations would build (Rahner 1967). What may have begun as merely a preparatory note to set the stage eventually developed into an essential foundation for all that was to follow. In the Ignatian Directory, he even suggested that the exercitant be kept meditating on this foundation, along with the particular and general examens for several days. Ignatius came to view it as an essential experience by which appropriate dispositions for the Exercises could be instilled.[1] This vision of divine purposes may reflect one of the profound insights Ignatius developed during the Manresa period (Cusson 1988). It was never far from his conscious mind — in a letter to Coimbra in 1547 he exhorted his brothers to distinguish themselves in learning and fraternal charity, "making yourselves perfect instruments of God's grace and co-laborers in the sublime work of leading God's creatures back to Him as their supreme end" (Epistolae I, 495-510, Letter 169; in Young (1959), p. 128).

From a psychological viewpoint, Ignatius here enunciates the fundamental principle of orientation, which serves as a reality criterion and a value-criterion for the activity of the self (Dir., XII, 1; Iparraguirre 1959). It is of fundamental importance that the principle be properly conceptualized and that it become effective as an operative principle for implementing the exercitant's efforts at self-organization and direction (Dir., XII, 7). As a principle of ego-orientation, it is operative at all stages of the Exercises (Rahner 1956),[2] and it is normative for all degrees of spiritual growth. Consequently, it does not represent or express a stage or degree of development in spiritual identity. Rather, the Foundation formulates the fundamental rule by which the ego disposes itself, under grace, to progress in spiritual growth at every stage in the process of development. Its importance, consequently, cannot be overestimated (Dir., XII, 3). In giving the Exercises, the Foundation is continually referred to and built on. The exercitant should repeatedly return to it and reflect on it so that its effective influence at successive stages not be diminished.

Ignatius also seems to have put a good deal of motivational weight on assimilation of the Foundation, envisioning that the exercitant would "be led to place himself entirely in the hands of God our Lord" (SpExMHSI, p. 792; cited in Cusson 1988, p. 135). Cusson (1988) adds: "Whether one takes a long or short time to prepare oneself for the retreat, the consideration of the Foundation should aim at a twofold result concerning our relationship with God: a lively consciousness of being in debt to him, and an immense desire of fidelity as our generous response to all his requests from us" (p. 135). Meditation on this Ignatian vision is intended to stir one to generosity and deepening desire for God.

In a certain sense, the Foundation encapsulates the entire program of spiritual development. The objective is stated in terms of

[1] These dispositions were those recommended in Annotation V [SE5].

[2] For an extended consideration of the place of the *fundamentum* in the *Spiritual Exercises*, see Tetlow (1989).

functions proper to spiritual identity — the praise, reverence and service of God (Dir., XII, 2). The means are set down in general terms as indifference, according to the norm of the "tantum quantum" and finally the disposition to choose only those things leading most to the objective of man's existence (Dir., XII, 3). This is Ignatius' statement of the primacy of freedom and faith under grace in spiritual development — the "path of freedom" (Fessard 1956). In general, then, Ignatian indifference and the "magis" sketch in broad lines the pattern for growth in spiritual identity. His indifference is not a matter of renunciation, but implies a reaching beyond all creaturely attachment for the divine, embracing the whole of God's creation in a spirit of love and service. It implies an existential distance between the self and all created things freeing one to reject even one's own prejudices and desires and to take responsibility for whatever one takes and uses and whatever one rejects or leaves behind. The first week of the Exercises concerns itself primarily with indifference, the following weeks, with increasing intensity, with the "magis." Cusson (1988) sums up this movement:

> Moreover, this constant rising above ourselves, which is required in the many daily choices we must make, and in the many ways of using creatures, demands a purification that is motivated above all by a stronger attachment to God, to his work, and to Christ, who is at the center of it all. An exact presentation of this outlook on human beings and their lives, which places the Foundation in the light of God's saving plan, necessarily leads to an awareness of our ceaseless need to bring order into our lives. We accomplish this by using all the natural means at our disposal, and by doing that with a view to surrendering ourselves more freely to the work of grace in us. (p. 79)

The structure of the *Exercises* hinges on two polar anchoring points provided by the Foundation and by the contemplation for attaining love in the fourth week [SE230-7]. These embrace the essential elements of the Ignatian vision: the movement of the world back to God. But between the vision and its fulfillment, between the ideal and its realization in the heart and mind of the retreatant, Ignatius will pose the obstacle of evil in the First Week, which diverts the movement of creation from its divinely appointed goal, and the call for the exercitant to freely join with Christ in the work of salvation, uniting himself with Christ in his passage through death to life (Third and Fourth Weeks) (Cusson 1988).

The Foundation provides a direct and condensed expression of Ignatius' ego-ideal. It expresses a profound and meaningful Christian view of man's purpose and his place in God's salvific plan. It also serves as the basic postulate for the rest of the Ignatian program of spiritual exercises. It enunciates an ideal of profound indifference encompassing the entire created order: nothing is allowed to stand between man and his divinely appointed destiny. The Foundation calls upon the exercitant to stand aside from everything intervening between himself and God — from all that in one way or another belongs to me but yet is not me — "not only material possessions, time, friends, but also my activity, my abilities, even my nature that has been formed by my own free decisions, health and sickness, honor and dishonor, thoughts and desires, and so forth. . . . This person ["the free, self-surrendering person posited by God"] has mastery over all other things, takes them or leaves them, and in this dealing with things finds God and itself and comes to an understanding of the relationship between God and self" (Rahner 1967, p. 19).

Yet human nature is not without its contradictions. The law of the flesh is forever at war with the law of the spirit. As Ramsey (1962) commented:

> Because of that other law that holds sway within, the resources for living as we ought may flow only from common grace and the grace of the Gospel — and beyond grace as power, from grace as forgiveness which brings in us who remain halt. lame and blind. Nevertheless, when by sin freedom injures itself and its life in love, there still remains a silent pressure toward love as the *vix sanatrix naturae* in the very constitution of man's transcendent spiritual freedom determining the *direction* in which alone health is to be found. Love belongs therefore to the nature of man. (p. 146)

## *Particular Examen* [SE24-31]:

This section describes details of the particular examen. The exercitant is to examine his faults three times in the day — first in the morning to guard himself against the particular sin or defect he wishes to correct [SE24]; second after dinner, asking God for grace to remember how often he has fallen into that particular sin or defect, and to amend himself in the future. The examen is to go over hour by hour, or period by period, and count the number of times he has fallen into that particular sin or defect, then resolve to amend himself in the future [SE25].

The method proposed here serves to concentrate ego energies at one point (Dir., XIII, 2) so that the work of countercathexis and control can proceed more effectively. The Ignatian propensity for mobilizing as many of the functions of the psyche as possible is noteworthy. Memory, imagination, critical judgment, affection, desire, resolution, and finally execution are all brought to bear in this brief exercise. Effectiveness of this technique depends on the capacity of the self to direct its attack in the right direction. This requires working-through of resistances and cognitive recognition of points of defective self-control. It should be clear that the technique of the particular examen has no effectiveness in itself, but only insofar as it provides a useful schema within which the person can take resolute action.

It should also be noted that the particular examen is regarded as an exercise which can be fruitfully continued beyond the Exercises in the rest of life (Dir., XIII, 4). This certainly was Ignatius' own practice (Meissner 1992b).[3] Implicit in this observation is the realization that efforts of spiritual man in self-control and organization never really reach a point of complete achievement, but require continual effort and application. This should be understood as a program of life-long spiritual growth. The *Directory* likewise suggests that the practice be inculcated as an effective means for right ordering of the exercitant's life (Dir., XIII, 5). Moreover, it can be questioned to what extent Ignatius would be concerned with actual examination of conscience and confession rather than a deepening awareness of personal sin within the perspective of the universal history of sin. The aim may better be taken as preparation for the retreat and achieving optimal dispositions for it than simply for confession (Cusson 1988); but we cannot forget that Ignatius himself was almost obsessionally devoted to frequent confession, even to frequent general confession in his more scrupulous moments. However, the exercitant who remains preoccupied with his sins and their external manifestations will fall short of encountering the full mystery of "Christ made sin" and a sense of communion with Christ in our sinfulness. In existential terms, this is the root of nonbeing within our being embedded within human freedom (Pousset 1971).

In the contemporary setting, a serious question has to do with the degree to which a focus on sin and sinfulness communicates effectively to modern men. We can wonder if the meaning of sin no longer touches a sensitive cord for postmodern man. Does meditation on the sin of the angels or of Adam and Eve carry much impact for modern consciences (Sievernich 1991)? Perhaps not — but this presents a problem for adapting the *Exercises* to modern concerns, not a question of the basic psychology involved. There are no lack of

[3] See chapter XXXII on Ignatius' ascetical practices below.

impressive examples of the presence, even pervasiveness, of evil in our modern world. We have lived through the Nazi Holocaust, through continuing fratricidal strife and even genocide, as much or more than any era of human history. The modern record of social injustice and prejudice leaves much to be desired.

It is common practice and frequently recommended by commentaries on the *Exercises* that the particular examen be employed in developing positive practices of virtue (Rickaby 1923). This is not mentioned in the *Exercises*, but seems to be thoroughly Ignatian in spirit and psychologically sound. The dominant theme in the *Exercises* is the loving and salvific plan of God; sin plays a secondary role only as a rejection or deviation from that plan. Ignatius does not seek negative immersion or depressive wallowing in guilt and shame, but develops them as the starting point of response to divine initiatives.

The third time recommended for self-examination is after supper, when the second Examen will be made in the same way, hour by hour, from the first Examen to the present [SE26]. Four additions follow [SE27-31] with recommendations for ridding oneself sooner of that particular sin or defect: (1) to feel grief for each time one falls into that particular sin or defect, which can be done even in the presence of many, without their perceiving what he is doing; (2) to check at night if there is any from the first to the second examen [SE28]; (3) to make a similar comparison from day to day [SE29]; and (4) also from week to week [SE30-1].

## GENERAL CONFESSION [SE32-44]:

Ignatius then proposes procedures for making a general confession:

> [32] GENERAL EXAMEN OF CONSCIENCE
>
> To Purify Oneself and to Make Ones Confession Better
>
> I presuppose that there are three kinds of thoughts in me: that is, one my own, which springs from my mere liberty and will; and two others, which come from without, one from the good spirit, and the other from the bad.

The movement of self-reflection here makes a demand that the exercitant appropriate his interiority, including thoughts and feelings. Ignatius' focus on conscious mental processes has no consideration for unconscious or even preconscious aspects of mental functioning. The appropriation of any mental content as my own rests on the connection with consciousness and freedom. But a variety of unconscious and dynamic processes can give rise to thoughts on the conscious level, but what is the connection between these unconscious levels and the individual's self-appropriation? Some would argue that they are "other" since they do not issue from freedom which Ignatius regards as essential to the personal self [SE5]. The psychoanalytic perspective would extend the range of self-appropriation to include the unconscious — in this view the unconscious is no less part of the self than the conscious.[4] These first distinctions are followed by a more or less traditional catalogue of sins in thought [SE33-37], word [SE38-41], and action [SE42]. The ways in which such sins can be mortal or venial and techniques for gaining merit from such temptations, by resisting and overcoming them, are discussed. Ignatius seems to have followed traditional confessional usages here. We can get a feel for the delicacy of Ignatius' conscience from the following:

> [40] One must not speak an idle word. By idle word I mean one which does not benefit either me or another, and is not directed to that intention. Hence words spoken for any useful purpose, or meant to profit one's own or another's soul, the body or temporal goods, are never idle, not even if one were to speak of something foreign to one's state of life, as, for instance, if a religious speaks of wars or articles of trade; but in all that is said there is merit in directing well, and sin in directing badly, or in speaking idly.
> [41] Nothing must be said to injure another's character or to find fault, because if I reveal a mortal sin that is not public, I sin mortally; if a venial sin, venially; and if a defect, I show a defect of my own.
>
> But if the intention is right, in two ways one can speak of the sin or fault of another:
>
> First Way. The first: When the sin is public, as in the case of a public prostitute, and of a sentence given in judgment, or of a public error which is infecting the souls with whom one comes in contact.
>
> Second Way. Second: When the hidden sin is revealed to some person that he may help to raise him who is in sin — supposing, however, that he has some probable conjectures or grounds for thinking that he will be able to help him.

Ignatius continued to utilize this method of examination of conscience throughout the rest of his life. Throughout the years of pilgrimage and study and during the years in Rome, until the day of his

[4] See Meissner (1986, 1993).

death, Ignatius remained faithful to the practice of the examens, apparently just as he had outlined them in the *Exercises.*[5]

Ignatius finishes the examens with some points on method:

> [43] METHOD FOR MAKING THE GENERAL EXAMEN
>
> It contains in it five Points.
>
> First Point. The first Point is to give thanks to God our Lord for the benefits received.
>
> Second Point. The second, to ask grace to know our sins and cast them out.
>
> Third Point. The third, to ask account of our soul from the hour that we rose up to the present Examen, hour by hour, or period by period: and first as to thoughts, and then as to words, and then as to acts, in the same order as was mentioned in the Particular Examen.
>
> Fourth Point. The fourth, to ask pardon of God our Lord for the faults.
>
> Fifth Point. The fifth, to purpose amendment with His grace.
>
> OUR FATHER.

The history of general confession is sketchy, certainly before Trent.[6] In Ignatius' day it was not common practice. He would probably have come into contact with it at Montserrat, through the work of Abbot Cisneros and the influence of the *devotio moderna*. The practice became more common through Ignatius' efforts and those of the early Jesuits. The practice of frequent confession and particularly general confession became a *leitmotif* of Ignatius' pastoral practice and a major vehicle for early Jesuit ministry (O'Malley 1993). They proposed it as an important instrument for renewal of spiritual life and turning away from sinful patterns. As was the practice in contemporary confessional manuals, lists of sins were intended to insure that consciences were sufficiently informed to include all confessable material so that all faults and failings could receive the healing balm of confessional forgiveness — Ignatius follows this traditional format.

The emphasis on renewal gave particular prominence to general confession, but the usage can be confusing (O'Malley 1993). In the sixteenth century it had several meanings — it could refer to a text, a detailed form of examination of conscience, or a type of confession.

[5] See the discussion of this practice in relation to his scrupulosity in chapter XVII below.

[6] See Calveras (1948) for a discussion of the role of extant confessional manuals not only on the confessional practice reflected in this text but on methods of prayer [SE238-260], particularly the first method.

As a form of confession it could mean the liturgical confession at the beginning of mass, or confession to a priest in the sacrament of penance, or, as recommended in the *Exercises*, a review of one's whole life to gain greater knowledge of oneself and turn more decisively away from sin to God. Nor was this to be a one-time effort. Ignatius himself made general confessions repeatedly at crucial junctions in his career and the practice was encouraged by his followers as an aid to spiritual growth. The *Constitutions* recommend the practice for Jesuit scholastics every six months "because of the many benefits it entails" [CS98]. The practice was followed presumably not out of obligation, but from a desire for spiritual progress.

Ignatius suggested that the exercitant make a voluntary general confession at the end of the first week. One reason he gives for this is that at the end of the first week the exercitant should have a more intimate knowledge of his sins than at any other time (Dir., XVI, 2). This serves to underline in part the objective of the first week, "namely an intimate knowledge of his sins together with true contrition" (Dir., XVI, 1). The sense of sinfulness and the accompanying guilt were significant aspects of Ignatius' own spiritual journey — the Autobiography testifies to his continual struggles with scruples and his frequent recourse to general confessions (Meissner 1992b). But clearly he also envisioned the confessional vehicle as a path leading toward God — the God who forgives and saves. As Leavy (1993) sagely notes, it is not merely the sense of forgiveness that seems to lift the burden of guilt, "but the opening of the imagination to hitherto abandoned symbols of redemption — in Christianity, for example, the suffering savior, or the interceding mother" (p. 420). Thus, seeking for forgiveness can become a vehicle for transference determinants participating in the dynamic constellation underlying the spiritual movement of the Exercises toward greater union with Christ and openness to God.

He added some comments pertaining to confession and communion:

> [44] General Confession with Communion
>
> Whoever , of his own accord, wants to make a general confession, will, among many other advantages, find three in making it here.
>
> *First.* The first: Though whoever goes to Confession every year is not obliged to make a General Confession, by making it there is greater profit and merit, because of the greater actual sorrow for all the sins and wickedness of his whole life.
>
> *Second.* The second: In the Spiritual Exercises, sins and their malice are understood more intimately, than in the time when one

> was not so giving himself to interior things. Gaining now more knowledge of and sorrow for them, he will have greater profit and merit than he had before.
> *Third.* The third is: In consequence, having made a better Confession and being better disposed, one finds himself in condition and prepared to receive the Blessed Sacrament: the reception of which is an aid not only not to fall into sin, but also to preserve the increase of grace.
> This General Confession will be best made immediately after the Exercises of the First Week.

The same dynamic forces that remained conflictual and unresolved in Ignatius' own lifelong spiritual struggles lie behind the obsessional, almost compulsive practices that played so dominant a part in his own spiritual career and that he proposed to any who undertook the Spiritual Exercises. A glance at his recommendations for the particular examen [SE24-31], the general examination of conscience [SE32-43], and the general confession [SE44], convey a sense of the detailed and programmed character of his efforts to ease the torment stemming from his relentlessly punitive superego. The language is frequently that of battle, struggle, and conquest, as for example, in his discussion of ways of overcoming sinful impulses or thoughts: the first method [SE33] is a sort of psychic knockout punch — we are reminded of his repressive banishment of all impure temptations after the vision at Loyola. The second way [SE34] resembles a bout of many rounds that is won only after numerous attempts, by a decision as it were. The image calls our attention to Ignatius' lifelong struggles with his disordered desires which became a preoccupation and focus for endless examinations, sorrow, confession, and self-demeaning protestations. But one should not see these experiences only through a pathological lens — what was at issue more deeply was purification. The agony of self-doubt and despair put Ignatius himself, and hopefully the exercitant who follows his lead, in touch with the mystery of the God who forgives and saves.

## Objective of the First Week

As the exercitant enters the first week, he undertakes the first phase in an extended program of spiritual growth. The objective of this first stage is variously described: shame and confusion for personal sin: "to put myself to the blush and to be confounded"; "great and intense grief and tears for my sins; "interior knowledge of my sins and a detestation of them"; "to feel the deordination of my actions: in order that abhorring it I may amend and order my self aright"; "knowledge of the world in order that, abhorring it, I may put away from myself worldly and vain things." To which the *Directory* adds: confusion and sorrow (Dir. XV, 1), withdrawing the soul from inordinate love of objects of sense (Dir. XV, 4), holy fear of God, bewailing sins and recognizing the turpitude and deformity of sin (Dir. XVII, 1). A summary statement takes this form: "The end and object assigned to the first week is principally the attainment of the knowledge that we have gone astray from the path which should lead us to the end for which we were created. Consequently, it also involves sorrow for aberration of such heinousness, and of such magnitude, and the kindling of an intense desire to return to that path and to persevere in it forever" (Dir. XVIII, 1).

The first week therefore is a confrontation with the problem of evil. For Ignatius, evil resides in the heart of man, where it derives from a disordered relation to and misuse of creation, thus subverting the divine order. Man's freedom, intended as the divine spark in man, is perverted into another path that runs counter to divine purposes and leads more deeply into the kingdom of Satan. Satan becomes the personification of evil — the enemy of human nature who seeks to undermine and destroy God's plan and kingdom. If the Ignatian perspective saw sin only in terms of the transgression of divine law, mere examination of conscience and confession would suffice. But it does not — sin goes more deeply to the heart of the relation between God and man. It is self-affirmation rooted in self-enhancement and pride that isolates the sinner not only from himself but from God — "you will be like God, knowing good and evil" (Gen 3: 5).

These narcissistically determined dynamics stand in opposition to man's essential dependence on God and on divine forgiveness. It is within this perspective that Ignatius shaped his view of human sinfulness and evil. The articulation of man's guilt within the matrix of divine forgiveness gives new meaning and transformation to the phenomenon of guilt. Ramsey's (1962) comment is to the point:

> From the point of view of forgiveness, what, then, is guilt? The answer to this question may be stated in the following four propositions, which, in the last analysis, are simply four ways of affirming a single idea: (1) Guilt is a forensic term for the difficulty of repentance; (2) guilt is a forensic term for unwillingness to receive forgiveness; (3) guilt is a forensic term for continuation in sin in the teeth of proffered forgiveness; (4) guilt is a forensic term for despair over sin and for despairing of the forgiveness of sin. The whole phenomenon of guilt receives itself into this single

> composite proposition; and this proposition about the nature of guilt, when seen in the light of forgiveness, is itself not capable of extension, variation, or more particular explication, and it affords no inference that affects human life in any other way than accomplishing the transmutation of guilt — which is indeed the goal of forgiveness. As often as God speaks or the gospel is spoken of, one can only give a plain assent to this understanding of what guilt means in the light of his Word. (p. 56)

This statement encapsulates some of the Ignatian perspective on guilt.

Special emphasis should be placed in this context on the crucial role of affective knowledge in Ignatius' thinking — an emphasis with parallels in psychoanalytic considerations of insight and its role in bringing about change in the patient. The "interior knowledge" in Ignatius' terms is synonymous with the affectively meaningful understanding at the heart of psychoanalytic insight. For Ignatius, affective experience accompanying a deepening awareness of sinfulness — the sense of confusion, sorrow, tears — comes as a result of grace guiding the soul to profound repentance and conversion leading to total surrender to God. He had a profound sense of the meaning of affectivity and its place in spiritual life. As Mouroux (1954) put it: "The fact that affectivity plays such an enormous part in the Christian life, arises mainly from man's structure. The spiritual life is essentially a matter of self-giving and the consecration of one's freedom to God. But affectivity prepares the way for it, then goes hand in hand with, and then crowns the movement of liberty; unless, conversely, it successively blocks it, paralyzes it, and dries it up" (p. 269). For Ignatius, the model was his own experience at Manresa in which his ambition, inordinate attachments, and pride had to be destroyed before they could be replaced with spiritual ideals and ambitions. These objectives of the first week are aimed at through a series of meditations on sin and hell.

Ignatius bases his self-assessment more on affective experience than on any merely cognitive aspect. His reliance on affect as the criterion of truth reflects something of his psychological style and orientation to his experience, especially the strength and vividness of his emotional life. Feelings for Ignatius were powerful sources of motivation and conviction, far stronger than the pale impact of intellectual insights and reasonings. As is often the case in the economy of affects, not only do emotions have a sense of inner force, but they often impress themselves unexpected, unannounced and uncontrolled, in such a way that they could not be contrived or devised in tune with self interest or assuagement, and so claim the stamp of authenticity. They could not have been made up and must be the real thing. This is especially so when the feelings are painful and tormenting.[7] Given our basic need to seek self-comfort and to opt for pleasure over pain, painful affects such as guilt or shame must have eluded the devices for comfort and concealment and thus reveal a fundamental truth about the self (Nussbaum 1988). This appreciation points the way to a fuller appreciation of the role of affective experience in Ignatius' rules for the discernment of spirits.[8]

## MEDITATIONS ON SIN

> [45] First Exercise
>
> It is a meditation with the three powers[9] on the first, the second and the third sin. . . .
>
> [46] Prayer. The Preparatory Prayer is to ask grace of God our Lord that all my intentions, actions and operations may be directed purely to the service and praise of His Divine Majesty.
>
> [47] First Prelude. The First Prelude is a composition, seeing the place.
>
> Here it is to be noted that, in a visible contemplation or meditation — as, for instance, when one contemplates Christ our Lord, Who is visible — the composition will be to see with the sight of the imagination the corporeal place where the thing is found which I want to contemplate. I say the corporeal place, as for instance, a Temple or Mountain where Jesus Christ or Our Lady is found, according to what I want to contemplate. In an invisible contemplation or meditation — as here on the Sins — the composition will be to see with the sight of the imagination and consider that my soul is imprisoned in this corruptible body, and all the compound in this valley, as exiled among brute beasts: I say all the compound of soul and body.

We can catch a sense of the central role Ignatius gives to the imagination in his meditative technique. Rahner (1967) observed:

> St. Ignatius is a man who thinks concretely and who has little time for things that can only be treated abstractly. He wants to move the whole man; he knows that, when a man has encountered reality, his true knowledge always occurs in a "conversion to the phantasm," or in a "conversion to history." Therefore, we

[7] So he thought, as did Freud (1900) in considering affects in dreams.

[8] See chapters XV and XVI below.

[9] The three powers are the traditional Augustinian division of the powers of the soul traditional at the time — memory, intellect, will. Rahner (1967) translates these into "spirit in its self-presence, in its self-intuition, and in its self-activity" (p. 43).

> always find in St. Ignatius' writings a union of idea and concrete image. We could almost say: a union of history and myth. What he says with an image is not only a dressed-up idea and an artificial image, it is also a turning toward the concrete truth that appears representatively in history. (p. 44)

In Lacanian terms, Ignatius strives to wed the symbolic and the imaginary to give greater force and meaning to both.

These vivid and imaginative reconstructions of the details of scenery and action are particularly prominent in the contemplations, where the exercitant is asked to immerse himself in concrete details of whatever subject he is considering. Even when the subject is more or less abstract, he still insists on construction of concrete sensory details — the so-called "application of the senses." Pruyser (1968) has commented on this aspect of the *Exercises*:

> Loyola's *Spiritual Exercises* are a form of religious thought control which makes a very deliberate use of the imagination. In certain phases of the systematic "meditations," as they are called, the retreat master urges the retreatant to imagine as vividly as possible the excruciating sufferings of Jesus at the various stages of the cross, to identify himself with the agonies of his Lord to the point of sweating, signing, or moaning, and to "live" for a time in these almost hallucinatory stages. In the first prelude of the *compositio* he is exhorted to see with the eye of the imagination the length, breadth, and depth of hell; to pray that he may feel deeply the pain suffered by the damned; to see the mass of fire; to hear the crying, shriekings, and weepings of the tortured souls and the curses they hurl at Christ and his angels; to smell the stench of rotting dirt and the smoke of sulfur. (p. 71)

The vividness of imaginative reconstruction brings the content of the meditation closer to the level of affective availability and thereby offers a better purchase on basic sources of motivation. As Rahner (1967) says, the more we look at brutality, treachery, meanness, cruelty, stupidity, pride, self-interest, malice, hatred, and in our own times genocidal destructiveness, the more we find our own world and the world of history shallow and repulsive. Imaginative vividness brings such evils closer to the core of our affectivity. If the imaginative vision tells us something about Ignatius' own guilt-ridden inner world (Meissner 1992b), it is also a graphic depiction of man's sinful state and the emptiness of his existence without God. As Cusson (1988) wisely notes, imagination and affectivity cannot carry the full weight of what Ignatius seeks. He requires spiritual understanding and a continually deepening grasp of the relation between the subject of each meditation and the overall plan sketched in the Foundation and the integration of its meaning with the personal meaning immediately relevant to each individual in respect to his relation to God and his place within the universal plan of salvation. The imagination can lead to a better grasp of the living Christ of history, but spiritual understanding is required to reach further to embrace the Christ of faith and his meaning in one's life. This latter aspect is the fruit of grace, for which Ignatius repeatedly begs.[10]

To continue with Ignatius' exercise:

[48] Second Prelude. The second is to ask God our Lord for what I want and desire.

> The petition has to be according to the subject matter; that is, if the contemplation is on the Resurrection, one is to ask for joy with Christ in joy; if it is on the Passion, he is to ask for pain, tears and torment with Christ in torment.
>
> Here it will be to ask shame and confusion at myself, seeing how many have been damned for only one mortal sin, and how many times I deserved to be condemned forever for my so many sins.
>
> [49] Note. Before all Contemplations or Meditations, there ought always to be made the Preparatory Prayer, which is not changed, and the two Preludes already mentioned, which are sometimes changed, according to the subject matter.
>
> [50] *First Point.* The first Point will be to bring the memory on the First Sin which was that of the Angels, and then to bring the intellect on the same, discussing it; then the will, wanting to recall and understand all this in order to make me more ashamed and confound me more, bringing into comparison with the one sin of the Angels my so many sins, and reflecting, while they for one sin were cast into Hell, how often I have deserved it for so many.
>
> I say to bring to memory the sin of the Angels, how they, being created in grace, not wanting to help themselves with their liberty to reverence and obey their Creator and Lord, coming to pride, were changed from grace to malice, and hurled from Heaven to Hell; and so then to discuss more in detail with the intellect: and then to move the feelings more with the will.

The confrontation with evil is fundamental in this contemplation in that sin is discovered in the sin of the angels without any prior context or history of evil — pride turned grace into malice. Grace does not absolve the person from the problem of freedom — even the angels who were created in grace had to confront the question of freedom and answer for consequences of their choice. Grace

[10] See also Pousset (1971) on this point.

cannot substitute for freedom in the movement toward salvation.[11] Were we to remove freedom and free choice from the picture, we would destroy that radical selfhood that is the basis for man's acceptance or rejection of God — such a removal is the work of the enemy of human nature. The *Exercises* pose the radical question — what do you want to do with your self, with your freedom? As Buckley (1984) comments:

> The Exercises come out of the appreciation of that issue, because the human person is fundamentally conditioned by a paradox: freedom is a question about yourself. It is not a question which the person has; it is a question which I am and with which I constitute what I am to become. To suppress this question is to destroy one's own humanity, for even the unfaced decisions of life — the choices that are made progressively determine what the answer to this question is. (p. 71)

Back to Ignatius:

> [51] *Second Point.* The second is to do the same — that is, to bring the Three Powers — on the sin of Adam and Eve, bringing to memory how on account of that sin they did penance for so long a time, and how much corruption came on the human race, so many people going the way to Hell.
>
> I say to bring to memory the Second Sin, that of our First Parents; how after Adam was created in the field of Damascus and placed in the Terrestrial Paradise, and Eve was created from his rib, being forbidden to eat of the Tree of Knowledge, they ate and so sinned, and afterwards clothed in tunics of skins and cast from Paradise, they lived, all their life, without the original justice which they had lost, and in many labors and much penance. And then to discuss with the understanding more in detail; and to use the will as has been said.

One piece of the puzzle of man's sinfulness portrayed in the Genesis account is, from a psychological perspective, the role of narcissism. It was man's wish to be like God that caused the trouble — not unlike the angels who rebelled against the authority of God and thereby separated themselves from God. The reflection drives home the point that in his pride, self-will, and disordered self-affirmation lies the root of man's sinfulness — qualities which find ready translation into terms of narcissistic self-inflation and omnipotence, familiar expressions in every psychoanalytic consulting room.

[11] See Ignatius' caution on insisting on grace to the detriment of freedom in SE369.

[52] *Third Point.* The third is likewise to do the same on the Third particular Sin of any one who for one mortal sin is gone to Hell — and many others without number, for fewer sins than I have committed.

I say to do the same on the Third particular Sin, bringing to memory the gravity and malice of the sin against one's Creator and Lord; to discuss with the understanding how in sinning and acting against the Infinite Goodness, he has been justly condemned forever; and to finish with the will as has been said.

[53] *Colloquy.* Imagining Christ our Lord present and placed on the Cross, let me make a Colloquy, how from Creator He is come to making Himself man, and from life eternal is come to temporal death, and so to die for my sins.

Likewise, looking at myself, what I have done for Christ, what I am doing for Christ, what I ought to do for Christ.

And so, seeing Him such, and so nailed on the Cross, to go over that which will present itself.

[54] The Colloquy is made, properly speaking, as one friend speaks to another, or as a servant to his master; now asking some grace, now blaming oneself for some misdeed, now communicating one's affairs, and asking advice in them.

And let me say an OUR FATHER.

The vividness of Ignatius' use of imagination here is impressive. Even more, the imaginative reconstruction has a quality of immediateness and personal intimacy emphasizing the closeness of the transitional space within which this prayerful dialogue takes place. The suggested dialogue has the quality of intimate conversation between friends, even lovers, and may convey some sense of the quality of Ignatius' own prayer experience.

SECOND EXERCISE [SE55-61]

It is a meditation on the sins . . . .

*Second Prelude.* The second is to ask for what I want. It will be here to beg a great and intense sorrow and tears for my sins.

[56] *First Point.* The first Point is the statement of the sins; that is to say, to bring to memory all the sins of life, looking from year to year, or from period to period. For this three things are helpful: first, to look at the place and the house where I have lived; second, the relations I have had with others; third, the occupation in which I have lived.

[57] *Second Point.* The second, to weigh the sins, looking at the foulness and the malice which any mortal sin committed has in it, even supposing it were not forbidden.

[58] *Third Point.* The third, to look at who I am, lessening myself by examples:

First, how much I am in comparison to all men;

Second, what men are in comparison to all the Angels and Saints of Paradise;

Third, what all Creation is in comparison to God: (— Then I alone, what can I be?)

Fourth, to see all my bodily corruption and foulness;

Fifth, to look at myself as a sore and ulcer, from which have sprung so many sins and so many iniquities and so very vile poison.

[59] *Fourth Point.* The fourth, to consider what God is, against Whom I have sinned, according to His attributes; comparing them with their contraries in me — His Wisdom with my ignorance; His Omnipotence with my weakness; His Justice with my iniquity; His Goodness with my malice.

[60] *Fifth Point.* The fifth, an exclamation of wonder with deep feeling, going through all creatures, how they have left me in life and preserved me in it; the Angels, how, though they are the sword of the Divine Justice, they have endured me, and guarded me, and prayed for me; the Saints, how they have been engaged in interceding and praying for me; and the heavens, sun, moon, stars, and elements, fruits, birds, fishes and animals — and the earth, how it has not opened to swallow me up, creating new Hells for me to suffer in them forever!

[61] *Colloquy.* Let me finish with a Colloquy of mercy, pondering and giving thanks to God our Lord that He has given me life up to now, proposing amendment, with His grace, for the future.

OUR FATHER.

The tone of Ignatius' exercise on sins is harsh and seems almost as though it were designed as an all-out attack on the exercitant's narcissism. Almost every facet of human existence that one might take pride in or that might in any way serve as the focus for pathological narcissism is subject to scrutiny and effort made to counter and confess it. He seeks shame, confusion, sorrow, even tears [SE48, 55] as leading to deeper personal knowledge of oneself and reform. The sin of the angels focuses the nature of sin — the use of freedom to reject and refuse the divine call to fulfill God's purposes. Their sin was a sin of pride, a refusal to submit to the will of their creator — a refusal that was treated with proportional justice.

The sin of Adam carries this reflection a step further — that man himself, in virtue of his freedom, has declined God's plan with dire consequences for the human race, including oneself [SE57-59]. It is an existential wasteland, a self-isolating and self-destructive isolation, a kind of self-incarceration, the immediate presence in us of death and nonbeing (Rahner 1967). The realization sinks in that I am connected to original sin as much as my first parents. Sin is a terrible and real possibility even in my life. Ignatius seems insistent on the most profound and penetrating realization of these truths — man is trapped within the mystery of evil and it is only through the beneficence and grace of God that he can escape from it. The following two exercises are largely repetitions, meant I would presume to drive the point home, and gain greater fruit, as Ignatius might say.

> THIRD EXERCISE [SE62-63]
> [62] This exercise repeats the two preceding, focusing on the points "in which I have felt greater consolation or desolation, or greater spiritual feeling" [SE62], and adds three colloquies [SE63] — the first to Our Lady, which is then repeated to Our Lord and to the Father.
> [63] First Colloquy. The first Colloquy to Our Lady, that she may get me grace from Her Son and Lord for three things: first, that I may feel an interior knowledge of my sins, and hatred of them; second, that I may feel the disorder of my actions, so that, hating them, I may correct myself and put myself in order; third, to ask knowledge of the world, in order that, hating it, I may put away from me worldly and vain things.
> And with that a HAIL MARY.

This colloquy sums up quite explicitly the objectives of the first week.

There is a difficult line to be drawn between sinful acts and faults that can be corrected by self-reflection and correction, as Ignatius suggests here, and those embedded in defects of character and psychopathology. One fruitful outcome of the Exercises may be recognition that one suffers from psychological impediments preventing one from gaining greater freedom and closeness to God, and that they may benefit from psychotherapeutic intervention. A wise director might be alert to such a possibility — recognizing that objectives of the Exercises are not psychotherapeutic but spiritual.

A fourth exercise summarizes the third, "that the understanding, without wandering, may assiduously go through the memory of the things contemplated in the preceding Exercises" [SE64]. Such repetitions, frequent in the course of the Exercises, call for prayer of greater simplicity without the discursive elaboration of preceding exercises. One could think of them as more important than the initial contemplations since they put the exercitant in a frame of mind more open to interior experiences and thus more available to the influence of grace (Buckley 1984).

We can get a sense here of the use Ignatius makes of the principle of repetition — apparently to gain a deeper impression on the exercitant and so to gain the greatest benefit from these meditations.

The objective is not simply sorrow for sins and repentance. He aims at something deeper and more meaningful — an "interior knowledge" of the reason for faults and shortcomings and sinful deviations, as rooted in my own fallibility and limitation, in the sources of evil within me which can be rooted out. Repentance should give way to further conversion — he begs "that I may feel an interior knowledge of my sins, and hatred of them; second, that I may feel the disorder of my actions, so that, hating them, I may correct myself and put myself in order" [SE63].

# CHAPTER X

# THE FIRST WEEK — HELL

In completing the exercises of the first week, Ignatius pushes more deeply into the mystery of human imperfection and potential for evil. His onslaught on the diabolical in man culminates in the mediation on hell.

## Meditation on Hell [SE65-72]

[65] *First Prelude.* The first Prelude is the composition, which is here to see with the sight of the imagination the length, breadth and depth of Hell.
*Second Prelude.* The second, to ask for what I want: it will be here to ask for interior sense of the pain which the damned suffer, in order that, if, through my faults, I should forget the love of the Eternal Lord, at least the fear of the pains may help me not to come into sin.
[66] *First Point.* The first Point will be to see with the sight of the imagination the great fires, and the souls as in bodies of fire.
[67] *Second Point.* The second, to hear with the ears wailing, howlings, cries, blasphemies against Christ our Lord and against all His Saints.
[68] *Third Point.* The third, to smell with the smell smoke, sulphur, dregs and putrid things.
[69] *Fourth Point.* The fourth, to taste with the taste bitter things, like tears, sadness and the worm of conscience.
[70] *Fifth Point.* The fifth, to touch with the touch; that is to say, how the fires touch and burn the souls.
[71] *Colloquy.* Making a Colloquy to Christ our Lord, I will bring to memory the souls that are in Hell, some because they did not believe the Coming, others because, believing, they did not act according to His Commandments; making three divisions:
*First, Second, and Third Divisions.* The first, before the Coming; the second, during His life; the third, after His life in this world; and with this I will give Him thanks that He has not let me fall into any of these divisions, ending my life.

Likewise, I will consider how up to now He has always had so great pity and mercy on me.

I will end with an OUR FATHER.[1]

If we reach beyond the imagery in this graphic and imaginative representation of hell, what does hell mean? Might we not think that it carries all the implications of isolating self-affirmation, self-aggrandizement, self-pursuit — the affirmation of self that ends paradoxically in self-negation? This non-sense of hell finds its concretization in images of fire, pain, tears, grinding of teeth and remorse. As Fessard (1956) comments: ". . . an absolute, eternal remorse, invading the entire field of my being, penetrating my consciousnesses through all its 'doors and windows,' and thus identifying itself with consciousness by way of my senses. That is how the I can complete the growth of sin, magnifying the non-being of its freedom to the absolute degree: by applying the senses to hell" (vol. I, p. 48) — to experience "bitter things, like tears, sadness and the worm of conscience" [SE69] — the ultimate in self-destructiveness.

We should be clear that Ignatius' objective here is not to sink the exercitant in this abyss of remorse and nonbeing. The aim is rather repentance and desire for reformation. The exercitant may find himself caught in the tension between remorse and repentance, a tension that should find its resolution in a deepening faith and trust in God. If an exercitant finds himself caught in the trammels of remorse, he is the victim of an overweening superego, and unless he can work his way through that impasse, his further progress in the Exercises may be doubtful. To the extent that he remains in that position, he will not be receptive to the further movements of the Exercises and the openness to grace they require.

We can draw a line between the dynamic of this exercise and pathological guilt. The remorse that leads to repentance carries the seeds of forgiveness and renewal of hope. In this lies the source of any true conversion, insofar as it runs counter to the superego dynamic underlying guilt. Use of the term "guilt" in this context is misleading — Ignatius seeks contrition rather than guilt. Guilt, in the sense of "sorrowful admission of sin, is the product of God's revelation and grace" (Rahner 1967, p. 38), is something quite different from the superego dynamic. Essential to the method of the Exercises is a constant drive to support and sustain the resources of the exercitant in confronting and defeating onslaughts of the superego, not to rein-

[1] A note [SE72] is added with directions for five times of meditation, taking account of the exercitant's age, disposition and physical condition.

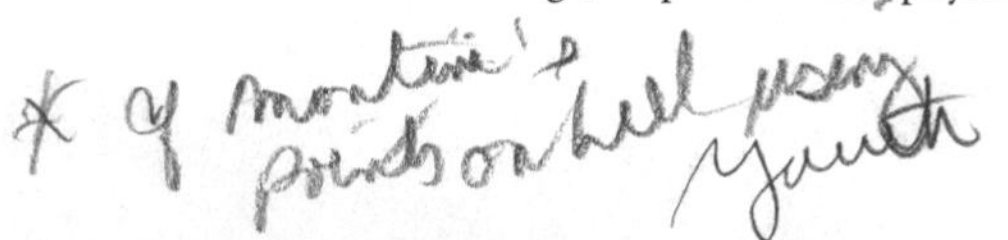

force it. This perspective will recur with particular significance in the rules for discernment.[2]

This exercise brings home the vivid and vigorous application of the senses Ignatius urges on the exercitant — the work of the imagination. The more vivid, concrete and detailed these images, the better. Ignatius has grasped a point that is also part of the wisdom of clinical psychoanalysis. Good analysts know that when patients are speaking a language that is general, vague, abstract, or nonspecific, they are distancing themselves from the hard and painful stuff of reality and are defending against painful or uncomfortable affects. It is in the realm of the factual, the actual, and the concrete that feelings and emotions have their play. Ignatius in these imaginative meditations is striving to generate a sense of the concrete sensible immediacy that connects with and generates meaningful affective responses.

The meditation on hell is one of the most vivid expressions of this technique. It culminates and concretizes the effort of the first week. It represents in the Christian mythological iconography the extreme and direst consequence of sin. Putting aside theological considerations of the basis of belief in hell, Ignatius uses this imagery to drive home the essential issue — the stark and penetrating understanding and realization of the reality of sin and the immense consequences both of the history of sin and my own personal sinfulness. The awareness of the meaning of hell — separation from God, exclusion from the divine salvific plan, loss of all that makes life worthwhile and meaningful — is a great grace to be sought with every diligence.

## Psychological Processes

We can formulate the psychological processes of the first week in the following points:

(1) *Recognition of the sources of libidinal and/or narcissistic gratification.* This is a work of ego self-analysis difficult to achieve without external assistance. Intimacy of contact and communication with the director are a help. It is particularly difficult in the preliminary stages of such introspective effort to achieve adequate disengagement of the observant ego from the participant ego. Here the director's intimate knowledge of the exercitant and his experience in dealing with psychological processes are very important. We know the tremendous difficulties, in the form of resistances, blind spots, and self-deceptions, encountered in psychoanalysis in trying to achieve a similar objective. However, in the present instance, unconscious elements

[2] See chapters XV and XVI.

are not presumed to be operating with the intensity found in neurotic disturbances, nor are they treated as offering such tremendous resistance to the efforts of the ego to come to grips with them as are encountered in the psychoanalytic process. As a general rule, then, frank, open and understanding discussion and inquiry between director and exercitant would seem to be sufficient to achieve the objectives of the Exercises. Moreover, in the matter of sin, the Christian with a reasonably well-formed conscience knows well enough where he has fallen in following God's law. The problem is more often one of directing one's efforts to overcoming such faults.

(2) *Estimation of such gratifications in relation to the value system of the spiritual life*. Estimation depends on recognition and involves a certain evaluation. In the meditations on sin, hell, death, judgment, etc., an implicit value system is presented for reflection. The Christian soul must face the stark realities of its spiritual existence, which constitute the framework within which the consequences of its failure to adapt to the demands of the Christian moral code are realized. It is necessary, therefore, for the exercitant to achieve through faith a certain reality-orientation, not only to the sensible world, but more pertinently to the spiritual world. The value system is reflected in God's revealed attitudes toward sin, in the terrible consequences of sin in itself, and as a turning against God.

Within that framework, the ego is called on to evaluate its own personal history of sin. The process here has a two-fold objective: realistic recognition of the sources of gratification in my own libido as deviations from this value system, and excitation of an appropriate affective response to this deviation.

(3) *Mobilization of psychic resources by the activation of sources of motivation*. Once the exercitant has achieved a realized awareness of his defections from realistically ordered action ("interior knowledge and detestation"), the matter cannot be permitted to rest there. Effective translation into action requires that potential for change be activated by proper motivation. The individual must feel shame, disgust, guilt, confusion, etc. Based on the previous evaluation, meditations of the first week call for a deeply felt affective response. We should be careful to note that there is no question of neurotic guilt here, which stems from the superego, escapes ego-control, and is neither appropriate nor reality-oriented. Consequently, quilt can be regarded as a disordered affection of a severely disabling nature. Strengthening of the hand of the superego in these contexts and a corresponding increase in the titration of guilt would become counterproductive. Rather, the detestation and sorrow which St. Ignatius

would have the exercitant seek, are controlled and directed by the ego; they are appropriately proportioned to the evil of sin, and are reality-oriented within the framework of the revealed realities upon which the exercitant meditates during the first week. The sorrow envisioned by Ignatius is thus reality-oriented rather than neurotic in origin. I am reminded of a similar stance recommended in Strachey's (1934) classic analysis of therapeutic action in psychoanalysis, in which part of the therapeutic effects of the analytic process are ascribed to the mitigation of the analysand's superego severity. In analysis as in spirituality, little is to be gained from feeding a neurotic superego.

The motivation presented to the exercitant and fostered in and by the ego is distinctively teleological and goal-oriented. The ultimate finality governing the exercitant's striving is set forth in the Foundation. From the point of view of intrapsychic dynamics, this finality is of the utmost importance. In turning against sources of instinctual gratification as motivating forces, the self must either reorient its sexual and aggressive energy or it must bring to bear its own energy resources. A source of proper motivation must be provided, and since all psychic striving is purposive, any effective motivation requires a clearly grasped goal.

(4) *Instinctual regulation and ego-control.* Another significant element in this first stage of spiritual development is the multifaceted insistence on mobilization of psychic resources, particularly the ego, in a concerted and concentrated effort toward countercathectic regulation of instinctual energies. The resolution and direction of ego-activities to regulate its proper functions and organize and direct them to a spiritual goal introduces a teleological dimension to the ego's activity and calls into play the capacity of the ego for what Allport (1955) called "propriate striving." This is related to the concept of "will," which seems to occupy a modest position in the hierarchy of psychoanalytic psychic processes (Waelder 1936; Fisher 1966; Meissner 1971b, 1984; Rangell 1989), but the central role of such functions in understanding the Ignatian perspective should not be underestimated.

The element of propriate striving together with regulation and control of libidinal energies are key elements in spiritual growth. The self begins to put into execution the regulation and control which is essential to its spiritual growth. At this point, processes of intrapsychic alteration, reorganization and synthesis begin to take effect. The person embarks on a life-long enterprise of self-reconstruction through progressive self-control and self-discipline. Insofar as control over instinctual drives is never definitive, and insofar as effort is always required not merely to extend or intensify the scope of regulation, but even to maintain previous gains, the process of spiritual growth is a never ending endeavor. Moreover, as it progresses it becomes progressively more difficult, since it begins to strike more deeply into the depths of the psyche and encounters more profound and resistant elements. Consequently, the negative aspect of instinctual control is largely dependent on the positive growth of the ego in strength and capacity to bring its resources to bear.

These meditations offer us a unique window into the tormented and guilt ridden inner world of the pilgrim. He saw himself as a "soul imprisoned in this corruptible body, and all the compound in this valley, as exiled among brute beasts: I say all the compound of soul and body" [SE47]. His intention was "to ask shame and confusion at myself, seeing how many have been damned for only one mortal sin, and how many times I deserved to be condemned forever for my so many sins" [SE48] and "to make me more ashamed and confound me more, bringing into comparison with the one sin of the Angels my so many sins, and reflecting, while they for one sin were cast into Hell, how often I have deserved it for so many" [SE50]. And again, in the meditation on personal sin, we hear: "The first Point is the statement of the sins; that is to say, to bring to memory all the sins of life, looking from year to year, or from period to period. . . . The second to weight the sins, looking at the foulness and the malice which any mortal sin committed has in it, even supposing it were not forbidden" [SE56-57]. These reflections lead to a colloquy with the Blessed Mother "that she may get me grace from Her Son and Lord for three things: first, that I may feel an interior knowledge of my sins, and hatred of them; second, that I may feel the disorder of my actions, so that, hating them, I may correct myself and put myself in order; third, to ask knowledge of the world, in order that, hating it, I may put away from me worldly and vain things" [SE63].

These images of sinfulness and inner evil certainly have theological underpinnings. But we might wonder whether the themes of guilt and shame enunciated here do not also reflect multiple levels of sinfulness in the levels of psychic integration within Ignatius himself.

Mingled with these guilt-ridden exercises is Ignatius' imaginative vision of hell. In the meditation on hell, the composition of place aims "to see with the sight of the imagination the length, breadth and depth of Hell" [SE65]. In this vision, he seeks an "interior sense of pain which the damned suffer, in order that, if through my faults, I should forget the love of the Eternal Lord, at least the fear of the pains may help me not to come into sin" [SE65]. He vividly details "the souls as in bodies of fire" [SE66], the "wailings, howlings, cries, blasphemies against Christ our Lord and against all His Saints" [SE67], the putrid smell of sulfur, and the taste of "bitter things, like tears, sadness and the worm of conscience" [SE69].

In developing these themes, Ignatius reveals some of the dark imagery that inhabited his mind. We should note the dominance of aggressive and destructive themes on the level of unconscious fantasy. There is little doubt that his accounts reflect the culturally reinforced spiritual and ascetic conventions of the day, but this context does not diminish the psychic impact of such images in Ignatius' mind. Cultural influences join with intrapsychic factors that absorb, respond to, and assimilate such peripheral influences into a pattern that reflects the dynamic and unconscious components operating within the individual psyche. These theologically impregnated themes took on personal reference and implication for Ignatius. They became the vehicle for transformed aggressive drive derivatives channeled through his more severely judgmental and punitive superego — the guilt that plagued his soul and the harsh images that crowded his mind reflect the punitive force of his superego-driven imagination.

## METHOD

If there is anything distinctively Ignatian about the *Spiritual Exercises*, it is methods he suggested for meditating. From a psychological point of view, his purpose was to activate psychic energies and bring them to bear on the objects of meditation. Thus, the imaginative function is activated through the composition of place and great vividness suggested in the application of the senses to the sensible aspects of these imaginative reconstructions (Dir. XX, 4). The retentive function is applied in recalling events and truths to be meditated on, and subsequently also powers of conceptualization and resolution are brought to bear. Ignatius seemed to be intent on focusing as many of the psychic capacities as possible on the matter of the meditation, thereby increasing the likelihood of penetrating understanding, meaningful affective response, and consequently purposeful and effective direction of action. To increase and intensify these intrapsychic shifts, repetitions of various exercises are suggested (Dir. XV, 2).

It is important in following through the program of the first week that the exercitant have clearly in mind what he should strive to achieve. The methods suggested for effectively obtaining objectives of the first week are of value only insofar as they actually bring about the anticipated modifications in operations of the self. Consequently, they are to be used or abandoned, emphasized or de-emphasized, insofar as they prove effective. The *Directory* offers a caution in use of the composition of place, for example, pointing out that it is merely a help to more effective utilization of other resources of the ego (Dir. XIV, 7).

## Further Points on Method in the Additions

Additions [SE73-86]: These are practical suggestions for concentrating the resources of the ego on the matter at hand.

> [73] I. The first Addition is, after going to bed, just when I want to go asleep, to think, for the space of a HAIL MARY, of the hour that I have to rise and for what, making a resume of the Exercise which I have to make.

The brief recapitulation prior to falling asleep is calculated to take advantage to some degree of workings of the unconscious mind during sleep. We know that functions of the ego are not totally suspended during sleep, but that it carries on a number of unconscious operations at several levels — e.g., in the complex function of dreaming, involving imagination, memory, affection, mentation. We also know that these functions can and often do carry on thought processes, even without awareness of the person. Studies of creative thinking among scientists and other intellectual workers suggest that problems which confounded and perplexed their conscious efforts at solution, yielded finally to a process of mentation continued in sleep. The situation here is analogous, where Ignatius would have the exercitant seek a penetrating understanding and a deep realization of spiritual truths. Filling the mind with ideas to be reflected on when the person awakens should serve to enlist processes of unconscious mentation in the service of the ego's objective.

> [74] II. The second:
> When I wake up, not giving place to any other thought, to turn my attention immediately to what I am going to contemplate in the first Exercise, at midnight, bringing myself to confusion for my so many sins, setting examples, as, for instance, if a knight found himself before his king and all his court, ashamed and confused at having much offended him, from whom he had first received many gifts and many favors: in the same way, in the second Exercise, making myself a great sinner and in chains; that is to say going to appear bound as in chains before the Supreme Eternal Judge; taking for an example how prisoners in chains and already deserving death, appear before their temporal judge. And I will

dress with these thoughts or with others, according to the subject matter.

These imaginings or considerations which Ignatius suggests are calculated to focus attention on the subject matter of the meditation. From this point of view, it is important that other considerations be avoided since they can only serve to distract the exercitant and divert his concentration from the objective of the moment. This assumes greater importance psychologically since further growth in spiritual identity is a function of the effective confrontation and resolution of each phase in the process of ego-orientation and synthesis.

[75] III. The third:
A step or two before the place where I have to contemplate or meditate, I will put myself standing for the space of an OUR FATHER, my intellect raised on high, considering how God our Lord is looking at me, etc.; and will make an act of reverence or humility.

Recollection is psychologically equivalent to the direction and organization of psychic functions. To place oneself imaginatively in the presence of God introduces a note of seriousness of purpose and of reverence which heightens effectiveness of the effort. Attention is a central factor since it is the measure of the ego's success in directing its powers to the object of the mediation. Recollection implies establishment of a psychological "set." The element of humility in this mind set is characteristically Ignatian.

[76] IV. The fourth:
To enter on the contemplation now on my knees, now prostrate on the earth, now lying face upwards, now seated, now standing, always intent on seeking what I want.

We will attend to two things. The first is, that if I find what I want kneeling, I will not pass one; and if prostrate, likewise, etc. The second; in the Point in which I find what I want, there I will rest without being anxious to pass on, until I content myself.

The degree of attention and concentration required in meditation of this sort is difficult to maintain over long periods of time. The reasons for this are physiological in part and psychological in part. Changing posture of the body from time to time can help to alleviate this tendency; movement of a gentle sort may also help. The biological organism also has certain innate rhythms which can be changed partially but tend to remain more or less constant and affect conscious functioning. They vary during the day so that the exercitant may find himself more vital and alert at one hour than at another.

Variations are also partly connected with stages of the sleep-wake diurnal cycle. These factors should also be considered. What is important is that the exercitant be able to engage in the process effectively.

> [77] V. The fifth:
> After finishing the Exercise, I will, during the space of a quarter of an hour, seated or walking leisurely, look how it went with me in the Contemplation or Meditation; and if badly, I will look for the cause from which it proceeds, and having so seen it, will be sorry, in order to correct myself in future; and if well, I will give thanks to God our Lord, and will do in like manner another time.

Ignatius' personal attention to method, an aspect of his own spiritual experience, is here apparent. Not only should the exercitant direct himself to the consideration of spiritual truths, but he is further requested to examine introspectively the intrapsychic processes by which he does so. Implicit in this recommendation of Ignatius is a fundamental apperception of ego-psychology. The ego is the autonomous and ultimate source of its own activities; it alone can direct its energies, it alone can organize and synthesize its own internal structure. This is a basic principle of psychotherapy as well as of spiritual growth. The introspective reflection and analysis recommended here introduces a sort of feedback mechanism into the activity of the ego. The inquiries of the director can help the exercitant to direct his attention to essential elements until the exercitant becomes sufficiently experienced to know what he is to look for.

> [78] VI. The sixth:
> Not to want to think on things of pleasure or joy, such as heavenly glory, the Resurrection, etc. Because whatever consideration of joy and gladness hinders our feeling pain and grief and shedding tears for our sins: but to keep before me that I want to grieve and feel pain, bringing to memory rather Death and Judgment.

The mood of the exercitant is important in bringing his affections into play. Since the first week aims at a sober realization of the reality of sin and seeks to develop a deep spirit of contrition, thoughts of pleasant, though holy, subjects must be regarded as distractions from the work at hand. Again, Ignatius seems to be seeking a full concentration of the exercitant's energies on the objectives to be gained here and now. Each step has its purpose which is to be sought after in its proper time and sequence.

> [79] VII. The seventh:
> For the same end, to deprive myself of all light, closing the blinds

and doors while I am in the room, if it be not to recite prayers, to read and eat.

Ignatius must have found this practice of darkening the room helpful to himself and others, but it should be employed with discretion. If darkness helps the exercitant to go about his work, well and good, but if otherwise, not.

[80] VIII. The eighth:
Not to laugh nor say a thing provocative of laughter.
In the light of what has been said, this observation is obvious. The mood of the first week is anything but light or frivilous.

[81] IX. The ninth:
To restrain my sight, except in receiving or dismissing the person with whom I have spoken.

What is of importance in all of these exercises is intrapsychic processes. For the mind to work effectively it requires attention and even concentration. Consequently, distractions arising from visual stimulation are to be controlled insofar as they draw the person's attention away from the work at hand. This is particularly relevant when there is opportunity for observing other people. But neither is the opposite extreme recommended. The exercitant is not to put himself in a state of sensory deprivation, since this too would impair efforts of the self to come to grips with its internal dispositions and reality.

[82-86] X. The tenth Addition is penance:
[82] This is divided into interior and exterior. The interior is to grieve for one's sins, with a firm purpose of not committing them or any others. The exterior, or fruit of the first, is chastisement for the sins committed, and is chiefly taken in three ways.
[83] First Way. The first is as to eating. That is to say, when we leave off the superfluous it is not penance, but temperance. It is penance when we leave off from the suitable; and the more and more, the greater and better — provided that the person does not injure himself, and that no notable illness follows.[3]
[84] Second Way. The second, as to the manner of sleeping. Here too it is not penance to leave off the superfluous of delicate or soft things, but it is penance when one leaves off from the suitable in the manner: and the more and more, the better — provided that the person does not injure himself and no notable illness follows. Besides. let not anything of the suitable sleep be left off, unless in order to come to the mean, if one has a bad habit of sleeping too much.

[3] See the rules for eating in chapter XVII below.

[85] Third Way. The third, to chastise the flesh, that is, giving it sensible pain, which is given by wearing haircloth or cords or iron chains next to the flesh, by scourging or wounding oneself, and by other kinds of austerity.
[86] Note. What appears most suitable and most secure with regard to penance is that the pain should be sensible in the flesh and not enter within the bones, so that it give pain and not illness. For this it appears to be more suitable to scourge oneself with thin cords, which give pain exteriorly, rather than in another way which would cause notable illness within.

He then added further notes on penance:

**Notes** [SE87-90]
[87] I. The first Note is that the exterior penances are done chiefly for three ends:

First, as satisfaction for the sins committed;

Second, to conquer oneself — that is, to make sensuality obey reason and all inferior parts be more subject to the superior;

Third, to seek and find some grace or gift which the person wants and desires; as, for instance, if he desires to have interior contrition for his sins, or to weep much over them, or over the pains and sufferings which Christ our Lord suffered in His Passion, or to settle some doubt in which the person finds himself.[4]

[89] Third note:
The third: When the person who is exercising himself does not yet find what he desires — as tears, consolations, etc. — it often helps for him to make a change in food, in sleep and in other ways of doing penance, so that he change himself, doing penance two or three days, and two or three others not. For it suits some to do more penance and others less, and we often omit doing penance from sensual love and from an erroneous judgment that the human system will not be able to bear it without notable illness; and sometimes, on the contrary, we do too much, thinking that the body can bear it; and as God our Lord knows our nature infinitely better, often in such changes He gives each one to perceive what is suitable for him.

Prudent caution in regard to the effective use of penance during the Exercises is recommended. The norm is always "tantum-quantum" and the effectiveness of penances in helping the ego obtain the objective. Ignatius lays down some prudent norms for the use of penances, particularly emphasizing the interior disposition of pen-

[4] The second note [SE88] deals with times and places for application of the additions.

ance — one of the objectives sought in the first week. But Ignatius also puts great stock in external penances as helps to achieving the interior disposition.[5]

> [90] Fourth note:
> The fourth: Let the Particular Examen be made to rid oneself of defects and negligences on the Exercises and Additions. And so in the Second, Third and Fourth Weeks.

This note gives us a sense of the utility Ignatius attached to the Particular Examen as an instrument for self-correction and self-improvement. It was a technique he implemented in his own life to an impressive degree.[6]

## PENANCE

The psychology of penance is little understood in our day and is generally regarded by psychologists as a form of masochism. By penance, I refer to the psychological disposition motivating performance of external penances. Thus, it is not identical with the virtue of penance which St. Ignatius described as "interior penance," but it forms an integral part of it. It is the prolongation of the basic attitudes proper to contrition into a more or less permanent disposition to take effective means to counter personal defects and failings and atone for past sins. Penance, then, represents a form of self-assertion in the face of forces tending to diminish one's autonomous functioning. It is equivalent to assuming responsibility for one's own self-direction and maturity, and thereby constitutes a decisive reinforcement of the independence of the self, particularly the ego subsystem, particularly vis-a-vis instinctual attachments and entanglements, through the execution of self-disciplinary action. The ego, in this process, assumes active mastery of instinctual impulses and desires, thus establishing and later maintaining its authentic control. When this dynamism has become an internalized and synthesized part of the functioning self, it can be said that the advance from contrition to penance involves a development in ego-capacity and another step towards self-maturation.

From the point of view of the dependance of penance on the capacity of the ego to take the initiative in the effective control of instinctual attachments, it would seem reasonable to expect that a defect in the resolution of this psychosocial crisis (e.g. initiative in

[5] See further discussion of penance in chapters XIX and XXXII below.
[6] See chapter XXXII on Ignatius' asceticism below.

the Eriksonian schema of developmental crises [Erikson 1959]) would impair ability of the self to achieve penance as a habitual ego-disposition in the spiritual life. Conversely, I would suggest, it would seem that the capacity of the person, under the energizing and guiding influence of grace, to achieve the level of authentic penance (I refer to real penance as opposed to false forms of penance which are nothing but manifestations of masochism) should have a reciprocal influence on the native capacity for initiative and personal responsibility.

Part of the moral perspective of psychoanalysis is that it extends the range of responsibility retrospectively to include actions and their consequences that might not have been consciously intended, that is, when the action was determined by some unconscious intention (Wallwork 1992). That responsibility for unconscious and harmful past actions rests on the fact that the self is the agent for actions, whether conscious or unconscious, and not some alien force. As soon as the subject becomes aware of his underlying intention, he has no choice but to accept responsibility for it (Freud 1925b). That sense of responsibility finds expression in a sense of regret and remorse for whatever harm one might have caused, and in a wish for atonement. It is this brand of regret and remorse that drives penitential behavior, and clearly differs radically from neurotic guilt. While the former impels toward forgiveness and repentance, the latter verges toward unforgiveness and punishment.

This distinction was basic to Freud's view of moral responsibility. He clearly distinguished between realistic remorse of actual misdeeds and neurotic guilt. Guilt connotes indiscriminate self-punishment that is often irrational, excessively harsh, and at times based on nothing more than fantasy; in addition it is self-defeating and self-diminishing, leads to greater defensiveness and becomes an obstacle to the very self-understanding that responsibility requires. In contrast to this, remorse, in the sense of self-reproach following recognition that one has committed some misdeed, is specific to the deed, does not apply to intentions or wishes, and is realistic and appropriate (Freud 1930). As Freud (1930) noted, "The superego torments the sinful ego. . . . The more virtuous a man is, the more severe and distrustful is its behavior, so that ultimately it is precisely those people who have carried saintliness furthest who reproach themselves with the worst sinfulness. This means that virtue forfeits some part of its promised reward; the docile and continent ego does not enjoy the trust of its mentor, and strives in vain, it would seem, to acquire it" (pp. 125-126).

In this sense, authentic penance is a direct counteragent to guilt. Properly understood, the "sense of penance" we are describing here is incompatible with a "sense of guilt," as that expression is understood psychiatrically in reference to neurotic guilt feelings. Psychodynamically, the former represents a decisive organization of the capacities of the self by which internal self-regulation and direction to spiritual goals are implemented; the latter represents the overpowering domination of the superego. The two are incompatible, and consequently, where penance is achieved on the spiritual level, its impact on functioning of the self should work in the direction of resetting the balance that was disturbed in the original working through of the psychosocial crisis of the phallic phase and oedipal conflict.

Ignatius lists three purposes of exterior penance [SE87]: satisfaction for past sin, control of sensuality, and seeking for grace. From a theological point of view, these purposes are well founded and meritorious; mortification has traditionally been recognized as a major means of satisfaction and impetration. We are concerned, however, with psychological aspects of penance, where there is no such clearcut agreement. Ignatius clearly recommended it as an efficacious means, but it is specifically a means and therefore must be subject to the demands of meaningful psychic integration and should be applied in terms of the basic Ignatian principle of reality-orientation in spiritual matters, the "tantum-quantum." This emphasis, of course, by which the practice of exterior penance is subject to the control of reason and the law of moderation, is precisely what distinguishes penance from masochistic self-punishment. The masochist is driven by a harsh superego which he can neither control nor satisfy. His self-punishment is masochistic precisely because he becomes the victim of it rather than its director. In structural terms, it is an acting out of the victim role (reflecting the internal demands of the victim introject) rather than a freely determined exercise of autonomous functions in the interest of spiritual objectives.

The mention of masochism raises a difficult question — to what extent could the pilgrim's penances be regarded as masochistic? The answer, as far as I can give one, falls far short of achieving any closure. Iñigo's severe penances probably represent a form of masochistic perversion reflecting a degree of intrapsychic conflict. These conflicts, which were recognizably libidinal, aggressive and narcissistic, were extreme in the early years of his pilgrimage, and it was only over time that his suffering gradually, and only partially, freed him from their grasp. Nonetheless, these conflicts required vigilance and strong repressive and other defensive countermeasures until the end of his life. His penances seemed to have been mitigated only in the face of severe and even life-threatening self-injury. But any analysis, based merely on a masochistic dynamism, will fall short of adequately understanding Ignatius' ascetical life.

Psychoanalytically speaking, masochism is a complex phenomenon (Berliner 1947). The sexual perversion of masochism is usually distinguished from moral masochism[7] in that the perversion involves sexual gratification derived from suffering. Freud regarded masochism as a turning of aggression against the self, linked to sadism, the two serving as opposite sides of the same coin. Often the sadomasochistic pattern takes place in an interpersonal context, in which one person takes the role of sadist and the other that of masochist — a pattern familiar enough in close interpersonal relations, e.g. marriages, the analytic relation. and so on. It can even rear its head in the confessor-penitent relation or even in the director-exercitant relation.

In the sphere of the sacred, the masochistic stance is articulated with a religious ego ideal and is often placed in the service of a spiritual set of values and objectives. In Ignatian terms, the masochistic stand might aim at countering the wish for wealth and pride — presumably desires that stirred in some form in the breast of the pilgrim against which he had to exercise continuing vigilance. The self-denial had the purpose of seeking love and approval from a divine object rather than a human one. We should not automatically assume that such religiously motivated masochism is pathological — it may or may not be. The masochism of the ascetic may elicit admiration or contempt; it may reflect psychic weakness or strength; it may be a vehicle for seeking or for expressing love. The masochistic surrender to God may serve as a way of avoiding reality, or the suffering and submission of the saint may serve as a vehicle for discovering increasingly meaningful levels of personal commitment and love of God. The mortification of the ascetic may reflect a profound love of God, it may alleviate guilt and expiate sin, it may be put to developmental uses — as, for example, growth in chastity and purity of mind and heart — or it may express a perversion that finds gratification in pain (Charmé 1983).

I think it is safe to say that Ignatius suffered from a rather extreme degree of moral masochism, but it was in many ways sublimated and adapted to a program of spiritual growth through the

[7] Masochism is a perversion insofar as the subject finds pleasure or gratification in humiliation or suffering. Moral masochism is a derivative form in which one seeks victimization or the position of victim out of an unconscious sense of guilt; sexual pleasure is not necessarily, or may be only indirectly, involved.

seeking of grace and an increasing love of God. Ignatius' penances were thus transformed into acts of love, driven more by seeking God's approval than by guilt or the need for punishment. If this is masochism, it is not simply the masochism of the neurotic or the moral masochist; it is masochism suffused with love and placed in the service of a highly narcissistically invested ego ideal, an ideal that is itself embued with the highest spiritual aims.

Penance, then, which is applied in order to satisfy for past sins may look very much like masochism to the pure behaviorist, but it does so only because the behaviorist ignores the fact that fervent souls, who have come to a deep realization of the seriousness and enormity of their sins, may try to plunge themselves into severe penitential practices — which practices could not be said to be out of proportion to the enormity of the offense against God — the same souls are constrained by other obligations to themselves (bodily health, etc.) and to others (capacity to work, sociability, etc.) from going beyond a prudently established moderation. It is, of course, the function of the ego to judge norms of moderation and to exert proper control over its execution. The function of the ego, then, is central in all true penance.

The application of external penances in order to overcome self and bring sensuality under the control of reason fits particularly well with objectives of the first week. But it is also a practice which has a wide range of application in the whole spiritual life. Maintenance of ego-control requires constant effort and penance can be of considerable help in this effort. As Ignatius points out in regard to food, if we refuse what is superfluous, this is not penance, but temperance; but if we go further and deny ourselves that which is within the limits of temperate moderation, we are practicing penance. If the libido gains particular gratification from food, the effort of the ego is to regulate food consumption by establishing limits and forcing the self to observe them. If one were to undertake penance, however, and deny himself even what would be considered a moderate portion of food, this is not only controlling the food impulse, but it is taking positive executive action in opposition to the impulse to oral gratification. Maintenance of control becomes a much easier matter of relaxation to the limits of moderation, rather than a striving against the unconquered resistance.

Penance and mortification are, along with prayer, suitable means for seeking and disposing oneself for God's grace. Psychologically speaking, penance undertaken in this fashion represents a translation into positive action of spiritual desires and purposes. Consequently, it requires directive activity of the ego, which conceives of the purpose, selects the means, directs and organizes its energies to seek its objective, and translates this energy into effective action by its executive capacity. All of this in the Ignatian perspective is energized and sustained by grace so that the individual proceeds from grace to grace, more surely because he or she has acquired internal dispositions for this purpose through the organization and coordination of psychic functions directed to this objective through penance.

# CHAPTER XI

# THE SECOND WEEK — IMITATION OF CHRIST

## Second Week [SE 91-189]

While the emphasis in the first week of the Exercises is on self-discipline and regulation of "inordinate affections," it remains a fact of psychological life that such regulation is not possible without a concomitant evolution in the resources and strength in the self. There must, therefore, be a positive growth in the self, over and above the sort of internal regulation we have been considering. Such growth involves a reorganization and reconstruction within psychic subsystems, both ego and superego. It is this project that Ignatius turns to in the second week of the *Exercises*.[1]

Internal growth and synthesis within the self are perhaps the most significant dimension of the process we are considering. This transformation within the self provides the major thrust and consequence of the action of grace, and it is by means of this internal reorganization that effective growth to spiritual identity is realized. The major impact of the first week of the Exercises is to orient the soul toward the schema of values proper to the spiritual order. Ignatius directs the exercitant to strive for a real and sincere internalization of these values resulting in a sincere sense of contrition and a purposeful organization of the exercitant's capacities to achieve an "ordering of life for the salvation of one's soul." Thus, the realm of spiritual values has in some incipient sense become an internalized norm of decision and judgment for the direction of the action of the self. This preliminary internalization is accompanied by a preliminary synthesis within the

[1] Staudenmaier (1994) comments, "If the First Week has gone well, I will have found my way to the failed, violent, and abandoned places of my own self and waited there long enough for God to meet and embrace me. Even to begin so perilous an inner journey, I need to be loved at the outset and to have sufficient emotional health to sustain my sense of being loved as I enter the places where love feels impossible. Absent a durable sense of self-worth, First Week dynamics easily drift toward masochism" (p. 17).

self representing an initial disposition in the direction of an evolving spiritual identity. It is this initial self-synthesis which Ignatius seeks to foster and nourish in the remainder of the Exercises. The interpretive principle in our deepening understanding of the hermeneutic of the *Exercises* takes on further meaning here — that the content of the meditations has both an objective and a subjective reference. They are both representative of as well as formative of the inner state of the exercitant's subjectivity — originally Ignatius' own subjectivity, and derivatively the exercitant's.

## OBJECTIVE

Up to this point, during the first week, the concern was not primarily with positive growth, but rather with reorganization and reconstruction of the self to the point where effective growth in spiritual identity becomes possible. The motivational currents here are in Ignatius' view both psychological and graceful, but caution and discretion are called for. As Imoda (1992) notes, "the first pitfall of the Second Week is that of an indiscreet enthusiasm which looks too exclusively to the positive, which lacks discernment and has the power to illude; St. Ignatius himself, at Manresa, could find it much more interesting to compete with the example of the saints than to seek the will of God (which might be different from his own)" (p. 54).

It is in connection with the intense affectivity and motivation that Ignatius seeks that the influence of unconscious dynamics has its privileged point of entry. The call to identify with Christ and his mission must be cast in terms that are individualized and pertinent to the life situation and capacities that have relevance and meaning for the subject (Iparraguirre 1959). Highly idealized spiritual ideals and fantasies can be highly misleading and can draw the individual down a false path lacking authenticity and personal relevance. Many a supposed vocation has arisen on such a basis only to falter and fade in time.

The entire process, as Ignatius conceived it, is guided and sustained by grace. But grace does not achieve its effects without active participation and engagement of the self. There are certain characteristics of the process which stem from activation of the ego. Our Lord provides such a rich source of aspects for imitation that the person must select. Selection will be partially determined by psychological factors in cooperation with and under the guidance of grace. From this point of view, identification with Christ is a very flexible concept, and its realization in various souls will follow highly individualized patterns.

An additional but by no means secondary consideration is that the second week culminates in an exercise of freedom in the election. The second week accordingly is structured to lead the exercitant to the threshold of that moment of choice and decision. The exercitant's deepening knowledge of himself and his relationship to God play a determinative role in this progression. His internalizing of God's plan, his growing capacity for discernment, his increasing openness to God's influence through grace, and his growing motivation to seek and fulfill God's will for him, are prime objectives of the second week.

## METHOD

In the exercises of this and the following week, the first prelude calls for presentation of the history of the particular mystery. This is to be a broad, cursory survey or calling to mind of the events in the particular mystery, followed by the usual procedure (composition of place, petition, etc.).[2]

A dominant theme of the second week is cast in terms of imitation. References to the imitation of Christ reverberate through the second week as a recurrent *leitmotif*. The theme of imitation works to synthesize universal and particular, objective and subjective, intellect and will, and focuses the exercitant's efforts toward a single end (Cusson 1988). Ignatius enunciates the theme in the meditation on the Kingdom — "I want and desire . . . to imitate Thee" [SE98] — the echoes of which can be heard throughout the week. Obviously Ignatius has more in mind than mere behavioral conformity which could border on the jejune, if not the delusional. Imitation here has more the meaning of the following of Christ, assimilation of his values and ideals, and identification with his role and mission in the divine plan of salvation.

The great meditations of the Second Week [SE91-189] draw us closer to the images of gallant chivalry that played such an elemental role in the psychic life of the young Iñigo and probably of the mature Ignatius. To further the soul's progress along the path of increasing identification with Christ and to bring the Christian values into clearer focus, Ignatius proposes a series of meditations that have become classic. The first of these, the meditation on Christ the King and the meditation on the Two Standards, set the stage for the spiritual struggle to follow, even as the ideas embedded in them provided the framework within which Iñigo carried on his own spiritual conquest. Cusson (1988) divides the rest of the week into three periods — the

[2] See the remarks on Method and the Additions in the first week.

first [SE101-134] devoted to mysteries of Christ's infancy and hidden life, the second [SE136-157, 164-168] introducing the election through the central material of the Two Standards, the Three Degrees of Humility, and suggestions for the election, and the third [SE 158-163, 169-189] returning to contemplations of the public life. The structure and pacing of these periods point up the importance of the election in the organization of the *Exercises*. Ignatius seeks the degree of autonomy and sense of responsibility that will enable the exercitant to make a binding choice that will be meaningful for how he lives his life. Therefore, the great meditations of the second week also carry forward the development in freedom and its linkage with divine freedom — facing the exercitant with the radical choice and enhancing his capacity to make that choice involved in the election (Fessard 1956; Pousset 1971).

## THE KINGDOM OF CHRIST [SE 91-100]

[91] THE CALL OF THE TEMPORAL KING

It Helps to Contemplate the Life of the King Eternal . . .

First Prelude. The first Prelude is a composition, seeing the place: it will be here to see with the sight of the imagination, the synagogues, villages and towns through which Christ our Lord preached.

Second Prelude. The second, to ask for the grace which I want: it will be here to ask grace of our Lord that I may not be deaf to His call, but ready and diligent to fulfill His most Holy Will.

[92] First Point. The first Point is, to put before me a human king chosen by God our Lord, whom all Christian princes and men reverence and obey.

[93] Second Point. The second, to look how this king speaks to all his people, saying: "It is my Will to conquer all the land of unbelievers. Therefore, whoever would like to come with me is to be content to eat as I, and also to drink and dress, etc., as I: likewise he is to labor like me in the day and watch in the night, etc., that so afterwards he may have part with me in the victory, as he has had it in the labors."

[94] Third Point. The third, to consider what the good subjects ought to answer to a King so liberal and so kind, and hence, if any one did not accept the appeal of such a king, how deserving he would be of being censured by all the world, and held for a mean-spirited knight.

[95] In Part 2

The second part of this Exercise consists in applying the above parable of the temporal King to Christ our Lord, conformably to the three Points mentioned.

> [96] First Point. And as to the first Point, if we consider such a call of the temporal King to his subjects, how much more worthy of consideration is it to see Christ our Lord, King eternal, and before Him all the entire world: which and each one in particular He calls, and says: "It is my will to conquer all the world and all enemies and so to enter into the glory of my Father; therefore, whoever would like to come with Me is to labor with Me, that following Me in the pain, he may also follow Me in the glory."
> [97] Second Point. The second, to consider that all those who have judgment and reason will offer their entire selves to the labor.
> [98] Third Point. The third, those who will want to be more devoted and signalise themselves in all service of their King Eternal and universal Lord, not only will offer their persons to the labor, but even, acting against their own sensuality and against their carnal and worldly love, will make offerings of greater value and greater importance, saying:
> "Eternal Lord of all things, I make my oblation with Thy favor and help, in presence of Thy infinite Goodness and in presence of Thy glorious Mother and of all the Saints of the heavenly Court; that I want and desire, and it is my deliberate determination, if only it be Thy greater service and praise, to imitate Thee in bearing all injuries and all abuse and all poverty of spirit, and actual poverty, too, if Thy most Holy Majesty wants to choose and receive me to such life and state."[3]

The two responses — one reflecting judgment and reason [SE97] and the other motivated by devotion and the wish to excel [SE98] — are suggested, but it is not clear whether Ignatius meant them to be separate or conjoined. They need not be taken as exclusive, but they may also reflect different and acceptable ways of responding to the call of Christ. They suggest the intersection of the natural and psychological with supernatural motivations (Imoda 1992). Some exercitants by reason of personality structure may not experience the fervor Ignatius might prefer, but their measured and reasonable response is nonetheless valid.[4] However, the question remains as to the weight attributed by Ignatius to the work of reason and intellect in relation to the impact of affective and emotional experience. Was his experience dictated more by the latter than the former, or in what ways might they have reinforced each other? In the *Exercises*, Ignatius seems to appeal in the first place to the intellect, seeking understand-

[3] Two notes follow, recommending making this exercise twice in the day [SE99], and reading the Imitation of Christ, the gospels, and lives of saints [SE100].

[4] See the discussion of this question in Cusson (1988) commenting on Clemence (1956).

ing of the revealed message and its import. But in practical terms the exercitant prays for enlightenment and affective movement, and these interior movements are prompted by the action of grace. The pattern is modeled on his own experiences, especially at Manresa. This points to the value he placed on affective experience and the importance he gave it, particularly in the matter of discernment where affects and grace are seemingly linked.

This meditation has been rightly regarded as a second foundation containing the central idea of the *Exercises* (Rahner 1956). Its appeal plays on a theme reflecting the deepest desires and aspirations — the figure of the noble king, in Jungian terms, is an archetype representing eruption of self from the anonymity and undifferentiation of the unconscious in an emerging process of development of self-consciousness and individuality. The theme, viewed in this perspective, would seem to be marvelously calculated to strike a chord of responsiveness in the self, emerging at this point in the *Exercises* from undifferentiation and subjection to instinctual forces to the differentiation and autonomy of spiritual identity. Such a king deserves the noblest and devoted service, so that anyone who would not respond generously would be nothing less than a "mean-spirited knight." Further the note of apostolic service begins to be sounded, shifting the ground from exclusive preoccupation with the inner world to the broader perspective of the kingdom (Staudenmaier 1994).

The imagery reverberates with echoes of the courtly life of Iñigo's adolescence, the magnificence and splendor of royal trappings, as well as his reverence for and devotion to old Velázquez and even the duke of Nájera — and beyond them, in the chain of associations, to his father Beltran. Clearly the imagery of soldierly conduct, chivalrous service, and dedication to the service of his appointed king never left the heart of Iñigo de Loyola.[5] They were transformed in the crisis and resolution of Manresa into ideals of the service of a heavenly king — inflamed by the imagery of Ludolph's *Life* and the power of his conversion experience (Meissner 1992b).[6]

The content of this meditation brings us back to an earlier day when the young hidalgo was caught up in visions of glory and heroic

[5] Ignatius' military mentality is central to the view advanced by Huonder (1932). But this aspect must be kept in perspective, along with his tact, diplomacy, sensitivty, empathy, and particularly his intensely affective and ecstatic mystical experience — a point made by Leturia (1933) in his critique of Huonder's work. See also Nicholau (1957).

[6] Leturia (1941) pointed to the influence of both the *Flos* and the *Vita Christi* on the Exercises, particularly in the meditations on the King and the Two Standards.

deeds in his king's service as the intrepid and valorous knight-errant whose sword was ever ready to serve its master. For Iñigo de Loyola such loyalty could not be cast in modest terms; it had to be writ large in terms of heroic sacrifice and courageous confrontation and conquest of even the greatest dangers and threats. Only such a spirit could have led him into the thick of danger and to face overwhelming odds with such reckless daring and courage. The military imagery evokes metaphors of fighting, battle and war.[7] These metaphors became the common language of Ignatius' followers, as exemplified in Nadal's exhortation to the scholastics at Alcala in 1576, referring to the mission of the Society as a campaign in a war against the forces of evil. The Formula of the Institute refers to the Jesuit "as a soldier of God beneath the banner of the cross." The "soldier of God" motif was common medieval usage for a member of a religious order, as in Erasmus' *Handbook of the Christian Soldier* (O'Malley 1993).[8]

If such had been the nature of his labors for his temporal king, we should not be surprised to find a similar quality in his service to a heavenly king. The same Iñigo who defiantly faced the French at Pamplona for the glory of Castile later entered into a deathly struggle with powerful psychic forces within the cave of Manresa. For that triumph in the name of Jesus Christ, no labor was too great, no pain too intense, no sacrifice beyond his reach. The ideals of conquest and glory had been transformed and sublimated and recast in a spiritual

[7] We can also recognize that the meaning of military metaphors has changed from the time of Ignatius to our own day. The military organization and professional codes of today bear little resemblance to their meaning in Ignatius' mind. In the age of chivalry, the central figure was the heroic knight on whose strength and prowess success in battle hinged. The dawn of modernity and the changing technology and tactics of war spelled the doom of such medieval images. And with Cervantes, the caricature of Quixote cast these diminishing idols in a more ludicrous light (Buckley 1993, 1995).

[8] Much of this rhetoric may have been a residue of the age of the crusades, imagery of which had captured the popular imagination and had its reverberations well into the fifteenth and sixteenth centuries. Ignatius spoke the language of the medieval and the age of chivalry that shaped much of his self-image. The long history of struggle to unify a kingdom, conquer and drive out the Moors, and the adventures of global exploration and conquest of the conquistadors (of which Ignatius' own brothers were an active part) would have had a deep and vivid impression on his imagination and fantasy. Buckley (1993) writes, "The chivalric symbols in the *Exercises* disclose an entire world in which one encounters pivotal emphases as upon *mas* and *senalar*, the absoluteness of personal choice, the greater likeness to the Lord, and the primacy of loyal, unflagging service" (p. 10). Buckley (1995) links this imagery to the theme of the *ecclesia militans* and Gregory VII's references to monastic life as the *militia Christi*, metaphors that would have sounded special resonances in the mind of Ignatius.

mold: the pilgrim saw himself as a warrior of God and of Christ. The warfare was not of this world, and the weapons and tactics were decidedly different. But the same desire for struggle, conquest, and glory burned in his soul as had been there from the first.

This meditation likewise marks an advance, or rather a first stage of advance over the first week. The *leitmotif* of this advance is cast in the words of Our Lord: "My will is to conquer the whole world, and all my enemies, and thus to enter into the glory of my Father. Whoever, therefore, desires to come with Me must labor with Me, in order that following Me in pain, he may likewise follow Me in glory" [SE 96], but these words of the meditation can be read as expressing Ignatius' own mind set. The entire program of the *Exercises* is thus laid before the exercitant (Dir. XIX, 1). His response will be in the form of a determination to imitate Our Lord in the bearing of insults, reproaches and poverty. The meditation is intended to generate a definitive readiness to follow Christ explicitly in choosing the difficult, suffering, and the humble and poor as essential aspects of the following.

The meditation involves a typically Ignatian technique. The self is seeking here a more penetrating insight into the nature of the forces opposed to Christ and into the values of the life to which it is called under the banner of Christ. The consideration effectively recapitulates and synthesizes much that has gone before — the need for self-control and the resolve on imitation of Christ in poverty and humility — but it also carries on the developmental momentum. It seems clear that Ignatius' effort here is to solidify and crystallize proceeding levels of self-synthesis. The effort of self-synthesis involves a progressive elaboration, dependent on the preceding level of synthesis at every stage of its progression. It involves an increasingly deeper and more penetrating realization of spiritual values and a progressive internalization and synthesis of these assimilations into an integral and meaningful construction. The process, then, is one of continual recapitulation and synthesis resulting in consolidation of previous synthetic achievements and a concurrent synthetic effort subsuming the previous level of synthesis in a contemporary resynthesis striving to reach a new level of spiritual realization and integration.

Psychologically, this is a decisive moment in the development of the *Exercises*. If the exercitant commits himself to this ideal and follows it generously and fervently, he will be drawn on through the succeeding phases of Ignatius' program. Likewise, in making his commitment and response to the call of Christ, the exercitant enters a new phase in his spiritual growth. The self up to this point has been engaged in a psychic reorientation and reorganization in relation to other facets of its non-ego psyche; it now sets itself decisively on the path to its own growth and development. This is attended by a new commitment, a reordering of patterns of ego-superego involvement and interaction, a new and more demanding value-orientation, and by a new synthesis of these elements into the expanding self-structure.

Stanley (1968) raised the interesting question whether the Ignatian method of detailed imaginative reconstruction of scenes from the gospel narratives can have the same motivational impact on modern exercitants as it might have had in Ignatius' day, especially given the marked shift of cultural interest from the imaginative to the literary. He argues that the residues of medieval piety are alien to modern consciousness, and that the shift from a cultural setting characterized by active use of the imagination antecedent to the invention and dissemination of printing would be offputting to the twentieth century mind. Thus the kind of immersion in historical detail and the exercise of pious imagination in recreating circumstances of Jesus' earthly life may not have the same implications and effect today as in Ignatius' time.

But the Ignatian *contemplatio* intends to engage the exercitant in the saving event constituted by the life of Christ and to elicit or facilitate his participation in that event and its consequences.[9] In order to collaborate in this salvific process, as Stanley (1968) recommends, "the Christian of the twentieth century must begin with the sacred text itself, the inspired expression of the religious experience of the Evangelist, the result of his personal confrontation (and that of the Apostolic Church, whose special witness he is) with the exalted Lord Jesus. To realize effectively here and now a similar confrontation, the modern believer must labor to grasp the significance of the words in which the Gospel scene is couched, appreciating the literary form of the narrative, penetrating the figures of speech, the peculiarities of idiom, perceiving (above all) the particular purpose or christological import of the passage" (p. 439). This recommendation can be added adaptively to the Ignatian methodology, but it should be recognized that it adopts a more intellectually based approach to contemplations than intended by Ignatius and that it can-

[9] The term *contemplatio* here in the second week has a specific meaning. Contemplation of the mysteries of Christ's life was a common practice in Ignatius' time, probably deriving from a Franciscan tradition. Ignatius had probably followed such a procedure in reading Ludolph the Carthusian's *Life of Christ* during his convalescence and conversion at Loyola. See Meissner (1994).

not substitute for the affective component that was so salient a part of his engagement in the process.

## The Incarnation [SE101-109]

[101] THE FIRST DAY AND FIRST CONTEMPLATION . . .
[102] First Prelude. The first Prelude is to bring up the narrative of the thing which I have to contemplate.

Here, it is how the Three Divine Persons looked at all the plain or circuit of all the world, full of men, and how, seeing that all were going down to Hell, it is determined in Their Eternity, that the Second Person shall become man to save the human race, and so, the fullness of times being come, They sent the Angel St. Gabriel to Our Lady ([SE 262]).

[103] Second Prelude. The second, a composition, seeing the place: here it will be to see the great capacity and circuit of the world, in which are so many and such different people: then likewise, in particular, the house and rooms of Our Lady in the city of Nazareth, in the Province of Galilee.

[104] Third Prelude. The third, to ask for what I want: it will be to ask for interior knowledge of the Lord, Who for me has become man, that I may more love and follow Him.[10]

[106] First Point. The first Point is, to see the various persons: and first those on the surface of the earth, in such variety, in dress as in actions: some white and others black; some in peace and others in war; some weeping and others laughing; some well, others ill; some being born and others dying, etc.

2. To see and consider the Three Divine Persons, as on their royal throne or seat of Their Divine Majesty, how They look on all the surface and circuit of the earth, and all the people in such blindness, and how they are dying and going down to Hell.

3. To see Our Lady, and the Angel who is saluting her, and to reflect in order to get profit from such a sight.

[107] Second Point. The second, to hear what the persons on the face of the earth are saying, that is, how they are talking with one another, how they swear and blaspheme, etc.; and likewise what the Divine Persons are saying, that is: "Let Us work the redemption of the Human race," etc.; and then what the Angel and Our Lady are saying; and to reflect then so as to draw profit from their words.

[108] Third Point. The third, to look then at what the persons on the face of the earth are doing, as, for instance, killing, going to Hell, etc.; likewise what the Divine Persons are doing, namely,

[10] A note here [SE105] prescribes the same preparatory prayer and the same three Preludes, for this and the following weeks, "changing the form according to the subject matter."

working out the most holy Incarnation, etc.; and likewise what the Angel and Our Lady are doing, namely, the Angel doing his duty as ambassador, and Our Lady humbling herself and giving thanks to the Divine Majesty; and then to reflect in order to draw some profit from each of these things.
[109] Colloquy. At the end a Colloquy is to be made, thinking what I ought to say to the Three Divine Persons, or to the Eternal Word incarnate, or to our Mother and Lady, asking according to what I feel in me, in order more to follow and imitate Our Lord, so lately incarnate.
I will say an OUR FATHER.

The meditation echoes the foundational themes of the principle [SE23] and speaks to Ignatius' imaginative vision of divine governance and providence over human affairs. This was a profound motif in Ignatius' belief system and served as a guiding norm for his sense of values and his desire to serve his Creator and Lord. The steps of the meditation serve to concretize the divine purpose and bring it to a fulfilling focus in the incarnational apperception. This setting and the *dramatis personae* will recur countless times in his spiritual rhetoric and imagery.

## THE NATIVITY [SE110-117]

[110] THE SECOND CONTEMPLATION is on the Nativity . . .
[111] First Prelude. The first Prelude is the narrative and it will be here how Our Lady went forth from Nazareth, about nine months with child, as can be piously meditated, seated on an ass, and accompanied by Joseph and a maid, taking an ox, to go to Bethlehem to pay the tribute which Caesar imposed on all those lands.
[112] Second Prelude. The second, a composition, seeing the place. It will be here to see with the sight of the imagination the road from Nazareth to Bethlehem; considering the length and the breadth, and whether such road is level or through valleys or over hills; likewise looking at the place or cave of the activity, how large, how small, how low, how high, and how it was prepared.[11]
[114] First Point. The first Point is to see the persons; that is, to see Our Lady and Joseph and the maid, and, after His Birth, the Child Jesus, I making myself a poor creature and a wretch of an unworthy slave, looking at them and serving them in their needs, with all possible respect and reverence, as if I found myself present; and then to reflect on myself in order to draw some profit.
[115] Second Point. The second, to look, mark and contemplate what they are saying, and, reflecting on myself, to draw some profit.

[11] The third prelude [SE113] is the same, as before.

[116] Third Point. The third, to look and consider what they are doing, as going a journey and laboring, that the Lord may be born in the greatest poverty; and as a termination of so many labors — of hunger, of thirst, of heat and of cold, of injuries and affronts — that He may die on the Cross; and all this for me: then reflecting, to draw some spiritual profit.[12]

[121] THE FIFTH CONTEMPLATION

Will be to Bring the Five Senses on the First and Second Contemplation

Prayer. After the Preparatory Prayer and the three Preludes, it is helpful to pass the five senses of the imagination through the first and second Contemplation, in the following way:

[122] First Point. The first Point is to see the persons with the sight of the imagination, meditating and contemplating in particular the details about them and drawing some profit from the sight.

[123] Second Point. The second, to hear with the hearing what they are, or might be, talking about and, reflecting on oneself, to draw some profit from it.

[124] Third Point. The third, to smell and to taste with the smell and the taste the infinite fragrance and sweetness of the Divinity, of the soul, and of its virtues, and of all, according to the person who is being contemplated; reflecting on oneself and drawing profit from it.

[125] Fourth Point. The fourth, to touch with the touch, as for instance, to embrace and kiss the places where such persons put their feet and sit, always seeing to my drawing profit from it. . .[13]

## NOTES

[127] First Note. The first note is to remark for all this and the other following Weeks, that I have only to read the Mystery of the Contemplation which I have immediately to make, so that at any time I read no Mystery which I have not to make that day or at that hour, in order that the consideration of one Mystery may not hinder the consideration of the other. . .[14]

[129] Third Note. The third: It is to be remarked that if the person who is making the Exercises is old or weak, or, although strong, has become in some way less strong from the First Week,

[12] Colloquy [SE117] and repetitions omitted. The third contemplation [SE118-119] repeats the first two, "noting always some more principal parts, where the person has felt some knowledge, consolation or desolation." The fourth contemplation [SE120] also repeats the first and second.

[13] Colloquy [SE126] omitted.

[14] The Second Note [SE128] dealing with times for repetitions of these meditations is omitted.

it is better for him in this Second Week, at least sometimes, not rising at midnight, to make one Contemplation in the morning, and another at the hour of Mass, and another before dinner, and one repetition on them at the hour of Vespers, and then the Application of the Senses before supper.

[130] Fourth Note. In this Second Week, out of all the ten Additions which were mentioned in the First Week, the second, the sixth, the seventh and in part the tenth have to be changed.

In the second it will be, immediately on waking up, to put before me the contemplation which I have to make, desiring to know more the Eternal Word incarnate, in order to serve and to follow Him more.

The sixth will be to bring frequently to memory the Life and mysteries of Christ our Lord, from His Incarnation down to the place or Mystery which I am engaged in contemplating.

The seventh will be, that one should manage as to keeping darkness or light, making use of good weather or bad, according that he feels that it can profit and help him to find what the person desires who is exercising himself.

And in the tenth Addition, he who is exercising himself ought to manage himself according to the Mysteries which he is contemplating; because some demand penance and others not.

All the ten Additions, then, are to be made with great care.

The changes in the additions are calculated to adapt them to the objectives of this second week. In the second addition, the exercitant not only recalls the material of the contemplation but excites in himself desires to know Our Lord more intimately in order to follow and serve Him better. Likewise, in the sixth, the exercitant does not try to feel sorrow and grief as in the first week, but calls to mind the mysteries he has already meditated on. Even his practice of penance should be regulated now not by desire for contrition and penance, but by the demands of each mystery and the fruit to be derived from it. This marks a shift away from the guilt-driven and masochistic origins of such penances toward a more sublimated and positively motivated use of penance in the service of love.[15]

[131] Fifth Note. The fifth note: In all the Exercises, except in that of midnight and in that of the morning, the equivalent of the second Addition will be taken in the following way: — Immediately on recollecting that it is the time of the Exercise which I have to make, before I go, putting before myself where I am going and before Whom, and summarizing a little the Exercise which I have

[15] See the comments on penance and masochism in chapter X above.

to make, and then making the third Addition, I will enter into the Exercise.

This recommendation is proposed as a help for the self to direct its energies to the kind of exercise undertaken in this week — contemplations of Our Lord's life.

[132] THE SECOND DAY

Second Day. For first and second Contemplation to take the Presentation in the Temple [SE 268] and the Flight to Egypt as into exile [SE 269], and on these two Contemplations will be made two repetitions and the Application of the Five Senses to them, in the same way as was done the preceding day.

[133] Note. Sometimes, although the one who is exercising himself is strong and disposed, it helps to make a change, from this second day up to the fourth inclusively, in order better to find what he desires, taking only one Contemplation at daybreak, and another at the hour of Mass, and to repeat on them at the hour of Vespers and apply the senses before supper.

[134] THE THIRD DAY

Third Day. How the Child Jesus was obedient to His Parents at Nazareth [SE 271], and how afterwards they found Him in the Temple [SE 272], and so then to make the two repetitions and apply the five senses.

## Preamble to Consider States [SE135]

First Preamble. The example which Christ our Lord, being under obedience to His parents, has given us for the first state, — which consists in the observance of the Commandments — having been now considered; and likewise for the second, — which is that of evangelical perfection, — when He remained in the Temple, leaving His adoptive father and His natural Mother, to attend to the pure service of His eternal Father; we will begin, at the same time contemplating His life, to investigate and to ask in what life or state His Divine Majesty wants to be served by us.

And so, for some introduction of it, we will, in the first Exercise following, see the intention of Christ our Lord, and, on the contrary, that of the enemy of human nature, and how we ought to dispose ourselves in order to come to perfection in whatever state of life God our Lord would give us to choose.

At this point in the *Exercises*, Ignatius introduces a parallel motif, namely that of the election of a state of life. I regard this as a parallel motif insofar as from a psychological viewpoint the election is secondary to the underlying growth process, that is to say, any election made in the course of a retreat comes about as a result of the process of psychological growth and takes the form of a specific expression of that underlying dynamic. Ignatius seems to recognize this dual movement in his remark about investigating God's will regarding state of life at the same time as contemplating the mysteries of Our Lord's life. Within this perspective, the election becomes a moment of decision and life commitment. Such life determining decisions are not only possible, but are central to Ignatius' intention. They are also congruent to a more existential understanding of freedom as the power of becoming oneself or of transforming nonbeing into being (Fessard 1956).

Although a case can be made for the structural centrality of the election (Fessard 1956), and although it is apparent that functionally one of Ignatius' main purposes seems to have been to help the exercitant determine his state in life or vocation, to limit the *Exercises* to this perspective is, in my opinion, to constrict them to only one facet of their utility. Not only can and should the *Exercises* be employed where there is no question of determining a state of life, but it seems that the election itself need not be regarded as functionally central when the *Exercises* are put in a broader context. Placing the election, whatever its object, in the central position is useful and helpful when the Exercises are employed in a compressed period of time and for this purpose. But when the Exercises are regarded as a process of spiritual development, the election as such is one of a series of more or less uniform progressions through which the self must pass on the way to a maturing spiritual identity. From this point of view, the centrality of the election is diminished, whether the process be projected over a short period or over a lifetime.

As Ignatius begins the development of the election, he presumes that the preliminary phases of the ongoing self-synthetic process have been accomplished. The exercitant has already enrolled himself under the banner of Christ and has begun to follow Christ. Not only has he determined to follow Christ, but he has decisively begun to seek identification with Him — he has chosen the way of spiritual perfection through the imitation of Christ, the leader.

# CHAPTER XII

# THE SECOND WEEK — FOLLOWING OF CHRIST

The latter portion of the second week, without diminishing the theme of imitation of Christ, shifts the emphasis more in the direction of choosing a path of life in which the issue is more than imitation — namely the active choice to follow Christ wherever he might lead — whether to a change of state of life or toward greater spiritual growth in one's already chosen path. The series of great meditations introduced here look forward to the central dynamic point of the Exercises — the election.

## The Two Standards [SE 136-146]

[136] The Fourth Day. Meditation on TWO STANDARDS The one of Christ, our Commander-in-chief and Lord; the other of Lucifer, mortal enemy of our human nature. . . .

[137] First Prelude. The First Prelude is the narrative. It will be here how Christ calls and wants all under His standard; and Lucifer, on the contrary, under his.

[138] Second Prelude. The second, a composition, seeing the place. It will be here to see a great field of all that region of Jerusalem, where the supreme Commander-in-chief of the good is Christ our Lord; another field in the region of Babylon, where the chief of the enemy is Lucifer.

[139] Third Prelude. The third, to ask for what I want: and it will be here to ask for knowledge of the deceits of the bad chief and help to guard myself against them, and for knowledge of the true life which the supreme and true Captain shows and grace to imitate Him.

[140] First Point. The first Point is to imagine as if the chief of all the enemy seated himself in that great field of Babylon, as in a great chair of fire and smoke, in shape horrible and terrifying.

[141] Second Point. The second, to consider how he issues a summons to innumerable demons and how he scatters them, some to one city and others to another, and so through all the world, not omitting any provinces, places, states, nor any persons in particular.

[142] Third Point. The third, to consider the discourse which he makes them, and how he tells them to cast out nets and chains; that they have first to tempt with a longing for riches — as he is accustomed to do in most cases — that men may more easily come to vain honor of the world, and then to vast pride. So that the first step shall be that of riches; the second, that of honor; the third that of pride; and from these three steps he draws on to all the other vices.

[143] So, on the contrary, one has to imagine as to the supreme and true Captain, Who is Christ our Lord.

[144] First Point. The first Point is to consider how Christ our Lord puts Himself in a great field of that region of Jerusalem, in lowly place, beautiful and attractive.

[145] Second Point. The second, to consider how the Lord of all the world chooses so many persons — Apostles, Disciples, etc., — and sends them through all the world spreading His sacred doctrine through all states and conditions of persons.

[146] Third Point. The third, to consider the discourse which Christ our Lord makes to all His servants and friends whom He sends on this expedition, recommending them to want to help all, by bringing them first to the highest spiritual poverty, and — if His Divine Majesty would be served and would want to choose them no less to actual poverty; the second is to be of contumely and contempt; because from these two things humility follows. So that there are to be three steps; the first, poverty against riches; the second, contumely or contempt against worldly honor; the third, humility against pride. And from these three steps let them induce to all the other virtues.

[147] First Colloquy. One Colloquy to Our Lady, that she may get me grace from Her Son and Lord that I may be received under His standard; and first in the highest spiritual poverty, and — if His Divine Majesty would be served and would want to choose and receive me — not less in actual poverty; second, in suffering contumely and injuries, to imitate Him more in them, if only I can suffer them without the sin of any person, or displeasure of His Divine Majesty; and with that a HAIL MARY.

Second Colloquy. I will ask the same of the Son, that He may get it for me of the Father; and with that say the SOUL OF CHRIST.

Third Colloquy. I will ask the same of the Father, that He may grant it to me; and say an OUR FATHER.[1]

This is another crucial meditation drawing the exercitant further along the path of spiritual development. The exercitant here is

[1] The note [SE148], dealing with times and repetitions of this meditation, is omitted.

directed to seek greater insight into the nature of the forces opposed to Christ and into the true life under the banner of Christ. The meditation reflects the conflict Ignatius saw as endemic to human history and as formed around the core of human existence — the endless struggle between the divine influence on human choice and the diabolical influence of the "enemy of human nature," between the joy and consolation characterizing the influence of God and the evil in the heart of man that is the work of the devil. It is not a manichean conflict between cosmic forces of good and evil, but a conflict between impulses leading toward God and the diabolical in man himself. It is the satanic, the diabolical, the anti-human, the destructiveness and self-centeredness in man that draws him away from God, and is thus the enemy of man's nature, which is created and ordered to God.

The technique is typically Ignatian in that the meditation recapitulates and synthesizes much that has gone before — the need to overcome instinctual gratification and establish ego control, the resolve upon the imitation of Christ in poverty and humility — while it also carries along the developmental momentum. It seems clear that Ignatius' effort here is to solidify and crystallize preceding levels of self-synthesis. The more effectively internalization and synthesis have taken place, the more solid is the foundation for preceding phases of growth. It is almost as though these meditations were a kind of cement being used to fix the simultaneously progressing identity formation. Significant identifications with Christ are thereby fused into the overall picture governed by the dominant theme of self-abnegation and indifference.

In this meditation, as in the meditation on the Kingdom, the program of Ignatius can be more clearly discerned. It is a progressive deepening of the realization of and commitment to the basic principle of indifference proposed in the foundation in the first week. Here the program of Christ is sketched as a progression firstly to poverty of spirit, secondly to desire of reproaches and contempt, and thirdly to humility. These are sketched as stages in a program of development, and from a psychological perspective they would seem to correspond to the progressive phases of spiritual self-synthesis constituting spiritual growth. The mechanism and motivation for this development are formulated in the words of the colloquy, "the better to imitate Him." Likewise, the program is set in relief by contrast with the process leading from inordinate attachments to pride.

Once again, the words of the meditation enable us to catch a glimpse of the old Iñigo, the soldier of honor and high ideals, guided by fidelity to his lord. It suggests that the old ego ideal has not perished, that there is something of the old Iñigo in the new Ignatius. But the very imagery of the chivalric ideal is transformed and elevated; no longer is the ideal of any lord in question, it is the ideal of service to a heavenly king through humility and suffering that is now proposed. It seems appropriate to conceptualize this transformation in terms of the transvaluation of identity.

We have some indication of the weight Ignatius placed on these meditations in later years. De Guibert (1964) quoted Manareo, one of the early members of the Society of Jesus, to the effect that Ignatius "applied himself chiefly to two exercises, namely, those of the two standards and of the king, thus preparing himself for the war against the infernal enemy and the world" (p. 118). Similarly, Nadal, writing in 1544 emphasized that Ignatius showed particular devotion to these same two exercises and felt that the objectives contained in these meditations were also to be goals of the Society he founded. De Guibert (1964) added that these texts seem to confirm the importance and influence of the *Flos Sanctorum* in Iñigo's conversion experience. Undoubtedly, they also reflect the spirit and frame of mind that influenced him at that time.

The meditation on the Two Standards particularly indicates the essentials of the Ignatian approach. Ignatius' thinking from beginning to end of the *Exercises* and his own life, is dominated by commitment to service, here the service of God under the banner of Christ. The lines of battle are clearly drawn; the enemy is known and identified. He is the devil, the tempter of men, who uses every device, exploits every weakness, and loses no opportunity to attack and destroy the souls of men. No man is secure from his ambushes. His subtlety and trickery are such that he often deceives men into doing evil in the name of good. He is a liar and a murderer, as he has been from the very first. Constant vigilance is mandatory, therefore, along unwavering resolution to do the opposite of what the evil one proposes. Only along this path lies the promise of wisdom, virtue, and salvation. The alternatives presented to man's free choice are stark — either to remain trapped in concupiscence or to do battle against it, to follow the standard of Satan or that of Christ, to choose between the nonbeing of sin and the being of grace. Freedom is to be achieved through a threefold renunciation — of riches and possessions through poverty, of worldly honor and power through insults, and of pride through humility — all deceitful seductions of the enemy. Moreover the appeal is personal and participative, rather than abstract and general — there is no place for spectators (Staudenmaier 1994).

And so, in this powerful meditation, the battle with the enemy is joined, but the followers of Christ have a superior force on their side. The arm of the Lord is not shortened, and his greater desire and power to save men overcomes any resource the demon can employ to destroy them. The enemy attacks the weaknesses of love of riches, care for the vain honor of the world, and finally pride. "And from these three steps," Ignatius tells us, "he draws on to all the other vices" [SE 142]. The discourse of Christ spells out the battle plan for countering these maneuvers of the enemy. Against the desire of riches, the soldier of Christ seeks spiritual or even actual poverty, should that be God's will. Against ambition and the desire for worldly glory, he seeks humiliation and contempt. And finally, against the threat of pride and narcissistic self-investment, he seeks humility.

The Ignatian technique of progressive recapitulation seems to reflect his own profound spiritual experience and growth. The stress on indifference and abnegation, proper to the spirit of the first week, returns again in the second week, now elevated to a new level in the following of Christ. In his own spiritual development, Ignatius seems to have mirrored this process, for at the end of his life, his spirituality was marked by presence of apparent extremes of the highest mystical gifts together along with intense and genuine concern for examination of faults and self-abnegation. Likewise, he never ceased to emphasize the need for abnegation in his followers (de Guibert 1964). It is as though he had never passed through and left behind any particular stage of his growth, but rather carried each phase along, subsuming it at each stage in a higher synthesis. I think we should consider the *Exercises* similarly with respect to the growth in spiritual identity. One never leaves the work of the first week behind, but carries it along into the second week and there integrates gains from the first week with the new fruits of the second week in a new synthesis which looses none of the gain.

Ignatius frames the meditation of the Two Standards in a graphic confrontation of Christ and Satan. In our supposedly advanced age of psychological sophistication, we are reluctant to accept the influences described as demonic; we much prefer to ascribe them to psychological dynamics of one sort or another. The confrontation between good and evil can be readily understood in terms of ambivalent and contradictory tendencies within the psyche. The influence of Iñigo's own experience is unmistakable here. It is as though in the portrait of the victim of the devil's machinations he was depicting himself before he was struck down by the French cannonball. Certainly, the young Iñigo de Loyola was not lacking in intense, consuming ambition and the willingness to sacrifice all in the search for worldly acclaim.

The meditation also suggests the basis for the pilgrim's approach in the transformed, spiritual conquest. Here the primary values and ideals that had governed his preconversion life now became the object of specific and unrelenting attack. Every vestige of worldly desire, ambition, the yearning for glory and recognition, and particularly pride — at once his family heritage and his own dominating passion — had to be rooted out and cast aside. In psychoanalytic terms, it seems clear that the spiritual program of the pilgrim was nothing less than an assault on his own narcissism and self-love, which he saw as the main impediment to his spiritual growth and conquest.

## THE THREE CLASSES [SE 149-155]

[149] The same fourth day let meditation be made on THREE PAIRS OF MEN in order to embrace what is best. . . .
[150] First Prelude. The first Prelude is the narrative, which is of three pairs of men, and each one of them has acquired ten thousand ducats, not solely or as they ought for God's love, and all want to save themselves and find in peace God our Lord, ridding themselves of the weight and hindrance to it which they have in the attachment for the thing acquired.
[151] Second Prelude. The second, a composition, seeing the place. It will be here to see myself, how I stand before God our Lord and all His Saints, to desire and know what is more pleasing to His Divine Goodness.
[152] Third Prelude. The third, to ask for what I want. Here it will be to ask grace to choose what is more to the glory of his Divine Majesty and the salvation of my soul.
[153] First Pair. The first Pair would want to rid themselves of the attachment which they have to the thing acquired, in order to find in peace God our Lord and be able to save themselves, and they do not place the means up to the hour of death.
[154] Second Pair. The second want to rid themselves of the attachment, but want so to rid themselves of it as to remain with the thing acquired, so that God should come where they want, and they do not decide to leave it in order to go to God, although it would be the best state for them.
[155] Third Pair. The third want to rid themselves of the attachment, but want so to rid themselves of it that they have even no liking for it to keep the thing acquired or not to keep it, but only want to want it or not want it according as God our Lord will put in their will and as will appear to them better for the service and praise of His Divine Majesty; and meanwhile they want to reckon

> that they quit it all in attachment, forcing themselves not to want that or any other thing, unless only the service of God our Lord move them: so that the desire of being better able to serve God our Lord moves them to take the thing or leave it.[2]

Ignatius strikes again while the iron is hot! He is striving in this meditation for the highest possible degree of detachment and drive control. The solemnity of this exercise is striking, indicating the pivotal role it played for Ignatius in moving the exercitant toward a more operational approach to issues of choice and commitment to freedom — an appeal to the will rather than to intellect or affectivity (Imoda 1992). Ignatius places the exercitant in the presence of the Divine Majesty and the heavenly court. He is asked to place himself in that disposition which would be best in the light of his previous commitment. The first two classes represent inadequate solutions of the problem which reflect the deficiency of ego-strength.

As Ignatius presents the parable, each class is presented with a conflict between their desire to save their souls and their attachment to money. The money is symbolic of any object to which libido can become attached in such a way as to make that object significant to the self. The solution of the first class is defective in that the individual is unable to pass beyond mere desire for resolution and execution. This is the solution of the self with a low degree of ego-strength, insufficient to counteract this particular desire. It does not have the resources to effect what it knows it must. The call to greater freedom calls for a renunciation they are unwilling to make or presents them with an inherent threat they prefer to avoid.

The solution of the second class is not altogether ineffective, but it is also defective insofar as the individual attempts to resolve the conflict by adopting a substitute attachment offering less resistance, or by a compromise with the demands of conscience. This is the solution of the ego lacking sufficient strength to assert its control over instinctual drives in this particular critical area of attachment where significant resistance is experienced. Consequently, it allows itself to be satisfied with a compromise. In an analytic perspective, compromise between ego and id can be adaptive, and in fact even the healthiest of structures are usually forms of compromise formation in some sense. But, as Ignatius well knows, compromise can mean capitulation, and such capitulation with the demands of inordinate desires is a defeat for the ego. They may be even more self-deceived than the first group, since they value and idealize freedom,

[2] The note [SE156], suggesting repeating the Three Colloquies from the Two Standards, is omitted.

but perversely cling to a hidden self-will and narcissistic self-investment. The two solutions, consequently, must be regarded as the solutions of the ego which has not effectively resolved the essential crisis of the first week. The meditation on the Three Classes is equivalently a testing of the progress of the exercitant.

The third solution is the only adequate one, since it represents the epitome of ego-control. The ego is so master of itself that the instinctual attachment is relatively powerless to affect it one way or another. Ignatius pictures the self as activated by a desire to attach or detach itself only insofar as attachment or detachment seems better oriented within the value-system of the spiritual life — God's will.

There is a nuance in this portrait which is of vital importance. None of the three classes of men actually surrenders the money. Surrendering the money is never in question directly. What is sought for is surrender of their attachment to the money. The first two classes fail in this, the third succeeds. But particularly to be emphasized is this: that the solution of the third class does not involve any repression or suppression of the impulse to gratification. The ego permits itself to wish for the money or not, but only insofar as the course of action it determines on is in conformity with its own internalized values. In this delicate nuance lies all the difference between domination of ego and that of superego. The strong ego, secure in its mastery of itself and its integration of instinctual drives and impulses, has no need to throw up rigid defenses or allow itself to be drawn into the opposite extreme of compulsive avoidance. From the point of view of autonomy of function, which is proper to the self and necessary for its spiritual growth, either extreme — inordinate attachment or compulsive detachment — is or can be an impediment.

Thus, as the *Directory* points out, the whole meditation bears on the single point of "what a shameful and wrongheaded thing it is to refuse to strip off inordinate attachments, and not merely that, but even if willing to strip them off, to will it only in the way that pleases oneself, instead of resigning oneself into the hands of God" (Dir. XXIX, 6). It is uncertain whether this meditation was part of the material gathered a Manresa; it may have been added subsequently. As Ignatius presents the three classes, each class is faced with a conflict between the desire to save their souls and their inordinate attachment to money or other material goods. We can read these descriptions as images of stages in his own spiritual growth. Only the third solution will do — it is the solution toward which the Exercises aim, and which Ignatius himself had achieved through his arduous spiritual discipline and ascetic self-denial.

[157] *Note*:

It is to be noted that when we feel a tendency or repugnance against actual poverty, when we are not indifferent to poverty or riches, it is very helpful, in order to crush such disordered tendency, to ask in the Colloquies (although it be against the flesh) that the Lord should choose one to actual poverty, and that one wants, asks and begs it, if only it be the service and praise of His Divine Goodness.

This note is of central importance to understanding the Ignatian method. He advises that, when under the influence of an inordinate attachment and repugnance is felt to its opposite, it helps in overcoming this attachment to beg that God chose us to the condition for which we feel the repugnance. The strategy here is to mobilize the countercathectic energies of the ego.[3] Repugnance is a form of libidinal resistance to ego-control, and is expectable considering the degree of self-denial and engagement Ignatius seeks. Where such resistance to efforts of the ego to establish control is too strong, Ignatius suggests a diversionary tactic. The ego, by begging that God order it to embrace that which it finds repugnant, can bring itself to a desire of it insofar as it sees that it is part of what it has already chosen and seeks with great desire, namely, God's will. Psychologically, this represents an activation of ego-energies and an intensification of motivation, which tend to break down or circumvent the resistance. The principle is practical and provides an insight into the concept of working-through ego-id conflicts which Ignatius employed. Spiritual writers shy away from seeing this movement in terms of acts of will, but more often attribute the effects to grace. We can at least question whether they are exclusive paradigms. This provides another example of Ignatius' tendency to take the bull by the horns.

The following sections suggests a series of topics for meditation based on events from Christ's life [SE 158-164] and makes recommendations for scheduling. These meditations covering from the fifth to the twelfth day lead up to the consideration of the Three Degrees of Humility.[4]

[162] First Note. The first note is that in the Contemplations of this Second Week according to the time each one wants to spend,

[3] See remarks on Annotation XVI in chapter VIII above.

[4] Two notes regarding repetition of the meditations [SE159] and use of the particular examen [SE160] are omitted. The omitted meditations include the baptism at the Jordan (fifth day) [SE158], the temptations in the desert (sixth day), calling of the disciples (seventh day), the Sermon on the Mount (eighth day), the walking on the waters (ninth day), preaching in the temple (tenth day), the raising of Lazarus (eleventh day), and Palm Sunday (twelfth day) [SE158].

or according as he gets profit, he can lengthen or shorten: if he lengthens, taking the Mysteries of the Visitation of our Lady to St. Elizabeth, the Shepherds, the Circumcision of the Child Jesus, and the Three Kings, and so of others; and if he shortens, he can even omit some of those which are set down. Because this is to give an introduction and way to contemplate better and more completely afterwards.

[163] Second Note. The second: The matter of the Elections will be begun from the Contemplation on Nazareth to the Jordan, taken inclusively, which is the fifth day, as is explained in the following.

[164] Third Note. The third: Before entering on the Elections, that a man may get attachment to the true doctrine of Christ our Lord, it is very helpful to consider and mark the following three Manners of Humility, reflecting on them occasionally through all the day, and also making the Colloquies, as will be said later.

## THE THREE DEGREES OF HUMILITY [SE 165-167]

[165] First Humility.

The first manner of Humility is necessary for eternal salvation; namely, that I so lower and so humble myself, as much as is possible to me, that in everything I obey the law of God, so that, even if they made me lord of all the created things in this world, nor for my own temporal life, I would not be in deliberation about breaking a Commandment, whether Divine or human, which binds me under mortal sin.

[166] Second Humility.

The second is more perfect Humility than the first; namely, if I find myself at such a stage that I do not want, and feel no inclination to have, riches rather than poverty, to want honor rather than dishonor, to desire a long rather than a short life — the service of God our Lord and the salvation of my soul being equal; and so not for all creation, nor because they would take away my life, would I be in deliberation about committing a venial sin.

[167] Third Humility.

The third is most perfect Humility; namely, when — including the first and second, and the praise and glory of the Divine Majesty being equal — in order to imitate and be more actually like Christ our Lord, I want and choose poverty with Christ poor rather than riches, opprobrium with Christ replete with it rather than honors; and to desire to be rated as worthless and a fool for Christ, Who first was held as such, rather than wise or prudent in this world.

[168] Note. So, it is very helpful for whoever desires to get this third Humility, to make the three already mentioned Colloquies

> of THE PAIRS, asking that Our Lord would be pleased to chose him to this third greater and better Humility, in order more to imitate and serve Him, if it be equal or greater service and praise to His Divine Majesty.

There can be little question that in proposing this consideration the inner psychological process involved in this development reaches a crisis. The humility Ignatius proposes is a complex notion which we might well translate as three degrees of love of God (Rahner 1967). I would also suggest that the degrees of humility are equivalent to degrees of spiritual identity. The first degree of humility is such that the self submits itself as far as it can to obey the law of God in all things so that it would never even enter into deliberation about violating that law seriously even though the greatest temporal enticements should be offered to it. This is another way of saying that the self would not consider a violation of its spiritual value system for the sake of some instinctual attachment. This is a reflection of an incipient but relatively undeveloped level of spiritual identity, but involving a generous complement of ego-strength. The second degree is an expression of Ignatian indifference proposed in the Foundation [SE23] and in the third class [SE155]. At this level the love of God puts the service and glory of God ahead of all personal desires and attachments. In his Directory, Ignatius specifies that without this degree of humility, one should not undertake the election — it is the essential condition of openness to the divine will (Cusson 1988).

The *Directory* suggested that this consideration should not be assigned to a fixed hour of meditation, but should be expounded simultaneously with the meditations of the Two Standards and the Three Classes (Dir. XXIX, 8). The reason given is that consideration of the third degree is to be continued throughout the entire day, even while the exercitant continues the series of meditations. Consequently, the almost casual manner in which Ignatius proposes this consideration should not mislead one in underestimating its significance.

The third degree of humility, in fact, marks a central and decisive crisis in the development of the Exercises and in the spiritual development programmed in them. In the context of a retreat of election, however, the focus of attention of the election can have the effect of overshadowing and diminishing effectiveness of the consideration of the third degree. Historically, of course, the election was the central point of the *Exercises*, the determination of state of life. And, in fact, the *Exercises*, as a series of compact exercises can also be centered around the election, not necessarily of one's vocation, but any other significant decision where the honor and service of God is at stake. Although centrality of the third degree can be overshadowed in this sort of employment, it does not lose its importance in the organic development of the *Exercises* (Iparraguirre 1959). When the Program of the *Exercises* is projected to the scale of life-long spiritual growth, the election fades into the background, and the third degree emerges as one of the most significant, if not the most significant, moments in the growth to spiritual identity.

The three degrees can also be interpreted as levels of resolution of disordered narcissism, as well as expressions of the spiritual maturity of the ego-ideal. In the first degree, Ignatius speaks of lowering and humbling myself so that any worldly desire will not stand in the way of keeping God's law. Self-aggrandizement and the sense of narcissistic specialness and exception thus give way to acceptance of one's position as subject to the divine will along with the rest of God's creatures. In the second degree, narcissistic retrenchment moves to a new stage — one becomes indifferent to all those things that might contribute to or feed a sense of specialness and self-glorification. The third degree carries the process forward to the point of embracing and preferring whatever brings self-devaluation and degradation — poverty, opprobrium, and humiliation — out of love for Christ and a desire to be more like him. The onslaught against pathological narcissism is complete and uncompromising.

Ignatius here seeks to strike a balance between reason and devotion, between humility and narcissism, and between love of God and love of self. The interweaving of these themes is evident in this comment of Fromm (1956):

> The faculty to think objectively is *reason*; the emotional attitude behind reason is that of *humility*. To be objective, to use one's reason, is possible only if one has achieved an attitude of humility. If one has emerged from the dreams of omniscience and omnipotence which one has as a child. In terms of this discussion of the art of loving, this means: love being dependent on the relative absence of narcissism, it requires the development of humility, objectivity and reason. One's whole life must be devoted to this aim. Humility and objectivity are indivisible, just as love is. (p. 120).

In the meditation of the Two Standards, Ignatius had sketched the program of Christ as a progression from poverty of spirit to a desire of contempt, and finally to humility. From there, the way was open to further growth as it pleased God to grant grace for it. Here, Ignatius probes more deeply into humility itself. The three degrees in themselves represent a recapitulation, according to the manner of Ignatius, of preceding levels of development and an important accretion. The first degree represents the maturity of spiritual identity attained at the end of the first week. It represents an intense realization of the value system of the first week, an effective internalization of it, and a level of self-resynthesis making this internalization an effectively functioning and organically integrated aspect within the self's own structure and with its intersystemic integration of the tripartite subsystems — ego, id, and superego — as part of the evolving self-system.

The second degree represents an advance over this, reflecting the maturity of spiritual identity reached in the second week in the meditations of the Two Standards and the Three Classes. The second degree, then, represents a new stage in spiritual growth in which a new crisis is faced, worked through and resolved. It entails acceptation and internalization of a new set of values, including previous values of the first week but adding to them a new perspective of spiritual perfection. Internalization of this new perspective, drawn on by guiding norms of the foundation and the kingdom, energized by the motivating power of love and grace, leads the exercitant to a new stage of synthesis in which the whole series of previous syntheses are recapitulated and elevated. Specifically, the second degree represents an advance to a level of more or less adaptive control over libidinal attachments and integration of a value system prohibiting the slightest capitulation to instinctual demands. This refinement over the first week intensifies the norm of adherence to God's will so that the self's effective sphere of operation now excludes any deviation from the full range of the moral order. It is not difficult to estimate the perfection of the degree and the level of psychic strength it requires, since so few, in fact, are able to live habitually in it.

This is the level of spiritual identity marked by that degree of autonomy of ego-functioning involved in Ignatian indifference. The evolution of spiritual identity is marked here by an increase of ego-autonomy and effectiveness of functioning. This growth within the self is accompanied by a consolidation and deeper penetration of the system of spiritual values. The concept of "indifference" is a difficult one to grasp, even by those schooled in the language of spirituality. This is perhaps because the word is its own worst enemy. To begin with, the word is negative, but the concept is not. As in so many facets of the psychology of the self, we find ourselves trapped into using negative words to express positive concepts of psychic functioning. Indifference is nonetheless a primary quality of autonomy. It is the quality of mastery — controlling rather than being controlled, directing rather than being directed. It represents that freedom from dependence on things, on the circumstances of life, on wealth, honor or a long life, which permits the self to determine itself independently by the free exercise of its own autonomy. It implies further a freedom from neurotic and narcissistic involvements and dependencies which serve as the nidus for so much human unhappiness and conflict. Indifference, then, is a strength in the sense of "inherent strength" or "active quality" which Erikson (1964) associates with the mature capacities of the self.

But Ignatius is not satisfied. For the demands of the election, the second degree is sufficient and to a certain extent necessary, but it does not represent the limit of spiritual growth. Ignatius opens a whole new order of development to the exercitant in the third degree. The first two degrees have presented a resumé of what has led up to this point. In the third degree we advance not simply to a new phase, but we enter the whole range of higher spiritual values which have no limit, no higher cut-off point, and in which the self proceeds to higher and higher levels of realization and synthesis. The self passes beyond indifference and control to a new level in which it is able to desire and chose poverty and contempt and all things opposed to the gratification of self in order the better to follow Christ our Lord and identify with Him.

This new orientation requires conceptualization of a whole new order of spiritual values, different from those which have preceded. The primary impulse through the second degree has been consolidation of ego-control in order that the exercitant might respond without interference from instinctual attachments or cathexes to the directives of God's will. With the third degree, however, we enter a totally new phase which sees the primary impulse directed toward ultimate realization of the life of Christ in us. This is the definitive crisis and commitment of the second week. Successfully resolved it can lead to the highest degree of spiritual growth. Insofar as it represents a higher degree of removal from narcissistic self-love and self-enhancement, it opens the way to a greater enhancement of freedom to follow the path of Christ, to join oneself with the standard of Christ.

The two most significant themes we have been developing in this consideration are conjoined in this formulation and raised to a new level of significance. I am referring to the themes of internalization of spiritual values and of identification with Christ. The identification with Christ is most concerned all through this second week with identification as a mechanism of value assimilation. The third degree of humility reflects a level of identification which has achieved a deep and meaningful internalization of the most profound Christian values. The internalization is complete in the sense that these values have become operative norms of judgment and behavior. They function in such a fashion as to turn unconsciously determined wishes into objectives flying in the face of all untoward libidinal gratification or narcissism. This level of spiritual identity implies an intense and profound identification with Christ and a deeply meaningful synthesis of the values of Christ into an integral synthesis extending even to unconscious levels of the psychic structure.

The moving dynamism supporting and energizing this entire process is the action of grace.[5] I have tried to bring the metapsychological aspects of this development into sharp relief in order to provide a basis in terms of which the dynamic action of grace can be formulated and understood psychoanalytically. The conceptualization of the action of grace emerging from these considerations is that, at least in one dimension, grace exercises an energizing effect on the self. But this energizing influence is not divorced from the loving influence of God on the soul, so that the activation of psychic resources is compounded with loving presence and communication between God and the soul. Under the influence of grace, therefore, the resources and capacity of the self are deepened and enlarged. In this very enhancement, the relationship of the soul to God is modified, intensified, developed and enriched (Meissner 1987). The extraordinary efforts of self-discipline and synthesis, which Ignatius describes, are within the realm of proper activity of the self, but they are not cast in the frame of reference of the unaided self struggling to gain spiritual ground on its own merits. But, given a source of activation and strength, along with the motivating power of love and communication of self to a divine other, the self becomes empowered to attempt extraordinary efforts. Ignatius himself is a living testimony to the validity of this conclusion.

It is important to remember that this third degree includes and recapitulates the previous two. It represents an advance, therefore, in which the value orientations of the previous degrees are elevated and resynthesized into a new level of synthesis. Consequently, one must be careful of expressing this progression in terms of self-annihilation; it is, in fact, an evacuation of lost remnants of self in the sense of the self as the object of pathological narcissism in all its forms. But at the same time, it is a product of the highest and most intense activity of the self (in the sense we have been using all along) in which a profound work of self-synthesis and organization is accomplished. It

[5] See the discussion of grace and nature in chapter V above.

achieves, therefore, more completely and more perfectly the objectives which have been leading the self from the very start.

Insofar as pride and narcissistic grandiosity hold such a central place in our reconstruction of the personality of Iñigo de Loyola (Meissner 1992b), it is hardly surprising that the opposite virtue, humility, should become a central facet of Ignatius' postconversion spiritual outlook. In fact, his consideration on humility [SE 164-168] is pivotal in the whole program of the *Exercises*. Spiritual commentators generally regard the so-called "third degree of humility" as the pinnacle of Ignatian spirituality (de Guibert 1964). The theme of the third degree echoes throughout his writings — in a letter to John III of Portugal, he wrote: "You will understand that, the more we desire to succeed, apart from offense on the part of our neighbor, in clothing ourselves with the livery of Christ our Lord which is woven out of insult, false witness, and every other kind of injustice, the more we shall advance in spirit and earn those spiritual riches with which, if we are leading spiritual lives, our souls desire to be adorned" (Epistolae I, 296-298, Letter 81; in Young (1959) p. 81).

In addition, the Ignatian principle of *agere contra*, so fundamental to Ignatian asceticism and spirituality, here reaches its apogee. Its application is part of the approach to overcoming "inordinate attachments" standing in the way of spiritual growth. The primary vulnerabilities of human nature, evident in the preconversion Iñigo, are here again put under attack by embracing their opposites. In the third degree of humility, the desire for riches is countered by the wish to be poor, excessive ambition and desire for worldly honors are countered by the wish for opprobrium, and the wish to be respected and praised in worldly terms is countered by the wish to be thought worthless and a fool for Christ's sake. These values dictated Ignatius' spiritual ascent, but they also underline the conflicting vulnerabilities that plagued his journey, particularly those that pertain to his narcissistic conflicts. These dynamics were embedded in the heart and mind of Ignatius from his earliest years, and they remained permanent fixtures of his psychic landscape until the moment of his death.

# CHAPTER XIII

# THE ELECTION

## Introduction

The election is in a way the centerpiece of the *Exercises*, representing the fundamental decision to abandon attachments and values that might draw man away from God and to follow the path of spiritual development leading ultimately to God. The preceding two weeks of the *Exercises* are intended to prepare the exercitant for this central and determinative choice, and in the succeeding two weeks consequences of the decision begin to unfold and subsequent steps along the path of spiritual growth begin to take form (Pousset 1971).[1] The election pursues the strategy of the Two Standards — freedom will determine itself by choosing poverty and humiliation in order to achieve humility, and through humility to find the way to God. In the election growth of authentic freedom is paralleled by the shrinking of narcissism in any of its pathological forms and its transformation into a renewed narcissistic investment in the self as integrated into the realm of spiritual values — identified here in respect to humility, particularly the third degree of humility. This is the fundamental Christian mystery of loss and gain — unless the seed dies there is no growth — unless a man loses his soul he cannot gain it — unless he dies to himself he cannot have life.

The meaning of the election is intimately connected to the problem of discerning God's will, a subject on which there is little consensus and considerable need for clarification of the meaning of God's will as an object of discernment and of the limitations of such discernment. The election refers to a complex of several factors — the process of seeking God's will, the decision to which the process leads, and the choice itself (Toner 1991).

[1] Opinions differ regarding the central position of the election in the *Exercises*; de Grandmaison (1920) saw them as a preparation for choosing a state of life; Fessard, Cusson, Iparraguirre and Egan saw it as an indispensable part of the dialectic of the *Exercises*. I prefer the latter view. I take the election to apply to any decision that has meaning for the individual's spiritual life and draws him closer to God and a deeper understanding of the Christian vocation and experience.

## The Election [SE169-189]

[169] Prelude for Making Election
First Point. In every good election, as far as depends on us, the eye of our intention ought to be simple, only looking at what we are created for, namely, the praise of God our Lord and the salvation of our soul. And so I ought to choose whatever I do, that it may help me for the end for which I am created, not ordering or bringing the end to the means, but the means to the end: as it happens that many choose first to marry — which is a means — and secondarily to serve God our Lord in the married life — which service of God is the end. So, too, there are others who first want to have benefices, and then to serve God in them. So that those do not go straight to God, but want God to come straight to their disordered tendencies, and consequently they make a means of the end, and an end of the means. So that what they had to take first, they take last; because first we have to set as our aim the wanting to serve God, — which is the end, — and secondarily, to take a benefice, or to marry, if it is more suitable to us, — which is the means for the end. So, nothing ought to move me to take such means or to deprive myself of them, except only the service and praise of God our Lord and the eternal salvation of my soul.

The election, as has been noted, was directed primarily to determination of one's state of life, but the method proposed by Ignatius is applicable to any important decision. The purpose throughout is to disengage the observant from the participant self and, in a condition of relatively tranquil and secure ego-control, make a determination according to the dictates of reason and in accord with a spiritual value-orientation. It is important, therefore, that the exercitant have achieved a certain amount of control of instinctual drives and desires so that these will not affect or interfere with the effort to make a reasonable decision. The *Directory* thus recommends that the exercitant seeking to make an election have achieved at least the second degree of humility (Dir. XXIII, 3). It is likewise of the greatest importance that the self apply itself carefully to this effort of self-determination (Dir. XXIII, 5). The success of the election in any case depends to a very large extent on the degree of achieved autonomy.

## Preparatory Notes [SE170-174]

[170] TO GET KNOWLEDGE AS TO WHAT MATTERS AN ELECTION OUGHT TO BE MADE ABOUT, AND IT CONTAINS FOUR POINTS AND ONE NOTE

First Point. The first Point: It is necessary that everything about which we want to make an election should be indifferent, or good, in itself, and should be allowed within our Holy Mother the hierarchical Church, and not bad nor opposed to her.

[171] Second Point. Second: There are some things which fall under unchangeable election, such as are the priesthood, marriage, etc. There are others which fall under an election that can be changed, such as are to take benefices or leave them, to take temporal goods or rid oneself of them.

[172] Third Point. Third: In the unchangeable Election which has already been once made — such as marriage, the priesthood, etc. — there is nothing more to choose, because one cannot release himself; only it is to be seen to that if one have not made his election duly and ordinately and without disordered tendencies, repenting let him see to living a good life in his election. It does not appear that this election is a Divine vocation, as being an election out of order and awry. Many err in this, setting up a perverse or bad election as a Divine vocation — for every Divine vocation is always pure and clear, without mixture of flesh, or of any other inordinate tendency.

[173] Fourth Point. Fourth: If some one has duly and ordinately made election of things which are under election that can be changed, and has not yielded to flesh or world, there is no reason for his making election anew, but let him perfect himself as much as he can in that already chosen.

[174] Note. It is to be remarked that if such election that can be changed was not made sincerely and well in order, then it helps to make the election duly, if one has a desire that fruits notable and very pleasing to God our Lord should come from him.

Ignatius casts his vote for fidelity to commitments and traditional values as accepted in his day. His view might have to be qualified by contemporary standards. To the extent that modern sentiments more readily accept the idea of temporary vocation or acknowledge impediments in choice of a definitive state of life, no such choices remain absolute. Marriage vows under certain circumstances can be reversed, priests can be defrocked and religious released from canonical vows. In any case, Ignatius recognizes that an election is not always made under optimal conditions. His advice is not to rework old ground, but to recognize the mistake and continue forward from the present moment to seek God's will. The issue of discerning God's will is central to the election process, a circumstance that raises a number of considerations regarding the function of this discernment and its relation to the discernment of spirits.[2]

## TIMES FOR AN ELECTION [SE175-177]

### *First Time*

> [175] Three Times for Making, in any one of them, a Sound and Good Election
>
> First Time. The first time is, when God our Lord so moves and attracts the will, that without doubting, or being able to doubt, such devout soul follows what is shown it, as St. Paul and St. Matthew did in following Christ our Lord.

St. Ignatius suggests three different times [SE175-177] in which a sound election can be made. The treatment of these three times compresses into a capsule a whole psychology of grace. Each "time", in fact, represents a way in which grace works its effects upon functioning of the self. In the first "time", the movement of grace is so overpowering and convincing that the self responds almost immediately and with perfect security and effectiveness. Ignatius cites biblical examples of the remarkable conversions of St. Paul and St. Matthew. It is to be noted that such a remarkable influence of grace is far from ordinary and deserves to be thoroughly tested before the exercitant undertakes any permanent or far-reaching changes in the external forum. From a psychological standpoint, however, what is effected in such a remarkable grace is related to the process of self-synthesis we have been describing. The response of the self is an essential aspect and is necessary for the effectiveness of the grace. The response, totally free and spontaneous, is itself, in fact, the effect of the grace. What is effected is the complete and effective mobilization of the self in relation to the relevant functions — whether judgmental, affective, executive, or what.

This presents a prime Ignatian model for how God acts on the soul. The claim is that God's presence is felt and his action recognized to be such — the experience is that of being chosen rather than choosing, but chosen in a way that leaves him free to respond as a matter of choice. The process here is similar to "consolation without previous cause" [SE330] in the rules for discernment.[3] If this first

[2] See the further discussion below and the analysis of discernment in chapters XV and XVI.

[3] See the discussion in chapter XVI below. Buckley (1973) points to the

time and CSCP are not synonymous, they have a good deal in common. As Egan (1976) emphasizes, "The First Time for Election, therefore, is a God-initiated, totally supernatural, irresistible, luminous revelation which so influences the person that he responds "without question and without the desire to question" (pp. 133-134). As Egan (1976) further observes:

> During the First Time, however, God controls the core experience and the echoes it produces throughout the different levels in he person's being. During the CSCP, on the other hand, God controls only the core experience, and may *begin* to control the echoes, yet the echoes eventually arise from the good angel, the enemy of our human nature or ourselves [SE336]. The CSCP can be the basis for Election, whereas the First Time is always an actual election or being-elected. The First Time, then is the CSCP in its ideal development from a God-given core experience, and nothing else, to a God-given core experience with God-given echoes. The First Time always includes a CSCP, but not vice versa. (p. 141)

In this experience, according to this interpretation, the divine initiative overwhelms the soul and leaves no room for human factors. This, of course, again leaves out of consideration the role of possible unconscious factors contributing to such an experience. Ignatius' formulation undoubtedly reflects his own experience in following this mode of decision-making, particularly in his conversion experience and in other revelatory moments (Egan 1976). Insofar as this mode of spontaneous inspiration may reflect unconscious dynamics, the Ignatian perspective would suggest that one channel of divine influence through grace may operate in and through the unconscious.

But Toner (1991) makes the point that Ignatius makes no mention of consolation in the first time, but that the role of consolation and desolation are explicit in the second time — distinguishing it from both the first and third times. It seems strange that if the distinction between the first and second times hinged on CSCP in the first and CCCP in the second, he wouldn't have said so. CSCP may or may not accompany a first time experience — if Ignatius' experiences of mystical illumination involved CSCP and first time elections, this does not argue to any necessary connection.

parallel: "The first time corresponds in some way to God's moving a man deliberately without the interplay of thoughts and affectivity, a movement in which, as with the *consolacion sin causa*, there is no possibility of doubt" (pp. 35-36). This sort of "first time" experience may also be analogous to many acute and dramatic conversion experiences (Conn 1986; James 1902; Meissner 1992b)

## *Second Time*

> [176] Second Time. The second, when enough light and knowledge is received by experience of consolations and desolations, and by the experience of the discernment of various spirits.

The second "time" is more ordinary and represents a more effective mobilization of the resources of the self. Here grace works in a more piecemeal fashion — gradually reinforcing efforts of the self in the direction of God's will and step by step withdrawing it from other interfering object involvements and attachments by the delicate interplay of consolation and desolation. The process in the end is the same, but whereas mobilization within the self was instantaneous and its response complete in the first "time," here in the second "time" the self must be led through certain resistances impeding spontaneous and freely autonomous self-commitment.

The second time simply refers to the rules for discernment of spirits, involving impulses from above and below.[4] Ignatius expands on this formula in the autograph directory:

> If, among the three modes of making an election, God does not move one in the first mode, let him seek persistently to find his vocation through consolations and desolations in the second mode of election. Here is the way to do this. Let him continue with his meditations on Christ our Lord and, while doing so, observe to which of the alternatives God moves him when he finds himself in consolation, and likewise in desolation. (Dir Autogr. 18; cited in Toner (1991), p. 131-132)

Ignatius focuses on the dialectic of affective responsiveness and the immediacy of emotional experience as determinative of the proper path of free choice and self-determination. We can hear echoes of his own conversion experience and the discernment of spirits he used to guide him on his own life path. Further details of this process are contained in the rules for discernment, especially rule five of the first week [SE318]. The psychology of these dynamic processes call for further exploration. As the 1599 Directory notes:

> The second "time" or occasion is of a more ordinary kind. This is when the mind is acted on by inspirations and internal motions

[4] The whole discussion of the election and the discernment of God's will is dependent on Ignatius' teaching about discernment of spirits, which is placed later in the *Exercises*. Readers may find it helpful to consult the chapters (XV and XVI) on discernment as background for the present discussion. The order here follows the sequence of these topics in the *Exercises*.

> so efficacious, that, without any intellectual effort or reasoning, or with scarcely any, the will is borne on to the service of God and to the state of perfection. . . . In the first and second "times" of Election, the will leads, the intellect follows, drawn by the will's attraction, without any discursive process of its own, yet without hesitation. (pp. 107-108; cited in Egan (1976))

While the affective element predominates, the role of the will is primary. Psychologically the will represents those executive functions attributed to the ego that are the basis for self-determination and choice. To the extent that appeal is made here to discernment, other cognitive and evaluative functions of the ego are brought into play and integrated with the determining operation of the will.[5] In psychological terms, the impulses underlying consolation and desolation would have to be considered as affective experiences involving to a significant degree unconscious determinants, while the function of decision making and choice falls to the ego functioning in both conscious and unconscious modes.[6] Other ego functions such as reasoning, judgment, and so on, are downplayed.

Caution is called for in interpreting such second time experiences, since the experience of consolation offers no guarantee that it comes from the good spirit. The possibility of purely psychic derivation or influence of an "evil spirit" means that no one second time experience can sustain a conclusion regarding God's will — Ignatius would look to a degree of enriched understanding and light resulting from many such experiences. Even then the conviction remains relative.

## *Third Time*

> [177] Third Time. The third time is quiet, when one considers, first, for what man is born — namely, to praise God our Lord and save his soul — and desiring this chooses as means a life or state within the limits of the Church, in order that he may be helped in the service of his Lord and the salvation of his soul. I said time of quiet, when the soul is not acted on by various spirits, and uses its natural powers freely and tranquilly.

[5] Buckley (1973) notes: "The second time corresponds to the movements of affectivity which demand the full work of discernment; here affectivity is made the criterion of the divine call" (p. 36).

[6] Some have suggested mystical components to this second time, e.g. locutions, but there is no support for this in the texts (Toner 1991). See the discussion of mystical phenomena in chapter XXXV below.

The third "time" is, of course, the most ordinary. In it the operation of grace never reaches the phenomenological level, exercising its influence presumptively in some unconscious fashion. The self is forced to labor its way along, following the norm of reason as the index of God's will. Ignatius insists that it is very important at this stage that the self be tranquil and undisturbed by the influence of emotion or undue attachment. It must be able to exercise its judgmental and evaluative functions freely and quietly. Methods proposed for making this election in the third "time" demand indifference and adherence to the determination of reason, which is the voice of ego, and not to any sort of self-gratification, which may be the voice of id. Grace imperceptibly supports and sustains the efforts of the self to achieve this.

There is a debate among students of the *Exercises* whether this last mode has any validity exclusive of the first two or whether it derives its validity from the second. For some the sequence of modes from first to third moves from the highest and most reliable in terms of identifying God's will to the lowest and most unreliable. This approach reflects a high valuation placed on movements of the spirit and a reliance on discernment of spirits as the preferred channel to finding God's will. Other opinions see the third mode of making an election has having an independent validity of its own, not necessarily dependent on discernment of spiritual consolation or desolation. Or, in other words, are these three modes distinct and autonomous channels of discernment or do they together form one complete mode of discernment (Toner 1991).[7]

## WAYS FOR MAKING AN ELECTION [SE178-188]

[178] If election is not made in the first or the second time, two ways follow as to this third time for making it.

THE FIRST WAY TO MAKE A SOUND AND GOOD ELECTION

It contains six Points.

First Point. The first Point is to put before me the thing on which I want to make election, such as an office or benefice, either to take or leave it; or any other thing whatever which falls under an election that can be changed.

[7] O'Sullivan (1990) has provided a discussion of aspects of decision-making processes, as delineated by psychologists, and their relevance for the times of election — primarily in the third time, but not exclusively so. He also makes the point that effective decision making usually involves some intermingling of cognitive and affective components, but in different fashion in each of the different times.

> [179] Second Point. Second: It is necessary to keep as aim the end for which I am created, which is to praise God our Lord and save my soul, and, this supposed, to find myself indifferent, without any inordinate propensity; so that I be not more inclined or disposed to take the thing proposed than to leave it, nor more to leave it than to take it, but find myself as in the middle of a balance, to follow what I feel to be more for the glory and praise of God our Lord and the salvation of my soul.

Ignatius states here the centrality of indifference in the structure of the Exercises — as an essential condition for election, particularly in the third time. The role of indifference was asserted in the Foundation [SE23] and is emphasized here on the brink of the election — a pivotal point in the Exercises and the state of mind aimed at in the consideration of the degrees of humility [SE167].

> [180] Third Point. Third: To ask of God our Lord to be pleased to move my will and put in my soul what I ought to do regarding the thing proposed, so as to promote more His praise and glory; discussing well and faithfully with my intellect, and choosing agreeably to His most holy pleasure and will.
> [181] Fourth Point. Fourth: To consider, reckoning up, how many advantages and utilities follow for me from holding the proposed office or benefice for only the praise of God our Lord and the salvation of my soul, and, to consider likewise, on the contrary, the disadvantages and dangers which there are in having it. Doing the same in the second part, that is, looking at the advantages and utilities there are in not having it, and likewise, on the contrary, the disadvantages and dangers in not having the same.
> [182] Fifth Point. Fifth: After I have thus discussed and reckoned up on all sides about the thing proposed, to look where reason more inclines: and so, according to the greater inclination of reason, and not according to any inclination of sense, deliberation should be made on the thing proposed.
> [183] Sixth Point. Sixth, such election, or deliberation, made, the person who has made it ought to go with much diligence to prayer before God our Lord and offer Him such election, that His Divine Majesty may be pleased to receive and confirm it, if it is to His greater service and praise.

The necessary indifference here requires more than simply making oneself indifferent. One must actually be indifferent — the state of mind must be realized rather than ambitioned or desired. Ignatius betrays his rationalistic inclinations. As Fessard (1956) noted, "Rational objectivity is here equivalent to the divine 'motion' of the other two times, and the whole concern of the I must be not to confuse it with any sensuous motion whatsoever" (I, pp. 81-82). Does that mean that human action is equivalent to divine action? Apparently so. The action here in the third time is envisioned as simultaneously an action of the subject and an object of divine action (Pousset 1971).

The frame of mind called for harkens back to the Principle and Foundation [SE23] providing the intellectual context for the whole of the Exercises. But, even here, Ignatius leans toward the model of the first or second times, relying on a feeling for whatever is "more for the glory and praise of God our Lord" [SE179]. And again in SE180, he seeks some divine movement along the lines of the first time. Clearly Ignatius put more stock in these putatively divine illuminations than in pure reason — reflecting the fact that he was himself more attuned to his affective life than reliant on intellectual processing alone. There is reason to think that as he grew older Ignatius was more inclined to lean on the third time as the modality for seeking God's grace, a tendency reflected perhaps in his appeal to reason and deliberation in the latter points.

The problem of the extent to which the third time is to be regarded as an independent and valid mode of discernment, exclusive of the first or second modes, remains a focal point of controversy. Rahner (1964), somewhat ambiguously, seemed to regard the tranquillity of the third time as a form of consolation. Egan (1976) carries the argument even further to suggest that the third time is deficient, depending for any validity on a movement of consolation of some form, even CSCP, as in the second or even first times. But Ignatius seems to rule out any movement from spirits in the third time, a quality that distinguishes it from the second time, and proposes it as a valid alternative for finding one's way to God's will (Toner 1991). Some of the directories even recommend that any third time election be postponed while any movements of the second time are still active. This is obviously a matter of relative degree, since minor fluctuations of feeling are inherent in the process. After the election is made, Ignatius seems to seek confirmation in prayer [SE183], presumably on the basis of some discernment of spirits. But this is after the fact, and does not concern the election process itself.[8]

By the same token, the lack of spiritual affects of consolation or desolation does not negate the influence of grace — grace can work its effects in unconscious ways as well as conscious. Grace can be operative in the individual's processes of reasoning, judging and weigh-

[8] Reliance on the third mode of discernment and election is also found in the *Deliberatio primorum Patrum*; see Toner (1991).

ing alternatives, just as readily as in so-called spiritual movements. As Toner (1991) notes, "There is no good reason within the framework of Ignatius' thought to assume that the Holy Spirit influences our will (volitional impulse) and affective sensibility (spiritual consolation) but not our memory, reason, and judgment or that in using these we are left on our own. Rather, Ignatius believes that whenever we open ourselves to the Holy Spirit, in spiritual consolation or desolation or in calm, he is present to help us find the Father's will" (p. 170).

> [184] THE SECOND WAY TO MAKE A GOOD AND SOUND ELECTION
>
> It contains four Rules and one Note.
>
> First Rule. The first is that that love which moves me and makes me choose such thing should descend from above, from the love of God, so that he who chooses feel first in himself that that love, more or less, which he has for the thing which he chooses, is only for his Creator and Lord.

Ignatius' basic reliance is on the influence and guidance of the Holy Spirit. That transcendental influence of loving guidance operates through changes in human subjectivity, specifically through a love that transforms human affectivity. It is this love from above (*de arriba*) that Ignatius has in mind here and which he indicates in the fifteenth annotation: ". . . it is more fitting and much better, that the Creator and Lord himself should communicate Himself to His devout soul, inflaming it with His love and praise, and disposing it for the way in which it will be better able to serve Him in the future" [SE15]. The metaphor is of immediate and intimate communication in love and is resonant with the contemplation on love in the fourth week [SE230-237].[9]

> [185] Second Rule. The second, to set before me a man whom I have never seen nor known, and I desiring all his perfection, to consider what I would tell him to do and elect for the greater glory of God our Lord, and the greater perfection of his soul, and I, doing likewise, to keep the rule which I set for the other.

[9] The argument regarding the autonomy of the third time seems unresolvable. Arguments that it refers to a second time experience for its validity seem questionable, despite this text. I would regard the third time, including both ways, as fully distinct and independent from first and second times, and the two ways as separate options not necessarily connected. Toner (1991) argues that the second way is dependent on the first for completion, but not the other way around. The first, then, can sustain itself without the second, but the second would presuppose the first. I do not find the argument suasive. In all these possibilities, various combinations of ways and times may come into play.

[186] Third Rule. The third, to consider, as if I were at the point of death, the form and measure which I would then want to have kept in the way of the present election, and regulating myself by that election, let me make my decision in everything.
[187] Fourth Rule. The fourth, looking and considering how I shall find myself on the Day of Judgment, to think how I would then want to have deliberated about the present matter, and to take now the rule which I would then wish to have kept, in order that I may then find myself in entire pleasure and joy.
[188] Note. The above-mentioned rules for my eternal salvation and peace having been taken, I will make my election and offering to God our Lord, conformably to the sixth Point of the First Way of making election.

The exercitant here no longer starts from indifference, but from preference — the original indifference must give way to a preference based in love, or this second method of choice cannot take place. The rules are meant to help determine whether the desire in question comes from disordered affectivity or from God. The love that drives this choice must come from above — from the love of God [SE184], again evoking aspects of the first and second times. Even so, Ignatius' advice is psychologically sound. The second rule [SE185] puts the subject in the position of an independent observer — a tactic calculated to enlist his observant capacities unencumbered by self-involved motivational considerations, opening the possibility for objectivity to outweigh subjective distortion. Other perspectives, the point of death [SE186] or the day of judgment [SE187], have a similar purpose, to gain perspective and put the exercitant in a frame of mind accentuating higher and more meaningful values that will guide his determination. Reasoned objectivity and perspectives of the meaning of life and salvation are intended to distance the self from any deceptive subjectivity on the verge of making this election — an objectivized perception of the self and its position in time and eternity.

## Reform of Life and State [SE189]

[189] TO AMEND AND REFORM ONE'S OWN LIFE AND STATE

It is to be noted that as to those who are settled in ecclesiastical office or in matrimony — whether they abound much or not in temporal goods — when they have no opportunity or have not a very prompt will to make election about the things which fall under an election that can be changed, it is very helpful, in place of making election, to give them a form and way to amend and

> reform each his own life and state. That is, putting his creation, life and state for the glory and praise of God our Lord and the salvation of his own soul, to come and arrive at this end, he ought to consider much and ponder through the Exercises and Ways of Election, as has been explained, how large a house and household he ought to keep, how he ought to rule and govern it, how he ought to teach and instruct it by word and by example; likewise of his means, how much he ought to take for his household and house; and how much to dispense to the poor and to other pious objects, not wanting nor seeking any other thing except in all and through all the greater praise and glory of God our Lord.
>
> For let each one think that he will benefit himself in all spiritual things in proportion as he goes out of his self-love, will and interest.

Consequently, in all three "times," the self must respond or else grace is without effect. Even the most efficacious grace does not violate man's most precious gift, his freedom, but rather works in and through the free response. Projecting this to the level of psychological growth of spiritual identity, such development is constituted by a progressive and continuing process involving at each stage autonomous activity of the ego and terminating in a fresh synthesis within the self. From a psychological perspective, there is no other agency which can effect this continuing and progressive resynthesizing (because it is an active, ongoing and continuing process which never reaches completion) than the self. Thus, growth in spiritual identity becomes a function of autonomous ego response to promptings of grace. Ignatius' insight here is profound — man becomes free and autonomous in the extent to which he can extricate himself from instinctual and narcissistic entanglements — "For let each one think that he will benefit himself in all spiritual things in proportion as he goes out of his self-love, will and interest" [SE189]. However valid this perspective may be psychologically, this is not Ignatius' focus — the surrender of narcissistic self-love is not the end point, as it might be in a psychotherapeutic context, but only a condition for embracing the love and service of God.

## Discerning God's Will

The election equivalently involves making a decision in accord with whatever the exercitant decides is God's will for him. The election, therefore, rests on discernment of God's will — an enterprise that is separate from but intimately related to the discernment of spirits. The meaning of Ignatian discernment of spirits has its own complexities and uncertainties,[10] discernment of God's will makes an even further advance into the realms of ambiguity. Clearly they are distinct enterprises — effective discernment of spiritual movements in the soul is not the same as discerning God's will, but the question as to whether and how they are related is subject to much controversy. An additional concern is the extent to which, having reached a clearly and unambiguous discernment, the decision can be regarded as certain or relatively probable.[11]

The whole question of seeking and following God's will was cast in the shadow of the Foundation in the *Exercises* [SE23], and took the form of seeking the glory, reverence, honor, and service of God. This motif formed a constant refrain in his writings and found expression in the motto of his Society, "*ad majorem Dei gloriam*," and in certain key Ignatian terms like the *magis* or his seeking to be *insignis*. It is not just the "glory" of God he sought, but the "greater glory." If the choice were between alternatives both equally for God's glory, then the decision would not matter and there would be no grounds for discernment. But Ignatius was constantly seeking the greater glory, so that his men were not to be just good servants of the Lord and their fellow men, but extraordinary, outstanding, distinctive. The emphasis echoes the strains of Ignatius' own personality, but also became central to his spirituality and his dedication to God's service. However, that goal could not be achieved without attaining a high degree of indifference and detachment from all created things. But the glory of God was not something abstract or intended only for God Himself; rather it was God's glory in us and for us — that glory was achieved in and through fulfillment of divine purposes in us as vessels of divine glory. For Ignatius the transcendent God was also immanent in all creation, particularly in human beings, in whom He was a living and loving influence.

Ignatius proposed a method for seeking God's will in concrete terms, that is as intended for the individual person with his capacities and strengths, limitations and weaknesses, with his resources of intellect, will, moral resources, affectivity, and the circumstances of his life and relationships, as well as his openness to grace. The emphasis on respect for the individuality of the person comes through

[10] See chapters XV and XVI below.

[11] I will follow here in large measure the detailed discussion of these issues in Toner (1991) — much of whose perspective I find compatible with my approach to these issues. I will make particular notice of points on which I might see matters somewhat differently.

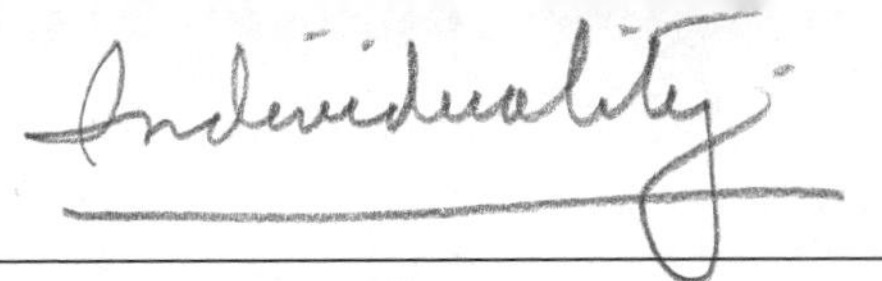



strongly in the *Constitutions*, where even the direction of the superior must adapted "according to the persons, times, places, and their contingencies" [CS64]. Similar phrases abound.[12] Thus, not every act of the person willed by God can be an object of discernment — only those freely chosen among possible alternatives. An important emphasis here is that God's will is not conceived as an antecedently determined plan that the exercitant sets out to discover; rather it is a plan that unfolds as one moves from decision to decision — God's will for each person in the near future may depend on what choices are made in the here and now.

Fundamental to Ignatius view is the idea that God is related to us in a union of personal and loving communion [SE231] and that his plan for each person is cast in terms of the overall purpose and meaning of creation [SE23]. Within this general framework, Ignatius held that God guides and facilitates our seeking his will. As Toner (1991) puts it:

> Thus, Ignatius says in the *Spiritual Exercises* that God moves or attracts us when we are seeking his will [SE175, 189], gives love from above to motivate choice [SE184], guides and counsels us [SE318], gives us light [SE176], and confirms or disconfirms our judgment [SE183]. In the Constitutions Ignatius speaks of God inspiring us [CS700], efficaciously bring our discernment to a right conclusion about his will [CS624a], enlightening us [CS711], teaching what that will is by the unction of the Holy Spirit [CS161, 414], indicating it [CS219], and communicating prudence to us [CS414]. (p. 37)

But all of this has no place unless and to the degree that we are seeking to do His will — any discernment must therefore be a collaboration between divine influence and human effort.[13]

Toner (1991) distinguishes different forms of discernment that might appear to be exceptions. Besides the direct and personal discernment of God's will for oneself, discernments can be consultative or entrusted. In a consultative discernment, the objective is to reach a conclusion as to what choice might be recommended to someone else who intends to make his own discernment and has sought assistance. Such a discernment is limited to the consultant's choice of recommendation, not to whether the consultee accepts or rejects the

[12] See CS66, 70, 71, 136, 211, 228, 238, 285, 287, 290, 297, 301, 343, 354, 395, 462, 471, 581, 671, 746.

[13] This theme was articulated clearly in the *Deliberatio primorum Patrum*, recounting the discernment leading to the decision to found the Society. See Toner (1974, 1991).

recommendation — the consultant can discern God's will only for himself, not for another. An entrusted discernment takes place when the subject seeks help in making a discernment and antecedent to the other's decision accepts the decision of the other resulting from a sound discernment process. In a consultative discernment, the subject reserves the right to make his own discernment, taking the result of the consultation into account. But in the entrusted discernment, that option is eliminated. Obviously, entrusted discernment is a court of last resort, when every reasonable effort of the subject has brought no success and the decision cannot be delayed. Without these conditions, entrusting a discernment to another would be avoiding responsibility and there would be no reason to expect any guidance from the spirit.

The enterprise of discerning God's will must be conditioned by qualifications and limitations. Limitations can be either objective or subjective. On the objective side, a fundamental principle of discernment is that only when the discernment is necessary for the discerner to freely choose the course that is for God's greater glory and to choose it because it is God's will, does the discernment have a role in finding God's will. Ignatius' own sense of such limits is reflected in his letter to Borgia regarding the issue of Borgia's becoming a cardinal — a move Ignatius staunchly opposed.[14] He wrote to Borgia:

> With regard to the cardinal's hat, I thought that to God's greater glory I should give you some account of what has gone on in me, speaking to you as to my own soul. It was as if I had been informed of the certain fact that the emperor had nominated you and that the pope was pleased to make you a cardinal. Immediately, I had this idea or inclination to prevent it in any way I could. However, I was not certain of the divine will; for many reasons on one side and the other occurred to me. So, I gave orders that all the priests in the house should celebrate Mass and those who are not priests should offer prayers for three days that I would be guided in the whole matter to the greater divine glory. Pondering on the matter and discussing it from time to time during this three day span, I perceived that certain fears came on me or at least that there was no liberty of spirit to speak against and prevent the project. I asked myself, "How do I know what God our Lord wishes to do?" Consequently, I did not feel entirely secure in [the thought of] obstructing it [the emperor's project]. At other times, during my customary prayers, I perceived that these fears had departed from me. Going on with prayer at various times,

[14] See the discussion of this episode in chapter XXIV below.

> sometimes with this fear and sometimes with the contrary, I finally found myself during my customary prayer on the third day, and always ever since, with a fully settled judgment that, as much as I could, I should turn the pope and the cardinals from their purpose. My judgment was so conclusive and my will so tranquil that I held and still hold for a certainty that if I did not act in this way, I would not give a good account of myself to God, but rather an entirely bad one. (Epistolae IV, 283-285 [Letter 2652]; cited in Toner (1991), pp. 47-48; also Young (1959), pp. 257-258.)

As Toner (1991) points out, discernment here is limited to finding God's will with regard to the discerner's own free and responsible choice, and only with choices that he has a right to make at that moment of decision. Thus the discernment was only about Ignatius' choice, not Borgia's; he did not forbid Borgia to accept the elevation, but only concluded to his own opposition. Further, Ignatius would have had no business making any discernment if he had no responsibility for it; and, finally, no discernment can reach a decision regarding God's will for the consequences of the choice.[15] Ignatius' decision might have influenced Borgia's or the pope's discernment and decision, but he could not discern what their decision might be. It would have been entirely possible that the pope would have discerned otherwise and insisted on elevating Borgia to the cardinalate. Thus, any such discernment can only be made in a Christian spirit of humility, mutual respect and love — recognizing that the spirit can move individuals to conflicting courses of decision and action. As Toner (1991) says, "What God wills this discerner to recommend may not be what God wills the other to choose" (p. 54). Thus, Toner (1991) warns against the misguided idea that discernment has any predictive or prophetic claim regarding the consequences of a choice. A decision, for example, to follow a life of consecrated celibacy or to become a lawyer is no guarantee that the choice will have a beneficial outcome.

Limitations can also arise on the subjective side. Obstacles, as far as Ignatius was concerned, included a lack of dependence on and trust in God's help and guidance, or correlatively, excessive reliance on human means, ambivalence, i.e. wanting on one hand to seek and follow God's will, while simultaneously wanting something else, and impatience, lassitude, or a need for gratification that shrinks from putting out the effort and enduring the uncertainty and patience

[15] A similar discernment was involved in Ignatius's attempt to resign as general; see chapter IV above. His reasons for resigning seemed clear and conclusive to him, but he could not discern what decision the group might reach in the matter.

required for a good discernment. Clearly, psychological indispositions, whether in the nature of conflict-and-defense or of character, can distort and frustrate any attempt to effectively discern God's will. A willing openness to divine input and a generous willingness to endure whatever sacrifice is required to follow the divine inspiration are mandatory for the Ignatian approach to this problem. This requires a singleness of purpose and a singular attachment to the love of God. In this respect, disordered narcissism is a major impediment to effective discernment — as it is the root of disordered attachment in all of Ignatius' spiritual teaching. As Toner (1991) observes:

> It is, Ignatius sees, egoistic self-love which ultimately roots all selfish desire and mainly divides the hearts of those who are striving to integrate their loves into one love for God. Therefore, he urges us to consider that "the measure of growth in the whole spiritual realm will be exactly the measure in which one has grown out of disordered self-love, self-seeking, and self-interest" [SE189]. Since Ignatius sees that freedom from disordered self-love [is] to be achieved by intensifying our love for God, the whole aim of the Spiritual Exercises up to the time of decision making and after is to grow in knowledge and love of God as revealed in Jesus Christ. (p. 77)

Also pre-existing prejudices, irrational beliefs, unconscious attitudes, affective dispositions, unconscious fantasy systems, and other unconsciously determined states of mind can interfere with or distort the discernment process.

## TESTING THE ELECTION

The question arises whether one can rely on any one time of election to effectively discern the will of God, or whether the times can be combined in order to achieve a more confident resolution. Toner (1991) takes the position that exerting one's best effort is required for sound discernment, and that therefore use of all possible and reasonable modes are called for in important decisions. As he puts it, ". . . in weighty decisions, when one has the time and energy, the first time experience should be tested by going though a second-time election, if God makes it possible, and also a third-time one. If strong second-time and third-time evidence should conflict with the first-time experience, the genuinity of the latter is at least suspect" (p. 123). The choice in these times of election is not between divine inspiration in the first and second and human reason in the third. The question of divine origin remains to be settled, and the whole point of the third time, as far as I can see, is that God can exercise his influence through human reason and will. While a first time experience may be subjectively characterized by absence of doubt, the actual determination of genuineness of the discernment may lie elsewhere. Toner (1991) concludes: ". . . there does not seem to be any solid evidence for denying that Ignatius thought the first-time election needs critical reflection. . . . In general, it can be said that reflecting on and testing any spiritual experience, especially one that points to choice and action, seems to be in accord with Ignatius' own practice and his instructions to others" (p.126).

Ignatius' recommendation that the result of any discernment be taken to prayer to seek confirmation indicates that no discernment can yield certain knowledge of God's will. Confirmation of the judgment is not the same as confirmation of motivation to put the decision into action. In the *Exercises*, there is a presumption, even prior to the election, that the discerner has already chosen to carry through whatever course he discerns as God's will. But, in the wake of an election, the result remains open to confirmation or disconfirmation. Ignatius provides an example of his own approach to such confirmation in the *Spiritual Journal*, in his deliberations over practice of poverty in the Society.[16]

Sources of confirmation are multiple. Presuming all the conditions for a sound discernment and decision, confirmation or disconfirmation may come from legitimate authority, from favorable or unfavorable circumstances, from success or failure in attaining the end intended, or from unintended or secondary effects. Legitimate authority has the power to allow or prevent a course of action, and carries a claim on obedience within proper limits. Prohibition of a course of action or command to do the opposite may make the discerned action impossible. This says nothing about the discerned judgment — the discernment of the authority may have been defective, or may simply have reasonably discerned something different than the subject. For Ignatius, there is no contradiction in the Holy Spirit inspiring two individuals to two entirely different and contradictory intentions. In his opposition to the pope's wish to elevate some of his men to episcopal status, there was no need to assume that the pope's decision was in accord with God's will — his discernment, if any, may have been careless, hurried, poorly informed, or otherwise ill-conceived.

When it comes to favorable or unfavorable circumstances, Ignatius has little to say. If a well discerned course of action is more

[16] See chapter XXXIV below.

for the greater glory of God, it is more likely that the forces of evil will come into play to oppose it. Similarly with success or failure of the enterprise — Ignatius is again silent. One reason, of course, is that the answer is all too obvious — success or failure means nothing. This is the fate of any discernment. If I decide after a complete and exhaustive discernment that I should devote my life to God in religious life, or that I should pursue a married life with the spouse of my love and choice, what guarantee might I have that the course of my subsequent life experience would be successful or disastrous? or that the opposite choice would be any more or less successful or catastrophic? Unfortunately — none! We would have to think the same about unforeseen or unintended effects. Medical treatment with drugs offers a model — all drugs have side effects and their occurrence is never predictable. Rare side effects may crop up in any case and cause trouble. This does not mean that the physician's decision to use the drug was ill-advised; the choice may have been entirely appropriate. But the fact is that all drugs, like all decisions in life, have side effects we cannot anticipate. But, like a good physician, when it is clear that the chosen course of action is having unanticipated or unintended, as well as deleterious, effects, the course of prudence is to reconsider and discern a further and adaptive alternative.

There is a strong tradition in Ignatian interpretation to the effect that the need for such confirmation is confined to the third time and that confirmation is necessary for any such valid conclusion. In this view, first time experiences need no validation and second time experiences need no added consolation or desolation to reach confirmation. Confirmation is gained exclusively through the movements of consolation and desolation. In his deliberation on poverty, Ignatius seems to have used a combination of second and third time methods, and still sought further confirmation, even though he had abundant consolation for confirmation in the second time mode. Clearly in that context he sought further confirmation after such a second time election and sought further consolation, probably along the lines of first time election to allow a conclusive resolution.[17] He put great trust in the guidance of the spirit, remaining convinced that the Holy Spirit would bring the well-intentioned and well-disposed soul to seek and find God's will, and that if what was discerned was not God's will, the spirit would give a sign to that effect. In effect, then, if a well made decision receives no sign of confirmation or disconfirmation, the decision should not be changed since it can be

[17] See the discussion of this process in chapter XXXIV below.

presumed that God wishes the person to find His will through rational discourse a la the third time (Toner 1991). Thus, by his own example, Ignatius teaches us that confirmation of a decision reached by discernment, but yet to be finalized, can be sought in further spiritual consolations, new reasons, a deeper sense of conviction regarding reasons already considered, intensification of movements of the will, and a sense of assurance that one has done all that he can reasonably do to find God's will and that God's will has, in fact, been found.

The conclusion on Ignatius' teaching regarding confirmation of the discernment process involves several points:[18] (1) confirmation concerns primarily the truth and soundness of the judgment regarding God's will, and only secondarily the resolve to carry out the action; (2) confirmation or disconfirmation of the tentative judgment reached by discernment does not rest narrowly on experiences of consolation or desolation, but embraces every kind of evidence and reasoning that can be brought to bear on the matter; (3) the confirmation sought excludes any need for confirmation in subsequent events or consequences resulting from the execution of the course of action thought to be God's will. Discernment provides no insight or perspective on any prospective course of future events. The best, most reasonable and thoughtful, even the most inspired and convinced conclusion regarding the will of God offers no guarantee that events will turn out as anticipated.[19]

[18] I am paraphrasing the conclusions drawn by Toner (1991).

[19] There is an added consideration regarding communal discernment, applied to group or institutional settings. An interesting specimen of group discernment can be found in the *Deliberatio primorum Patrum*. See Toner (1974, 1991). However, this lies beyond the scope of my discussion. See Toner (1991) and Futrell (1970) for further discussion of communal discernment.

# CHAPTER XIV

# THE THIRD AND FOURTH WEEKS

## Third Week [SE190-217]

### Objective

The objective of the third week is usually set down as confirming the election (Iparraguirre 1959). From the point of view of a retreat of election, this would signify that the exercitant offers his election to God and seeks to strengthen his motivation for carrying it through by meditating on the Passion. This applies also in the broader context of spiritual growth. The exercitant, entering the first phases of the third week, has merely set foot on the vast continent of the third degree. He must now begin exploration and settlement of that vast region.

The self has been set on a path leading toward identity formation by way of identification in the second week. The motivating force behind this process is a growing and deepening love of the person of Christ. The context for this activity has been meditation and contemplation of the mysteries of the life of Christ. In progressing into the third week, this entire process shifts to a new level of greater intensity and depth. Paralleling this shift, Ignatius turns attention from the mysteries of the rest of Our Lord's life to the culmination of that life in the Passion and Death. Here is the most sublime expression of all that Christ stood for and the consummate sacrifice of His love. The great saints and mystics of the Church have always turned to the Passion as the great lesson of love and self-sacrifice, the consummate realization of the third degree of humility.

Consequently, the third week strives to confirm and solidify previous gains. These are all subsumed and ratified by identifying with Christ crucified. But at the same time, the most powerful motives for spiritual growth are brought to bear. Ignatius remarks: "the peculiar grace to be demanded in the Passion is sorrow with Christ, Who is full of sorrow, anguish with Christ in anguish, tears and interior pain for the great pain that Christ has suffered for me" [SE203]. Thus, the psychological process of identification with Christ, begun in the second week, is here continued and extended on the most sublime and intense level.

One of the powerful motifs brought into focus here is relating oneself and one's death to the suffering and death of Christ. Death is the consequence of sin, so that the third week in effect recapitulates immersion in the mystery of evil of the first week, with particular focus on the mystery of sin and death. The message is that through union and identification with Christ suffering and dying, we also share in Christ's ultimate victory over death and sin. As Cusson (1988) observes: "Christ will transform temporal death by integrating it into his "creaturely homage" to the Father. Thus he makes of it an act of perfect obedience which is both adoration and an expression of the greatest love. Instead of guarding it jealousy in order to save that life which he too had received as a gift, Christ will lose it and give it freely: "Father, into thy hands I commend my spirit!" (Lk 23: 46). And through this act, man's death in Christ becomes life again. It is a passage from the servitude of sin and death to the eternal liberty of the divine life" (p. 279).

Accordingly, the subjective dispositions Ignatius seeks in the third week also reverberate with the affective dispositions acquired as fruit of the first week — grief, affliction, interior pain and distress [SE195], sorrow and shame [SE193, 203]. As in the first week, the root of these subjective dispositions lies not simply in reflecting on the intensity of physical and mental pain of Christ's sufferings, but more deeply in profound awareness of the meaning of sin and its consequence of death. Ignatius follows here the pauline theme of death as the wages of sin (Rom 6: 23) — even for Christ himself who "from Creator He is come to making Himself man, and from life eternal is come to temporal death, and so to die for my sins" [SE53].

Amplifying the emphasis of Ignatius, the *Directory* puts particular stress on the affective response to the Passion. Besides compassion with Christ crucified, it itemizes the objectives to be striven for: hatred of sin, knowledge of God's goodness, confirmation of hope, love for God, incitement to imitation of Christ, and zeal for souls (Dir. XXV, 4-10). Underlying these objectives is an activation of emotional responsiveness, now organized and directed by the ego to objectives and purposes it has made its own. This affective reorganization has proceeded apace with synthesis within the ego itself, so that through transformation of the ego, the entire psychic structure is reorganized and directed to objectives of spiritual growth.

In the logical structure of the *Exercises*, two lines of force are brought into conjunction at this point — deep realization of the meaning of sin and my sinfulness of the first week, and the desire to know, love, and serve Christ of the second — in a sense joining the history of sin with the history of salvation (Cusson 1988). They provide the intellectual and affective substratum for entering into and identifying with Christ suffering and dying, for recognizing that the basic cause of that suffering is in ourselves, in our sinfulness. Christ embraced that sinfulness in order to change the sorrow and despair of the human condition to life and joy. Therefore, in terms of this logic, Christ's suffering becomes our own, and only through union with his suffering does love deliver us from evil and make our suffering redemptive. The election itself involves a conversion, a turning from sin to grace, from self-absorption to love, from sinfulness to forgiveness.

## FIRST CONTEMPLATION [SE190-199]

[190] THE FIRST CONTEMPLATION AT MIDNIGHT IS HOW CHRIST OUR LORD WENT FROM BETHANY TO JERUSALEM TO THE LAST SUPPER INCLUSIVELY ([SE289]) . . . .

[191] First Prelude. The first Prelude is to bring to memory the narrative; which is here how Christ our Lord sent two Disciples from Bethany to Jerusalem to prepare the Supper, and then He Himself went there with the other Disciples; and how, after having eaten the Paschal Lamb, and having supped, He washed their feet and gave His most Holy Body and Precious Blood to His Disciples, and made them a discourse, after Judas went to sell his Lord.

[192] Second Prelude. The second, a composition, seeing the place. It will be here to consider the road from Bethany to Jerusalem, whether broad, whether narrow, whether level, etc.; likewise the place of the Supper, whether large, whether small, whether of one kind or whether of another.

[193] Third Prelude. The third, to ask for what I want. It will be here grief, feeling and confusion because for my sins the Lord is going to the Passion.

[194] First Point. The first Point is to see the persons of the Supper, and, reflecting on myself, to see to drawing some profit from them.

Second Point. The second, to hear what they are talking about, and likewise to draw some profit from it.

Third Point. The third, to look at what they are doing, and draw some profit.

[195] Fourth Point. The fourth, to consider that which Christ our Lord is suffering in His Humanity, or wants to suffer, according to the passage which is being contemplated, and here to commence with much vehemence and to force myself to grieve, be sad and weep, and so to labor through the other points which follow.

Pain is meaningless divorced from intentionality. What gives meaning to Christ's suffering is his redemptive intention and the free choice with which he made his sacrifice. The pain and sorrow of the exercitant likewise have meaning to the extent that they join in the suffering of Christ. That pain can only become redemptive to the extent that it chooses and wills what God wills, joins its suffering with the intentionality of Christ suffering.

[196] Fifth Point. The fifth, to consider how the Divinity hides Itself, that is, how It could destroy Its enemies and does not do it, and how It leaves the most sacred Humanity to suffer so very cruelly.
[197] Sixth Point. The sixth, to consider how He suffers all this for my sins, etc.; and what I ought to do and suffer for Him. . . .[1]
[199] Note. It is to be noted, as was explained before and in part, that in the Colloquies I ought to discuss and ask according to the subject matter, that is, according as I find myself tempted or consoled, and according as I desire to have one virtue or another, as I want to dispose of myself in one direction or another, as I want to grieve or rejoice at the thing which I am contemplating; in fine, asking that which I more efficaciously desire as to any particular things. And in this way I can make one Colloquy only, to Christ our Lord, or, if the matter or devotion move me, three Colloquies, one to the Mother, another to the Son, another to the Father, in the same form as was said in the SECOND WEEK, in the meditation of the THREE PAIRS, with the Note which follows THE PAIRS.

The emphasis here falls on the freedom with which Christ delivers himself to his accusers and executioners, surrendering himself to the love and will of the Father [SE195]. His sacrifice originates in love and is meant to be redemptive [SE197]. In the words of Paul, "For our sake he made him to be sin, so that in him we might become the righteousness of God" (2 Cor 5: 21). Thus Christ's freedom becomes the model for our freedom through self-renunciation and self-sacrifice out of love and faith — divine freedom made manifest in the world is inexorably linked with human freedom. In the fundamental choice of the election, then, the act of autonomous human freedom is simultaneously an act of human freedom and of divine freedom.

[1] Colloquy [SE198] omitted.

## SECOND CONTEMPLATION [SE200-207]

[200] SECOND CONTEMPLATION IN THE MORNING IT WILL BE FROM THE SUPPER TO THE GARDEN INCLUSIVELY . . . .
[201] First Prelude. The first Prelude is the narrative and it will be here how Christ our Lord went down with His eleven Disciples from Mount Sion, where He made the Supper, to the Valley of Josaphat. Leaving the eight in a part of the Valley and the other three in a part of the Garden, and putting Himself in prayer, He sweats sweat as drops of blood; and after He prayed three times to the Father and wakened His three Disciples, and after the enemies at His voice fell down, Judas giving Him the kiss of peace, and St. Peter cutting off the ear of Malchus, and Christ putting it in its place; being taken as a malefactor, they lead Him down the valley, and then up the side, to the house of Annas.
[202] Second Prelude. The second is to see the place. It will be here to consider the road from Mount Sion to the Valley of Josaphat, and likewise the Garden, whether wide, whether large, whether of one kind, whether of another.
[203] Third Prelude. The third is to ask for what I want. It belongs to the Passion to ask for grief with Christ in grief, anguish with Christ in anguish, tears and interior pain at such great pain which Christ suffered for me. . . .[2]

The agony can be seen as an expression of Christ's immersion in human sinfulness and the inherent opposition of human willfulness to God's will. Through sin, human freedom opposes itself to God, but it does not become painful until the sinner becomes aware of his separation from God. The malice of sin and its consequences are played out in Christ's agony on the stage of his inner world and the wrenching opposition between his humanity drenched in sin and his divinity (Pousset 1971). He embraces here his role as the "Man of Sorrows", a role imposed by God as part of his salvific mission in total acceptance and free commitment to fulfilling divine purposes. Ignatius again calls for the "application of senses" to help the exercitant not only consider, but experience, with Christ the sense of lonesomeness and forsakenness that go with his separation from the Father who has abandoned him to suffer this agony that is part and parcel of his humanity as it is ours (Rahner 1967). Ignatius then notes changes in the additions for this week:

[2] Two notes are omitted, one dealing with repetitions of the meditation [SE204] and the other with adaptations for age or physical indisposition [SE205].

[206] Third Note. In this THIRD WEEK the second and sixth Additions will in part be changed.

The second will be, immediately on awaking, to set before me where I am going and to what, and summing up a little the contemplation which I want to make, according as the Mystery shall be, to force myself, while I am getting up and dressing, to be sad and grieve over such great grief and such great suffering of Christ our Lord.

The sixth will be changed, so as not to try to bring joyful thoughts, although good and holy, as, for instance, are those on the Resurrection and on heavenly glory, but rather to draw myself to grief and to pain and anguish, bringing to mind frequently the labors, fatigues and pains of Christ our Lord, which He suffered from the moment when He was born up to the Mystery of the Passion in which I find myself at present. . . .[3]

[209] Note. It is to be noted that whoever wants to dwell more on the Passion, has to take in each Contemplation fewer Mysteries; that is to say, in the first Contemplation, the Supper only; in the second, the Washing of the Feet; in the third, the giving of the Blessed Sacrament to them; in the fourth, the discourse which Christ made to them; and so through the other Contemplations and Mysteries.

Likewise, after having finished the Passion, let him take for an entire day the half of the whole Passion, and the second day the other half, and the third day the whole Passion.

On the contrary, whoever would want to shorten more in the Passion, let him take at midnight the Supper, in the morning the Garden, at the hour of Mass the house of Annas, at the hour of Vespers the house of Caiphas, in place of the hour before supper the house of Pilate; so that, not making repetitions, nor the Application of the Senses, he make each day five distinct Exercises, and in each Exercise take a distinct Mystery of Christ our Lord. And after thus finishing the whole Passion, he can, another day, do all the Passion together in one Exercise, or in different ones, as it will seem to him that he will be better able to help himself.

Ignatius urges more than mere contemplation of these episodes, but asks the exercitant to share concretely in the suffering of Christ

[3] The fourth note [SE207] prescribes the particular examen as before. Meditations for the succeeding days are suggested covering events of the trial of Jesus before the Sanhedrin and Pilate, the crucifixion and burial, and finally a review of the whole of the Passion [SE208], during which "one will consider all that day, as frequently as he can, how the most holy Body of Christ our Lord remained separated and apart from the soul and where and how It remained buried. Likewise, one will consider the loneliness of Our Lady, whose grief and fatigue were so great: then, on the other side, the loneliness of the Disciples."

through penance and to thus intensify the sense of identification with the painful destiny of Christ who has humbled himself to share our human destiny — a theme that had been central in Ludolph's *Life* and the *Flos Sanctorum*.

## FOURTH WEEK [SE218-237]

### Objective

Even more than was the case in the third week, the psychoanalytic model of the mind and method of investigation begin to overreach themselves in trying to analyze what transpires in this fourth week. We have entered a more specifically spiritual realm in which what is effected is on a transcendent plane stretching to the limit the capacity of mere psychological understanding. Grace utterly dominates the picture. Ignatius himself has so little to say that this must have been the nature of his own mystical experience.

The exercitant is directed to seek "grace to be intensely glad and to rejoice in such great glory and joy of Christ our Lord" [SE221]. Just as the exercitant has been drawn to seek identification with Christ crucified and anguish with Christ anguished in the third week, so now he is encouraged to rejoice with Christ resurrected and triumphant. While the emphasis of the third week fell on consolidation of previous gains and intensification and development in the third degree of humility through identification with Christ in His supreme moment of contempt, sacrifice and humility, the emphasis of the fourth week falls rather on the ultimate facet of the perfection of spiritual identity — the positive union of love with God. This is accomplished through intensification of the theological virtues of faith, hope and especially love. The meditation on the mysteries of the resurrection and exaltation of Our Lord bring the exercitant ever more deeply into the mystery of God's love. In the resurrection, the soul finds assurance of faith and confirmation of hope. These virtues have been dynamically operative at every phase of spiritual growth, and each progression has been accompanied by an intensification of them so that they have come more and more to dominate the orientation of the ego. Here in the fourth week they emerge to the full flowering of their potentiality, becoming dynamic foci at the very core of this highest phase of self-synthesis. In this lofty plane of spiritual identity, all the rest is brought to a new level of synthesis and perfection.

## FIRST CONTEMPLATION [SE218-225]

[218] The First Contemplation
HOW CHRIST OUR LORD APPEARED TO OUR LADY . . . .
[219] *First Prelude.* The first Prelude is the narrative, which is here how, after Christ expired on the Cross, and the Body, always united with the Divinity, remained separated from the Soul, the blessed Soul, likewise united with the Divinity, went down to Hell,and taking from there the just souls, and coming to the Sepulchre and being risen, He appeared to His Blessed Mother in Body and in Soul.
[220] *Second Prelude.* The second, a composition seeing the place; which will be here to see the arrangement of the Holy Sepulchre and the place or house of Our Lady, looking at its parts in particular; likewise the room, the oratory, etc.
[221] *Third Prelude.* The third, to ask for what I want, and it will be here to ask for grace to rejoice and be glad intensely at so great glory and joy of Christ our Lord. . . .[4]
[223] *Fourth Point.* The fourth, to consider how the Divinity, which seemed to hide Itself in the Passion, now appears and shows Itself so marvellously in the most holy Resurrection by Its true and most holy effects.
[224] *Fifth Point.* The fifth is to consider the office of consoling which Christ our Lord bears, and to compare how friends are accustomed to console friends. . . .[5]

It is not accidental that Ignatius places the appearance to Mary at the head of his reflections on the resurrection — in his mind the images of the Blessed Mother and the Resurrection were intimately linked.[6] Just as he closed the third week with "the loneliness of Our Lady, whose grief and fatigue were so great" [SE208], the first contemplation of the fourth week [SE218] draws attention to her again, as though she were the connecting link between the passion and death and the resurrection. The experience of the resurrection seems absorbed into this reunion of the suffering son and the grieving mother. Beyond theological considerations (Fessard 1956; Pousset 1971), the reason may lie buried in the recesses of Ignatius' unconscious fantasy life. I have speculated (Meissner 1992b) on the linkage between his mystical experiences and the unconscious association with the theme of the loss and restitution of the connection with his mother — an

[4] Omitted points [SE222] repeat those from above [SE194].
[5] Colloquy [SE225] omitted.
[6] See Cusson's (1988) somewhat labored effort to explain this connection, especially pp. 302-306.

echo of the maternal deprivation he suffered soon after birth. Is it possible that one resonance of his mystical experience was the unconscious sense of reunion with the lost mother? Is the inference that the connection between Mary and the Resurrection echoes this theme in that Mary has held the place in his unconscious fantasy life of the lost, yearned for, still loving although remote, mother of his infancy, and the resurrection carries further meaning of the return of the lost mother to life and the promise of reunion in mystical ecstasy? If so, the "joy of the resurrection" may also carry the added significance of a "joy of reunion." The movement here is directly derivative from Ignatius' own conversion experience in which the Blessed Mother played such a salient role (Meissner 1992b), so that by implication similar dynamics operative in that setting may well underlie the options Ignatius follows in proposing the structure of the fourth week.[7]

## NOTES [SE226-229]

[226] *First Note.* In the following Contemplations let one go on through all the Mysteries of the Resurrection, in the manner which follows below, up to the Ascension inclusive, taking and keeping in the rest the same form and manner in all the Week of the Resurrection which was taken in all the Week of the Passion. So that, for this first Contemplation, on the Resurrection, let one guide himself as to the Preludes according to the subject matter; and as to the Five Points, let them be the same; and let the Additions which are below be the same; and so in all which remains, he can guide himself by the method of the Week of the Passion, as in repetitions, the five Senses, in shortening or lengthening the Mysteries.

[227] *Second Note.* The second note: Commonly in this FOURTH WEEK, it is more suitable than in the other three past to make four Exercises, and not five: the first, immediately on rising in the morning; the second, at the hour of Mass, or before dinner, in place of the first repetition; the third, at the hour of Vespers, in place of the second repetition; the fourth, before supper, bringing the five Senses on the three Exercises of the same day, noting and lingering on the more principal parts, and where one has felt greater spiritual movements and relish.

[228] *Third Note.* The third: Though in all the Contemplations so many Points were given in certain number — as three, or five, etc. — the person who is contemplating can set more or fewer

[7] In addition, the suggestion that the risen Christ first appeared to his mother appears in Ludolph (ch. 70) following the authority of Ambrose, Anselm, and Ignatius of Antioch. See Cusson (1988, pp. 303-4, fn. 52).

> Points, according as he finds it better for him. For which it is very helpful, before entering on the Contemplation, to conjecture and mark in certain number the Points which he is to take.
> [229] *Fourth Note.* In this FOURTH WEEK, in all the ten Additions the second, the sixth, the seventh and the tenth are to be changed. The second will be, immediately on awaking, to put before me the Contemplation which I have to make, wanting to arouse feeling and be glad at the great joy and gladness of Christ our Lord. The sixth, to bring to memory and think of things that move to spiritual pleasure, gladness and joy, as of heavenly glory. The seventh, to use light or temporal comforts — as, in summer, the coolness; and in winter, the sun or heat — as far as the soul thinks or conjectures that it can help it to be joyful in its Creator and Redeemer. The tenth: in place of penance, let one regard temperance and all moderation; except it is question of precepts of fasting or of abstinence which the Church commands; because those are always to be fulfilled, if there is no just impediment.

Ignatius suggests that the last meditation of the fourth week ought to be on the Ascension. The Ascension of Christ symbolizes through our identification with Christ our return to God through the mediation of the Incarnate Word. Just as the exercitant joined himself to Christ in suffering and death, so he shares in the glory of the resurrected and ascended Christ. This is the salvific moment toward which the Exercises have been aimed from the beginning and in the call to the Kingdom, "Whoever would like to come with me is to labor with me, that following me in the pain, he may also follow me in the glory" [SE96].

## CONTEMPLATION TO GAIN LOVE [230-237]

> [230] CONTEMPLATION TO GAIN LOVE
> *Note.* First, it is well to remark two things: the first is that love ought to be put more in deeds than in words.
> [231] The second, love consists in interchange between the two parties; that is to say in the lover's giving and communicating to the beloved what he has or out of what he has or can; and so, on the contrary, the beloved to the lover. So that if the one has knowledge, he give to the one who has it not. The same of honors, of riches; and so the one to the other. . . .

The theme of love permeates the entire work but carries here a pragmatic accent that looks to the integration of love and the actualities of life and work. Love is to be objectified in deeds and actions rather than in affects and words. But Ignatius goes further to specify that love expresses itself in mutual liberality and communion. The love of God, then, is a mutual sharing of the liberality of the person with the liberality of God distilled into the meaningful conjunction of grace and freedom. This is equivalently commitment of self insofar as the person is his freedom. This freedom finds the pinnacle of its expression and liberality in the election in which one not only finds but embraces God's will (Buckley 1984).

> [232] *First Prelude.* The first Prelude is a composition, which is here to see how I am standing before God our Lord, and of the Angels and of the Saints interceding for me.
> [233] *Second Prelude.* The second, to ask for what I want. It will be here to ask for interior knowledge of so great good received, in order that being entirely grateful, I may be able in all to love and serve His Divine Majesty.
> [234] *First Point.* The First Point is, to bring to memory the benefits received, of Creation, Redemption and particular gifts, pondering with much feeling how much God our Lord has done for me, and how much He has given me of what He has, and then the same Lord desires to give me Himself as much as He can, according to His Divine ordination. And with this to reflect on myself, considering with much reason and justice, what I ought on my side to offer and give to His Divine Majesty, that is to say, everything that is mine, and myself with it, as one who makes an offering with much feeling:
>
> Take, Lord, and receive all my liberty,
> my memory, my intellect, and all my will —
> all that I have and possess.
> Thou gavest it to me: to Thee, Lord, I return it!
> All is Thine, dispose of it according to all Thy will.
> Give me Thy love and grace,
> for this is enough for me.
>
> [235] *Second Point.* The second, to look how God dwells in creatures, in the elements, giving them being, in the plants vegetating, in the animals feeling in them, in men giving them to understand: and so in me, giving me being, animating me, giving me sensation and making me to understand; likewise making a temple of me, being created to the likeness and image of His Divine Majesty; reflecting as much on myself in the way which is said in the first Point, or in another which I feel to be better. In the same manner will be done on each Point which follows.
> [236] *Third Point.* The third, to consider how God works and labors for me in all things created on the face of the earth — that is, behaves like one who labors — as in the heavens, elements, plants, fruits, cattle, etc., giving them being, preserving them, giving them vegetation and sensation, etc.

Then to reflect on myself.

[237] *Fourth Point.* The fourth, to look how all the good things and gifts descend from above, as my poor power from the supreme and infinite power from above; and so justice, goodness, pity, mercy, etc.; as from the sun descend the rays, from the fountain the waters, etc.

Then to finish reflecting on myself, as has been said. . . .

The culmination and pinnacle of the spirituality of the *Exercises* is reached in the famous Contemplation for Obtaining Love. It is the final contemplation toward which the whole of the Exercises have been aiming — the final point in which, together with the Principle and Foundation [SE23], the Exercises are framed and defined (Pousset 1971). From the beginning it is plain that all things about him spoke to Ignatius of the immediate presence and love of God — the typically Ignatian theme of finding God in all things. At the beginning of the Exercises he urges the retreatant to strive for immediate communion with his Creator [SE15], such that the entire enterprize is driven or drawn by the love of God. And in the meditations on the kingdom [SE91-100] and on the three classes of men, the love at issue is loving surrender to God and Christ as the ultimate desire (Rahner 1967). We know of his great power of reflection and the facility with which he could put himself in the presence of God. These qualities are a recurrent motif throughout the *Exercises* but find unique reflection in the words of the contemplation.

The contemplation sounds another typical Ignatian note when he says ". . . love ought to be found in deeds rather than words." The love of God was a theme recapitulating and subsuming all other phases of spiritual growth. For the love of God was the ultimate foundation of spiritual growth and the ultimate test of spiritual identity. Whatever else a man might be, if he did not have charity, he was a tinkling cymbal and a sounding brass (1 Cor 13). De Guibert (1964) recalls a comment of Nadal, who perhaps knew the mature Ignatius better than anyone, to the effect that Ignatius' special grace was "to see and contemplate in all things, actions and conversations the presence of God and the love of spiritual things, to remain a contemplative even in the midst of action" (p. 45). This contemplation brings to the threshold of Ignatius' mystical experiences — a subject to which we shall return.[8]

This is unquestionably the *terminus ad quem* of the *Spiritual Exercises* and the summit of spiritual development. It is, moreover,

[8] See chapter XXXV below.

characteristically Ignatian in that it weaves together the dominant themes on which he has played throughout into a magnificent synthesis (Iparraguirre 1959). The initial emphasis is placed on effective action and the desire to give, as hallmarks of true love. The theme of mutuality articulates the capacity of both lover and beloved to freely share with each other — particularly the freedom to share knowledge, honors, and riches — the reverse of the snares of the devil described in the Two Standards [SE142]. This recapitulates the theme of service sounded in the Foundation and re-echoed through every succeeding phase. The same theme is woven into the third and fourth weeks, when the exercitant is told to ask for an "interior knowledge of so great good received, in order that being entirely grateful, I may be able in all to love and serve His Divine Majesty" [SE233]. The two dominant themes of love and service thus rise together to a thundering climax.

To these are added the third major motif which Ignatius has been improvising from the beginning of the first week. "Take, O Lord, and receive all my liberty . . ." The theme of self-denial, of surrender to the will of God, thus reaches its fullest realization. The most perfect act of that liberty, which has been growing apace within the developing self, is the free surrender of that liberty, along with its complete identity, to Him Who has fashioned and sustained them in being. Ignatius here reaches out to the last and highest peak of spiritual attainment and the summit of spiritual identity in the love and grace of God. It is at this level that the psychoanalytic view has run its course and can say no more.

The most authoritative commentators restrict the Contemplation to the fourth week, at times linking it to the unitive way — Nadal's view. Polanco linked it more directly to the meditations on the resurrection and ascension, also including pentecost, rather than any considerations of the unitive way. Others have sought to divorce it from the context of the *Exercises*, as though it had a separate reference to the mystical life. My own view is that it is the culmination of the spiritual program embedded in the *Exercises* and provides a powerful distillation of Ignatius' spiritual dynamism in the driving force behind his ascent of the mystical and ascetical mountain. It provides a point of transition to ever deeper appreciation of the meaning of divine immanence in the created world, and even, as was the case for Ignatius himself, the mystical experience of divine transcendence.

Many spiritual writers base the approach to Ignatian spirituality on the indifference of the *Exercises*, since it opens the way to greater receptivity to God's grace and to fulfilling his will. The themes are authentically Ignatian, but as Cusson (1988) notes, it may put the accent in the wrong place. He writes:

> But it considers the problem from the wrong end, in regard to both the theoretical and the practical aspects of the spiritual life which it is describing. What is true or important of someone as a point of arrival is not always equally so at the starting point. To put the emphasis on this indifference as the foundation without which the edifice cannot be built is to run the risk of concentrating all one's spirituality on effort. As history has often shown, it interprets Ignatius in a voluntaristic sense. (p. 331)

Cusson opts, and I think correctly, for contemplation of the divine plan founding and animating the entire process. He closes his penetrating study of the *Exercises* with these words:

> Ignatian contemplation is an intelligent and respectful opening of oneself to the divine truth and the radiant splendor of glory expressed there about the Father, the Son, and the Holy Spirit. Such loving contemplation engenders spiritual desire, which is itself a gift from God. This desire in turn raises the person above his or her entangling natural attachments (and thus arises indifference, the freedom from disordered attachments); and then it plunges him or her into the following of Christ with an interior thirst for fidelity and union, for imitation and service (and hence arise the three kinds of humility). Through exercises like those of Ignatius, the retreatant, with attention now centered on the divine salvific plan, St. Paul's "mystery of Christ," and on the mediation of Christ, disposes himself or herself with understanding and generosity sustained by grace, to welcome these divine gifts: the light which enlightens and the desire which draws and commits. In this way he becomes interiorly docile to the motions of the Holy Spirit, who now leads such a person, closely associated with Christ, to move with discernment through the possible ways of service, self-gift, and charity — all set in order according to the divine good pleasure. And the rest of life becomes an effort to make oneself a part of this same circular movement: God down to creation and back up again to God. This is a meaningful effort, based on the action of grace and fidelity to it; and it is purused through a life attentive to seeking God in all things, to contemplating his radiant power and goodness, and to honoring and serving his Divine Majesty. It is a life all to the great glory of God. (p. 332)

So it seems to have been for Ignatius, and so he desired to make it for others.

The primary place in Ignatius' thinking about the role of man before God was given to freedom — in the *Suscipe,* for example, freedom is offered before anything else. This culminating prayer of the *Exercises* does little more than echo the motif of the fifth annotation [SE5] — calling for the generous offering of one's will and liberty — which was presented to the exercitant even before the Foundation. The theme finds an echo in the thoughts of Modell (1993), writing from a psychoanalytic perspective:

> . . . the individual creates his or her own interests. These interests can be thought of as emergent *values* of greater intensity, which can be powerful motives in directing the individual's life. . . . It is not too far-fetched to say that such passionately held interests are a form of loving. . . . The passion that some individuals invest in ideas, in moral values, in specified activities is analogous to a kind of love. There is something very useful in the idea of a free-floating libido that can attach itself to nearly anything. In this sense, a hyperinvestment of libido, expressed as a *Besetzung* (cathexis), is an expression of love. We could say that the private self generates private space through interests that claim attention and love. (p. 130)

It is this dynamic that we can assume, from a theological perspective, is subsumed and transcended through the action of grace. In this sense, grace interpenetrates the dynamic self-generating action of the self in the passionate self-investment in Ignatius' call to a loving service of Christ in the *Exercises.*

In an effort to bring a psychoanalytic reflection to bear on this material, there are unavoidable tensions. Tension arises between the themes of love and service as Ignatius articulates them and the psychological perspective on human love and its permeation with narcissistic issues. While Ignatius propounds a pure love of God that pours itself out in selflessness, self-denial and service to others — a vision of love without any self-interest, if you will — the analyst, based both on his theory and his experience of the actualities of human loving experience, tends to hold to a view of human love as never completely or fully divorced from narcissistic issues or from the entanglements of ambivalence. If Ignatius preaches attainment of love through self-denial and detachment from any inordinate self-investment, the analyst would maintain that the capacity for mature object love is always mingled with a degree of narcissistic self-investment and self-interest, and even further, that if such self-investment is lacking the capacity for love of another is correspondingly compromised. By extension, this argument would lead to the conclusion that even love of God is never completely without self-interest and narcissistic self-investment. If only to the extent that the ideals of self-abnegation and service were mobilized in the service of Ignatius' own ego-ideal, he serves as an case in point (Meissner 1992b).

The theologian, in this case, would charge the analyst with a failure to understand fully the basic human need for love, both receiving and giving love. If man is divinely ordained to participate in divine love, does not the strains of narcissism in him divert him from that destiny or at least complicate his achievement of it? What does it mean to say that this divinely given capacity for love is attuned to underlying needs for narcissistic satisfaction? If love is linked to self-love, or hatred to self-hatred, is man then doomed to self-love and self-hatred? I would argue that this tack bypasses the understanding of narcissism as essential to human wellbeing and psychological integrity, assuming that the translation of narcissism into self-love and attaching pejorative spiritual connotations to that term covers the ground; but it does not. I would turn the argument around to say that the effect of grace is in some measure to lead the individual away from pathological narcissism in the direction of healthy narcissism, following the course of narcissistic transformation (Kohut 1966). The transformation in Ignatius' ego-ideal, as developed in my previous study of his personality (Meissner 1992b), resulted in a refashioning of the ideals of courtly romantic love and chivalrous service into the spiritualized themes of love and service of God and man. In his case, the components of the ego-ideal were not abandoned or lost, but were transformed into a spiritualized ideal that became the basis and animating spirit of his spiritual career and teaching.

## THREE METHODS OF PRAYER [SE238-260]

We have seen the central role occupied in Ignatius' spiritual life by prayer. It was a staple of his spiritual and ascetical enterprise and a subject to which he returned countless times — in his spiritual exhortations to others, and in the *Constitutions*, in which he advanced prescriptions for the prayer life of his followers.[9] The methods of prayer he describes here have become classic, but they yield little in the way of psychological insight. They do suggest the extent to which his approach to spiritual matters was organized and systematized, reflecting some of his more obsessional control. But we cannot fail to remind ourselves that his entrance into the realms of mystical transport could not have rested simply on this basis, nor could his appar-

[9] See chapter XIX below and further discussion of Ignatius' prayer life in Meissner (1992b).

ent disregard of spontaneity lend itself to adequate understanding of the freedom of the spirit that seemed so central to his teaching about the spiritual life and responsiveness to the movements of grace. The recommendations are practical and stem presumably from his own experience. Also, much of the procedure in the first method is reminiscent of his technique in the examens, while the techniques recommended in the second and third — focussing on the meaning of words in the prayer and the use of rhythm — approximate meditative techniques of some Eastern religions. Their purpose is to facilitate the concentration of attention on the matter of prayer and to minimize external distractions.

[238] And First on the Commandments
First Method

The first Method of Prayer is on the Ten Commandments, and on the Seven Deadly Sins, on the Three Powers of the Soul and on the Five Bodily Senses. This method of prayer is meant more to give form, method and exercises, how the soul may prepare itself and benefit in them, and that the prayer may be acceptable, rather than to give any form or way of praying.

I. The Ten Commandments
[239] First let the equivalent of the second Addition of the SECOND WEEK be made; that is, before entering on the prayer, let the spirit rest a little, the person being seated or walking about, as may seem best to him, considering where he is going and to what. And this same addition will be made at the beginning of all Methods of Prayer.

[240] *Prayer*. A Preparatory Prayer, as, for example, to ask grace of God our Lord that I may be able to know in what I have failed as to the Ten Commandments; and likewise to beg grace and help to amend in future, asking for perfect understanding of them, to keep them better and for the greater glory and praise of His Divine Majesty.

[241] For the first Method of Prayer, it is well to consider and think on the First Commandment, how I have kept it and in what I have failed, keeping to the rule of spending the space of time one says the OUR FATHER and the HAIL MARY three times; and if in this time I find faults of mine, to ask pardon and forgiveness for them, and say an OUR FATHER. Let this same method be followed on each one of the Ten Commandments.

[242] First Note. It is to be noted that when one comes to think on a Commandment on which he finds he has no habit of sinning, it is not necessary for him to delay so much time, but according as one finds in himself that he stumbles more or less on

that Commandment so he ought to keep himself more or less on the consideration and examination of it. And the same is to be observed on the Deadly Sins.

[243] Second Note. After having finished the discussion already mentioned on all the Commandments, accusing myself on them and asking grace and help to amend hereafter, I am to finish with a Colloquy to God our Lord, according to the subject matter.

[244] II. On Deadly Sins

About the Seven Deadly Sins, after the Addition, let the Preparatory Prayer be made in the way already mentioned, only with the difference that the matter here is of sins that have to be avoided, and before of Commandments that have to be kept: and likewise let the order and rule already mentioned be kept, and the Colloquy.

[245] In order to know better the faults committed in the Deadly Sins, let their contraries be looked at: and so, to avoid them better, let the person purpose and with holy exercises see to acquiring and keeping the seven virtues contrary to them.

[246] III. On the Powers of the Soul

*Way*. On the three powers of the soul let the same order and rule be kept as on the Commandments, making its Addition, Preparatory Prayer and Colloquy.

[247] IV. On the Bodily Senses

*Way.* About the five bodily senses the same order always will be kept, but changing their matter.

[248] *Note.* Whoever wants to imitate Christ our Lord in the use of his senses, let him in the Preparatory Prayer recommend himself to His Divine Majesty, and after considering on each sense, say a HAIL MARY or an OUR FATHER.

And whoever wants to imitate Our Lady in the use of the senses, let him in the Preparatory Prayer recommend himself to her, that she may get him grace from Her Son and Lord for it; and after considering on each sense, say a HAIL MARY.

[249] SECOND METHOD OF PRAYER

It is by contemplating the meaning of each word of the Prayer.

[250] *Addition*. The same Addition which was in the First Method of Prayer will be in this second.

[251] *Prayer*. The Preparatory Prayer will be made according to the person to whom the prayer is addressed.

[252] *Second Method of Prayer*. The Second Method of Prayer is that the person, kneeling or seated, according to the greater disposition in which he finds himself and as more devotion accompanies him, keeping the eyes closed or fixed on one place, without going wandering with them, says FATHER, and is on the consideration of this word as long as he finds meanings, comparisons,

relish and consolation in considerations pertaining to such word. And let him do in the same way on each word of the OUR FATHER, or of any other prayer which he wants to say in this way.

[253] *First Rule*. The first Rule is that he will be an hour on the whole OUR FATHER in the manner already mentioned. Which finished, he will say a HAIL MARY, CREED, SOUL OF CHRIST, and HAIL, HOLY QUEEN, vocally or mentally, according to the usual way.

[254] *Second Rule*. The Second Rule is that, should the person who is contemplating the OUR FATHER find in one word, or in two, matter so good to think over, and relish and consolation, let him not care to pass on, although the hour ends on what he finds. The hour finished, he will say the rest of the OUR FATHER in the usual way.

[255] *Third Rule*. The third is that if on one word or two of the OUR FATHER one has lingered for a whole hour, when he will want to come back another day to the prayer, let him say the above-mentioned word, or the two, as he is accustomed; and on the word which immediately follows let him commence to contemplate, according as was said in the second Rule.

[256] *First Note*. It is to be noted that, the OUR FATHER finished, in one or in many days, the same has to be done with the HAIL MARY and then with the other prayers, so that for some time one is always exercising himself in one of them.

[257] *Second Note*. The second note is that, the prayer finished, turning, in few words, to the person to whom he has prayed, let him ask for the virtues or graces of which he feels he has most need.

[258] THIRD METHOD OF PRAYER

It will be by rhythm.

*Addition*. The Addition will be the same as in the First and Second Methods of Prayer.

*Prayer*. The Preparatory Prayer will be as in the Second Method of Prayer.

*Third Method of Prayer*. The Third Method of Prayer is that with each breath in or out, one has to pray mentally, saying one word of the OUR FATHER, or of another prayer which is being recited: so that only one word be said between one breath and another, and while the time from one breath to another lasts, let attention be given chiefly to the meaning of such word, or to the person to whom he recites it, or to his own baseness, or to the difference from such great height to his own so great lowness. And in the same form and rule he will proceed on the other words of the OUR FATHER; and the other prayers, that is to say, the HAIL MARY, the SOUL OF CHRIST, the CREED, and the

HAIL, HOLY QUEEN, he will make as he is accustomed.

*First Rule.* The First Rule is, on the other day, or at another hour, that he wants to pray, let him say the HAIL MARY in rhythm, and the other prayers as he is accustomed; and so on, going through the others.

*Second Rule.* The second is that whoever wants to dwell more on the prayer by rhythm, can say all the above-mentioned prayers or part of them, keeping the same order of the breath by rhythm, as has been explained.[10]

[10] Sections [SE261-312] containing points for additional suggested meditations during the second, third and fourth weeks are omitted.

# CHAPTER XV

# THE DISCERNMENT OF SPIRITS — FIRST WEEK

## Introduction

Ignatius' spiritual journey was in effect a progressive development of his capacity for discerning movements of grace and spiritual affects. We catch a glimpse of the beginnings of this sensitivity during his conversion at Loyola, when he became aware of the differential effects of his thoughts and imaginings. The process continued apace at Manresa, and became more refined and developed as he grew in spiritual experience and reflected on his thoughts and feelings. Discernment became the centerpiece of his spiritual doctrine, as it had been the core of his own spiritual odyssey. He distilled the fruits of that experience into the sets of rules in the *Exercises* that play such a central role in the experience of anyone making the Exercises.[1]

A central distinction in these rules, often overlooked, is between discerning the movement of spirits and discerning the will of God. Toner (1982) insists that Ignatius' rules have a limited scope and cannot be extended without considerable theological elaboration to discerning the will of God — despite the fact that seeking and following the will of God was primary in Ignatius' mind. We would have to look elsewhere for his ideas about determining God's will — to begin with, at the end of the Foundation [SE23] and in the directives for the election [SE169-189] and elsewhere — which extend well beyond discernment of spirits and call for great understanding of times and contexts, consultation, assimilating lessons of past experience, and calculating consequences of any projected course of action as to what is more conducive "to the greater glory of God" (K. Rahner 1977). Ignatius had no illusions about where the responsi-

[1] However derivative from his own experience, Ignatius' views regarding discernment are quite consistent with traditional teaching on spiritual discernment (H. Rahner 1977; Toner 1982). Buckley (1973) notes that although these rules are consistent with traditional teaching, Ignatius' work seems stems not from the tradition but from his own experience as reflected in the *Autobiography*.

bility lie for making expeditious use of the rules for discernment — as he wrote Teresa Rejadell in 1536: "I am not going to save myself by the good works of the good angels, and I am not going to be condemned because of the evil thoughts and weaknesses which the bad angels, the flesh, and the world bring before my mind. God asks only one thing of me, that my soul seek to be conformed with His Divine Majesty" (Epistolae I, 107-109 [Letter 8]; in Young (1959) p. 25).

Ignatius was concerned in these rules, more narrowly and specifically, with detecting and identifying those promptings of the Holy Spirit within the soul — promptings that found expression within the hidden depths of the human soul and were known only to God and the subject.[2] His intention was to filter these promptings out from those influences coming from the outside world, from the evil spirit, or from the spontaneous promptings of the human spirit. From the point of view of the psychology of grace, the latter exclusion could be questioned — I would take the position that promptings of the spirit, good or evil, cannot be distinguished from natural psychological wishes and desires. But to dichotomize grace and nature in this sense may be misleading, since, in whatever way God chooses to move the soul by his grace, it may be through and not independently of the powers of the psyche.[3] The very effort and success of discernment itself may be an integrated result of grace and human potential for understanding and judgment.

Not only does Ignatius offer us the fruits of his own experience of discernment, but he offers us an example as well. His descriptions of his efforts at discernment, beginning with his early reflections during his convalescence at Loyola, continuing with his tortured efforts to discriminate between temptations and movements of the Holy Spirit at Manresa, and in his prolonged deliberations over the role of poverty in the Society, provide a sense of the role of discernment in his own life and how central it was to his spiritual development. What he tells us about discernment in the *Exercises* must be placed in context with his teachings in the *Constitutions* and in other spiritual writings and letters. But also he set an example in his frequent seeking for help from others to facilitate his own reflections and reading of his inner movements. His oft repeated consultation with confessors were used to complement his own discernment in order to gain

[2] Consistent with the analytic view of the unconscious, I would extend this to include promptings as yet unknown to the subject, that is allowing room for the influence of grace in and through the unconscious.

[3] This issue will return in considering "consolation without previous cause" in the next chapter.

a better sense of God's will. His use of such help in deciding whether to accept the role of general of his new Society, and in determining to undertake writing of the *Constitutions* only after his confessor convinced him that it was God's will. The process of discernment even in the *Exercises* is complemented by the function of the director, who can add a dimension of objectivity and perspective that the exercitant may not be able to achieve unassisted. The rules themselves were intended originally and primarily for the director, and only to others who have been instructed in their application. Ignatius left it to the director, in conjunction with the retreatant, to determine the extent to which the rules could be applied or adapted flexibly to the needs of the individual.

Toner (1982) adds a further caution — that these rules have nothing to do with exceptional mystical experiences or anything resembling diabolical possession. Their scope is intrapsychic, pertaining to thoughts and feelings that might arise even before any action might be taken. Likewise, we have to remember that Ignatius had no concept of unconscious motives or affects, that the frame of his considerations is entirely conscious and self-aware. Part of the problem in recasting these rules in more modern garb is that we would also take consideration of unconscious motives and forces that might play a role in determining in some part the nature and quality of the exercitant's experiences on which the process of discernment would focus. This adds considerably to the complexity and uncertainty of the discernment process — such that any absolute certainty remains a distant goal that retreats even further the more we grasp for it.

## RULES FOR THE DISCERNMENT OF SPIRITS [SE313-336]

These rules, together with the rules on scruples, provide an encapsulation of Ignatius' psychology of spirituality. Spiritual growth requires the capacity to interpret experiences of affectivity, intentionality and purpose as a kind of language by which God guides the soul to greater perfection and union with Himself. Discernment is the reading of such signs, a hermeneutic of religious experience (Buckley 1984). The *Exercises* lay great stress on the importance of these rules in implementing the progress of the exercitant. He is to keep the director continually informed of the character of his experiences as the retreat progresses, and the director is to apply his experience in dealing with souls to discern whether the exercitant is making real progress or whether he is being drawn out of the path of progress by some form of self-deception. The same characteristics of openness and honesty are likewise required for the fundamental rule of free association in psychoanalysis. The rules for discernment of spirits are the guiding norms for such determinations.

Ignatius structures the Exercises so as to induce a degree of regression in the exercitant. He is isolated from all other human contacts except his involvement with the director — and this for a period of thirty days. This arrangement can only have the effect of stimulating and intensifying transference dynamics. The retreat is carried on in an atmosphere of abnegation and deprivation — the exercitant is expected to undertake certain penances, to deprive himself of food, sleep, even light — as means for facilitating the work of the exercises and gaining greater fruit. These are all practices which can have the effect of weakening the operative secondary process functioning of the ego and inducing a degree of what analysts call "topographical regression." The exercitant's schedule is tightly regulated, with specific periods designated for prayer and meditation. His attention is turned within, and he is asked to become introspective and preoccupied with himself in a way that is quite divergent from his usual everyday practice. Together with the intensity and intimacy of the relationship to the director and the exercitant's dependency on him, the stage is set for regression that might well bring with it feelings and fantasies, unconscious and otherwise, that the exercitant would not otherwise have so readily available. He is placed in an infantile position that draws his attention and emotions back toward infantile levels of experience, the more so when these early experiences may have been somewhat traumatic and conflictual.

The principles of relative sensory deprivation and lack of gratification also have their effect. As Pruyser (1968) commented:

> Abstinence can be practiced in many different ways and to different degrees. . . . Practitioners of the ascetic way know that it is not only a means of coming to grips with moral issues, but also a royal road to the emotions. It is, however, not the only way, or the most effective method. Ignatius of Loyola's *Spiritual Exercises* coupled selective asceticism with a zealous and imaginative engagement in special passions . . . . The retreatant is both "toned down" and "keyed up" by a combination of abstinence and total emotional surrender to the torments and glories of Jesus Christ with whom he is to make a positive identification. (p. 152)

This relaxation of ego-controls is another feature that the Exercises share with the psychoanalytic method.

The framework of application is precisely concerned with the influences of good and evil spirits on the soul. Although the rules as we have them undoubtedly represent a distillation of Ignatius' own soul-searching experiences during his convalescence at Loyola and later at Manresa, they reformulate teaching that has deep roots in the tradition of Christian spirituality (Rahner 1956). Care is called for, however, in any psychological application or interpretation of these rules, since their evidential base must be presumed to consist in almost exclusively well-adjusted subjects psychologically. Ignatius' recommendations do not, nor should they be expected to, take into account the dynamics of neurotic and other pathological conditions that are the province of clinical psychoanalysis and psychiatry. Even if appeal can be made to Ignatius' own ordeal of scruples and suicidal thoughts during the Manresa period, it would be extremely rash to try to make this the basis for projection of these rules to the pathological realm. Moreover, it seems quite clear that the requirements which Ignatius laid down for those who were to be admitted to the Exercises call for a certain degree of maturity and autonomy which would be incompatible with neurotic maladjustment (Beirnaert 1964).

But it should be made clear that this limitation does not thereby exclude unconscious influences from the picture. From a psychoanalytic point of view, the unconscious has a function in determination of all behavior to a greater or less extent. Hence, Ignatius' rules must be interpreted in the light of the dynamics operating within the psyche at whatever level. We are dealing here with responses of the total psychic structure. Moreover, my objective here is quite conservative — I will not attempt any valuation of these rules, but rather merely attempt to fit them into the psychological context of the *Exercises* and interpret them within that framework.

## RULES FOR THE FIRST WEEK [SE313-327]

[313] RULES FOR PERCEIVING AND KNOWING IN SOME MANNER THE DIFFERENT MOVEMENTS WHICH ARE CAUSED IN THE SOUL
The Good, to Receive Them, and the Bad to Reject Them.
And they are more Proper for the First Week[4]

[4] Toner (1982) notes that designating the rules as appropriate to the first or second week may be misleading. The first set of rules were not meant to be restricted to the first week, nor the second to the second, even though they may find greater application in that connection. Both sets are complementary, not exclusive; the rules of the second week presume those of the first. He also points out the distinction between essential and contingent consolation — the continuum of spiritual consolation extends from the essential pole, in which enduring peace results from a fundamental life choice moving towards God, to the contingent pole marked

The good and bad movements of which Ignatius speaks are the *inclinaciones y mociones* of the *Constitutions* [CS92, 144]. They represent impulses or inclinations of the mind or will, and can derive from from God or an angel, from the evil spirit, or from our own human nature. They can refer to thoughts, judgments, images, associations, as well as feelings and affective states. Right choices come from the good spirit — Ignatius' repeated prayer is that God "be pleased to move my will and put in my soul what I ought to do regarding the thing proposed" [SE180].[5]

These rules of the first week are not all immediately concerned with discernment, but include practical counsels to deal with situations in which discernment may be obstructed or complicated, e.g. during periods of temptation or desolation when the influence of evil spirits or disordered attachments may be stronger.

> [314] Rule I:
> First Rule: In the persons who go from mortal sin to mortal sin, the enemy is commonly used to propose to them apparent pleasures, making them imagine sensual delights and pleasures in order to hold them more and make them grow in their vices and sins. In these persons the good spirit uses the opposite method, pricking them and biting their consciences through the process of reason.

This first rule provides a structure integrating various approaches to religious experience. Three levels of influence — preternatural (superhuman, spirits), thoughts and intentionality (rationality), and affectivity — are causally connected and expressed in experiential terms. Contradictions prevail — good vs. evil spirit, sensual pleasure vs. conscience, attraction to sin vs. remorse. The causal lines can move up or down, here the downward movement from preternatural to affective prevails; the opposite takes place in the fourth and fifth rules [SE317, 318]. Affective states (consolation and desolation) can give rise to corresponding thoughts — a danger cautioned against in rule five (Buckley 1973).

by the waxing and waning of intensity of feelings toward God. The focus of Ignatian discernment is on contingent consolation.

[5] Ignatius uses these terms with his own characteristic meanings. The *inclinaciones* are tendencies arising naturally — e.g. "thoughts" in SE32. *Mociones* are spiritual experiences or interior motions within the soul produced by good or evil spirits and thus are objects of discernment [SE313; also SE6, 227, 316, 317, 330 and CS92, 144, and 627]. The latter is Ignatius' normal usage, but occasionally *mociones* can refer to thoughts or inclinations coming spontaneously from natural sources, as in SE32 and 182. See also Calveras (1958), pp. 460-468.

The case described in this rule is that in which the ego has established little or no control over libidinal or other impulses and the pattern of behavior is dominated by libidinal or destructive gratifications of one sort or another. These subjects' lives are dominated by capital sins, rooted in pride, covetousness, lust, anger, and so on (Buckley 1973). In such a condition, whatever fulfills the demands of libido brings with it gratification, under dominance of the pleasure principle, and satisfaction of motivating drives and impulses. The channelization of libido and its attachments can have multiple determinants, including those which are unconscious and refer to the deepest strata of psychic structure and the most primitive levels of experience. Any determinants, interfering with the pattern of gratification, are either absent or sufficiently suppressed to avoid conflict.

When ego-systems begin to interfere in this pattern, conflict arises.[6] Activation of the ego may arise from renewed comprehension of previously accepted value criteria or from a concurrently internalized value system. The basic reality-and-reason orientation of the ego is inevitably set at odds with the pleasure-dominated orientation of libidinal attachments. Evaluative and judgmental functions of the ego set in motion other ego systems mobilizing ego-energies in a countercathectic direction. The effort is directed toward bringing the drive capacities underlying libidinal attachments under sufficient ego-control to permit their adaptation and regulation according to the dictates of reason and the reality principle. This effort runs counter to the energy currents of libidinal cathexes (object-attachments) from which the conflict arises. The stronger the libidinal attachments, the stronger the resistance to ego-control, the sharper the conflict, the deeper the desolation. The sinners described here have drifted away from God and adopted a pragmatic atheism in which God no longer counts and has been replaced by an idolatry of the self (Toner 1982) — a form of narcissistic perversion that would fit the picture of the preconverion Iñigo.

The sting of conscience and remorse to which Ignatius refers is not to be taken in the sense of neurotic guilt. Rather it should be understood in the penitential sense we have previously discussed,[7] that is, the penitential spirit introduces a note of discontent and signal guilt moving the person toward repentance and forgiveness. Neu-

[6] Ignatius describes the opposite tendencies as contrary, not merely different or mutually negating, but diametrically opposed. By implication, any mean between them would involve negation of both contraries (Toner 1982).

[7] See above, pp. 168-173.

rotic guilt reflects the working of a pathological superego poised as an impediment to spiritual progress and development. Conscience and remorse are here concerned with realistic and appropriate responses to past failings and faults. It is a form of signal guilt which draws the penitent on to the path of sorrow and regret, and thus to forgiveness. Seeking of forgiveness reflects the workings of a benign superego, adequately integrated with the functioning ego. The pathological superego will have none of forgiveness; it seeks punishment and retribution, and that often unremittingly. The guilt-ridden or scrupulous neurotic can only find relief when he is able to seek and give forgiveness. Forgiveness must come within before it can be accepted from without. As we have seen above, this was a continuing problem for Ignatius in that he had to deal throughout his life with a remorseless superego.

> [315] Rule II:
> Second Rule. In the persons who are going on intensely cleansing their sins and rising from good to better in the service of God our Lord, it is the method contrary to that in the first rule, for then it is the way of the evil spirit to bite, sadden and put obstacles, disquieting with false reasons, that one may not go on: and it is proper to the good to give courage and strength, consolations, tears, inspirations and quiet, easing and putting away all obstacles, that one may go on in well doing.[8]

The subjects of this rule are on the path toward God, turning away from sin and seeking God's greater service, much like Ignatius himself at the beginning of his conversion or even later in his trials at Manresa. Their consciences are more developed, moving toward progressive purification and ordering to God, and more attuned to the demands of reason and spiritual values. From a psychological perspective, if the effort to establish ego-control is continued and sustained, the level of libidinal resistance gradually decreases and the ego begins to experience its own form of gratification in the adaptation of other ego-systems with the reality-oriented value system it has accepted (conscience). In this phase, however, ego-control is not so thoroughly established or so consistently maintained that it does not run into both pockets of strong resistance from unresolved libidinal attachments and significant regressions of ego-control, where libidinal energies have reasserted themselves and re-established a

[8] Another description of the effects of the evil spirit can be found in the letter to Teresa Rejadell of 1536. See chapter XXXIII below.

degree of resistance. The resistance can manifest itself under all the forms of desolation, depression, anxiety, confusion, excuses, dejection, etc.

Against this continued resistance, there is required a stronger organization and direction of ego-energy — renewal of resolution and purpose, renewal of conviction from the basic motives for ego-control — anything which subserves the bringing to bear of the ego's energy and resolve upon the task at hand. The greater the degree of ego-strength, the more effective will this mobilization be, the more readily will it find consolation in its efforts.

The basic struggle here can be depicted as between ego and id — Freud's (1923) monograph of that title provides the theoretical backstop for this Ignatian perspective. In the relatively normal personality, the experience of consolation in the resolution of the ego-id conflict in favor of ego would imply a state of more or less peaceful coexistence between ego and superego. This would not be unexpected, since the normal superego has developed along lines not very far removed from that proper to the ego. In other words, internalized norms of conduct derived from parental and other early childhood authority figures are for the most part conformed to norms of reason and reality. Where there is disjunction between ego and superego, there will develop conflict in this direction also, usually from the defect in superego formation. This is very likely the case in persons of scrupulous tendency, including, of course, the pathological condition of obsessive-compulsion — a feature of Ignatius' postconversion personality. The function of the ego is to bring about a working compromise between the demands of id, superego and reality. The operative norm in the present instance is represented by reality: here reality includes a set of spiritual realities (knowledge of which is had through revelation and theology) and a set of values derived from that reality. Consolation derives from harmonious functioning of self-systems relative to the reality standard; desolation stems from resistance of the id to ego-control or from excessive demands of superego.

Ignatius does not address them here, but other obstacles to spiritual movement can arise from the world, particularly from family or friends to whom the effort to find God is alien or strange. He touches on some of these difficulties in his letter to Teresa Rejadell, and again we can hear echoes of his own conversion experience. More than one person who has felt himself called to serve God in a religious vocation has met such opposition. The doubts and uncertainties aroused by such objections can be as forceful as any interior resistances or lingering attachments.

In any case, focussing on consolation and desolation should not interfere with keeping perspective on the essentials of Ignatius' teaching — that growth in the spiritual life does not depend on consolations, nor need it be impeded by desolations. He would write Bartholomew Hernandez: "It is not surprising that all the scholastics do not experience that relish for devotion which is desirable, for He who dispenses this grace does so when and where He thinks fit. . . . if one does nothing to endanger the solid virtues and gives the time to prayer required by the Constitutions, with few or many consolations, he should in no way be disturbed, but accept from God's hand what He disposes in the matter, always making more account of what is really important; that is, patience, humility, obedience, charity, and other virtues" (Epistolae VII, 268-270 [Letter 4619]; in Young (1959) p. 342). Thus spiritual consolation should not be sought for or made an end in itself, since the evil spirit or our own self-deception, particularly when rooted in narcissistic need, can use it to deceive us. Ignatius urges indifference to consolation or desolation, as in all other things.

Toner (1982) properly calls attention to the phrase "*animo y fuerzas*" — "courage and strength" — another recurrent theme in the *Exercises* [SE 7, 16, 323, 324] and other Ignatian writings. Spiritual growth requires action, determination, strength, and courage — it is not for the faint of heart. As Toner notes: "Ignatius seems to have both strength and energy in mind, force and vigor in using it. . . . In these texts, Ignatius is always referring to energy or active power *under control of the agent*, to be used as he chooses. This energy is *volitional* rather than corporal. It is *directed to activating desirable affections and thoughts* [SE116, 195], and *to deactivating or at least restraining the influence of undesirable thoughts and spontaneous affections already in act* [SE16, 155], or both [SE7, 323, 324, 327]. Putting all these qualifications together, we see that *fuerzas* refers to courageous volitional energy (force or active power) which is subject to the agent's decision" (p. 65). This usage is accurately descriptive of the psychoanalytic meaning of "ego-energy" or "ego-strength."

These dispositions play a critical role in Ignatius' psychology. Such ego-dispositions do not of themselves produce consolation, but they are effective in dispelling desolation. They are directly reflective of Ignatius' own psychology and tell us something about his approach to the spiritual life. This is the side of Ignatius redolent with strains of phallic narcissism and the transformations of aggression that formed such a dominant aspect of his personality (Meissner 1992b). The language and metaphors of the *Exercises* repeatedly speak to the activity of the exercitant in disposing himself to better receive God's grace. We could argue also that one possible effect of grace is to instill or elicit just this sort of *animo y fuerzas*, without any necessary connection with the pathological influence of phallic or narcissistic determinants.

> [316] Rule III:
> Third Rule. The third: Of Spiritual Consolation. I call it consolation when some interior movement in the soul is caused, through which the soul comes to be inflamed with love of its Creator and Lord; and when it can in consequence love no created thing on the face of the earth in itself, but in the Creator of them all.
>
> Likewise, when it sheds tears that move to love of its Lord, whether out of sorrow for one's sins, or for the Passion of Christ our Lord, or because of other things directly connected with His service and praise.
>
> Finally, I call consolation every increase of hope, faith and charity, and all interior joy which calls and attracts to heavenly things and to the salvation of one's soul, quieting it and giving it peace in its Creator and Lord.

## SPIRITUAL CONSOLATION

The term "consolation" became a watchword for Ignatian spirituality; the goal of the *Spiritual Exercises* was to bring the exercitant to experience such consolation authentically. Ignatius probably acquired the idea from the *Imitation of Christ*, since it was the governing idea of Kempis' late theology, but even so the term was common in sacramental usage. The difference between this consolation and sensual gratification (sensible consolation?) should be noted. Ignatius insists here on the distinction between spiritual consolation and any other form of consolation; whenever the term is used in the Ignatian vocabulary, it means "spiritual consolation."[9] It does not refer sim-

[9] In the Autograph Directory, he indicates "spiritual gladness, love, hope of heavenly things, tears and interior movement which leaves the person consoled in our Lord," and again, "interior peace, spiritual joy, hope, faith, love, tears and elevation of mind, which are all gifts of the Holy Spirit" (DirSpExMHSJ 11 and 18; cited in Toner 1982, p. 82). Ignatius does not get more explicit, characteristically avoiding definition. However, clearly spiritual consolation is *de arriba*. Ribadenyra recounted Ignatius' observation that he could not live without consolation; when asked what he meant, he replied that consolation was "something he sensed in himself that was not his own, nor could be his own, but was purely from God" (cited in Veale (1996), p. 26). This reflects the degree to which Ignatius relied on subjective experiencee, but also the disparity from an analytic perspective according to which no experience is possible that is not in some sense psychic. If a

ply to any positive, satisfying, delightful, or uplifting emotion, even if experienced in a religious context — prayer or liturgy for example — otherwise the Holy Spirit would be behind every euphoric affective response that wasn't sinful. But they remain fundamentally affective experiences involving psychological processes.[10] Sensible consolation depends on libido and follows the pleasure principle, while the former depends on ego and follows the reality principle as determined previously. The emotional component of the experience of consolation is prompted and brought into play by the ego, and therefore remains under ego-control.[11] Consequently, it is always an appropriate emotion and is always reality-oriented, i.e., sadness in contemplation of personal sins or the sufferings of the Passion, but joy in the thought of God and salvation. Tears, sadness, or sorrow are forms of consolation in that they are rooted in faith and love of God, and they draw the soul to repentance and forgiveness that draws it closer to God. Consolation, therefore, is never opposed to the reality orientation of the ego, as in the case of sadness or tepidity in relation to spiritual things and elation in the thought of earthly things.[12]

Nor should we make the mistake of thinking that Ignatius means to limit the action of the Spirit to consolation and desolation. The action of the Spirit is not limited and can exercise multiple effects not included in consolation or desolation. Nor is consolation synonymous with an increase of the theological virtues, since they can grow through desolation as well.[13] Rather Ignatius' focus remains on

consolation comes from above, it can only do so by finding its expression in natural psychic processes.

[10] Buckley (1973) insists on a specific meaning of consolation and desolation in the Ignatian context, dissociating them from affective connotations, whether positive or negative, and divorced from considerations of pleasure and pain. What is determinative is the direction of the movement, to or away from God. Toner (1982) objects to this reading of the rules, insisting — I think properly — on the centrality of affectivity in Ignatius' perspective. Buckley's argument, focusing other aspects of the rules, has independent merit.

[11] This should not be interpreted to mean that such consolation is the result of autonomous voluntary control of the ego. Consolation may result from the response of the ego to grace, but then it is the ego's receptive capacity that carries the burden of "control." The question of control here does not refer to causality, but to the locus of experience. Similarly, the feeling or affective experience is a form of action on the part of the ego. The attempt to distinguish affect as passive from (motoric) action as active (Toner 1982) would miss the point. For a discussion of affect as activity, see Schafer (1976).

[12] Egan (1976) notes that the consolation in question here is either CCCP or consolations experienced in the wake of CSCP.

[13] On the meanings of "increase of hope, faith and charity" see Toner (1982), pp. 104-107.

the affective component involved in experiences of faith, hope, and charity — even to the point of encouraging the subject to stir up such feelings to overcome desolation [SE319-322]. Nor are they the most fundamental of criteria for discernment of the will of God — teachings of the church and scripture, directives of proper authority, the demands of charity, for example, may prove to be more reliable and override experiences of consolation and desolation. They can provide a testing ground for discerning consolation and desolation (Toner 1982). As O'Sullivan (1990) notes, "There is wisdom in the fact that, in both the rules of discernment and the times of choice, Ignatius spends considerable time discussing the use of conscious reflection, calling for its integration with sensibility and emotion before judging the soundness of choices/decisions" (p. 20).

It is important to note here the acute attention Ignatius pays to affective movements that the exercitant is experiencing. This is the touchstone of his method, just as it is a central aspect of the psychoanalytic method (Modell 1973, 1984). Ignatius uses the flow of affects to track the exercitant's progress and as basic elements of his discernment of spirits. A second important question is whether these affective dispositions reflect in any sense transference dynamics. In his discussion of this question, Newman (1985) emphasizes the analogy between consolation and positive transference to God. He points to the association between consolation and love of God, the exclusivity of this loving attachment, and even defines the shedding of tears for past sins as consolation when they lead to increased love of God. This is analogous to Freud's notion of positive transference as a form of love which also endows the object with idealized qualities — the overvaluation of the love object usually involving narcissistic elements. In the *Exercises*, God serves as such an idealized object — indeed infinitely so. The ideal that Ignatius proposes is the total submission and surrender of self to this omnipotent love object. If there are elements of transference in such authentic consolation, there would have to be more involved than the transference model would be able to sustain. The love of God may incorporate transference, but it involves more than transference. The issue here is the same as that involved in the question of whether religion is merely a form of obsessional neurosis, or whether — even when it becomes a vehicle for the expression of obsessional defenses and behaviors — it does not mean and signify something beyond obsessionality (Meissner 1984).

To Ignatius' mind, there is no doubt that movements of spiritual consolation can come from God. The first movement he names is specifically the fruit of the Spirit — charity that ignites the soul with love of God. In 1536, he wrote to Teresa Rejadell: "If you look closely, you will easily see that those desires of serving Christ our Lord do not come from you, but are given you by our Lord. Thus when you say: "The Lord has given me increased desires to serve him", you praise him, because you make his gift known and you glory in him, not in yourself, since you do not attribute that grace to yourself" (Epistolae I, 99-107 [Letter 7]; in Young (1959), 18-24, p. 20). He had a profound sense of being guided and moved by the hand of God, and without exception attributed every good outcome, every good wish or desire to the influence of the good spirit through grace. This is a love that contradicts self-love, even loving God more than oneself, or loving oneself in relation to God. The transformations of narcissism play a critical role here insofar as pathological forms of self-love are at the root of inordinate attachments that draw one away from the love of God, but constructive transformations of the ego-ideal are necessary for growth to spiritual perfection and identity and for love of God. Ignatius' description of consolation speaks to a high degree of intensity of feeling in experiencing the love of God.

## SPIRITUAL DESOLATION

> [317] Rule IV:
> Fourth Rule. Of Spiritual Desolation. I call desolation all the contrary of the third rule, such as darkness of soul, disturbance in it, movement to things low and earthly, the unquiet of different agitations and temptations, moving to want of confidence, without hope, without love, when one finds oneself all lazy, tepid, sad, and as if separated from his Creator and Lord. Because, as consolation is contrary to desolation, in the same way the thoughts which come from consolation are contrary to the thoughts which come from desolation.

Spiritual desolation is both qualitatively and quantitatively diverse and can manifest itself in many forms. Ignatius is intent on formulating desolation specifically as spiritual and not in general terms. He uses the logic of contraries to make his point. He underlines the contrast with consolation in his Autograph Directory: "Prompted by the evil spirit and his gift, desolation is the contrary [of consolation]: contrary to peace, conflict; contrary to joy, sadness; contrary to hope in higher things, hope in base things; contrary to heavenly love, earthly love; contrary to tears, dryness; contrary to elevation of mind, wandering of mind to contemptible things" (DirSpExMHSJ 12; cited in Toner (1982) p. 125). The essential note, however, of spiritual desolation is that it tends to undermine and destroy faith, hope and charity.

But he did not have a clinical concept of depression to complicate his thinking. If we can clearly state that his meaning of spiritual desolation is not the same as depression, the term can also be used to describe depression, as is often the case in nonclinical spiritual writings. If they are not synonymous, that does not mean that spiritual desolation may not be accompanied by and include depression where there is a question of conflict between the striving ego and a demanding and self-punishing superego.

Actually the distinction between spiritual desolation and depression can be a difficult matter. Often they overlap to considerable degree, and each may give rise to the other. Spiritual directors need to be on the alert for clinical depression, since efforts to overcome desolation cannot be expected to deal with an underlying depression. Moreover, depression will hinder real spiritual growth. An individual can be trapped in both depression and desolation, but he may also be depressed without being in desolation, and he may be desolate without being depressed. The signs of desolation given by Ignatius do not help discrimination since they can also be found in depression. In depression, it is particularly the depressive mood (sadness, lethargy, mourning, discouragement, loss of hope) in conjunction with neurotic guilt and poor self-esteem that gives the lie to a pathological condition. Feelings of worthlessness, inadequacy, self-degradation, and shame, are hallmarks of narcissistic pathology and can be symptomatic of depression. Desolation can occur in conjunction with any or all of these — or without them. Whatever mixture of desolation and depression the exercitant might experience, it has the marks of desolation to the extent that it has an antispiritual effect, drawing the soul away from God and tending to a decline of faith (Toner 1982).

We can also point to a certain analogy between desolation and negative transference. They both involve negative feelings toward the respective authority figure. Ignatius seems to conceive of desolation as based on negative feelings toward God — the exercitant may feel  desolate, abandoned and rejected by God, alienated and alone, worthless and unloved. These feelings and their connection with God may remain relatively unconscious, and find their way into expression in more or less symptomatic terms. But God may not be the only object of such transference feelings. We should not forget the director. He occupies a rather unique position as the only figure to whom the exercitant communicates during the Exercises. He becomes an object in some degree of infantile attachments, dependence, and even love. He may also become the target for negative feelings that derive from infantile levels, as in the classic displacement transference. Directors are also well advised to keep in mind the vicissitudes of the subject's relations to other significant objects in his life as sources of depressive or desolate reactions.

> [318] Rule V:
> Fifth Rule. In time of desolation never to make a change; but to be firm and constant in the resolutions and determination in which one was the day preceding such desolation, or in the determination in which he was in the preceding consolation. Because, as in consolation it is rather the good spirit who guides and counsels us, so in desolation it is the bad, with whose counsels we cannot take a course to decide rightly.

Ignatius here moves beyond definitional concerns and begins to address practical measures applicable to subjects advancing in virtue. The advice is solid and echoes one of the principles found useful in psychoanalysis — that the patient should be encouraged not to make any important decisions during analysis until he and the analyst have adequately explored and understood its meaning and consequences. In a state of consolation, ego-systems are functioning properly and harmoniously, and the ego is maintaining adequate control. It is the function of ego to perceive and evaluate situations and determine the course of action to be followed. When a decision or resolution has effects which are of some consequence, the time to make them is when the ego is in control of its resources and it is not under the influence of conflictual forces within or without itself. The latter is the situation in desolation and the ego could not be expected to come to a right decision, i.e., one determined by the norms of reason and reality according to the proper function of ego.

There are three steps for dealing with desolation: (1) recognize it for what it is, (2) resist any impulse to change any prior decisions leading to spiritual growth, and (3) do what seems advisable to deal with the desolation and its causes (Toner 1982). This is the burden of rules V-IX for the first week. These points resonate with a therapeutic perspective on depression. Similar emphasis can be made in helping patients deal with depression in psychotherapy or analysis.[14] More specifically, the patient must first recognize his condition as a depression, but even more importantly he must accept and bear the pain and anguish connected with it. Then he should take hold and not allow his tormenting feelings and the discouragement and hope-

[14] On the capacity to bear depression, see Zetzel (1965).

lessness of his condition to lead to any significant changes in his life situation or any other important decisions. And lastly, he has to find a way to mobilize himself and his resources to deal with the causes of his depression and to work himself out if it. The process involves, therefore, both passive and active components — passive in bearing the painful feelings, active in doing something about them. Even the reflection of the first aspect brings into play a split in the ego, mobilizing the self-observant capacity to take a position vis-a-vis the suffering part of the self. The subsequent steps build on and reinforce this dynamic. Ignatius' counsels in rules VI-IX echo the third step. It also resonates with the spirit of the *agere contra* [SE13, 97, 157].[15] This would seem to be another reflection of the Ignatian paradox — trust completely in God, but act as though the result depended on your own effort.

> [319] Rule VI:
> Sixth Rule. Although in desolation we ought not to change our first resolutions, it is very helpful intensely to change ourselves against the same desolation, as by insisting more on prayer, meditation, on much examination, and by giving ourselves more scope in some suitable way of doing penance.

Desolation implies that the effort of the ego to establish control and achieve proper organization and integration has run upon a snag of some sort, some form of resistance which it is not able to overcome. The suggestions offered here are intended to help the exercitant to bring his effort to bear on that area of resistance and overcome it. In prayer, for example, we not only beg God's help to bolster the energy of the ego, but in the very act of prayer we have begun to mobilize some of those very energies. Self-analysis can help to discern the source of the resistance and direct the capacities of the ego to overcoming it. Likewise the use of penances implies and reinforces the disposition of ego resources in countering desolation. The reinstitution of ego control and autonomy and the integration of self-systems is accompanied by the experience of consolation. The role of grace, working in and through created power and effort, may be synonymous with the effort of the subject in willing a change. While some spiritual writers would insist that such effort, unaided by grace, cannot undo spiritual desolation (Toner 1982), the ques-

[15] See also CS265: "Temptations ought to be anticipated by their opposites, for example, if someone is observed to be inclined toward pride, by exercising him in lowly matters thought fit to aid toward humbling him; and similarly of other evil inclinations."

tion to my mind remains open. Perhaps, the issue hinges on the extent to which desolation and depression may be mingled — the one responsive to spiritual means, the other to natural. But, practically speaking, it makes little difference, especially since we cannot know when grace is playing a part. In fact, as I have argued, the self-conscious mobilization of natural resources may be one expression of grace-sustained motivation. What counts is the mobilizing of resources to counter the desolation — another expression of *agere contra*.

Moreover, the principle of counteracting desolation may not call for an intensification of spiritual effort, but a lessening of it out of considerations of discretion and moderation. The lesson was clear in Ignatius' letter to Borgia, whose saintly excesses were considerable, responding to Borgia's request for Ignatius' opinion regarding prayer and penance: Ignatius counsels moderation and prudence in an effort to soften the duke's penetential passion.[16] From an analytic perspective, the principle of such diminished intensity would involve softening of the overburdening superego.

> [320] Rule VII:
> Seventh Rule. Let him who is in desolation consider how the Lord has left him in trial in his natural powers, in order to resist the different agitations and temptations of the enemy; since he can with the Divine help, which always remains to him, though he does not clearly perceive it; because the Lord has taken from him his great fervor, great love and intense grace, leaving him, however, grace enough for eternal salvation.

A device for stirring the subject to autonomous activity in overcoming resistances underlying desolation. The ego can come to depend too much on grace in overcoming such resistances and allow employment of its own resources to grow slack. This underlines the centrality in the mind of Ignatius of effective effort on the part of the person, reflecting his tendency to assume an more active position in the face of desolation.

> [321] Rule VIII:
> Eighth Rule. Let him who is in desolation labor to be in patience, which is contrary to the vexations which come to him: and let him think that he will soon be consoled, employing against the desolation the devices, as is said in the sixth Rule.

Ignatius offers a penetrating insight into the psychology of spiritual development, and into intrapsychic dynamics. In the conflict of

[16] Portions of the letter are reproduced in chapter XIX below. See also Young (1959) 179-182.

desolation, one might think that, given his characteristic penchant for action, he would recommend a strong offense as the best defense. In other words, the course of ego-action would be direct counterattack or repudiation. However, psychotherapists have long since become acquainted with the stubbornness and ingenuity patients can manifest in resistance. Ignatius wisely counsels rather a more indirect tactic — strive rather to hold the ground that has been gained and maintain a spirit of equanimity and patience with the assurance that the period of trial will pass. This basic disposition combined with the pattern of activity recommended in Rule VI describes a rather effective program for support of the ego and disengagement of non-ego dispositions. This is also related to the capacity to bear the desolation and/or depression mentioned previously.

> [322] Rule IX:
> Ninth Rule. There are three principal reasons why we find ourselves desolate.
>
> The first is, because of our being tepid, lazy or negligent in our spiritual exercises; and so through our faults, spiritual consolation withdraws from us.
>
> The second, to try us and see how much we are and how much we let ourselves out in His service and praise without such great pay of consolation and great graces.
>
> The third to give us true acquaintance and knowledge, that we may interiorly feel that it is not ours to get or keep great devotion, intense love, tears, or any other spiritual consolation, but that all is the gift and grace of God our Lord, and that we may not build a nest in a thing not ours, raising our intellect into some pride or vainglory, attributing to us devotion or the other things of the spiritual consolation.

The three principal reasons for desolation can be interpreted psychologically in the following terms: (1) desolation is due to ineffective mobilization of ego-resources and the consequent failure to establish adequate ego-control; (2) insofar as ego-activity is sustained and energized by grace, its interruption permits ego-energies to diminish; (3) the more or less integrated functioning of the ego in consolation can induce a state of premature self-satisfaction, before the ego has attained the full flower of its maturity. There is no better way to attain a knowledge of its deficiencies and weaknesses than for the ego to encounter the resistance of non-ego forces in the psyche or to come to grips with discrepancies in its own areas and levels of functioning. This encounter is the substance of the experience of desolation.

Part of what is in question here also has to do with the proper orientation of the ego to the total reality within which it functions. Grace is a substantial part of that reality; for the ego to think itself capable in itself of what it effects, in fact, through grace is in reality a fundamental deception. Ignatius' preoccupation with narcissism shines through here. To the extent that the continuing flow of consolations may feed into the sense of self-enhancement and even spiritual pride or grandiosity attendant on archaic narcissism, desolation can serve as a valuable corrective. In Ignatius' view, the first reason may reflect human failing and limitation, but the others would be God's doing. There is tension here between a theological perspective and a more limited psychological understanding.

> [323] Rule X:
> Tenth Rule. Let him who is in consolation think how he will be in the desolation which will come after, taking new strength for then.

The stability of ego-control is short-lived and requires constant effort to maintain. Ignatius here recommends that some part of the ego's effort be directed to preparation for future regression and disruption of that control. The ego is thus able to dispose itself to deal more effectively with desolation when it does materialize. This also makes good sense in dealing with depression — the realization that the depression is time-limited, that it had a beginning and will have an end, can help to restore a sense of perspective and hope to the patient suffering from the pain of depression.

Ignatius also seems to be offering a hedge against narcissistic self-enhancement or spiritual grandiosity. The risk of self-inflation accompanies the enhancement of spiritual consolation. These can readily take the form of "peak experiences" described by Maslow (1971); but such peak spiritual experiences can carry within them certain risks. As Lifton (1961), addressing himself to the effects of brainwashing, commented:

> Ideological totalism itself may offer a man an intense peak experience: a sense of transcending all that is ordinary and prosaic, a freeing of himself from the encumbrances of human ambivalence, of entering a sphere of truth, of reality, trust, and sincerity beyond any he had ever known or ever imagined. But these peak experiences, the result as they are of external pressure, distortion, and threat, carry a great potential for rebound and for equally intense opposition to the very things which initially seem so liberating. Such imposed peak experiences — as contrasted with those more freely and privately arrived at by great religious leaders and mys-

> tics — are essentially experiences of personal closure. Rather than stimulating greater receptivity and 'openness to the world,' they encourage a backward step into some form of 'embeddedness' — a retreat into doctrinal and organizational exclusiveness, and into all or nothing emotional patterns more characteristic (at least of this stage of human history) of the child than of the individuated adult. (p. 435)

Even in the realms of grace-induced spiritual consolation, these same risks are operative. The analyst here would be alert to issues of underlying conflict and ambivalence and wary of defensive or compromise formations that may be embedded in the consolation and serve as defensive against the opposite more depressive undercurrents that may contribute to repressed, concurrent, or subsequent depressive affects associated with desolation.

> [324] Rule XI:
> Eleventh Rule. Let him who is consoled see to humbling himself and lowering himself as much as he can, thinking how little he is able for in the time of desolation without such grace or consolation.
>
> On the contrary, let him who is in desolation think that he can do much with the grace sufficient to resist all his enemies, taking strength in his Creator and Lord.

Ignatius' recommendation again touches on the risk of narcissistic deviation attendant on consolation — humility is called on to keep things in balance. His message is that one in consolation should be aware that desolation lies not far down the path — in other words, all consolation is time limited — and likewise for one in desolation — it too is limited and consolation may not be far away. For both consolation and desolation, the basic Ignatian strategy of *agere contra* is again the order of the day. His tendency is consistently to adopt a active posture regarding anything that would draw the soul away from its Creator. If consolation begins to bleed over into self-enhancement or pride, counteractive measures are taken. And desolation can be countered by consoling thoughts of God's grace.

Also, this observation formulates the basic principle of reality orientation in the spiritual order. The ego must recognize and accept its utter dependence on grace and must realize that growth in spiritual identity is entirely beyond its capacity without the assistance of grace. Also a critical facet of such growth is related intimately with the growth of the ego in humility. Any other orientation for the ego is a form of deception and results in a separation of it from the system of values and the framework of reality in which spiritual identity is to mature. The tendency to fall into this deception is heightened by consolation, where it takes the form of a subtle pride. The same deception lies at the root of Ignatius' advice to one in desolation, since the tendency to lose sight of the basic reality orientation needs to be counteracted here too.

> [325] Rule XII:
> Twelfth Rule. The enemy acts like a woman, in being weak against vigor and strong of will. Because, as it is the way of the woman when she is quarrelling with some man to lose heart, taking flight when the sun shows her much courage: and on the contrary, if the man, losing heart, begins to fly, the wrath, revenge, and ferocity of the woman is very great, and so without bounds; in the same manner, it is the way of the enemy to weaken and lose heart, his temptations taking flight, when the person who is exercising himself in spiritual things opposes a bold front against the temptations of the enemy, doing diametrically the opposite. And on the contrary, if the person who is exercising himself commences to have fear and lose heart in suffering the temptations, there is no beast so wild on the face of the earth as the enemy of human nature in following out his damnable intention with so great malice.

We can pass over the gender stereotypes displayed here — not uncommon for a Spanish hidalgo of the sixteenth century. They should not distract us from the basic Ignatian psychology expressed here. The contending images can be translated into psychological terms reflecting conflictual and oppositional tendencies within the human psyche. It should be noted that the insights into the nature of intrapsychic dynamics which Ignatius offers in this and the following rules are applicable only within the context for which they were intended: the mature personality with a considerable degree of ego strength and struggling to grow in spiritual identity. Within this narrow context, the effort of the ego to maintain control over desires and urges attributable to the evil one is a never ending process in which attachments, repugnances and resistances are overcome, reassert themselves, shift to new objects and conditions, are overcome again and again, only to assume new and more subtle forms. The ego is constantly challenged to ferret out, analyze, recognize and counteract each new manifestation. Ignatius suggests here that it is necessary for the ego to make a strong and determined effort to bring such resistant impulses under control. There is unquestionably enough clinical evidence to suggest what drive-dependent forces can do against a weak and neurotic ego. When the ego, however, has sufficient strength to take resolute action to break down the resistance and bring it to heel, it is quite a different story. The emphasis on effective action speaks to

Ignatius' characteristically assertive, forceful, and energetic approach to the spiritual battle — unrelenting and desirous of yielding little or no ground to the enemy. The spirit of Pamplona lives on!

> [326] Rule XIII:
> Thirteenth Rule. Likewise, he acts as a licentious lover in wanting to be secret and not revealed. For, as the licentious man who, speaking for an evil purpose, solicits a daughter of a good father or a wife of a good husband, wants his words and persuasions to be secret, and the contrary displeases him much, when the daughter reveals to her father or the wife to her husband his licentious words and depraved intention, because he easily gathers that he will not be able to succeed with the undertaking begun: in the same way, when the enemy of human nature brings his wiles and persuasions to the just soul, he wants and desires that they be received and kept in secret; but when one reveals them to his good Confessor or to another spiritual person that knows his deceits and evil ends, it is very grievous to him, because he gathers, from his manifest deceits being discovered, that he will not be able to succeed with his wickedness begun.

The pattern which resistance can follow is often extremely subtle, and unless the ego has a strong and clear grasp on basic principles and objectives of the spiritual life, deception can easily be its lot. The ego can easily find itself seduced into some worthy preoccupation, quite praiseworthy in itself, but nonetheless diverts its energies and attention away from the crucial area of resistance. The further the ego progresses in establishing its rightful domain of ego-control, the more subtle and deceptive are the forms which resistance assumes. It is precisely for this reason that psychotherapy is often such a long drawn out process; the resistances must be sufficiently worked-through so that the control of the ego is stable and secure enough to insure healthy adjustment. So Ignatius recommends that the best way for one to uncover and recognize these resistances is to take counsel with someone experienced in the spiritual life who will be able to recognize and point them out and suggest means for overcoming them.

We can note that a similar phenomenon can be recognized in the context of psychotherapy or psychoanalysis. The patient may be tormented by internal impulses, wishes, and fantasies which seem to him despicable, shameful, ugly, repulsive and disgusting. He strives mightily to ignore, suppress, repress these evil inclinations. When he reaches a point of trust in his therapist that such material can be revealed and discussed without fear of judgment or retribution, he finds great relief in sharing this toxic material. When the context of his instinctually derived thoughts and feelings is brought into the dispassionate light of consciousness and reason, they can be looked at objectively and discovered to be little more than understandable aspects of his own humanity. The neurotic conflicts and the pathogenic affects connected with them are thus undercut. From the point of view of resistances, however, such revelation and detoxifying are countered by the neurotic need to preserve the pathological *status quo*. Ignatius' recommendation in this rule is connected with his extension of the principle involved in the manifestation of conscience he incorporated in the *Constitutions*.

> [327] Rule XIV:
> Fourteenth Rule. The fourteenth: Likewise, he behaves as a chief bent on conquering and robbing what he desires: for, as a captain and chief of the army, pitching his camp, and looking at the forces or defences of a stronghold, attacks it on the weakest side, in like manner the enemy of human nature, roaming about, looks in turn at all our virtues, theological, cardinal and moral; and where he finds us weakest and most in need for our eternal salvation, there he attacks us and aims at taking us.

From what has been said, we would expect the resistance of instinctual forces to manifest themselves at that point at which ego-control was least secure or weakest. This is not always the case, since even minor diversions of ego-energy can be the occasion for the recurrence of libidinal or narcissistic resurgence. But, in general, the weaker the ego, the stronger we can expect instinctual resistance to be.

# CHAPTER XVI

# THE DISCERNMENT OF SPIRITS — SECOND WEEK

## Rules for the Second Week [SE328-336]

The rules for the second week are intended for those who have advanced beyond the level of the first week, in which libidinal attachments and drive-defense conflicts between ego and id have assumed a more or less gross form depending on the level of refinement of the exercitant. The motivational framework for these individuals has moved beyond polarities of pleasure and pain to a level of development in which instinctual satisfaction is no longer the goal; rather they become open to the temptation of the good. The obviously evil can no longer draw him, but he is much more vulnerable to temptation under the appearance of good. Desolation is no longer as pressing a concern since it is an affectivity drawing the soul away from God. Rather the good, even the obviously good, becomes more potentially destructive. "What is at issue here is the discrimination between that movement of affectivity which is genuinely and organically towards God, and that which is deceptive" (Buckley 1973, p. 33).

When ego-control has been fairly securely established, however, more and more of the energies of the ego are directed to the effort of spiritual growth rather than to defensive needs. Consequently, instinctual resistances are offered a certain scope for resurgence — a variant on the theme of the "return of the repressed." Their appearance usually takes a somewhat different and much more subtle form than the original attachment, just as the return of the repressed must find a modified form of expression to circumvent more effective and adaptive defenses — e.g. finding expression in dreams rather than symptoms. Ignatius has this more refined level in mind in proposing this second set of rules. Depending on the exercitant's capacity and level of development, it may be that some of these rules of the second week would be applicable in the first week. The director should use discretion, for if the rules of the second week should confuse rather than clarify, this would not help the exercitant's efforts. The rules are a help to clearing up confusion, not to creating it.

Toner (1991) adds the caution that we should not give undue significance to details without keeping any particular point in perspective in the context of Ignatius' overall teaching on the discernment of spirits and God's will. The focus of this second set of rules is on the "apparent reasons, subtleties and continual fallacies" which the spirit of darkness uses to undermine consolation. Toner (1982) argues that keeping this limited context in mind reduces the significance of the distinction between consolation with and without previous cause — since the latter is hardly mentioned elsewhere. The point is arguable and will be taken up separately.[1] A further element added to these rules of the second week is temporal in the sense that we must look to the historical ends toward which consolations may lead us. As Buckley (1973) notes, "The introduction of evil into good is subtle and slow, carried on over a gradual devolution [SE332]. For this reason, one must attend to the process itself as well as to the first moment of consolation. It is no longer enough to know how to deal with attractions towards the good by analysis of the entire beginning, middle, and end" (p. 32). Even the first moment of CSCP must be distinguished from the period following after it (Buckley 1973).

We can also observe that the rules for discernment provide a schema of interpretation enabling the exercitant to gain a sense of meaning and relevance in the flow of his experiences. The parallels here to the psychoanalytic process are noteworthy — especially in the aspects of the structure of the Exercises that might induce a degree of regression in the exercitant with the emergence of thoughts and feelings that he must reflect on and bring into some form of meaningful psychic resolution and integration. The interpretive resources of the rules for discernment are an important facilitating framework for helping him to accomplish this purpose. The role of the director as the facilitator of interpretations thus becomes central to the process. Here the factors contributing to consolidation of the alliance between exercitant and director, and the interplay of transference dimensions, enjoy a powerful determining role in the degree to which the interpretive potential of the rules for discernment can be realized. For the most part, the literature on the *Exercises* makes the transference relation to God a primary focus; there is a tendency to underestimate or even ignore the role of the director and the position he holds as the immediate focus of transference dynamics.

[1] See below, pp. 277-284.

[328] RULES FOR THE SAME EFFECT WITH GREATER DISCERNMENT OF SPIRITS

And They Help More for the Second Week

[329] Rule I:

The first: It is proper to God and to His Angels in their movements to give true spiritual gladness and joy, taking away all sadness and disturbance which the enemy brings on. Of this latter it is proper to fight against the spiritual gladness and consolation, bringing apparent reasons, subtleties and continual fallacies.

For the ego engaged in the process of spiritual growth, this enunciates the general rule for discernment and is substantially the same norm laid down in rule II of the first week [SE315]. As observed there, consolation derives from increasing integration of self-systems and their conformity with internalized values of the spiritual order; conversely, desolation will stem from disruption of that process by drive resistances, or disjunctions within the ego between certain of its subsystems (intrasystemic conflicts), or from impositions from the side of the superego (intersystemic conflicts). It is primarily with exceptions to this general rule that the rules of the second week are concerned. Discernment becomes more complex — the evil spirit can induce consolation that leads deceptively to desolation, or mislead advancing souls in other subtle ways.

[330] Rule II:

Second Rule. The second: It belongs to God our Lord to give consolation to the soul without preceding cause, for it is the property of the Creator to enter, go out and cause movements in the soul, bringing it all into love of His Divine Majesty. I say without cause: without any previous sense or knowledge of any object through which such consolation would come, through one's acts of understanding and will.

Ignatius introduces a distinction here that has become a *cause celebre* for Ignatian interpreters, particularly with reference to its implications for Ignatian mysticism. The distinction is between "consolation with preceding cause" (*consolatio cum causa praevia* — CCCP) and "consolation without preceding cause" (*consolatio sine causa praevia* — CSCP). I will argue that, where consolation arises with no preceding cause in the conscious order, the effect must be presumed psychologically to have unconscious determinants. Consequently, the operation of grace in this instance would presumably exercise its effect through the unconscious. As I would read Ignatius' usage here, he seems to be referring explicitly to conscious preceding causes. Commentators on the *Exercises* often write as though the unconscious either did not exist or had no consequential role to play in the dynamics of the Exercises. Egan (1976), for example, commented, "Essential to the inner rhythm and dynamics of the Exercises is the exercitant's radical return to himself as subject, the active disposition of his entire person, his creative self-presence, his presence to his own deepest mystery as man, a self-presence which sums up, concentrates and fulfills the expectations of his own created self-transcendence to surrender itself to loving Mystery in Jesus Christ" (p. 66). Without gainsaying this perspective, we must add that unconscious dynamics are at work within this idealized schema, whether congruently with the deepest and most authentic spiritual desires, or acting with impeding or interfering effect on the basis of Ignatius' inordinate desires or underlying unknown and unheeded defensive needs.[2]

> [331] Rule III:
> Third Rule. The third: With cause, as well the good Angel as the bad can console the soul, for contrary ends: the good Angel for the profit of the soul, that it may grow and rise from good to better, and the evil Angel, for the contrary, and later on to draw it to his damnable intention and wickedness.

This is the first refinement on the general rule of discernment in consolation and desolation (rule I) — the evil spirit can produce consolation as well as the good. In psychological terms, such false consolation may reflect the fact that persistent instinctual resistance or formation of an instinctual attachment can take a form closely enough adapted to the contemporaneous functioning of the ego that the basic disjunction between the resistance and/or attachment and the internalized objectives of the ego is not immediately apparent.[3] Under such circumstances, the integral functioning of the ego is not disturbed and the ego would then experience consolation; only when the disparity is recognized can the issue be joined effectively. The norm of judgment for the ego remains inherent in its reality orientation. Such false consolation carries some analogous connotations to positive transference acting as a resistance in psychoanalysis. In such a circumstance, the patient seems involved and positively engaged in the analytic work, but this serves only to mask an underlying resistance rooted in his positive attachment to the analyst. What seems to be positive turns out to be negative.

[2] For a more extended discussion of this difference in perspectives, see my contrapuntal contretemps with Egan's arguments rejecting any role for the unconscious in the CSCP (Meissner 1992b, chapter XX). The question is taken up more at length below in this chapter.

[3] Such an attachment would be ego-syntonic.

> [332] Rule IV:
> Fourth Rule. The fourth: It is proper to the evil Angel, who forms himself under the appearance of an angel of light, to enter with the devout soul and go out with himself: that is to say, to bring good and holy thoughts, conformable to such just soul, and then little by little he aims at coming out drawing the soul to his covert deceits and perverse intentions.

Substantially the same point as in rule III. The dividing line between authentic ego-control and realignment of the drives to avoid open conflict with the ego should be observed. The drives are capable of considerable modification to ego demands, thus giving the appearance of real ego-control; this superficial placation may, however, mask gratification at another level or in terms of a substitute object. The guiding norm for the ego must remain the internalized value system by which its spiritual growth is regulated.

Ignatius fosters a high degree of introspection and attention to inner affective and cognitive states. The rules for discernment are acutely attuned to and dependent on the retreatant's capacity to recognize and interpret these inner states of mind. The exercitant is not only directed to identify specific states of mind, but also to recognize patterns in the progression of thoughts and feelings — as is evident in the next rule. But this was a capacity Ignatius himself had to develop through difficult and at times wrenching experience. That an impulse could first manifest itself as consolation and later stand revealed as deceptive and undermining of spiritual progress undoubtedly reflected his own experience — possibly at Manresa in many forms. One that he specifically tells us about was the vision of the serpent — at first immensely consoling, and later discerned to be from the evil spirit.[4] Similar discernments evidently played a role in his determination that his intense devotion and experiencing of spiritual insights were deceptive in that they distracted him from his studies. His insight here was further articulated in a letter to Salmeron and Broet in 1541 describing the tactics of the enemy:

> He enters through the other's door and comes out his own. He enters with the other by not opposing his ways but by praising them. He acts familiarly with the soul, suggesting good and holy thoughts which bring peace to the good soul. Later he tries, little by little, to come out his own door, always suggesting some error or illusion under the appearance of good, but which will always be evil (Epistolae I, 179-181 [Letter 32]; in Young (1959), p. 51-52).

[4] See the discussion of this vision and its psychological implications in chapters XXXV and XXXVI below.

> [333] Rule V:
> Fifth Rule. The fifth: We ought to note well the course of the thoughts, and if the beginning, middle and end is all good, inclined to all good, it is a sign of the good Angel; but if in the course of the thoughts which he brings it ends in something bad, of a distracting tendency, or less good than what the soul had previously proposed to do, or if it weakens it or disquiets or disturbs the soul, taking away its peace, tranquility and quiet, which it had before, it is a clear sign that it proceeds from the evil spirit, enemy of our profit and eternal salvation.

Ignatius proposes here the basic norm for discernment and the orientation of the ego in dealing with subtleties of the various forms of resistance. The self, which is growing spiritually and gaining in a sense of spiritual identity, can be expected to experience consolation as long as it continues uninterruptedly on that course and continues to grow. Such growth involves the ever increasing development and integration of resources of the ego and a constantly improved organization and synthesis of self-systems. The self, as it were, feeds on the realities of the spiritual order, known through revelation and the inspiration of grace; internalizes the value system inherent in that order of reality; and through a subsequent and continually renewed synthesis, grows in spiritual identity. Consequently, that system of values must remain definitive for its progress and growth. Any deviation from it, therefore, even if it is cloaked in the guise of consolation, must be regarded as detracting from authentic spiritual growth and as stemming from forces opposed to the development of the self.

Fessard (1956, 1966) noted the extent to which Ignatius appealed to both intellectual and affective criteria in detecting motivations that might be less good — the choice is not between good and evil, but between the less good and the better. The values involved are not simply objective, but pertain to a subjective evaluation involving different meanings or paths of progression — from a less good past to a better future, or from a better past to a less good future. Ignatius' distrust of reliance on intellectualization — vulnerable as he thought it to be to self-deception or self-serving — shows through here. He was more inclined to put his trust in affects which he regarded as the locus of movements of the spirits. The psychoanalytic perspective might seek to balance this appraisal by a greater degree of caution with respect to affects and their potential for misleading.

There is a certain analogy here to the process of free association in analysis. The analysand is encouraged to follow the flow of his thoughts and/or feelings wherever they may lead. The fuller and more amplified meaning of the patient's experience becomes more evident as the picture evolves and a broader range of associations come into play. Ignatius' "wait-and-see" recommendation has similar merit, especially when discernment is uncertain and the subtleties of the experiential currents more complex. To do otherwise would not only not serve the purposes of discernment, but could at times be spiritually or psychologically deleterious (Toner 1989).

> [334] Rule VI:
> Sixth Rule. The sixth: When the enemy of human nature has been perceived and known by his serpent's tail and the bad end to which he leads on, it helps the person who was tempted by him, to look immediately at the course of the good thoughts which he brought him at their beginning and how little by little he aimed at making him descend from the spiritual sweetness and joy in which he was, so far as to bring him to his depraved intention; in order that with this experience, known and noted, the person may be able to guard for the future against his usual deceits.

Ignatius places great value on the capacity of the ego to reflexively analyze its own operations, at least those on the conscious level. It is more than likely that future manifestations of resistance will follow a more or less similar course, and that they will appeal to the same needs and drives appealed to in the previous case. The ego can only profit from careful analysis of this process, since it gains thereby in self-knowledge and humility. The process described here echoes Ignatius' experience at Loyola and Manresa, and his own personal history of deceptions and missteps along the way. Reflection on experience thus gives one a more secure grasp of the process and his ability to evaluate it.

> [335] Rule VII:
> Seventh Rule. The seventh: In those who go on from good to better, the good Angel touches such soul sweetly, lightly and gently, like a drop of water which enters into a sponge; and the evil touches it sharply and with noise and disquiet, as when the drop of water falls on the stone.
>
> And the above-said spirits touch in a contrary way those who go on from bad to worse.
>
> The reason of this is that the disposition of the soul is contrary or like to the said Angels. Because, when it is contrary, they enter perceptibly with clatter and noise; and when it is like, they enter with silencing as into their own home, through the open door.

When the drives are operating with little restraint, the interference and countercathectic activity of the ego disrupts the situation and creates intrapsychic conflict and even, as we have seen (rule I of first week [SE314]), desolation. The continuation of instinctual gratification, however, would create no conflict and no disruption. Conversely, when the ego has established a fairly extensive control over instinctual impulses and self-systems are functioning integrally, the interference of drive forces or demands will have a disruptive effect, even possible desolation (rule II of first week [SE315]).

> [336] Rule VIII:
> Eighth Rule. The eighth: When the consolation is without cause, although there be no deceit in it, as being of God our Lord alone, as was said: still the spiritual person to whom God gives such consolation, ought, with much vigilance and attention, to look at and distinguish from the following, in which the soul remains warm and favored with the favor and remnants of the consolation past; for often in this second time, through one's own course of habits and the consequences of the concepts and judgments, or through the good spirit or through the bad, he forms various resolutions and opinions which are not given immediately by God our Lord, and therefore they have need to be very well examined before entire credit is given them, or they are put into effect.

Ignatius offers here a cautionary note that we are well advised to keep in mind regarding the CSCP. There is a tendency on the part of some interpreters to view the CSCP as though it were its own validation, that the experience is such that it can be accepted without hesitation or question as coming from God and as moving the soul toward fulfilling God's will. Ignatius here makes it clear, however, that even the CSCP should not escape discernment and should be subjected to careful scrutiny before any significant action is taken, to be more certain that the proposed course of action be in keeping with spiritual growth and fulfilling God's will. The question of how to interpret CSCP from a more explicitly psychological perspective remains pressing and demands our attention.

## CONSOLATION WITHOUT PREVIOUS CAUSE (CSCP)

Rule II [SE330] presents the idea of the CSCP, according to which God alone acts on the soul to give it consolation. Thus God and God alone can enter the soul and convert its love into a total love of God Himself. Although the idea does not occupy a large place in the *Ex-*

*ercises*, it is significant nonetheless.[5] It is also a view that Ignatius espoused repeatedly throughout his life — it occurs, for example, in the letter to Teresa Rejadell[6] and in his *Spiritual Journal*.[7]

In considering Ignatius thoughts regarding CSCP, we run into a thicket of troublesome questions. Toner (1982) has summarized these quite conveniently:

> Does it differ from consolation with preceding cause intrinsically or only extrinsically? That is, does it differ by reason of some features in the content of the experience or only by its mode of originating? If the difference is intrinsic, is the cognitive element in the consolation conceptual or non-conceptual? If non-conceptual, is it mystical in the strict sense of the word? Does it bear within itself an objective guarantee of its immediate origination from God alone, without any created mediation? Is there a subjective certitude in the recipient that it does so originate and is an experience of God? Can there be any divine communication about a created object during such consolation, for example, about something which God wills the person to do? Do the answers about the cognitive side of the experience and about the description which Ignatius gives of the affective side allow for its being a frequent, even relatively ordinary, experience of good Christian life, or is it a rare experience of a few persons? What is its relation to consolation with preceding cause? What role does it play in discernment of spirits? and then, in discernment of God's will? (p. 291)

I will touch on nearly all of these questions in the ensuing discussion.

Ignatius' distinction between CCCP and CSCP has become a focal point for discussion and controversy ever since he proposed the ideas. He pointed out two differences: (1) that one form of consolation arises from preceding acts of the person, while the other does not, and (2) that CSCP can come only and immediately from God. The differences are concerned with origin of the consolation and do not indicate any difference in the nature of the consolation. Interpreters have split over the question of whether the nature of the consolation might be different — does the consolation coming directly from God differ from that from any created source, whether the person himself or other sources? For some such an intrinsic difference is implied, and for others not. With regard to the first difference, the

[5] Major commentators on the *Exercises* regard CSCP as the essential and fundamental experience of the effects of grace in the Exercises — including Cusson (1988), Egan (1976), Fessard (1956, 1966), Gil (1971), Przywara (1938-1939), H. Rahner (1968), and K. Rahner (1964).

[6] See the discussion of this letter in chapter XXXIII below.

[7] See the discussion of the *Journal* in chapter XXXIV below.

key issue for our purposes is whether the consolation can count unconscious motives among its determining sources or not. For Ignatius, it seems clear that the preceding cause is not any separate agent acting on the person to produce consolation (good or evil spirit), but rather some antecedent conscious activity on the part of the subject effecting the consolation. But Ignatius had no concept of the unconscious as we might understand it psychoanalytically. Does that leave open the possibility that, at least in CCCP, if not in CSCP, unconscious determinants might contribute to the experience?

The problem becomes a bit more complex with regard to the CSCP. Here such preceding causes are eliminated, so that the sole source of consolation is God himself acting on the soul. Does this eliminate unconscious motivations? I will argue that it does not, that because Ignatius knew nothing of unconscious causality he was left with a dichotomy of conscious or divine causality. On his terms, if a preceding cause was recognized, there remained an ambiguity as to its cause — God alone, a good spirit, or even an evil spirit. But if it was experienced as a CSCP, then there was no doubt — the cause was God alone and nothing else (Toner 1982). This leaves open the possibility that CSCP may reflect unconscious influences, whether or not God is active in causing them, but it also leaves open the possibility that when they occur God is an active agent operating in the soul through grace. Even in this latter instance, however, God's direct action through grace does not bypass the nature of the creature and the order of secondary causes. The influence of grace psychologically may have its effects on an unconscious or conscious level. This latter question can only be resolved in terms of a more developed psychology of grace — an effort that lies beyond the scope of this work.[8]

One view of CSCP makes it a first principle for any spiritual discernment or discernment of God's will — primarily Rahner and Egan. Rahner (1964, 1977) essentially recast the place of CSCP in Ignatian spirituality in his view of the existential logic of the *Exercises*. He wrote: "This consolation is nothing other than the clear awareness of man's free, grace-elevated transcendentality which has not been distorted by any categorical object. . . . one should certainly not evaluate this "consolation without previous cause" as a singular mystical phenomenon open only to a select few, but as the foundation and highpoint of "normal" Christian life" (1976, p. xv). Following Rahner's lead, Egan (1976) extended the transcendental theology of Ignatian discernment to its implications for Ignatian mysti-

[8] My best effort to articulate such a psychology can be found in Meissner (1987).

cism, and offered the thesis that CSCP is fundamental to the Christian experience of grace and the basis for a mysticism of everyday life. As he puts it, "Because the CSCP is the pure openness of subjective transcendence which draws the exercitant wholly into God's love, it contains *within itself* the evidence of its divine origin. . . . The CSCP, therefore, cannot in itself be measured or tested, but provides in itself the basic measure against which all other consolations are to be measured" (p. 43). Toner (1982) takes an opposite tack, pointing out that, if such was Ignatius' intention, he did not indicate it in rule VIII and in rule V seems to accept CCCP as a reliable sign of the spirit as long as there is no sign of the influence of the evil spirit — especially in the afterglow.[9] Even an experience of CSCP can lead one into deception in the time immediately after the actual consolation. So Ignatius is careful to make the distinction between actual consolation and the period following on it, since the actual consolation remains open to many *post factum* influences coming from a variety of sources other than God. By implication, thoughts and intentions may be given by God in the consolation itself and that these can be accepted without subjecting them to the usual tests involved in discernment.[10]

Ignatius puts great reliance here on the quality of the experience, since it is only in experience that discrimination between CCCP and CSCP lies. But he does not tell us what that experience is, that is, he does not give us any sense of what it is about the experience that would discriminate it from CCCP — other than a lack of awareness of any preceding cause. If the discrimination rests on this slender reed, acknowledging that Ignatius had no concept of unconscious causes, it seems problematical to attribute the certitude and lack of

[9] Toner also indicates that he finds no evidence in Ignatius' writings to support Rahner's view of CSCP as a first principle of all discernment, and that there are numerous indications that effective discernment is possible, probably more frequently and ordinarily, without CSCP — a position with which I concur. Toner also points out that Ignatius gives no indication of the frequency of CSCP. The Rahner-Egan approach, leaning on CSCP as a first principle of all discernment, forces them into seeing it as a frequent component of Christian spirituality, a view not readily assimilable to the major effect of CSCP, being drawn so completely and totally into the love of God (Toner 1982). Rahner's effort to salvage this point by appealing to degrees of CSCP seems to dilute the experience to the point that his other stipulated characteristics of CSCP pale into insignificance, i.e. how can a low degree CSCP retain all the qualities of certitude, total absorption in love of God, and so on, that the basic thesis requires?

[10] Rahner (1964) discounts any communication regarding any created reality during the CSCP; Egan (1976) opts for such communication.

deception to it that he does. Toner (1982) raises the question, but does not answer it. In his view, Ignatius neither asserts nor denies such certitude, and since we are not sure about what goes on in CSCP beyond a total love for God, we can make no reliable conjecture.[11] Ignatius himself warns about deceptions arising afterwards [SE336] which require careful scrutiny and discernment. But nowhere does he question deception in the CSCP itself.

Ignatius regarded CSCP as an effect of grace (rule II [SE330]), and nothing else. Egan (1976) sees this text as stating "the unequivocally and exclusively divine nature of this consolation," and concludes: "The CSCP, therefore, is not simply one consolation among many, but *the* God-given consolation. Only God, and He alone, can and does console in this precise way" (p. 33).[12] From a psychoanalytic perspective, this is an assumption that is at least questionable, since the effect could be attributed to purely natural causes working through unconscious motivation. The understanding of the dynamics of grace need not exclude a conjunction with and assimilation of natural psychic resources, including the unconscious (Meissner 1987). If we could maintain that consolation without any known cause was a product of grace, we should still be able to interpret the action of grace as producing its effect through unconscious processes. Ignatius was skilled enough in dealing with intrapsychic dynamics to realize that, even granted the operation of grace, there was wide scope for the operation of other psychological determinants. Due to the subtle patterns of resistance, then, such periods of consolation need careful scrutiny, particularly when under the influence of such consolation the ego makes certain resolutions for future external action.

In the Rahner-Egan transcendental theology of CSCP, the natural openness of human consciousness to transcendental elevation (supernatural transcendence) is the cornerstone of their thinking. Supernatural transcendence makes CSCP possible insofar as it makes

[11] An opposite tack is taken by Gil (1971) who rejects any differentiation between CCCP and CSCP on the basis of the awareness of God, whether conceptual or nonconceptual, mystical or nonmystical, and looks to something extrinsic and antecedent to the consolation. For him, contrary to Rahner, absolute certainty is impossible, so that only a degree of prudential judgment can be reached. This leaves open the question whether causality of CSCP is divine or psychic, i.e. unconscious.

[12] The preceding cause in this text has been interpreted as meaning without any conceptual object (Rahner 1964), or without any created cause (de Tonquedec 1953), or without any sort of created operation, even unconscious (Peeters 1931). Clemence (1951- 1952), however, opines that a psychological phenomenon that is neither conscious nor unconscious seems unthinkable, if not contradictory.

this transcendence explicit as the center of consciousness and as a function of supernatural elevation through grace. Human intellect and will are directed toward God as the goal of natural transcendence, so that, in effect, God is always implicitly present as the horizon of consciousness. In every act of knowing and loving, the human spirit has a vague awareness of God as its term, and it is this natural transcendence that is elevated to the supernatural through grace. This awareness is not conceptual but existential, so that "the concrete, unique, intrinsic orientation toward God which constitutes the innermost essence of man" (Rahner 1964, pp. 160-161) becomes conscious and therefore is no longer simply implied as the horizon of consciousness. For Egan (1976), movement from conceptual transparency to transcendental awareness results in "an inexpressible non-conceptual experience of his Christ-affected and supernaturally elevated transcendence" (p. 40) which is synonymous with CSCP.

The conceptual experience thus transcended is equivalent to CCCP experienced during meditations on the life of Christ, as in the *Exercises*. This allows for a shift from CCCP to CSCP and renders the christocentric orientation of human transcendence thematic and conscious. This shift can take place only when the meditative CCCP becomes transparent of supernatural transcendence. But this movement is often difficult to recognize and to distinguish CCCP from a bonafide CSCP. One criterion Egan suggests is discrepancy between the intensity of the experience of being drawn into God's love and whatever consolation is desired or expected from the given exercise. We cannot fail to be impressed by the extent to which the discernment process, following Ignatius' lead, hinges on subjective experience and affectivity.

Egan's (1976) stance is more accommodating to psychological perspectives than Rahner's rather apodictic claim that the CSCP carries an inherent certitude of its divine origin and is thus irreducibly self-evident.[13] Egan makes the helpful clarification that CSCP is certain to be *objectively* from God, but the recipient's *subjective* experience may be open to a wide variety of certainty or doubt depending on the quality of the consolation and the subject's capacity for discernment. As Egan (1976) put it:

[13] This line of thinking is followed by Coathelem (1971), who also declares CSCP to be a mystical experience — Rahner (1964) would take a more conservative line allowing CSCP in lower degrees that need not be mystical. For Coathelem, every spiritual consolation has mystical overtones, a view that puts it beyond the range of common Christian experience and, therefore, cannot serve as a basic principle of all Ignatian discernment.

> We maintain, therefore, that the CSCP offers the exercitant a supernatural first principle for the application of a supernatural logic to find God's Will. This first principle, moreover, is *objectively* certain, because this consolation flows from God alone. Because the CSCP, however, is rarely given in an absolutely pure state and always maintains itself in a dialectical relationship with the CCCP and the time-after consolations, it renders only a *greater or lesser subjective* evidence, depending upon the exercitant's maturity, the depth and quality of the CSCP, and the exercitant's own gifts for discernment. (p. 45)

The psychological perspective would have to go even further to say that, if we can acknowledge the claim that the consolation may be objectively from God, there is no subjective experience that can validate that claim. We simply do not, and cannot, know. Any claim that a given CSCP is both objectively and subjectively certain cannot be sustained.[14] Subjective experience of CSCP is not so qualitatively different from that of CCCP that one can be certain of the difference, and in neither case does the quality of the experience exceed the range of potential psychic experience.

The issue for our psychoanalytic reflection is whether the unconscious plays any role in this process. We must remind ourselves that the issue of transcendental subjectivity and supernatural elevation are subjects beyond the scope of analytic competence. They are theological issues which the psychologist can only accept through faith or reject, and, if he accepts, respect. Nonetheless, speaking of the transcendental horizon of human consciousness, Egan (1976) wrote:

> Because this horizon usually remains horizon, it is not one object among the many objects of our consciousness. Overlooked, denied or often confused with the unconscious, this supernaturally elevated horizon does not ordinarily emerge into express, thematic consciousness. Implicit, however, to the experience of self always concomitantly present to all conceptual knowing is a simple grasp of God as the Whither of transcendental subjectivity and as the Ground of the active self-identity of one's own spirit. (p. 39)

Theologians may argue the transcendental thesis, but I have no grounds for doing so. I would note, however, that the horizon concept lies very close to and is entirely compatible with an understanding of the unconscious. Egan properly notes that the transcendental horizon should not be confused with the unconscious, but they may also be compatible and noncontradictory. But, I might also argue,

[14] This assertion, which I would regard as a psychological given, would tend to undercut Rahner's position and Egan's refinement of it.

that if there is such an existential transcendental horizon of human consciousness, it may well have its influence on the human unconscious and that it might even conceivably serve as a mediating conjunction between the action of grace on one hand and the psychological effects of grace on the other. This would offer some ground for sustaining a hypothesis that one possible effect of grace psychologically comes through its influence on the unconscious.[15]

## Desolation and the Dark Night

A particular case in which Ignatius' rules for discernment encounter a significant degree of complexity is the relation between spiritual desolation and the so-called "dark night of the soul" described so vividly by John of the Cross and other mystics. The painful aridity, darkness of mind, anxiety, and the feeling of abandonment and separation from God fit the Ignatian formula for spiritual desolation, but the dark night is a path through which the Spirit guides those who are straining toward the heights of mystical experience. It would clearly seem to be a case of spiritual desolation drawing the soul closer to God. In Ignatian terms, we would have to acknowledge the possibility of the good spirit as the agent of spiritual desolation — the counterpoise to the role of the evil spirit as the agent of spiritual consolation in the rules for discernment [SE331, 332]. This latter possibility is not considered by Ignatius in any of his rules. Consideration of the dark night calls for a more sophisticated understanding of the rules for discernment (Toner 1989).

The desolation of the dark night in a sense goes beyond Ignatian desolation, coming at a highly advanced stage of spiritual development and not in relation to the influence of the evil spirit. Thus it is a form of desolation not considered by Ignatius, although it seems clear from his own mystical experiences that he was no stranger to it. In St. John's terms, the dark night is a form of purification to which the soul is subjected in drawing near to the mystical union. The pain induced in this state is involved in the discipline required to purge the soul of the last residues of narcissistic self-investment and egoism and any remnants of sensual attachment. The pain of this purification may be alloyed with elements of spiritual consolation, of joy in

[15] This issue touches on the dichotomous logic of posing the question of the relation of grace and psychological processes, including the unconscious processes, in terms of divine as opposed to psychic causality. For an extended discussion of this issue, see Meissner (1992b), especially the responses to Egan's (1976) usefully articulated refutations of the role of the unconscious in chapter XX.

the conquering of self and the sense of intense love of God and openness to His grace. John's directives for enduring this purgation, particularly in his *Ascent of Mt. Carmel*, are not dissimilar to Ignatius' thrust in the *Spiritual Exercises*.

John describes an infusion of divine light independent of any effort of the subject and leading to his illumination and an increase in faith, hope and charity. This is a form of infused contemplation filling the soul with love and deepened understanding — the soul is entirely passive in this experience. One cannot help but be reminded of Ignatius' intense illuminations at Manresa and on the bank of the Cardoner. This illumination is called "dark night" paradoxically in that the illumination exceeds the capacity for human understanding and it afflicts and torments the soul. While this desolation bears certain similarities to Ignatius desolation, the differences are marked. The illumination in John is both painful and oppressive or joyful and enlightening depending on how it is received and the condition of the soul receiving it.

The increase in theological virtues in the dark night attains an extraordinary level — a level that can be attained only by one who has passed through the active night of the sense and of the spirit to achieve a deep understanding of theological mysteries and docility to the Holy Spirit. Any effort at active cooperation with these movements is insignificant or can be counterproductive. The soul can only passively submit to movements of the spirit which become all-encompassing.

John describes an increase of "esteeming love" for God which he distinguishes from "burning" or passionate love — a valuing of God above all creatures and an urgent longing for God along with a willingness to suffer anything for the love of God. To this can be added a passionate spiritual love resembling but quite different from sensual love. This love becomes all-encompassing so that all human appetites are absorbed in it and God is loved completely with mind, heart, soul and strength. There is a sense of presence that strengthens, but without satisfaction, and brings with it a tormented sense of frustrated longing for the beloved. During early stages of purification, during the dark night, this torment cannot be borne for long, but serves to prepare the soul for the greater purification to come in mystical infusion and contemplation. This purgation draws the soul on to the final stage of mystical illumination, an experience of union with God that is immensely enlightening and enriching. It seems more than likely that Ignatius' efforts to describe his mystical experience both in his *Autobiography* and in his *Spiritual Journal* reflect similar experiences at Manresa and later in Rome.

However, in Ignatius' descriptions of spiritual desolation, the anti-spiritual aspect with overtones of separation from God and increasing discouragement seems to predominate. The overlap with John's description of negative aspects of the dark night is evident. But John's account is more complex. The torment in the dark night is induced by the sense of presence, more promised than fulfilled, so that it is the sense of frustrated longing and unfulfilled desire that gives rise to dysphoric affects. The closeness of the beloved object, along with the need for greater purification and purgation, creates a sense of inflamed yet unassuaged desire — this is the note that Ignatius leaves out. Whatever illumination the soul experiences, it pales in the face of its aroused but unsatisfied desire, so that all seems darkness and the absence of God predominates over the presence.

Given these points of similarity and difference, I would appeal to the comparative psychology of these great mystics to explain the contrast. John is one of the main exponents of the idea of mystical union and the loving embrace of the mystical marriage as enunciated in the Canticle of Canticles. This element is entirely lacking in Ignatius, whose mystical rhetoric is cast in the language of loving service rather than mystical union. The contrast is clear in rule six of the first week [SE319] where the typical Ignatian attitude is displayed — he prefers the active path of exercising himself in the effort to overcome desolation by greater spiritual effort, in the spirit of the *agere contra*. This is entirely alien to John, whose recommendation to the soul in the dark night counsels passivity, quiet, waiting patiently in the darkness of faith and hope for God to make himself known. There are perhaps essential elements of psychological disposition differentiating kataphatic and apophatic mysticism and finding expression in the differential approaches to the mystical mountain and to mystical experience in two of the greatest mystics in Christendom. I have no doubt that both experienced something quite similar in the peak moments of their mystical ascent, but that their capacities to describe the experience and the metaphors available to them for thinking about it differed as a function of their respective psychological orientations.

# CHAPTER XVII

# VARIOUS RULES

Ignatius introduces several series of "rules" dealing with various aspects of spiritual and ascetical practice. Rather than "rules," they are meant to be practical and prudent directives or recommendations — largely based on Ignatius personal experience. The "rules" pertain to eating, that is to say fasting, distributing alms, understanding scruples, and finally for thinking with the church.

## Rules for Eating [SE210-217]

[210] RULES TO PUT ONESELF IN ORDER FOR THE FUTURE AS TO EATING]
First Rule. The first rule is that it is well to abstain less from bread, because it is not a food as to which the appetite is used to act so inordinately, or to which temptation urges as in the case of the other foods.
[211] Second Rule. The second: Abstinence appears more convenient as to drinking, than as to eating bread. So, one ought to look much what is helpful to him, in order to admit it, and what does him harm, in order to discard it.
[212] Third Rule. The third: As to foods, one ought to have the greatest and most entire abstinence, because as the appetite is more ready to act inordinately, so temptation is more ready in making trial, on this head.[1] And so abstinence in foods, to avoid disorder, can be kept in two ways, one by accustoming oneself to eat coarse foods; the other, if one takes delicate foods, by taking them in small quantity.
[213] Fourth Rule. The fourth: Guarding against falling into sickness, the more a man leaves off from what is suitable, the more quickly he will reach the mean which he ought to keep in his eating and drinking; for two reasons: the first, because by so help-

[1] This rule enunciates a time-honored ascetical practice, often carried to extremes in the live of the great saints, including Ignatius (Meissner 1992b). There is reason to suspect pathological influences on such practices, at least in some cases, e.g. St. Wilgefortis (Lacey 1982; Parry-Jones 1985) and St Catherine of Siena (Rampling 1985) may have involved forms of anorexia nervosa. Ignatius suggests moderation rather than extremes.

ing and disposing himself, he will many times experience more the interior knowledge, consolations and Divine inspirations to show him the mean which is proper for him; the second, because if the person sees himself in such abstinence not with so great corporal strength or disposition for the Spiritual Exercises, he will easily come to judge what is more suitable to his bodily support.

[214] Fifth Rule. The fifth: While the person is eating, let him consider as if he saw Christ our Lord eating with His Apostles, and how He drinks and how He looks and how He speaks; and let him see to imitating Him. So that the principal part of the intellect shall occupy itself in the consideration of Christ our Lord, and the lesser part in the support of the body; because in this way he will get greater system and order as to how he ought to behave and manage himself.

[215] Sixth Rule. The sixth: Another time, while he is eating, he can take another consideration, either on the life of Saints, or on some pious Contemplation, or on some spiritual affair which he has to do, because, being intent on such thing, he will take less delight and feeling in the corporal food.

[216] Seventh Rule. The seventh: Above all, let him guard against all his soul being intent on what he is eating, and in eating let him not go hurriedly, through appetite, but be master of himself, as well in the manner of eating as in the quantity which he eats.

[217] Eighth Rule. The eighth: To avoid disorder, it is very helpful, after dinner or after supper, or at another hour when one feels no appetite for eating, to decide with oneself for the coming dinner or supper, and so on, each day, the quantity which it is suitable that he should eat. Beyond this let him not go because of any appetite or temptation, but rather, in order to conquer more all inordinate appetite and temptation of the enemy, if he is tempted to eat more. Let him eat less.

Throughout these rules, the institution and maintenance of ego control over eating behaviors and appetite is evident. Ignatius aims at mastery over appetites and regulation of inordinate desires. Important to insist that these rules are not meant as guidelines for dieting, but are intended as guides for deriving spiritual benefit from regulation of eating habits.

## DISTRIBUTING ALMS [SE337-344]

[337] IN THE MINISTRY OF DISTRIBUTING ALMS

The Following Rules Should be Kept

First Rule. The first: If I make the distribution to relatives or friends, or to persons for whom I have an affection, I shall have four things to see to, of which mention was made, in part, in the matter of Election.

[338] The first is, that that love which moves me and makes me give the alms, should descend from above, from the love of God our Lord, so that I feel first in me that the love, more or less, which I have to such persons is for God; and that in the reason why I love them more, God appears.

[339] Second Rule. The second: I want to set before me a man whom I have never seen or known, and desiring all his perfection in the ministry and condition which he has, as I would want him to keep the mean in his manner of distributing, for the greater glory of God our Lord and the greater perfection of his soul; I, doing so, neither more nor less, will keep the rule and measure which I should want and judge to be right for the other.

[340] Third Rule. The third: I want to consider as if I were at the point of death, the form and measure which then I should want to have kept in the office of my administration, and regulating myself by that, to keep it in the acts of my distribution.

[341] Fourth Rule. The fourth: Looking how I shall find myself on the Day of Judgment, to think well how then I should want to have used this office and charge of administration; and the rule which then I should want to have kept, to keep it now.

[342] Fifth Rule. The fifth: When some person feels himself inclined and drawn to some persons to whom he wants to distribute alms, let him hold himself back and ponder well the above-mentioned four Rules, examining and testing his affection by them; and not give the alms until, conformably to them, he has in all dismissed and cast out his disordered inclination.

[343] Sixth Rule. The sixth: Although there is no fault in taking the goods of God our Lord to distribute them, when the person is called by God our Lord to such ministry; still in the quantity of what he has to take and apply to himself out of what he has to give to others, there may be doubt as to fault and excess. Therefore, he can reform in his life and condition by the above-mentioned Rules.

[344] Seventh Rule. The seventh: For the reasons already mentioned and for many others it is always better and more secure in what touches one's person and condition of life to spare more and diminish and approach more to our High Priest, our model and rule, who is Christ our Lord; conformably to what the third Council of Carthage, in which St. Augustine was, determines and orders — that the furniture of the Bishop be cheap and poor. The same should be considered in all manners of life, looking at and deciding according to the condition and state of the persons; as in married life we have the example of St. Joachim and of St. Ann, who, dividing their means into three parts, gave the first to the poor, and the second to the ministry and service of the Temple,

and took the third for the support of themselves and of their household.

These norms were intended for a more privileged group of exercitants possessing wealth and resources beyond the ordinary, especially those with certain responsibilities toward the poor stemming from ecclesiastical benefices or inheritance. The basis for decisions in sharing such wealth reflect the value-orientation of the *Exercises* and the mind of Ignatius. These same principles found their way into the *Constitutions* in relation to matters concerning the vow and practice of poverty. Candidates for admission to the Society were to distribute all their temporal goods to the poor and to renounce and dispose of any they might receive [CS53, 54], even ecclesiastical benefices [CS59]. The same norm is applied to novices under the guidance of the superior [CS254].[2]

Uppermost in Ignatius' mind was the motivation with which such divestments were made. Alms given to churches or houses of the Society were accepted only on the basis of charity directed to the service of God [CS564], and when begging had to be done for support of the Society, contributions were to be sought only on the basis of love of God [CS569]. In cases where malfeasance was involved, as for example use of Society revenues for personal advantage, dismissal from office or even from the Society was the remedy [CS774]. This was especially the case when Society resources were diverted to relatives [CS776] — alms to needy or deserving relatives was one thing, illegitimate channeling of funds another.

## RULES FOR UNDERSTANDING SCRUPLES [SE345-351]

[345] THE FOLLOWING NOTES HELP TO PERCEIVE AND UNDERSTAND SCRUPLES
And Persuasions of our Enemy

These rules form an extension or application of the rules for discernment of spirits to the particular case of scrupulosity. Undoubtedly, here again we are dealing with the fruit of Ignatius' own experience and introspective analysis. His own scrupulosity came to a head during the terrible episodes of conscience which beset him during his stay at Manresa — probably from August to October of 1523 (de Guibert 1964). It is very likely, however, from what we know of Ignatius' own spirituality, even in his mature years, that it did not

[2] See the discussion of poverty in the Society in chapter XVIII and of Ignatius' deliberation on poverty in his *Spiritual Journal* in chapter XXXIV.

lack a certain quality of obsessiveness, suggesting at least that Ignatius was in some degree able to master his scrupulosity and obsessionality and bend it to the objectives of his spiritual growth, but that it was never completely eliminated.

> [346] Rule I:
>
> First Note. The first: They commonly call a scruple what proceeds from our own judgment and freedom: that is to say, when I freely decide that this is sin which is not sin, as when it happens that after some one has accidentally stepped on a cross of straw, he decides with his own judgment that he has sinned.
>
> This is properly an erroneous judgment and not a real scruple.

Distinction of scruple from erroneous judgment of conscience. The erroneous judgment makes a mistake, but is quite definite about it. The scrupulous conscience is unable to attain this level of decision. The example of stepping on a straw cross would be typical of a scrupulous conscience, but Ignatius' emphasis is on the distinction, not the example.

> [347] Rule II:
>
> Second Note. The second: After I have stepped on that cross, or after I have thought or said or done some other thing, there comes to me a thought from without that I have sinned, and on the other hand it appears to me that I have not sinned; still I feel disturbance in this: that is to say, in as much as I doubt and in as much as I do not doubt.
>
> That is a real scruple and temptation which the enemy sets.

Ignatius' description of a scruple. Scrupulosity implies fear and insecurity, endless doubt, magnification of trivialities, sometimes to the point where it constitutes real psychopathology. This type of behavior is usually ascribed to an overly severe superego which is self-punishing and demanding to the extent that it tends never to allow the demands of conscience to be satisfied, but continually afflicts the ego with doubts, hesitations, and anxieties that it has failed to conform to the moral norm. Thus, scrupulosity is often classified as a form of obsessive-compulsive neurosis. Scrupulosity, however, can occur in all degrees from the slightest to the most intense. Here again, we must remember that in the context of the *Exercises*, Ignatius is prescribing for normal persons who have, in fact, achieved a considerable degree of ego development. Ignatius puts his finger on the core elements of ambivalence, obsessional doubting, and undoing so characteristic of this form of pathology.

> [348] Rule III:
>
> Third Note. Third: The first scruple — of the first note — is much to be abhorred, because it is all error; but the second — of the second note — for some space of time is of no little profit to the soul which is giving itself to spiritual exercises; rather in great manner it purifies and cleanses such a soul, separating it much from all appearance of sin: according to that saying of Gregory: "It belongs to good minds to see a fault where there is no fault."

Ignatius observes that scrupulosity can be put to good advantage by the ego engaged in the work of the first week. The psychiatrist would hesitate to designate this form of scrupulosity as pathological. The behavior is scrupulous only in a general sense, implying attention to detail and careful examination of faults, etc. Since the situation in question is one in which the individual is presumed to have sufficient ego-strength, there is less of a problem in the operation of the superego. In these cases, the superego is sufficiently mature to support efforts of the ego rather than coming into conflict with them. As in any work requiring assiduous effort and attention to detail, a touch of compulsivity is helpful — as long as mastery of the situation is in the hands of the ego and the compulsivity (or in this case, scrupulosity) is being directed to the objectives of the ego. These theoretical considerations aside, the extent to which the individual can use this characteristic for spiritual growth is the central issue; in pathological scrupulosity the self is the victim of superego attacks so that any question of use is excluded. The subject is used by the drives and their derivatives, rather than being the active user.

> [349] Rule IV:
>
> Fourth Note. The fourth: The enemy looks much if a soul is gross or delicate, and if it is delicate, he tries to make it more delicate in the extreme, to disturb and embarrass it more. For instance, if he sees that a soul does not consent to either mortal sin or venial or any appearance of deliberate sin, then the enemy, when he cannot make it fall into a thing that appears sin, aims at making it make out sin where there is not sin, as in a word or very small thought.
>
> If the soul is gross, the enemy tries to make it more gross; for instance, if before it made no account of venial sins, he will try to have it make little account of mortal sins, and if before it made some account, he will try to have it now make much less or none.

The person, who is "gross" in Ignatius' terminology, is one whose ego is caught up in the struggle with drive-related impulses and has not sufficiently established ego-control over them, and whose superego is overly lax or permissive. The "delicate" person, on the other hand, is one whose ego has established a sufficient degree of control over instinctual forces so that it remains relatively independent of instinctual derivatives, yet not completely securely. The control tends to be more defensive than autonomous. Where ego-control is inadequate, the danger to spiritual growth lies in the direction of failure to establish adequate control and thereby permitting drive influences to gradually reassert themselves and strengthen their position. Where ego-control is more adequate, the danger is rather that the ego will become prey, not to impulses of the id, but to demands of the superego. These demands can begin by pursuing the disposition of the ego to follow the norm of morality; but it soon begins to extend that norm beyond that which is required by the dictates of reason or revelation. In either case — capitulation to drive impulses or to superego demands — that which is essential to spiritual growth, the autonomous and integral functioning of the ego, is compromised. The norm for the ego's functioning and development remains the reality-based-and-oriented criteria of reason. Deviation from this norm in either direction can be fatal. Thus, scrupulosity can become a danger for the ego which has attained a more advanced level of development. The extent to which it will become a real danger depends on the level of mature formation of the superego and the intensity of unresolved infantile conflicts underlying its punitive severity.

> [350] Rule V:
> Fifth Note. The fifth: The soul which desires to benefit itself in the spiritual life, ought always to proceed the contrary way to what the enemy proceeds; that is to say, if the enemy wants to make the soul gross, let it aim at making itself delicate. Likewise, if the enemy tries to draw it out to extreme fineness, let the soul try to establish itself in the mean, in order to quiet itself in everything.

A simple rule; and, presuming that the ego has sufficient strength to deal effectively with unruly drives or demanding superego, effective. As has been observed several times, the ego is the principle of reality orientation and adjustment. Whatever detracts it from that basic function is interfering with its development. Therefore, the ego must exercise itself to grasp clearly the values and conditions of its operation which constitute the structure of reality. For the ego engaged in spiritual growth, that reality is determined by judgments of reason and by realities of the spiritual milieu as known through faith. Once the ego loses this basic orientation, it is prey to a whole range of impeding deceptions and illusions. This is a basic factor underlying the Ignatian insistence on interior knowledge of religious truths and realities.

> [351] Rule VI:
> Sixth Note. The sixth: When such good soul wants to speak or do something within the Church, within the understanding of our Superiors, and which should be for the glory of God our Lord, and there comes to him a thought or temptation from without that he should neither say nor do that thing — bringing to him apparent reasons of vainglory or of another thing, etc., — that he ought to raise his understanding to his Creator and Lord, and if he sees that it is his due service, or at the least not contrary to it, the ought to act diametrically against such temptation, according to St. Bernard, answering the same: "Neither for thee did I begin, nor for thee will I stop."

Ignatius' recommendation here is simply a reformulation of the two basic movements in the operation of the ego in opposing a scruple: first, evaluating the word or deed in the framework of the complete reality of the spiritual life; second, mobilizing ego-efforts to diametrically oppose anything opposed to that reality and its inherent values. We might wonder whether, behind this rule, there lay the various contexts in which he had felt such ambivalence and conflict — when he violated the order of the Franciscan superior in Jerusalem by his subterfuge in revisiting some of the holy places? or when he was accused by the Inquisition and confronted with the choice of defending his cause before the tribunal or capitulating and accepting their judgment? or when he decided to address that fateful letter of protest to the irascible and future Pope and then head of the Theatines, Gian Pietro Carafa? These were all possible instances of obsessional doubt rooted in ambivalence that to some degree reflect the underlying conflicts over authority and obedience that preoccupied Ignatius even as General, and may have served as a focus for his scrupulous afflictions. Such a line of reasoning may have helped him to resolve his ambivalence in these and other instances, whether the outcome was advantageous or not. We might think that often enough in his brilliant career, especially with respect to the founding and advancement of the Society of Jesus, this approach had served him well.

It is well to remind ourselves that these recommendations were written in the first quarter of the sixteenth century, nearly five centuries ago. They are distillations of Ignatius' own experience in the course of his spiritual struggles, and they give us some sense of his psychological acumen at work in the midst of the agony and torment that he describes. Even as he was experiencing these conflicts and struggles, he was also an observant participant — capable of reflecting on the experience even as he endured it. The parallel examples that come to mind are, of course, Augustine in his *Confessions*, although the analysis he provided came from later in his life looking back at his early life and conversion, but also Sigmund Freud, who carried on the work of analysis even while he immersed himself in the psychic flow not merely of his experiences with suffering patients, but more pertinently and poignantly, in his own self-analysis. Ignatius' rules, therefore, can be regarded as the result of a process of self-analysis that he carried on primarily, but not exclusively, at Manresa.

## IGNATIUS' SCRUPULOSITY

Ignatius' persistent scrupulosity was a characteristic feature, not only of his personality, but also of his ascetical practice. We cannot ignore the impact of this piece of pathology on his ascetical life and on the ascetical doctrine he propounded to his followers. This affliction apparently appeared for the first time in the crisis at Manresa in the form of doubts that he had adequately confessed and atoned for his former sins. In the course of the spiritual struggle and torment provoked by these scruples, he brought into play all his spiritual resources to gain victory — fasting, penances, long hours of prayer, repeated confessions and consultations with his spiritual director.

One reflection of this scrupulous tendency was his having devised the method of examination of conscience as part of the *Spiritual Exercises* and his continued utilization of the method of the examens continually throughout the rest of his life. Laynez observed in 1547 that Ignatius took "so much care of his conscience that each day he compared week with week, month with month, day with day, seeking daily to advance" (de Guibert 1964, pp. 39-40). Ribadeneyra added: "He had always kept this habit of examining his conscience every hour, and of asking himself with careful attention how he had passed the hour. If at the end of it he happened upon some important matter, or a task that prevented this pious practice, he postponed the examen, but at the first free moment, or the following hour, he made up for this delay" (de Guibert 1964, p. 66). The occasional breakthrough of obsessional doubts, frequently taking the form of intense scruples, plagued him, not only in the early years of his pilgrimage, but even into his advanced years as General of the Society in Rome.

This obsessional practice was driven, at least on the conscious and manifest level, by his obsession with sin and a fearful desire to root out any least semblance of fault. In 1554 Ribadeneyra reported an instance of extreme tenderness of conscience: "I heard from himself that he once had his confessor come to hear his confession for a single fault. It was for having made a certain father's fault known to three fathers, when to remedy his difficulties it would have sufficed to tell two. And yet these difficulties were numerous and not unknown to the third father, so that there was no danger of his conceiving a wrong idea of the father from this single communication" (de Guibert 1964, p. 67). One effect of this degree of obsessional control was the impression of complete dominion over his passions and impulses. Witnesses from later years expressed their amazement at the degree of this mastery and control over his emotions and their expression — all the more remarkable in a man who was born with the full complement of Basque passion and affective vitality. De Guibert (1964) summarized this impression: "We should also add his examens, continued until his death with their incessant effort to keep his violent passions in check. The Diary of 1544 gives us a glimpse of their secret reawakenings, and he overcame them to such an extent that his most familiar witnesses remembered him only as one who had an absolute mastery over himself" (pp. 72-73).

This scrupulosity provides a pathological expression of the underlying obsessional structure of his personality (Meissner 1992b). Psychoanalysts would understand this aspect of his character as due to the excessive severity of his superego — the need for obsessional control based on the threat of breakthrough of instinctual impulses. The leakage of such impulses into consciousness is accompanied, in the classic freudian model, by guilt from both libidinal (incestuous) and aggressive (destructive) wishes. In Ignatius' case I think we can add narcissistic impulses, resulting in shame more than guilt.

The obsessiveness is striking in his own spiritual practice and directives. Examination of his conscience, carried on almost hourly and with obsessive intensity, even to the point of compulsion, is notable. His spiritual teaching and direction, as evidenced in the *Spiritual Exercises*, for example, are highly structured and organized to the point that many have found them repellant and difficult to emulate. Study of his spiritual teaching, in both the *Exercises* and the *Constitutions*, conveys a sense of discipline, tenacity to the point of stubbornness or obstinacy, and an impressive emphasis on control — especially emotional control and self-mastery. We can find evidence of defense mechanisms — isolation, intellectualization, and reaction formation, among others.

These considerations strike an important chord in that they tell us something of the psychological dispositions distilled into the *Exercises* and Ignatius' spiritual teaching. These behavioral reflections give us some hint of the conflictual struggles that permeated his inner life and powered the rigid self-discipline that characterized him in later years. One might argue as well that this need for inner control spilled over into his style of governing the Society, with his passion for establishing regulations (reflected in his obsessional immersion in the writing of the Constitutions) and his insistence on unquestioning blind obedience from his followers — no doubt related to his authoritarian conflicts and character. It is worth noting in this context that the one area of his experience that seemed exempt from this consuming obsessionality was his prayer life and mysticism.

## RULES FOR THINKING WITH THE CHURCH [SE352-370]

These "Rules for Thinking with the Church" [SE 352-370] were composed toward the end of and after Ignatius' time in Paris (Ravier 1992), some around 1534-1535 and some even later before coming to Rome, possibly in 1539-1541. The rules have been thought to derive from the summary appendix of the Council of Sens in 1528, just before Iñigo arrived in Paris.[3] As late additions, they remain peripheral to the main drift of the *Exercises*. They are often interpreted as antidotes to contemporary heresies, and were downplayed even in the early Directories. But they were included by Ignatius and are thus relevant to the entire body of the *Exercises*.

The "church" here has an obvious and concrete reference to the church of Rome and its hierarchical organization and structure. But to interpret these rules in that frame of reference would be a form of simplistic fundamentalism. The referent here is rather the community of followers gathered under the banner of Christ and engaged in the fundamental historical struggle against the forces of evil in the world (Buckley 1993, 1995) — imagery proposed in the meditation on the Kingdom. The church is understood as carrying on the struggle against the "enemy of human nature', cast in military metaphors. The exercitant's election would have led him, in some sense, to join in that struggle against the dehumanizing and diabolical, and therefore, on the side of the church. Ignatius does not have in mind primarily the canonical codes and disciplinary structure of the church, but is thinking more ecclesiastically and spiritually.

[3] Some comparisons are offered by Buckley (1993, 1995).

But the rules for thinking with this militant church are also cast in more feminine images of the spouse and mother, countering the more masculine and phallic quality of chivalric images. For Ignatius, the church is the "true spouse of Christ" and "our holy mother" [SE353] — the only place where nuptial imagery enters the picture (Buckley 1995).

The purpose of these rules was possibly to buffer his newborn Society from suspicions of heresy or even to counter threats of the fanatical adherents of Carafa. In any case, they must be read as reflecting the mind of Ignatius as he assumed the reigns of government of the Society and the context of belief and practice of the sixteenth century in which they were written. They were presumably intended to counter Lutheran influences, and take positions contradicting the views of the *alumbrados*, Ignatius' nemesis. They may have been provoked by anti-Erasmian sentiment, which reached fanatical intensity among certain Roman churchmen connected with the Inquisition. If they can be read as a manifesto of Ignatius' own orthodoxy, they were also an indictment of what were thought to be current heretical positions (O'Malley 1993).

[352] TO HAVE THE TRUE SENTIMENT
Which We Ought to have in the Church Militant
Let the following Rules be observed.

[353] First Rule. The first: All judgment laid aside, we ought to have our mind ready and prompt to obey, in all, the true Spouse of Christ our Lord, which is our holy Mother the Church Hierarchical.

[354] Second Rule. The second: To praise confession to a Priest, and the reception of the most Holy Sacrament of the Altar once in the year, and much more each month, and much better from week to week, with the conditions required and due.

[355] Third Rule. The third: To praise the hearing of Mass often, likewise hymns, psalms and long prayers, in the church and out of it; likewise the hours set at the time fixed for each Divine Office and for all prayer and all Canonical Hours.

[356] Fourth Rule. The fourth: To praise much Religious Orders, virginity and continence, and not so much marriage as any of these.

[357] Fifth Rule. The fifth: To praise vows of Religion, of obedience, of poverty, of chastity and of other perfections of supererogation. And it is to be noted that as the vow is about the things which approach to Evangelical perfection, a vow ought not to be made in the things which withdraw from it, such as to be a merchant, or to be married, etc.

[358] Sixth Rule. To praise relics of the Saints, giving veneration to them and praying to the Saints; and to praise Stations, pilgrimages, Indulgences, pardons, Cruzadas, and candles lighted in the churches.
[359] Seventh Rule. To praise Constitutions about fasts and abstinence, as of Lent, Ember Days, Vigils, Friday and Saturday; likewise penances, not only interior, but also exterior.
[360] Eighth Rule. To praise the ornaments and the buildings of churches; likewise images, and to venerate them according to what they represent.
[361] Ninth Rule. Finally, to praise all precepts of the Church, keeping the mind prompt to find reasons in their defence and in no manner against them.

It is well to remember that such rules were generated in a context of intense strife in the Church and under conditions of the Reformation and Counterreformation. Ignatius was a true and devoted son of the Church which he saw as the visible representation of Christ's kingdom on earth. His respect for the Church was less an act of abject submission and mindless conformity than a sense of mission and dedication to the service of his king. As Cusson (1988) notes, "The fervent and realistic ideal of the service of Christ made Ignatius "a man of the Church" in the fullest sense of that term. It would be a betrayal of his thought and experience to present "a Kingdom of God" which did not lead to the service of the Church of Christ" (p. 210).

[362] Tenth Rule. We ought to be more prompt to find good and praise as well the Constitutions and recommendations as the ways of our Superiors. Because, although some are not or have not been such, to speak against them, whether preaching in public or discoursing before the common people, would rather give rise to fault-finding and scandal than profit; and so the people would be incensed against their Superiors, whether temporal or spiritual. So that, as it does harm to speak evil to the common people of Superiors in their absence, so it can make profit to speak of the evil ways to the persons themselves who can remedy them.
[363] Eleventh Rule. To praise positive and scholastic learning. Because, as it is more proper to the Positive Doctors, as St. Jerome, St. Augustine and St. Gregory, etc., to move the heart to love and serve God our Lord in everything; so it is more proper to the Scholastics, as St. Thomas, St. Bonaventure, and to the Master of the Sentences, etc., to define or explain for our times the things necessary for eternal salvation; and to combat and explain better all errors and all fallacies. For the Scholastic Doctors, as they are more modern, not only help themselves with the true understanding of the Sacred Scripture and of the Positive and holy Doctors,

> but also, they being enlightened and clarified by the Divine virtue, help themselves by the Councils, Canons and Constitutions of our holy Mother the Church.
>
> [364] Twelfth Rule. We ought to be on our guard in making comparison of those of us who are alive to the blessed passed away, because error is committed not a little in this; that is to say, in saying, this one knows more than St. Augustine; he is another, or greater than, St. Francis; he is another St. Paul in goodness, holiness, etc.
>
> [365] Thirteenth Rule. To be right in everything, we ought always to hold that the white which I see, is black, if the Hierarchical Church so decides it, believing that between Christ our Lord, the Bridegroom, and the Church, His Bride, there is the same Spirit which governs and directs us for the salvation of our souls. Because by the same Spirit and our Lord Who gave the ten Commandments, our holy Mother the Church is directed and governed.

This rule undoubtedly reflects the mindset of sixteenth century orthodoxy. Church definitions could at times contradict sensory evidence; the critical case was the eucharist which was interpreted to be the body and blood of Christ, despite the appearances of bread and wine. Theologians might take a different tack in our day, emphasizing that the essence of the doctrine is the real presence of Christ in the eucharist. The fathers of Trent had no other intellectual resources to assert this belief than by appeal to thomistic categories of substance and accident — the sacrament was thus substantially Christ's body and blood and only accidentally gave the appearance of bread and wine. In terms of the language of Trent, black was white. Nonetheless, this rule does address and to a degree reflect the authoritarian strains in Ignatius' personality that found their way into his spirituality.[4]

> [366] Fourteenth Rule. Although there is much truth in the assertion that no one can save himself without being predestined and without having faith and grace; we must be very cautious in the manner of speaking and communicating with others about all these things.
>
> [367] Fifteenth Rule. We ought not, by way of custom, to speak much of predestination; but if in some way and at some times one speaks, let him so speak that the common people may not come into any error, as sometimes happens, saying: Whether I have to be saved or condemned is already determined, and no other thing can now be, through my doing well or ill; and with this, growing

[4] This subject has relevance for understanding Ignatius' views on obedience. See my discussion in chapters XXII, XXIII, and XXIV.

lazy, they become negligent in the works which lead to the salvation and the spiritual profit of their souls.

[368] Sixteenth Rule. In the same way, we must be on our guard that by talking much and with much insistence of faith, without any distinction and explanation, occasion be not given to the people to be lazy and slothful in works, whether before faith is formed in charity or after.

[369] Seventeenth Rule. Likewise, we ought not to speak so much with insistence on grace that the poison of discarding liberty be engendered.

So that of faith and grace one can speak as much as is possible with the Divine help for the greater praise of His Divine Majesty, but not in such way, nor in such manners, especially in our so dangerous times, that works and free will receive any harm, or be held for nothing.

[370] Eighteenth Rule. Although serving God our Lord much out of pure love is to be esteemed above all; we ought to praise much the fear of His Divine Majesty, because not only filial fear is a thing pious and most holy, but even servile fear — when the man reaches nothing else better or more useful — helps much to get out of mortal sin. And when he is out, he easily comes to filial fear, which is all acceptable and grateful to God our Lord, as being at one with the Divine Love.

The authoritarian elements are unmistakable. The first rule reads: "All judgment laid aside, we ought to have our mind ready and prompt to obey, in all, the true Spouse of Christ our Lord, which is our holy Mother the Church Hierarchical" [SE352]. Again, in rule nine: "Finally, to praise all precepts of the Church, keeping the mind prompt to find reasons in their defence and in no manner against them" [SE361]. Complete submission of intellect and judgment is recommended in rule 13: "To be right in everything, we ought always to hold that the white which I see, is black, if the Hierarchical Church so decides it, believing that between Christ our Lord, the Bridegroom, and the Church, His Bride, there is the same Spirit which governs and directs us for the salvation of our souls. Because by the same Spirit and our Lord Who gave the ten Commandments, our holy Mother the Church is directed and governed [SE365]. The rest of the rules are concerned with opposing any questioning, doubting, or criticism of the Church and its practices.

Whatever their theological prudence in the context of the heretic-baiting and fanatic counter-reformational dynamics that flourished in Rome and elsewhere, these rules breathe a spirit of authoritarian control and the suppression of freedom of thought or expression. They share the spirit of Ignatius' letters and directives concerning absolute and blind obedience. They would have to be considered as expressions of Ignatius' own authoritarian characteristics and conflicts. But this dictum would have to be tempered by a word of caution. These rules were far from controversial in the sixteenth century, so that the note of exaggerated orthodoxy should be muted. Moreover, their connection with the *Exercises* is peripheral; Nadal, in his Directory for the *Exercises* (1573-75), lumped them with the other rules (for almsgiving, scruples, and the use of food) and opined: "About these four the following can be said in general. They should be proposed not to everybody, but only to persons who seem to need them and for whom it is worth the effort" — a sentiment endorsed by the official *Directory* in 1599. They are practical pastoral guides, cautions to be followed in the treacherous currents of Reformation religious practice (O'Malley 1993).

# SECTION III

# THE *CONSTITUTIONS* AND OBEDIENCE

# CHAPTER XVIII

# THE SPIRITUALITY OF THE *CONSTITUTIONS*

## Introduction

When Paul III established the Society of Jesus as a canonical order, the bull already contained a rough outline of regulations governing the order, derived from the early deliberations of Ignatius and his companions in 1539. The so-called *Formula*, based on the *Prima Societatis Jesu Instituti Summa*, was included with some modifications in the papal bulls *Regimini militantis Ecclesiae* of 1540, establishing the Society, and *Exposcit debitum* of 1550, confirming it. The bulls also established the right of the order to draw up constitutions by which it was to be governed and directed.[1]

On 4 March 1541, Ignatius and his companions divided the material into forty-nine points. Even though this revision was provisional, Ignatius regarded it as having the force of law and promulgated the articles in a letter to Laynez (Epistolae I, 246-247 [Letter 61]; in Young (1959) pp. 67-68). But this only brought Ignatius to the threshold of what might well be his most important work. The rapid growth of the Society and the signs of papal favor made it mandatory that constitutions be written. The companions had imposed this burden on Ignatius and Codure, but Codure died on 29 August 1541. Ignatius had to struggle with this monumental labor on his own. Very likely, he was occupied (indeed preoccupied) with it from 1543 on. It was a long and difficult labor, made all the more complex by his many other obligations as General and by his continuing ill health (Dudon 1949).

[1] Coemans (1932) concluded that Ignatius and the companions had intended to create formal constitutions from the time they decided to establish a religious order. See also de Aldama (1989). The *Formula* was expanded in the bull *Exposcit debitum* of Julius III in 1550; this third version is the one usually printed at the head of the *Constitutions* as the definitive version.

As early as 1542, certain decisions had to be made, particularly regarding poverty and the endowment of colleges. Pietro Codazzo's gift of the Church of della Strada raised the question of whether the church could possess property independently of the Jesuit community. The answer was at first the traditional one observed by mendicant orders — that it could — but this did not satisfy Ignatius. He continued to struggle with the matter, studying rules of other religious institutes and seeking divine inspiration in prayer. The *Spiritual Journal* of 1544-1545 records his fervent effort to resolve the issue of the poverty appropriate for professed houses of the Society.

By the end of 1546, the first section of the *Constitutions*, the *Examen Generale*, dealing with admission of candidates to the Society, was completed (Aldama 1973). The work went slowly, partly because of Ignatius' plodding style and the care he took over each detail, but also presumably because of other demands on his time. The situation changed in 1547, when Polanco became Ignatius' secretary and provided him with valuable and effective assistance for the last decade of Ignatius' life (Aldama 1973).

## The First Draft

By August 1548, enough progress had been made to allow Ignatius to call a meeting of the professed fathers in 1550. The flood of correspondence between Rome and the provinces brought questions, problems, and suggestions about matters pertaining to the vows, ministries, issues of poverty and obedience. He and Polanco managed to pull together a provisional draft by the end of 1550. The meeting of the professed fathers lasted from the beginning of November 1550 until the beginning of February 1551. There were a good many criticisms: Bobadilla thought it was too long and that there should be a summary that would be easier to assimilate. Laynez and others objected that divesting oneself of all possessions before profession was unfair and risky, and they thought it would be better for the Pope rather than the General to decide if and when to send religious to foreign countries. Salmerón objected to the length and some points pertaining to the vows.

Despite these reservations, the fathers voted their overall approval of the draft, but Ignatius was not yet satisfied with the version of the Constitutions his companions had approved, known as Text A. He continued testing its provisions, gathering fresh data and impressions, rewriting, and clarifying. Nadal brought back observations and criticisms from Sicily, Spain, and Portugal; Ignatius and Polanco examined them closely, considered their relevance, and made whatever modifications were called for. The resulting text, known as Text B, reflects the efforts of Ignatius and Polanco to refine and perfect the document. The task continued until Ignatius' death (Aldama 1973; Ganss 1970). Ignatius had wanted his *Constitutions* to become not a lifeless document, but a living and meaningful guide. But he had to rely increasingly on those he commissioned to promulgate it — for the most part Nadal, but also Laynez and Ribadeneyra (Ravier 1987).

## The Hand of Ignatius

No doubt Ignatius needed the help he got from Polanco and also Nadal. It is probably safe to say that without their assistance the work might never have been completed. In October 1547 Polanco wrote to Spain: "One responsibility has cost our Father a great deal of time. It is his work on the Constitutions, which with God's grace will keep our Society in good estate and greatly advance it. It is necessary work, but it demands a large amount of time and is laborious" (von Matt and Rahner 1956, p. 88). The Spanish text B — the text in Spanish and Latin that Nadal carried on his promulgating missions — was still being revised when Ignatius died.[2] But Ignatius undoubtedly put his unique stamp on the Constitutions. Essential points had already been decided before his collaborators came into the picture, and even after 1551 the manuscripts bear unmistakable marks of Ignatius' revisions. As Aldama (1989) concludes:

> There is, then, no doubt that the Constitutions express the *thought* of Ignatius, though this does not mean that we can analyze each word and sentence as if they were all spoken or written by the saint himself. Only in those passages where the textual history indicates a direct intervention by Ignatius is such analysis justified. In general, the actual words and phrases are the means used by Polanco to express the mind of the founder. Doubtless some, or even many, of them came directly from Ignatius in conversation with his secretary, though we cannot be certain which ones these are. (p. 11)

The last word throughout was his, and there is no question but that writing the *Constitutions* became his major preoccupation. Nadal was fond of quoting Ignatius' comment: "I have asked God to grant me three graces before I die, in the first place the confirmation of the

[2] By the time of Ignatius' death, the *Constitutions* had been promulgated in every province of the Society except France where political conditions did not permit it.

Society of Jesus by the Holy See, secondly a similar approval of the *Spiritual Exercises*, and thirdly that I might be able to write down the Constitutions" (cited in von Matt and Rahner 1956, p. 89).

Ignatius had founded not only a new order but a new kind of order, distinctly different from the Franciscans, Dominicans, Benedictines, and others. The prevailing style of religious life included wearing of identifying habits, performance of the office in choir, observance of feasts and penances imposed by rule, and so on. Ignatius abandoned these traditional practices, prolonged the trial period of the novitiate, postponed solemn vows to the end of a long and rigorous course of training, and instituted the practice of the account of conscience.[3] The habit, choir, austerities of rule, acceptance of ecclesiastical benefices, and the capitular system[4] were all abolished. Ignatius' work has become the model for constitutions of many subsequent religious groups. Through the *Constitutions*, more than any other single work, Ignatius placed his mark on the history of the Church.

At the same time, the *Constitutions* incorporate and adapt many aspects of traditional spiritual wisdom. This was undoubtedly due to the efforts of Polanco to glean material from the Rules of St. Augustine, St. Benedict, and the constitutions of the Franciscans. Many such details were included, but as de Guibert (1964) notes most of these pertained to particular aspects of community discipline. But the primary source that far outweighs all others was Ignatius' own personal experience and his vision of the total giving of oneself in the service of Christ's kingdom. Others, particularly Laynez and Polanco, made suggestions, but as de Guibert comments:

> . . . it remains true that the large directive ideas and the most characteristic formulas are from Ignatius and from him alone. And this is the case to such an extent that sometimes in the midst of a text which is clarified and smoothened by the expert pen of Polanco, we meet with a paragraph that is strained, distorted, and difficult, but full and strong, which is the work of Ignatius. The secretary did not dare to polish so vigorous and personal a passage. (p. 161)

[3] The account of conscience was the manifestation by the subject to his superior of his mind and heart not only for his own spiritual progress but to enable his superior to better guide and direct him in his apostolic work. Ignatius made this a regular practice in the Society.

[4] The term "capitular system" refers to the practice in older religious orders for the community to gather regularly to hear a reading of a chapter of the rules of the order — thus being referred to as "chapter." Ignatius did not want to confine his men by imposing the obligation of chapter.

Composition evolved over four stages: (1) 1546-1547 — the first draft of the Examen (text alpha), (2) 1549-1550 — the first draft of the *Constitutions* (text a) and a second text of the Examen (text A), (3) 1550 — text A of the *Constitutions*, essentially a rough draft, and text B of the Examen, and (4) 1551-1553 — definitive text of the *Constitutions* (text B) (Aldama 1989).[5] At Ignatius' death in 1556, the text of the *Constitutions* was left in manuscript form — essentially four separate treatises: the General Examen, the explanations entitled Declarations on the Examen, the text of the Constitutions proper, and the explanatory Declarations on the Constitutions. This autograph manuscript edition, text B, in a newly corrected Spanish version (text C) by Polanco, received final approval and confirmation from the First General Congregation assembled in 1558 to elect Ignatius' successor as General (Aldama 1989; Ganss 1970).[6]

Our interest in this enormous effort is here confined to what the document tells us about the aspects of Ignatius' spirituality he sought to institutionalize in his Society. The task is not made easier by the style of the *Constitutions*. They are legal documents, regulations meant to govern the organization and works of the Society for all time. They are to that extent without emotion, personal reflection, nuance, or suggestion about the man who poured his life's blood and even dying breath into them. We are forced to read between the lines to discern something of Ignatius' spiritual vision.

The first point to note is that the guiding spirit throughout is the *Spiritual Exercises* (Leturia 1941). The powerful spiritual insight Ignatius gained at Manresa had never left him, and even three decades later, after years of pilgrimage and study, and even in the course of his ongoing experience as General of the Society, the same inspiration seemed to come to the fore in his writing of the *Constitutions*. The same spirit of submission to God's will, prayerful devotion to advancement of God's kingdom, humble acceptance of God's graces, and self-sacrifice that comes through so vividly in the *Exercises*, appears in the pages of the *Constitutions* — now transformed into prescriptions, directions, rules, and guiding norms. The spirit of the

[5] Text A was written under Polanco's direction, but Ignatius' handwriting appears in 230 places, correcting words and phrases, adding or subtracting even whole paragraphs. Text A was presented to the fathers in January 1551, amended to Text B as a result of their reflections (Aldama 1989).

[6] Ganss' translation will be followed throughout and referred to henceforth as *Constitutions*. Subsequent versions include a new Latin text ordered by the 4th General Congregation, and a new Spanish text (D) by the 5th Congregation. Summaries were not long in coming — Laynez prepared one in 1560, and an official summary, ordered by the 3rd General Congregation, appeared in 1580.

Foundation in the *Exercises* [SE23] breathes on every page of the *Constitutions.* The spirit of the pilgrim of Manresa remains alive in the founder and legislator.

What has changed is the man Ignatius, mellowed and made wise by his years of experience. He is no longer the fanatical extremist with a burning desire to take the kingdom of heaven by storm. The tone is measured, prudent, holding up ideals and lofty ambitions, while at the same time urging moderation. He had ruined his health and destroyed his body in his impatient and immoderate zeal for self-abnegation and severe penances; he did not wish his sons to make the same mistake and render themselves less, rather than more, fit for God's work. The same progression can be seen in his directions regarding poverty, which strive for balance between the ideals of evangelical poverty and practical matters of supporting large houses and many laborers in the vineyards. He had to feed his men, maintain houses where they lived and worked, support novices and others still in training, foot the bill for advanced degrees in the great universities, keep the doors of the colleges open, and so on. The ideals and practices of the pilgrim years had to give way to more prudent arrangements and procedures.

In writing the *Constitutions*, Ignatius had dominantly in mind the apostolic mission of the Society and his desire to mold it into an effective instrument to do God's work. The stamp of papal approval and reconfirmation [CS1, 134] was significant not only for juridical reasons, but because it confirmed the line of authority linking the Society to the divine will. Ignatius repeatedly refers to the Society as "least" [CS1, 134, 190, 638],[7] as if to undercut any suggestion of pride or privilege. But there is no doubt that he was at the same time zealous to build his Society on the firmest foundation he could find.

In the background, there was a pervasive conviction that the career of Ignatius, as reflected in his *Vita*, the Society of Jesus and the *Constitutions*, were all divinely inspired and guided. So it was seen by Polanco, Laynez and especially Nadal. God was the true founder of the Society and Ignatius was his instrument. Nadal probably took this line in the face of the crises of 1553 and 1556-7, when Rodrigues and Bobadilla argued that the founding of the Society was a collaborative venture of the first companions (O'Malley 1993). For some, it seemed that the *Constitutions* began to take on the aura of a revelation rather than a piece of human legislation.

[7] Ganss (1970) cites Laynez (FN II, 131-133) to the effect that Ignatius called the Society "least" because of the weakness of its human foundation, out of humility, and because of its late origin in the history of the Church.

## The *Constitutions* and Ignatian Spirituality

As de Guibert (1964) tells us, the *Constitutions of the Society of Jesus* is no less important for the light it sheds on Ignatian spirituality than the *Spiritual Exercises*. In fact, the spirit of the *Exercises* breathes on every page of the *Constitutions*. Not only in the sections dealing with interior spiritual life does one find expressions of Ignatius' spiritual views, but spiritual principles are brought into play in prescriptions on training of novices, studies, apostolates and the manner of governing in the Society. The guiding spirit throughout is provided by Ignatius' ideal — "to wander through the world and, where they did not find the desired spiritual fruit in one part or another, to go on to another and another in succession, going through towns and other particular places, to the greater glory of God our Lord and for the greater spiritual benefit of souls" (MI Const I, 160; cited in Aldama (1989) p. 14).[8] Images of the primitive church and the mission of so-called "wandering charismatics" (Theissen 1978) prevail.

The *Constitutions* themselves embrace ten divisions, preceded by two preliminary documents, the *Formula of the Institute* ([FI1-10], Ganss (1970), pp. 63-73)[9] and the *General Examen* [CS1-133]. The *Formula*, as noted above, was the original document drawn up by Ignatius and the first companions in proposing a new religious order for papal approval. The *General Examen* contains material pertaining to the admission of candidates to the Society — the questions they should be asked, the qualities required, any impediments, tests required for admission, and especially the life the candidate can expect to lead in the Society [CS53-103]. Spiritual issues touched on include renunciation [CS53-63], the role of obedience and the openness it requires [CS80-96], and finally a typically Ignatian emphasis on humility and the experience of humiliations [CS101-3].[10]

Buckley (1984) commented on the influence of the *Exercises* on the Examen. The process is similar to the *Exercises* in its care for

[8] The theme is repeated in the General Examen: "The end of this Society is to devote itself with God's grace not only to the salvation and perfection of the members' own souls, but also with that same grace to labor strenuously in giving aid toward the salvation and perfection of the souls of their fellowmen" [CS3].

[9] [FI#] will refer to the *Formula* in Ganss' edition to distinguish these sections from those in the *Constitutions* proper.

[10] Ignatius began the *Examen* shortly after approval of the Formula in 1540, and subsequent revisions were made for succeeding papal approbations. The *Jesuiten Lexicon* noted that the *General Examen* was "a complete innovation at that time, demonstrating the great importance which the founder of the order attached to the selection of candidates" (Koch 1934, p. 63).

withdrawal, direction, and discernment, over an extended period of solitude allowing the applicant to sound the depths and test the validity of his election of this way of life. Whereas the Exercises are directed to making an election for disposing of one's life, the Examen provides a testing of whether such an election has been made, has been made freely and with full cognizance of the consequences. Its intent is to raise the level of reflective consciousness of the candidate's religious context and self-awareness. As Buckley (1984) notes:

> The candidate is asked to take what has existed so "subjectively" and give it a new "objectivity" — an objectivity that is obtained as one explains or attempts to explain to another what has perhaps up to this time only been inarticulately present to oneself. This new "objective" mode of existence makes this situation and these experiences present to the candidate in a new way and gives both him and his director the opportunity to judge whether the charism of his life indicates a movement into the Society of Jesus. This new mode of personal existence is, consequently, a new mode in which he possesses his own freedom. . . . In the *Spiritual Exercises* the election is followed by the third and fourth week, the cost and glory of discipleship; in the *General Examen*, this confirmation that an election has been made is followed by one of the most profound descriptions of this cost ever written by Ignatius, the great fourth chapter of the *General Examen*. In both the Exercises and the Examen, this is the moment in which the disciple hears and lives with the words, "If anyone will come after me." (pp. 76-78)

The remaining ten sections contain prescriptions for living in the Society and for governing it. The doctrine contained therein can be taken as Ignatius' final statement of his formulated spirituality — the spiritual vision he wished to instill in the hearts and minds of his followers and to institutionalize in the structure and mission of his Society.

## Theological Context

The primary orientation is to the glory and service of God [CS133, 508] — the primary consideration, together with the universal good, that serves as the norm of all judgment and rule in the Society [CS258].[11] The spirit on which the Society was based was

[11] The phrases reflecting this intention are sprinkled liberally throughout the text — "greater service of God and good of souls" [CS605], "for the glory of God and the good of souls" [CS616], "what is of greater service to God and of universal good" [CS618, 622], "greater honor to God and the more universal good" [CS623], "the greater edification of the neighbor and the service of God our Lord" [CS625], "the honor and glory of God and the universal good" [CS626], and so on.

first of all the love of God [CS288] and secondly what Ignatius refers to as "the interior law of charity and love" [CS134]. It was this spirit of love that served as the basis for obedience [CS547, 551] and the underlying motivation for seeking the glory of God in all things [CS602] and ensuring the bond of union in the Society [CS671]. Ignatius seeks "a love and desire of all perfection and a desire that greater glory and praise of Christ our Creator and Lord may follow" [CS602]. Everything decided or accomplished in the Society is to be directed to this end [CS305] without exception; Ignatius' abiding conviction is that firm adherence to this norm is the guiding light on which the well being and effectiveness of the Society for God's service depends [CS134, 812, 825]. This theme has become such a dominating motif in the life and history of the Society that the motto "*ad majorem Dei gloriam*" has become synonymous with the name and work of Jesuits the world over. Hardly a logo or banner or sigillum representing the Society does not carry the familiar AMDG.

In addition to seeking and promoting the kingdom of God, Jesuits are enjoined to seek personal perfection and holiness in all things [CS250, 288]. The path to such holiness is through centering themselves on the love of God and eliminating all creaturely attachments that might stand in the way of that. Ignatius wrote:

> [CS288] All should make diligent efforts to keep their intentions right, not only in regard to their state of life but also in all particular details. In these they should always aim at serving and pleasing the Divine Goodness for its own sake and because of the incomparable love and benefits with which God has anticipated us, rather than for fear of punishment or hope of rewards, although they ought to draw help also from them. Further, they should often be exhorted to seek God our Lord in all things, stripping off from themselves the love of creatures to the extent that this is possible, in order to turn their love upon the Creator of them, by loving Him in all creatures and all of them in Him, in conformity with His holy and divine will.

We can recognize here the delicate balance between the highest ideals and the practicality of Ignatius, acknowledging the limits and imperfection of the human condition. The love of God is held out above all other motives, but the need for reward and the fear of punishment may have a place too, since no practical man would anticipate their complete elimination. These goals can also find support and encouragement in familiarity with God in prayer [CS288, 723, 813], and by confidence in the help and guidance God will provide for those who trust in Him [CS67, 414, 555, 812, 814]. They can know God's will since it is expressed through the superior who stands in the place of Christ [CS284, 547, 619]. Wisdom and prudence in making decisions and pursuing courses of action come from seeking inspiration of the divine wisdom through prayer [CS711, 746]. The more one seeks the divine will and devotes himself to it, the more generous will he find God with His graces and spiritual gifts [CS282, 283]. Love and reverence for God is to be encouraged in whatever work is undertaken [CS111, 114, 118, 130, 132, 251, 547].

Corresponding to the goal of personal sanctification, another end of the Society is leading others to greater love and service of God. The *Formula* states the purpose of the Society — "to strive especially for the defense and propagation of the faith and for the progress of souls in Christian life and doctrine" [FI3]. Jesuits, therefore, are encouraged to have a spiritual care for the advancement in holiness of their fellow men [CS115], seeing in them the image of God [CS250], and seeking constantly to assist them to gain the goal for which they were created by example and learning — this provided the rationale for the Jesuit commitment to higher education in colleges and universities [CS307, 446]. Zeal for the spiritual progress and salvation of souls played a prominent role in Ignatius' vision of the Society [CS114, 115, 156, 163, 204, 258, 603, 813]. The preferred means to this objective were those that united to God and made them more effectively a human instrument to be wielded by the hand of God, rather than any merely human resources [CS813]. Reliance is placed throughout on guidance and inspiration of the Holy Spirit [CS134, 219, 414, 624, 700, 701] and the place of the Society in the arrangements of divine providence [CS134, 304, 547, 555, 812, 814]. Here again we can glimpse the long shadow cast by the vision at La Storta — "I will be propitious to you at Rome" — and Ignatius' unwavering conviction that he was doing God's work.

Consistent with this profound dedication to God's will, the attachment of Ignatius and his Society to the figure of Christ was a powerful theme in the spirituality of the order. For starters, Ignatius gave his Society the name of Jesus [CS1] as though to signify the special dedication of the Society to the work of the kingdom of Christ — Ignatius' order was to be enlisted under the banner of the Christ of the meditation on the Two Standards [SE136-148]. Trust in Christ and His continuing support was fundamental to the Ignatian vision: "The Society was not instituted by human means; and neither is it through them that it can be preserved and developed, but through the omnipotent hand of Christ, God and our Lord. Therefore in Him alone must be placed the hope that He will preserve and carry forward what He deigned to begin for His service and praise and for the aid of souls" [CS812]. Consequently those who enter the Society are to put away all prior attachments and dedicate themselves wholly to the service of Christ [CS61, 62, 66], seeking to imitate Christ and devote themselves to His service [CS101, 193], exercising themselves in virtue and following the counsels of Christ [CS50, 53, 54, 254] in poverty, chastity and obedience. The dedication to the service of Christ is to be sought even in sickness [CS272] and even further to the end of life itself [CS595, 586, 602]. For Ignatius, it was love of Christ that provided the essential bond of union among the members of his Society [CS671].

Permeating this theologically impregnated milieu of the life and mission of the Society was the reality of divine grace — the means by which Ignatius envisioned divine assistance being given to his men [CS774, 814]. Ignatius' trust in God and His providence is such that he is confident that God will provide His grace as it is necessary to promote His service [CS686] and to enable the Society to perform its mission in the world [CS3, 79, 308, 555, 624, 638, 814]. The necessary graces are gained through intimacy with God in prayer [CS723], by generosity in devoting oneself to God's service [CS282, 283], and by offering prayers and masses beseeching God's help and guidance [CS11, 790, 812]. The measure of God's grace will be proportional to their devotion [CS277] and cooperation with grace [CS814], which is the root and source of all spiritual progress [CS3, 93, 94, 101-3, 282, 283, 343, 360, 414, 540, 553, 662, 723, 789, 790].

## SPIRITUAL MEANS

The end and purpose of the *Constitutions* seems singular and singleminded — achieving the greater glory of God. Nadal wrote: "Our Father was a magnanimous, noble and generous soul . . . . He resolved to serve Our Lord in the best way possible and accomplish things for his greater glory. And that was his first principle. That is why in the *Constitutions* you will find in every chapter and every paragraph 'for the greater glory and service of God our Lord!'" (MonNad V, 270; cited in Clancy 1976, p. 108). The means were geared to this end — spiritual means, of course, but also human means that would offer promise of successful work and accomplishment, especially solid learning, the ability to teach and preach, and "the art of dealing with and conversing with men" [CS814].

## Vows

As an approved religious order, the Society of Jesus was bound to the observance of religious vows of poverty, chastity and obedience. Since the vow and virtue of obedience plays such a central role in Ignatius' spiritual vision and psychology, I will consider its place in the *Constitutions* in the next chapter.[12]

*Chastity*. As for the vow of chastity, Ignatius makes short work of it. "What pertains to the vow of chastity does not require explanation, since it is evident how perfectly it should be preserved through the endeavor in this matter to imitate the angelic purity by the purity of body and mind" [CS547]. Ganss (1970) offers an explanatory note to the effect that the sixteenth century had more or less unquestioningly accepted the ideal of chastity and the problems pertaining to celibacy that so trouble our times had not yet arisen. Ignatius, then, was not any different than other spiritual writers of his day who tended to brush over the vow of chastity without comment. For de Aldama (1989), chastity was taken for granted, as was consistent with patristic and medieval tradition. On the other hand, there is enough evidence to suggest that Ignatius was continually troubled by sexual and libidinal impulses even in his mature years. The massive repression of sexuality he claimed at the time of his conversion[13] leaves many questions unanswered and suggests that his more or less unconscious libidinal urges may have played themselves out in more repressed and indirect ways (Meissner 1992b). Here we are confronted with the iron curtain. Other references to chastity in the *Constitutions* are simply juridical [CS4, 13, 14, 119, 121, 527, 532, 535, 540].

*Poverty*. Ignatius' statements regarding the vow of poverty are much more extensive and elaborate. The issue of poverty was one that preoccupied him profoundly. The first section of his *Spiritual Journal* was taken up with his lengthy deliberations and prayerful reflections on this subject. The guiding inspiration was to follow Christ poor — the ideal that Ignatius had embraced from the beginning of his spiritual journey (Dudon 1949; Dalmases 1985; Meissner 1992b) — "If thou wilt be perfect, go, sell all that thou hast, and give it to the poor . . . and follow me" (Mt 19: 21) [CS53, 54]. Most of the

[12] The reflection on Ignatian obedience encompasses study of his own writings on obedience, in the *Constitutions* (chapters XXI, XXII and XXIII) and other writings (chapter XXIII), and of his practice of obedience (chapter XXIV), My effort to analyze the virtue and practice of obedience in psychological terms consistent with Ignatian principles is contained in section V below.

[13] See chapter II above.

references to poverty in the *Constitutions* are concerned with juridical specifications regarding the vow and prescriptions for fiscal management, specifically for renunciation of possessions on taking the vow and for receiving and disposing of revenues. Our focus here falls on spiritual aspects of the virtue of poverty, the poverty of the spirit that Ignatius so prized. In the *Formula*, we read: "From experience we have learned that a life removed as far as possible from all infection of avarice and as like as possible to evangelical poverty is more gratifying, more undefiled, and more suitable for the edification of our fellowmen" [FI5]. Ignatius felt that his men, during the course of their training, should actually experience poverty [CS287] and suggested experiences for this [CS66-71]. He regarded poverty as the "strong wall of religious life" [CS553]; it was against this protective shield that "the enemy of the human race generally tries to weaken this defense and rampart which God our Lord inspired religious institutes to raise against him and the other adversaries of their perfection" [CS553].[14] We are hardly a step removed from the meditation on the Two Standards [SE 136-148] — Lucifer tries first to tempt men to the desire for riches [SE 142] as the first step toward worldly vices, while Christ urges his followers "to want to help all, by bringing them first to the highest spiritual poverty, and — if His Divine Majesty would be served and would want to choose them — no less to actual poverty" [SE 146]. So important was this issue to the mind of Ignatius that he insisted on a special vow of the professed not to alter the *Constitutions* in this regard, unless to make the regulations more strict [CS553, 554] (de Aldama 1989).

However, tension persisted between the evangelical ideal of the pilgrim and the necessity for the General to have revenues, endowments of colleges, properties, and so on. Ignatius tried to resolve the tension by creating two classes of members — the professed would strive to live the evangelical ideal, and the rest could live on revenues from endowments and investments. But as the role of the professed gradually eroded over the years, the pragmatic effect of this solution seemed to dwindle. The subsequent history of the Society's efforts to manage the issue of poverty continue to express this tension between the need for resources to support corporate apostolic enterprises and the individual call to the spirit of personal poverty inherent in the vow. These tensions have become especially acute in the modern era.

[14] See also CS816.

## Virtues

Much of Ignatius spiritual teaching regarding virtues flows along familiar and traditional lines. He held out the ideal of Christian perfection as part of the end and purpose of the Society [CS3, 156, 307, 813]. The path to this perfection lie in imitation of Christ [CS101-103], as had been the ground plan for the second week of the *Exercises*. Important aspects contributing to this goal were observation of the prescriptions of the institute [CS547, 602, 813] and renunciation of possessions [CS55, 256, 258, 259]. Continual cultivation of the virtues was essential to this program [CS813] and for the preservation of union of hearts in the Society [CS671] and edification of the neighbor [CS637].

The primary place was given to the theological virtues of faith, hope, and charity. Faith was an essential ingredient to a vocation and a basic motivation for all that followed. Besides expectable cautions regarding heresy and schism due to the religious crisis of the mid-sixteenth century [CS22, 24, 165-7], Ignatius appeals to the spirit of faith in seeking spiritual direction [CS263], and in sickness and death [CS272, 595]. Hope found expression in the confidence that God would provide whatever was required for any mission they were assigned [CS67, 82] and that He would preserve and guide the Society in its divinely inspired mission [CS812, 814].

But by far the greatest place in Ignatius' thinking and in his spiritual vision was given to charity and love of God. He stressed the "interior law of love and charity" [CS134] and emphasized again and again its importance for the life of the Society [CS671, 813, 821]. It was the pervasive and implicit norm for every judgment and action [CS209, 237, 269, 582, 727]. The union of his followers in the spirit of love and charity was essential to the enterprise of the Society and its mission that Ignatius held so dear. He wrote:

> [CS671] The chief bond to cement the union of the members among themselves and with their head is, on both sides, the love of God our Lord. For when the superior and the subjects are closely united to His Divine and Supreme Goodness, they will very easily be united among themselves, through that same love which will descend from the Divine Goodness and spread to all other men, and particularly into the body of the Society. Thus from both sides charity will come to further this union between superiors and subjects, and in general all goodness and virtues through which one proceeds in conformity with the spirit. Consequently there will also come total contempt of temporal things, in regard to

which self-love, the chief enemy of this union and universal good, frequently induces disorder.

## Other Christian Virtues

It is not surprising, considering the central place given to humility in the *Spiritual Exercises* [SE165-168], that we should find Ignatius placing humility at the heart of his spiritual vision in the *Constitutions*. He emphasizes how necessary and essential a role humility plays for life in the Society, particularly for the union of hearts that he so prized [CS659]. He insisted that the humility and self-abnegation of candidates and those in training be tested [CS83, 101, 102, 250, 265, 282, 516] and found adequate. Humility was essential for the manifestation of conscience [CS93], including manifestation of errors and defects [CS63], for the indifference Ignatius recommended as to the grade or position one might be assigned in the Society [CS11, 130]; similarly in the choice of studies [CS289], in acquiring academic degrees [CS390], in manner of living [CS576-80], in begging [CS82] and even sickness [CS89].

Humility played a special role for him in the exercise of obedience — he wished his men to submit themselves to the orders of superiors with readiness and humility [CS284], even when the orders were in some way repugnant. And they were to show the same respect and humility to even the most lowly officials [CS84]. This degree of self-abnegation and humility was prescribed for all levels in the Society — for novices [CS66, 68, 98, 297], coadjutor brothers [CS114, 117, 118, 132], tertians [CS516], spiritual coadjutors [CS116], admonitors of the general [CS770], superiors [CS423, 659], and even the general himself [CS725]. It was the essential ingredient in the indifference that Ignatius insisted on, whether it was a matter of accepting the decision of a superior [CS292, 543], accepting and being content with the grade to which one was assigned [CS72, 111, 116, 117, 130, 542], or even accepting the ministries to which one was assigned [CS606, 618, 619, 633].

The role of humility in Ignatius' thinking has a specific focus, viewed from a psychoanalytic perspective — namely it is the counterpoise and bulwark against inroads of narcissism, particularly in its pathological forms of pride and ambition. These were the target, along with desire for riches, of the third degree of humility in the *Exercises* — "in order to imitate and be more actually like Christ our Lord, I want and choose poverty with Christ poor rather than riches, opprobrium with Christ replete with it rather than honors; and to desire to be rated as a fool for Christ" [SE167]. Here in the *Constitutions*, ambition or seeking honors or power are regarded as serious evils [CS695, 696, 720] that are to be expunged with all diligence — "It will also be of the highest importance toward perpetuating the Society's well-being to use great diligence in precluding from it ambition, the mother of all evils in any community or congregation whatsoever" [CS817]. This casts some light on the energy and determination with which Ignatius opposed efforts to have any of his men appointed to ecclesiastical dignities.[15] He dreaded that this practice would open the door to ambition — "the mother of all evils."

The same theme can be found echoed in his letters, especially where involvement of his men in matters related to worldly preferment was in question. Not only was ambition to be avoided, but even the appearance of ambition was contrary to the purposes of the Society. On one occasion Araoz wrote asking advice about participation of scholastics studying in universities in public functions. Ignatius wrote:

> Rome, April 3, 1548
>
> You ask whether our scholastics should vote in elections to various chairs and offices. Do not permit this. Rather inform them that they are not to do this at all, as their own peace of mind and the spirit of our Institute will be thus better preserved. This spirit requires of us to withdraw from every appearance of ambition and to remain on terms of peace and affection with all. We will thus avoid making adversaries of those whom we do not favor. Give orders also that in Valencia, and wherever degrees are taken, they who are under your authority should occupy no special place, either first or last, but they should take part in academic functions and pass their examinations, which will show whether they have studied well or not. Should they happen to be present when others are nominated, let them withdraw, and they can pass later extra numerum. I consider this procedure advisable not only to free ourselves from every appearance of restless ambition, as I hope we shall be in our Lord, but also for the good example and edification of others. Although they take part in university functions and accept degrees to encourage themselves to study or to arm themselves with authority so that they can place at the disposal of others what God has shared with them, this matter of special places, because it involves more danger than profit, is, I think in our Lord, not suitable for Ours, nor in keeping with the spirit of poverty and humility by which we should be characterized. Yours in our Lord . . . (Epistolae II, 71-73 [Letter 302]; in Young (1959) 172-173)

[15] See the examples of Ignatius' opposition to these efforts in chapter XXIV below.

The situation was much the same with regard to pride. We hear again the echoes of the *Exercises*:

> [CS101] . . . to how great a degree it helps and profits one in the spiritual life to abhor in its totality and not in part whatever the world loves and embraces, and to accept and desire with all possible energy whatever Christ our Lord has loved and embraced. Just as the men of the world who follow the world love and seek with such great diligence honors, fame, and esteem for a great name on earth, as the world teaches them, so those who are progressing in the spiritual life and truly following Christ our Lord love and intensely desire everything opposite. That is to say, they desire to clothe themselves with the same clothing and uniform of their Lord because of the love and reverence which He deserves, to such an extent that where there would be no offense to His Divine Majesty and no imputation of sin to the neighbor, they would wish to suffer injuries, false accusations, and affronts, and to held and esteemed as fools (but without their giving any occasions for this), because of their desire to resemble and imitate in some manner our Creator and Lord Jesus Christ.

The qualifying phrases remind us that Ignatius is addressing himself both in the *Exercises* and the *Constitutions* to an internal disposition rather than to external behavior. Ignatius did not want his men running around making fools of themselves; in fact he sought every means to fashion them into effective and dynamic instruments for the work of the kingdom. What he had in mind was that internal disposition to self-abnegation and humility that could allow for the greatest diligence and application to the work of God and the preservation and promotion of the Society and its work. It was a balance that Ignatius had sought for himself throughout his own spiritual odyssey. We have only to recall the vicissitudes of his pilgrim years to be impressed by the extent to which he lived out these recommendations. But he had also to come to the realization that the accoutrements of the beggar and the fool for Christ would not accomplish the spiritual goals he envisioned. In part the problem he faced was to find a way to combine the simple virtues of the pilgrim with the kind of encounter with the forces of the world that he sought to influence and bring to the cause of Christ and His Church. The resulting balancing act has its pluses and minuses that remain a source of unresolved tension in Jesuit life.

Among the means for attaining such virtue, to which Ignatius gives an important place, is the control and appropriate regulation of affections [CS288] — again echoing the spirit of the *Exercises*. Candidates were counseled to renounce any untoward affection for relatives [CS54, 61] or for possessions [CS55, 256, 258]. This degree of personal maturity and integration was recommended for those admitting candidates [CS143], for tertians completing their spiritual training [CS516], for superiors generally [CS423], and especially in the general [CS725, 728]. By the same token, inordinate affections are to be regarded as impediments to admission [CS179] or, when passions or vices prove incorrigible, as grounds for dismissal [CS210]. Such attachments Ignatius regarded as destructive of the spirit of unity and the wellbeing of the Society [CS657].

# CHAPTER XIX

# METHODS FOR SPIRITUAL GROWTH IN THE *CONSTITUTIONS*

## Spiritual Ideal

Ignatius himself provides a vivid idealized portrait, in the *Constitutions*, of the character and spiritual stature he thought any future General of the Society should possess [CS723-735]. But it can be argued that it represents his portrait of his ideal of the good Jesuit, since there is nothing here that he does not prescribe for all Jesuits, especially the professed and superiors (de Aldama 1989). The description is embodied in ten points:

> [CS723] 1. In regard to the qualities which are desirable in the superior general, the first is that he should be closely united with God our Lord and intimate with Him in prayer and all his actions, that from God, the fountain of all good, the general may so much the better obtain for the whole body of the Society a large share of His gifts and graces, and also great power and efficacy for all the means which will be used for the help of souls.
> [CS725] 2. The second quality is that he should be a person whose example in the practice of all virtues is a help to the other members of the Society. Charity should be especially resplendent in him, toward all his fellowmen and above all toward the members of the Society; and genuine humility too should shine forth, that these characteristics may make him highly lovable to God our Lord and to men.
> [CS726] 3. He ought also to be independent of all passions, by his keeping them controled and mortified, so that in his interior they may not disturb the judgment of his intellect and in his exterior he may be so composed, particularly so self-controlled when speaking, that no one, whether a member of the Society who should regard him as a mirror and model, or an extern, may observe in him any thing or word which does not edify him.

[CS727] 4. However, he should know how to mingle rectitude and necessary severity with kindness and gentleness to such an extent that he neither allows himself to swerve from what he judges to be more pleasing to God our Lord nor ceases to have proper sympathy for his sons. Thus although they are being reprimanded or punished, they will recognize that in what he does he is proceeding rightly in our Lord and with charity, even though it is against their liking according to the lower man.

[CS728] 5. Magnanimity and fortitude of soul are likewise highly necessary for him to bear the weaknesses of many, to initiate great undertakings in the service of God our Lord, and to persevere in them with constancy when it is called for, without losing courage in the face of the contradictions (even though they come from persons of high rank and power) and without allowing himself to be moved by their entreaties or threats from what reason and the divine service require. He should be superior to all eventualities, without letting himself be exalted by those which succeed or depressed by those which go poorly, being altogether ready to receive death, if necessary, for the good of the Society in the service of Jesus Christ, God and our Lord.

[CS729] 6. The third quality is that he ought to be endowed with great understanding and judgment, in order that this talent may not fail him either in the speculative or the practical matters which may arise. And although learning is highly necessary for one who will have so many learned men in his charge, still more necessary is prudence along with experience in spiritual and interior matters, that he may be able to discern the various spirits and to give counsel and remedies to so many who will have spiritual necessities.

He also needs discretion in exterior matters and a manner of handling such diverse affairs as well as of conversing with such various persons from within and without the Society.

[CS730] 7. The fourth quality, one highly necessary for the execution of business, is that he should be vigilant and solicitous to undertake enterprises as well as energetic in carrying them through to their completion and perfection, rather than careless and remiss in such a way that he leaves them begun but not finished.

[CS731] 8. The fifth quality has reference to the body. In regard to health, appearance, and age, on the one hand account should be taken of propriety and prestige, and on the other hand of the physical energies which his charge requires, that in it he may be able to fulfill his office to the glory of God our Lord.

[CS733] 9. The sixth quality pertains to extrinsic endowments. Among these, preference ought to be given to those which help more toward edification and the service of God in such a charge. Examples are generally found in reputation, high esteem, and whatever else aids toward prestige with those within and without.

> [CS735] 10. Finally, he ought to be one of those who are most outstanding in every virtue, most deserving in the Society, and known as such for a considerable time. If any of the aforementioned qualities should be wanting, there should at least be no lack of great probity and love for the Society, nor of good judgment accompanied by sound learning. For in regard to other things, the aids which he will have . . . could through God's help and favor supply to a great extent for many deficiencies.

This passage has also been long regarded as a self-portrait, whether consciously or unconsciously created. His biographer da Camara wrote in 1555: "How often I observed that in his whole manner of proceeding, the Father observes with exactitude all the rules of the Exercises. Thus he appears to have planted these rules in his own soul and then to have drawn them from his own interior acts. The same thing can be said of Gerson [i.e., of the *Imitation of Christ*], to such an extent that to converse with the Father seems to be nothing else than to read John Gerson put into practice. I must remember to write down many instances from which this universal statement can be drawn. The same thing is true of the Constitutions, especially of the chapter in which he portrays the general, in whose case he seems to have portrayed his own self" (FN I, 656).[1] The question remains as to how far we can go in accepting this description as an unself-conscious self-revelation rather than an idealized model. Clearly any prospective general would have to be a paragon of all conceivable virtues and psychic strengths.

Certainly half-measures or compromise were not congruent with Ignatius' spirit — if ideals were unattainable they were no less to be striven for. He wrote the scholastics at Coimbra:

> For his encouragement each one should keep before his eyes, not those who he thinks will accomplish less but rather those who are active and energetic. Do not ever permit the children of this world to show greater care and solicitude for the things of time than you show for those of eternity. It should bring a blush to your cheek to see them run to death more unhesitatingly than you to life. Hold yourselves as little worth if a courtier serve with greater care merely to have the favor of an earthly prince than you do for the favor of the King of Heaven, and if a soldier for the honor and glory of a victory and a little booty gets himself ready and battles more bravely

[1] Cited in Ganss (1970), p. 309. The idea was espoused by Ribadeneyra as well; see Becher (1977) and de Aldama (1989). The reference to Jean Gerson as the author of the *Imitation of Christ* reflects the knowledge of the time. The authorship was long uncertain and frequently attributed to Gerson who wrote other spiritual works. Modern scholarship attributes the *Imitation* to Thomas a Kempis.

> than you do for the victory and triumph over the world, the devil, and yourselves, with the kingdom of heaven and everlasting glory as your prize.
>
> For the love of God, therefore, be not careless or tepid. For if tautness breaketh the bow, idleness breaketh the soul; while on the contrary, according to Solomon, "the soul of them that work shall be made fat" [Prov 13: 4]. Try to maintain a holy and discreet ardor in work and in the pursuit of learning as well as of virtue. With one as with the other, one energetic act is worth a thousand that are listless, and what a lazy man cannot accomplish in many years an energetic man usually achieves in a short time. (Epistolae I, 495-510 [Letter 169]; in Young (1959) 120-130, 123)

Yet, withall, Ignatius was also insistent on flexibility, especially in the formation of the young scholastics with whom the method was often necessarily adapted to the subject rather than the subject to the method. This was often the case "especially with some who do not advance spiritually by one method, that with the grace of God they may be helped more by another" (CS343).

## SPIRITUAL EXERCISES

Ignatius not only proposed to his followers an ideal of religious virtue that he thought essential to the work of the Society and the kingdom of God, but he was also attentive to concrete practices of piety and virtue that he thought would help mould his followers and lead them along the path to increasing virtue and spiritual growth. The first instrument for such development was, not surprisingly, the *Spiritual Exercises*. Those in training were to make the Exercises in their entirety during the novitiate [CS65] and again in tertianship (the year of "third probation") [CS98]. Further, all were to study and reflect on them and have the experience of giving the Exercises to others [CS408, 409, 437]. This was one of the specific ministries of the Society [CS623, 648].

### *Prayer*

Devotion to a life of prayer was one of the primary means to spiritual growth and Ignatius' own devotion to prayer was one of the most striking aspects of his spiritual life.[2] But his own devotion to prayer and what he might recommend to his followers were quite

[2] See the discussion of Ignatius' prayer life and asceticism in chapter XXXII below; see also Meissner (1992b).

different matters. His discretion and prudent judgment, based largely on his won experiences, counseled moderation and subordination of immersion in prayer to the requirements of the love and service of God. He had to hold the line against those who in their fervor sought to devote long hours to prayer and to insist that others in the Society be required to do the same. In 1548, he had to deal with two Spaniards, Oviedo and Onfroy, who wished to retire into solitude for seven years in order to better prepare themselves for their later apostolate by a life of prayer. They regarded only one or two hours a day as insufficient and insisted that more time should be given to prayer. Ignatius sent a long instruction to Borgia refuting this "unsound teaching." Ignatius' view was that long periods of time were not necessary for effective prayer. Students must devote themselves to learning and need to preserve their strength for this purpose. Greater service can at times be given through other means than by prayer (de Guibert 1964; Stierli 1977; de Vries 1971).

He generally counseled moderation in prescribing the time spent on prayer by young scholastics during their studies [CS340-343]. He was not slow to urge his followers to fervor and seeking of perfection and exhorted scholastics at Coimbra to greater heroism in God's service, but not without prudent discretion. Their studies were the work at hand for the greater glory of God — the way to balance fervent devotion to prayer with the demands of God's service was through faithful adherence to obedience (Epistolae I, 496-510). In 1548 he learned that at Valencia and Gandia the practice of at least two hours of daily prayer had crept in, some even spending as much as eight hours at prayer. He at once wrote the provincial Araoz that this was an aberration and threatened to take action against them if they did not abandon this delusion. He even directed Araoz to set an example by reducing his customary three hours of prayer to one (Epistolae II, 46-47). Similar directions were issued to Oviedo, the rector at Gandia (Epistolae II, 54-65).

Along the same line, Polanco responded to questions from the Portugese novice master:

> As to prayer and meditation, if there are no bothersome or dangerous temptations . . . I notice that he rather approves the effort to find God in all things than that one should spend a long time in prayer. It is this spirit he desires to see in members of the Society, that if possible they find no less devotion in any work of charity or obedience than in prayer or meditation. As a matter of fact, they should do nothing at all except for the love and service of God our Lord, and each one should find greater satisfaction in

> what he is commanded, for then he can have no doubt that he is acting in conformity with the will of God our Lord. (Epistolae III, 499-503 [Letter 1848]; in Young (1959), p. 236)

In 1551, Antonio Brandao, a Portugese Jesuit, raised doubts about the appropriate prayer life for those engaged in studies. Ignatius responded point by point: Mass on Sundays and feast days and twice during the week would suffice; unordained scholastics could devote an hour a day to prayer along with two daily examinations of conscience and recitation of the Little Office of the Blessed Virgin or similar prayers; ordained scholastics should be content with daily Mass, recitation of the breviary, two examinations of conscience, and another half hour for whatever special devotion they might have. Mental effort and study were their principal concern, but they should try to seek the presence of God in all things. Study performed out of love of God and offered to Him for his greater glory and service would be their best prayer. They can find as much devotion in works undertaken for the love of God and under holy obedience as in prayer (Dudon 1949; Epistolae III, 506-513 [Letter 1854]; in Young (1959) 237-243, 240-241). These were basic principles written into the *Constitutions*.

For a time some uncertainty remained about whether the single hour of prayer Ignatius recommended for those in studies was meant to include examens and other prayers. The issue was decided when Ignatius corrected in his own hand the earlier rule in the *Constitutions* given to Nadal to promulgate in 1553: "In addition to confession and Communion . . . and Mass which they will hear every day, they will have one hour. During it, they will recite the Hours of Our Lady, and examine their consciences twice each day, and add other prayers according to the devotion of each one until the aforementioned hour is completed, in case it has not yet run its course. They are to do all this according to the arrangements and judgment of their superiors, whom they oblige themselves to obey in place of Christ our Lord" [CS342].

Once Ignatius made his views on this subject clear, he was not about to change them. In 1553, the Spaniards complained to Nadal that they had only an hour each day for prayer and asked for permission to extend the time. Nadal brought the request to Ignatius, recommending that it be granted, but Ignatius reprimanded him, "For a truly mortified man, a quarter of an hour is enough to unite himself with God in prayer." At other times, he was heard to say, "Of a hundred persons making profession of lofty prayer, ninety at least are deluded." In general he felt that the methods of prayer outlined in the *Exercises* were enough for prayerful formation of the scholastics, and that long hours of prayer were not necessary (Dudon 1949). We can guess that Ignatius was speaking from his own experience, particularly from the time at the University of Paris, when he had to learn from bitter experience that he could not continue long hours of prayer and penance and devote himself to study at the same time. He had to moderate his ascetical practices and shortened the time he devoted to prayer. Shortly before his death, he wrote: "One should reflect that man does not serve God only when he prays. Otherwise all prayer would be too short that does not last twenty-four hours daily (if that were possible), since everyone indeed should give himself to God as completely as possible. But in reality, God is served better at certain times through other means than prayer or, *a fortiori*, if he shortens it" (Epistolae XII, 652).

In the *Constitutions*, the place of prayer was given great prominence; Ignatius wanted his sons to be men of prayer. He stressed the central role of prayer in promoting the life of virtue and insuring the wellbeing and adaptability of the Society to carry out its mission in the world [CS812-3]. It was an important aid to good government [CS424], particularly for the general [CS790]. In general, the members of the Society will be better adapted to the work of the kingdom and be more effective in bringing souls to God in the degree to which they are united to God in prayer [CS723, 813]. Thus specific provisions are laid down for instructing and training novices [CS65], and recommendations for those in probation [CS277, 279], scholastics [CS340-5], the professed and formed coadjutors [CS582-3], and for temporal coadjutors [CS344, 345].[3]

## *Penance*

It seems quite clear that prayer itself was subordinated in Ignatius' mind, as well as in his practice, to self-denial and abnegation. Da Camara reported that when he reprimanded Nadal, "the Father said that his opinion, from which no one would ever move him, was that for the scholastics one hour of prayer is sufficient, it being supposed

[3] The simplicity of Ignatius' norms for prayer gradually yielded to pressures for longer prayer. Borgia, as General. specified an hour of prayer daily in addition to mass and two examinations of conscience (de Guibert 1964; Buckley 1979). Litanies were added in 1566 — contrary to Ignatius' opposition to any form of common prayer. Other accretions were gradually added that changed the complex of community life as Ignatius envisioned it from an emphasis on the interiority of grace and solitude to collective expectations and rules (Buckley 1979).

that they are practicing mortification and self-denial; and that such a one would easily accomplish more prayer in a quarter of an hour than another, who is not mortified, would do in two hours" (FN I, 676-677; Stierli 1977, p. 146). This was the basic principle that governed Ignatius' spiritual journey and was embedded in his *Spiritual Exercises*. They are "Spiritual Exercises to conquer oneself and to order one's life without making a decision through any disordered attachment" [SE21].

Consequently, Ignatius put a strong emphasis in his list of spiritual practices on mortification and the performance of penances. Mortification was proposed as an ideal — "as one who is dead to the world and to self-love and who lives only for Christ our Lord" [CS61]. As Ignatius put it, "The better to arrive at this degree of perfection which is so precious in the spiritual life, his chief and most earnest endeavor should be to seek in our Lord his greater abnegation and continual mortification in all things possible" [CS103]. Self-abnegation and mortification was recommended with regard to food, clothing, living circumstances, and other bodily needs [CS296, 297], and was to be sought especially in those wielding authority [CS423, 671, 726]. However, moderation was urged for those still in formation [CS263, 340, 362, 363, 582]. Penances for all should not be extreme so as not to interfere with personal health and effectiveness [CS300]. The question of fasting was particularly sensitive, since Ignatius' own excesses had undermined his health. The moderation of maturity was distilled into the *Constitutions*, emphasizing that the body and health were gifts of God to be taken care of and employed for God's service.

Ignatius urged discretion and moderation in ascetical practices, as in other matters. He wrote at one point to the scholastics at Coimbra:

> Yet I would not have you conclude from this that I am displeased, or at all disapprove of what has been written me on the subject of some of the mortifications practiced among you. For these and other holy follies, I well know, have been used by the saints with great profit to their souls. They help one in the work of self-conquest, and progress in virtue, especially in the beginning of one's change of life. But when with God's grace you have gained some mastery over self-love, it is better, I take it, that you follow out what I have said in this letter on the necessity of discretion. (Epistolae I, 506; cited in Doncoeur 1959, p. 37)

In 1547, he wrote at length to Borgia in an effort to moderate the Duke's excessive penitential enthusiasm:

> With regard to fasting and abstinence, I would advise you for the love of God to guard and fortify your stomach and your other natural forces, and not to weaken them. For when the soul is disposed and firmly determined to die rather than commit the least deliberate offense against the Divine Majesty, and when besides it is not harassed by any particular temptation of the enemy, the world and the flesh, mortification is no longer so necessary. . . . because we should care for the body and love it in proportion as it obeys and serves the soul more perfectly. On its part the soul finds in this obedient aid of the body more force and energy to serve and glorify our Creator and Lord. . . .
>
> With regard to the chastisement of the body, instead of trying to shed a drop of blood, rather seek our Lord more closely in all things, I mean His holiest gifts: intensity of faith, hope and charity, joy and spiritual repose, tears and intense consolation, elevation of the spirit, divine illuminations and impressions, and all the other spiritual sweetness and feeling which flows from such gifts. . . . Of all these holy gifts, there is not one which should not be preferred to all bodily acts which are only good when they have for their aim the acquisition of these graces. . . . So, when the body finds herself in danger as a result of laborious exercises, the best thing is to seek these gifts by mental acts, or by other moderate exercises. For not only is the soul restored to serenity, but when a healthy mind is in a healthy body, all becomes healthy and fitted to a better service of God. (Epistolae II, 233-237 [Letter 466], 234; in Young (1959) 179-182; cited in Doncoeur 1959, p. 37-39)[4]

Penances in the Society were not prescribed, but were left to the discretion and prudence of subjects, as long as they were undertaken with approval of the superior [CS8, 580]. At the same time, the su-

[4] Mannaerts (1523-1614) relates (*Exhortationes*, II, 613-614) that "a few years after the foundation of the Society, when . . . Ignatius observed that many, shortly after their entrance, were wasting away and dying, he called a meeting of physicians." When they learned of the austere life many were leading, they marveled that the number of those who had died was not greater. Then they urged that seven hours of sleep should be common to all each night; that mental prayer should not exceed an hour, except for the examens of conscience at their appointed times; that there should be an hour of rest after eating; that study should not be prolonged beyond two hours; that there should be time each week for a walk and other proper recreation. Many of these recommendations, harmonizing with the ordinary schedule and tempo of life in Mediterranean countries, were incorporated into the *Constitutions*. Ignatius appealed to "temperate restraint in spiritual and bodily labors . . . [which] will help this entire body to persevere in its good state and to be maintained in it" [CS821-822].

perior might impose certain penances as a means of correcting errors or defects [CS90, 269, 270, 754], and these should be accepted with good spirit and a desire for improvement [CS98, 269, 291].

Just as in the *Exercises*, Ignatius has constantly before his mind's eye the enemy whose efforts to undermine and frustrate efforts to follow the path of service and love of God must be guarded against at all costs. His wiles are directed to drawing men away from devotion to strict poverty [CS553, 816]; he can prompt them to indiscreet devotions [CS182] that draw them away from the path of true virtue [CS260] — his attacks are most vehement when the soul is most weakened and vulnerable at the time of death [CS595]. Countering the influence of the devil was even a criterion for deciding on apostolic missions — where the evil one had sown his cockle (Mt 13: 24-30), especially where he had stirred up ill will against the Society, there is where greater effort to do Christ's work is called for [CS622f]. In similar fashion, the path of virtue required that those who answer the call of Christ to enter the Society must turn their backs on the world [CS50, 53], leaving behind all emotional attachments [CS61], abandoning all the pomps and vanities of the world [CS66, 297], and to abhor whatever the world loves and embraces [CS101, 671].

Uppermost in his mind was the necessity to eliminate inordinate attachments and control unruly passions by means of self-denial and imitation of Christ. Denial of self is the essential foundation stone of all spiritual life and progress. No one could conquer the devil and preach to others until he had conquered himself. The fire of divine love and the ardent desire to serve God's kingdom had to be nourished by self-contempt and self-hatred; the path to spiritual growth lay in denial of self out of love for the suffering and humiliated Christ. Contemplation of the events in Christ's life in the *Exercises* focuses on the lowliness, poverty, and humiliations of the Savior. The exercitant is urged to follow Christ in his impoverishment and insults, to imitate Him in his lowliness and humility — "Let him desire and seek nothing except the greater praise and glory of God our Lord as the sum of all he does. For everyone must keep in mind that in all that concerns the spiritual life his progress will be in proportion to his surrender of self-love and of his own will and interests" [SE189].

Self-abnegation, the essential condition of Christian perfection, is his constant theme, enjoined on his followers and practiced personally day in and day out. Overcoming of self is the secret of all virtue, to be sought and achieved through the practice of poverty, chastity, and obedience to the will of God and His service (Dudon 1949). Ignatius' goal was radical abnegation of self through complete renunciation of comfort, honor, and especially one's own judgment (de Guibert 1964). In a letter to Fernandez on qualities of candidates for admission to the Society, Polanco wrote:

> With those who are received, I note that what the Father concerns himself most to make sure of, and what he thinks we must be most careful to secure, is obedience. . . . Individuals who are hard-headed, who upset and disturb others, even in slight things, he cannot put up with. In the matter of mortifications, I see that he wishes and esteems more those that touch one's sense of honor and self-esteem rather then those that make the flesh suffer, such as fasts, disciplines, and hair shirts. (Epistolae III, 499-503 [Letter 1848], 501; in Young (1959) 233-237)

The ideal he proposed to his followers also appears in the *Constitutions* in the form of a portrait of the apostle of Christ:

> Men crucified to the world, and to whom the world itself is crucified, such would the rule of our life have us to be; new men, I say, who have put off their affections to put on Christ; dead to themselves to live to justice; who with St. Paul (2 Cor 6: 5-8) in labors, in watchings, in fastings, in chastity, in knowledge, in long-suffering, in sweetness, in the Holy Spirit, in charity unfeigned, in the word of truth, show themselves ministers of God; and by the armor of justice in the right hand, and on the left by honor and dishonor, by evil report and good report, by good success finally and evil success, press forward with great strides toward their heavenly country. (Constitutions, Preface)

### *Sacraments*

Another extrapolation from the *Exercises* is the place Ignatius gave to examination of conscience and participation in the sacraments, particularly confession and communion. It was in part his urging of frequent communion that drew the attention of the Inquisition in his pilgrim years (Dudon 1949; Dalmases 1985; Meissner 1992b). Daily examination of conscience and confession and communion at least every eight days was urged for novices [CS261] as well as scholastics [CS342], temporal coadjutors [CS344], and formed coadjutors [CS584]. Da Camara describes Ignatius' implementation of some of these practices:

> These ordinary means [for making progress in virtue] were: to make the examens, to make one's prayer, to have correctors (*sindicos*), and to give an account daily to someone about the profit which one was drawing from these means. . . . Sometimes to cor-

> rect someone for a fault, our Father made him the corrector (*sindico*) for this fault, and to all others he was to point out their defects in this manner, just as they in turn were to point out his own to him. Toward the same end Ignatius also had the custom of having him examine himself several times every day about this fault, and, before dinner or before retiring, to tell someone whether he had made this examen at the prescribed times. (Memoriale 23, in SdeSI, I, 541; cited in de Guibert (1964), p. 95).

The practice of mutual correction follows the pattern set by Ignatius himself who repeatedly sought out spiritual guides and confessors to help him along his often tormented path toward sanctity. The practice would require good will and charity or it could have unfortunate effects. We know that Ignatius was not slow to expose his own faults and limitations, even as general. In this same spirit, a general confession was urged for those making the *Spiritual Exercises* during the first probation and before taking vows [CS98, 200]. They should also have a regular confessor to whom they can open their consciences completely [CS261, 278]. Frequent attendance and celebration of mass were encouraged [CS80, 584]. Devotion to Our Lady had a special place, particularly in the form of recitation of the Hours of Our Lady [CS342-5] to which Ignatius had always had a profound personal devotion.

Especially characteristic of Ignatius' spiritual practice was frequent reception of the eucharist. He was probably first exposed to this practice at Montserrat, and at Manresa received the sacrament every Sunday. There too, he came to know the *Imitation of Christ*, in which frequent communion is encouraged. The early Jesuits often cited Gerson, then thought to be the author of the *Imitation*, in support of the practice. The idea gradually caught on, not merely because of the efforts of Ignatius and his men, but in good measure. Their insistent encouragement of this devotion even brought suspicion and denunciations down on their heads (O'Malley 1993). This high valuation of both frequent confession and communion, so integral a part of Ignatian spirituality, found its way inevitably into the *Constitutions*.[5]

We can be impressed, in this brief survey of the spiritual teaching embedded in the *Constitutions*, by the degree of consistency that Ignatius' spiritual outlook expresses — stretching from the early years of the Manresa experience and the origins of the *Spiritual Exercises* to the final formulations inscribed in this magisterial document intended

[5] Ignatius nowhere insisted that every Jesuit say his own mass. He himself would either say or attend mass before his customary meditation (Buckley 1976).

for his spiritual posterity and as the expression of his vision for the Society that was to continue his crusade for the kingdom of Christ. If the lines of continuity are clearly etched, we can also observe a degree of progression from the early almost fanatical intensity of the pilgrim to the measured and matured spirituality of the founder and superior general. Ignatius had learned painful lessons that taught him the wisdom of moderation and the need to temper his spiritual fervor in the interest of adapting himself and his followers to the demands of the work that lay ahead of them.

# CHAPTER XX

# AN ETHIC OF SERVICE AND LOVE

## Introduction

In his magisterial treatise on Jesuit spirituality, Joseph de Guibert (1964) wrote:

> One very clear and noteworthy characteristic of Ignatius' diary, as of all the documents we have of his interior life, is the total absence of what could be called the "nuptual" aspect of the mystical union. In the *Spiritual Exercises* [SE353-365] he presents the Church as the spouse of Christ; but nowhere does he represent the individual soul as the spouse of God or of Christ. Ignatius' union with the Trinity and with Jesus is described in multitudinous ways and presented as something intensely intimate; yet nowhere is it envisaged as a "spiritual marriage." Neither does his mystical union appear as a "transforming union" which gives the life of the soul a foundation in the life of God, and in some way causes a man's own personal life to disappear within that of the Christ who lives in him. There is nothing in Ignatius which resembles the lyricism of the *Spiritual Canticle* and the *Living Flame* of St. John of the Cross. The magnificent poetic gifts of the Carmelite Doctor are totally lacking in the founder of the Society. (pp. 55-56)

De Guibert underscored one of the paradoxes of Ignatian mysticism. Insofar as mystical union plays such a central role in mystical experience, its relative absence from Ignatius' mystical spirituality is something of a puzzle. It is clear from a careful study of Ignatius' descriptions of his own mystical ecstasies that both in his mystical baptism at Manresa, as conveyed in his *Autobiography*, and in his mature years of intense mystical experience in Rome, as portrayed in the *Spiritual Journal*, he was a recipient of the highest mystical gifts and experienced the loftiest transports of mystical union — as intense and transforming as any conveyed by the powerful and poetic descriptions of John of the Cross or Teresa of Avila. But also clearly,

Ignatius followed his own path in climbing the mystical mountain and gave his spiritual doctrine a unique and characteristic stamp. The themes of mystical union are decisively underplayed and in their place the characteristically Ignatian themes of humility and service become code words for expressing his profound love of God and man.

## LOVE IN THE *Spiritual Exercises*

It has been noted that the *Exercises* have little to say about love, but a good deal more about service. Yet at the very end of the *Exercises*, Ignatius refers to "the zealous service of God our Lord out of pure love" [SE370] as a goal to be prized above all else. Motifs of love and service are thus fused into a common and mutually sustaining theme pervading all of his spirituality. If there is justice in de Guibert's (1964) distinction between mysticism of love or union and mysticism of service, the balance tilts in Ignatius from one to the other — if the motif of service dominates the *Exercises* and the *Constitutions*, the companion motif of love emerges as the dominant theme in his *Spiritual Journal*.[1] Yet it may also be fairly claimed that de Guibert's classic distinction between the "mysticism of union" and the "mysticism of service" may not do justice to pivotal statements about union with Christ and God in the annotations [SE15] and in the second mode of election [SE184]. The only explicitly nuptial reference is to the union of Christ and the church as his spouse [SE353].

We have previously discussed aspects of love in the *Exercises*, specifically with reference to their development in the fourth week.[2] The essence of Ignatius' teaching on love is contained in the contemplation on gaining love [SE230-237] and is expressed in two points: that love is found in deeds rather than words [SE230], and that love is a matter of mutual exchange between lover and beloved [SE231]. Ignatius joins two central themes here, namely his emphasis on humble service in the kingdom of God as the preferred expression of love for God — the theme that found such dramatic expression in the meditations on the Two Standards and on Christ as king — and the note of mutuality in giving and receiving that takes on special relevance in the context of returning love for love in response to the loving initiative coming from God as creator, lord and redeemer. These themes become *leitmotifs* echoing throughout all of Ignatius' spiritual teaching and practice.

[1] See chapter XXXIV below.
[2] See chapter XIV above.

One of the more thoroughgoing discussions of love from a psychoanalytic perspective was provided by Erich From (1956). He pointed out that love was an activity, not merely a passive emotion. Moreover, it consisted in giving rather than receiving. One common misunderstanding is that such giving means giving something up, being deprived, sacrificing. People, whose character has not developed beyond the receptive, exploitative or hoarding orientations, experience any giving in this vein. Some would be willing to give, but only with he understanding that they will receive something in return. Some make a virtue out of the sense of sacrifice involved in giving — virtue lies in accepting the sacrifice. For them, if it is better to give than receive, it really means that it is better to suffer deprivation than experience satisfaction in giving. But for more fully developed personalities, giving is an expression of potency, strength, of the cup overflowing with bounty and joy. Giving is better than receiving because it expresses my vitality and activity.

However, it is worth noting at this point that in the *Exercises* Ignatius is somewhat cryptic about the question of love of God, but that it is present in a decisive form nonetheless — embedded in certain condensed formulae that effectively make a central point but say little more, as though the matter of love was to be left between the exercitant and his God — as if the role of that love that could be spiritually transforming and elevating was too personal, too intimate, too much a matter of the intercourse between God and the soul to permit any further descriptive or prescriptive statements. In the fifteenth annotation [SE15], Ignatius wrote, ". . . in the Spiritual Exercises, when seeking the Divine Will, it is more fitting and much better, that the Creator and Lord Himself should communicate Himself to His devout soul, inflaming it with His love and praise, and disposing it for the way in which it will be better able to serve Him in future."

Thus, love of God, so central to Ignatius' spiritual life, was not a matter of human desire or passion, or not merely that. The love that inflamed the soul with spiritual desire and drew it into closer loving union with God came from God as a gift of divine grace. The theme recurs even more explicitly in his treatment of the second mode of election — "that love which moves me and makes me choose such thing should descend from above, from the love of God, so that he who chooses feel first in himself that that love, more or less, which he has for the thing which he chooses, is only for his Creator and Lord" [SE184]. Clearly Ignatius had something more in mind than is implied by the rhetoric of service. For him the love of God reached ecstatic, encompassing, all-consuming proportions, and if the unitive themes are not explicitly enunciated, they are palpable as matters of powerful presence and realized amplitude.

The meaning of love and charity in Ignatius' spiritual vision were intimately linked to the meaning and place of freedom and its correlative relation to the dynamics of grace. Love, along with freedom and grace, were gifts of divine generosity and love, which, for Ignatius, should call forth a response of loving self-surrender and service. The theological connotations of this vision are complex and immersed in the density of the supernatural and mystery. Let us listen to Karl Rahner (1969):

> The act of apprehending God as love by love is the acceptance of a love which is wholly without ground in ourselves, but rather most radically and incalculably free. There is no prior lovableness in us to explain it (though that love confers such a quality). It depends totally and eternally on God's freedom; it has no other ground than his freedom itself. In this radical sense it is, and eternally remains, "grace". The "possession" of God, if one may still use the word, is the radical self-transcendence and ecstasis of man's dynamism towards truth, into the abyss of mystery. It is the radical self-abandonment and self-transcendence of a love which by no self-giving can win the love of the beloved, but which lives wholly by his love which has no ground but itself. It is purely receptive and only by being so is it the basis of the mutual exchange of .love. It is not based on that exchange. (p. 27)

Yet in Ignatius' hands these profound themes have a strikingly human quality — he does not speak of mysteries and transcendence, but of service and mutual exchange. In a unique and powerfully intimate sense, the love of God was for Ignatius a form of object relation between the person of the loving believer and the person of the loving God.[3] In this sense, he stands firmly in a thomistic tradition founded on an idea of a personal relation between God and man through grace.

At the same time, specifically in terms of such a relation, the human and psychological dimensions have their place. Fromm (1956), for example, connects the need to love with the need to compensate for the anxiety of our human separateness by seeking loving union — in strictly human terms, but also in religious terms in union with God. The quality of love of God is a function both of the personal

[3] I do not mean to introduce a trinitarian obscurity here — the persons of the triune divinity should not be confused with this humanistic language. I mean only that as Ignatius speaks of his love of God and of God's love for him he uses a language that could as well apply to the love between two human persons.

qualities the individual brings to this connection and the nature of the image of God or the God-representation (Rizzuto 1979) in the mind of the believer. In some cultures, the maternal qualities of the godhead predominate, in others the paternal. And in others, some amalgam of these qualities prevail. The love of the mother is unconditional, protective, enveloping; it is also a love that cannot be acquired — the mother loves her children because they are hers, not because of what they do or accomplish. Paternal qualities, however, make demands, establish laws and regulations, demand obedience. The child is loved best who is most like the father and most obedient to his commands. As Fromm (1956) commented:

> In the matriarchal aspect of religion, I love God as an all-embracing mother. I have faith in her love, that no matter whether I am poor and powerless, no matter whether I have sinned, she will love me, she will not prefer any other of her children to me; whatever happens to me, she will rescue me, will save me, will forgive me. Needless to say, my love for God and God's love for me cannot be separated. If God is a father, he loves me like a son and I love him like a father. If God is mother, her and my love are determined by this fact. (p. 67)

But there is also question of the degree to which these patterns of relation to God remain embedded in relatively infantile terms and what would constitute more mature and psychologically coherent orientations toward the love of God. One shift is from a anthropomorphic view of God to one that is more philosophically sophisticated. As Fromm (1956) noted:

> The God of Abraham could be loved or feared as a father, whether he be angered and punitive or forgiving and loving. In this sense, if God is a father, then I am a child, still wishing for an omnipotent and omniscient father to protect me from the consequences of my human limitations, my ignorance and helplessness. As he observes: "I still claim, like a child, that there must be a father who rescues me, who watches me, who punishes me, a father who likes me when I am obedient, who is flattered by my praise and angry because of my disobedience. Quite obviously the majority of people have, in their personal development, not over come this infantile stage, and hence the belief in God to most people is the belief in a helping father — a childish illusion" (p. 70).

This may not serve as the final word, however, insofar as the depiction of God in New Testament terms is precisely as a loving and forgiving father. The connotation that this view is infantile and to be superseded remains open to question. A further consideration would center on the question of the integration of the gospel presentation of God and the related imagery with more theologically elaborated and abstract considerations and how they relate to the psychodynamic considerations raised in Fromm's comments. The question remains open, as far as I can see.

A further comment, however, may help to bring this reflection back to the Ignatian paradox. Fromm (1956) wrote:

> In contemporary religion we find all the phases, from the earliest and most primitive development to the highest, still present. The word "God" denotes the tribal chief as well as the "absolute Nothing." In the same way, each individual retains in himself, in his unconscious, as Freud has shown, all the stages from the helpless infant on. The question is to what point he has grown. One thing is certain: the nature of his love for God corresponds to the nature of his love for man, and furthermore, the real quality of his love for God and man often is unconscious — covered up and rationalized by a more mature *thought* of what his love is. (p. 82)

There is an added problem, however, in bringing Ignatius' insights to bear on modern consciousness. God has changed over the centuries, so that the God to which modern man might address himself is not the same God as Ignatius envisioned. In our time, the idea of God has undergone a series of transformations at the hands of Christian philosophers and theologians; he has become more profoundly subjectivized with contradictory effects. The meaning of God has been used as a means of self-defense in the face of the overpowering contradictions of modern life, as a basis for creative inspiration along with tragic illusions, a form of spiritually based life insurance, and as an opiate for the disillusioned and desperate masses. God no longer has a single and unequivocal meaning, but his place in human consciousness is more varied and variable. It has become overburdened by the hopes for the betterment of human nature that seem frustrated and defeated by the present perversity of human nature. As Krejci (1969) commented:

> Christian infinity and God do not bear only one uniform meaning; they are distinguished by their content; there is a difference, for example, between the longing for absolute religious justice, for an absolute end to the religious conflict between good and evil, and the longing for transcendence, which mirrors the idea of man's finding rest in God as compensation for the insufficient humanization of the world and the harsh self-sufficiency of nature. . . . The idea of God becomes an instrument in the struggle against the dehumanization of man and the defence of his concrete indi-

> vidual existence (Gabriel Marcel), a means to the integral humanization of the present and to the integral presence of Christianity (J. Maritain). The idea of God is purified from certain ancient prejudices, the sanctification of lack of education, intimidation, absolute subjection, ignorance of science, etc. The orthodox God of the Middle Ages, the God of Thomas Aquinas, has been subjected to differentiation within Christianity. It can be seen that the idea of God has been strongly dechristianized, for its manifold development has often been so great that it is no longer compatible with the basis of Christianity. God is not regarded at all as an opiate; many Christians in fact understand the idea of God as an instrument in the struggle for a progressive alteration in the world (Teilhard de Chardin, Paul Chauchard). God or Christian infinity no longer bears one uniform meaning to the same extent as formerly. (pp. 86-87)

However one resonates with these themes, my reading of Ignatius locates him in a transitional phase, as though his thinking was rooted in classical thomistic doctrine whereas the dynamism of his spirit and inspiration pointed more toward the world of modernity that was only beginning to peak over the horizon in his day. The motifs of service and love find a more compatible resonance in the modern context, even given the degree of subjectivization and humanization the ideas of God and of his love may have undergone. But Ignatius allowed little room for illusion — his God could not serve as any kind of opiate and basis for illusions of the betterment of the human condition. The vision called for the realization of Christ's kingdom in this world — and to this extent it carried with it elements of a vision of a more hopeful, even millennialist, future as embodied in the triumph of the kingdom of Christ. But the vehicle lie in the human response to divine initiatives, in devotion to the cause of Christ and self-immolating service — not in any transforming action of God exclusive of human participation and cooperation. The theme echoes the Ignatian paradox — we depend totally on God and his sustaining grace for any effectiveness or achievement, but we act as though the outcome was totally dependent on our own initiative and effort.[4]

## Love and Charity in the Constitutions

For a more expanded reading of Ignatius' views on the place of love in Ignatian spirituality and particularly love of God, we can turn to the *Constitutions*, where the highly schematic and lapidary formu-

[4] See my earlier discussion of the paradox in chapter VIII above.

lae of the *Exercises* have been translated into explicit and practical terms. Ignatius is not slow to put the principle of love at the very root of the inspiration and vitality of the Society — ". . . it must be the Supreme Wisdom and Goodness of God our Creator and Lord which will preserve, direct, and carry forward in His divine service this least Society of Jesus, just as He deigned to begin it; and although what helps most on our own part toward this end must be, more than any exterior constitution, the interior law of charity and love which the Holy Spirit writes and engraves upon hearts . . ." [CS134].

Ignatius leaves little doubt as to the importance he attributed to the principle of love and how closely linked it was to his idea of service.

> For the preservation and development not only of the body or exterior of the Society but also of its spirit, and for the attainment of the objective it seeks, which is to aid souls to reach their ultimate and supernatural end, the means which unite the human instrument with God and so dispose it that it may be wielded dexterously by His divine hand are more effective than those which equip it in relation to men. Such means are, for example, goodness and virtue, and especially charity, and a pure intention of the divine service, and familiarity with God our Lord in spiritual exercises of devotion, and sincere zeal for souls for the sake of glory to Him who created and redeemed them and not for any other benefit" [CS813].

The need for a pure intention played a primary role in Ignatius' spiritual outlook, since he associated it with the movement of the Spirit: in the *Exercises*, it took the form of "the love that moves and causes one to choose . . . descends from above, from the love of God, so that before one chooses he senses that the greater or less attachment for the object of his choice is solely because of his Creator and Lord" (SE184). Thus he could write, "In the midst of actions and studies, the mind can be lifted to God; and by means of this directing everything to the divine service, everything is prayer" (Epistolae, letter 4012), and again to the beleaguered Manuel Godhino who was complaining of his distracting involvement in temporal matters, "By your good and upright intention you turn everything you do into something spiritual for God's glory" (Epistolae, letter 2383; cited in Veale, 1996).

It is striking the degree to which these explicitations of the law of charity in the *Constitutions* echo themes of the *Exercises*. Cusson (1988) adds a comment that makes it clear how much Ignatius' views on love and charity reverberate with the themes of the Foundation [SE232] in the *Exercises*:

> However, if we are to be correct and complete, we must add that Ignatius perceived this view of the service of God in a dynamic context, that of the lover who gives himself and seeks to be loved for the good of the one beloved. That is why Ignatius' attitude will ripen into a sort of obsession for serving God. To refuse this service, to take it lightly, or to separate any part of one's life from it, is not only to neglect a tremendous responsibility or to hamper the work of the salvation of souls; but even far more, it is to be ungrateful, and thereby to fail to respond fully to the Love who has given himself without measure. Ignatius writes: "How he, the Creator, has become man, and has passed from eternal life to death here in time, and death for our sins" [SE53]. If, from now on in his life, Ignatius reaches out to everything, commits himself to everything, makes use of everything, the reason is, we might say, that everything should return to God. There is still more: The love of God becomes involved in everything. The interest of His Divine Majesty is playing a part everywhere, since everything exists for God. (p. 68)

Ignatius goes on to ask "What have I done for Christ? What am I doing for Christ? What ought I to do for Christ?" [SE53].

The echoes of these themes and their connection are heard throughout the pages of the *Constitutions*: ". . . in the eyes of our Creator and Lord those gain greater merit who with greater charity give help and service to all persons through love of His Divine Majesty . . ." [CS13]; and again, ". . . they should always aim at serving and pleasing the Divine Goodness for its own sake and because of the incomparable love and benefits with which God has anticipated us, rather than for fear of punishments or hope of rewards. . . . Further, they should often be exhorted to seek God our Lord in all things, stripping off from themselves the love of creatures to the extent that this is possible, in order to turn their love upon the Creator of them, by loving Him in all creatures and all of them in Him, in conformity with His holy and divine will" [CS288]. This spirit was meant to infuse everything the men of the Society undertook, even teaching of extern students: teachers were urged to "make it their special aim, both in their lectures when occasion is offered and outside of them too, to inspire the students to the love and service of God our Lord, and to a love of the virtues by which they will please Him" [CS486].

The same spirit of loving service — of love of God and devotion to His divine service — was sought in applicants to the Society [CS148, 156] from the very beginning of their engagement with the Society in the work of the Lord, no less than in those who held the highest office in the Society, pre-eminently in the General [CS725,

728, 735, 790], but also in those who hold the rank of superior in the Society. The love of God was the pervasive watchword in all dimensions of Society life and provided the basic motivational force for that life. It was the motivation underlying obedience — as Ignatius wrote, "They should keep in view God our Creator and Lord, for whom such obedience is practiced, and they should endeavor to proceed in a spirit of love and not as men troubled by fear" [CS547]. And again, addressing the manifestation of conscience, "Likewise, it should be strongly recommended to all that they should have and show great reverence, especially interior reverence, to their superiors, by considering and reverencing Jesus Christ in them; and from their hearts they should warmly love their superiors as fathers in Him. Thus in everything they should proceed in a spirit of charity, keeping nothing exterior or interior from the superiors and desiring them to be informed about everything . . . [CS551]. On his part, the superior was urged to use "all the love and modesty and charity possible in our Lord, so that the subjects can dispose themselves to have always toward their superiors greater love than fear" [CS667]. Even in giving corrections and penances, when discipline or correction required, the norm was charity, love and kindness [CS269, 270, 727].

Charity was, then, the measure of merit in all undertakings [CS13] and the guiding norm for all decisions and actions, both on the part of superiors [CS729, 735] and subjects. Discreet charity was the norm in dismissals [CS209, 213, 225, 226, 237], in the choice of prayers, devotions and penances [CS582], and in decisions related to choice of ministries and apostolic commitments. Such fraternal charity was especially necessary in the face of sickness and death [CS595, 601].

## Charity and Humility

Love and charity are intimately linked in the *Constitutions*, but use of the term "charity" tends to elicit connotations of the theological virtue. The virtue was prized by Ignatius above all others, including humility which occupies such a pervasive place in his spiritual writings and practice. In his mind, charity and humility were inextricably joined and mutually interdependent. In the *Constitutions*, charity occupies a much more central place in that it was the determinative principle that generated all the efforts of the Society and directed them to their end in finding and fulfilling the will of God. It was the "interior law" [CS134] that governed everything else and joined the Society and its members to God in seeking their supernatural end [CS813].

The link between charity and humility in Ignatius' mind finds expression in his view that charity finds its expression in the performance of even the humblest tasks [CS114], since they are performed out of the love and service of God. He wrote: "It will be very specially helpful to perform with all possible devotion the tasks in which humility and charity are practiced more, and, to speak in general, the more one binds himself to God our Lord and shows himself more generous toward His Divine Majesty, the more will he find God more generous toward himself and the more disposed will he be to receive graces and spiritual gifts which are greater each day" [CS282]. So prized was this virtue for Ignatius that he urged that it be a special subject for exhortations and preaching [CS280], and that it be regarded as a basic motivation for manifestations of conscience to the superior [CS63].

The balance and integration of charity and humility that Ignatius idealized has not always been effectively achieved by his followers.  The rhetoric of the *magis* or an uncompromising dynamism that puts no limits or restraints on finding and doing the will of God can open the way to illusions and blunders that smack of excessive zeal or grandiosity. The early Jesuits did not always meet with unalloyed enthusiasm and acceptance of their apostolic efforts (Clancy 1976; O'Malley 1993). They often enough met rejection and vilification as a response to their unbridled presumptuousness or well-meaning but ill-advised efforts to influence either churchmen or laymen to pursue paths of greater virtue. The same drives drew them into the political arena — into political and diplomatic missions at the behest of the Holy See or into royal courts where they sought to influence kings and elicit royal favors. Mannaerts would take Ribadeneyra to task for writing that "the Society ought to employ itself in great things." He commented, "I think it would be better to cut out both these phrases; because in every nation among all peoples we are falsely accused of interfering in great affairs which rightly belong to princes or states. Therefore, we must not give fuel for scandal" (FN IV, 991; cited in Clancy (1976), p. 115).

## The Bond of Fraternal Charity

When Ignatius sought to emphasize the necessity of an internal bond that would unite the members of his Society in ties of mutual support and trusting commitment, it was the law of charity that he cited.

> The chief bond to cement the union of the members among themselves and with their head is, on both sides, the love of God our Lord. For when the superior and the subjects are closely united with His Divine and Supreme Goodness, they will very easily be united among themselves, through that same love which will descend from the Divine Goodness and spread to all other men, and particularly into the body of the Society. Thus from both sides charity will come to further this union between superiors and subjects, and in general all goodness and virtues through which one proceeds in conformity with the spirit. [CS671]

And again: "Whatever helps toward the union of the members of this Society among themselves and with their head will also help much toward preserving the well-being of the Society. This is especially the case with the bond of wills, which is the mutual charity and love they have for one another" [CS821].

The subject was sufficiently central to his thinking to have an entire chapter (Part VIII, chapter I [CS655-676]) devoted to it in the *Constitutions.* He stressed union of the members with the head and mutual union among the members as essential to preservation of the Society and for attainment of its goals [CS655, 821]. This required that considerable care be exercised in the choice of those who desired to enter the Society [CS657]. Also, as we have seen in discussing Ignatius' views on obedience, he gave to holy obedience a central role in regard to the preservation of the union of hearts and minds in the Society [CS659, 662, 821]. In this connection, superiors played a vital part in contributing to the union of charity and love, since in the hierarchical model of authority Ignatius held they were bearers of authority and provided the structure within which obedience was exercised [CS666, 789], but also in virtue of the love, modesty and charity with which they dealt with their subjects [CS667].

Ignatius prized the union of hearts and minds as essential to the bond of charity and took a stand against divisive opinions and divergent doctrines as sowing seeds of discord. "This union and agreement among them all ought to be sought with great care and the opposite ought not to be permitted, in order that, being united among themselves by the bond of fraternal charity, they may be able better and more efficaciously apply themselves in the service of God and the aid of their fellowmen" [CS273]. Any who were found to be the cause of division, discord or estrangement were to be separated from that community as if "a pestilence which can infect it seriously if a remedy is not quickly applied" [CS664], either by expulsion from the Society or by transfer to another community [CS665]. The norms of preservation of charity and avoidance of controversy and discord applied equally to relationships with persons outside the Society with whom members of the Society had dealings [CS163, 318, 489, 572, 593, 823].

## Pauline Perspective

To a remarkable degree, the Ignatian doctrine on love and charity finds a note of resonance with the teaching of St. Paul. If we integrate the themes of love, humility and self-sacrifice dominating the *Spiritual Exercises* with the chords of love, charity, humility, service. and fraternal union reverberating through the pages of the *Constitutions*, we arrive at a systematic elaboration of the same elements embedded in the great apostle's letter to the Corinthians:

> If I have all the eloquence of men or of angels, but speak without love, I am simply a gong booming or a cymbal clashing. If I have the gift of prophecy, understanding all the mysteries there are, and knowing everything, and if I have faith in all its fullness, to move mountains, but without love, then I am nothing at all. If I give away all that I possess, piece by piece, and if I even let them take my body to burn it, but am without love, it will do me no good whatever.
>
> Love is always patient and kind; it is never jealous; love is never boastful or conceited; it is never rude or selfish; it does not take offense, and is not resentful. Love takes no pleasure in other people's sins but delights in the truth; it is always ready to excuse, to trust, to hope, and to endure whatever comes.
>
> Love does not come to an end. But if there are gifts of prophecy, the time will come when they must fail; or the gift of languages, it will not continue forever; and knowledge — for this, too, the time will come when it must fail. For our knowledge is imperfect and our prophesying is imperfect; but once perfection comes, all imperfect things will disappear. When I was a child, I used to talk like a child, and think like a child, and argue like a child, but now I am a man, all childish ways are put behind me. Now we are seeing a dim reflection in a mirror; but then we shall be seeing face to face. The knowledge that I have now is imperfect; but then I shall know as fully as I am known.
>
> In short, there are three things that last: faith, hope and love; and the greatest of these is love. (1 Cor 13: 1-13)

## A Psychoanalytic Note

The theme of love in its sublimated and spiritualized guise strikes sympathetic chords that resonate with ideas of sexuality considered within a psychoanalytic framework. It would lie beyond the scope of the present consideration to try to develop an adequate psychoanalytically based understanding of love that would allow for integration with the themes of love and charity in the spiritual realm. That would be a major undertaking — one that has yet to find satisfactory expression or formulation within psychoanalysis. Certainly such a theory could not call itself psychoanalytic without maintaining clear connections and derivations from the basic libido theory that distinguishes psychoanalysis from most other psychologies.

But the difficulties lie precisely in how one can understand libido and its functions in terms that allow for the spiritual dimensions of love that find expression in the love of God, in mystical union, or in selfless devotion and self-surrender for the good of others that is the hallmark of authentic charity. The great commandment of the law echoes throughout these considerations — "You must love the Lord your God with all your heart, with all your soul, and with all your mind. This is the greatest and the first commandment. The second resembles it: you must love your neighbor as yourself" (Mt 22: 37-39). Whatever contribution analysis might make to understanding this love, it cannot be reductionistic; but by the same token love at any level or in any guise cannot be fully comprehended exclusively from the basic drive capacities of human nature. I would argue that without libidinal capacity, the love of God is either impossible or meaningless.

The difficulty lies in connecting the love of which the great commandment of the law speaks with the libidinal drive so central to the analytic perspective. It is one thing to say that they are connected, but another to say precisely how. Freud's view of sexuality is rather complex, with at times divergent connotations. In some contexts it referred to ordinary usage having to do with genital sexual activity and orgasm, and the pleasure related to such activities or other psychic processes related to them. This is the narrowest usage, reflected for example in his pointing to the loss of sexual interest resulting from castration anxiety. But in more extended usages, all sensual pleasure was viewed as connected to the sexual sphere and derivative from sexual pleasure in the first sense — in this sense all positive and loving affection, even tenderness, was regarded as basically sexual (Freud 1916-17, 1925a). Then again, at other points, Freud drove a wedge between the sexual and the genital that seemed to relax any connection between them (Freud 1905, 1913, 1925a).

In this broadest usage, his view of the sexual was not too dissimilar from Plato's Eros, representing those forces supportive of life, increasing structuralization and psychic synthesis (Freud 1905). As Freud commented in the 1920 preface to the fourth edition of his *Three Essays* (1905):

> . . . some of what this book contains — its insistence on the importance of sexuality in all human achievements and the attempt that it makes at enlarging the concept of sexuality — has from the first provided the strongest motives for the resistance against psychoanalysis. . . . And as for the 'stretching' of the concept of sexuality . . . anyone who looks down with contempt upon psychoanalysis from a superior vantage-point should remember how closely the enlarged sexuality of psychoanalysis coincides with the Eros of the divine Plato. (p. 134)

Not only are we confronted with multiple connotations of the term 'sexual,' but the sexual drive is also subject to various forms of defensive and adaptive modification and direction, including sublimation and aim-inhibited modifications. The degree to which in any given context the sexual component is sublimated[5] or aim-inhibited[6] makes the influence of sexual drive components in any context of human endeavor quite complex indeed. What emerges more clearly from these considerations is that the psychoanalytic perspective on love and sexuality are in no sense constrained to the ordinary connotations of genital sexual expression or pleasure. However, as I have discussed more fully elsewhere (Meissner 1992b), there is good reason to think that in Ignatius himself the intense affective experiences that marked his devotion and mystical transports reflect the residues of a repressed and only partially sublimated sexuality. The massive libidinal repression that accompanied his conversion would seemingly have left a portion of his powerful sexual dynamism relatively unintegrated, at least to a degree allowing for a return of the repressed that found further sublimation into his profound mystical affective

[5] That is, diverted to apparently nonsexual and/or socially valued aims.

[6] That is, the quality of instinctual satisfaction is altered by external or internal obstacles resulting in attenuated pleasure from activities or relationships more or less remote from the original sexual aim.

life, if not elsewhere.[7] Consequently, we have reason to regard the profound spiritual doctrine on love and charity that he proposed as guiding norms for life in his Society as reflecting some of these sublimated libidinal components transposed into an elevated and spiritualized register. This is all the more striking in view of the sparse treatment given to sexuality in the *Constitutions*, especially in view of the fact that commitment to a religious life required a vow of celibacy and chastity. He seems to dispatch the question with a wave of the hand — "What pertains to the vow of chastity does not require explanation, since it is evident how perfectly it should be preserved through the endeavor in this matter to imitate the angelic purity by the purity of the body and mind" [CS547]. Was this just the spirit of the times (Ganss 1970) or does it reflect an extension of his need to maintain his usual defensive posture regarding sexuality.[8]

The love Ignatius had in mind for his Society was this kind of sublimated and aim-inhibited libidinal capacity distilled into the form of fraternal charity, love and service of one's fellowmen, and love of God. Fraternal charity in the Society was the bond of union joining the members into an effective instrument for accomplishing God's purposes in this world. From one point of view, love of God and love of one another out of love of God was the primary unifying force in the Society. This fraternal charity encompassed acceptance, support, friendship, tolerance for one another's faults and shortcomings, a willingness to share for the good of one another, and above all a willingness to sacrifice oneself and all one has for the good of another and for the love and service of God our Lord.

If there were distillations of sublimated homosexual and/or heterosexual libido in the mix, the psychoanalyst would not be abashed to think so. But this way of viewing the matter does not seem to cover the ground adequately, nor does it offer much in the way of insight. The love or charity that pervaded Ignatius' thought and desire was not merely a natural love, but a love that comes as a gift of God, as a resultant of divine grace and benevolence, and while it may be congruent with reductively derived forms of libidinal expression, seems to reach beyond them to embrace a more sublime spiritual

[7] In his psychobiography (Meissner 1992b), I discussed the vicissitudes of this drive related economy in Ignatius' life, especially in his dealings with women, but also in his libidinal involvements with many spiritual sons and daughters, expressed largely in his charismatic presence and the intensity of emotional involvement on many fronts.

[8] Other references to chastity are no more than passing references to the vow itself as a canonical requirement.

love that transcends, even as it does not divorce itself from, the sublimated forms of libidinal expression. We stand here at the point of the mystery of the interplay of grace and nature, of the human and the divine, and the quality of the interrelation between man and his God. The troublesome question remains as to how the impulse of grace drawing the human soul to an elevated and supernaturalized love of God is integrated with the roots of libidinal experience drawn from man's natural and fundamental libidinal capacity.

The question that this problematic inevitably raises concerns the psychological meaning of the God who is so loved. Whatever dynamic we can envision that speaks to the presence of God to the human mind and heart, from the side of the experiencing human the imagery that is stirred draws on basic transference material that is organized and transformed into some form of God-representation (Rizzuto 1979). The affective currents deriving from these transference elements become distilled into the love experience even at the highest spiritual or even mystical levels. I have argued at length (Meissner 1992b) regarding the role of these derivatives in Ignatius' mystical experience and the determinative influence they may have played in coloring his affective responses in states of mystical elevation and transport.

The idea that elevation to mystical heights, with the transcendent power of the affective experiences associated with that state, may simultaneously draw upon fundamental affective resources that might have arisen developmentally in more primitive, even preoedipal, phases, is perfectly consistent with what we know and understand about the other vicissitudes of human loving in more natural and familiar contexts. This understanding, it should be noted, does not reduce the love of God to some simplistic form of translation of the libidinal investment in transference objects, any more than an analysis of the color work and brush techniques of van Gogh is an adequate basis for understanding the meaning of one of his canvases. A reductive explanation is not necessarily reductionistic. So, if we can trace some of the roots of spiritual affective experience to more natural and human derivatives, we have not exhausted the intelligibility of the experience — at the least we would also have to take into account the role of the divine agent, acting not only as the object of love but as in some sense moving and sustaining the love experience in the human lover through grace. Ignatius touches on this question in his insistence on the mutuality of love, especially in the love of God above all other loves of which man is capable.

# CHAPTER XXI

# MODES AND METHODS OF GOVERNANCE

## The Manner of Governing

The structure of governance holds a prominent place in these legal prescriptions, but of even greater import was the manner of governing. Ignatius and his companions drew from their early experiences together and in some part from the inspiration of Ignatius the impetus to form not just a new religious order, but a new form of religious life. This required that institutionalized norms for this undertaking should be both firm and flexible — the unique modality referred to as "our way of proceeding," marked by a communal form of organization with diffuse sharing of responsibility and a formal hierarchical authority structure. The authority invested in individuals was directed to promotion and preservation of unity and implementation of effective apostolic works. The style of governance was consultative rather than autocratic or authoritarian, and the function of obedience was primary — "this virtue must always be maintained in its vigor" [CS659], but was to be exercised "in such a manner that the superior on his part uses all the love and modesty and charity possible in the Lord" [CS667].

The *Constitutions* provide ample directives for the general and other superiors regarding their manner of exercising their authority. De Guibert (1964) cited from Ribadeneyra's work on *Ignatius' Manner of Governing* to this effect:

> Our Father taught that authority is of course necessary to help the neighbor and to do him good, and ought therefore to be sought after; that this authority, however, is not acquired by anything that recalls or smacks of the world, but by contempt of the world, and through true humility, and through showing more by deeds than by words that one is a disciple and imitator of the humble Christ, and that one wishes for and seeks only His glory and the salvation of the souls whom He Himself came to seek. And for this reason one does not look down on anything, however small it

> may be or worthless in the eyes of men, if one can draw from it some glory for God. One should always begin with what is lowly if one wishes to arrive at what is high and to be favored by the Lord who resists the proud and exalts the humble. (p. 150)

Ribadeneyra's emphasis recalls for us the central place of humility in Ignatian spirituality and the critical place he gave it in the *Spiritual Exercises*. If the exercise of authority was not rooted in humility, it was not the authority Ignatius envisioned in his Society. At all levels, the burden of governance can be sustained more easily with the help of consultors, as Ignatius recommends [CS810].[1] But after such consultation has been heard, the responsibility for making the decision remains with the superior.

The art of governing is thus one of guidance and discernment. The superior enters into a relationship with the subject in which he becomes the participating guide of his subject's spiritual and personal development, always attuned to his personal situation and potential for growth, and to the dynamic influence of the Spirit inspiring not only his vocation to the Society but his desire for greater service. As Emonet (1990) writes:

> The *Constitutions* were born of a discernment; their application also presumes an ongoing discernment, which is the superior's task to effect. The yardstick against which he must constantly measure the exercise of his authority is *discreta caritas* — a "discerning love." This major virtue entails a specific tension within the heart of the person who must govern. On the one hand there is love, which is by nature absolute, which intends to give all immediately and is not satisfied with good desires but looks for deeds [SE230]. On the other, there is discernment, which takes account of the real and actual situation, the limited capacities and the slowness of progress, without for all that giving vent to frustration or abruptness towards the companion who is on his journey. Government in the Society thus relies more on an openness of hearts and spirits and on a fraternal discernment than on the compelling force of laws and purely formal structures. (pp. 115-116)

## Manifestation of Conscience

One vehicle for the more effective exercise of the superior's authority and the subject's obedience was the manifestation of conscience.

[1] See also [CS432, 490-2].

> [CS91] Through reflection in our Lord, what follows has seemed good to us in His Divine Majesty. It is a matter of great and even extraordinary importance that the superiors should have a complete understanding of the subjects, that by means of it they may be able to direct and govern them better, and while looking out for the subjects' interests guide them better into the paths of the Lord.
>
> [CS92] Likewise, the more completely the superiors know these subjects' interior and exterior affairs, just so much the better will they be able, with greater diligence, love, and care, to help the subjects and to guard their souls from various inconveniences and dangers which might occur later on. Further still, in conformity with our profession and manner of proceeding, we should always be ready to travel about in various regions of the world, on all occasions when the supreme pontiff or our immediate superior orders us. To proceed without error in such missions, or in sending some persons and not others, or some for one task and others for different ones, it is not only highly but even supremely important for the superior to have complete knowledge of the inclinations and motions of those who are in his charge, and to what defects or sins they have been or are more moved and inclined; that thus he may direct them better, without placing them beyond the measure of their capacity in dangers or labors greater than they could in our Lord endure with a spirit of love; and also that the superior, while keeping to himself what he learns in secret, may be better able to organize and arrange what is expedient for the whole body of the Society.

Ignatius emphasizes the importance of this manifestation of conscience for implementation of obedience and for union of judgment and will so central to his vision of obedience [CS551]. It was both an exercise in self-abnegation and sincerity of purpose, but rooted in the charity that was to pervade all relationships in the Society [CS63].

This corresponds to the exhortation to members of the Society to openness and communication with superiors [CS551]. Ignatius envisions here a union of superior and subject binding them together in a common cause and purpose. The manifestation of conscience is intended both for the benefit of the subject, insofar as it enables the superior to understand him better and accommodate to his individual needs better, and the superior, insofar as it provides him a better sense of what is required in adapting the capacities of his men to the apostolic goals of his community. The spirit of the manifestation is one of charity and seeking the optimal good of the individual and the group. Within this spirit, manifestation of conscience is one expression of the mutuality and collaboration that can be and should be the mark of an authentic authority relation.[2] Noteworthy [CS92] also is the stress on the superior's knowing the positive side of the subject's character. In Ignatius' view, manifestation of conscience included the whole consciousness or general attitude, not merely a series of faults (as the English term "examination of conscience" too often connotes).[3]

## THE IDEAL OF GOVERNANCE

Ignatius directed his effort in the *Constitutions* to fashioning a mode of governing that embraced the spiritual ideals that he had sought so assiduously on his own spiritual journey and that he recognized as related to essential Christian virtues. As Ganss (1970) commented:

> Ignatius wanted superiors to rule much as kindly fathers and as taking the place of Christ, so that as far as possible the relations between subjects and superiors would be firm but characterized by love [CS551, 727, 810], mutual esteem [CS423, 551, 667], and cordial and open communication [CS91-93]. According to Ignatius' ideal, therefore, government by superiors should be paternal in the sense of their being kindly and inspiring the "filial confidence" . . . but not in the sense that a superior should either exercise his authority in an authoritarian manner or bear himself toward his subjects as if they were still immature minors. (p. 250)

The ideal of governance that Ignatius espoused and the kind of superior he envisioned as exercising the authority of Christ in his Society was specified in his idealized portrait of the superior general.[4]

## IGNATIUS' STYLE OF GOVERNING

Ignatius' basic methods of governing are reflected in the *Constitutions*, as we have seen. A primary principle was the centrality of the vow of obedience to the Pope whose voice was the voice of God [CS603-617, 633]. And where the Pope gave him a free hand, Ignatius responded to requests from bishops, cardinals, and princes who had been benefactors of the Society and to whom he owed a debt of gratitude. Beyond that, his ears were attuned to any situation of spiritual

[2] See my discussion of the authority relation in chapter XXVI below.

[3] In 1611 Covarrubias defined *conciencia* as "knowledge of one's self, certain or nearly certain knowledge of that which is in our soul, whether good or bad" (p. 346). See also [CS263, 551].

[4] See the portrait of the general in chapter XIX above.

need or human misery. As Ravier (1987) notes, "The voice of misery was for him the Voice of God" (p. 330). In addition to the papal will, the principles of discernment that Ignatius had evolved at Manresa were constant guidelines.

Ignatius retained a somewhat simplistic ideal, derived from the spirit of the first fathers, that he tried to impose on his growing Society. It was a zealous ideal, filled with magnanimity, generosity, and zeal for souls. His harshness often came into play in his efforts to mold the Society according to this image, when the material was not sufficiently pliant to suit his tastes. His idealism and rather rigid expectations did not always serve well in dealing with emotional difficulties and weaknesses of others, particularly around the question of admitting or even readmitting candidates to the Society. Ravier (1987) comments:

> We should acknowledge that he needed some time to realize that not all candidates for the Society had his strength of character nor the dynamism of his grace. To the extent that one can discern an evolution in his *ars gubernandi* it is toward a more indulgent appreciation of human fragility, of "the weakness of many" which takes place. Was it without a certain regret of thus seeing the idea devalued which he was creating of the "companion of Jesus Christ"? Must we not necessarily perceive a certain disenchantment in this avowal offered at the end of his life: "If he wished," reports Polanco, "to live longer, it would be to prove himself more severe in admissions into the Society." (p. 339)

## Hierarchical Structure

Ignatius created a structure of governance that incorporated wide distribution of responsibility along with clear lines of authority. At the pinnacle stands the General, from whom authority is communicated to subordinate superiors. The General was

> . . . to be for all the members a head from whom descends to all of them the impulse necessary for the end which the Society seeks. Thus it is that from the General as the head flows all the authority of the provincials, and from the provincials that of the local superiors, and from that of these local superiors that of the individual members.[5] Thus too from that same head come assignments to missions, at least by his mandate and approval. The same should be

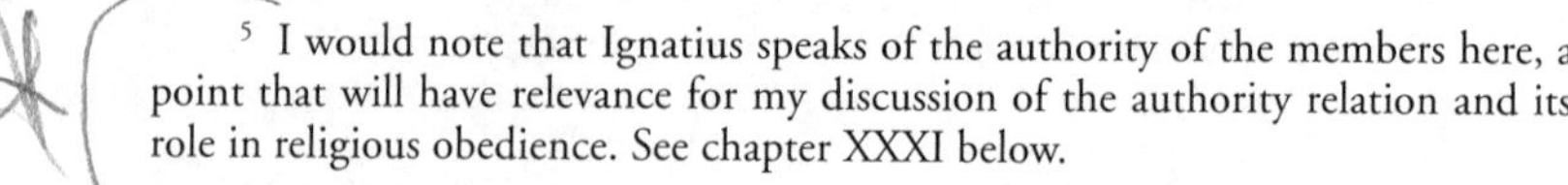

[5] I would note that Ignatius speaks of the authority of the members here, a point that will have relevance for my discussion of the authority relation and its role in religious obedience. See chapter XXXI below.

> understood about communication of the graces of the Society; for the more subjects are dependent upon their superiors, the better will be the love, obedience, and union among them be preserved. [CS666]

The structure of the Society was organized around a series of grades or ranks to which the members were assigned. The professed were regarded as the highest rank in the Society, men who realized the best qualities envisioned by the founders and who were marked by special gifts of nature and learning. They were priests who, in addition to the solemn vows of poverty, chastity and obedience,[6] took a special fourth vow of obedience to the Holy Father. Ignatius looked on the professed who took the fourth vow as men of mission, especially prepared to carry out the most difficult of apostolic efforts, men of maturity who could take the place of the founding fathers and were prepared to go to any place and undertake any responsibility for the good of the Society and the Church [CS12, 511].[7]

Creation of this special rank opened the door to rivalry and ambition from the beginning. As always, preferment brings its inevitable weight of narcissistic investment, intensified by the selectivity of the honor. Of the few professed at the time of Ignatius' death, most held positions as superiors or provincials,[8] and a few, like Canisius, were advanced to profession on the basis of exceptional virtue and learning. Another group were missionaries destined for particularly difficult or dangerous missions — such as Ethiopia, the Indies, Bohemia, or Brazil. Ignatius also had additional missioners advanced to full profession in situations of crisis to strengthen and confirm the place of the Society in these perilous regions.

A second rank or grade in the Society was held by spiritual coadjutors. They too were ordained priests, but with less learning or edu-

[6] The distinction between solemn and simple vows of religion is canonical and refers to whether the vows were strictly those of a religious order in the full sense or not. The solemn vow of poverty, for example, meant surrender of both ownership and use of possessions, while the simple vow meant only surrender of the use (Ganss 1970).

[7] At the time of Ignatius' death there were about 40 professed in the Society out of about 1,000 Jesuits. The professed houses were part of Ignatius' ideal vision of the Society. The professed were to live apart in separate communities in which prescriptions of the Institute and the Constitutions were to be observed with special care and devotion. The professed fathers were to live entirely on alms and were to dedicate themselves to apostolic labors.

[8] Ravier (1987) notes that one reason for this was the juridical requirement in some countries that religious superiors be "professed" in order to accept donations, make contracts, and so on. The legal meaning of profession and its implications for the Society were not synonymous; the easiest way to avoid difficulties was to profess superiors in such circumstances.

cation than the professed, who carried on a spiritual ministry. The third grade of temporal coadjutors or lay brothers who were neither ordained nor learned, but were employed in material and temporal activities. Beyond these formal grades, the scholastics were students, who had completed two years of novitiate and had taken simple but perpetual vows of poverty, chastity and obedience; they were engaged in studies and were destined for the grade of professed or spiritual coadjutor. The novices were young men who had recently entered the Society and were undergoing their first probation lasting two years, after which they were allowed to take simple vows.

One interesting question is why Ignatius took the trouble to set up these various grades at all.[9] It was clear to Ignatius that few of the recruits to his Society would have had sufficient theological training. Also it would take time for the young men who came to him to acquire the theological training necessary for the work of the Society. His solution was original (de Aldama 1989). He would admit some candidates who, although ordained as priests, would have little theology and/or little aptitude for it, but who could do valuable work in the Society in carrying on spiritual ministries, celebrating mass, hearing confessions, catechizing, and so on. He called them "spiritual coadjutors." But he also needed men to devote themselves to the work of taking care of material needs; these were the "temporal coadjutors." The papal brief approving these arrangements stipulated that these grades could be bound by simple vows as long as the general needed their help. Ignatius required the professed to have sufficient theological knowledge to be obtained in the stipulated four-year theological curriculum. But he allowed the spiritual coadjutors, like many priests of the time, to function with little more than a basic knowledge of grammar and matters of conscience sufficient to hear confessions. These were probably stopgap measures for Ignatius, presuming that, as enough scholastics finished their theological training, the role of spiritual coadjutor would be diminished and finally eliminated. But after his death, exactly the opposite came about — the number of spiritual coadjutors increased until the grade was made permanent by the general congregation in 1615. The grade continued to cause difficulties and dissatisfaction, so that the numbers decreased steadily, and probably would have been eliminated if the Society had not been suppressed in 1773.

The men in all of these grades were members of the Society and Ignatius' companions in Christ, allied with the General by ties of

[9] Ganss (1970) summarizes the research of Lukacs (1968) on this question, and I take the liberty of summarizing Ganss' summary.

obedience. The members had all responded to the call of Christ to a life of self-sacrifice and service. Ignatius was particularly concerned about whom to admit to the Society and laid special emphasis on the capacity to undertake the difficult work of the Society and on the candidate's free choice in committing himself to the Society for life. Candidates were admitted only after a long and careful examination and trials that put their devotion and motivation to the test. Ignatius was ever available to help candidates by his prayers and often lengthy conversations and offered every spiritual help he could devise when they might be tempted.

## THE EXERCISE OF OBEDIENCE

Following the precepts of obedience requires the exercise of considerable virtue and self-denial. As Ignatius put it:

> [CS284] To make progress, it is very expedient and highly necessary that all should devote themselves to complete obedience, by recognizing the superior, whoever he is, as being in the place of Christ our Lord and by maintaining interior reverence and love for him. They should obey entirely and promptly, not only by exterior execution of what the superior commands, with becoming energy and humility, and without excuses and murmurings even though things are commanded which are difficult and repugnant to sensitive nature; but they should try to maintain in their inmost souls genuine resignation and true abnegation of their own wills and judgments, by bringing their wills and judgments wholly into conformity with what the superior wills and judges, in all things in which no sin is seen, and by regarding the superior's will and judgment as the rule of their own, in order to conform themselves more completely to the first and supreme rule of all good will and judgment, which is the Eternal Goodness and Wisdom.

And this mind set is to be applied not only to the superior but to any minor officials that have authority from him [CS286].[10]

Despite his at times apparent severity, Ignatius sought to implement a spirit of loving self-communication in his followers [CS547, 551]. In matters pertaining to apostolic work he encouraged his followers to work within the framework of authority — what was accomplished through recourse to the will of superiors was the work of God, and what was not in accord with the will of superiors was not [CS552].

[10] See also [CS434, 84-86].

## REPRESENTATION

But room had to be made for some form of feedback from subjects, taking into consideration that the superior's judgment was not infallible or irreversible and that he might not have a clear understanding of all aspects of a given situation. This form of flow of information from subject to superior has become known as "representation," and was incorporated in Ignatius' provisions.[11] In the *General Examen* intended for candidates to the Society, he wrote: "However, when something occurs constantly to these candidates as being conducive to greater glory to God our Lord, they may, after prayer, propose the matter simply to the superior and leave it entirely to his judgment, without seeking anything more thereafter" [CS131]. The formulas are expanded in recommendations to novices:

> [CS292] Just as an excessive preoccupation over the needs of the body is blameworthy, so too a proper concern about the preservation of one's health and bodily strength for the divine service is praiseworthy, and all should exercise it. Consequently, when they perceive that something is harmful to them or that something else is necessary in regard to their diet, clothing, living quarters, office or the manner of carrying it out, and similarly of other matters, all ought to inform the superior about it or the one whom he appoints. But meanwhile they should observe two things. First, before informing him they should recollect themselves to pray, and after this, if they perceive that they ought to represent the matter to him who is in charge, they should do it. Second, after they have represented it by word of mouth or by a short note as a precaution against his forgetting it, they should leave the whole care of the matter to him and regard what he ordains as better, without arguing or insisting upon it either themselves or through another, whether he grants the request or not [A]. For the subject must persuade himself that what the superior decides after being informed is more suitable for the divine service and the subject's own greater good in our Lord.
>
> [CS293] A. Even though the subject who represents his need ought not personally to argue or urge the matter, nevertheless if the superior has not yet understood it, and if he requests further explanation, the subject will give it. If by chance he forgets to provide after he has indicated his intention to do so, it is not out of order to recall it to his memory or to represent it with becoming modesty.

[11] See also the section on representation in the letter on obedience to Portugal — in chapter XXIII.

The theme is stressed repeatedly that any such representation should be preceded by prayerful reflection and consideration, and, after representation has been made, whatever the superior decides is to be regarded as better. Even in missions of importance, undertaken at the request of the Holy See, complete disposition of oneself to direction of the superior is sought without any efforts to influence such dispositions exclusive of the superior's approval. "The part of him who is sent will be, without interposing himself in favor of going or remaining in one place rather than another, to leave the disposition of himself completely and freely to the superior who in the place of Christ our Lord directs him in the path of His greater service and praise. In similar manner, too, no one ought to try by any means to bring it about that others will remain in one place or go to another, unless he does so with the approval of his superior, by whom he should be governed in our Lord" [CS618]. The same principle would apply even to the general, should he disagree with the directive of the pope — representation is appropriate, but the final decision is to be left to His Holiness [CS607]. And Ignatius adds for emphasis, "For someone to propose the motions or thoughts which occur to him contrary to an order received, meanwhile submitting his entire judgment and will to the judgement and will of his superior who is in the place of Christ, is not against this prescription" [CS627].

## THE IDEAL OF OBEDIENCE

The overall impression conveyed by the treatment of obedience in the *Constitutions* is that Ignatius was proposing, indeed, prescribing an idealized form of obedience that he would have regarded as optimal for management of his Society. The treatment of obedience in the *Constitutions*, therefore, mirrors themes enunciated in Ignatius' other writings on the subject — particularly the letter to the Society in Portugal. His insistence is on the hierarchical, indeed, monarchical, structure of authority in the Society and on the requirement of complete, unquestioning, and absolute obedience of will and judgment on the part of subjects.

Spiritual writers have agonized over these formulas. There is a profound paradox, not only when these prescriptions are held up against Ignatius' own behavior,[12] but when one considers the dynamic activity and accomplishment of the Society of Jesus for which these prescriptions were intended. The role of the Society in history and in

[12] See chapter XXIV below.

the mission of the Church has repeatedly and constantly called forth the initiative, responsibility, dedication, and active commitment of Ignatius' sons that dictates something quite different from the picture of indifference and passive resignation characteristic of his formulations on obedience. There is a gap here between theory and practice apparently. The conceptual challenge confronting us, in our effort to probe and understand more deeply the complex spirituality of this great saint, is to come to an understanding of obedience that has the potential of encompassing and providing a context of meaning that would embrace not only the rhetoric of obedience that Ignatius proposed in these documents, but also the dynamic expressions of his implementation of the virtue of obedience in his own experience and practice, and in the dynamic and forceful initiatives demonstrated by his sons in the course of the history of the Society.

While the challenge before us is clear, and I will undertake to meet it in some degree in the ensuing pages, I am also suggesting that the issue is not merely a dialectical one of reconciling paradoxical opposites. I would suggest that part of the problem is that we are confronted with residues of a basic conflict in Ignatius himself, that he struggled with a conflict within himself over issues of authority and obedience, and that these issues were never satisfactorally or completely resolved. The result is that different aspects of the authority conflict came to expression in different aspects of his self-expression. In one context, he was the responsible superior, the overseer of the mission of the Society in the world, and the saintly founder and lawgiver of a new and struggling religious institution. As such his emphasis fell on the need for hierarchical organization and the prerogatives of order and authoritative control. In another context, he was struggling to break new ground, to carve a path deviating from traditional norms and attitudes, to create a new kind of religious institution flying in the face of established interests and traditional investments. In this context, he felt a sense of mission, of calling to a cause in which he took his inspiration directly from God — as reflected significantly in the vision at La Storta. The emphasis thus fell on his initiative, his determination to carry on his crusade in the face of all opposition, on insistence that his vision of what was right and good had to carry all opposition before it, and that in the service of that cause every resource, every initiative, every means available had to be called into action in order to achieve the goal — hardly a context calling for conformity, resignation, or even blind obedience. The contradiction between these latter dispositions of Ignatius in action and the prescriptions of his writings on obedience could not be more stark.

The centerpiece of this spiritual vision was the whole question of obedience and the place Ignatius gave it in his plan for the organization and functioning of his Society. The special position of obedience in his religious and spiritual vision is reflected in the pages of the *Constitutions*, but it presents us with a paradoxical issue requiring further exploration and understanding in terms of the psychology of obedience. It is to this subject that we turn in the next section.

# CHAPTER XXII

# THE SPIRIT OF OBEDIENCE IN THE *CONSTITUTIONS*

## Introduction

Ignatius' insistence on total and perfect obedience is one of the major themes he instilled into the *Constitutions*. Not only does this teaching reflect his own spiritual practice, but as he developed the idea in these pages it is intimately connected with his vision of the Society of Jesus and an integral part of its apostolic mission.[1] In his treatment of apostolic missions from the pope or other religious superiors (part VII), he developed a practical approach to obedience in the exercise of the apostolate. The concept of "mission" for him included any form of apostolic work the pope might impose on a Jesuit in virtue of the special vow of obedience by which the Jesuit had placed himself at the pontiff's disposal. As de Guibert (1964) comments:

> It is here that we find with the greatest clearness the fundamental concept of Ignatius in the founding of the Society: to place at the disposal of the Holy See a group of apostles thoroughly formed by the tests in their training, provided with sound learning and accustomed to deal with men, always ready to be off at a simple sign to wherever authority designates a more urgent, more painful, more difficult and delicate work to be accomplished. (pp. 149-150)

## Monarchical Culture

Ignatius' apostolic vision, as Ganss (1970) reminded us, was articulated in the monarchical culture of the sixteenth century in which he lived, with its general acceptance of the divine right of kings. The feudal system that had dominated the European continent for centu-

[1] Blet (1956) pointed out that the two currents in Ignatius' views on obedience — one reflecting the monastic tradition, the other an ideal of religious and apostolic perfection — reflect the dual end of the Society: personal perfection and salvation of others.

ries was giving way to powerful centralized governments. The organization of smaller provincial structures into nations, as in the Spain of Ferdinand and Isabella, led to the vesting of greater power in the hands of the monarch who ruled through intermediaries in the farflung territories under his jurisdiction. The reach of Spanish power in the sixteenth century was global. As Ganss commented:

> Not far different was to be the system of government which Ignatius devised for his new supranational apostolic order which he intended to give service anywhere on earth. The authority which a superior general held under the pope in Rome would descend through a provincial superior into its respective provinces. Yet within this monarchic structure, Ignatius was going to include democratic functions and processes to a degree truly surprising for his era, that of absolute monarchs. (p. 11)

The world in which Ignatius' religious vision came to fruition was a world in turmoil. The structures of religious unity and stability were crumbling. Abuses at all levels of the Church were rampant and cried out for reform. Whether Luther ever nailed his 95 theses to the Wittemberg church door or not, the Lutheran reform and rebellion was well on its way. The crisis both within and outside the Church called for moral and administrative reforms. Despite the best efforts of Pope Paul III to convoke a general council to address these needs, the squabbling among Catholic kings frustrated his designs for more than a decade. When the bishops finally assembled at Trent and officially opened the Council on 13 December 1545, the stage was set for the massive undertaking that was to become the Counterreformation. None of this was lost on Ignatius and it played a significant role in his emerging views. Above all, he was impressed by the need of the papacy for men dedicated to carrying out its commands and supporting its initiatives for meaningful reform. Ignatius meant to fashion such a corps of dedicated soldiers in the struggle for God's kingdom.

## Spiritual Vision

The spiritual vision guiding Ignatius' thinking can be expressed in terms of the vision at La Storta as Ignatius was making his way toward Rome. That vision may have crystallized his idea of an intimate companionship with Christ, the divine mediator of God's redemptive plan for the world. Ganss (1970) noted:

> In no small measure Ignatius' later stress on obedience arose from his desire to secure among the members of his order effective and charitable cooperation toward apostolic success in the service of this Christ and His mystical body. The founder expected the members of his Society to Love their lord in contemplation and to manifest their love by deeds. He was singularly successful in motivating men to volunteer in the crusade for Christ's kingdom and to strive for distinguished service in it. In his view their apostolic effectiveness was to arise from their being human instruments intimately united with God [CS813]. (p. 22)

The model of authority in Ignatius' mind was hierarchical and monarchical. Authority in the Church came through the pope [CS1, 603], and that authority in the Society was exercised through the superior general who possessed complete authority over it [CS618, 737-65, 789] or those who would take his place were he incapacitated [CS786-8]. Authority in the Ignatian perspective, then, comes ultimately from God, and in the Church was communicated through Christ to his vicar, the Pope, and hence to the hierarchy governing the Church [CS7, 527, 529, 603]. For Ignatius the line of authority in the Society ran from pope to superior general, from him to the local provincial, then to the rector or superior of each local community, and by extension to any minor official he might appoint [CS286, 434, 662, 666, 765, 791]. Orders of such officials are obeyed only because they derived their authority from Christ, so that submission in obedience to any legitimate authority — even the cook — is obedience to Christ. Thus Ignatius wrote:

> Therefore it is better that the cook should not request the one who aids him to do this or that, but that he should modestly command him by saying, "Do this" or "Do that" [D]. For if he requests him, he will seem more to be speaking as man to man; and it does not seem right and proper for a lay cook to request a priest to clean the pots and do other similar tasks. But by commanding him or saying "Do this" or "Do that," he will show more clearly that he is speaking as Christ to man, since he is commanding in His place. Thus the person who obeys ought to consider and weigh the order which comes from the cook, or from another who is his superior, as if it were coming from Christ our Lord, that he may be entirely pleasing to His Divine Majesty. [CS 85]

The note D [CS86] cited here adds: "To request and to command, each is good. Nevertheless, at the beginning one is aided more by being commanded than by being requested." And greater abnegation and humility can be found in the most menial and humble tasks [CS83].

## Obedience in the Society of Jesus

The primary text on obedience occurs in Part VI of the Constitutions, devoted to the personal lives of the members of the Society. The section on obedience reads as follows:

> Chapter 1: What pertains to obedience
> [CS 547] — 1. In order that those already admitted to profession or to membership among the formed coadjutors may be able to apply themselves more fruitfully according to our Institute in the service of God and the aid of their fellowmen, they themselves ought to observe certain things. Although the most important of these are reduced to their vows which they offer to God our Creator and Lord in conformity with the apostolic letters, nevertheless, in order that these points may be further explained and commended, they will be treated in this present Part VI. . . .
>
> All should keep their resolution firm to observe obedience and to distinguish themselves in it, not only in the matters of obligation but also in the others, even though nothing else is perceived except the indication of the superior's will without an expressed command. They should keep in view God our Creator and Lord, for whom such obedience is practiced, and they should endeavor to proceed in a spirit of love and not as men troubled by fear. Hence all of us should exert ourselves not to miss any point of perfection which we can with God's grace attain in the observance of all the Constitutions [A][2] and, in our manner of proceeding in our Lord, by applying all our energies with very special care to the virtue of obedience shown first to the sovereign pontiff and then to the superiors of the Society.
>
> Consequently, in all the things into which obedience can with charity be extended [B], we should be ready to receive its command just as if it were coming from Christ our Savior, since we are practicing the obedience to one in His place and because of love and reverence for Him. Therefore we should be ready to leave unfinished any letter or anything else of ours which has been begun and to apply our whole mind and all the energy we have in the Lord of all that our obedience may be perfect in every detail [C], in regard to the execution, the willing, and the understanding. We should perform with great alacrity, spiritual joy, and perseverance whatever has been commanded to us, persuading our-

[2] Letters in brackets [ ] refer to Declarations — usually more specific explanations of points in the main text; they have the same force as the rest of the Constitutions. They were originally intended as a help to superiors in interpreting the text, and add a degree of flexibility (de Aldama 1989). The text of the declaration is at the end of the respective section.

selves that everything is just and renouncing with blind obedience any contrary opinion and judgment of our own in all things which the superior commands and in which . . . some species of sin cannot be judged to be present. We ought to be firmly convinced that everyone of those who live under obedience ought to allow himself to be carried and directed by Divine Providence through the agency of the superior as if he were a lifeless body[3] which allows itself to be carried to any place and to be treated in any manner desired, or as if he were an old man's staff which serves in any place and in any manner whatsoever in which the holder wishes to use it. For in this way the obedient man ought joyfully to devote himself to any task whatsoever in which the superior desires to employ him to aid the whole body of the religious Institute; and he ought to hold it as certain that by this procedure he is conforming himself with the divine will more than by anything else he could do while following his own will and different judgment.

[CS 548] — A. These first Declarations which are published along with the Constitutions bind with the same authority as the Constitutions. Therefore in the observance, equal care should be bestowed upon the Declarations and the Constitutions.

[CS 549] — B. Such things are all those in which some sin is not manifest.

[CS 550] — C. The command of obedience is fulfilled in regard to the execution when the thing commanded is done; in regard to the willing when the one who obeys wills the same thing as the one who commands; in regard to the understanding when he forms the same judgment as the one commanding and regards what he is commanded as good. And that obedience is imperfect in which there does not exist, in addition to the execution, also that agreement in willing and judging between him who commands and him who obeys.

[CS 551] — 2. Likewise, it should be strongly recommended to all that they should have and show great reverence, especially interior reverence, to their superiors, by considering reverencing Jesus Christ in them; and from their hearts they should warmly love their superiors as fathers in Him. Thus in everything they should proceed in a spirit of charity, keeping nothing exterior or interior hidden from the superiors and desiring them to be informed about everything, in order that the superiors may be the better able to direct them in everything along the path of salvation and perfection. For that reason, once a year and as many times more as their

[3] This somewhat distasteful sentiment echoes the view of Francis of Assisi — see Bonaventure, *Opera*, VIII, 520-1: "He (St. Francis) being one time demanded who was to be judged truly obedient proposed the similitude of a dead body for an example" (cited in Clancy 1976, p. 346).

> superior thinks good, all the professed and formed coadjutors should be ready to manifest their consciences to him, in confession, or secret, or in another manner, for the sake of the great profit this practice contains . . . . Thus too they should be ready to make a general confession, from the last one they made, to the one whom the superior thinks it wise to designate in his place. [CS 552] — 3. All should have recourse to the superior for the things which they happen to desire; and without his permission and approval no individual should directly or indirectly request, or cause to be requested, any favor from the sovereign pontiff or from another person outside the Society, either for himself or for someone else. He should be convinced that if he does not get that which he desires from the hands of the superior or with his approval, it is not useful to him for the divine service; and that if it is useful for that service, that he will get it with the consent of the superior, as from the one who holds the place of Christ our Lord for him.

The spirit behind this text was an integral part of Ignatius religious vision and sense of mission from the first.[4] This magisterial text echoes the sentiments of the Formula of the Institute, based on the propositions drawn up by the first companions in 1539 and confirmed by the papal bull *Exposcit debitum* on 21 July 1550. The chapter on obedience [FI4] reads:

> All who make the profession in this Society should understand at the time, and furthermore keep in mind as long as they live, that this entire Society and the individual members who make their profession in it are campaigning for God under faithful obedience to His Holiness Pope Paul III and his successors in the Roman pontificate. The Gospel does indeed teach us, and we know from the orthodox faith and firmly hold, that all of Christ's faithful are subject to the Roman pontiff as their head and as the vicar of Jesus Christ. But we have judged nevertheless that the following procedure will be supremely profitable to each of us and to any others who will pronounce the same profession in the future, for the sake of our greater devotion in obedience to the Apostolic See, of greater abnegation of our own wills, and of surer direction from the Holy Spirit. In addition to that ordinary bond of the three vows, we are to be obliged by a special vow to carry out whatever the present and future Roman pontiffs may order which pertains to the progress

[4] The influence of the inspiration of St. Onuphrius (Humphrey), whose exploits Iñigo read in the *Flos Sanctorum*, are noteworthy. Referring to his conversion, Ignatius wrote Nadal that "At that period of my life I was filled with desire to do great things in the service of God, such as had been dome by St. Humphrey and other saints who gave themselves unreservedly to Him" (MonNad V, 270; cited in Clancy 1976, p. 5).

> of souls and the propagation of the faith; and to go without subterfuge or excuse, as far as in us lies, to whatsoever provinces they may choose to send us — whether they are pleased to send us among the Turks or any other infidels, even those who live in the region called the Indies, or among any heretics whatever, or schismatics, or any of the faithful. Therefore before those who will come to us take this burden upon their shoulders, they should ponder long and seriously, as the Lord has counseled [Lk 14:30], whether they possess among their resources enough spiritual capital to complete this tower; that is, whether the Holy Spirit who moves them is offering them so much grace that with His aid they have hope of bearing the weight of this vocation. Then, after they have enlisted through the inspiration of the Lord in this militia of Christ, they ought to be prompt in carrying out this obligation which is so great, being clad for battle day and night [Eph. 6: 14; 1 Peter 1: 13]. However, to forestall among us any ambition of such missions or provinces, or any refusal of them, all our members should have this understanding: They should not either directly or through someone else carry on negotiations with the Roman pontiff about such missions, but leave all this care to God, and to the pope himself as God's vicar, and to the superior general of the Society. This general too, just like the rest, should not treat with the said pontiff about his being sent to one region or another, unless after advice from the Society. All should likewise vow that in all matters which promote the observance of this Rule they will be obedient to the one put in charge of the Society. (He should be as qualified as possible for this office and will be elected by a majority of the votes, as will be explained in the Constitutions. Moreover, he should possess all the authority and power over the Society which are useful for its good administration, correction, and government. He should issue the commands which he knows to be opportune for achieving the end set before him by God and the Society. In his superiorship he should be ever mindful of the kindness, meekness, and charity of Christ and of the pattern set by Peter and Paul, a norm which both he and the afore-mentioned council should keep constantly in view. Assuredly, too, because of the great utility to the order and for the sake of the constant practice of humility which has never been sufficiently praised, the individual subjects should not only be obliged to obey the general in all matters pertaining to the Society's Institute but also to recognize and properly venerate Christ as present in him.

The views expressed here undoubtedly belong to Ignatius, but were accepted without reserve by the first companions, so that it must be taken as reflecting their consensus. There is no single point that seems to have loomed with as great significance in the mind of Ignatius than the emphasis on obedience. Obedience had no other meaning for him than complete submission of the will at a minimum, and, at a higher level, of the judgment to any command or directive of the superior (de Aldama 1989).

The hierarchical structure of the Society in the order of obedience also loomed large on Ignatius' horizon.

> [CS662] To this same virtue of obedience is related the properly observed subordination of the superiors, one to another, and of the subjects to the superiors, in such wise that the individuals dwelling in some house or college have recourse to their local superior or rector and are governed by him in every respect. Those who are distributed throughout the province refer to the provincial or some other local superior who is closer, according to the orders they received; and all the local superiors or rectors should communicate often with the provincial and thus too be directed by him in everything; and the provincials in their turn will deal in the same way with the general. For this subordination, when well observed in this manner, will preserve the union which is attained chiefly through it, with the help and grace of God our Lord.[5]

The primary and supreme guiding norm was the will of God [CS284, 547]. What might be determined as the divine will was to be sought out and followed in all things [CS288], even in dismissals [CS211, 220, 226]. The guiding ideal was the congruence of one's own will to the will of God, resulting in complete obedience that found expression in "genuine resignation and true abnegation of their own wills and judgments, by bringing their wills and judgments wholly into conformity with what the superior wills and judges" [CS284]. This union of wills and subjection of self was realized on the basis of charity, mutual consideration and care, which was the bond of union [CS273, 671, 821].

Mere execution would simply not do. The theme echoes throughout his letters. Polanco's letter to Araoz in 1547 touched on Ignatius' judgment about whom to accept in the Society: "Obstinate attachment, stubbornness of judgment and of self-will in any manner, even when they are greatly compensated for by other good qualities, cannot be tolerated in this house. Here, even though one has abundant occasion to justify one's desire for poverty and for the stern mortification of the inclinations of self-esteem, one must practice especially the submission of the will and judgment, and in general everything

[5] See also [CS791] and [CS424].

connected with obedience" (Epistolae I, 615; cited in de Guibert (1964), p. 91).

The forms of obedience described here [CS547] mirror the description of levels of obedience in the Letter on Obedience to the Society in Portugal.[6] Ignatius' clear preference is for obedience that is complete and perfect — not merely execution, but also "in willing and judging between him who commands and him who obeys" [CS550], calling for a significant degree of self-abnegation. The same emphasis is made in his recommendations for obedience to the novices — the most desirable condition is complete abnegation of one's own will and judgment and conformity with the will and judgment of the superior [CS284]. The reference to "blind obedience" calls to mind an ancient monastic tradition,[7] but its meaning here [CS547] — the only one in the *Constitutions* — has been much disputed. Ganss (1970) commented:

> Blind obedience surely entails a willingness to obey cheerfully and a propensity to presume that the superior's order is right and prudent until some cogent reason to the contrary has become manifest. If Ignatius' metaphor should be pressed too far, he could be taken to mean that the subject should abdicate his judgment, responsibility, and initiative — something which no man may do and which is incompatible with the dignity of the human person. But such an interpretation falsifies Ignatius. His own texts and example reveal that the "blindness" was not total. The subject was expected to keep his eyes sufficiently open to see that there was no sin [CS549], and whether there were factors which should be represented to the superior (see [CS92, 131, 543, 627]). (p. 248)

Behind these considerations regarding obedience in the Society lies the imagery of the meditations on the Kingdom of Christ and the Two Standards in the *Spiritual Exercises.* In those meditations Ignatius raised the banner of crusade to conquer the world for Christ. The imagery is redolent with the echoes of the ideals of romantic chivalry and the dreams of military glory that had filled the preconversion head of the young hidalgo. The ideals of dedication to the cause, of complete humility and self-abnegation, were essential requirements for participation in that crusade. They were the goals instilled in the *Exercises* and they serve no less as compelling motives for the spirit of obedience here in the *Constitutions.*

[6] See the discussion of the letter in chapter XXIII.

[7] References to the lifeless body can be found in Sts. Nilus and Francis of Assisi (Aldama 1989).

Humility, as Ignatius envisions it in the *Exercises*, comes to mean the stripping away of all narcissistic residues and attachments that would stand in the way of total commitment to Christ's service. Ignatius sought to establish this principle as central to the workings of his Society — the practice of renunciation of possessions and of self-love through the practice of humility were essential to the kind of self-sacrifice and service he had in mind. As de Guibert (1964) observed:

> Now all his experience as a director had convinced Ignatius that the only truly effective means of bringing souls to reach this decisive point lies in the effective practice of these renunciations and humiliations. Just as he had only a mediocre confidence in the obedience of one who never had to break his will and bend his judgment before a difficult and disconcerting command, so he always had doubts about the depth of the humility of one who never had to accept painful reprimands and sharp affronts. Grace awaits cooperation from ourselves in order to establish us in these lowly opinions of ourselves. Ignatius felt instinctively that such cooperation is given more frequently because of the concrete experience of our lowliness, or because of the practical devaluation practiced in real humiliations which are accepted with generosity, than because of thoughts which are beautiful but abstract. (p. 94)

Ignatius was deeply concerned with the preservation of the Society, and the union of hearts and minds among its members as vital to this end. He wrote:

> [CS821] Whatever helps toward the union of the members of this Society among themselves and with their head will also help much toward preserving the well-being of the Society. This is especially the case with the bond of wills, which is the mutual charity and love they have for one another. This bond is strengthened by their getting information and news from one another and by having much intercommunication, by their following one same doctrine, and by their being uniform in everything as far as possible, and above all by the link of obedience, which unites the individuals with their superiors, and the local superiors among themselves and with the provincials, and both the local superiors and provincials with the general, in such a way that the subordination of some to others is diligently preserved.

The stress on conformity and unity in this passage can be read with authoritarian overtones; but not without the Ignatian emphasis on charity and the bond of wills that provided the essential substratum for the whole. Conformity in Ignatius' view, however desirable, was not to be imposed, but was to arise out of the mutual bonds of a common purpose and a common cause embraced as much by subordinates as by superiors. Obedience was both the product of unity and a safeguard for it. It was suggested "that they should have and show great reverence, especially interior reverence, to their superiors, by considering and reverencing Jesus Christ in them; and from their hearts they should warmly love their superiors as fathers in Him" [CS551]. Ignatius returns repeatedly to the theme of obedience as promoting the union of hearts and minds (de Aldama 1989). "Since this union is produced in great part by the bond of obedience, this virtue should always be maintained in its vigor; . . . Those who are more important in the Society should give a good example of obedience to the others, by being closely united to their own superior and by obeying him promptly, humbly, and devoutly" [CS659].[8]

Thus the meaning of obedience in the *Constitutions* derives from the love uniting the companions with one another and formulated in the concrete following of Christ for both superior and subject. The relation between them never takes the form of dialectical opposition, nor is it an ascetical exercise of humility. "It is first of all a mutual fraternal assistance with a view to *mejor acertar*, that is, finding the will of God more surely in all things, and in this sense it expresses the bond that holds the whole body together," as Emonet (1990, p. 113) puts it. Ignatius' own example of exercising his authority is instructive. As we find in the *Fontes Harrativi*, "Ignatius showed his love for his subjects in that he never burdened his sons beyond their strength. He sought rather to bring them relief than to weigh them down. He showed his love again, in striving to discover and understand their talents" (FN III, 618).[9] At the same time, he constantly promoted discernment in preference to merely following rules or instructions; to Oliver Manareo, he wrote, "Man bestows the function, but God bestows discernment. In future I want you to act without scruples, judging what should be done according to the circumstances, even if the rules and instructions say something different" (FN III, 434); and to Gregory Rosephius, "When obedience orders you to do something, it does not suppress your prudence and your discernment"

[8] Ignatius so highly valued a union of hearts and minds that he had little time for any who would affect it adversely. He wrote: "One who is seen to be a cause of division among those who live together, estranging them either among themselves or from their head, ought with great diligence to be separated from that community, as a pestilence which can infect it seriously if a remedy is not quickly applied" [CS664]. See also CS212-215.

[9] See CS161, 219, 222, 423, 624, 729.

(FN III, 540). This style has important implications for the manner of exercising authority in the Society — "In practical terms, when any important decision has to be taken, the superior will invite the companions concerned to embark on a process of discernment with a view to reaching a consensus, so that the solution adopted will be both viable and effective" (Emonet 1990, p. 117).

## OBEDIENCE TO CHRIST

Central to Ignatius' notion of obedience is the concept that the superior's voice is the voice of Christ and obedience to the order of the superior is equivalent to obedience to the will of Christ. "They should keep in view God our Creator and Lord, for whom such obedience is practiced. . . . we should be ready to receive its command just as if it were coming from Christ our Saviour" [CS547]. The echoes of the visions at the Cardoner and La Storta can be heard here — the mission of the Society was the service of Christ and every Jesuit was to be an instrument of Christ in the world (Ganss 1970). Thus the authority of the general in the Society was that of Christ — "At all times he should be obeyed and reverenced as the one who holds the place of Christ our Lord" [CS765]. The phrase echoes the terms of the Formula [FI4]. Regarding training of novices, Ignatius wrote, "To make progress, it is very expedient and highly necessary that all should devote themselves to complete obedience, by recognizing the superior, whoever he is, as being in the place of Christ our Lord and by maintaining interior reverence and love for him" [CS284]; even with respect to minor officials, "They should accustom themselves to consider not who the person is whom they obey, but rather who He is for whose sake they obey and whom they obey in all, who is Christ our Lord" [CS286].[10] And for the scholastics, "His [the superior's] subjects ought to hold him in great respect and reverence as one who holds the place of Christ our Lord" [CS424]. As Emonet (1990) reflects, the Christ constantly before Ignatius' mind's eye is Christ carrying his cross. The image finds application to both superior and subject:

> Superior and subject thus find themselves side by side, like two companions committed to the following of Christ carrying his cross — each one, however, with a different kind of service. The subject has the specific mission entrusted to him, which is his share of the cross; the superior has the concern for the body as a

[10] See also [CS342, 434, 765].

whole, with its ever-present danger of splitting up — this is *his* share of the cross. Each intervention on the part of the superior should refer the Jesuit back to his deepest identity and make him come to grips with the situation on the basis of the original experience that constituted him a member of the Society of Jesus, a companion of Jesus (cf. *Formula Instituti*, nos.1, 3-4, 6). In this perspective, we can understand Ignatius' words: "Anyone who knows how to command well and worthily is almost always obeyed" (FN III, 272). (pp. 114-115)

# CHAPTER XXIII

# IGNATIUS' OTHER WRITINGS ON OBEDIENCE

## Introduction

Ignatius' thinking about obedience began to take shape early in the course of creating the Society. Obedience and submission to God's will had been a prominent theme since the days at Manresa and were central ideas in the *Exercises*. Later, when the companions of Paris had banded together, the idea of submission to the authority of the Pope was central in their considerations. And in the discussions of March-June 1539, culminating in the *Deliberatio primorum Patrum*, one of the central questions was whether they should commit themselves to one of their number under a vow of obedience. The decision "to obey one among us" did not come easily — the deliberation consumed several weeks (Ravier 1987, pp. 84-89, 369-374). The outcome undoubtedly reflected Ignatius' views, but was wholeheartedly endorsed by the companions.

## Variations on the Theme

After his election to the office of General, Ignatius was not slow to promulgate his views on obedience. In August 1542, he wrote to Giovanni Battista Viola, who was having difficulties with his studies in Paris and had imprudently ignored Ignatius' advice:

> I received your letter but I fail to understand it. In two different places you speak of obedience. In the first you say that you are ready to obey me, and in the second you say: "Because I would rather die than fail in obedience, I submit to the judgment of your reverence." Now, it seems to me that obedience seeks to be blind, and is blind in two ways: in the first it belongs to the inferior to submit his understanding, when there is no question of sin, and to do what is commanded of him; in the second it is also the inferior's duty, once the superior commands or has commanded something, to represent to the superior whatever considerations

> or disadvantages may occur to him, and to do so humbly and simply, without any attempt to draw the superior to either side, so that afterwards he can follow, with peace of mind, the way pointed out to him or commanded. (Epistolae I, 228-229 [Letter 52]; in Tylenda (1985) p. 4)

In July 1547, a letter to the Jesuits at Gandia directed them to elect a superior and gave reasons for the necessity for obedience of a high order. The following year, he had Polanco draft a letter to Andres de Oviedo, responding to his request to spend seven years in retirement and solitude. The message was to obey the provincial, but Ignatius was concerned about setting a precedent that ran counter to the Society's mission (O'Malley 1993). The idea began to take form that, while others might engage in severe austerities and long hours of prayer, Jesuits were to practice self-denial by obedience to their superiors.

Again in 1550, Ignatius ordered that a directive be delivered to all Jesuit houses in Rome on the subject of obedience. He made it clear that the obedience he exacted from his sons was to be prompt and unquestioning — blind obedience. The text is Polanco's:

> Our reverend Father Master Ignatius wishes for God's greater glory and the greater spiritual progress of all of Ours (as he has already partly declared in other ordinances), that in the future, when his reverence or father minister summons anyone, whether he be a priest or not, or the subminister calls one who is not a priest, they should all answer the call at once, as though it was the voice of Christ our Lord, and practice this obedience in the name of His Divine Majesty. In this way obedience should be blind and prompt. If one is at prayer, he should leave his prayer. If he hears the voice of his superior, or rather the voice of Christ our Lord, when he is writing and has begun a letter, say A or B, he should not wait to finish it.
>
> In like manner, if he happens to be with anyone at all, even a prelate (supposing he owes him no obedience), he should come if he is called by any of his superiors. Should one be called who happens to be taking some bodily refreshments of any kind, whether he be at table or in bed, or busy with an invalid, serving a drink or a medicine, or engaged in a service which could not be interrupted without harm to the patient, such as helping to bleed him, or should he be going to confession or about to receive Communion, or hearing the confessions of others, if a priest, in all such cases he should send word to the superior and ask whether he wishes him to leave his meal, his bed, or whatever else it may happen to be.

Given at Rome, August 24, 1550. (Epistolae III, 156 [Letter 1326]; in Tylenda (1985) pp. 36-37)

## THE LETTER ON HOLY OBEDIENCE

Other communications about obedience stemmed from the persistent problems in Portugal. The crisis could not have come at a less propitious time — in 1553, Pedroche launched his attack on the *Exercises*, echoing earlier criticisms of Cano and the Archbishop Siliceo; then Carafa ascended the papal throne as Paul IV. The crisis in Portugal reflected organizational complexities pointing to the need for greater cohesion if the Society was to survive; it was a crisis of authority and self-understanding (O'Malley 1993). Events in Portugal would absorb Ignatius' attention for most of 1552 and into 1553. Early efforts to establish the Society in Portugal had enjoyed great success, partly because of the favorable disposition of King John III who generously supported the works of the Society, and because of the enormous influence of Simon Rodriguez who founded several colleges and accomplished other works. Rodriguez had been acting as superior and reports began to come to Ignatius regarding his arbitrariness and inconsistency. For reasons which are obscure, deviations soon developed from the pattern of religious life Ignatius had laid down for the Society. The variations followed two extremes: severity of excessive prayer and penances ("holy follies") on one hand, and too much attention to physical comfort on the other. Younger Jesuits were openly challenging orders of superiors. Ignatius' insistence on obedience was at risk.

The situation had reached the point at which some Portugese Jesuits had begun to attract followers and gained considerable influence at the Portugese court. A movement arose to form a separate religious order and withdraw from the Society and obedience to Ignatius. One source of the difficulty had been Rodriguez, who seemed to prefer his own counsel to Ignatius'. Near the end of 1551 Ignatius decided to remove him from office as provincial of Portugal and move him to Aragon, where he would have less influence. Rodriguez refused to go and remained in Portugal. There was a flurry of orders and counter-orders, letters that never arrived or arrived too late, miscommunications, and orders and decisions that were never implemented. For a time Ignatius did not even know who the Provincial of the Portugese province was. He had named Miguel de Torres to the post at the beginning of 1552, but Aragon still had no provincial and Rodriguez never arrived there. Confusion reigned! Borgia, who knew the situation well, intimated to Ignatius on 19 September 1552 that, if he had known the situation better, he would have acted differently.

The group at Coimbra were shocked and confused, friends of the Society were disedified, and rumors circulated that the Society in Portugal was being dissolved. John III, ever a friend of the Society, tried to bolster the order by appointing a Jesuit to be his confessor. This also proved abortive. Departures and dismissals from the Society followed, to the consternation of many, especially when some of those dismissed continued their apostolic work to good effect. Ignatius was finally able to pour some oil on these waters by recalling Torres, but the agitation continued for well over a year. He also recalled da Camara from Portugal to get some sense of what was going on there. The whole affair was painful and difficult, particularly the behavior of Rodriguez, Ignatius' old companion, whom he was forced to recall and subject to ecclesiastical discipline. As Ravier (1987) comments:

> The balance sheet of the crises, departures and dismissals was not encouraging. In July, one hundred five companions remained in Portugal. The dissidents dreamed of founding a new Society. The King dissuaded them. For Ignatius, the refusals and equivocations of Simon Rodriguez were very painful: he was torn between his friendship for his former companion of the early days and what he thought to be his duty as Superior General. Should he expel Simon Rodriguez from the Society? (p. 178)

Rodriguez finally arrived in Rome on 10 October. At his trial the following February, the ecclesiastical court imposed a series of penances which Ignatius dispensed. Rodriguez submitted at first, then rejected the decision since he felt it was unjust. He vacillated, finally appealed to Cardinal Carpi, protector of the Society, for exemption from his vow of obedience. The affair came to naught and he remained in the Society, saving Ignatius the pain and embarrassment of dismissing him.

Historians have not been kind to Rodriguez. Dudon comments: "This man is not an insolent rebel, strutting about and blowing his trumpet to rally his friends against his leader. But he is shockingly disobedient all the same. With his humble and gentle words, he sticks to what he wants; and to cover his resistances, he does not lack quibbles or suspicious moves or a sort of shameless daring" (1949, p. 344). Brodrick wrote: "Father Simon went on being the big man at court and the adored man at Coimbra. His Jesuit subjects loved him intensely, partly because he deserved to be loved, and partly for the less noble reason that he allowed them to do pretty well as they listed. It all went to his head, never a very wise head, and he gradually came to think and act almost in independence of St. Ignatius" (1940, pp. 242-243).

For Dalmases (1985), probably quite correctly, the issue was obedience, so dear to the heart of Ignatius. Rodriguez had his problems, but the rift between Ignatius' central government and one of his subordinate administrators, also an early companion, was central. There was a decided clash between Ignatius' notions of obedience and Rodriguez' inclinations. But the fundamental role of Ignatian obedience had not really been established — the authority of the founders, Rodriguez among them, had not been fully explicated, and the principle was not yet in place in any institutional sense (Endean 1987). The threat to Ignatius may have been more in his own anxieties over questioning of his authority. His vision of the structure of the Society and the essential role of unquestioning obedience would have been challenged by Rodriguez's relative independence. We might conjecture that, in addition, Ignatius was getting a bit of his own medicine; at least in his persistence and his independent mind, Rodriguez was not that far from offering a mirror to the saint.

Ignatius had appointed Diego Miro to replace the troublesome Rodriguez. But this only gave rise to further tensions. Where Rodriguez' manner of governance had been mild and relaxed, Miro was strict and demanding, exacerbating tensions and resentments for the treatment of Rodriguez. Some of Rodriguez' adherents refused to obey the new provincial. Ignatius had sent Miguel de Torres to implement the transition, but Torres' reports were disturbing — Ignatius could not tolerate such disobedience. He wrote a stern letter to Miro, demanding complete, unquestioning submission to orders of superiors. Ignatius' terms were harsh — those who will not submit to the superior as if to Christ himself are to be expelled or delivered to Rome, where they will have to deal with Ignatius himself. The letter reads in part:

> According to information coming to us from Doctor Torres, whom I sent to the province of Portugal as my representative and visitor in the Lord, I understand that there is a notable failing, among not a few of Ours, in that virtue which is more necessary and essential in the Society than anywhere else, and in which the vicar of Christ, in the bulls of our Institute, most carefully recommends that we distinguish ourselves. I mean the respect, reverence, and perfect obedience to our superiors who hold the place of Christ our Lord, even of His Divine Majesty. . . .
>
> I command you in virtue of holy obedience to take the following step with regard to the safeguarding of that virtue. If there is

anyone who is unwilling to obey you — and I say this, not to you alone but to all superiors or local rectors in Portugal — do one of two things: either dismiss him from the Society, or send him here to Rome if you think that a particular individual can, by such a change, be helped to become a true servant of Christ our Lord. If necessary, keep their highnesses informed, who I doubt will make any objections, in keeping with the spirit and holy good will which God our Lord has bestowed upon them. To retain one who is not a true son of obedience does no good for the kingdom. Nor is there any reason for thinking that such a person, his own soul being so destitute, can help other souls, or that God our Lord would wish to accept him as an instrument for His service and glory.

We see from experience that men, not only with average talents but even less than average, can often be the instruments of uncommon supernatural fruit, because they are completely obedient and through this virtue allow themselves to be affected and moved by the powerful hand of the author of all good. On the other hand, great talent may be seen exerting great labor with less than ordinary fruit, because being themselves the source of their activity, that is, their own self-love, or at least not allowing themselves to be moved by God our Lord through obedience to their superiors, they do not produce results proportionate to the almighty hand of God our Lord, who does not accept them as His instruments. They achieve results proportioned to their own weak and feeble hands. . . . And while we have enough to do here without burdening ourselves with this additional task from Portugal, we will not decline the added burden because of the special charity which God our Lord causes us to feel toward Portugal." (Epistolae IV, 559-563 [Letter 3105]; in Tylenda (1985) pp. 65-67)

The situation plagued Ignatius for several years and caused him considerable annoyance with the continuing difficulties. Part of the problem was Rodriguez, whose style of governing created favorites and fostered intense devotion in his followers, as well as inspiring equally intense sentiments among his opponents. All this was upsetting to Ignatius, who saw his Portugese sons straying badly from the path of virtue that he envisioned for his Society.

Ignatius' efforts to rekindle the spirit of obedience in the divided province mere far from successful. In January 1553 da Camara described the sad state of affairs and begged Ignatius to address members of the province on the subject of obedience. Ignatius did so in March. In the letter, drafted with the help of Polanco, Ignatius achieved a magisterial and classic pronouncement on the subject of holy obedience. This letter stands as the most developed statement of Ignatius' views on the vow of religious obedience. His understanding of the virtue, essentially unchanged throughout his career, was the view that was incorporated in the somewhat lapidary and legalistic formulae of the Constitutions.

The letter reads as follows:

Letter to the Members of the Society in Portugal — 26 March 1553
On Perfect Obedience

May the perfect grace and everlasting love of Christ our Lord greet and visit you with his most holy gifts and spiritual graces.

1. *Obedience Is To Be the Characteristic Virtue of the Society*

It gives me great consolation, my dear brothers in our Lord Jesus Christ, when I learn of the lively and earnest desires for perfection in His divine service and glory which He gives you, who by His mercy has called you to this Society and preserves you in it and directs you to the blessed end at which His chosen ones arrive.

And though I wish you all perfection in every virtue and spiritual gift, it is true (as you have heard from me on other occasions), that it is in obedience, more than in any other virtue, that God our Lord gives me the desire to see you signalize yourselves. And that, not only because of the singular good there is in it, so much emphasized by word and example in Holy Scripture in both Old and New Testaments, but because, as Saint Gregory says: "Obedience is the only virtue which plants all the other virtues in the mind, and preserves them once they are planted." And insofar as this virtue flourishes, all the other virtues will flourish and bring forth the fruit which I desire in your souls, and which He claims who, by His obedience, redeemed the world after it had been destroyed by the lack of it, *becoming obedient unto death, even death on a cross* [Phil. 2:8].

We may allow ourselves to be surpassed by other religious orders in fasts, watchings, and other austerities, which each one following its institute holily observes. But in the purity and perfection of obedience together with the true resignation of our wills and the abnegation of our understanding, I am very desirous, my dear brothers, that they who serve God in this Society should be conspicuous, so that by this virtue its true sons may be recognized as men who regard not the person whom they obey, but in him Christ our Lord, for whose sake they obey.

2. *The Foundation of Obedience*

The superior is to be obeyed not because he is prudent, or good, or qualified by any other gift of God, because he holds the place and the authority of God, as Eternal Truth has said: *He who hears you, hears me; and he who rejects you, rejects me* [Luke 10:16]. Nor on the contrary, should he lack prudence, is he to be the less obeyed in that in which he is superior, since he represents Him who is infallible wisdom, and who will supply what is wanting in His minister, nor, should he lack goodness or other desirable qualities, since Christ our Lord, having said, *the scribes and the Pharisees sit on the chair of Moses*, adds, *therefore, whatever they shall tell you, observe and do; but do not act according to their works* [Matt. 23:2-3].

Therefore I should wish that all of you would train yourselves to recognize Christ our Lord in any superior, and with all devotion, reverence and obey His Divine Majesty in him. This will appear less strange to you if you keep in mind that Saint Paul, writing to the Ephesians, bids us obey even temporal and pagan superiors as Christ, from whom all well-ordered authority descends: *Slaves, obey those who are your lords according to the flesh, with fear and trembling, in singleness of heart, as to Christ, not serving to the eye as pleasers of men, but as the slaves of Christ doing the will of God from your heart, giving your service with good will as to the Lord and not to men* [Eph. 6:5-7]. From this you can judge, when a religious is taken not only as superior, but expressly in the place of Christ our Lord, to serve as director and guide in the divine service, what rank he ought to hold in the mind of the inferior, and whether he ought to be looked upon as man or rather as the vicar of Christ our Lord.

### 3. *Degrees of Obedience*

Obedience of Execution and of the Will

I also desire that this be firmly fixed in your minds, that the first degree of obedience is very low, which consists in the execution of what is commanded, and that it does not deserve the name of obedience, since it does not attain to the worth of this virtue unless it rises to the second degree, which is to make the superior's will one's own in such a way that there is not merely the effectual execution of the command, but an interior conformity, whether willing or not willing the same. Hence it is said in Scripture, *obedience is better than sacrifice* [1 Sam. 15:22]. for, according to Saint Gregory, "In victims the flesh of another is slain, but in obedience our own will is sacrificed."

Now because this disposition of will in man is of so great worth, so also is the offering of it, when by obedience it is offered to his Creator and Lord. How great a deception it is, and how dangerous for those who think it lawful to withdraw from the will of their superior, I do not say only in those things pertaining to flesh and blood, but even in those which of their nature are spiritual and holy, such as fasts, prayers, and other pious works! Let them hear Cassian's comment in the Conference of Daniel the Abbot: "It is one and the selfsame kind of disobedience, whether in earnestness of labor, or the desire of ease, one breaks the command of the superior, and as harmful to go against the statutes of the monastery out of sloth as out of watchfulness; and finally, it is as bad to transgress the precept of the abbot to read as to contemn it to sleep." Holy was the activity of Martha, holy the contemplation of Magdalene, and holy the penitence and tears with which she bathed the feet of Christ our Lord; but all this was to be done in Bethany, which is interpreted to mean, the house of obedience. It would seem, therefore, that Christ our Lord would give us to understand, as Saint Bernard remarks, "that neither the activity of good works, nor the leisure of contemplation, nor the tears of the penitent would have pleased Him out of Bethany."

And thus my dear brothers, try to make the surrender of your wills entire. Offer freely to God through his ministers the liberty He has bestowed on you. Do not think it a slight advantage of your free will that you are able to restore it wholly in obedience to Him who gave it to you. In this you do not lose it, but rather perfect it in conforming your will wholly with the most certain rule of all rectitude, which is the divine will, the interpreter of which is the superior who governs you in place of God.

For this reason you must never try to draw the will of the superior (which you should consider the will of God) to your own will. This would not be making the divine will the rule of your own, but your own the rule of the divine, and so distorting the order of His wisdom. It is a great delusion in those whose understanding has been darkened by self-love, to think that there is any obedience in the subject who tries to draw the superior to what he wishes. Listen to Saint Bernard, who had much experience in this matter. "Whoever endeavors either openly or covertly to have his spiritual father enjoin him what he himself desires, deceives himself if he flatters himself as a true follower of obedience. For in that he does not obey his superior, but rather the superior obeys him." And so he concludes that he who wishes to rise to the virtue of obedience must rise to the second degree, which, over and above the execution, consists in making the superior's will one's own, or rather putting off his own will to clothe himself with the divine will interpreted by the superior.

### Obedience of the Understanding

But he who aims at making an entire and perfect oblation of himself, in addition to his will, must offer his understanding, which is a further and the highest degree of obedience. He must not only will, but he must think the same as the superior, submitting his own judgment to that of the superior, so far as a devout will can bend the understanding.

For although this faculty has not the freedom of the will, and naturally gives its assent to what is presented to it as true, there are, however, many instances where the evidence of the known truth is not coercive and it can, with the help of the will, favor one side or the other. When this happens every truly obedient man should conform his thought to the thought of the superior.

And this is certain, since obedience is a holocaust in which the whole man without the slightest reserve is offered in the fire of charity to his Creator and Lord through the hands of His minister. And since it is a complete surrender of himself by which a man dispossesses himself to be possessed and governed by divine providence through his superiors, it cannot be held that obedience consists merely in the execution, by carrying the command into effect and in the will's acquiescence, but also in the judgment, which must approve the superior's command, insofar, as has been said, as it can, through the energy of the will bring itself to this.

Would to God that this obedience of the understanding were as much understood and practiced as it is necessary to anyone living in religion, and acceptable to God our Lord. I say necessary, for as in the celestial bodies, if the lower is to receive movement and influence from the higher it must be subject and subordinate, the one body being ordered and adjusted to the other, so when one rational creature is moved by another, as takes place in obedience, the one that is moved must be subject and subordinated to the one by whom he is moved, if he is to receive influence and energy from him. And, this subjection and subordination cannot be had unless the understanding and the will of the inferior is in conformity with that of the superior.

Now, if we regard the end of obedience, as our will so our understanding may be mistaken as to what is good for us. Therefore, we think it expedient to conform our will with that of the superior to keep it from going astray, so also the understanding ought to be conformed with his to keep it from going astray. *Rely not on your own prudence* [Prov. 3:5], says Scripture.

Thus, they who are wise judge it to be true prudence not to rely on their own judgment even in other affairs of life, and especially when personal interests are at stake, in which men, as a rule, because of their lack of self-control, are not good judges.

This being so, we ought to follow the judgment of another (even when he is not our superior) rather than our own in matters concerning ourselves. How much more, then, the judgment of the superior whom we have taken as a guide to stand in the place of God and to interpret the divine will for us?

And it is certain that this guidance is all the more necessary in men and matters spiritual, as the danger in the spiritual life is great when one advances rapidly in it without the bridle of discretion. Hence Cassian says in the Conference of the Abbot Moses:

"By no other vice does the devil draw a monk headlong, and bring him to death sooner, than by persuading him to neglect the counsel of the elders, and trust to his own judgment and determination."

On the other hand, without this obedience of the understanding it is impossible that the obedience of will and execution be what they should be. For the appetitive powers of the soul naturally follow the apprehensive and, in the long run, the will cannot obey without violence against one's judgment. When for some time it does obey, misled by the common apprehension that it must obey, even when commanded amiss, it cannot do so for any length of time. And so perseverance fails, or if not this, at least the perfection of obedience which consists in obeying with love and cheerfulness. But when one acts in opposition to one's judgment, one cannot obey lovingly and cheerfully as long as such repugnance remains. Promptitude fails, and readiness, which are impossible without agreement of judgment, such as when one doubts whether it is good or not to do what is commanded. That renowned simplicity of blind obedience fails, when we call into question the justice of the command, or even condemn the superior because he bids us do something that is not pleasing. Humility fails, for although on the one hand we submit, on the other we prefer ourselves to the superior. Fortitude in difficult tasks fails, and in a word, all the perfections of this virtue.

On the other hand, when one obeys without submitting one's judgment, there arise dissatisfaction, pain, reluctance, slackness, murmurings, excuses, and other imperfections and obstacles of no small moment which strip obedience of its value and merit. Wherefore Saint Bernard, speaking of those who take it ill when commanded to do things that are unpleasant, says with reason: "If you begin to grieve at this, to judge your superior, to murmur in your heart, although outwardly you fulfill what is commanded, this is not the true virtue of patience, but a cloak for your malice."

Indeed, if we look to the peace and quiet of mind of him who obeys, it is certain that he will never achieve it who has within himself the cause of his disquiet and unrest, that is, a judgment of his own opposed to what obedience lays upon him.

Therefore, to maintain that union which is the bond of every society, Saint Paul earnestly exhorts all *to think and say the same thing* [1. Cor. 1:10], because it is by the union of judgment and will that they shall be preserved. Now, if head and members must think the selfsame, it is easy to see whether the head should agree with the members, or the members with the head. Thus, from what has been said, we can see how necessary is obedience of the understanding.

But how perfect it is in itself, and how pleasing to God, can be seen from the value of this most noble offering which is made of the most worthy part of man; in this way the obedient man becomes a living holocaust most pleasing to His Divine Majesty, keeping nothing whatever to himself; and also because of the difficulty overcome for love of Him in going against the natural inclination which all men have of following their own judgment. It follows that obedience, though it is a perfection proper to the will (which it makes ready to fulfill the will of the superior), yet, it must also, as has been said, extend to the understanding, inclining it to agree with the thought of the superior, for it is thus that we proceed with the full strength of the soul - of will and understanding - to a prompt and perfect execution.

4. *General Means for Attaining Obedience*

I seem to hear some of you say, most dear brothers, that you see the importance of this virtue, but that you would like to see how you can attain to its perfection. To this I answer with Pope Saint Leo, "Nothing is difficult to the humble, and nothing hard to the meek." Be humble and meek, therefore, and God our Lord will bestow His grace which will enable you to maintain sweetly and lovingly the offering that you have made to Him.

5. *Particular Means for Attaining Obedience*

In addition to these means, I will place before you three especially which will give you great assistance in attaining this perfection of obedience.

Seeing God in the Superior

The first is, as I said at the beginning, you do not behold in the person of your superior a man subject to errors and miseries, but rather him whom you obey in man, Christ, the highest wisdom, immeasurable goodness, and infinite charity, who, you know, cannot be deceived and does not wish to deceive you. And because you are certain that you have set upon your own shoulders this yoke of obedience for the love of God, submitting yourself to the will of the superior in order to be more conformable to the divine will, be assured that His most faithful charity will ever direct you by the means you yourselves have chosen. Therefore, do not look upon the voice of the superior, as far as he commands you, otherwise than as the voice of Christ, in keeping with Saint Paul's advice to the Colossians, where he exhorts subjects to obey their superiors: *Whatever you do, do it from the heart, as serving the Lord, and not men, knowing that you will receive from the Lord the inheritance as your reward. Serve the Lord Christ* [3:23-24]. And Saint Bernard: "whether God or man, his substitute, commands anything, we must obey with equal diligence, and perform it with like reverence, when however man commands nothing that is contrary to God." Thus, if you do not look upon man with the eyes of the body, but upon God with those of the soul, you will find no difficulty in conforming your will and judgment with the rule of action which you yourselves have chosen.

Seeking Reasons to Support the Superior's Command

The second means is that you be quick to look for reasons to defend what the superior commands, or to what he is inclined, rather than to disapprove of it. A help toward this will be to love whatever obedience shall enjoin. From this will come a cheerful obedience without any trouble, for as Saint Leo says: "It is not hard to serve when we love that which is commanded."

Blind Obedience

The third means to subject the understanding which is even easier and surer, and in use among the Holy Fathers, is to presuppose and believe, very much as we are accustomed to do in matters of faith, that what the superior enjoins is the command of God our Lord and His holy will. Then to proceed blindly, without inquiry of any kind, to the carrying out of the command, with the prompt impulse of the will to obey. So we are to think Abraham did when commanded to sacrifice his son Isaac [Gen. 22:2-3]. Likewise, under the new covenant, some of the holy Fathers to whom Cassian refers, as the Abbot John, who did not question whether what he was commanded was profitable or not, as when with such great labor he watered a dry stick throughout a year. Or whether it was possible or not, when he tried so earnestly at the command of his superior to move a rock which a large number of men would not have been able to move.

We see that God our Lord sometimes confirmed this kind of obedience with miracles, as when Maurus, Saint Benedict's disciple, going into a lake at the command of his superior, did not sink. Or in the instance of another, who being told to bring back a lioness, took hold of her and brought her to his superior. And you are acquainted with others. What I mean is that this manner of subjecting one's own judgment, without further inquiry, supposing that the command is holy and in conformity with God's will, is in use among the saints and ought to be imitated by any one who wishes to obey perfectly in all things, where manifestly there appears no sin.

6. *Representation*

But this does not mean that you should not feel free to propose a difficulty, should something occur to you different from his opinion, provided you pray over it, and it seems to you in God's presence that you ought to make the representation to the superior. If you wish to proceed in this matter without suspicion of attachment to your own judgment, you must maintain indifference both before and after making this representation, not only as to undertaking or relinquishing the matter in question, but you must even go so far as to be better satisfied with, and to consider as better, whatever the superior shall ordain.

7. *Final Observations*

Now, what I have said of obedience is not only to be understood of individuals with reference to their immediate superiors, but also of rectors and local superiors with reference to provincials, and of provincials with reference to the general, and of the general toward him whom God our Lord has given as superior, his vicar on earth. In this way complete subordination will be observed and, consequently, union and charity, without which the welfare and government of the Society or of any other congregation would be impossible.

It is by this means that Divine Providence gently disposes all things, bringing to their appointed end the lowest by the middlemost, and the middlemost by the highest. Even in the angels there is the subordination of one hierarchy to another, and in the heavens, and all the bodies that are moved, the lowest by the highest and the highest in their turn unto the Supreme Mover of all.

We see the same on earth in well-governed states, and in the hierarchy of the Church, the members of which render their obedience to the one universal vicar of Christ our Lord. And the better this subordination is kept, the better the government. But when it is lacking everyone can see what outstanding faults ensue. Therefore, in this congregation, in which our Lord has given me some charge, I desire that this virtue be as perfect as if the whole welfare of the Society depended on it.

8. *Final Exhortation*

Not wishing to go beyond the limits set at the beginning of this letter, I will end by begging you for the love of Christ our Lord, who not only gave us the precept of obedience, but added His example, to make every effort to attain it by a glorious victory over yourselves, vanquishing the loftiest and most difficult part of yourselves, your will and understanding, because in this way the true knowledge and love of God our Lord will possess you wholly and direct your souls throughout the course of this pilgrimage, until at length He leads you and many others through you to the last and most happy end of bliss everlasting.

From Rome, March 26, 1553.

The servant of all in our Lord,

Ignatius [Epistolae IV, 669-681 [Letter 3304]; in Tylenda (1985) pp. 72-83]

The metaphors, echoing the earlier text of the *Constitutions* [CS 550-559], are drawn from traditional treatments of religious obedience, based on material gathered from Polanco's ongoing study of writings on obedience of more traditional religious groups. Ignatius' views remain totally consistent and unwavering throughout his years as general. The same motifs found in his more formal statements on obedience are scattered generously throughout letters he wrote as General. The maintenance of unity [Epistolae I, 558], the impossibility of maintaining social order and effective functioning in the Society without strict obedience [I, 599, 688; IV, 560], the necessity for proper authority to direct the work of the Society as in any well-ordered government [I, 553, 560; II, 55, 56], a harsh and rigid attitude toward any disobedience [IV, 561], are recurrent themes. The supernaturalization of the authority hierarchy (the idea that the will of the superior was the will of God and that the superior gave his orders *in loco Christi*) appears repeatedly in the *Constitutions* [CS84, 85, 424, 434, 547, 603, 633, 659, 701] as well as in the letters [Epistolae I, 561, 689, 691; II, 56; IV, 671, 672], along with the insistence on blind obedience [I, 228; XII, 662]. As Bertrand (1985) noted regarding Ignatius' writings on obedience: "The circumstances that motivated the *Letter on Obedience*, and all the other letters dealing with this subject as well, are always the same. It is never a question of defending the central power, but of rousing or sustaining the peripheral power, either in local terms or at the level of great nations. This is a constant that suffers no exception — at least during Ignatius' lifetime" (p. 77). They reflect the sixteenth century perspective in which the universe was ordered from top to bottom and all authority derived ultimately from God.

## Obedience in Ignatian Spirituality

In these passages, as in other aspects of his spiritual teaching, the Ignatian inspiration harkens back to the *Exercises* and their roots in the Manresa experience. The context here derives from the meditations on the Two Standards and the Three Degrees of Humility. The field of battle is that of the kingdom of Christ versus that of the Devil, waging war for men's souls and the establishing of God's kingdom. The good soldier surrenders himself in total self-abnegation and humility to the will and commission of Christ, the ideal and loving leader.

Ignatius' vision reverberates with echoes of the illuminations on the banks of the Cardoner and at La Storta. Ignatius saw himself and his company as engaged in a struggle to achieve God's redemptive plan, to follow Christ and the earthly representation of His Vicar the Pope and all who derive jurisdiction from this authority down to the lowest superior in the Society. He envisioned a company of dedicated soldiers, ready with prompt and unquestioning obedience to pursue any task or mission set before them by the Vicar of Christ. Obedience was thus the essential principle of unity, action, and coordination. The authority to command such obedience came directly from God, so that the least command of the superior was synonymous with the will of God. The command of the superior, then, was given *in loco Christi*, "in the place of Christ."

Ignatius' approach, drawn from his own military background and experience, is the spirit of command and obedience characteristic of Iñigo the warrior. He was, we can presume, a courageous leader who demanded unquestioning obedience and tolerated no insubordination in his men. The military objective was all-important and overruled any obstacles. This was the spirit and determination that led him to ramparts of Pamplona. Part of Ignatius' rigor may also have been due to a diffuse crisis over both obedience and poverty throughout the Society. Ravier (1987) noted the increasing split between Ignatius the spiritual director and Ignatius the administrator, especially after 1552, when the Portugese scandal broke. But Ignatius' view of obedience was not unlike that of Xavier from his post on the other side of the world. They both took a fairly severe position in matters of obedience. But then it could be said that they were cut from the same cloth. There seems to be little question, however, that the situation in Portugal had tried Ignatius' patience and prudence to the breaking point and that he saw the root of the difficulty in the failure of holy obedience.

# CHAPTER XXIV

# IGNATIUS AND OBEDIENCE

## Psychoanalytic Perspective

To the psychological eye, Ignatius' repeated and unremitting emphasis on the centrality of obedience plays rather oddly alongside the pattern of his own life and career. Ignatius throughout his life remained rather headstrong, determined to follow his own course without much regard for the wishes and expectations of those around him, and in good hagiographic style, his biographers have cast this independence and strong will in a spiritually positive light — that in following his own idiosyncratic path he was merely following directives of the Holy Spirit guiding him toward his divinely inspired destiny. This may well have been the case. Ignatius seems to have possessed an unerring sense of the guidance of divine providence in all that pertained to obedience, that whatever the superior commanded under holy obedience — *in loco Christi* — was guaranteed by divine influence (Blet 1956). But from a psychoanalytic perspective, we cannot be sure.

## The Paradox

Divine guidance aside, we are left with a psychological paradox. The spiritual mentor and Superior General, who so avidly counselled absolute, immediate, unquestioning, perfect, and blind obedience, may not have been especially noteworthy for his own display of obedience throughout his career. He was not following the laws and mores of his home country when he got into trouble as a rambunctious youth; it was not compliance with the decisions of his commanders that made him defy the French, when the commander of the garrison at Pamplona was prepared to surrender; nor was he responsive to the needs and wishes of his family when he turned his back on the castle of Loyola to seek his destiny as a beggar of Christ. Time and again he defied expectations of superiors, mentors, and officials of both church and realm, insisting on his own approach, his own inspiration, his own view of things. He refused to submit to the wishes of the superior of the Franciscans in Jerusalem, insisting on doing things his own way until the poor friar had to invoke the power and authority of the Holy See. In his repeated confrontations with the Inquisition, he proved rather a brazen, contentious, almost defiant defender of his views and practices. One might guess that this less-than-compliant attitude may have contributed to the suspicions and reactionary posturing of the judges.

Perhaps most striking, when Ignatius was deciding what manner of religious order he would found, he again struck out on an independent course. He would follow none of the prescribed and approved models of religious community extant in the church. He had to go his own way. His order was to be different, unique, special. From this perspective, his counsel to the Portugese scholastics at Coimbra, is ironic: "It is a great delusion in those whose understanding has been darkened by self-love, to think that there is any obedience in the subject who tries to draw the superior to what he wishes. Listen to Saint Bernard, who had much experience in this matter. "Whoever endeavors either openly or covertly to have his spiritual father enjoin him what he himself desires, deceives himself if he flatters himself as a true follower of obedience. For in that he does not obey his superior, but rather the superior obeys him" (Tylenda 1985, p. 7).[1]

Ignatius had flagrantly contradicted this advice on countless occasions in the course of gaining papal approval for his vision of a new religious order. If there were ever a case of bending the superior to one's own wishes, of drawing him into obeying one's own views and desires rather than submitting in unquestioning obedience to the wishes and directives of the superior, Ignatius' behavior would be hard to beat.

## PAPAL NEGOTIATIONS

Other examples can be found in Ignatius' dealings with the Popes during his time in Rome.[2] Ignatius was not slow to exert himself in having things his way. Not long after their arrival in Rome, serious rumors were spread by Mainardi and his friends in the papal curia to the effect that Ignatius' companions were really disguised Alumbrados or Lutherans — the same charge Ignatius had met in his previous brushes with the Inquisition. The accusations charged them with immoral lives, teaching heresy, and attempting to found a religious

[1] This quotation is from the letter on obedience cited fully in chapter XXIII.

[2] I am indebted to the contribution of J.W. Padberg (1993) from which this series of examples is drawn.

order without papal approval. Witnesses were advanced to support the charges, abetted by Michael Landivar, who had originally joined the companions in Paris but then left the group. The charges were serious and ate into the base of Ignatius' support. The companions were threatened with dire punishments and with being expelled from their house. Ignatius decided to fight fire with fire. He confronted Cardinal DeCupis, who was behind some of the threats, and convinced him of his innocence. He then took his case directly to the governor of Rome and demanded a trial. The trial was decided in Ignatius' favor and Landivar was expelled from Rome.

But a month later, the word reached Spain that his men were regarded in Rome as heretics. Again Ignatius demanded a formal proceeding, citing his accusers in the papal court. Despite opposition and delays in gaining his objective, he persisted stubbornly until the ringleaders were summoned to court, where they quickly pleaded total ignorance and praised Ignatius and his men. Ignatius was counseled to drop the matter at that point because of the power and influence of these men, but the stubborn Basque would not yield an inch. He pressed his case and demanded a written judgment clearing him once and for all from charges of heresy. He met official recalcitrance — the cardinal and the governor turned a deaf ear, their refusal to act backed by curial officials. Ignatius responded by rounding up letters and testimonials to the good works and orthodoxy of his companions from prelates and important figures in places they had worked. When the matter was presented to Paul III, probably through Cardinal Contarini, a supporter of the Society, the matter was laid to rest — but no written declaration. Ignatius then followed the Pope to his villa at Frascati. The Pope responded favorably to Ignatius' request, and, after some delay, a formal declaration was issued by Conversini, the governor of Rome, clearing the companions of all charges and praising their work. The slanderers were given rigorous sentences. Padberg (1993) comments that "Ignatius was undoubtedly and thoroughly committed to the service of the Church and of the pope as the person who had universal responsibility for that Church; but he was at the same time as tenacious as a bulldog in seeing that those relations were based on fact and truth about himself and his companions" (pp. 17-18).

Ignatius' views at certain points came into opposition to papal wishes, especially around the question of receiving ecclesiastical dignities. Ignatius opposed the efforts of several popes — Paul III, Julius III, Marcellus II, and Paul IV — to impose such honors on Jesuits. A case in point was that of Claude Jay, who was offered the See of

Trieste by Ferdinand, king of the Romans, brother of Charles V and later emperor in his stead. Jay refused but the pressure continued. Appeals were sent to Paul III. Ignatius intervened — a memorandum was sent to the king demonstrating how acceptance of such dignities would harm the Society. Ignatius himself paid visits to a number of influential cardinals, and then explained the situation at length to the pope. The pope was sympathetic, but said that the appointment had been made and he could not reverse his decision. Ignatius was not to be put off. He pestered the cardinals, especially Cardinal Carpi, the protector of the Society, and prayed. Results were slow and unpromising. Ignatius spent day and night visiting every cardinal in Rome to press his case and persuade the pope to change his mind. The evening before the consistory announcing the appointment, Ignatius turned in desperation to Margaret of Austria, seeking her help to delay the announcement. The family influence finally paid off; the pope agreed to Margaret's request — Ignatius had bought some time. Then a barrage of letters was launched by the viceroy, Margaret, Carpi and Ignatius to king Ferdinand. The king finally relented and called off the effort. Ignatius wrote on 22 December 1546, "More by divine grace than by human diligence, though efforts have not been wanting on our part with God's help, a stop has been put to this matter for the time being and we are hopeful for the future" (Epistolae I, 454, cited in Padberg, p. 23).

The case of Francis Borgia provides another example. Borgia, who was the duke of Gandia and viceroy of Catalonia, secretly joined the Society, but for three years continued his princely life and role. In the interim he settled his affairs and completed his theological studies. When he visited Ignatius in October 1550, a move was afoot to make him a cardinal — the move was supported by Julius III and the college of cardinals, all at the urging of Borgia's longtime friend, Emperor Charles V. When Ignatius found out about it, the matter was a closed issue as far as the pope and the cardinals were concerned. Nonetheless, Ignatius went into action — special prayers were offered by the Jesuit community and Ignatius bent every effort to oppose this promotion. Borgia discretely fled the city in February 1551, and as soon as permission was received from the emperor began to follow a Jesuit life openly. Ignatius by this time was able to persuade the pope to give up the plan.

But the emperor was not so easily dissuaded. In the following year, he again pressured the pope to elevate Borgia to the cardinalate, and Ignatius again presented his case successfully to Julius III. But the question surfaced again in 1554, this time urged by the new

Spanish king, Philip II. Ignatius countered by ordering Borgia to take a special vow against accepting ecclesiastical dignities — probably the first Jesuit to do so. Borgia himself enlisted the help of Philip's sister, Princess Juana, who had herself taken vows as a Jesuit scholastic (Rahner 1960; Meissner 1992b), to persuade her brother to give up the idea. Efforts on Borgia's behalf finally ceased. Ignatius wrote to him in 1552:

> I held and now hold that it is the divine will for me to oppose this [appointment], even though others might think otherwise and bestow this dignity on you. There would be no contradiction at all involved; for the same Divine Spirit is able to move me to that action for certain reasons, and for other reasons to move others to the contrary action and to bring about the result to which the emperor was pointing. May God our Lord always in everything do what will be to his greatest praise and glory. (Epistolae IV, 283-285 [Letter 2652]; cited in Toner (1991), pp. 47-48; also in Young (1959), pp. 257-258.

The story was similar in the case of Laynez. Laynez, one of the Paris companions, was offered several ecclesiastical dignities, all of which he resolutely declined. But in 1555, the newly elected Pope Marcellus II planned to make Laynez a cardinal. His untimely death brought a temporary halt to the process. But when Ignatius' nemesis, Cardinal Gian Pietro Carafa, ascended the papal throne as Paul IV, the threat was renewed. Despite his antipathy toward Ignatius, Carafa admired and respected Laynez. Apparently Laynez was intended to play a pivotal role in the new pope's plans for reform of the Church. Laynez was ordered to prepare himself for any responsibility and to take up residence in the papal palace. Laynez did move in, but as it turned out stayed there for only one night. In the meantime, Ignatius was busily exerting his efforts to put a stop to this effort. Again special prayers were requested and the influence of important figures brought into play — both Ignatius and Laynez enlisted the help of influential cardinals. Paul IV finally thought better of it, and soon after Ignatius died. His successor as general of the Society was Diego Laynez. Padberg (1993) recalls a comment of Nadal regarding Ignatius' view on accepting papal appointments:

> Only the Supreme Pontiff can compel the Society in this regard. In such instances, every manner and means of resisting and impeding such an intention of the pontiff is to be expended and exercised, every stone (as they say) to be turned lest such a dignity be imposed. We are not to cease working toward this end or give up our efforts until we have exhausted every possibility. This will

> not be verified until the Apostolic See expressly obliges us under pain of mortal sin and will obviously brook no further resistance. (p. 28)[3]

A variant on the theme is found in the case of Ottaviano Cesari. His family had vigorously opposed his entrance into the Society, so he fled from his home in Naples and entered the Society in Sicily. Ignatius wrote a series of letters in an effort to preserve Cesari's vocation from family pressures. After he had joined the Society, his mother still wanted him back in Naples and besieged the Sicilian superiors in Palermo and Ignatius in Rome. Ignatius' promise to assign him to Naples after his training did not satisfy her. She appealed to Julius III who appointed a commission of three cardinals, one Carafa. They issued a *monitorium* directing Ignatius to send the young man to Naples. Ignatius gave the permission, but then had Polanco write the Sicilian provincial that Cesari was not obliged to go to Naples and that Ignatius himself was still against the idea. Another letter to the provincial put the matter in even stronger terms — Ignatius regarded the *monitorium* as invalid and illicit since it came only from Carafa rather than the full commission and Ignatius thought the return to Naples would pose a threat to Cesari's vocation. He would grant the permission as ordered, but his mind was not changed. Ottaviano did go to Naples and soon after Ignatius' death left the Society.

Ignatius' behavior in these contexts, in which he was confronted by demands of the ultimate ecclesiastical authority, should not surprise us. This is the same Ignatius who confronted the Franciscan provincial in Jerusalem, who argued his case before the judges of the Inquisition on several occasions, in each bending every effort to justify his position and in the end yielding to no more than the letter of the judgment. One would be hard pressed to claim any more than mere obedience of execution in any of these examples. From the perspective of five hundred years of history, we can salute this rebellious quality as salutary and providential. We can allow ourselves to believe that God was using the unique qualities of this saintly warrior to achieve great wonders for the church and for the advancement of His kingdom on earth. But this consideration does not diminish the paradox: can these observations be taken to suggest an underlying unconscious conflict over authority in Ignatius? To what extent do Ignatius' own attitudes toward authority and obedience determine the place of the virtue of obedience in his spiritual vision. As Padberg (1993) observes:

[3] The quotation is from Nadal (1976), p. 500; see O'Malley (1993).

> But, simply put, examples such as these are very important for our understanding of how Ignatius really understood reverence for the pope, obedience to his wishes, service of the Holy See, and "thinking with the Church." For the first and thirteenth of the Rules for Thinking with the Church should not be read as if they gave the only and the definitive answer to the theory and practice of Jesuit obedience, or even to the theory and practice of that obedience as understood by Ignatius; instead, those rules must be interpreted in the context of concrete examples of Ignatius' practice of thinking with the Church and responding to the wishes of the Holy See. (p. 30)[4]

## Ignatius' Authority Conflicts

In my previous study of Ignatius' personality (Meissner, 1992b), I explored possible grounds for persistence of certain of his authority conflicts. One consideration pertains to the extent to which he manifested characteristics similar to the authoritarian personality (Adorno et al. 1950).[5] Individuals with this personality profile tend to adhere rigidly to conventional and generally accepted values; they tend to be uncritically submissive to whatever moral authorities exist in the group to which they belong, authorities whom they frequently idealize; they tend to turn their aggression against anyone violating or rejecting the values they espouse, so that their attitudes are often harsh, condemnatory, and punitive; they tend to be tough-minded rather than tender-minded, so that they usually reject a subjective or imaginative approach to things; their thinking tends toward superstition and stereotypes, often in the form of belief in more or less mystical determinants of individual fate and a tendency to think in rigid categories; they frequently seem preoccupied with power and control, emphasize issues of power and submission in regard to authority, and identify with powerful figures; their attitudes are often hostile and cynical, tending to view the world as dangerous and threatening and projecting strong negative emotions to the outside; and finally sexual fantasies tend to be a source of excessive concern (Adorno et al. 1950; Meissner 1971a).

Ignatius' personality may have shared some of these characteristics. He certainly adhered to the conventional values of his time, especially the religious values that so strongly dominated his culture. He was, with the exceptions noted above, respectful and submissive

[4] See chapter XVII above regarding the Rules for Thinking with the Church.

[5] See the further discussion of authoritarian attitudes in relation to the pathology of obedience in chapter XXIX below.

to authority, both ecclesiastical and civil; the regime he instituted in the Society, however, was far from totalitarian. He was capable of delegating authority and more often than not deferred to the judgment of local superiors, who could understand the circumstances of a given case much better than he could. As Bertrand (1985) has observed about all Ignatius' writings on obedience: "The circumstances that motivated the *Letter on Obedience*, and all the other letters dealing with this subject as well, are always the same. It is never a question of defending the central power, but of rousing or sustaining the peripheral power, either in local terms or at the level of great nations. This is a constant that suffers no exception — at least during Ignatius' lifetime" (p. 77).[6]

His attitude toward church authorities, popes and bishops, was in some respects submissive and idealizing, but not without a degree of manipulation and "managing" on his part, as we have seen. One would hardly place Ignatius among the tender-minded; his approach was usually pragmatic and concrete, except for his mystical experience, which was exquisitely tender and affective. His mystical inclination was broad and deep, and the wish to submit himself totally and without reserve to the power and direction of the divine will was uncompromising and complete. His view of the world as threatening tended to focus on the spiritual realm, where he saw dangers on all sides — a fantasy of the evil one carrying on his diabolical campaign for destruction of the Church and pious souls that played such a determinative role in the *Spiritual Exercises*. Finally, we have noted the role of sexuality in Ignatius' emotional life: the powerful repressive barriers he was forced to erect against any sexual impulses, and the displacement and sublimation of his libidinal inclinations into apostolic and even mystical paths.

Freedom is threatening because it allows for unpredictability; it cannot be controlled. The tendency of the authoritarian disposition is to suppress freedom — in the name of any other noble investment — but unequivocally to suppress freedom. In whatever guise, authority concerns itself with achieving a balance between the demands of order and the demands of freedom. While authoritarians may find themselves driven to an emphasis on order that sacrifices freedom,

[6] My translation. The original reads: "Les circonstances qui ont motive la *Lettre sur l'obeissance* et, aussi bien, tous les autres documents epistolaires quit en traitent, sont dans leur structure toujours les memes. Il ne s'agit jamais defendre le pouvoir central, mais de susciter ou de soutenir le pouvoir peripherique, soit sur le plan local, soit a l'echelon de grandes aires nationales. Il y a la une constante qui ne souffre aucune exception, au moins du vivant de saint Ignace."

libertarians may surge to the opposite extreme of complete license to the detriment of order. Functional authority operates somewhere between the extremes. There is no one point on the continuum at which maximal freedom is guaranteed along with order. There is an optimal point, however, for each authority relation, operating within the distinctive requirements for order and commitments to individual freedom characterizing the group (Meissner 1971). In Ignatius' dealings with the Portugese problem, his problem was not merely bringing dissident and recalcitrant followers back into line, but in allowing the degree of freedom that allows for initiative and self-actualization in undertaking and carrying through apostolic works, while keeping in place the prescriptions of obedience that serve the purposes of coordination and sustaining of the works and directions of the Society as a whole. He was forced to ease the reins when the Portugese provincial was too strict and severe, and tighten his grip on them when faced with rebelliousness and recalcitrance.

In some degree, freedom carried a threat in the mind of Ignatius, and he sought to regulate the risks of his own inner freedom by obsessive devices, constant self-examination and accusation, self-denial, repression of all inordinate desires. He imposed on himself, both psychically and externally, a pattern of discipline that minimized spontaneity, and sought to impose a similar order on the lives of his sons in his *Constitutions*. If we were to regard these aspects of his behavior in authoritarian terms, they might pass for an elaborate form of "escape from freedom" (Fromm 1947).

It is hard to escape the impression that there are aspects of Ignatius' character that fit the authoritarian mold to some degree. The question is how much. I have argued (Meissner 1992b) that these authoritarian trends may have found their way into the formulas of the *Constitutions*. If so, they were tempered significantly by other elements in Ignatius' complex personality and his practical genius as an administrator. As his letters and directives make clear, he relied greatly on the judgment and prudence of his subordinates, particularly when the problems existed far from Rome and when he had no direct knowledge of the situation. The authoritarian strain was also tempered by Ignatius' capacity for drawing men to him in a spirit of devotion and companionship. The love and generosity, that pervade his writings and seem to have been an important part of his everyday dealings with his fellow Jesuits, may have gone a long way toward moderating the severity and obsessive perfectionism revealed in his more authoritarian utterances. We have some inkling of this from the reports of da Camara. In his *Memorial*, he tells us, "Our Father strongly deplored and punished the lack of obedience not only in essential matters, . . . but also in every other matter" (Memorial, n. 3; cited in Ravier 1987, p. 373). But he also strikes certain other notes suggesting that Ignatius was slow to appeal to obedience and much preferred to call upon the mature judgment and good will of men he could trust:

> Our Father was accustomed, in all that he could have others do with gentleness and without recourse to obedience, not to let obedience intervene; on the contrary, when he could have someone do something, not because the person had seen the wish of His Reverence, but because the individual did it of his own free will — that pleased Ignatius much more than if the individual did something because he had realized Ignatius' wish but without anyone's telling him to do so — that pleased him more than to have to give the order, finally, for the same reason, [it pleased Ignatius more] when the matter was ordered without its being under pain of obedience. (Memorial, n. 262; cited in Ravier 1987)

In his later years, Ignatius could sometimes invoke holy obedience over seemingly trivial matters, but the overriding impression is that he tended to respect the judgment of those on the scene. They were to use their own judgment, even when he advised or prescribed some course of action. On occasion he would send a blank sheet of paper with his signature, so that the local superior could fill it in as he thought best. Rules were meant to be interpreted flexibly and reasonably. Nadal described governance in the Society as combining firmness and sweetness — firm in its goals, sweet in dealing with individuals, taking into account their physical and psychological needs and exercising patient, moderation and understanding. Phrases like "I command" or "I order" were never to be used. If Nadal was setting norms for the practice of obedience, he was also reflecting the tenor of actual practice (O'Malley 1993).

We have good reason to wonder whether in his strong statements on obedience — for example, in his letter to Father Miro on the dismissal of disobedient subjects[7] — Ignatius was not responding to the impulse to erect a kind of authoritarian system of governance within the Society. In such a system, the more authoritarian the tendencies of those participating, the more evolved the social defense system becomes. The superior becomes punitively aggressive toward his inferior, and the inferior becomes masochistically submissive to this superior. Thus the pattern and structure of the system derive

[7] Cited in chapter XXIII above.

from and in a sense depend on the interaction of authoritarian intrapsychic forces. However we balance these various elements, we cannot forget that this was nonetheless the same Ignatius who tangled with the Inquisition and stalwartly argued his case, the same Ignatius who founded a group of which he was the guiding spirit, the leader, and until the end of his life the primary authority.

## Authoritarianism

I have discussed the issue of Ignatius' authoritarianism at length elsewhere (Meissner 1992b); my purpose here is merely to fit this piece into the overall puzzle. There is no escaping the contradictions and conflicts in this aspect of his personality. His submissiveness and resignation to authorities, especially within the church, were prominent in his postconversion spiritually oriented demeanor. He tended to rationalize such directives as the will of God — the same will of God that he sought to come to know and follow as a central theme of his spirituality. But this profession of submissive obedience has to be considered side-by-side with his stubborn and almost willful pursuit of his objectives regardless of opposition, his unwillingness to accept any lawful decision or order of ecclesiastical or royal superiors without bending every effort to have things turn out as he wished and mobilizing every resource to mold the decision or order to suit his purposes. Ignatius evidently played the cards on both sides of the game.

If we detect a certain disparity between his thinking and rhetoric about the exercise of authority and obedience on the one hand, and some of his actions, on the other, there is also some suggestion of ambivalence about having and using power and authority. He was reluctant to accept the role of General, even though he was the obvious and universal choice; he remained ambivalent about continuing to carry the burdens of office and even tried unsuccessfully to resign. In the light of these factors, we would be hard pressed to avoid the impression that Ignatius had to deal with significant conflicts over the issue of authority.

I suggest that these conflicts were underlain by the basic conflict of identifications at the very foundation of his inner psychic life. The ideal of submission, self-denial, and the complete commitment of self to the will of another in holy obedience would in this view reflect the maternal identification that played a dominant part in shaping his postconversion ego ideal and personality. The image of the authority figure, the possessor of power and influence, the one who commands and is obeyed, reverberates with the masculine and paternal identification that remained as the persistent residue of the image of Beltran de Loyola.

These two powerful sources of internalized structure played out their conflictual and ambiguous roles in the heart and mind of Ignatius. Try as he might, he was never able to resolve or integrate these warring factions. The dominance of one or the other, as well as the precarious balance between them, found various expressions in his relationships with fellow Jesuits, in his governance of the Society, in his relationships with authority figures in the church and the body politic, and even in his mystical life.

# SECTION IV

# THE PSYCHOLOGY OF OBEDIENCE

# CHAPTER XXV

# TOWARD A PSYCHOLOGY OF OBEDIENCE

## Introduction

It may not be immediately evident why an extended analysis of the psychology of obedience might be relevant to understanding Ignatian spirituality. But there is no way to circumvent the appreciation that the virtue of obedience was and is one of the core dimensions on which Ignatius erected his spiritual edifice. The immediate context for development of his ideas about obedience in the *Spiritual Exercises* was obedience to the will of God, which he saw as primary and essential to any religious life or growth in virtue. The context shifted somewhat in the *Constitutions*, where the immediate focus was on religious obedience, emphasizing aspects of the religious vow of obedience. The focus on the vow built on and incorporated all of his thinking about the virtue, but went further in institutionalizing requirements of the vow and specifying its role in the religious organization.

However, Ignatius' thinking was conditioned not only by his own psychological dispositions and inner conflicts, as suggested previously, but also took shape in a culture that was inherently monarchical and in cultural terms envisioned a direct line of power and authority coming from God to the king in the secular sphere, so that the authority of the king was backed by the authority of God — the "divine right" model of royal authority — and a similar direct line extending from God to the Pope in the religious sphere. Ignatius' thinking about religious obedience, then, was articulated within this framework and accordingly his sense that the voice of the superior was the voice of Christ or God made immediate sense. Our contemporary culture, now half a millennium away from the late medieval culture of sixteenth century Spain, no longer accepts these cultural postulates. Our view of authority is more horizontal than vertical, more democratic than monarchical, more egalitarian than authoritarian. If Ignatian spirituality is to have any relevance to modern concerns and sympathies, the understanding of authority and obedience must be reformulated and recast in contemporary terms.

## Religious Crisis

Needless to say this evolution has been and is attended by crisis. The problem of obedience in contemporary religious life is one of the central issues confronting the working out of the religious vocation. In the contemporary scene the religious vocation is in crisis. Large numbers of religious have left and are leaving their orders and congregations and returning to secular life. The exodus of priests, particularly young and energetic ones, who have abandoned their vocations and have been laicized and married has become a problem of serious and worrisome proportions, creating a serious crisis in the church. The questions which are being seriously raised in this crisis of religious life have to do with the meaning and vitality of religious life as a way of life within the Church. The inner meaning and purposefulness of the religious vocation is being brought under scrutiny — and the inquiry has led many to conclude that there is no identifiable merit or functional utility to the religious vocation.

We might ask ourselves what some of the reasons for this attitude and the crisis related to it might be. There can be little question that the decree of Vatican II on the renewal of religious life provided an auspicious starting point. The decree of the council called for renewal and updating of religious practices and a reorganization of religious life more in accord with the needs and demands of the contemporary world. It also underlined the need for experimentation in finding new and more useful ways to achieve the goals of religious communities. The direction of change and experimentation was toward secularization. There was a perceptible tendency to drop more traditional and formalistic aspects of the religious life. Religious garb was either dropped or modified in the direction of more modern styles. Traditional forms of community exercise or community prayer were modified or eliminated. The organizational structure of many religious enterprises changed in the direction of a more secular pattern of organization.

## Secularizing Forces

One can point, for example to the secularization of religious educational institutions. There are a wide variety of influences which came together to force religious groups to alter their involvement and affiliation with educational institutions. The traditional pattern had been one in which the institution was founded, owned and run by the religious group. Individual religious were assigned by their respective superiors to live in the religious community and to work in the educational institution. The religious worked without direct salary — their investment in the work of the institution was religiously motivated and was seen as a direct expression of their religious vocation. The religious' personal sacrifice could be envisioned and understood in terms of religious vocation and direct service of the Church's work and God's kingdom.

Secularizing forces changed that. The increasing size of educational institutions served to dilute the specifically religious impact of religious personnel on the campus. Their role became increasingly nonreligious and their work became more and more formally educational — whether in terms of teaching or administration — so that the religious purposes of their activity became increasingly less apparent. The advancing pattern of mass education also meant that the size and cost of educational facilities had to increase. Thus the proportional contribution to Catholic education made by nonsalaried religious became less significant — as they began to represent a smaller and smaller proportion of the personnel of the institution. The institution was forced to look elsewhere for financial support — particularly to government funding. The subsequent step of turning the ownership of the institution over to a nonreligious board of trustees was predictable, if not unavoidable.

The upshot was that a separation was introduced between the structure of the religious community and the structure of the institution. The commitment of religious personnel to the institution was thereby irrevocably altered. They became salaried employees of the institution. The institution could no longer be seen as clearly or convincingly in terms of a religious purpose. The inevitable result was that the goals, direction and structure of the religious community had to undergo significant changes. Participation in the life of the religious community was no longer *ipso facto* connected with a religious commitment to the institution. The religious employed by the institution was a salaried employee like any layman. His religious commitment was shifted to the community — it no longer specifically included the institution.

## Deinstitutionalization

One can easily see that this shift in direction and structure raises important questions. The dissociation of community and institution leaves a potential gap. What is the function of religious groups serving secular institutions which have no identifiable religious purpose? The situation is similar in hospitals run by religious. If individual religious can be assigned to teach or work in such a secular institution, why should not they be assigned a whole broad range of secular involvements — some of which may have more directly realizable apostolic goals? Further, if the religious community can no longer identify its purpose and function in relation to the support and service of such institutional structures, what is the nature and function of the religious community without such institutional affiliations? It appears that the shock waves from such inevitable structural changes have not stopped having their effect.

It can be seen, therefore, that in the face of social pressures, institutional changes, needs for adaptation and experimentation, the pattern of religious life began to shift more and more toward a secular model. It has become increasingly difficult for the religious to identify what is different about his pattern of life as distinguished from his lay colleague — in such a way as to justify his living a religious life in religious community. The problem is a serious and difficult one — but I only mean to raise it here as an indication of the problems that it raises for the consideration of obedience. For the changes in the structure of religious life have had their inevitable effects on all aspects of religious life — of which obedience must be regarded as central.

## The Crisis of Authority

Obviously, the problem of obedience is closely related to the problem of authority. Shifts in attitudes toward and understanding of authority have undergone a significant evolution — particularly in the last few years. The general political climate has a direct bearing on this phenomenon. The twentieth century has seen the rise of the democratic spirit as in no other era of history. This is particularly true in the Western world. It is correlated with the gradual rise in level of education and political sophistication in the general populace — a phenomenon particularly of western cultures — and of the increasing impact of mass communication media in the transfer of information. In a situation in which the populace at large is much better prepared to form an independent judgment about matters of common concern and in which the availability of information is so great and rapid, we are forced to recognize that divergent opinions are going to be formed more readily. We must also recognize that ready acceptance of a point of view or directive from any authoritative source is more liable to be questioned and critically appraised.

In the post-Tridentine era, the combination of ignorance and the necessity for defensive mobilization of the Church's resources in the face of doctrinal and persecutory onslaughts gave the need for authority and hierarchical organization within the Church a certain urgency. It also created a climate within which the exigency of obedience was apparent. Organization of the Church's resources under the Pope in a hierarchical and authoritarian structure had the advantage of tightening the structure and protecting the Church and its members from the heretical onslaughts of its enemies. This apprehension undoubtedly contributed significantly to Ignatius' desire to dedicate his Society to the service of the Pope — ready to travel to any corner of the globe or to undertake any mission that the Pope should desire — papal shock troops, if you will. But in the post-Vatican era, such exigencies have lost their force. The result is that the structures of the Church — once historically purposeful and vital — have become inapt and constraining in the modern context. The structures evolved over preceding centuries are calculated to serve the functions of conservation and preservation of doctrine, of holding on to faithful adherence to such doctrine, of reinforcing the discipline of the Church to insure solidarity and adherence of the faithful to the formal body of the Church. It is apparent even in our own day that the values and priorities which generated and consolidated this more conservative and authoritarian organization is still adhered to by many in the Church — particularly among those who are participants in the hierarchical structure, or among those who have come to depend on that structure and to regard it as necessary. Many in the Church who have known no other pattern of organization cannot conceive of the Church without its hierarchical structure.

It is our position here that the structures, which had once served purposeful and meaningful goals in the life of the Church, may no longer be adaptive in the contemporary life of the Church. They therefore need modification and reorganization in relation to contemporary needs of the Church and the culture within which it must function. Older, traditional structures and patterns of organization can become constricted and provide obstacles and hindrances to the advancement of the Church's work. However, structures are never easy to change; one might offer some hope for changing attitudes and understanding of the meaning and purpose of such structures.

It was in part this realization that prompted the work of Vatican II. The council fathers were responding to something that they themselves were only vaguely and hesitantly aware of. The inexorable cultural and dynamic forces that they were responding to have continued to work in the Church and in society at large. The Church has begun to adapt to the needs and demands placed on it in the modern world. Religious life — insofar as it reflects and embodies the life and work of the Church — must organize itself in new patterns and styles of carrying out its life and work. This is a work of renewal and adaptation. The wheels have been set turning and it can safely be said at this point that there is no turning back.

What we are witnessing is a process of gradual secularization and deinstitutionalization. Along with this pattern we are finding pressures and forces building up which move us in the direction of increasing decentralization and democratization of a broad spectrum of social structures. There is an increasing emphasis and exigency for localized control of social processes, for increasing autonomy on the personal level and particularly for loosening of authoritarian and bureaucratic forms of organization. At the same time, the counterforces of increasing industrial potential and technological sophistication are driving in the direction of greater institutionalization and removal of sources of control to higher organizational levels. It is not clear at this point how the social organism will respond to and resolve these conflicting and diverging forces. It is plain, however, that the crisis of modern society and social structures is related to the intensifying sense of anomie and displacement and alienation that these conflicting forces create.

Consequently one cannot be sure that the emerging directions of change are all to the good. It is important, therefore, that we do not allow ourselves to make the predictable error of the swinging pendulum — to rush to an opposite extreme that may in the balance be worse than the position we have vacated. Whatever evaluation one can make of social pressures and forces working on the structure of the Church and religious life, we cannot afford to ignore them. They must be acknowledged and adapted to. That is the law of social life. Institutions that fail to adapt in the face of social and cultural change are doomed to wither and die.

## ADAPTATION

In our efforts to adapt and change, however, neither can we afford the opposite error of thinking that the structures and patterns that have evolved through the years have been valueless or useless. There is a tendency among those who speak of the need for change and adaptation to reject and abandon all the practices and patterns of organization of the past. In conjunction with contemporary pressures toward deinstitutionalization and the emphasis on individualism and personalism, there is a tendency to react to and rebel against all forms of institutionlization and organization. Since institutions and organizations are structured through and in terms of authority, there evolves a revolt against all forms of authority and structure.

It is a mistake to think that all forms of institution or authority are not desirable. Human life on a social level requires organization and structure. Institutions are part of the life blood of society — and institutions without authority are meaningless. It is a mistake, as well to think that authority is intrinsically authoritarian — or conversely that all obedience is submission. The work of adaptation, therefore, is not accomplished through rebellion and overthrow of pre-existing forms and structures. It does, however, require modifications of our understanding of how such structures are functionally organized and motivated. The patterns and styles of our activity and responsiveness to and within such structures must undergo significant changes. What we are proposing here, then, is a view of the structure of authority and obedience within the Church which is broader than the more traditional view, but which does not reject or abandon the view of authority and obedience that has emerged in the Church since the council of Trent. Rather what we are proposing and trying to formulate would view the attitudes and styles of the exercise of authority in the Church and in religious life as a special case, which was conditioned by historical and social pressures to express itself in more authoritarian patterns. Those attitudes and styles cannot be condemned since they were historically adaptive and socially necessary within their respective contexts. But they cannot be regarded as absolute or essential to the Church's organization and functioning. In the face of contemporary contexts and demands, the Church's adaptive capacity must be further called forth to bring the Church's organization and structure closer to the context of the contemporary world.

As John Murray (1966) put it so well, in recent centuries the Church found it necessary to emphasize and to structure itself in terms of the vertical dimension of authority. Implicit in this was the view that the Church's authority was derived from a divine source and that the organization of the Church reflected a hierarchical principle according to which that authority and the power associated with it was distributed successively from higher to lower levels. The Pope was below God, the bishops below the Pope, the priests were under the bishops and the people under the priests. Each level owed absolute and faithful obedience to the level above it, and exercised absolute and direct authority over the level below it. In such a rigidly hierarchical structure, there was little room for human decision-making, human initiative or responsibility, or for the exercise of autonomy and judgment. The stamp of divine origin and authority seemed somehow to permeate the whole. The directives that came from higher levels were proposed and to be regarded as God's will.

What is emerging in our time is an increasing emphasis on the horizontal aspects of authority. We are beginning to acknowledge that the exercise of authority involves human structures and forms of organization. We are beginning to realize that there is room and need in human structures for personal responsibility and initiative, for implementation of decision-making processes on a broader and more democratic basis — in short that authority and obedience cannot violate human autonomy and maturity. The horizontal dimension of authority in the Church and in religious life has not been absent. It was there in minor but real ways. The Church has held sacred the dignity and inviolability of the human personality. It has been the guardian of the rights and privileges of human conscience and judgment. Religious institutes have cherished the principles of representation and conscience. But these elements remained in the background more or less and were somehow absorbed in the larger picture of hierarchical and authoritarian organization in which divine prerogatives and absolute obedience were central. The imbalance is being redressed currently. The horizontal dimension is finding increasing emphasis and recognition. The declaration on religious liberty of Vatican II stands as a monument to the modern world of the Church's traditional and continued insistence on the primacy of human conscience and freedom.

## The Psychology of Obedience

Thus the view of obedience we are considering here — particularly from a psychological perspective — is based on an understanding of the human personality that views human growth and development and functional maturity as correlative to and integrated with personal autonomy, individuality, responsibility, initiative and freedom on one hand, and on the other as a process that builds on, maintains, and integrates forms of interrelationship, dependence, and participative belonging consistent both with mature and adaptive adult functioning and more autonomous aspects of human personality. In this perspective, authentic obedience, and particularly religious obedience, is an achievement of mature human development. The capacity for mature obedience is related to and derived from the individual's level of personal maturity and capacity for growth. The more capable the individual is of true autonomy, of authentic responsibility, of real initiative and judgment, and of adaptive relationships with others, the more capable he is of true obedience. The capacity for free self-determination is thus essential to the notion and to the exercise of obedience. I would view this understanding as not only consistent with Ignatius' understanding of spiritual development and obedience, but as inherently essential to it.

Obedience then, is subject to growth and can attain a level of development which depends on the individual's life history and pattern of personal experience. The development of obedience can also fall short of full maturity; it may be stalled or fixed at one or other level of the developmental process. Obedience can be more or less mature, more or less developed. It can express itself in less mature forms corresponding to earlier and less mature levels of development. It is also be clear that obedience is subject to developmental vicissitudes not only in individual terms, but that the pattern of organization of authority and obedience in institutions can assume a variety of more or less mature forms, usually resulting from the relative immaturity of those engaged in the authority relation.

The child grows in obedience. The obedience of a child to its parents is less mature and less developed than the obedience an individual might show in more adult forms of social structure — for example, the obedience of an employee in a corporation, or that of a mature religious in the context of religious obedience. The persistence of more infantile patterns of obedience in the latter situation reflects a developmental defect or a regression to more infantile patterns. The defect may involve personal dynamics of either a subject or of a superior. But when the defect is institutionalized in structured forms of interaction reinforcing less mature patterns of obedience, then other factors must be taken into account. There may be expedients, external social and cultural influences, which prompt and reinforce less mature patterns of interaction, but they must be recognized as less mature nonetheless.

As we have already indicated, less mature patterns of obedience may have an adaptive value in given historical contexts or circumstances. But we must recognize at the same time that less mature patterns are temporary and contingent and that they serve an immediate function, which is at once transient and demands to be superseded by more mature forms and patterns of obedience. I believe this is the direction of the present drive toward an enlargement and deepening of the concept of obedience. There is an inexorable pressure, both individual and institutional, calling for an advancement of patterns of obedience toward more mature levels. There is an implicit ethical demand in human social organization and functioning which calls for movement toward more mature and developed forms of action and interaction. We can tolerate fixation at less mature levels only in the interest of other gains and objectives — other contingencies and adaptive necessities. But when these are not present or recognizable, pressures for more developed patterns exert themselves. The kind of disciplined and unquestioning obedience in the military, for example, has its purposes, but in a democratic society they are strictly limited and qualified by constraints regarding personal dignity and freedom.

In turning to the psychology of obedience, then, we will base our considerations primarily on a developmental perspective (chapter XXVII). This will enable us to see more clearly the components and levels of organization within the obediential response. We will then consider some of the pathological types or styles in which the more deviant forms of obedience can express themselves (chapter XXIX). It is important to see not only how obedience grows and what goes into it, but also to see what is involved in its deviant forms. In this connection, we will take up the difficult question of disobedience (chapter XXX) — for we can really only grasp what it is that constitutes real obedience by clearly separating it from what passes for disobedience. We will also consider some of the functional aspects and problems of obedience in its implementation and exercise in religious life (chapter XXVIII). Finally we will consider religious obedience specifically in terms of its structure and objectives (chapter XXXI). Here the question of the relationship between the individual and the corporate aspects of obedience must be considered. And finally we will offer some reflections on the ethical dimension of religious obedience, specifically in terms of the psychological and developmental perspectives that have gone before (chapter XXXI). It is hoped that in this way we will be able to present a fairly comprehensive view of the nature of obedience in its psychological dimension which will broaden the understanding and scope of the nature of obedience — and hopefully provide some deeper perspective for understanding the role of obedience in the spiritual teaching of Ignatius.

# CHAPTER XXVI

# THE AUTHORITY RELATION

## Authority as Relation

The immediate context of obedience, the matrix out of which it develops and within which it manifests itself, is the authority relation. I have attempted to analyze and explore the authority relation in detail elsewhere (Meissner 1971a); in the present consideration, I would like to focus on some of the central aspects of the authority relation and their relevance for the exercise and functioning of obedience.

The authority relation refers to the complex interaction between a superior and his subject or subjects, based on a continuing process of mutual regulation. It is a relation in which superior and subject have certain determinable roles and functions they carry out in reciprocal interaction. Authority as such constitutes the superior's role in this relation — a role involving responsibility for decision-making, leadership, direction of group resources to shared goals and purposes, etc. The limits and effectiveness of the superior's functioning are to a large measure determined by acceptance of the group and their responsiveness to his initiatives and directives. In the concrete order (as opposed to the formal and legitimate order), the group determines the extent and degree to which the superior is regarded and responded to as superior and in what areas of the exercise of his authority.

The subject's participation in and responsiveness to the authority relation is what constitutes his obedience. Obedience, therefore, emerges as a specific role and function within the authority relation. It is defined and operates in relation to authority and its exercise. It does not take place in a vacuum — nor is it a phenomenon that can be considered as an isolated human response flowing from intrapsychic determinants alone. It is a response to a stimulus coming from outside — particularly response to an initiative from the superior. And more than a response, it is a sharing and a participation in a relationship. It represents an engagement in a continuing process of mutual regulation and responsiveness. In terms of loyalty, obedience can be viewed as the continuing engagement in and perduring commitment to the mutual responsiveness and regulation that is the essence of the authority relation.

## SUBJECTION AND AUTHORITY

What, then, constitutes the subject's participation in and responsiveness to the authority relation? The essential concept that I would like to articulate here is the notion of subjection. In framing this concept, I will try to situate it as the basic core of obedience — the essential action and process that constitutes and shapes obedience and without which we cannot be said to have obedience at all. Subjection is the act by which one becomes a subject — by which one enters into and becomes a participant in the authority relation under obedience. In the first place, it should be noted that subjection is an action — it is an active commitment and engagement of oneself. It is, therefore, an act of self-direction and determination. Subjection must consequently be rooted in freedom. The direction and determination of self, as well as the engagement and commitment implicit in subjection, are inconceivable without a basic root of such action in freedom.

The act of subjection is in part an act by which the authority relation is established. A relationship can be established only through involvement and responsiveness of more than one individual. Subjection is an act by which the subject responds to and takes part in the authority relation. Subjection is, therefore, responsive and from the beginning takes on the form of an interaction. However, it is a response of a particular kind. It is a response to an initiative coming from the superior. If it is to constitute the relation of authority, subjection must answer in a manner consistent with the structure of the authority relation. That is to say, subjection must take the form of an engagement in the essential process of mutual regulation central to the authority relation. Subjection is a commitment to mutual regulation. Subjection thus, insofar as it is a response to the superior's initiative, must express itself in the form of a comparable initiative — the subject's initiative responding to the initiative of the superior. Subjection is an expression of the willingness and readiness to take responsibility within the authority relation. There can be no mutual regulation without the assumption of responsibility in both sides of the relation. Mutual regulation requires a willingness to stand over against the superior — to exercise autonomy and judgment, to take an independent or critical or oppositional stand when necessary and indicated. A necessary aspect of mutual regulation is a dialogue of participating agents in which they exercise a mutual influence. Subjection is thus an action that requires initiative and responsibility, embracing autonomy and independence of thought and judgment, and rooted in the freedom of self-direction and determination.

Insofar as subjection is in part constitutive of the authority relation, it becomes an act by which authority itself is constituted and shaped. Subjection is thus a source of authority. It is the reciprocal act by which the subject becomes a subject, and by which he thereby establishes the superior as superior. Subjection emerges as one of the roots of authority. What I am pointing out here may come as a surprise to some — but it has been implicit in all that has preceded. The traditional view of authority has been hierarchical and vertical in its conceptualization. Authority was seen as originating in a higher source — in the religious context in the will of God — from where it extended itself to lower levels of the organization. The lower was thereby subordinate to the midmost and the midmost to the highest. The structure was clear and unequivocal. The view I am presenting here, however, views the organization of authority as essentially horizontal and interactional. It is constituted in part in and through the interaction of individuals within a group process.

## SOURCE OF AUTHORITY

The roots of authority, then, are multiple. Authority is not a quality or force originating in a single source and then magically distributed. It is an aspect of human interaction and of social structures and can be understood and analyzed in terms of such human processes. We can point to some of the roots of authority. First of all, authority is resident in the structure of the organization. Human organizations have a structure which implies that certain functions and roles are distributed throughout the organization. There is a process of division of labor within human groups and organizations which increases the capacity of the group to achieve and work toward those goals for which the organization exists. Functions of direction, policy-making and decision-making are aggregated to certain individuals. Other functions are centered in different individuals. The priority and selectivity of these functions imposes a necessary hierarchization on the group and dictates in some measure the structure of authority. Thus authority is resident in the structure and is ascribed to individuals by reason of the function or position that they hold. This form of authority is legitimate authority. It is the form of authority that was almost exclusively regarded as acceptable and valid in more traditional approaches to authority. Thus, in the religious group, authority is vested in the superior — an authority he acquires by virtue of his appointment to a given office.

But the roots of authority go deeper and reach further. There is an authority resident in the community itself. The community can give itself a sense of direction and purpose, it can evolve a consensus — whether that be done formally and in a consciously organized manner through meetings and voting procedures, or whether it be accomplished in informal and less conscious ways through the interaction and processes that unfold within the group — which directs the group as whole to certain goals, in certain directions of activity and purpose. Part of the superior's function is to integrate this capacity and force within the group with his own initiatives. But it is clear that the group has an autonomy setting it apart from the superior and his legitimate authority. The group consensus bears with it the stamp of authority because it has a direct influence on the responsiveness of the group to the superior's initiatives — either accepting and integrating them or resisting and rejecting them. Often the superior's initiatives or directives go unanswered and unobserved because the consensus of the group either does not accord him effective authority over such matters or because his initiative runs counter to the consensus of the group.

The community itself, therefore, has a power of direction and effective decision-making which serves as a source of authority. The community in this view is seen as acting by consensus. Where such consensus is lacking, the opinions or sense of direction involved become fragmented and diverse. The authority of the community is then compromised and must be integrated with other sources of authority in order to attain authoritative status. The sense of group direction does not always achieve clear definition, but when it does it must be reckoned with as a source of direction and initiative having considerable influence on the pattern of activity that the group will actually follow.

## INDIVIDUAL AUTONOMY AND AUTHORITY

As we have suggested in our discussion of subjection, there is a third root of authority that must be placed alongside the legitimate authority of the superior and the authority of the community as a major source of authority. The authority that derives from subjection is an authority rooted in the autonomy and maturity of the individual. The individual's act of subjection is an expression of his own inner autonomy and identity. His subjection is a reflection of his own inner sense of subjectivity — his awareness of his own inner strength and resourcefulness which allows him to enter into the process of mutual regulation. His own inner subjective strength and autonomy becomes a root of and resource for the authority relation — and lends to it a strength and purposefulness marking it as authoritative. Subjection thereby brings to the authority relation those inner strengths of will, purpose, intention, commitment and valued striving which vitalizes the authority relation and gives it the character of purposeful direction and valued commitment.

The individual, autonomous and independent, becomes, in and through the act of subjection, a root and source of authority. His subjection involves as we have seen an enduring commitment to and faithful engagement with certain shared values that he accepts as his own and which he verifies and confirms in his acceptance and commitment. His freedom, initiative and responsibility, are thereby made available to the authority relation and become inner resources by which authority gains strength and conviction. His acceptance and responsiveness to the goals and values of the group contributes a source of strength to the integration of group striving to fulfill and achieve these goals and values.

## THE DIALECTIC OF AUTHORITY

It is plainly essential for the working out of authority that these multiple sources and roots of authority be integrated and brought into congruence. The sources of authority can stand in opposition to each other. The effectiveness of the exercise of authority and of the striving to fulfill shared goals and to realize common values is impaired by such opposition and divisiveness. However, the tension and conflict among sources of authority are also a source of vitality and strength for the group. As in any human process, there is bound to be conflict and divergence. The strength of the group lies in its capacity to bring these sources of authority into meaningful interaction and to permit them to engage each other in a meaningful process of mutual regulation. There must be a continuing and ongoing dialectic among all the sources of authority — legitimate, communal and personal. The dialectic must take place in a horizontal dimension — each source of authority recognizing itself and the other sources as respective roots of authority with a valid and real function in the dialectic. The dialectic of authority, then, requires that each source recognize and accept its own autonomy and responsibility — and that each enter into the process of mutual regulation with the willingness to exercise its responsibility and initiative and to respond to and accept the initiatives and responsible engagement of other roots. Only then can an effective and realistic dialectic ensue which is based in and derivative from the authority relation.

In the context of such a relation, it is apparent that the structure and implicit assumptions about the nature and functioning of obedience have considerable impact on the way in which the interaction of superior and subject works itself out. The implicit requirements generated within the relationship serve as determinants of the manner of functioning of the participating individuals. This is relevant not only for consideration of particular interactions — the way in which superior and subject interact or carry out a particular negotiation — but it also has relevance for the total style of the pattern of interaction which gives the relationship its quality and perduring style. This more perduring aspect of the authority relation can have important implications for the functioning and adaptation of the participants.

We can entertain at least two possibilities — one that a certain style of interaction might appeal to and mobilize certain personality dispositions of the participants, and the other that the pattern of interaction within the authority relation might have a part in determining or producing such response patterns that characterize the functioning personalities. Thus we can ask whether a certain style of interaction within the authority relation brings out and exploits certain aspects of the individual's already established personality — or whether the establishment of a certain style of interaction contributes to establishment of certain personality characteristics. The former question is more easily answered. The latter question is more problematical.

## COMPLIANCE

There can be little doubt that the establishment of certain patterns of interaction in any human organization plays into the personality dispositions of those who participate in it. If the style of interaction in the authority relation is set up along authoritarian lines and the expectation is set — whether implicitly or explicitly — for the subject's compliance to be maximal, this puts into action certain inevitable pressures toward compliant behavior. Where submission and compliance are selected as valued response patterns and subtle pressures and rewards set to work to reinforce such behavior, one can expect compliant behavior to be increased. This is not merely a matter of social conditioning. Rather it is a matter of a more basic appeal to underling dependency needs. Every human being has such needs, but in some the need is stronger and can exercise a certain regressive pull. The need to rely on others, to be dependent and to be taken care of by others — as one was as a child — can be a powerful influence on one's behavior and thinking. The posture of compliance and submission also serves the function of avoiding any aggressive self-assertion or autonomy. For some individuals the expression of aggression in any form is threatening because it is associated with hostile and destructive wishes and fantasies. Such individuals adopt and cling to a position of passivity and dependency precisely to avoid any confrontation with their own aggression. Further the threat of self-assertion and autonomous behavior is linked to the threat of abandonment, of being rejected and thrown out, of losing the valued esteem and affection of others. For such individuals, the demand for compliance and submission in the authority relation meets a deeper inner need within their own personalities.

Erich Fromm (1955) brought this issue into focus in his discussion of irrational authority. He commented:

> As long as there was overt authority, there was conflict, and there was rebellion — against irrational authority. In the conflict with the commands of one's conscience, in the fight against irrational authority, the personality developed — specifically the sense of self developed. I experience myself as "I" because I doubt, I protest, I rebel. Even if I submit and sense defeat, I experience myself as "I" — I, the defeated one. But if I am not aware of submitting or rebelling, if I am ruled by an anonymous authority, I loose the sense of self, I become a "one," a part of the "It."
> The mechanism through which the anonymous authority operates is *conformity*. I ought to do what everybody does, hence, I must conform, not be different, not "stick out" . . . (p.153)

The same strictures are operative in any context in which the reponsibility of mature obedience is avoided.

By the same token, the presumption within the authority relation of the subject's initiative and responsibility can be quite threatening to such individuals. The valuation and expectation of initiative and responsibility thus avoids the regressive pull and appeal to dependency needs, but it also runs the risk of mobilizing aggressive self-assertion and even adolescent rebelliousness. Structures which mobilize potential for growth also mobilize potential for regression — as will become evident in our discussion of developmental processes.[1] If the presumption of initiative opens the way to a more mature form of obedience, it also opens the way to the excess of willfulness and hyperautonomy. It is difficult to tread the way of mature and adaptive functioning in any human endeavor. There is a natural human tendency to distort in the direction dictated by inner subjective needs and infantile fixations. There is a tendency for subjection to be drawn regressively into forms of submission and dependency — there is also a tendency for autonomy to become willfulness and rebelliousness. In either case, the controlling element in the authority relation has to be found in the process of mutual regulation which can serve in a healthy and productive manner to temper willfulness into willingness and to bring mere submission to the level of subjection. This, however, presumes both the concern and the mature capacity of those involved to seek out a more mature pattern of relationship.

## THE PERSONAL EQUATION

From this point of view it is interesting to note that the patterns of interaction between superiors and subordinates are largely determined by personality characteristics of the participants. A recent study of patterns of interaction between superiors and subordinates at a number of levels of organization suggests that the communication process is perceived in predictably distorted ways, depending on the role of the persons involved and their relative passivity or activity as personality dimensions. Generally persons who initiate communications in such interactions tend to exaggerate the amount of communication, while those who receive the communications tend to underestimate it. Superiors generally tend to exaggerate the amount of communication which they initiate to subordinates, while subordinates tend to underestimate the amount of this same communication. Individuals with relatively passive personalities tend to exaggerate the amount of all communications — initiated or received — and particularly any communications from relatively active comunicators. Thus a relatively passive subordinate tends to feel that he is close to his superior and tends to exaggerate his initiations to the superior and the superior's initiations to him. This may not reflect the reality at all. On the other hand, a relatively active subordinate, even if he is in a position to receive many communications, is more likely to feel isolated or independent from the superior and tends to underestimate the amount of initiating or responding to his superior (Webber 1970).

[1] See chapter XXVII below.

Such findings are of interest because they suggest that the patterns of interaction and more particularly the way in which the patterns of interaction are perceived are closely related to personality factors. The exaggeration of passive personalities, in which they see the amount of communication with the superior as greater than it really is, can be readily seen as reflecting their own inner need for acceptance, closeness, and dependence in relation to the superior. Similarly, the tendency of active personalities to minimize the amount of communication can be seen as reflecting their inner need to reject such dependency and to see themselves as more independent and autonomous.

Thus the authority relation becomes in many ways the focus for a spectrum of inner needs, wishes and attitudes. This aspect of the authority relation can be usefully considered in relation to a phenomenon that is quite familiar from the practice of psychoanalysis, namely the phenomenon of transference. In the psychotherapeutic setting, the transference phenomenon is intensified and takes a particular form quite specific to that setting. But the phenomenon of transference is much broader than that. It forms a normal human process influencing every significant relationship that human beings enter into. The authority relation is particularly susceptible to transference response bias.

The basic notion of transference is that individuals carry around in their heads a set of images and associated emotional patterns of response which are completely unconscious and derive from early levels of their childhood experience — particularly in relation to their parents. These unconscious residues are activated in any relationship in which these elements are stimulated. Thus patterns of feeling and behavior which were originally experienced with the important figures of childhood are displaced onto figures in current relationships. This brings about an activation and a repetition of attitudes, fantasies, feelings of love, hate, anger, etc. — all of which derive from earlier relationships but are brought to life in the context of a real current relationship.

In the context of the authority relationship, the structure of the relationship unavoidably taps into transference elements that derive from the individual's previous experience of authority. This can relate to any of a variety of developmental contexts in which obedience was demanded or imposed, but the obvious and most significant context is the child's obediential relation with the parents. The subject's interaction with the superior, then, can be profoundly affected by a displacement into the relation of these earlier transference elements.

The transference elements may be positive or negative. The subject may respond to the superior positively as a good and loving father. Or he may respond in negative terms — as to a harsh and demanding or punitive father. Or his response may reflect both elements, together or in sequence as the relation works itself out. Depending on how the transference elements come into play, the authority relation and the subject's obediential response will tend to reflect some prior level of development.

The authority relation can be subject to distortion from the side of the superior as well. But from this perspective, although transference elements can play a role, one must also take into consideration the identification of the superior with authoritative figures from his own past. This adds to the transference elements another aspect of functioning, that is that human beings tend to assimilate the roles and patterns of action of significant persons they have experienced in such positions. The superior then may play out in his own role as superior elements that derive from authoritative figures from his own early experience. The parents again are primary figures in this unconscious identification — although other figures may be involved. In the exercise of his authority, the superior may then become like his father in the exercise of his authority — he may be firm and consistent and kindly or he may be strict and severe and punitive — depending on how the father was and how he was perceived by the superior at that stage of his life. We shall have more to say about identification in the following section in regard to its role between subject and superior as a central structuring aspect of the authority relation, but here we are concerned with its role in determining the superior's participation in the interaction.

The situation is considerably more complex — for we must remember that these elements work themselves out in a relational context. The superior who has a need to identify with a punitive and rigid parental figure will also have a need to see his subordinates as willful and rebellious — and thus requiring severity and punitive responsiveness on his part. He may thus misinterpret autonomous independence for disobedience. Such a response may play into the transference distortions of the subject and provide him with a verification that justifies and confirms his anger and wishes to rebel. All of this can take place at a completely unconscious level, so that superior and subject are caught up in a mutual hostility which disrupts the authority relation and for which neither is aware of the real reasons for their failure — and in which the essential process of mutual regulation is distorted and impaired.

# CHAPTER XXVII

# DEVELOPMENTAL ASPECTS OF OBEDIENCE

## Introduction

As we turn to this specifically psychological consideration, it is well to remind ourselves that such a consideration has its limitations. The problem of religious obedience touches the human person at many levels. A psychology of obedience can approach the problem at the level of patterns of behavior and of the inner motives and meaningfulness of the human experience of obedience. Its conclusions and implications have a limited validity and applicability within the sphere of its own empirical base and theoretical constructs. The problem of religious obedience, however, reaches beyond the narrow range of psychology. The understanding of intrapsychic processes and motivations must be complemented by and integrated with a broader context of specifically religious and theological understanding.

Moreover, the problem of obedience is not one that modern psychologists have paid a great deal of attention to in its own right. There is a vast body of information and conceptual analysis derived from study of group processes, leadership, power relations, and other dimensions of group organization and structure that have a bearing on the problem of obedience — but they have not been specifically focused on this question. There is, nonetheless, an abundance of findings, insights, and theoretical formulations which can serve as the basis for at least a tentative formulation of the psychology of obedience.

It is obvious from the start that religious obedience is not simply a matter of behaviors. It involves and reflects all levels of the organization of personality. The psychology of obedience, then, must provide a basis for understanding the intrapsychic functioning related not only to various levels and forms of obedience, but also to deviations and pathological manifestations of obedience. We are approaching the psychology of obedience in the first instance through a descriptive analysis of the developmental process and its relation to obedience, since that seems to offer the surest ground on which to try to meet these multiple demands.

We approach this analysis, therefore, in a spirit of inquiry and investigation. Our approach is heuristic and not conclusive. We can safely assert that the findings we shall be discussing rest on a firm basis in experimental and clinical experience — and they can be ignored only at great cost. What requires cautious assessment and reflection is the analysis and its conclusions. The complexity and motivational subtlety of human behavior and human personality requires that psychological formulations be advanced with an eye to their need for qualification. Psychological principles can be stated only in more or less relative terms, which acknowledge the limitations imposed by wide variations in individual differences and the inevitable exceptions. With these conditions of our analysis in mind, we can proceed.

## THE DEVELOPMENTAL PROCESS

The importance of the developmental process for an understanding of human psychology has become increasingly apparent in recent years. The impetus to this insight was given by Freud's early formulations of stages in instinctual development. The psychoanalytic approach is intrinsically historical and genetic; it rests on the fundamental idea that the organization and functioning of the human personality results from a process of organic development deriving from the interaction of intrinsic biological factors of growth and maturation and of experiential factors modifying and influencing each step of the developmental progression. Following in Freud's footsteps, the interest in and investigation of the behavior and development of infants has mushroomed until it now forms one of the most active and productive areas of psychological interest.

The insight into the nature and relevance of developmental processes is essential for any adequate understanding of human behavior or activity. This is due not simply to the fact that early life experiences have a determinable influence on the personality, but also to the fact that developmental residues are built into the functioning personality in ways that make it possible for their influence to actively shape the ongoing current of behavior and experience. Each developmental phase, each developmental crisis, each developmental achievement, leaves a specific residue in the structure of the emerging personality as a vital component of the functioning self. Psychologically obedience expresses intrapsychic processes that do not take place in a vacuum — they are subject to complex interpersonal and social interactions. The psychology of obedience, then, cannot rest simply with an intrapsychic vantage point, but must be seen as socially conditioned and embedded. The response of obedience takes place within the context of authority, the structures of which arise out of specific types of interactions in all human organizations.

From the beginning of the child's experience, he is caught up in a social process. From the very first contact with other humans, he is immersed in a social and interactive matrix which actively shapes his responses and responds to him in a variety of highly influential and determining ways. The child's inner psychic development and his social interaction come together in a process of mutual influence and support. From the first contact with the mother's breast, the child is interacting socially, and within that social matrix undergoes those experiences in terms of which his own inner development is shaped and progresses (Galatzer-Levy and Cohler 1993).

## The Beginning

We must begin our analysis, however, where the child begins — at the beginning. When adults think of children, they tend to make the mistake of thinking that the child's experience is somehow similar to the experience of the adult. In fact we know very little about what the infant's experience is like — we can only infer it from his behavior. A great deal of effort has gone into studying the newborn infant's experience of the world. Such studies indicate that the infant's organism and its functioning is relatively disorganized in many ways, and in many ways surprisingly organized. General reactivity is relatively unstable; physiological regulations are subject to relatively wide fluctuations; autonomic responsiveness is less stable and tends to fluctuate; other bodily functions of temperature regulation, ingestion, elimination, sleep, etc., are poorly and only gradually regulated. The infant's perceptual world is also poorly organized, he does not at first recognize boundaries between himself and the outside world. His behavior shows an overall lack of organization, a certain diffusion of responsiveness, a lack of differentiation and specificity.

At the same time, even from the first moments of life, the infant's behavior and experience are not without significant organization and structure (Stern 1985). Eye movements are not random but tend to follow and seek out more complex visual patterns. Attention studies, for example, reveal a preference for complexity in newborn infants of only a few hours of age. The infant thus starts with some degree of structure in his psychic functioning. Structure emerges and develops from the very beginning of life. The infant is caught up in and responds to processes that sustain and foster that development. The most significant dimension of the infant's developmental matrix is the human caretakers who surround, protect, feed, nurse, and communicate in countless ways with the child. Important interactions are occurring from the first moments of the child's experience which, if successful, can elicit and foster processes of normal growth and development — and, if unsuccessful, can impair the developmental process and seriously affect the child's future adaptive capacities (Galatzer-Levy and Cohler 1993; Stern 1985).

## Trust

The most significant interaction in the child's earliest experience is with the mother. Mother and child are involved from the beginning in a continual and continuing process of give-and-take, each influencing and accommodating to the other in a multitude of subtle as well as obvious ways. In the successful mother-child unit, there takes place a process of mutual regulation which Erikson (1963) has pointed to as crucial for the child's development. The mother's mothering and caring activities will optimally mesh with and respond to the child's needs and emerging capacities. On the child's part, optimal adaptation will enable him to respond to the mother's mothering and find gratification in it.

In the beginning of their career together there, is an initial phase of mutual adaptation between mother and child — the first of several discriminable phases of their progressive interaction. These successive phases focus on a series of developmental issues — each of which reflects the child's stage of development and lays the groundwork for future steps. Each developmental issue becomes the focus of a real negotiation between mother and child. The success of the negotiation of any one of the earlier issues influences the child 's development as it organizes itself around that issue and also influences the relative success of subsequent negotiations of future issues.

The period of mutual regulation between mother and child deals with the primary adaptive task of establishing a suitable meshing of mothering activities and the infant's cues. The child emits certain signals of his inner distress and states of need that have an important adaptive function because the infant's continuing well-being depends on the correct reading and responding of significant adults. The infant is not self-sufficient. He depends in critical ways on the caretaking activity of others to maintain a homeostatic balance of his natural bodily functions. Such a homeostatic balance is essential not merely for maintaining vital functions, but for providing him with a sense of well-being and security. Only by maintaining that inner balance can the infant thrive.

Thus mother and child are caught up in a mutual negotiation over matters of basic processes — feeding, eliminating, sleeping and waking. Successful negotiation of these matters is usually achieved within the first few months. It is reflected in the extent to which the child is able to establish a stable rhythm of these activities. The child's capacity for discrimination in responding to the mother's handling also increases. He responds more readily to her than to anyone else and will quiet more readily for her than for anyone else. For the mother, success of the negotiation is reflected in her assurance that she knows her baby and understands him as no one else does. At the same time, her anxieties over providing these important life-sustaining ministrations for the child also diminishes.

It is vitally important that mutuality be established in this early phase. The mother must be sensitive to and responsive to the cues the child emits. A balance between her empathy with what she feels the child needs and her objectivity in viewing him as an independent unit apart from her own thoughts and feelings is essential. A certain measure of objectivity is crucial if the mother is to be able to pick up the unique qualities that characterize the individual infant. These qualities are present from birth and her mothering activities must somehow be adapted to them. If she fails to do this, she runs the risk of missing the child's cues and thus responding more in terms of her own needs and feelings which she begins to mistake for the child's.

The most striking aspect of this whole process is that for the basic regulation of his inner states and the balancing of vital processes the infant must depend on another human being — the mother. He must learn to depend on her for the control of inner distressful states. The degree to which he can count on her, rely on her, find assurance that she is a constant and reliable object for him to relate to and depend on for these necessary and life-sustaining functions, and more specifically the extent to which he comes to know her as sensitive and responsive to his inner needs and states of discomfort, are vital elements in this early interaction (Stern 1985). The child's primitive and vaguely undifferentiated sense of wholeness, goodness and internal security and comfort are strongly influenced by how this basic interaction proceeds. This is the basis for what Erikson (1959, 1963) described as "basic trust." The baby's trusting is reflected in his ease in feeding, in the confidence that what is being taken in from another is good and comforting, in the depth of sleep which can be entered with the assurance that the needed and sustaining object will be there when he awakens, and in the ease of elimination. The infant's trusting familiarity with the mother becomes, as Erikson (1963) put it, an inner certainty as well as an outer predictability.

This mutual regulation leaves a fundamental residue in the child's emerging personality which will shape his basic orientation toward other persons in his environment. The rudiments of basic trust or basic mistrust are thus laid down — and the question of which direction and what degree of either trust or mistrust the child carries with him is decided within the context of this earliest interaction. The capacity to trust is fundamental to any kind of human relatedness, and the extent to which that capacity is impaired will determine much of what later passes for psychopathology the inability to relate to and get along with other people.

The meaning of these early developments for the problem of obedience is central and crucial. Trust is essential to any meaningful and mutually rewarding human relationship. Human interactions — at least any that are of significance or that last for any significant length of time — are impregnated with the seeds of ambivalence, of hate and love blended in conflicting and interlocking manner. Our ability to find satisfaction and gratification in other human beings depends on our capacity to trust others and to have a basic sense of the reliability of their good intentions. The alternatives are basic and devastating — either paranoid suspicion or schizoid withdrawal. Obedience is such a significant human interaction that calls in profound and meaningful ways on the individual's capacities for trusting relatedness.

The commitment of oneself and one's personal resources to a course of action prescribed by another requires a considerable degree of trust of that other. We must be able to put our trust in his judgment, his knowledge, his good intentions, and so on. There was a time in the operation of obedience — as in the religious culture of the sixteenth century that Ignatius knew —when an appeal to the will of God as manifested in the superior's decision — whether royal or religious — could be made to substantiate a claim to trust and trustworthiness. But the naive simplicity of that view of authority and obedience is no longer adequate, nor does it elicit the sense of inner security and confidence that it once might.

But the need for trust persists. One of the strengths of the traditional view of obedience was that it provided an acceptable rationale and a source of trust. No matter what the leader or superior decided or how unreasonable or foolish his decision seemed, one could always take recourse to a deeper logic and a deeper purpose that was insured by an appeal to divine purposes. The authority of kings was based on divine right and that of religious superiors on the will of God. If one could not find the basis of trust in the superior, one could at least put one's trust in his authority and the grace of his office. The same rationales do not carry the same impact or conviction in our day, so that the basis for trust must vary accordingly.

## DEVIATIONS IN TRUST

At this point we can ask what the effect of an impairment in basic trust might be on the functioning of obedience. The impairment of each developmental aspect that we shall consider can take place either by way of defect or by way of excess. Each aspect of development has an optimal range within which issues can be resolved in such a way as to allow for maximal growth and to optimally serve the needs for further development and adaptation. The resolution of each developmental crisis may be impaired by a relative excess or a relative deficit in the aspect in question. Each of these deviations from the optimal range of developmental solutions carries with it certain impediments and risks for the development of obedience and has a characteristic expression within the life of obedience.

The deviations in trust can take the form of either a deficit in trust — Erikson's "basic mistrust" — or of an excess of trust. The influence of mistrust on obedience can be pervasive, profound and insidious. In its most deviant and disruptive form, as an expression of paranoid pathology, the defect of basic trust impairs all human relationships and makes any contact with other people a dreaded threat to one's own existence. At less pathological levels, however, mistrust introduces a chronic hesitation and uncertainty into relationships of all kinds. Lack of trust carries with it an element of suspicion and doubt into the authority relation. Thus the individual's capacity to respond willingly and spontaneously to directives of another become qualified — from minor to rather severe degrees depending on the measure of trust the individual has been able to attain. The lack of trust introduces a basic flaw into the authority relation that impedes its effectiveness and workability.

If the relationship between a superior and a subject is governed by mistrust, it becomes impossible for the authority relationship to work itself out in any terms except those of power and position

(Meissner 1971a). The authority relation depends on and derives from a mutual regulation between superior and subject. In order for a balance to be struck in the authority relation, there must be an input of trust on both sides. Each of the participants — leader and follower, superior and subject — must enter and share in the relation with a sense of trust in the trustworthiness of the other and with a sense of his own trustworthiness. Mistrust undercuts both. It inhibits the subject's capacity to trust his superior. He is unable to open himself to determination of his own will by the superior without a sense of loss, of impediment, of diminution of self, of loss of control and even dread — all of which reflects the basic uncertainty of a state in which the organism had to depend on the significant other for life-sustaining operations and in which the failure of trust threatened the loss of self and a sense of impending disaster. Similarly, mistrust undercuts the subject's sense of his own trustworthiness of his own capacity to deal with the demands of his environment, to take the measure of reality and deal with it, to compensate for deficiencies and failures of others where necessary, to achieve an optimal result in a cooperative context of a directive taken in faith.

If we approach the relationship from the leader or superior's perspective, his mistrust will also have certain deleterious effects on the workings of obedience. If the superior has only a limited trust in the maturity, reliability and responsibility of the subject, his capacity to rely on the subject's judgment and good intentions will suffer. Their interaction will be pervaded with a sense of insecurity and uncertainty. The leader will entertain an uneasy sense of things going wrong unless he assumes responsibility for their being carried out. He will have difficulty in assuming any comfortable reliance on the subject and will lack any sense of the subject's trustworthiness. The picture is familiar in political leaders, who have difficulty delegating responsibility to subordinates and feel compelled to supervise even trivial details of day-to-day governance — the syndrome of micromanagement. In the face of such mistrust, both superior and subject have no recourse but to retreat to more secure and defensive positions. Such defensive positions represent a failure of the attainment of trust and constitute less mature levels in the development of obedience. Trust, therefore, provides a basic substratum on which obedience builds and without which the capacity for mature and genuine obedience is severely limited — if not impossible.

Trust can also err in the direction of excess — and that deviation also carries with it certain impediments to the exercise of mature obedience. If the subject is excessively trusting, his obedience becomes naive, thus undercutting his own sense of self-reliance and capacity to take a critical and relatively objective view of his own and the superior's actions. The excess of trust can lead him into an unquestioning acceptance of the superior's decisions — and to the assumption that, whatever and however the superior should decide, his decision is good and right. We have reason to question whether the Ignatian insistence on blind obedience might not tend in this direction. Certainly the more traditional view of obedience tended to idealize this deviation. In that view, an excess of trust was impossible — the more the better. The model of obedience, as hierarchically organized and as based on power vested in the superior, worked best when the subject's trust was maximized. His response in obedience would thus tend to be unquestioning accepting, and uncritical. In the Ignatian view of obedience, this model seems to claim strong endorsement, but not unequivocally — the subject's responsibility for judgment and evaluation, including the necessity for representation, as well as the terms of mature discernment — would tend to modulate this more authoritarian approach

This ideal of obedience is presumably still alive and well in military circles. Such obedience, whatever its rationale and advantages, runs the risk of becoming fixated at an early developmental level so that the individual is prevented from moving on to more mature and meaningful levels of obedience. The difficulty with such an excess of trust is that it tends to impede the capacity for autonomy and thus tends to undermine the individual's sense of initiative and responsibility. It involves trust excessively contaminated by dependence. A more mature form of obedience, as we are envisioning it here, reflects and depends on more mature levels of personality development and represents an integration of the elements of trust, autonomy, responsibility, initiative and freedom. The excess of trust, therefore, freezes the developmental process in obedience at a relatively immature and regressive level.

Trust can be excessive in the superior as well as in the subject. Excessive trust on the superior's part can effect a failure in his own exercise of responsibility. In the authority relation the superior's function demands that he accept and exercise his proper responsibility in decision-making and direction. It is possible for him to vacate that responsibility by an excessive trust in his subordinates. Within each respective level of the structure of authority the superior has responsibility for certain functions. If he leaves such functions in the hands of subordinates out of a false sense of excessive trust, he can run the risk of violating those subordinates by imposing a responsibility on them which is properly his own. He can thus undercut and disrupt the proper functioning of authority. The balance and distribution of responsibility is upset with resulting confusion and impairment. This is quite different from the situation in the exercise of subsidiarity in which the superior does not avoid his responsibility, but in fact meets it with the assistance of subordinates.

## Autonomy

As the developmental process proceeds, the child gradually begins to assume some initiative in the social exchange with the mother, introducing another significant developmental issue. The child gradually increases the scope of his initiatives and becomes involved in actively eliciting responses from the mother. He tries to focus her responses to meet his needs. The degree to which his attempts to elicit her feeding and comforting activities are successful serve as the initial root for the development of his own inner sense of autonomy. He begins to develop a sense of his own capacity to bring about responses in the significant others in his environment. A sense of his own inner resourcefulness and capacity to control the discomfort and tension arising from his unfulfilled needs develops through his increasing capacity to focalize the mother's caring activity. He becomes more aware of himself as an active agent in his own inner regulation and the balancing of inner states. Not only does he find a familiar trust in the caretaking figure, but he can to some extent succeed in eliciting those trustworthy responses as a result of his own action.

At this stage of development, the child enters on a period of self-assertion. Every parent knows very well the negativism of the second year of life. The child learns to use the word No as an expression of his emerging and increasing assertion of himself as separate from and over against everything else — including his parents. The child seems sometimes almost driven to carry out his own intentions and to try to extend the area of his control over his environment. Before this his initiatives had been primarily in the direction of eliciting supportive and caring responses from the mother. Now he begins to make his attempts even in the face of her opposition. A battle of wills may develop. The important issue that must be successfully negotiated for the child's continuing emotional growth is whether and in what areas the child is able to establish his self-assertion and in what areas not. He must gain some sense that his winning out and having his way is in certain areas acceptable to the trusted and needed parent.

Mahler (Mahler et al. 1975) attributes these developments to the practicing phase of separation-individuation.

The typical situation, within which the traditional analytic view and its concern with instinctual derivatives focused much of this conflict, was toilet-training. There is a great deal of mythology about toilet-training, but it has to be regarded as only one of the areas of interaction between parent and child that it can serve as the focus for significant developmental issues — these issues are not restricted to the toilet-training context but are much more general in the child's pattern of responsiveness and reaction with his parents. The maturation of the child 's physical organism and the gaining of a capacity for sphincter control gives him an increasing capacity to hold on to or let go of feces, making bowel training a natural for working out issues of control and willfulness (Erikson 1963).

It is crucial at this stage that the mutual relation between child and parent be maintained. The child still needs the support of outer controls, but if the outer controls are exercised too rigidly or prematurely they deprive the child of the opportunity to exercise his own control. If the child's attempts to exercise control over his own bodily functions are interfered with, he may develop a sense of frustration and powerlessness which forces him to resort regressively to earlier and less mature patterns of behavior or to progress prematurely to a pretended and fragile autonomy. Such children often regress to whining and demanding behavior or to regressive forms of oral gratification like thumbsucking. Or, conversely, the child may become willful and hostilely resistant — assuming a pretended autonomy which expresses a resistant wish not to depend on or rely on anyone.

The development of a sense of basic autonomy depends on and extends the previously acquired sense of basic trust. The child learns that his sense of trust in himself and in the world will not be jeopardized by his emerging wish to have a choice and to exercise his own willingness or willfulness. His willfulness and potential disruptiveness must be met by parental firmness to protect him from his own destructive wishes and guide and support him in his effort to gain greater self-control and self-assertion. If this crisis is not well negotiated, the development of real autonomy can become prejudiced — by either shame or self-doubt. The developmental objective of this stage is to acquire and establish a sense of self-control without loss of self-esteem.

If the child is to be encouraged to stand on his own feet, he must also be protected from those experiences which threaten him with doubt or shame. The child not only tests out his capacity for self-assertion, but at the same time begins to explore and discover the extent to which he can express destructive and aggressive wishes — particularly in the presence of the mother or father. The manner in which such aggressive assertions are responded to by the parents is central to the whole development of autonomy. If the child 's aggression is met with too much permissiveness, the child will develop a sense of the dangerousness of his inner impulses which neither he nor the powerful parents can control. If his aggression is met with an overly controlling or punitive response, the child will develop a sense of his own inner wickedness and badness. In either case he can easily fall prey to shame and doubt.

It is in this context that the mutual regulation between the child and his parents takes on vital significance in determining how the child's development in autonomy is to proceed. The parent's function is to blend firmness with permissiveness in order to help the child to find the area and degree of the appropriate exercise of his emerging autonomy — and thus save him from embarrassment or uncertainty of overreaching his independence and suffering corresponding loss of self-esteem. If the child's natural drive toward increasing autonomy and self-expression achieves sufficient latitude, it will permit him to find his own level of optimal expression and assertion. If his attempts to attain a degree of independent functioning are met with punitive restrictiveness or loss of love, his development will be frustrated. He must be able to integrate these tentative explorations into a growing sense of autonomy without threat of loss of support or loss of that measure of dependence necessary for him to maintain his emerging independence. The dynamics of this process are reflections of the rapprochement crisis (Mahler et al. 1975).

All of this is a schooling in obedience. The character of the child's obedience alters as he grows in autonomy. The area of obedience is the vital ground on which issues of autonomy are played out and in which they obtain their most pertinent expression. From the very beginning, even in its most rudimentary expression, obedience is a matter of mutual regulation and exchange. Even the earliest exchange between the newborn infant and his mother can be formulated in terms of a relationship of authority. Mother and child work out certain necessary tasks in a relationship in which one is superior and the other is submissive and dependent. If the mother treats the relation in an unilateral or authoritarian manner, the effects on the child will be profound and will undermine some of the most vital aspects of his personality development. Mutual regulation is central and essential if the developmental tasks are to be accomplished. Thus obedience from its earliest expression involves mutuality and depends on mutual regulation as a vital element in its inner structure. The principle of mutual regulation extends through the full range of obedience.

## AUTONOMY AND OBEDIENCE

Similarly, the issue of autonomy is an integral part of the problem of obedience at all levels. Obedience must thus be seen as a process involving an interchange in mutual regulation between relatively autonomous persons. Obedience — particularly religious obedience — is built on a basis of autonomy and derives from it. Thus any form of the exercise of authority which violates autonomy is to that extent a violation of and a deviation from authentic obedience.

The point of view that views obedience as characteristic of children and that sees obedience as less necessary or useful as one grows to maturity reflects an extremely limited notion of both autonomy and obedience. Such a position sees autonomy and obedience as somehow opposed. This assumption was central to more traditional views of obedience postulating a childlike lack of autonomy in subordinates along with reservation and restriction of autonomy to the superior. Obedience in such a formulation becomes a form of submission, expressing the optimal exercise of obedience in the complete surrender of personal autonomy. In the present view, obedience and autonomy are intrinsically related and mutually interdependent. To the extent that real autonomy is lacking in the authority relation — which serves as the matrix of obedience — obedience is deprived of its true meaning and relevance.

Obedience, then, is not viewed here as involving the directive of an autonomous superior to a nonautonomous subject whose only modality of acceptable response is submission and acceptance. Mature and authentic obedience is rather based on a relationship between autonomous individuals relating to each other in virtue of their respective roles as superior and subject, and who work out the issues of direction and action by a process of mutual regulation which respects the autonomy and responsibility of their respective positions. Their mutual participation in the relation of authority imposes on each a set of responsibilities prescribed under the obligations of obedience inherent in the framework of their interaction.

The interaction of these respective responsibilities constitutes the essence of obedience. The specifics and limits of the authority relation are determined by the social structure in which they take place. Thus the terms of authority and obedience in the military are not the same as in a corporate structure or in a religious order. Regardless these respective responsibilities cannot be met or accepted except by a free and autonomous action of the individual. Consequently, there is a cluster of related and mutually dependent elements that depend on and are intrinsically proportioned to each other regardless of the social structure and character of the authority relation — freedom, responsibility, autonomy, and obedience.

The successful interaction between superior and subject in the authority relation depends on the relative capacity of each to function in maturely autonomous manner and thus to allow each other to exercise their respective responsibilities. Mature autonomy involves not only acceptance and acknowledgment of one's own independence and responsibility, but also the capacity to accept and acknowledge the other's proper independence and responsibility. This delicate and complex relationship is susceptible to all of the conflicts and developmental impairments that can mar the growth in obedience. The developmental aspects of obedience are thus not merely interesting history — they provide a present and often determining aspect of the exercise of authority and obedience. In this deeper sense, the superior may come to represent, in an unconscious and overdetermined way, all those figures in the subject's life experience who have held the position of controlling authority. Thus the subject's response to the exercise of the superior's authority comes to reflect a complex integration of previously experienced levels of obedience and related developmental influences.

## DEVIATIONS IN AUTONOMY

Deviations in autonomy can undermine real obedience, perhaps more effectively than any other developmental parameter, either by an hypertrophy or an atrophy of autonomy. The parent's failure to meet the child's emerging sense of self-direction with firm guidance can drive the child to an extreme of willfulness and stubbornness. The struggle for autonomy takes the form of a desperate withholding or stubborn refusal to respond, except on one's own terms and in one's own time. Such autonomy reflects its fragility and insecurity in its excessive need to assert itself all the more absolutely and arbitrarily.

Mature autonomy takes a somewhat different course. It is central to the notion of autonomy that one have not only a sense of one's own independence and capacity for inner direction and control, but also that one have a respect for and responsiveness to the independence of others. Autonomy implies an independence that does not find it necessary to deny or exclude a healthy dependence on and interrelationship with others, and does not find it necessary to ignore the dependence of others on oneself. Mature autonomy maintains a sense of inner direction and control which is available as a potential resource when needed and does not depend on or need constant affirmation and reassertion from others. The truly autonomous person can open himself to direction and control from outside himself without a loss of self-esteem and without feeling that his subjection to the will of another represents a subjugation or submission. Where there is a deficit of too much — yielding to the will of another must be cast in terms of power, of winning or losing, of domination and humiliation. These are the concerns of defective autonomy.

The authority relation for people who are defective in autonomy becomes a threat, cast in terms of power and control. But for the truly autonomous person, the authority relation and obedience do not represent a limiting or a lessening of autonomy. Autonomous obedience is neither a mere acceptance of an authoritarian directive nor a submission of one's will to the will of another — even to the will of God. It is rather a form of stimulus or engagement eliciting the individual's response to some common effort, to participate in and contribute to the achievement of shared group goals. The individua1's response involves assumption of a basic responsibility derived from his own inner sense of autonomy and free initiative. The obedient response requires a sense of responsible self-commitment and self-involvement. Such obedience is violated by a willful and rebellious refusal, just as much as by the unthinking and unquestioning acquiescence and submissive acceptance of the directive. Both rebellion and compliance are a violation of the individual's responsibility and autonomy — and in both true obedience is diminished and mitigated.

The atrophy of autonomy similarly undermines obedience. Such a lack of autonomy is expressed in the individual's failure to achieve a sense of his own independence and in his insecurity and uncertainty about his own capacity to control inner impulses and to direct himself to meaningful and constructive goals. He cannot assert himself without a sense of inner doubt and shame. This inner insecurity and lack of autonomy undermines his capacity for responsibility and initiative, and he is forced to seek security and reliability in the judgment and direction of others. He tends to regard himself as powerless and others as powerful. His relation to and involvement in the authority relation is not a struggle for power — it is a struggle that he has already lost. His position is not to react against and defend against the loss of power by willful stubbornness or rebelliousness — he has no power to lose and nothing to defend. His only recourse is submission and acceptance of direction and control from others. Only thus can he avoid and alleviate the anxiety that independence or self-assertion brings with it. Such a personality would find self-effacement, self-sacrifice, self-immolation and total submission to the will of the superior — and to God's will — totally gratifying and comfortable.

Such an individual — despite the fact that traditional views of obedience often regard this attitude as the most virtuous form of obedience — is incapable of mature obedience. Mature obedience derives from the individual's capacity to see himself as an independent source of responsible judgment and action. Without that inner sense of self-reliance and autonomy, he cannot respond to and meet the impress of authority. He cannot exercise "responsible subjecthood" (Meissner 1971a), nor can he engage himself in that process of mutual regulation that is the essence of the authority relation and of the subject's participation in it through obedience. Without a sense of himself as responsible and autonomous and without a sense of his own inner resourcefulness, the individual has no recourse but to cling to the sources of stability and strength around him. This is not mature obedience — it is a caricature of obedience according to the infantile model.

Deviations in autonomy can affect the superior's role and function as well. When the superior's sense of autonomy is hypertrophied, it tends to undermine obedience by overriding the subject's autonomy. Such hypertrophied autonomy is often a false autonomy that really covers an underlying sense of insecurity and uncertainty. In these circumstances the superior tries to extend his shaky control to all levels of the decision-making process. He thus tends to leave little room for his subordinates to exercise their own proper judgment. Such hyperautonomy is unable to recognize or acknowledge the respective autonomy of others. Such leaders and superiors tend to be rigid, controlling, arbitrary, repressive and authoritarian. They tend to cast the model of authority in terms of power and power conflicts. The position of such a leader is the reciprocal of the atrophy of autonomy in the subject. Where the subject sees little or no power in himself and vests all power in the superior, the hyperautonomous superior tends to see all power in himself and views any exercise of autonomy in the subject as a threat and challenge to his power. Such a superior will inevitably be severely threatened by a hyperautonomous subject — so much so that the authority relation between them will tend to degenerate into a willful and stubborn struggle for control and the exercise of power. The exercise of authority and obedience in such a relation becomes marked by reciprocal repressiveness and rebelliousness. Mutual regulation and responsible autonomy is severely undermined on both sides of the relation.

The superior's autonomy can also suffer from an atrophy that undermines responsible exercise of his authority. The appropriate exercise of authority demands that the superior also see himself as an independent and responsible source of influence on others. He must see himself as capable of making meaningful decisions and of directing others to meaningful goals. If the superior lacks this sense of inner reliance and resourcefulness, it represents a deficit of autonomy such that his capacity to act responsibly and effectively is impaired. Such a superior is unable to fulfill his role as leader. He must rely on the responsibility and initiative of others to fill in the vacuum of authority that his own insecurity creates. Mutual regulation thus fails and the subject is put in the position of inappropriate decision-making. In such circumstances, the subjects' exercise of self-direction and autonomy is no longer obedience, since it takes place in a context of defective authority. True obedience derives from a matrix of authentic and effective authority. Obedience must take place within the context of an authority relation or else it ceases to be obedience.

## INITIATIVE

The rudiments of initiative derive from early interactions with the significant caretakers in which the issues are focused around the degree to which the infant can succeed in controlling and focalizing the mother's caretaking activity. The initial stages of the development of initiative are therefore closely interwoven with and dependent on the establishment of basic trust as well as an emerging sense of autonomy.

It is only gradually that initiative becomes a central issue in the developmental process. Its emergence as a developmental issue is related to the maturation of a number of areas of the child's functioning. Along about two or three years of age, the child seems to become more integrated in the organization of his capacities and behavior. Locomotion is no longer a skill to be acquired or a task, but it becomes an assured capacity to be relied on and unconsciously assumed. The child's locomotion becomes an exploration and testing of the limits of his capacity to run or walk. He propels himself into space and begins to assert his sense of mastery over it. He begins to develop parallel sense of mastery over the elements of language. His talking becomes a sheer exercise of function — but also increasingly in the service of an unquenchable curiosity. The use of language takes the form of an endless series of questions. The child's mind becomes as curiously intrusive as is his locomotion in space. These corporal and linguistic developments are accompanied by a remarkable development of the child's imaginative capacity. Children at this stage are caught up in the imaginative world of fantastic stories and fairy tales. The imagination is unleashed — and the child's world takes on an animistic and magical quality which is at once fantastic and often indeed frightening.

The entire complex of interlocking phenomena set the stage for the emergence of conscience. This aspect of the child's inner development is essential for the understanding of obedience. Emergence of the child's inner capacities and their relatively more advanced integration allow for development of a sense of internal control and regulation. Elements of the child's emerging conscience take shape at first around parental prohibitions. These prohibitions are at first simply extrinsic, but little by little the child begins to take them in and makes them his own. This gradual internalization is prompted and sustained by the child's increasing need to foster his own emerging sense of initiative and to extend his own capacity to originate and control his own behavior. The necessity for making parental prohibitions his own is based on his inner need to guarantee that his increasing initiatives are carried out in a manner which will find acceptance from the important and powerful figures upon whom he is still so dependent. Since his initiatives involve and express both aggressive impulses and sexual interests and curiosity, they run the risk of disapproval, punishment, and the threat of abandonment. Initiative, thus, runs the risk of loss of love. The development of conscience, a system of internal controls and prohibitions, serves as insurance against such loss.

## RESPONSIBILITY AND FREEDOM

With an emerging sense of initiative, the child develops a sense of his own capacity for self-direction and self-determination without incurring the threat of disapproval or loss of love. It is in this aspect of the emergence of initiative that we can begin to look for the rudiments of responsibility. The sense of responsibility declares the reality of one's self and one's uniqueness as different from everybody else and as capable of responding to the areas of endeavor on one's own terms. Subjective responsibility rests on the acknowledgment of man as the initiator of his own acts.

Responsibility recognizes the reality of choice and freedom, as well as the individual's capacity to direct his own purposeful actions to specific ends. The capacity that each individual attains to accept responsibility both for himself and his own actions as well as for the world in which he lives depends in large measure on the pattern of his growth in initiative. If he has experienced the emergence of initiative without excessive guilt, if he can achieve a sense of inner trust in his own capacity to regulate, control and direct his emergent impulses and interests, if he can achieve a sense of mastery and competence in the exercise of his powers without encountering severe restrictions and punitive retaliations — only then does the sense of responsibility have a chance to establish itself in the mature personality.

Mature obedience builds on and evokes the individual's capacity for initiative, freedom and responsibility. These are correlative dimensions of the human response emerging from the same developmental roots. The pattern of development in obedience we are tracing here follows a course of increasing autonomy, increasing initiative, increasing freedom and increasing responsibility. Along this development course, there are innumerable pitfalls and pressures which can subvert or fixate the developmental progression at one or other level. In the exercise of obedience — given this basic developmental organization of the personality structure — there are functional influences and pressures that tend to disrupt and interfere with the mature obediential response. Both the residues of developmental vicissitudes and functional aspects of the interaction within the context of the authority relation can undermine and distort the exercise of responsible obedience. The response of obedience, therefore, is subject to regressive pulls and influences from many sides which can cause it to operate at less than mature levels — levels in which elements of initiative or responsibility or freedom are diminished or distorted.

Initiative is the reflection of the child's impulses to self-expression and aggressive intrusiveness into his environment — an intrusiveness that rests on the assurance that the child may be allowed to explore the limits of his capacities and reach out into the unknown without loss of the needed assurances of continuing love and support and without loss of an inner sense of self-reliance, reliability and competence. Competence here has a special meaning implying the individual's sense of capability for more or less competent performance along with a sense of mastery of the necessary skills for the adequate performance of what he seeks to do. Initiative expresses itself as the capacity for self-direction without the fear of a loss of competence and without a sense of guilt.

## Regressive Risks

The regression to less mature levels of obedience is a constant risk and temptation. Maintaining the authority relation on a level of mature obedience is considerably more difficult than regressing to less mature and less demanding levels of response. In addition, there are often institutional pressures at work which reinforce or foster more regressed modes of response. From this point of view, the more or less institutional view of obedience that has long been operative in religious groups must be seen as an expression of a more dependent and less developed stage. It rests on a model of obedience in large measure based on the denial of initiative, freedom, autonomy and responsibility. The developmental process, however, teaches us that human beings normally grow beyond the constraints of the limited levels of their development, and that the process of development itself is open-ended and continuous. Development does not stop — one is always capable of continued growth.

## Initiative in the Group

Mature initiative is embedded in a social structure — specifically in the authority relation, and is thus caught up in the interaction of multiple initiatives. One individual's initiative is limited by the initiative of others in the group — just as the individual's autonomy is also limited by the autonomy of those around him. Conversely, one's own initiative derives from the initiative of others and in a sense depends on it. Excessive initiative can ride roughshod over the initiative of others — it can place a high value on its own prerogatives while disrespecting the prerogatives of others. Excessive initiative can thus violate obedience by removing itself from the context of authority and by expressing itself as a form of hyperindividualism ignoring the goals, objectives and needs of other members of the group. This form of excessive initiative is linked with the sort of hyperautonomy we have already discussed.

Optimally initiative functions within the context of the intermeshed initiatives of the group and its members. In the responsible exercise of initiative, however, there is room for the initiative of individuals to be brought to bear on the group. The expression and implementation of such initiatives is a central aspect of the group's continuing vitality. Every group needs to maintain the sources of its own renewal and revitalization in order that it continue to serve a meaningful purpose in the social context. Adaptation in the group and the continued refocusing of its goals and objectives can be attained only through the influence of individual initiatives operating in and through the group.

The initiative that brings with it new life and vitality often stems from the younger generation in any group or culture. This is particularly true in religious groups in which vital initiatives must come from younger members who are more attuned to the needs for change and adaptation. Thus the religious group has a stake in sustaining and encouraging the initiative of its younger members, since its own survival and relevance is closely linked with such renovating initiatives. The strength of institutions lies in their capacity to foster and nurture the initiative of younger members — giving it at the same time the support and guidance which allows that initiative to integrate itself constructively with the inner dynamisms of common goals and values. The community, whether socially, politically or religiously conceived, must find within itself the resources to offer that guidance along with the acknowledgement and acceptance of the possibility that the integration of new initiatives may bring with it the alteration and perhaps growth of the structures, values, and goals with which the group identifies itself.

Our view of obedience is that it is essentially a call to initiative. In obedience, the leader's initiative reaches out to elicit a response from the subject's own initiative. The subject's initiative becomes congruent with the initiative of a superior or of the group to the extent that the subject identifies with the group and has internalized the goals and values of the group as his own. To that extent his initiative becomes part of the group's initiative. The excess of initiative, however, can set itself up in opposition to the initiative of the group and thus becomes divisive. There is a fundamental distinction between initiative that opposes itself to the group and initiative that contributes to a new sense of direction within the group initiative — the difference between revolution and evolution. The latter is a form of responsible initiative providing a constructive force within the group and serving adaptive needs of the group. Such constructive and responsible initiative is what is elicited through mature obedience.

The lack of initiative, therefore, can be severely detrimental to the functioning of obedience. It represents a violation of obedience in that it is an evasion of the responsibility to which one is called by obedience. Each member of the religious group, for example, has a responsibility to contribute his initiative to the religious group. One's personal initiative is a valuable resource of the group, as a source of its continued adaptation and vitality. Individual members can be at fault in withholding their responsible initiative. The religious group itself can also be at fault by refusing to acknowledge or encourage the initiatives of its members. Initiative must be met with initiative. The exercise of individual initiative must be met by a responsive initiative in the group, if it is to be at all meaningful or if it is to be able to effect anything. The failure of the group to respond to the initiative of its members has been a frequent failing of religious groups in the past. But the failure of initiative at one level requires suppression of initiative at another level. In such a situation individuals tend to withhold their initiative and to leave all initiatives in the hands of superiors. The result is an inevitable atrophy of individual initiative. The response of obedience comes to be little more than an obedience of execution — simply doing what one was told.

## Initiative in the Superior

The initiative of the superior is closely tied with his function as leader — at least the exercise of leadership is the primary channel by which his initiative can be expressed toward the group. The patterns and functions of leadership within religious groups are undergoing some significant shifts. Traditionally the superior was primarily a decision-maker who was responsible for making the important policy and other operational decisions which other members of the religious group carried out under obedience. The superior is less and less in that position. The increasing complexity of matters of decision makes it more and more difficult or foolhardy to have the decision-making process rest in the hands of one man or woman. The process of making decisions is thus becoming more diffuse and comes in more meaningful ways to involve more and more of the members of the religious group in it.

Thus the superior's role is gradually changing. In the current setting he still holds the formal decision-making responsibility, but his function has become more and more to organize and lead the decision-making activity of others. In the period of rapid and radical change in religious life that we are now experiencing, the function of leadership becomes crucial for the adaptability and effectiveness of the religious group. At least one dimension of the current crisis in religious life can be traced to a failure of effective leadership within the religious group. Superiors in part see themselves functioning in terms of the older model of leadership and have not generally responded to the demand for leadership in the broader and more personal sense.

Leadership in the context of obedience is best envisioned in terms of the interaction of respective initiatives. The superior is functioning most effectively as leader when his own initiative operates in such a way as to elicit and stimulate the initiative of his subjects. If he errs in the direction of excess, he can easily override and discourage the initiative of his subjects. This creates a vacuum of initiative among members and an inevitable drift of initiative toward a centralization in superiors. If the superior errs by way of defect, he fails to assume his own responsibility as leader and the group runs the opposite risk of a diffusion of initiative away from group concerns and objectives. Individual initiative thus can become increasingly divisive and becomes directed toward individual goals rather than to group goals. The superior's leadership is required to organize and direct the initiatives of individuals toward group goals. It should be obvious that such leadership cannot take the form of merely making decisions and giving orders. It requires even more the eliciting of personal interest and investment from the members of the group — a much more difficult and complex function than was envisioned under the more traditional views of obedience.

## IDENTITY

The term "identity" expresses a sense of psychological continuity and integration in the self; in terms of the development of the self, its roots reach back to the earliest levels of self-awareness (Stern 1985). The term was popularized by Erikson (1959, 1963) who regarded it as a developmental achievement of adolescence. In this sense identity referred to the integration of the achievements of preceding phases of development into a more or less stable and autonomous sense of self, conveying an assured sense of personal sameness and continuity and including a sense of meaningful integration into a social context. This implies that the continuity and meaning of oneself to oneself is matched by the continuity and meaning of oneself for others.

Certain aspects of identity are immediately relevant to the consideration of authority and obedience. Adolescents, by and large, are caught up in inner struggles of self-definition and identity formation. Identity formation requires not only a degree of inner integration and definition of self, but also the necessity for integrating oneself within a given social and cultural context. The adolescent period is one of earnest searching for ideas, ideals, purposes, goals, and values, to which one can actively and meaningfully commit oneself and with which one can meaningfully identify. It is period of affiliation, of self-commitment and of ideological conviction. This aspect of the process by which youth seeks to consolidate its sense of identity Erikson (1964) called fidelity. Fidelity integrates the purposeful energies of youth with pre-existent social structures and institutions. The strength of social institutions and their culture is measured by the ideals and values and functional roles that it is able to provide for young institutions are able to inspire is an index of their vitality.

A secure sense of identity and fidelity are essential for continual development beyond the level of adolescent turmoil to a level of more mature and meaningful existence. In the religious life, for example, the religious organization provides the content and the substance of faithful commitment and identification as a guarantee that the strengths of religious traditions are responsive to the needs of youth for faithful affiliation. The central task of religious formation is nourishment of a sense of personal religious identity. Such a development involves several parameters. Inner personality growth requires that residues of earlier developmental accomplishments be integrated into a coherent and consistent sense of self. It requires that the individual develop a sense of meaning within himself as well as a sense of his meaningfulness to the community within which he functions and whose life and goals he accepts as his own. He must integrate into a meaningful whole the roles and functions and patterns of behavior that constitute a pattern of life he can embrace and internalize. This will result hopefully in a sense of congruence between one's own personal goals and values and the shared goals and values of the religious group.

In its specifically religious meaning obedience, is a commitment to such a religious context. It involves a sense of meaningful participation in and commitment to God's work and God's purposes as implemented through the goals and functions of the religious group. Growth in religious obedience is not simply, therefore, a matter of inner psychological development. The extent to which prior developmental crises have been resolved and the basic elements of trust, autonomy, initiative, etc. integrated will determine the resources available to the individual as he comes to meet the expectations of his religious vocation. His search for meaningful commitment and his potentiality for identity and fidelity in that commitment must be met through mutual regulation. The religious group offers him the context and necessary structures and value-orientations to allow his emerging sense of identity to find expression and sustenance. It provides an organized framework of purposeful and meaningful existence that he can make his own in the conviction of fidelity and the assurance of trust.[1]

The mature sense of obedience, then, derives from a secure sense of identity and fidelity. This implies that residues of trust, autonomy, and initiative have been integrated into an adequately functioning sense of identity, and that these developmental achievements are articulated within a stable and meaningful social and institutional context. Thus the functional aspects of obedience are intimately related to developmental influences, but are also responsive to and interacting with organizational and institutional influences. In the understanding of the development to genuine identity, we can also begin to appreciate that, in many complex ways, developmental achievements themselves are dependent on social and cultural factors. Emergence of a mature sense of religious identity is as much a reflection of developmental achievements as it is a reflection of the strengths and meaningfulness of the religious group.

Thus the problem of identity brings into focus many complex issues involved in the relationship and interaction between the individual and the group, by which the individual identifies himself as belonging to a certain group and, conversely, by which the group identifies him as one of its members. The group thus becomes an object of self-commitment as well the locus of self-interest and investment. The degree to which the individual religious attains a sense of religious identity — a sense of his belonging to the religious group even as the group belongs to him — reflects the degree to which he identifies with group values and objectives. Through identification the individual makes the group his own and thus internalizes the group values. Group goals thus become invested with personal self-interest with the result that in some degree group goals and purposes become congruent with personal goals and purposes.

## DEVIATIONS IN IDENTITY

The risk in such identifying is overidentification. The individual can become overidentified with group goals, values, and patterns of action with a resulting failure of objectivity in which the individual

[1] Similar statements could be made with respect to the issues of identity, fidelity, and obedience in other social structures — corporations, academic institutions, even the military — but *mutatis mutandis.*

can surrender his sense of critical judgment and evaluation. Autonomy is thus eroded and the individual's participation in group processes tends to drift in the direction of compliance and conformity. Group standards and norms are rigidly and unquestioning adhered to. While a genuine sense of identity derives from a sense of fidelity to the group and its values, the excess expresses itself in hypercommitment in which any sense of individuality is absorbed in the more or less independent attachment to the group. This serves to turn fidelity into fanaticism and undercuts initiative and responsibility.

Such overidentification can take rather subtle forms. The individual's own inner sense of identity can become linked with a certain set of patterns of action, structure or ideological commitment within the group. Consequently, any attempt to change or alter the existing organization of the group presents a severe threat to the fragile sense of identity. Often this form of overidentification is expressed in terms of adherence to more traditional and familiar models of obedience. Many religious identify themselves as religious in terms of a modality of obedience that requires passive conformity and self-sacrificing acceptance as essential. This attitude and its adherence is reinforced by a well-established rhetoric of obedience which holds up the model of the obedient Christ — obedient even to the death of the cross. At a deeper level, however, it is a basic psychological law that one cannot violate the sense of identity, autonomy, and responsibility without stirring up anger, resentment, and hostility. Overidentification and the submission of obedience is incurred at the cost of unconscious hostility. Such unconscious hostility can be channeled into rigidity, discontent, punitiveness, and especially hypermoralism. But not infrequently such regressive impulses are directed inward in the form of depression, poor self-esteem, self-defeating, or self-destructive practices, alcoholism, work inhibition or gradual alienation from the religious community.

As opposed to the excess of identity, the defect of identity takes the form of a lack of identification and a relative unclarity in the definition of roles and functions by which one defines his place in the group. The failure to achieve a sense of identification with the religious group serves to undermine the individual's capacity for commitment and fidelity to group goals and values. His sense of belonging and sharing is diminished. The danger is then that the individual will shape a divergent identity for himself — a negative identity. He may set himself up as the antagonist to the views and value of the group. He may set himself against anything that is traditional or valued by the life of the religious group. Such a posture represents not merely a divergence and disagreement with pre-existent forms and structures, but it is driven by the inner need to define a meaningful identity where that identity has failed to develop. This does not mean that every opposition to traditional views and values represents a failure of identity. There is real distinction between the pressure toward negative identity deriving from failure to form a religious identity and opposition to group processes deriving from a more autonomous sense of identity. The former is divisive and destructive; the latter is an expression of mature initiative that can bring new life and vitality to the group.

## GENERATIVITY

The developmental process, as we are envisioning it here, extends beyond the coming to maturity, and extends throughout the life course from beginning to end. Throughout the course of life, man is confronted with the need for adaptation and growth. In this sense development is an open-ended and continuous process in which the developmental achievements of previous stages are continually integrated in the service of new needs and adaptive challenges in the course of life.

One of the significant aspects of mature development, especially relevant for the life of obedience, is generativity. Generativity which reaches beyond the confines of concern for self-meaning and self-integration, beyond the limits of self-interest, to a concern for the development of others and of the group. It is a quality enabling one to move beyond learning to teaching, beyond following to guiding, beyond dependence to caring. It is a basic life concern that focuses on the guidance of the next generation to maturity. Generativity expresses itself in a specifically intergenerational concern. It thus reaches beyond productivity or creativity and directs these capacities into a concern for the establishment and guidance of the coming generation (Erikson 1963, 1964).

Generativity is an aspect of mature personality development which broadens and deepens the sense of belonging. It leads to a concern for establishing those conditions within which the next generation will be able to grow to the fullness of identity and maturity. As such, it represents an enlargement of personal commitments and resources. In achieving true generativity, the individual gains a deepening of his own sense of capacity and of the meaning of his existence. He comes to acknowledge himself as a responsible possessor of a tradition and a trust that must be communicated to and shared with the young as a condition of their achievement of the rudiments of trust, autonomy, and responsible initiative. True maturity embraces not merely becoming responsible for oneself, one's judgments and actions, but also becoming responsible for a tradition and a faith. In achieving generativity, one also becomes responsible for transfer of that tradition and faith to the next generation as a meaningful heritage of strength and trust.

Generativity thus emerges as a most important aspect of the life of obedience. Obedience in the fullness of its meaning is much more than a response to a directive of a superior — it is a life form and expression of an inner sense of identity and fidelity and of belonging to a community. More than a pattern of action, it is a structure of meaning in one's life that becomes a part of one's own inner sense of identity. It is a sharing in the life of a community with specific goals and commitments — a shared commitment that lends meaning and direction to one's own life and activity. Since obedience is so central to the formation of religious identity, generativity emerges as an essential ingredient in the maturity of religious obedience. The fullness of mature obedience reaches beyond the immediate concern for one's own obeying or of one's own sense of religious belonging or sharing. It extends to concern for the meaningful continuity of the religious group, and to the meaningful integration of young religious into the shared religious experience of the group. Generativity extends to the concern for providing younger members of the religious organization with the guidance and support which would enable them to grow in a sense of religious identity and fidelity. It involves a commitment of oneself to guaranteeing the vitality and meaningful continuity of religious traditions — so that the coming generation of members of the religious group has available institutions and structures permeated with a sense of strength and purpose and guided by an inner conviction of fidelity to God's purpose and God's will.

## Deviations from Generativity

Generativity is thus a natural prolongation and extension of the sense of identity — along with its attendant element of achieved internalization of and identification with the goals and values of the religious group. The risk of excessive overidentification can extend into an excessive commitment and rigid adherence to existing structures resulting in a willed imposition of such structures on younger members of the group. Such adherence to pre-existent forms and structures can be imposed on fledgling members of the religious group with a rigidity that overrides the essential individuality and initiative of younger religious. Authentic generativity aims at fostering genuine and mature obedience — implying growth in trust, autonomy, initiative, responsibility and freedom. The excess of generativity, however, can direct itself to the preservation and prolongation of pre-existent structures of the religious group rather than to fostering mature identity in those who seek to find their lives within the religious group. Such a rigid adherence to and imposition of the past can actually impede real growth to religious identity. Mature obedience is impeded because what is sought is submission to and acceptance of previously established structures rather than growth or adaptation.

Generativity is more frequently seen in its defective form, reflecting an underlying failure in the sense of identity. Older religious may lose a sense of their position as bearers and transmitters of the tradition of the group. They can thereby lose a sense of their own value as participating members of the group and become subject to a loss of self-esteem. Older religious can thus begin to feel lost and useless, begin to devalue themselves and become depressed and apathetic. This depressive condition is relatively common among older religious who feel left out and bypassed by the currents of change within the religious group. Not only is there a current of change around them, but the inevitable internal changes of advancing age and increasingly impaired capacity produces a gradual loss of function that severely threatens their self-esteem and sense of value. It is little wonder, then, that such individuals cling to pre-existent forms and patterns of organization. But it is also apparent that such a picture reflects a failure to achieve a sense of generativity. Older members of the religious group are pre-eminently bearers of the tradition within the group. They owe to the group and to its younger members the guidance and the confirmation of trust that is and has been their possession.

The failure of generativity may result in a form of self-absorption and self-pity that undermines the individual's own capacity to function effectively, and also injures the strength and adaptive vitality of the group. The group's continuing potentiality for adaptation and change in the face of the many pressures and influences that come to bear on it is derived not only from the influx of new members and new initiatives, but it is also dependent on the continuity with the strengths of the past and the guidance of the wisdom and experience that only the older generation can offer. The importance of generativity for the life of obedience is both a matter of the mature realization of obedience in the life of the mature religious and a matter of the preservation and continuation of the life of religious obedience as a meaningful expression of the vitality and purposefulness of the group itself. The group must draw its strength from the wisdom of the past and the hope for the future. If it is denied either, it cannot hope to survive the present.

## Conclusion

The view of obedience from a developmental perspective places it more in the context of personal growth than in the more limited context of response to directives from the superior. I have tried to bring into focus an idea of obedience that is shaped in the course of development insofar as man is responsive to and participating in the social interaction and structures that sustain and give meaning to his life. Obedience has a special relevance in the religious context, however, since it is an essential part of the individual's sense of religious identity as well as an essential element in the purposeful organization of the religious group. Such obedience has a history and a course of development; it builds on and incorporates important developmental attainments and achieves an integration of the elements of trust, autonomy, initiative, responsibility and generativity. Its functioning is dependent on the degree to which each of these developmental parameters has been successfully achieved and integrated into the functioning personality. A developmental impairment or a regressive return to any of these preceding levels — for whatever reason, whether personal and individual or institutional and organizational — will undermine and distort the mature expression and capacity for obedience and will thus contribute to the persistent problem of obedience in all of its many forms.

# CHAPTER XXVIII

# FUNCTIONAL ASPECTS OF OBEDIENCE

## Introduction

Our considerations of obedience to this point have centered on the development and organization of those intrapsychic dimensions having important and immediate relevance for the growth and patterning of obedience. Obedience develops in contexts which either give it life and vitality or constrain and stifle it. This dynamic reflects the manner in which intrapsychic elements of human personality display themselves in complex patterns of interaction within social structures. The behavioral pattern is not merely an expression of intrapsychic determinants, but it is a product of the interaction of intrapsychic resources and developmental attainments with an ongoing pattern of influence stemming from other individuals and from forms of social organization. We can consider some of these patterns of interaction — specifically identification and ritualization.

## Identification

Identification is a basic mechanism which I consider to be central to the functional integration of obedience. In preceding chapters, I described some of the elements of the authority relation and the manner in which the structure of the authority relation derives from, focuses, and in many ways interacts with aspects of psychic structure and functioning considered from a developmental perspective. The essential psychic mechanism or process, by which an individual comes to engage in and becomes an active participant in the authority relation, is identification.

The notion of identification has been badly abused since Freud first articulated it, so that its real meaning has become quite confused and its explanatory utilization diffuse. In psychoanalytic usage, the term "identification" has a number of connotations particularly in relation to the structural organization and development of the personality. The internalization in question results in an internal structural change by which the self-structure of the individual acquires attributes and qualities derived from relationships with significant objects. These identifications become integrated as part of the autonomously functioning organization of the self. The locus for such identifications is the ego and superego, insofar as the respective aspects internalized from external objects are relatively unencumbered by instinctual, drive-derivative, or defensive needs or conflictual pressures (Meissner 1972, 1981).

I am using the term in the present context to refer to those inner psychic processes by which the individual identifies himself as a member of the group and by which the group reciprocally identifies him as belonging to itself. This sense of belonging involves recognition of oneself as sharing in a common set of values, goals, objectives, purposes and intents. Membership in the group is constituted by real sharing of the common value system which gives the group its unique stamp and provides it with a sense of inner vital purpose. Real membership, then, in this sense, is not merely a matter of joining the group, of carrying a membership card. It is rather a matter of realized sharing of values.

## INTERNALIZATION OF VALUES

Identification, therefore, is in some part a process of internalization of values. The individual becomes truly a member of the group insofar as he has internalized group values so that they have become a real and vital part of his own personal internal value structure. This internalization of values in a general sense is closely linked to the formation of identity. Identification, in this sense, involves a sharing in and assimilation of values which produces an internal modification of the self. The individual's sense of identity is closely linked to the set of values he has internalized and which form the operative and integrative core of his personality. Identification of oneself as belonging to and sharing in the inner life and valued commitments of a group thus can become an integral part of one's own individual identity. In this way the member of a religious group identifies himself as belonging to the group and has a realized sense of congruence between his own inner values and the values embedded in the group structure and process.

From another point of view, membership entails an engagement in and an active participation in the authority relation. The identification by which an individual achieves membership and the integration of values thus engages him in the authority relation. Since obedience, as we have defined it, represents the subject's engagement and responsiveness within and to the authority relation, identification assumes a significant role as central to the understanding of obedience.

The effect of identification is to make it possible for the individual to enter the authority relation within the context of shared values. Superior and subject are both members of the group and their interaction and mutual regulation takes place within the larger context of shared values both have internalized. The interaction is not based on power or power relations, but on an essential dialectic between autonomous sources of authoritative interaction. The authoritative nature of the participation of each individual is based in part on the fact that through his identification his response derives from and expresses in his own personal terms some aspect of the value system shared within the authority relation which is in fact constitutive of the group process. The process of mutual regulation at the heart of the authority relation, therefore, is in some sense a dialectic of value systems — operating within an overriding context of shared group values.

At this point, I would like to make some clarifications. The sharing of values cannot be construed as the basis for conformity. Values, by reason of their internalized aspects unique to each personality structure, are never identical. The individual's value system is always highly personal and unique. The sharing of values as constitutive of a group is based on an integration of essentially divergent value systems which find some areas of congruence and convergence. The integration of values must always involve a process of dialectical and mutual regulation. The integration of shared values rests on a consensus of value-orientations that cannot be achieved except by a continuing dialogue of intents, meanings, purposes, goals, attitudes, etc. Without the integration of values and its attendant necessity for mutual regulation, the authority relation could not survive. It would have only two diametric alternatives — conformity or rebellion.

Without the process of identification and the context of values it implies, the authority relation degenerates into a power relation. The sharing of values sets the conditions for meaningful dialogue and mutual regulation. The influence of superior on subject and of subject on superior takes place within the context of mutually shared values. As long as the value context is operative, each participant must identify with the other — subject with superior and superior with subject — and each must recognize the other as autonomous sources of the sense of valued conviction in which each of them shares and which each has internalized. Without the context of value, the meaningful basis for mutual regulation has been withdrawn and the roots of identification have been removed. The basis for sharing and real mutuality no longer pertain. The participants are set in basic opposition to each other and the focus of power becomes sharper and determinative. The interaction, if there be any, can only persist in terms of power — either submission or rebelliousness on one side and authoritarian control on the other.

## SUBJECTION

It should be clear that the internalization and sharing of values does not leave room for conformity or for rebellion. It does not make much sense to rebel against oneself. One does not rebel against one's own internalized values. This does not mean that there is not a meaningful dialectic of values — as we have suggested, such a dialectic is central to the mutual regulation of the authority relation. But rebellion is a rejection and overthrow of values — it is a destructive resort to power and an evacuation of values. From the opposite perspective, the internalization and integration of values is a process requiring autonomous engagement and free self-determination. This is not consistent with mere submission or subjugation to the force of extrinsic power. Subjection within the authority relation is an active process of self-commitment and engagement — a process embracing and basing itself on the underlying mechanism of identification and the integration of values. As we have already pointed out, subjection is in no sense to be equated with submission or subjugation. The latter are devalued and valueless terms that have relevance only to a relationship of power. Subjection takes place in a context of internalization of values within the authority relation.

It can be seen, therefore, that identification is essential to the working out of mature obedience. The identification provides a meaningful step in the integration of individual personality which builds on and derives from developmental attainments contributing to obedience. The mature religious must identify himself with the religious group and the religious group with him. He must achieve a sense of religious identity in order for the integration of developmental aspects to emerge. The identification brings about an integration within the individual's own personality that allows each of the constitutive elements deriving from the individual's developmental history to emerge and play its respective role in the mature capacity for obedience. Without such an integrative identification, mature obedience is impaired. We can also conclude that subjection without identification is equivalent to submission.

## RITUALIZATION

I would like to bring into focus at this point a concept that has enjoyed considerable elaboration in the study of human cultural and behavioral systems. Anthropologists have long been interested in the developmental function of rites and rituals in primitive communities. Recent ethnological studies have described ceremonials among social animals. In clinical sciences, ritualization has long been recognized as characteristic of obsessional behavior and as having highly magical and idiosyncratic meanings to the patient. But ritual can also have its positive aspects. Fromm (1955), for instance, regarded ritual, along with art, as basis measures enabling man to come in contact with the essence of reality. As he put it: "Aside from art, the most significant way of breaking through the surface of routine and of getting in touch with the ultimate realities of life is to be found in what may be called by the general term of "ritual." . . . Whether we think of the Greek drama, the medieval passion play, or an Indian dance, whether we think of Hindu, Jewish or Christian religious rituals, we are dealing with various forms of dramatization of the fundamental problems of human existence, with an *acting* out of the very same problems which are *thought* out in philosophy and theology (pp. 144-145). While all of these origins and applications of the concept of ritualization have their specific relevance, they also provide the basis of derivation for the concept as applied here.

Ritualization in this study derives from the remarkable insight of Erik Erikson in his genial paper on the ontogeny of ritualization (1966). He defines the concept in these terms: ". . . we should, therefore, begin by postulating that behavior to be called ritualization in man must consist of an agreed-upon interplay between at least two persons who repeat it at meaningful intervals and in recurring contexts; and that this interplay should have adaptive value for the respective egos of both participants" (pp. 602-3). The fabric of social life is woven by ritualizations permeating almost every phase of everyday life. Ritualization, therefore, does not refer to an aspect of human behavior that is unusual or rare in any sense. Ritualization is in effect the patterning of human interactions taking place in countless ways and in countless contexts of human living. Erikson used the example of the mother's approach to her awakening child in the morning. The mother's response becomes a repeat performance which elicits predictable responses in the infant and is carried out by both participants with great enjoyment. The routine is highly individual and adapted to the individual peculiarities of the child, yet it is at the same time highly stereotyped according to a pattern dictated within the context of a family tradition and a culture.

## Authority and Ritualization

I would suggest that the interplay of authority and obedience within the authority relation is a form of ritualization reflecting elements basic to any form of human ritualization, but also with characteristics unique to itself. As in any ritualization, obedience involves a certain mutuality. We have discussed the role of mutuality and its centrality in the authority relation. The mutuality is based on the reciprocal needs of both participants, and its quality changes with the quality of the relation. In mature obedience, mutual regulation involves mutual responsiveness of initiatives and responsibilities. Mutual interaction is neither divisive nor disruptive, but rather unites both superior and subject in a common enterprise, in a cooperative venture, in which each has his proper yet reciprocally complementary roles and functions to contribute and mesh with that of the other in symbolic actuality. The symbolic actuality thus carries within itself significance and purposefulness for both participants.

The ritual quality of obedience also underlines the fact that the participation in the authority relation through obedience is highly personal — even as the mother's response to the child's morning initiative is highly individual and personal. The authority relation is not an abstract structure — it is a human relation and interaction. At the same time it is group-bound. It takes place within a context of shared purposes, intents and specifically values. The mutual regulation and interaction between superior and subject is not governed exclusively by idiosyncratic needs and concerns on either side. It is embedded in and responsive to and functions in terms of values mutually shared and reinforced. The interaction is based on and specified by the context of group values which both participants have internalized and which provides the common ground of their participation in the relation.

The ritualization, therefore, has a twofold effect. It both enhances the individual's sense of belonging and at the same time enhances his sense of distinctiveness. The individual's participation in the authority relation gives him a sense of increased sharing in group values. His subjection in the authority relation is equivalently an engagement with group values and confirms his sharing in them — as it fortifies his own internal sense of possession of them. The engagement at the same time must bring into focus the tension between the perspective of values as internalized and values as shared. These are always in dialectical counterposition precisely because internalization is both an assimilation but at the same time an adaptive synthesis. What is internalized is not simply taken in — as the old analytic model of incorporation might have had it — but it is creatively synthesized into a new configuration which is unique and personalized. One cannot engage, therefore, in the dialectic of values without having an increased sense both of what is shared and what is personally possessed.

## Ritualization and Spontaneity

The ritual of obedience is formalized — both in the details of its specific contexts and in the whole of its organization within the religious group — and yet it retains an element of playfulness and spontaneity. The formality of obedience has perhaps been too much emphasized in the past, and its playfulness too little. One of the functions of formality is to underline the familiarity of procedures through repetition of the same elements. Formality and an emphasis on it helps to support that need. Familiarity eases the strain and anxiety of uncertainty and provides an assurance of predictability. Yet sheer formality and utter familiarity would reduce ritual to mere routine. Obedience, instead of being a form of ritualization would become a form of routinization. Consequently, the element of playfulness or surprise carries with it important implications. The interaction in the authority relation is after all highly personalized — personalized in terms of the individuality of both participants. It must preserve that individuality in some way. It must preserve the element of mutual recognition which provides the basis for effective responsiveness. The mutual responsiveness in obedience is not mechanical or inhuman. It is uniquely and specifically human responsiveness — and therefore it is affective. It is an engagement — and engagement without emotion is unimaginable. There is room, therefore, for playfulness and spontaneity in the authority relation. It would seem to be necessary both as an affirmation and as a recognition of meaningful human participation.

It should be stressed that such forms of ritualized affirmation are an indispensable aspect of periodic experience. It is essential to preserve the sense of meaningful belonging and sharing and to foster and confirm the inner sense of personal value and self-esteem. Elements of affirmation bridging over into reaffirmation, of formality melding and modulating into familiarity, and of recognition, provide a bulwark and a defense against a sense of estrangement. I think this aspect of the functioning of obedience is paramount. The basic elements of subjection, identification and meaningful ritualization provide a sense of belonging, meaningful sharing and valued engagement and commitment that underlie religious perseverance. They are essential to a sense of continuing vocation for the individual religious. When they fail, they incur a sense of estrangement, a sense of separation, of not belonging, of not being recognized or accepted or valued, that is intolerable to any human being. One has to suspect that these basic derangements in the functioning of obedience lie behind many of the disillusionments, disaffections and defections in contemporary religious life.

## Functions

It can be easily seen, then, in the light of this discussion, that ritualization fulfills several important functions. It serves to bind instinctual energies into patterns of mutuality which are relatively convincing and which tend to simplify otherwise complex and difficult patterns of interaction. Interactions, which would otherwise be ladened with difficulty and strain, become familiarly pleasurable. Ritualization also provides channels by which individuals can function in highly personal and individual ways and at the same time function as the bearer and representative of a group ethos. The patterning of responses and the patterning of mutual interactions protects the individual from both impulsive excesses and from instinctual arbitrariness. Ritualization also provides the groundwork and context within which lasting and meaningful identifications can take place.

This last function of ritualization is most important. We have already seen the central role of identification for obedience and the authority relation. But it must be kept in mind that identification does not simply happen in some mysterious way. It does not take place as a derivative of something happening within an individual psyche as an isolated phenomenon. It has a context of meaning which is essentially social and which requires the appropriate setting conditions. Ritualization, insofar as it fosters the sense of belonging and familiarity and to the extent to which it provides the person with a context for spontaneous and meaningful self-expression without risk of instinctual excess or impulsive destructiveness, provides the conditions within which meaningful identifications can emerge. Thus ritualization is an essential precondition for the formation and preservation of a sense of religious identity and belonging without which faithful commitment is impossible.

A further important function of ritualization is the role it plays in the regulation of ambivalence. Ambivalence is a state of mind in which opposite feelings toward the same object or situation exist side-by-side — positive and negative, love and hate, libidinal and destructive. No meaningful human relationship is without ambivalence — whether it be an engaging working relation, a relation of parent and child, a marriage relation, or the relation of superior and subject. Ambivalence is therefore resident in the authority relation. Participation in the authority relation stirs sometimes deep feelings of a positive nature — trust, pleasure, admiration, attachment and even dependency — along with deep feelings of a negative nature — anger, rage, resentment, hate, rebelliousness, dislike, rejection. These feelings, both positive and negative, can exist side by side — but they are often the occasion of considerable conflict and anxiety to those who experience them. Ritualization offers secure and expectable channels by which such basic emotions can be expressed and usefully modified without running the risk of excess or of losing control. This is particularly true of hateful or destructive feelings. Ritualized patterns of interaction permit the expression of sentiments of opposition, objections, even resentments and hostility without disruptive or destructive consequences.

When such patterns of ritualization break down, the buffering social controls are diminished with an inevitable result that aggressive impulses are felt to be more threatening and more disruptive. The breakdown in patterns of ritualization has the correlative effect, therefore, of increasing anxiety. The obsessive clinging to forms of obedience and the rigid adherence to familiar and highly formalized structures of authority that was often seen in the past had the important function of binding and controlling such disruptive impulses. In the same light, our experiences, in more recent contexts, of rising anxiety in the face of shifting structural configurations can be seen as involving a need to deal with the anxiety aroused by the disorganization and reorganization of ritualized patterns of interacting and responding within the group.

## Ritualization and Generativity

As a last comment on ritualization, I would like to emphasize that the individual needs not merely to take his place as a participant of the ritualization process, but that he needs to function in the last analysis as a ritualizer. He needs to be reinforced in his role as ritualizer so that he can become both a transmitter of traditional ritual as well as an innovator of adaptive ritualization for the future. This capacity is an expression of his generativity (Erikson 1966). In a sense, subjection to the authority relation — embracing all the elements that are involved in it — means that one becomes both a participant in and a shaper of the ritual. The ritual, as we observed, is not reducible to mere routine or mere formality. It has scope for individual spontaneity and self-expression. Subjection is in this sense a creative participation that both creates the ritual as it responds to it, and makes it possible for the ritual to remain adaptively relevant. Through obedience, then, the individual religious becomes both a possessor and a creator of ritual. He thus also becomes the transmitter of ritual and creative ritualization which provides the context within which younger members of the religious group can achieve a sense of identification, by which they in turn become sharers in and creators of ritual. Erikson (1966) underlined these important considerations in his seminal comment:

> At any rate, there can be no prescription for ritualization, for far from being merely repetitive or familiar in the sense of habituation, any true ritualization is ontogenetically grounded and yet pervaded with a spontaneity of surprise: it is an unexpected renewal of a recognizable order in potential chaos. It thus depends on that blending of surprise and recognition which is the soul of creativity, reborn out of the abyss of instinctual disorder, confusion of identity, and social anomie. (p. 621)

# CHAPTER XXIX

# THE PATHOLOGY OF OBEDIENCE

## Introduction

We can approach the problem of obedience from a number of viewpoints. The developmental perspective allowed us to gain some appreciation of elements contributing to mature and functional obedience. We have also looked at the manner in which some of these elements can be distorted and the effects of such deviations on the operation of obedience. We can turn our attention at this point to several forms of personality organization of particular interest for the manner in which they express themselves in the life of obedience. The following discussion of pathological types of obedience will overlap the preceding discussion of specific deviations in some measure, but the focus of our interest in this consideration is on the overall pattern of personality functioning and its impact on the problem of obedience. In this light I will discuss authoritarian, obsessive, paranoid and narcissistic personalities to explore implications of these types of personality organization for obedience.

It should be immediately added by way of prefatory note that we are dealing with types of personality organization labelled as pathological. Such forms of personality organization are frequently seen in the psychiatrist's practice and in more pronounced forms might well receive a DSM-IV diagnosis as one or other form of personality disorder. But it must also be remembered that these are forms of organization of human personalities, and therefore they can be found broadly distributed in any large group of human beings in more mitigated or less deviant patterns. These patterns are not exclusive, and they are present in all degrees of intensity or qualitative variation in relatively normal populations. A given individual may show a more or less obsessive and narcissistic and paranoid pattern in his personality functioning at one and the same time or in different situations or in response to different stimulating conditions or stress. An individual can show any or all of these patterns and still be able to carry on his life quite effectively and relatively normally. These patterns can also be quite disturbing and disruptive. We are interested at this point in trying to see what the effect of such patterns might be — regardless of their degree of intensity or their pathology — on the exercise of obedience.

## The Authoritarian Personality

The authoritarian personality was first studied in Germany during the early Hitler years and was intended as a study of anti-Semitic attitudes. In the post-war years, this interest in anti-semitism and ethnocentric attitudes was extended in the work of a group at the University of California (Adorno et al. 1950). A variety of tests were developed and together with other behavioral data suggested a certain consistent pattern of personality characteristics related to anti-semitic and ethnocentric attitudes. This pattern, called the "authoritarian personality," included such characteristics as rigid adherence to conventional middle-class values, generally submissive and uncritical attitudes to idealized moral authorities, a tendency to be sensitive to any violation of conventional values along with punitive attitudes toward anyone responsible for such a violation, a generally tough-minded attitude and an insistence on objectivity, a tendency to think superstitiously about the deterministic power of fate, a tendency to think in rigid categories and stereotypes, a general preoccupation with issues of power-control or strength-weakness, a tendency to identify with powerful or influential figures, a more general attitude of hostility and punitiveness, a tendency to project hostile or destructive impulses and to believe dangerous things are happening or could happen, and finally an excessive concern with sexual fantasies.

The California study demonstrated that these characteristics tended to correlate with each other and tended to cluster together. Whether such covariance can be taken to indicate an underlying personality type or not, these characteristics do have a certain consistency that allows us to refer to them as authoritarian characteristics or attitudes. Such attitudes, however, can be found in varying degrees in the normal population and could well represent aspects of almost any human personality. Such attitudes can be manifested in varying degrees by individuals — without any one of them actually having a personality organization quite like that described in the study. The authoritarian personality, therefore, is a construct providing us with a typology that may be difficult to identify in reality. But as with any typology, the elements of the type can usually be found distributed in the general population.

The authoritarian attitude derives from feelings and a conviction of inner inadequacy and weakness. The threat of autonomy and independence for such individuals is too great, so that the authoritarian seeks to adhere to something outside of himself that he hopes will provide the strength he lacks in himself. His inner conviction can take a sadomasochistic form expressed in strivings for domination or submission. The authoritarian attitude rests on an essentially masochistic base involving feelings of inferiority, powerlessness and insignificance. Sadistic impulses are often present in the same person expressing themselves in a tendency to make others dependent on oneself, seeking power and influence over others, and even to making others suffer. Such tendencies often remain at an unconscious level, defended against by reaction formations and rationlizations of excessive concern for the welfare of others. These concerns can then find expression in more or less paternalistic attitudes sometimes found in those in authority. But the authoritarian attitude does not try to dominate others out of a genuine sense of care and concern; rather the authoritarian cares for others and is concerned about them only insofar as and to the extent that he can dominate them.

The authoritarian need for power is not rooted in strength, but in weakness. The authoritarian admires power and authority and tends to submit to it, but at the same time he wishes to have and exercise power and to have others submit to him. The authoritarian conceives and responds to authority in terms of power. As Fromm (1941) cleverly put it, for the authoritarian character there are only two sexes — the powerful and the powerless. His admiration for power and his willingness to submit to it are aroused by any source of power — whether it be a person or an institution. He is fascinated by power for its own sake. Just as powerful figures arouse his admiration, so the powerless arouse his contempt and the wish to dominate and humiliate.

The authoritarian attitude sees the world and all relationships and all structures in terms of power. His role in life is to submit to the inexorable forces of fate — in the form of destiny, or providence, or law, or even in the religious context the will of God. He seeks out a higher power in the face of which he has no other recourse but submission. The authoritarian does not lack courage or strength of conviction, but his existence is rooted in powerlessness, so that action can only be taken in the name of the higher power. Any action in his own name is taken only at great risk. Thus courage takes the form of the strength to endure and to accept whatever the higher power designates as his lot. Thus suffering becomes the highest virtue and heroism is translated into the submission to the dictates of fate. The leitmotif is submission to the forces of fate or destiny or the will of another rather than changing the course of things and taking responsibility for one's own life.

The central conflict for the authoritarian personality is over the issue of aggression — whether in its constructive or destructive guise. The authoritarian cannot tolerate his own aggressive and destructive impulses. He lacks a sense of inner mastery and control of such impulses and the primitive and destructive quality of these impulses can be terrifying. The issue of control thus becomes a major one for such personalities — the control of inner impulses, but in addition the control of impulsiveness or aggressiveness in and from others. Thus it is no surprise that authoritarian types should be preoccupied with matters of power and control.

These inner insecurities over the control of aggression have large implications. In the struggle to gain and maintain control the individual allies himself with the sources of power and control in his environment. The inner sense of fragility and lack of control is supported by a psychic alliance with the centers of power outside. Submission to moral authorities thus tends to assume a rigid and uncritical quality. There is an investment for the individual in supporting and maintaining the power and influence of external authorities. Whenever anything threatens the structure of power around him or the basis of his alliance with such power sources, his anxiety and insecurity are aroused. Any changes in the power structure or the structure of authority become a threat to his internal security and need for control. Similarly, if he should have to exercise authority, he feels insecure and threatened by anything that might challenge or question the absoluteness of his power and the security of his control. His anxiety can be allayed only by unquestioning submission from subordinates. It is easily understood how any initiative other than his own can be severely threatening to such a personality.

Such tendencies are widely distributed — and widely denied as well. Conflicts over aggressive impulses, particularly those that are hostile or destructive, are the common human lot. The authoritarian solution to such basic conflicts is not infrequent. Their influence on the exercise of obedience can be quite significant. The authoritarian attitude approaches the authority relation in terms of power. It is relatively impossible for authoritarians to conceive or respond to the authority relation in any other terms than those of power. They see the authority relation as a relation of dominance and submission. It is difficult for them to see the structure of authority in any but vertical and hierarchical terms. They tend to see power as vested in the superior and as totally lacking in the subject. The view of the authority relation as involving a process of interaction and mutual regulation between autonomous, free and responsible individuals is entirely foreign to the authoritarian attitude. Genuine and mature obedience has little place for the authoritarian mind.

Authoritarian attitudes undoubtedly have a profound effect on the exercise of obedience in religious life. The authoritarian need to find external sources of strength can find a congenial context in the hierarchically organized structures of some more traditionally organized religious communities. The ultimate appeal to a need for submission to and an acceptance of a divinely dictated fate behind which there stands the infinite assurance and insurance of God's will is admirably suited and responsive to authoritarian needs. In such a context, so intensely held and promoted in the traditional rhetoric of obedience — and not an insignificant component of one interpretation of Ignatian obedience — the authoritarian attitudes can take root and flourish. Such a context may also prove attractive to individuals whose authoritarian needs might find corresponding satisfaction. On this basis we would not find it surprising that the structure of religious groups has often tended to assume an authoritarian form.

## THE OBSESSIVE PERSONALITY

Like authoritarian traits and attitudes, obsessive characteristics can manifest themselves across a broad range of degrees of intensity and relative pathology. Many individuals have significant obsessive and compulsive elements in their personalities, but these traits are sufficiently well integrated into their overall functioning and are useful in making them relatively productive and hardworking members of society. In certain areas of human endeavor obsessive traits are valued and rewarded. Such is the case in many areas of scientific endeavor, in academic scholarship, in areas of business accounting, etc. Wherever attention to detail, thoroughness, consistency and perseverance are useful and productive characteristics, one can expect a certain social value to be attached to obsessive traits. Indeed a certain moderate degree of obsessiveness is relatively adaptive — particularly in our society — and consistent with normal adult personality functioning.

Obsessional traits, however, can be manifest at a greater degree of intensity and pathology. At more severe levels, they can combine into an obsessive personality pattern. At this level of organization, obsessional traits come to dominate the style and organization of the individual's life and behavior and give a definite quality to his experience and activity. At the more severe extreme, obsessive and compulsive elements can take over the individual's functioning and cause considerable discomfort and impairment, as in obsessive-compulsive neurosis. Neurotic obsessionals are overwhelmed with doubt and guilt. To overcome these feelings and the intense anxiety associated with them, obsessional patients are driven to carry out elaborate rituals which they feel compelled to complete in exact and often exhausting detail. The failure to carry out these exacting rituals would result in terrible consequences, so that they live in constant dread and anxious doubt generated by their fear of omitting any part of these rituals. The rituals thus have a magic significance — the magical quality of obsessional thought processes is quite characteristic — masking underlying wishes to carry out the consequences they consciously fear. The purpose of the rituals, therefore, is to magically undo or control underlying sexual or aggressive impulses and wishes. The elaborate rituals and controlling mechanisms represent attempts to avoid and control instinctual impulses that are somehow frightening or disturbing.

In addition to the patterns of compulsive and ritualized activity, the obsessive syndrome also involves disturbed thinking as well. These patients are afflicted with periods of obsessive brooding in which they alternate between the pros and cons of any question or decision without being able to reach any firm conclusion. Their thinking is permeated with doubt and uncertainty. A severely obsessional individual cannot affirm any belief, thought, proposition, observation, recollection or conviction without doubt and hesitation. He begins to doubt his own perceptions and memory. Severely obsessional patients will return again and again to make sure that a cigarette or match is put out, or that a gas jet is turned off, or a door locked. The uncertainty is generated by the underlying wish for the consequences of not putting out the cigarette or not turning off the gas jet or not locking the door to occur.

The elements of doubt, indecision and uncertainty of obsessional thinking are quite familiar in religious circles in the form of scruples.[1] Scrupulous individuals also reflect the characteristic magical quality of obsessional thought. They are tormented by guilt and doubt. They are driven to confess and reconfess their "sins" — even though frequently enough what they are concerned about cannot be regarded

[1] See the discussion of Ignatius' scrupulosity and his rules for scruples in chapter XVII above.

as sinful by any reckoning. Their guilt, doubt and uncertainty, however, are generated by their constant struggle with unconscious instinctual impulses. The seemingly endless repetition of their obsessional ruminations and acts expresses the underlying failure of their instinctual conflicts to find resolution. Occasionally such troubled people experience the breakthrough of instinctual impulses in the form of a wish or fantasy or temptation to commit some evil deed — often to kill or hurt someone, usually someone close to the individual. The material may frequently be sexual as well, expressing itself in wishes to exhibit, seduce, rape, etc. These instinctual disruptions often throw the patient into a paroxysm of guilt and anxiety. They represent a failure of obsessional defenses.

The obsessive personality has a style and an organization that is quite characteristic. They tend to be conscientious, concerning themselves with the minutest details and with careful observance of rules and regulations. The obsessive tends to treat relatively minor or trivial prescriptions with the same concern and care that he gives to more significant and meaningful ones. He often seems to lack a sense of proportion or discrimination between what is important and what is not. His investment in detail runs the constant risk of ignoring what is essential. He tends to miss the forest for the trees. He pours considerable effort into maintaining orderliness and neatness — often to the detriment of any really creative or productive output. He tends to be perfectionistic — he is not satisfied unless he has completed what he has set out to do in every detail. His standards are usually high — for performance and for moral behavior — while he can at the same time be harshly critical, demanding and devaluing of the efforts of others. Imagination plays little role in his life. He puts little value in art, literature, music or poetry — and gives these interests little room in his life. His preferred realm is the world of common sense and hard facts. He prefers mathematics, technology, exact sciences. He is proud of his intellectual capacity and resorts to it as a means of dealing with reality and with his own inner conflicts. He defends against inner impulses and feelings by resorting to defenses of intellectualization and rationalization.

The organization of obsessional cognitive functioning is characteristically rigid — rigid in thinking, in attention, and in interests. The range of attention tends to be narrowed rather than broadened. He prefers to focus on a relatively small area of interest and to try to explore it in exquisite detail. His interest is primarily in technical details. Attention tends to be rigidly and intensely directed to its object. There is a tendency for the obsessive's activity in general to be organized and directed toward purposeful objectives and goals. This overriding purposefulness and goa1-directed character is usually aimed at accomplishing work. The obsessive lives for work — and his investment in it is driven by an inner necessity. They tend to be stubborn, unvarying, self-willed. They can often be quite stubborn and obstinate. There is little room in their lives for spontaneity or relaxed enjoyment — little room for affection or emotional involvement and expressiveness. They tend to try to narrow their subjective experience of emotion — a defense that psychiatrists call "isolation of affect."

The pressure of conscience is constant in their lives. If they should fail to continue to work for serious goals or if they should allow themselves some measure of relaxation and enjoyment, or if they should loosen some of their rigid control over feelings, they inevitably fall victim to feelings of guilt and remorse. There is a sense of moral obligation that hovers over every facet of their lives — a feeling of obligation and resignation to duty. In relation to authority, they generally assume a posture of ambivalent submission — often on a moralized basis. Obsessional morality tends to be harsh, rigid and demanding — a form of hypermorality which serves as a defense against underlying instinctual impulses even as it offers a channel for their expression. In this regard the obsessive and the authoritarian personalities are similar. Both are deeply conflicted over inner impulses of aggression. Both are trapped by issues of power and control. The authoritarian, however, tends to submit to authority as a means of allying himself with an external source of power. The obsessive submits out of a fear of his own inner power and destructiveness which he feels he must overcome and over which he must exercise a rigid and unvarying control. The authoritarian submits out of a sense of his own inner weakness — the obsessive submits out of a fear of his own inner power and destructiveness.

In this light it is not difficult to see that obsessive traits fit quite congenially with the traditional model of obedience. There are many aspects of the more or less idealized pattern of traditional obedience that can be described as obsessive-compulsive. There was a strong emphasis on the observance of the religious rule, along with an obsessive concern with the details of the rule and their minute observance. There was an emphasis on work and productivity and an expression of self-denial — to the exclusion of pleasure and enjoyment. Art, literature, and the fine arts in general were held in suspicion and were given little place. The life of the religious community was organized and highly structured. The need for self-direction or decision was minimized. Virtue lie in the observance of the daily order, the rules, and the customs. The obsessive personality and style would tend to find such a structured milieu most responsive to inner obsessive needs for structure and control.

The obsessive style of obedience takes the form of rigid adherence to the superior's directives or to the religious rule. His adherence is to the letter of the law rather than to its spirit. He prefers to have things spelled out in specific detail. He then tends to follow out these details in a compulsive and often ritualized manner. The obsessive does not feel comfortable with opportunities for initiative. He leaves little room for it — or if he does bring himself to show some initiative, it is in contexts in which the safeguards are secure and well-established. Initiative is threatening to the extent that it calls for self-direction and allows room for spontaneity. Spontaneity is threatening since it involves a disruption of established patterns of regulation and control. Initiative opens the way to the expression of inner impulses and wishes. The obsessive personality will tend to support and cling to the established order of things — insofar as that order supports his need for control and structure.

While the obsessive style has little tolerance for initiative, it also tends to pursue a distorted form of autonomy. The obsessive tends to be rigid, stubborn, and willful in the exercise of obedience. He will follow the superior's directives rigidly and carefully as long as what the superior orders follows an established and organized pattern. Should the superior direct him toward change, toward new and uncertain paths, the obsessive subject becomes stubbornly resistant. Obsessional defenses and change — like oil and water, perhaps like gasoline and alcohol — do not mix. The obsessive clings to the established and well-ordered pattern of things — out of an inner necessity. Such willfulness should not be mistaken for simply wanting to have his own way. The true obsessive does not want his own way — he avoids having his own way even though his willfulness can often give that appearance. What he wants is an established, secure, familiar and predictable way of doing things. Change is threatening because it confronts him with the unknown — and in the unknown lurks the possibility of loss of control, of loss of the established structure on which he depends to deal with disruptive and dangerous inner impulses. Change for the obsessive provokes anxiety and he is forced to set himself against it. The obsessive outlook thus tends to be inherently conservative.

Obsessional traits can also be found in the exercise of the superior's function. Obsessive superiors tend to emphasize and rely on order and organization. They distrust and cannot tolerate initiative. Initiative disrupts and imperils the necessary control that is reinforced by order and regulation. The obsessive superior tends to be hyperresponsible. He often feels that he himself is personally responsible for whatever happens as a result of the activity of his community or its members. He tends, therefore, to concentrate as much responsibility as possible in his own hands. The more effectively he can do this, the less anxious he feels. This inevitably leaves less room for the exercise of responsibility on the part of subjects and tends to reinforce a paternalistic framework for obedience. The potentialities for initiative, autonomy and freedom in the exercise of obedience are minimized. The basic insecurity forcing the obsessive superior to concentrate responsibility in this way derives from his own inner conflicts, particularly conflicts over responsibility.

This pattern of behavior becomes understandable if we remind ourselves that every human being is capable of responsible judgment and activity, but at the same time every human being has inner impulses to act irresponsibly and impulsively. The obsessive is threatened by these impulses since they are often associated with destructive consequences or loss of control. One of the ways of defending himself against such impulses is to deny them and then project them on to others. By such a mechanism the superior would be able to see himself as totally responsible — without any such irresponsible impulses — and he would then tend to see others, particularly his subordinates as less responsible than they might actually be. However, he sees them in terms of the irresponsible impulses that he denies in himself and projects upon them. The mechanism works in the opposite direction as well. While he tends to see subordinates as irresponsible and impulsive, he also tends to see those who are above him, his own superiors, as excessively rigid and demanding and punitive and as imposing responsibility on him. But this is again a projection — not of instinctual impulsiveness but of punitive and moralistic superego attitudes. The projection operates in both directions. Irresponsibility is projected toward lower levels in the structure, and excessive demands for responsibility are projected upwards.

Where obsessive individuals are interacting in a social system, there is a tendency for them to split their conflicts over responsibility in this way and project them at each level of the system. There can arise an interlocking system of projections in which superiors are seen as rigid, demanding, and repressive, and inferiors are seen as immature, impulsive, and irresponsible. This has been referred to as a "system of social defense' (Meissner 1965, 1971a). It serves to reinforce intrapsychic defense mechanisms. It also has the inevitable effect of shifting the locus of responsible judgment and action from lower levels of the organization to the upper levels. Subjects who are viewed and treated as less mature and responsible tend to become less mature and responsible. Thus the projections begin to verify themselves. It thus becomes obvious that obsessional concerns can have severe and farreaching effects on the modality of obedience in the religious group.

## THE PARANOID PERSONALITY

Paranoid traits are usually seen in more pathological form, expressed in rather severe personality disturbances such as the paranoid psychoses or paranoid schizophrenic conditions. But paranoid traits — like other groups of traits we have been considering here — can exist in less intense and less pathological forms. In their milder forms, paranoid traits may form a constituent in relatively normal and adequately functioning personalities.

The paranoid personality is marked by suspiciousness and a tendency to blame others for one's own inadequacies and failures. Paranoid individuals are usually actively and intensely attentive to details. Their attention is sharp and focused, much like the obsessive, but it is usually much more intense. In addition, paranoid attentiveness to detail has a different motivation than the obsessive. Paranoid attentiveness is always searching the environment, always on the lookout for something, constantly scanning in a tensely purposeful and directed manner. This style of relating and attending to reality has been described as "rigidly intentional." The paranoid is intent on finding what he is looking for. His attentive scanning of reality is not intended to find out what might be out there in his environment. Rather it is intended to find what he is already convinced to be out there. He searches intently for confirmation for his inner convictions and anticipations. The strength of these rigid anticipations and convictions allows him to disregard or discredit anything contrary to or contradicting his inner view. Consequently, he finds what he is looking for — regardless of what there may be for him to find. His resources of perceptiveness and judgment are employed not in the service of identifying and adapting to reality, but rather in the service of reinforcing and confirming his inner convictions and biases.

With this sort of selection operating in his perception of reality, the paranoid can arrive at nearly any conclusions he wishes. He can be — at one and the same time — quite correct in his perception of things and absolutely wrong in his conclusions. Their interpretation of the data of reality is governed not by the information supplied from reality, but by their inner needs and convictions. The paranoid interpretation of reality may thus be quite divergent from anyone else's. Often they will seize upon some minor aspect of a situation, which to others seems trivial and unimportant or irrelevant, and give it a central importance and significance. Normally we give significance and evaluate facts and events by some reasonably objective standard. But the paranoid attributes significance and judges the value of events in terms of an inner frame of reference. He sees his own perceptions as valid and cannot admit anyone else's different perception as in any sense valid. The rigidly paranoid individual has a great deal of difficulty accepting the fact that events in the real world can be seen in different ways by different people. He lacks sufficient flexibility to be able to leave room for another's point of view. He accepts only his own perceptions and finds it necessary to discredit or devalue any other. The continuity of paranoid traits with prejudice — a relatively widespread social phenomenon — can be appreciated on these terms.

For the paranoid person, whatever presents itself as different thereby becomes threatening and must be held in suspicion. Anything unexpected, the surprising or unusual, or even simply new, presents a provocative challenge for any rigid person. This is particularly the case for the suspicious paranoid individual. Such elements are disruptive and must be reconciled with the paranoid's rigidly inflexible inner convictions and view of the world. The rigid or dogmatic obsessive can ignore or avoid the new or unusual, but the paranoid cannot. The paranoid can afford to ignore nothing. He must deal with the possibility of the new or unusual by anticipating it. He is thus constantly alert and attentive to its possibility. He is constantly scanning his environment searching out anything that might be unexpected or unanticipated. When such elements are discovered — as they must — he must scrutinize and cautiously evaluate them to make sure that they do not violate his inner scheme.

This characteristic hyperalertness and hypersensitivity of the paranoid is particularly noteworthy in areas of experience in which there is a great deal of ambiguity and uncertainty. Human interactions and the problem of judging the inner attitudes and motivations of others is one of the most important of such areas. The paranoid individual is thus prone to attributing attitudes and motivations to others on the basis of his own inner frame of reference rather than on the basis of information coming from them. He may ignore direct information opposite to his view — because he regards it as untrustworthy and because that data does not fit into his preconceived notion of others' real intentions. Evidence of any kind is accepted or rejected not on the basis of its objective validity, but on the basis of its congruence with his inner scheme and his own biased perceptions related to it. The organization of paranoid thought processes is governed not by objective evidences, but by inner subjective needs.

This tendency, so common in paranoid individuals, has been described as projection. But projection is not exclusively a paranoid mechanism, even though it is found characteristically in paranoid personalities. The paranoid attributes thoughts and motives to other people around him, but the thoughts and motives are in fact derived from his own inner impulses and unconscious wishes. He is prone to project hostile and destructive wishes or intentions, thus interpreting the behavior of others as in indicating evil intentions to hurt or harm him in some way. The projection of hostility in this way serves as a defense against his own hostile impulses and wishes that he must avoid and repress.

Projection at the same time serves a blaming function. It enables the paranoid to avoid taking responsibility for his own life and misfortune and enables him to blame others for his difficulties. He can attribute these difficulties and disappointments to the evil intentions of others who want to undermine and hurt him. This also allows him to avoid facing his own inner weakness and ineffectualness and his own inner feelings of frustrated inadequacy. He need not face up to the fact that his failures are due to his own limitations and inadequacy.

The distortion of autonomy reflected in these paranoid distortions is considerably more severe and more pathological than that in obsessive-compulsive states. For the normal individual, a genuine sense of autonomy carries with it a feeling of competency, pride and self-respect. But the paranoid becomes either arrogantly hyperautonomous or furtively ashamed — and sometimes his behavior embraces both of these extremes of distorted autonomy. Paranoid autonomy is a constantly threatened autonomy. His sense of self-direction and mastery is in constant jeopardy. He does not have a sense of being in charge of his own life. He is constantly threatened by external forces and sources of influence. He constantly dreads external control and external influences on his behavior, thoughts and intentions. A well-established autonomy can allow itself a certain degree of comfortable relaxation. It can tolerate a degree of inner relaxation consistent with a certain amount of spontaneity or even constructive regression. That amount of flexibility is essential for any initiative to have room for expression. A relatively secure sense of autonomy can also allow a degree of relaxation — externally — it can open itself without threat or suspicion to listen to and take into account someone else's point of view, that might be different from one's own. The really autonomous person can even comply with or submit to another's will without a sense of shame or humiliation or loss. The paranoid individual can do none of these things.

Paranoids cannot tolerate giving-in, either to themselves or to any external source of influence. They must maintain a rigid hyperautonomous position — a fragile and defensive position at that. The paranoid must cling to his inner convictions — part of which includes his view of reality and his conviction of his own place and function within it. Any directives from an external authority — a source of often powerful influences — are a threat precisely because they derive from someone else's perception and judgment about reality. Thus the paranoid posture in relation to authority is apprehensive, suspicious, anxious, defensive and antagonistic. Authority is seen as threatening and hostile — due to the operation of projective defenses — and he must be continually preoccupied with defending himself from this attack. In this aspect of their interaction with authority, paranoid and authoritarian traits bear a certain resemblance. They differ, however, in that the authoritarian sees authority as a power to which he must submit and with which he must ally himself as a protective measure — while the paranoid sees the external authority not simply as powerful, but as filled with evil and hostile intent toward himself. The paranoid's defensive need is therefore considerably greater.

It is not difficult to see that the paranoid's difficulties with obedience would be considerable. He would be quite incapable of entering into the process of mutual regulation and interaction, so essential to a mature authority relation. He is so immersed in his own inner needs and preoccupations that effective sharing in and identification with the group's needs and values is remote. The paranoid can allow himself a degree of slender affiliation only where participation in the group serves his inner subjective needs for support and defense. There may, in fact, in such circumstances develop a form of hyperidentification with the group. The individual thus overidentifies with the group and excessively idealizes and values its goals, objectives and aspects of its functioning. Correspondingly, there is a devaluation and hostile rejection of other groups and their functioning. Paranoid mechanisms can thus become mobilized in the service of attacking and rejecting the other group. These are the processes that are operative in prejudice of all kinds. Prejudice and paranoia have a great deal in common — particularly the need to reject, exclude, devalue, and demean the objects of hostility. Both paranoia and prejudice rest on the determining force of inner needs and convictions.

Paranoid traits, therefore, make the life of obedience extremely difficult and precarious. For genuine obedience to function at all, there is required a sense of basic trust and mutually reinforced autonomy. The paranoid has neither. His constant sense of threat and danger and his everpresent need for suspicious self-protection undermines any capacity for trust. The capacity for such individuals to participate in and share in a group process and to engage in meaningful and reciprocal relationships with others through obedience is minimal at best. To expect them to enter into a life of meaningful obedience is in effect to ask them to surrender the internally elaborated scheme which dominates their lives and enables them to preserve their fragile and precarious autonomy. Through obedience they would place themselves in a position in which they could no longer rely on themselves — their own perceptions and judgments — but would have to accept and rely on the judgments and perceptions of others. These would seem to be incompatible.

## THE NARCISSISTIC PERSONALITY

The last form of deviant personality that we shall consider is the narcissistic personality. The designation "narcissistic personality" stands for a spectrum of personality types that have retained strong narcissistic components in their personality structure. These types of personality organization are currently the object of considerable interest and psychiatric study, inasmuch as they form a large group of patients seen in psychiatric practice and are often found in rather creative and productive individuals.

The understanding of such personalities derives from Freud's basic notion of narcissism. Freud saw the infant as starting life in a condition of a]most complete narcissism. He saw the course of libidinal development as entailing a gradual process of modifying the basic condition of narcissistic self-love in the direction of an emerging capacity to love others. Narcissistic personalities retain a significant component of narcissism in their make-up with resulting impairment of their capacity to love others meaningfully, to relate to others in meaningful and productive ways, and to grow to fuller and more mature levels of personality functioning and emotional stability. Narcissistic individuals love others only as an extension or reflection of themselves, or insofar as the other contributes to the well-being or stature of oneself. They never really grow to that level of maturity in which they become capable of loving others for their own sake rather than for oneself. Their interest, investment, gratification and love remains centered on themselves.

Individuals with narcissistic personalities are not infrequently found in groups and organizations. They can and do commit themselves to causes of various kinds. But the commitment is at root based on self-interest and self-enhancement. Such individuals are found quite frequently in religious groups, but religious life for them is somewhat paradoxically a means for enhancing self-esteem and self-regard. Rather than becoming a life of self-sacrifice and service to others, the religious life becomes for the narcissistic individual a way of supporting self-esteem and self-interest. As we have seen, a measure of self-interest and self-esteem is essential for emotional growth and maturity of personality development. But in the narcissistic personality, this aspect of the personality takes on an excessive and central concern. There is a line to be drawn between normal narcissism and pathological narcissism — we are dealing with the latter here. The narcissistic character bases most of his interest and activity on self-reference, even when it is a matter of interacting with and responding to other people. They are dominated by the need to be loved and admired. There is a basic contradiction at the root of their personalities between their often inflated concept of themselves and their abilities and their importance on the one hand, and the inordinate seeking and need for recognition and praise from others on the other.

Real empathy for the feelings of others has little place in the narcissistic personality. Their personal rewards are derived primarily from the plaudits of others and from their own sometimes grandiose fantasies. When the applause diminishes and the sources feeding the inner hunger for approval and admiration dry up, then the narcissistic person becomes restless and bored with what he is doing. Without a constant supply of praise and approval from others, the narcissistic individual becomes dissatisfied and often depressed. They tend to be easily aroused to jealousy or envy. They see the reward and praises going to others as somehow taken away from them. Moreover, they often think of themselves as somehow owed rewards and praises — even the rewards and praises that go to others. They will often idealize and value highly others from whom they expect tribute and admiration. They also devalue and treat contemptuously those who do not admire or pay them tribute. They tend strongly to exploit or manipulate others to their own interest and advantage — feeling that they are somehow entitled to exploit others for their own enhancement and advancement. The narcissistic personality is thus capable of being quite charming and engaging — in the interest of engaging others to his advantage.

The efforts of narcissistic individuals to enhance their sense of self-esteem and value is a form of defense against their underlying feelings of worthlessness and inferiority. Frequently the grandiosity, self-centeredness and self-reference covers an underlying paranoid or depressive core. Feelings of inadequacy and inferiority may alternate with rather grandiose and omnipotent fantasies. Behind these feelings and fantasies, there lies at a deeper level a rather infantile sense of entitlement — the conviction that the world owes them something, particularly that the world owes them recognition, admiration, rewards and love. When he doesn't get what he feels entitled to, the narcissistic person can become quite enraged. The anger that flows from his offended sense of entitlement can lead to more or less paranoid projections serving to justify the underlying sense of rage and deprivation that he feels. He may feel that he is not getting what he is entitled to because of some fancied conspiracy against him. He may feel that the conspiracy is based on the envy and jealousy that others have for him and his accomplishments. At this level the sense of offended narcissism has emerged into a full-blown paranoid distortion. The paranoid construction and the accompanying projections serve to bolster and preserve the injured sense of self-esteem and the narcissistic core that is so badly threatened.

Such pathological elements may be found in some degree in most narcissistic personalities, but for the most part many such individuals are capable of functioning at a rather high level. Generally they show good intelligence, they have a well-developed social capacity, they can maintain rather good control of their impulses, and they often manifest a remarkable capacity for consistent application and work. They are able to mobilize their resources quite effectively in areas offering them scope for their ambitions and in which they can satisfy their needs for admiration and acclaim. Because of their abilities and ambition, such individuals are often found in positions of influence and leadership. They frequently become outstanding performers in artistic fields. The theatre is a major focus of the interest and investment of such individuals — it provides them with a context of display and offers them a ready source of applause, admiration and notoriety.

Narcissistic personality structure is not incompatible with real talent or even genius — Goethe was a severely narcissistic individual. But the pattern more frequently seen in narcissistic individuals is that they are too interested and eager for easy rewards. The result is often that their work is marked with a certain brilliant superficiality, intended more to impress than to make a solid and meaningful contribution. Their careers are more often marked by promise than solid attainment or accomplishment. They are often the promising young talents who never seem to reach their potential — in whom the promise remains a promise.

The attention of psychiatrists has increasingly been drawn to the problem of the apparently well-functioning and adequate personality that may in fact cover underlying developmental defects. Zetzel (1970) has referred to such personalities as the "so-called normal" personality types. In many such cases there is a failure of libidinal development and a fixation at levels of narcissistic personality development. A characteristic profile, in which disordered narcissism seems to play a significant role, was characterized as the "Nobel Prize complex" (Tartakoff 1966). Patterns of personality development that are able to pass for relatively "normal" reflect not only intrinsic developmental factors, but also the limits set within a given culture and the diversity of personality patterns generated and reinforced by a given culture. Our own American culture places a high premium on performance and productivity. The narcissistic personality can find a remarkably adaptive fit between his own inner needs for reward and recognition and the cultural dispositions that respond to such needs by providing rewards for attainment and performance and by providing esteem and admiration for those who strive for them.

The Nobel Prize complex is manifested in students, teachers, professional men, scientists, performers, etc. who entertain highly narcissistic and ambitious life goals. They wish to become President, to gain great wealth and influence, to become a great leader or thinker, to become a person who can influence men's minds and actions. More important to them than these accomplishments, however, is their ambition to gain the acclaim and admiration of others. They wish not merely to attain, but even more so to be a acclaimed for their attainments. Many of these persons are intellectually or artistically highly gifted and thus they tend to elicit considerable admiration and acclaim from others. Objective achievement, however, is often overshadowed or even inhibited by their preoccupation with acclaim and recognition. Their ambition sees the alternatives as all-or-nothing. If they do not gain the highest level of acclaim, they regard it as nothing. Not to gain the Nobel Prize is failure.

Many such individuals are firstborn — many are only children. They cherish a double fantasy — the omnipotent fantasy of having power and influence, and the impotent fantasy of being special and being chosen out by reason of exceptional gifts. Individuals who have been singled out from childhood as exceptionally bright tend to be more competitive — they seek recognition rather than love. Those who have been singled out as attractive or as artistically gifted tend to seek love and affection rather than recognition. Disappointments loom large in the experience of such individuals. They become excessively sensitive to even minor disappointments. Their narcissistic expectations and feelings of entitlement are bound to be disappointed in the confrontation with harsh reality. The problem in the developmental experience of so many of these individuals is that in so many settings of their early life experience — at home, in the family, in school, and often even in the early phases of their work or careers — their expectations of success and recognition have been continually reinforced. Expectation becomes a way of life which is built into their personalities.

When these narcissistic expectations and fantasies are disappointed and go unfulfilled, these individuals are plunged into feelings of failure and worthlessness. Thus disappointment can drive them to the very opposite of their excessive feelings of entitled self-enhancement and self-regard. They become despondent and depressed. They often develop a variety of psychosomatic or hypochondriacal complaints. The inflated self-image is rapidly deflated — self-esteem and any sense of self-value is lost.

Narcissistic personalities, and particularly the configuration of the Nobel Prize complex, are seen frequently enough in religious life. They tend to be seen more frequently when the religious group enjoys a certain esteem and regard in the life of the Church. Members of such highly esteemed and acclaimed orders are seen as having a special position in the Church, as living lives of special service and special dedication. The religious state generally is viewed as somehow more sacred and more elevated than the ordinary lay state. This element varies as a factor in respective religious groups — but remains a relevant factor for all of them. Similarly the priesthood is accorded respect and recognition as a special state of dedication and consecration to sacred things. Such states of life are viewed as sacred — as somehow set aside and removed from worldly concerns and accorded special religious acclaim. Participation of individuals in these states — by reason of special vows of religion or by reason of a special ordination rite — carries with it, then, the privilege of special status and special regard in the life of the Church. In these terms the religious life acquires a certain narcissistic appeal.

Narcissistic personalities can find a certain response to this basic appeal. Additional narcissistic appeal can be found in the trend in many religious groups to give their members special professional training. The opportunities for the expression and implementation of basic narcissistic needs and wishes are not lacking in religious life.

What, then, might the impact of excessive narcissism be on the life of obedience? Narcissistic individuals do not generally fit well into any pre-established framework. They tend to manifest a high degree of autonomy, initiative, and responsibility — they may in fact appear to all intents and purposes to possess a stable and well-functioning identity. But the underlying motive and quality of their world remains narcissistic. They are often capable of extraordinary initiative and are often willing to take on significant responsibilities — but they do so in the interest of narcissistic objectives of self-enhancement and self-aggrandizement. Their performance may reflect unusual talent or extraordinary capacity for organization and leadership. But their efforts and their accomplishments are always directed toward the narcissistic goal and expectation of acclaim and recognition.

The tendency of such individuals in the exercise of obedience is toward excessive initiative, autonomy, and responsibility. Difficulties arise when it becomes necessary for the narcissistic individual to mesh his initiative with the initiative of the superior or the initiatives of the rest of the religious group. They tend to assume excessive responsibility. In so doing, they tend to undermine the exercise of responsibility or the capacity for responsibility in others. The basic reason for this accumulation of responsibility is that along with responsibility goes recognition, influence, acclaim, and admiration. This hyperresponsibility in such narcissistic characters is associated with a hyperautonomy which tends to violate the autonomy of others. A narcissistic autonomy feeds off the autonomy of others — as it increases they must diminish.

Narcissistic difficulties in the exercise of obedience may also come at the level of the integration of identity. Such individuals may be capable of developing a sense of fidelity sufficient to permit them to establish a working sense of their own identity, not only as a free and autonomous self, but also as a functioning and participating member of the religious group. They may, however, have considerable difficulty with this. If participation in the religious group offers them certain narcissistic rewards, then such affiliation becomes meaningful for them. One risk they run under these conditions, however, is the risk of overidentification and overcommitment. The resulting identification comes not out of a sense of real commitment to the group and its goals as a major focus of purposeful activity, but flows out of the expectation and anticipation of recognition and acclaim resulting from one's contribution to the group and its goals.

This aspect of the narcissistic defect can become most telling at the level of generativity. Real generativity requires a capacity to transcend self and the interests of self to direct one's efforts toward enhancement of the group and toward bringing to full potential the new members of the coming generation within the group. The narcissistic fixation would make such a step of self-transcendence relatively difficult. But even here, if the group offers sufficient rewards and sufficient acclaim for going through the motions of generative interest, the narcissistic person may be able to give the appearance of generativity. The inner reality, however, is beyond him.

The narcissistic personality has difficulty in any meaningful or real relation with other people. He is so focused and intent on his own inner needs for acknowledgement and his own ambition for attainment and acclaim that meaningful interaction and relationship with others is impaired. He cannot enter any relationship as a subordinate or equal and be comfortable in the relationship. His difficulties with the authority relation are characteristic. He cannot engage in the process of mutual regulation and mutual regard essential to the workings of the authority relation — and correlatively of obedience. The superior's directive can come to the individual as a request to subordinate the individual's goals and ambitions to the objectives of the group. The narcissistic individual may be able to integrate such a request and respond to it, if it can somehow be turned to narcissistic ends. If not, there is bound to be a tension and conflict between narcissistic ends and group ends and purposes. Frequently in discussions of obedience, the subject arises of a confrontation between the will of the superior and the will of a subject. This is usually regarded as the ultimate test case of obedience. But what is usually involved in such extreme and hypothetical cases is a confrontation between the hyperautonomous and hyperresponsible will of the superior on one hand and the hyperautonomous and narcissistic will of the subject on the other. Such a confrontation becomes an expression of willfulness on both sides — and on both sides it is a violation of real obedience.

The whole area of the influence of personality types on obedience is large and little explored. We have tried to explore some of the personality styles and types that seemed to have more immediate relevance to the workings of obedience. These particular personality patterns have the advantage of revealing some of the basic personality dynamics and conflicts which can have an effect on the exercise of obedience — rather than on its formal organization. They are also patterns of personality organization and traits that enjoy a certain incidence in religious groups. There is an advantage, too, in viewing influences on obedience from the point of view of pathology in that it offers another perspective which can enrich our understanding of what goes into the complex workings of obedience.

The major emphasis of this consideration, however, is on the fact that obedience, particularly in the religious context, is not simply a matter of commands issued and responses made in a sort of psychological vacuum. Rather obedience is the complex product and process of a life-long development whose roots and whose implications reach far beyond the immediate context of an order from a superior, and whose patterns and resolutions are complex integrations of multiple influential factors and determinants. Obedience is a derivative of and an expression of the individual's inner personality structure. That structure represents the moving end point of a continual process of growth and integration that begins at birth and does not reach any conclusion as long as there is life.

CHAPTER XXX

# THE PROBLEM OF DISOBEDIENCE

## Introduction

There are many facets to obedience — all of which can contribute in some measure to our understanding of obedience and what it entails. In the preceding chapter, we have been considering deviations of obedience from the perspective of personality organization and the developmental defects lying behind them. In this chapter, I want to focus on deviance in obedience itself. In our effort to understand obedience, it is imperative that we take account of disobedience — for it is only in a dialectic of opposites that certain aspects of the exercise of obedience can emerge with the needed clarity. In short, if we are to understand obedience, we must also try to understand disobedience.

The problem of obedience can be approached from several perspectives. I would like to treat the problem of obedience here in a broader context of meaningful change and adaptation as it affects the group. In so doing, the developmental considerations we have already discussed[1] will play an important part. Deviations in authority and obedience reflect deeper and broader considerations than merely the immediate execution of a given order in the concrete context — or in the case of disobedience, the failure to execute such an order. But even more important for the understanding of disobedience is the clear understanding of what disobedience is not. In terms of our preceding discussion, it is no longer adequate to define disobedience in merely operational terms. Failure to execute the superior's commmand or positive opposition to the superior's expressed will are not necessarily expressions of disobedience. Our analysis removes the reflection on disobedience from a merely operational or behavioral level to a deeper and broader level of intention and ethical commitment.

[1] See the discussion of developmental aspects in chapter XXVII above.

## Obedience and Social Process

It will be helpful in this regard to look at the problem of disobedience from the point of view of social process and social change. Social changes and the processes involved in it can be looked at from two more or less polar points of view. One can evaluate and maintain attitudes toward social change based on either the primacy of order or the primacy of conflict. The point of view stressing primacy of order would hold a view of society as a unified system of action. The unity of the social organism is insured by a shared culture embracing a certain general consensus about values and goals and about the means for achieving them. This social organization is consolidated by specific means of communication and by a certain form of political organization. Society in this perspective is viewed as a form of natural organism whose function is maintaining social control. Social control is a necessary good for which society exists. The view of human nature in such a perspective is that man is a creature of composite drives and needs requiring socialization and extrinsic regulation. From a religious point of view, the view of social process based on order would seem to imply a distinction between morally superior and morally inferior men. The morally superior would be expected to exercise control over and maintain social constraints on the morally inferior. Social process would be the organizational action by which the social control of superior over inferior was to be established and maintained.

The primary objective and major value to which such a society directs its efforts is maintenance of social order, balance, stability, and authoritative control. The norm of positive and healthy participation in the society is acceptance of extant values and conformity to present social structures and forms of organization. The ideology implicit in existing social structure thus becomes normative. Any deviation from this framework is seen as pathological. The society moves to correct deviations from the established norm through the extension of social control and the more effective institutionalization of existing values. The system places an emphasis on the need for rehabilitation of deviant individuals and helping them to overcome their pathology by healthy acceptance of existing norms. Examples of this form of social control could be found in the Soviet use of psychiatric diagnoses and institutionalization to control political deviants under the former communist regime. There is stress in such a system on the need for maintaining the system itself and for working within it. Correction of evils in the social system is implemented by way of administrative reorganization and extension of control, rather than by any real change in the system. The primary value is placed on maintaining order — which comes to be identified with preservation and extension of the existing ordering structures of the society. The operative presumption is that if some control is good, more is better.

It is possible to view social process and social change from the opposite perspective of conflict. The view of society based on order took the view that order and the preservation of order — implicitly this order, the present order — was the primary objective and highest value of society; the view of society based on conflict takes an opposite stand. Rather than maximizing the advantages of order, it tends to minimize them and prefers to emphasize the need for conflict and freedom in the social system. It views the social organism not as a unity, but as a heterogeneous aggregate of subgroupings, each with divergent and conflicting goals, points of view and values. Society is not a unified and transcendent system of structures and values to which its members must adjust. It is a creation of those who take part in it — an expression and extension of their wishes, needs, purposes and actions. Man is not made for society — society is made for man, and by man. If it does not suit his needs and purposes, if it does not accomplish what he wishes it to accomplish, he can change it. The attitude to change, therefore, is quite positive in this view. It sees change as a necessary and vital part of social processes. Change and the processes of change become a primary value in this view of society. Moreover, this view places man in the center of the schema — man, as a freely autonomous and functional participant in social processes, becomes the architect and arbitrer of social organization and change.

The approach from the point of view of conflict, then, puts a high value and an emphasis on the free and autonomous action of the members of society — rather than the insistence on order and social control that characterizes the point of view of order. Striving of individuals toward ever-evolving standards and satisfaction of unfulfilled aspirations and goals of subgroups within the society are viewed as positive and healthy processes. This point of view is often governed by a more or less utopian view of the ideal organization and functioning of society — an ideal toward which society is constantly seen as striving. In this light, deviant behavior is not seen as necessarily destructive or pathological, but rather as potentially having a positive and adaptive function insofar as it enables the society to progress toward the social ideal. Where deviant behavior results in the challenging or overthrow of existing social structures or institutions, it is seen as part of the necessary process of change. Conversely, any impediments to the realization of the social ideal are seen as an illegitimate obstruction to necessary process. Extension of existing forms of organization or institutional control are regarded as illegitimate extensions of social control, as violations of individual rights, or as exploitations of minority subgroups who lack the resources for social control.

The mechanisms for correction of social ills that this view would endorse involve disruption of social organization and radical transformation of existing structures and forms of social interaction. The objective of social reformation is often put in the extreme form of revolutionary overthrow of the existing system. Norms of social direction and control, therefore, tend to be based on the objectives and ambitions of underprivileged and subordinate minorities — who are striving for greater status and power in the social structure. The underlying philosophy of change contains as part of its credo the belief that meaningful change cannot take place without destruction of the existing system. Change within the system is regarded as impossible — or at least involving too much effort or too much time. The philosophy of change is also based on the belief that change is an end in itself — that any change must somehow be a change for the better.

## COMPETING IDEOLOGIES

Both of these persuasions — polarized as they are — represent ideological positions. As ideologies they demand unreserved commitment from their adherents. Ideologies have an internal dynamism toward polarization. The determinants of whether an individual is to embrace one or the other of these ideologies are multiple and complex, but the psychological factors play a predominant role. Whether an individual stresses the need for order or whether he stresses the need for change stems in large measure from the history of his life experience, particularly with authority figures. We have already discussed at length some of the developmental aspects of attitudes toward authority and obedience. It is inevitable that the attitude toward disobedience should be critically influenced by one's personal inclinations and persuasions about the relative necessity for order or for change.

The central problem for any authority — whether it be civil, ecclesiastical, or religious — is not to commit itself to either ideology, but to find a way to maximize both elements within the struc-

ture of the social organization and function. It is the function of authority to maximize both order and change. Authority strives for the maximal degree of order within the social structure that is consistent with a minimal degree of freedom. At the same time, it strives for the maximal degree of freedom that is consistent with a minimal degree of order. The order-perspective tends to emphasize the need for order to the detriment of freedom. The conflict perspective tends to emphasize the need for change and freedom to the detriment of order. Our objective in our consideration of obedience in general, and specifically in the discussion of disobedience, is to avoid the ideological seduction of either polarity. We are striving to achieve a balanced view in which the need for freedom and change are proportioned to the need for order, and in which the need for order does not violate the necessities of freedom and progress.

## THE MEANING OF DISOBEDIENCE

The problem of disobedience, then, is in large measure a problem of identifying it and not confusing it with other elements that may have a legitimate and proper place in the life of the group. I will be using the term "disobedience" here with specific reference related directly to the overall context of the present study. If we can think of obedience as the response that a subject makes to the superior's initiative within the functional context of an authority relation, we can include under the label of "disobedience" the subject's refusal to make such a response, his avoidance of such a response for whatever reason, his withdrawal from a meaningful participation in the authority relation — including, therefore, his involvement in those processes that constitute the essence of the authority relation, namely mutual regulation and interaction, autonomous self-commitment, responsibility and initiative. Disobedience, therefore, can take the form of rebellious refusal and withdrawal, or it can take the form of excessive conformity and unquestioning and irresponsible subordination and submission.

It is critically important, therefore, that we establish the distinction between disobedience and dissent. Disobedience is a failure of obedience — a failure that may, as we have seen, have developmental antecedents as well as situational determinants. Dissent, however, is not a failure of obedience. Acknowledge of this principle is implicit in Ignatius' recognition of representation[2] in both the *Constitutions*

[2] See the discussion of representation in chapter XXII above.

and in his own exercise of obedience. As regarded here, it is rather an expression of obedience and a necessary part of it. I would like to focus at this point on the necessity of dissent for the functioning of religious obedience.

## RELIGIOUS DISSENT

We can see that in any society, then, meaningful dissent is essential to continuing vitality and adaptive functioning of the group. This is no less true for the religious group. If we put ourselves in the position of equating disobedience with dissent, we thereby condemn ourselves to a static posture and run the risk of stagnation and decay. If Ignatius' formulations regarding obedience were taken literally, the religious group would be exposing itself to this risk. If meaningful dissent is an essential part of the process by which social groups bring about change within themselves, we cannot thereby think that all dissent is constructive or progressive. Dissent may be — and often is — counterproductive or destructive. One does not always know when dissent is productive and when it is not.

The productive effects of dissent do not necessarily result from the dissent itself, but involve the complex interplay of a variety of factors. Potentially productive and meaningful dissent can be subverted and turned to destructive purposes by other forces at work in the group over which the dissenter may have no control. But the risk of negative effects is part of the price one must pay for the potentiality of growth and the continued vitality of the group. Thus one can view dissent from either of the alternative perspectives of order or change. Those who look at it from the perspective of order will see it in more destructive terms. Those who look at it from the perspective of change will see it as more positive and productive. Plainly it can be either. It is important, however, to realize that a polarization of one's view or ideological commitment can determine how one looks at it.

## DISSENT IN SOCIAL STRUCTURES

This discussion takes the point of view that dissent is a necessary part of the functioning of any social organization. Democratic societies, in fact, make dissent an integral part of the institutionalized social process. The essence of the democratic process is not only that the social order is governed by the will of the majority — but more importantly that the mechanisms exist by which the minority can effectively influence the majority to change its opinion and adopt the point of view of the minority. Democratic political organization, therefore, is based on an institutionalized means by which the will of the minority can influence and change the will of the majority. The process is more difficult for autocratic or totalitarian regimes in which the means for social change are not so readily available. In such highly structured and ordered societies, the mechanisms of social change are restricted with the result that revolution and rebellion become more necessary as means of social revision.

There is a history of meaningful dissent within the Church. The inviolability of the Christian conscience has been an essential part of Christian belief from the beginning. This remains true even though the theological rationale by which the primacy of conscience was defended, even in the face of and against the community of belief, was not always secure. There was an emphasis on "thinking with the Church" which reflected a basic order-perspective and which was part of the traditional hierarchical (vertical) view of authority in the Church. This mentality found partial expression in Ignatius' rules for thinking with the Church in the *Spiritual Exercises* [352-370].[3] But there has also been a persistent acknowledgement of the *consensus fidelium*, reflecting a dialectical process in the Church, along with an acknowledgment of a prophetic tradition that extends through all ages of the Church.

The Church's capacity to integrate diverse life styles and intellectual currents is a tribute to its resiliency and inner strength. It has achieved through the centuries a striking unity in diversity at all levels of its organization. The history of the great councils is a marvelous record of capacity for inner dialectic within the Church and of its capacity to embrace divergent cultures and modalities of thought. The argument was often divisive, but also integrative. The essential transition from an historically embedded and discursive modality of the revelation to the theological reflection, based on an essentially Greek and Western modality of thought and expression, was a cultural and religious achievement of the first order. It was wrought through the vicissitudes of dissent and debate — and ultimately provided an essential basis for the continued intellectual vitality of the Christian dogma, as well as the enrichment of Christian belief.

The dynamic process of dissent can be traced through every age of the Church's life. Closer to our own experience, Vatican Council II provided an unparalleled example of the effective operation of meaningful dissent. The council fathers refused to accept the Roman

[3] See the discussion of these rules in chapter XVII above.

schemata of the first session. They refused to submit to this form of doctrinal imposition and insisted on their prerogatives to question and debate. They acted with responsibility and initiative, and their dissent set an example of Christian independence in keeping with the best tradition in the Church. Their dissent was the basis on which a new consensus was evolved that has had profound effects on the life of the Church.

## Dissent and Obedience

The ideological commitment to order has a tendency to view dissent as threatening and to respond to it with a polarizing attitude of repression. It tends to view dissent as a form of disobedience. At the same time, it tends to idealize the lack of dissent and to characterize obedience in those terms. The ideology of order, therefore, tends to push dissent in the direction of disobedience, and to push obedience in the direction of submissive conformity. The impact of the argument that we have been developing here, however, is that real obedience and dissent are not at all incompatible. We must recognize, it seems to me, that dissent may be an expression of disobedience — but we must also recognize that it may be an expression of obedience.

The essential discrimination lies in the basic notion of true obedience — as embracing trust, autonomy, responsibility, initiative, fidelity, identity, and ultimately generativity. True obedience embraces and builds itself out of these elements. Any posture that violates or eliminates these qualities represents a deviation from true obedience. Consequently, dissent that serves as an expression of hyperautonomy is to that extent a deviation from obedience. Similarly submission, which violates responsibility and initiative, represents another deviation from obedience. Dissent that does not stem from an inner sense of identity and fidelity is disobedience. Conformity that stems from a lack of identity and responsible initiative is also disobedience.

We can express some of this aspect of the problem of disobedience in terms of the question of loyalty. Dissent and loyalty are by no means opposed — even though the opposition is often postulated. Loyal dissent is an aspect of true obedience and can be meaningfully productive. Disloyal dissent, however, is divisive and destructive and runs the risk of being counterproductive. Loyalty is in effect an expression of an inner sense of fidelity. Loyalty is the outer face of the inner fidelity linked closely with and expressing the consolidation of identity.

Fidelity is the inner capacity, the inner strength, which makes it possible to pledge and sustain loyalties (Erikson 1968). Loyalty, thus, is the external expression of the capacity to commit oneself in meaningful and purposeful ways to abiding relationships with other persons, to social structures, institutions and values that provide a supportive context for the emergence and sustaining of individual identity. Loyalty in this sense is far from a submission of oneself or a conformity to environmental structures. Essentially it involves an affirmation of one's self, one's individuality, one's identity. Loyalty implies that essential developmental tasks have advanced to such a level and at such a pace that the emerging sense of one's self has been integrated with social and cultural realities. The integration with these realities and structures gives rise to and sustains the inner sense of meaning of the self which reflects the mutual regulation and reinforcement of man's inner identity and the cultural forces that shape his world.

Fidelity is a commitment of oneself in meaningful and sustained ways. But we must also be clear about what objects one can commit oneself to with such abiding loyalty. We should not confuse loyalty with conformity to existing structures and patterns of action — just as we should not confuse disloyalty with a challenging of existing order or a wish to change it. Fidelity and loyalty pertain to abiding aspects of human relations and structures intimately related to the maintenance of identity. This aspect of social structures is embodied in those dimensions of social experience that carry and sustain the inner meaning which gives them life, purpose and vitality. That aspect of social structures and organizations which conveys and embraces their inner meaningfulness and purposefulness is values. It is the respective value-systems which embody, express, integrate, and ratify the existence of social structures. Social structures exist in a sense as an embodiment of and for the sustaining of certain values. Sharing in such social structures and their respective functions involves at its deepest level a sharing in the value system that vitalizes and gives purposeful existence to these structures. Fidelity and loyalty, as abiding and identity-sustaining commitments of self, are directed to the perduring values that generate and give reality and form to social structures and institutions.

Loyalty, then, is not a matter of acceptance, conformity to, or commitment to existing structures and patterns of organization. It is not a matter of commitment to the shape or form to the superficial and accidental aspects of social realities. It is rather a commitment to the abiding realities and valued ideals lying behind and vitalizing social structures. It is a commitment to sustain existing structures and their functioning, only insofar as they embody and express in real and meaningful ways the inner reality, the valued goals and ideals for which the structure was created and for whose attainment the structure continues to exist. Fidelity and loyalty, then, are sources of strength in social institutions. They bring a new strength and new vitality which reinforces and sustains the intention of the group toward meaningful goals and values. The strength of organizations is in the striving for and sustaining of such meaningful values and goals.

## FIDELITY AND FREEDOM

Fidelity and freedom are correlative — one cannot exist without the other. There cannot be fidelity without freedom — and there cannot be freedom without fidelity. If man is not free, his loyalty becomes mere conformity. Freedom enables him to sustain a commitment to those values which are an expression of his own inner identity — and which form the bond by which he shares in the life of the group and is identified with its goals and intents and purposes. Without freedom there is no valuing, no valued intention, no purposeful striving and self-direction. There is only submission and conformity. And if man is not faithful, his freedom becomes only a negative potentiality — a freedom to rebel. Freedom that has only the potentiality for rebellion is destructive and hopeless. It falls short of real freedom which is exercised in responsibility and valued purposefulness. It becomes license. Thus fidelity without freedom is mere conformity. Freedom without fidelity is rebelliousness and license. These are both forms of disobedience.

If loyalty can be viewed as an affirmation of self, it is at the same time an affirmation of that to which one commits oneself. The commitment is specifically to sustain, vitalize, and take responsibility for that to which one is committed. It involves a willingness to take appropriate initiatives so that the values inherent in the object of loyalty be sustained or grow. Implicit in such commitment is a readiness to foster and improve the group or organization — not only because it is a significant expression of and support for one's own identity, but precisely because its preservation and development are linked to the extension and enhancement of the values inherent in it. Personal commitment in loyalty to a group or structure guarantees preservation of these values as well as their continued availability to those who are to come after. Thus issues of loyalty and fidelity extend themselves to the concerns of generativity. Care and concern for future generations is maintained by loyalty to the social institutions which preserve and sustain those values to which one has committed oneself, with which one identifies, and which serve as sustaining resources for one's own inner sense of identity. Thus the strengths and beliefs of one generation are made available to the coming generation.

## DISSENT AND GROWTH

Growth reflects the process of change, and as such it involves risks and dangers. Any change from the old to the new must involve a surrender of the old and an acceptance of the new. There is inevitable conflict in this and it cannot be escaped. The individual will unavoidably be torn between attachment and allegiance to the past and desire for what is new. One must learn to give up the past, to suffer loss of the old and familiar, and to commit himself to the uncertainty and risk of the new and unfamiliar. The risk in growth is great. The potentialities for progression and improvement also carry with them potentiality for regression to earlier or less mature solutions. All growth — biological or psychological or social — involves both progression and regression. If we seek the benefits of progression and development, we must tolerate the risk of regression. Psychologically, the processes of progression and regression are closely intertwined. Psychological development and the resolution of conflict require a capacity or a productive regression to inner sources of strength to provide the resources for continued growth.

Dissent is the social analogue of internal conflict. It provides the stimulus and the motive for social growth. It is likewise not without risks. Dissent runs the risk of disloyalty. It is advisable, therefore, that we guard ourselves against the mistaken identification of dissent and disloyalty. Dissent and loyalty, as we have observed, are not only opposites, but their coexistence and mutual interaction are essential to the continuing process of social growth. We can understand, then, that dissent is not to be equated with disloyalty, just as we can also understand that the interaction of dissent and loyalty in the process of obedience is not only desirable, but in many ways necessary.

## LOYALTY AND DISSENT

But I would like to advance the argument a step further. In the view I am proposing here, dissent is a necessary and essential part of true loyalty. Without it true loyalty cannot exist. Loyalty involves not so much a commitment to an institution or organization as it presently exists, but rather a commitment to a set of values that the organization or institution embodies, preserves and promotes. It is a commitment to improve and develop the organization so that it more effectively embodies and expresses the values for and by which it exists. Such a commitment constitutes a commitment to continuing growth, change, development, progress. It involves a willingness and a readiness to dissent. Without it loyalty becomes an empty shadow — partial and ineffective — mere conformity. With it loyalty becomes a source of strength and vitality for the group or institution. Loyalty and dissent, therefore, form a necessary dialectic in which each is dependent on the other — a dialectic in which, optimally, each embraces and modulates the other in a continuing process of mutual regulation.

The dialectic of loyalty and dissent is not without risks. The primary threat to this delicate balance of modulating processes stems from ideology and ideological commitments. Ideological commitment involves a closure on accepted truth and an intolerance of ambiguity that derive from an inner insecurity and lack of strength. The conflict and tension inherent in the dialectic becomes intolerable. The anxiety can only find relief by suppression of either dissent or of loyalty. Suppression of dissent pushes in the direction of authoritarian repressiveness and rigidity.

Suppression of loyalty produces destructive rebelliousness. Thus ideological commitment tends to destroy the dialectic. As a consequence, it leads to polarization of extremes. Dissent is radicalized and becomes disloyalty. Loyalty is radicalized and becomes submissive conformity. In either case, real obedience is destroyed. Ideological commitment creates and fosters disobedience. We must somehow come to realize that in true obedience there is room for loyalty and there is room for dissent. Moreover, there is room for dissent in loyalty and room for loyalty in dissent. The young — in addition to all those who are subject to obedience — must learn that there is room for loyalty in their need to dissent. Their elders — particularly those who hold and exercise authority — must come to recognize that dissent does not necessarily imply disloyalty, but that it may indeed be an expression of a genuine loyalty.

## CONCLUSION

In evaluating the problem of disobedience, then, we must look beyond mere behaviors and patterns of activity. We must look to the level of inner intentions and convictions and values. Obedience reaches into the innermost recesses of the human psyche and our consideration of it must touch it at its most relevant and meaningful level. The traditional identification of disobedience with dissent or deviance cannot now be sustained. The presumption that disobedience and disloyalty are coextensive is no longer operative. Obedience is, in effect, the subject's participation in the authority relation. Within that relation he must respond with freedom, responsibility and initiative — or else his response is not obedience at all, but a caricature of obedience. Obedience is an engagement of the subject's autonomous and responsible initiative. Without it, any human group and its structures — including the religious group — will wither and die.

# CHAPTER XXXI

# RELIGIOUS OBEDIENCE

## Introduction

Ignatius was deeply concerned about the quality of obedience. He made it a central tenet of his *Constitutions* and insisted on it as a primary dimension of his religious vision. The motif of obedience resonates throughout the *Spiritual Exercises*, and we might imagine that the primary direction of the Exercises themselves was to draw the exercitant toward ever greater responsiveness to divine initiatives and thus to ever greater obedience to God's will and grace. Our understanding of the vicissitudes of obedience is an essential aspect of our delving into the psychological roots of Ignatian spirituality.

The structure of authority and obedience Ignatius created in his *Constitutions* was more along the model of a team than anything authoritarian, as would be suggested in a military model. Authority and obedience were necessary since they provide efficiency in the organization and direction of corporate enterprises. Ignatius buffers the tendency of authority to become authoritarian by subjection of the General to a congregation representing the whole Society and by mandatory consultation with official consultors and other advisers. He desired that decisions of superiors be made in the most sensible and informed way possible, meaning that the superior governs best when he functions in collaboration and consultation with his fellow Jesuits working supportively and cooperatively as a team. Neither the exercise of authority nor individual initiative should operate in isolation, but but rather in a harmonious integration characteristic of a fellowship of workers in the vineyard of the Lord bound together in love and work, in freedom and initiative, together with authority and mutual dependence.

A model for this kind of relationship can be found in the fellowship of Ignatius and his first companions. They began by taking stock of the sources of their union, especially the companionship they experienced, despite their obvious differences, and the attraction to following in the footsteps of Christ and working together for the good of souls. It was this experience that was distilled into the *Exercises* and later codified in the *Constitutions.* As far as the authority relation goes, then, superior and subject were not bound together by a mandate of authority, but as companions sharing a spiritual venture based on a deep bond of fellowship in the Lord (Emonet 1990).

## THE RELIGIOUS CONTEXT

I would like to make a few comments about the nature and functioning of religious obedience as such. These reflections move beyond the limits of psychology, but they are implicit in and derivative from the discussion of psychological elements in obedience that goes before. In this sense these comments can be regarded as at least derivatively psychological.

Religious obedience functions in a specifically religious context which has theological relevance and meaning. The values called into focus in this context are specifically religious. Subjection in religious obedience has particular intents and purposes that have to do with an individual's earnest commitment of himself to the fulfillment of God's will. Subjection and identification in the religious context are in part motivated by grace and constitute a response not merely to human initiatives, but to the salvific initiatives of grace as well. Thus the operation of obedience takes place not merely in terms of the dialectic of human intents and values, but also in terms of the inner silent dialectic of the human with the initiatives and movements of grace. The supernatural consideration lends an added dimension that raises considerations of mere psychological relevance and impact to a more profound and meaningful level.

The concept of obedience presented in the preceding pages bases itself on certain critical elements in the mature personality — specifically on the capacity for trust, autonomy, initiative, responsibility and faithful commitment. It is basic to my view of the action of grace and the responsiveness to grace of the human personality that grace does not violate nature, but in fact perfects it. Grace does not diminish human freedom, but confirms and enhances it (Meissner 1966, 1987). If grace is a basic motivating force in religious obedience, obedience must embrace and express that freedom. Moreover, I presume that where grace is operative, freedom must be enhanced — and conversely, where freedom is curtailed, grace (or at least its effects) is diminished. The dimensions of human personality that I have delineated here are the elements of personality that I consider essential to the capacity for free action and determination of self. The view of personality development that has been presented carries as an implicit and underlying theme the notion that increasing maturity involves an emerging capacity for autonomous judgment and action and an increasing capacity for free self-expression and self-direction. The correlation of levels of development with aspects of the integration of obedience carries the implication that development toward mature obedience is at the same time a development in the inner freedom and autonomy of the human person.

The burden of the preceding analysis is also that obedience implies a capacity for responsibility and initiative. Initiative, responsibility and freedom are all correlative — and constitute essential aspects of mature obedience. The defect of any one of these elements means a diminution, an impairment, a regression in the capacity for mature obedience.

## GOD'S WILL

Obedience, as a religious phenomenon, is often cast in terms of the acceptance and submission to God 's will. More traditional views of obedience have tended to understand that proposition in terms of a divine will that was somehow prior to human action and separate from it. God's will was conceived as existing in the mind of God prior to any human thought or decision. God's will was mysteriously communicated to those who held positions of authority, who subsequently communicated the divine intentions to subordinate levels of the hierarchy. At each level, the divine purpose was accepted and responded to with compliant fulfillment. That was at least the idealized conception. However, such a conception left no room for human motives and functioning. It was never quite clear how divine intentions were communicated. Nor was any acknowledgement made of the obvious contribution of human thought and action — in the form of basic human motives, mistakes, ignorance, misconceptions, errors in judgment and intention, stupidity — and all the imperfections that flesh is heir to. This was all perfectly obvious, of course, but it was somehow submerged in a theological frame of reference that left no room for human purposes and processes to play themselves out.

One can also view the divine will as expressing itself in and through human thought and action, through human purposes and intentions. In this latter view, the divine will is no longer seen as transcendent and preceding human intentions, but rather as immanent within human actions and as expressing itself concurrently through human operations. There is certainly less security in this. There is less clarity and force — for one can no longer say with unquestioning and unquestionable conviction "This is God's will!" The process is less one of possessing God's will than it is a process of seeking God's will.

Obedience, therefore, becomes no longer merely a process of accepting and submitting to God's will, but a process of finding God's will by active engagement and dialectic within the authority relation. Finding God's will calls upon the initiative and responsibility of each individual religious, because only through active subjection does God's will for him in the present set of concrete circumstances become available to him. God's will becomes manifest only through the mutual regulation and responsible responsiveness of the authority relation. If a superior or a subject avoids, for whatever reason, the essential dialectic of the authority relation, they are avoiding the immediate context within which God's will is to be sought and found.

## DISCERNMENT

God's will and its seeking and finding, therefore, is a matter of discernment.[1] It is a matter of personal discernment, but also of mutual discernment within the authority relation. Discernment, then, is an essential ingredient in the process of mutual regulation central to the authority relation. There has been a great deal written about discernment so that I need not go into it here, except to note that the Ignatian notion of discernment is integral to his whole approach to finding the will of God. Ignatian discernment, however, was conceived in the framework of the individual soul standing before God. That framework embraces only part of the total context. The relevant discernment for the working out of obedience, since obedience is essentially the subject's response and responsiveness to authority, must take place in the interaction among the respective sources of authority — superior, subject and community. Ignatian discernment is thus conceived here as an integral part of the overall discernment process relevant to obedience. It is an essential ingredient, but it must be integrated with other interpersonal and group processes of discernment.

Pointing out the larger context of discernment leads to a further aspect of religious obedience. It underlines the fact that obedience is

[1] This assertion can only be made in the light of previous qualifications regarding the limitations of discernment in determining the will of God, as contained in chapters XV and XVI, and especially chapter XIII above. See also the more extended treatment of the relation of discernment to determining God's will in Toner (1991).

always in some degree corporate — whether obedience be exercised in a family context, an institutional context, or a social context. Obedience functions within the authority relation which forms a part of a social structure, a group. This is particularly relevant in religious obedience which is always embedded in and part of the religious group process. Obedience is thus never simply a matter of mutual regulation and discernment between an individual subject and an individual superior. The very interaction is group based and group derived. It is governed by values that are shared values in the group context. It necessarily involves reference to group goals, intents, purposes, objectives, attitudes, etc.

The authority relation is the primary point at which individual values and intents are brought into interaction with and integration with group values and intents. What superior and subject bring to and contribute to the authority relation are in part derivative from and expressive of group influences and group processes providing the context within which the authority relation functions. The corporate aspect of religious obedience is considerably more prominent than in any other context of obedience, precisely because it is the intention of the group organization to place specifically designated and acknowledged group goals above relevant but divergent individual goals. The integration and congruence of individual and common goals is all the more important in that religious life and religious obedience is a total life commitment which embraces all of the individual's energies and capacities. No other functional context of obedience makes such a claim.

## OBEDIENCE IN THE RELIGIOUS GROUP

This tension, articulated around the office of Provincial in the Society of Jesus, is well expressed by Emonet (1990):

> In practical terms, for the Provincial this means "works" to be looked after, apostolic mandates to be honoured and new paths to be opened up, while always respecting the vocation of his fellow Jesuits, their personal talents, their spiritual freedom and the deep desires which inspire them and which at times do not necessarily fit in with the overall plan of the Province. This leads to considerable tension, which is lived out on the level of each individual Jesuit's personal membership in the Society. On the one hand there is the body, which finds its unity in the bond of charity and expresses it in the relationship of obedience, while on the other there is the personal life-commitment of each member. There is a two-

> fold temptation lurking for the person who is responsible for the whole group: that of reducing the tension by overly unilateral recourse to authoritarian measures in order to safeguard the common good, and that of favouring personal projects at the risk of splitting the group. (p. 111)

Religious obedience is, then, uniquely a matter of an inner dialectic between the elements of individuality and corporality or community. Both the individual and the corporate entity stand over against each other as independent and autonomous sources of authority. The authority of the individual does not derive from or depend on the authority of the group — and the authority of the group does not derive from or depend on the authority of the individual. The vitality and capacity of the religious group for effective functioning, however, depends on the dialectical integration of both in the practical and concrete working through of authority and obedience.

It seems to me that in some of his most insightful and provocative writing, Rahner (1964) has articulated the theological foundation which carries immediate relevance for the consideration we are offering here. He has brought into focus the role of individuality in the structure and functioning of the Church. This is directly relevant to what we have been saying in terms of the psychological structure of authority and the function of obedience. The individual emerges in the maturity of his autonomy and identity and, by the validity of his faithful commitment and engagement in the authority relation, as an authentic source of authority in the group structure. Rahner has delineated the role of individuality in the Church expressed in terms of a charismatic element and in terms of the prophetic role. Authentic charisma, guided and guaranteed by the inspiration of the Spirit, is not limited to the authoritative structures of the community or of legitimate authority. It is likewise resident in the individual and thereby provides an authentic expression of and channel for the recognition of God's will. Charisma, moreover, cannot be regulated or determined by legitimate authority. It carries within itself an authority that is independent of the recognizable legitimate authority of the Church and its formal structure. Its validity and authenticity derive from the inner effects of the Spirit rather than from the formal and official designation of the Church.

Thus those who hold legitimate authority must recognize that it is not they alone who guide and rule. The effective action of the Spirit guarantees that they should not — and in significant matters do not. The charismatic element means that subjects cannot be conceived of simply as members of the organization whose function is to

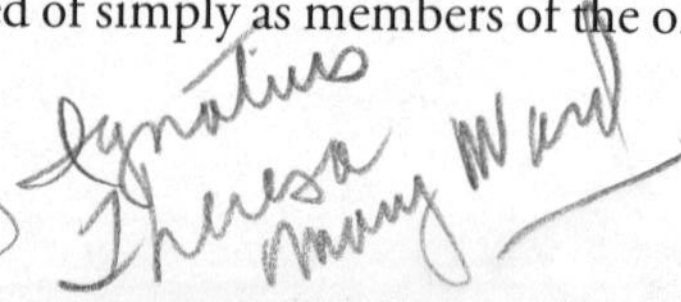

carry out and submit to orders from above. They are guided and responsive to inner promptings and initiatives. These promptings can be viewed in a theological perspective as reflecting the direct action of the Spirit who can and does guide his Church directly and who is not limited to communicating his divine will through ecclesiastic or legitimate channels. Rahner writes:

> In the Church there are not only movements that have to owe their origin to higher authority in order to be legitimate. The official hierarchy must not be surprised or annoyed if there is stirring in the life of the spirit before this has been scheduled in the Church's ministries. And subordinates must not think they have nothing definite to do until an order is handed down from above. There are actions that God wills even before the starting signal has been given by the hierarchy, and in directions that have not yet been positively approved and laid down officially. . . . Executive authority in the Church must, therefore, always cultivate the awareness that it is not, and may not be, the self-sufficient planner, as though in a totalitarian system, of all that is done in the Church. It must keep alive the consciousness that it is a duty and not a gracious condescension when it accepts suggestions from 'below'; that it must not from the start pull all the strings; and that the higher, and, in fact, charismatic wisdom can sometimes be with the subordinate, and that the charismatic wisdom of office may consist in not shutting itself off from such higher wisdom. Ecclesiastical authority must always realize that a subject's duty of obedience, and the fact that such authority has competence to determine what its competence is, neither makes the subordinate devoid of rights as against authority, nor guarantees that every action of authority in the individual case is correct and the one willed by God. (Rahner 1964, pp. 70-71)

The charismatic element is expressed in the subjection that is integral to mature obedience. The act and process of subjection is internally rooted in individual freedom and fidelity. Charisma and human freedom are thus inextricably linked. The respect for the function of charisma within the Church is equivalently respect for the function of human freedom. It cannot legitimately be limited or programmed within the directives of legitimate authority. The operation of these various elements and their interplay is no less relevant in the immediate context of the religious group than in the broader context of the Church. The charismatic element is at work in the religious group as well and plays itself out in the workings of obedience. It is resident in the free subjection by which the subject establishes and confirms his subjecthood and subjectivity.

## THE ETHICS OF RESPONSIBILITY

There is an ethical dimension to these concerns which is fundamental. We can harken back to the distinction that Max Weber drew between an *ethics of responsibility* and an *ethics of ultimate ends*. The ethics of responsibility looks to the consequences and verifiable results of action. It concerns itself with personal consequences in the immediate present and concrete circumstances. An extreme expression of the ethics of responsibility can be seen in so-called "situation ethics." The ethics of ultimate ends, on the other hand, concerns itself with principles rather than with consequences. An act is right and good insofar as it is consistent with certain grasped and articulated moral principles. Traditional moral theology has tended to emphasize principles rather than consequences.

The ethics of responsibility recognizes and acknowledges the ethical validity of the individual judgment and the particular existential circumstances — as having ethical relevance and impact quite independently of the deductive derivation from ethical principles or the general case. As Rahner has pointed out in his reflections on the place of the particular and individuality in the election of St. Ignatius,  Ignatius presupposes a philosophy of human existence and an ethical position according to which moral decision in its unique individuality is not reducible to general normative ethical principles. Moral judgment and decision involves an element which is positive and unique and cannot be regarded as a negative limitation of the general. The object of an election, therefore, in an Ignatian perspective, contains a universal element. But its content cannot be limited to that, nor can it simply be discerned in terms of a syllogistic deduction from previously enunciated and apprehended moral principles. Otherwise the structure and integration of Ignatian elective activity becomes empty and meaningless. There is need to integrate this basic insight into the Ignatian election with his views on obedience. Insofar as election involves individual discernment and discrimination as well as the exercise of responsibility as autonomously grasped and expressed, obedience to God's will cannot be conceived merely in terms of submission and acceptance. It must be discerned and personally responded to. The rhetoric of obedience, expressed for example in the famous letter on obedience from Ignatius to the community at Coimbra, is not immediately congruent with this aspect of the election.

Subjection, then, rooted in responsible initiative, identity and fidelity is an expression of free individuality and autonomy. As such it is intrinsically ordered to the specific existential concerns of an ethic of responsibility. Subjection, however, becomes meaningless unless it is considered in the context of the authority relation. Subjection, as we have seen, is governed by and guided by the values that permeate and in part constitute the ethical matrix of the authority relation. The dialectic between personal values and communal values is intrinsic to the functioning of obedience. The shared values of the group are in this sense prior to the responsible subjection of the individual and must be integrated in the functioning of obedience. Thus the ethics of responsibility, which is resident in individual subjection and discernment, must engage the ethics of the community and its pre-existent structures. The dialectic to which we have addressed ourselves as essential to mature obedience is thus a dialectic embedded in a value matrix and specific concerned with ethical functions.

The view of obedience which has been dominant in the Church and religious groups and which stresses the vertical and hierarchical nature of authority is based on and functions in terms of a more or less rigid ethics that is closer to the ethics of ultimate ends. It places an emphasis and high value on more bureaucratic forms of organization and operation. The functioning of obedience was dictated and governed by an adherence to form and principle. In such a situation, the religious superior could declare unilaterally that a given course of action was God's will. The implicit ethic acknowledged only passive acceptance as the appropriate response of subordinates. The forces of change and democratization in religious life no longer permit such a pattern to be acknowledged as valid and authentic. The ethical concerns which direct and support religious life are broader and more meaningful. The functioning of obedience can no longer take the shape of linear adherence or the arbitrary appeal to absolute principles and absolute ends. The ethical foundations of obedience have shifted to include human freedom, responsibility and the structural ingredients of mature human personality.

## Conclusion

The view of obedience which we have presented here is one that embraces the total functioning of the human personality. I have tried to show the connections between certain central developmental vicissitudes and their influence on the emerging configuration of the personality. These central developmental aspects are rooted in maturational givens which are specified and critically influenced by the pattern of experience that is made available to the growing child.

These developmental achievements become the organic building blocks of the mature personality — and serve to introduce and integrate the child in dynamic fashion into the structure and fabric of social interactions. We have tried to articulate the relevance of these developmental considerations for an understanding of obedience.

Obedience, therefore, has been viewed less in terms of specific interactions of command and response — and more in terms of a pattern and a context of religious living. Instead of seeing obedience as matter of specific actions, decisions and patterns of behavior, I have preferred to view it in the light of deeper motivations, intentions, and specifically in relation to the inner structures and capacities of the human personality that form the substructure of obedience. I felt that this deeper perspective offers a clearer entrée to the inner meaning and the more significant aspects of obediential functioning. It also serves to broaden and deepen the context of our consideration of obedience. Obedience can thus be seen in more meaningful contexts as related to the inner structure of personality and as involving a dynamic process which bears immediate implications for personality functioning and integration. Our view of obedience, then is one that sees it in developmental perspective — as being capable of growth, of having the potentiality of functioning at different levels of integration and maturity, as being capable of regression and maladaptive responsiveness. Obedience is not merely a process whose focus is restricted to the immediate context — but it has a history and a more complex deviation that reaches back into the past. And the past is not merely historical nor is its relevance merely an historical relevance — but it presents itself in the form of developmental residues that form the present constitutive elements of the integration of the functioning personality and therefore of the capacity for obedience. Developmental residues thus become present realities in the responsiveness to present contexts of authority and obedience.

To place the consideration of obedience in this perspective — the perspective of inner realities and determinants of personality functioning — has the disadvantage of not making immediately available a set of maxims or directives that say how things should be done or what things need to be changed or improved. Consequently, it is not an answer to many urgent questions — at least not directly. But it does offer a wider context of understanding that may serve as a frame of reference as we strive for what we seek. What we have stressed is that obedience is a matter of the inner structure of human personality and its delicate, yet complex interplay with social structures and values that form the context of communal concerns. Inner structures express and form themselves in this complex interaction with the social environment. Human interactions cannot be programmed or prescribed. They must be worked out and worked through by the participants in the existential setting. We can only hope to bring into focus some of the ingredients of that interaction and some of the hidden influences to which it may be responding — the rest must be achieved by the actual participants in the reality of their interaction.

This view of obedience takes its position over against the traditional attitudes to obedience — and offers in the first instance an empirical and conceptual basis for the understanding of obedience which places it in opposition to older and more traditional views. I have tried to suggest that the implications of this more psychologically based view were consistent with a valid theological perspective. The theological perspective, however, is divergent from traditional views in that it rests on an active, immanent presence and interplay of divine intents and purposes within and through human processes. Grace perfects nature — and acts through it. Human initiatives, purposes, and intents are thus conceived as graceful and grace-related. God's will is sought and found, in human purposefulness and striving — rather than merely given and conformed to.

In speaking of the basic human encounters by which a man becomes a man, John Murray wrote as follows:

> The third great encounter in which man becomes a man is the encounter with his own spirit. Meeting his own spirit, he meets a power within him that can give purpose to his life — the power to choose a destiny, and to summon all his energies for its pursuit. Meeting his own spirit, he meets the responsibility for the choice of purpose, and for the success or failure in the achievement of his chosen purpose in this world and in the next. . . . . In this wrestling with his own spirit, and with all the alternatives presented to it by circumstances and his own desires, a man becomes a man. He enters into possession of his powers and of himself — becomes self-directed, self-controlled, able to think his own thoughts, feel his own feelings, meet his own friends with love, and his enemies without fear. By choosing his purposes, he becomes purposeful, and to that extent a man, strong and gentle, clear in mind, able to mobilize his energies; such a man in his own degree, as our Lord was when he emerged from his lonely desert struggle, in which he had encountered the alternatives that life would have to offer him, and made his choice. Through his life runs that thread of purpose, which is the mark of virility: I am come for this, I am not come for that . . . . (Murray 1967, pp. 424-425)

No better expression could be found of the radical meaning of obedience and responsible subjection as presented in the above pages. But it was the tragedy of John Murray's age that he could go on to say — as a child of his age — " . . . by the vow of obedience one declines the most bruising encounter of all — that of man with himself, with his own spirit and its power of choice, with his own powers and the problem of their full exercise, towards the achievement of a determined purpose" (1967, p. 427). Even he, who became the architect of the Vatican II decree on religious liberty, saw obedience as a retreat from the basic encounter which is essential to the development of a mature self. Even so, he was right — the danger of obedience is the risk of irresponsibility, childish immaturity, and purposelessness.

But the risk is not the loss of responsibility and purposeful initiative in obedience. The risk is rather in the loss of and distortion of obedience itself — in the failure of growth to mature obedience or in the regressive retreat to less than mature forms of obedience. For — contrary to Father Murray's view — obedience is that basic encounter, not merely of man with his own spirit and inner purposes — but it is also that basic encounter with God's Spirit and God's purposes which summons human resources and initiatives more profoundly and more searchingly than any encounter of man with himself.

But the question has been seriously raised whether contemporary currents do not lead in the direction of a growth of idiosyncratic talents and personal aspirations that have become more individualistic than personal. Can such individualism coexist with a sense of corporate responsibility and purpose? To what extent can the Society or any religious group summon its members to common enterprizes of importance to the service of the church, when such service involves the sacrifice individual plans and ambitions and the hope of otherwise promising and productive careers? The dynamic of such commitment is only possible to the extent that individuals from the days of their probation have achieved a deeply personal grasp of their own religious experience and a vision of their vocation as extending beyond immediate personal interests to the broader stage of the kingdom to which obedience calls them. As Buckley (1984) observes, "It is primarily a question of personal freedom, of religious experience, of the charism of a person's life, of the contours grace has assumed in the candidate's life and of the election with which he has particularized and given shape to his future" (p. 80).

# SECTION V

# ASCETICISM AND MYSTICISM

# CHAPTER XXXII

# PRAYER AND ASCETICAL LIFE

The spiritual life of Ignatius rested in part on an ascetical substructure that was essential to sustaining his lofty mystical experiences, and provided an aspect of his spirituality that he was better able to articulate than his mystical transports. His discussions and directives regarding his ascetical practice were cast in more descriptive terms that bring his experience closer to our own, or at least to experiences that we can recognize as within the scope of describable behaviors and motives. We can turn our attention to Ignatius' life of prayer and penance to try to grasp another dimension of the complex dynamic forces at work at the roots of his spiritual vision.

The most salient point to be grasped here is that Ignatius proffered no method of spiritual growth other than that contained in the *Exercises*. The program of spiritual exercises sketched therein was the foundation stone on which he built the rest of his spiritual edifice — in other words, the *Exercises* laid out the program of ascetical praxis which led toward mystical elevation. Through the exercises and their inherent asceticism, the soul striving and seeking for God would become increasingly receptive to grace and finally to the divine initiatives of ever greater spiritual growth culminating on the mystical level. For Ignatius, asceticism could never cause authentic mystical effects since these were wholely the work of grace. The ascetic could only direct his efforts to making himself more receptive by self-abnegation, correction of inordinate attachments, and striving to achieve the third degree of humility. The soul could do more than humbly await the divine disposition through grace.

Following the examples of the great saints, asceticism played a central role in Ignatius' spiritual struggle. Asceticism in the strict sense is essential to any spiritual life. As Rahner (1967) put it:

> This asceticism is Christian self-abnegation in the true sense — an abnegation which gives up positive values in this life, and not just useful things that are a mere means to the end . . .; it also gives

> up (preserving, of course, the proper relationship and subordination to higher values) personal values . . ., such as marriage and the freedom to develop one's personality by disposing of material possessions that make for independence. (p. 71)

Such renunciations are motivated by the love of God and make no sense from the limited perspective of this world and its values. Only a spiritual value-orientation can justify it. It lies beyond the bearing of the "slings and arrows of outrageous fortune" that is the common human lot. It surrenders what otherwise would be valued and desired, but to the extent that it is so, stands in the way of greater love and service of God. This was the driving force behind Ignatius' consuming passion that found such powerful expression in his ascetical life.

## LIFE OF PRAYER

From the first days of his conversion in the sick bed at Loyola, Iñigo devoted himself to prayer in imitation of the great saints he had read about in the *Flos Sanctorum*. This prayer gradually became more intense and extensive. Throughout his life, he would spend long hours at night gazing at the vast wonders of the heavens, lost in thought and prayer. He told da Camara that "the greatest consolation he received was to look upon the heavens and the stars; and that he did it frequently and for long periods" (Vita 11).

This devotional practice reached heroic proportions at Manresa. He assisted at Mass daily and attended vespers and compline in the local priory. When he moved into the Dominican priory he could also assist at matins in the early hours of the morning. In private, he would then recite the hours of our Lady from the little book he brought from Loyola. Adding to this ascetical burden, he devoted himself to seven hours of prayer each day, usually on his knees. The rest of the day was devoted to spiritual reading, specifically the *Imitation of Christ*, but probably also the *Ejercitatario* of Cisneros given him by the saintly Dom Chanon, and perhaps even the *Flos Sanctorum*.

He maintained the intensity of his prayer life unabated after he left Manresa. In Barcelona, for example, most of the day and half the night were devoted to prayer. He attended Mass, vespers, and compline every day. He could be found frequently at prayer in the crypt of the chapel of St. Eulalia in the cathedral. He would kneel with arms outstretched or lie face down on the ground before the crucifix, uttering groans and prayers. At night, he would arise when others were asleep and spend the long hours of the night in prayer and ecstasy. Dudon (1949) summed up his life of continual prayer:

> From the day of his conversion Ignatius of Loyola was a man of prayer. Daily Mass, the recitation of the Hours of our Lady, the rosary, visits to the most venerated sanctuaries of Manresa, long solitary prayers in the chapel of Villadordis and in the cave which thereafter took his name, were his familiar practice, and, as it were, a need of his heart. All through the ups and downs of Alcala, Barcelona, Jerusalem, Salamanca, Paris, Azpeitia, and Venice, he changes his program only to enrich it. As the days follow one another and he walks toward his true destiny, Christ becomes more and more necessary and actual to him. Priest and Founder of an order, his spirit of prayer becomes purer and brighter to the point that he himself can remark to Laynez: "Manresa was but a beginning." (p. 365)

Even in his last years in Rome, when his ascetical excesses had begun to take their toll, he said mass daily except when he was too ill. As his strength diminished, he was forced to limit this practice, at first he limited himself to saying mass only on Sundays and feasts, but increasingly found it necessary to conserve his strength even more. Even so, when he was unable to celebrate mass himself, he would always attend mass said by another. or even at times would often have mass celebrated for him in his private chapel. Da Camara recalled that he would recite the prayers that had been designated for him as a substitute for the divine office, then he would retire to the little chapel next to his room to say or hear mass. After mass, he would spend the next two hours lost in prayer — a time when he did not wish to be disturbed (de Guibert 1964).

Without question, one of the central and principal features of Ignatius' life was his constant immersion in prayer. At the same time, he did not urge long hours of prayer on his followers, but he maintained a persistent insistence on habitual recourse to and familiarity with God through prayer, even in the midst of work. He constantly turned to prayer for guidance for all his own problems and for any decisions he had to make of any importance, seeking for light and grace from God. As Ravier (1987) puts it, "No decision . . . was made except before God, or better, in God; it was preceded, "enveloped," prolonged by prayer" (p. 326). The formulas enuntiating this theme of turning to God appear everywhere in the *Constitutions* and his letters — "to judge in the Lord," "to do what will seem best in Our Lord," "for the greater glory of God." At the end of his life, he wrote to Ramirez de Vergara, who was hesitant about entering the Society:

> The Holy Spirit will teach you better than anyone else the means for tasting with relish and for executing with sweetness that which reason dictates to be for the greater service and glory of God. Although it is true that for our pursuing the better and more perfect things the activity of the reason is sufficient, the other activity, that of the will, could easily follow this activity of the reason, even though this emotion in the will does not precede the decision and the execution, with God our Lord thus recompensing the confidence which one has placed in His providence, and recompensing too the abnegation of one's whole self, and the sacrifice of one's own comforts — indeed, with God compensating for these generous acts by much contentment and relish, and with an abundance of spiritual consolations which is the greater the less one has sought it, and has instead the more purely sought His glory and pleasure. (De Guibert 1964, p. 97)

These phrases suggest that these words of advice flow out of Ignatius' own experience and that he is simultaneously telling us something about his own inner life of prayer.

## PENANCES

Ignatius' teachings about self-denial, abnegation, and mortification came full blown from his own ascetical practice. He preached nothing that had not been implemented and realized fully in his own spiritual struggles. From the time he left Loyola, he practiced the most severe mortifications and penances with the two-fold aim of atoning for his past sins and demonstrating his love of God by imitating the austerities of the saints. The discipline became a nightly practice; fasting became his ordinary routine, measured by the characteristic intensity with which he approached every facet of his spiritual commitment. He often did not eat for days, reducing his strength and even endangering his health. The long watches, penances, and fasts took their toll. Once at Villadordis, he collapsed during one of his prayer vigils. Some pious women found him unconscious on the floor, revived him and took him to a hospital where he could be cared for (Dudon 1949). His excessive austerities, continued so unremittingly at Manresa, resulted in the abdominal ailment that turned out to be biliary lithiasis, the severity of which was only appreciated at his autopsy. The severe, at times excruciating, pains accompanied him along the rest of his journey. We do not hear much of them during his trip to Jerusalem, but once back in Barcelona, the pain resumed with vengeance. For the most part during those pilgrim years, he begged his food, and gave the best part of his collections to the poor, and ate little himself.

His ascetical practice embodied the program he had laid out in the *Spiritual Exercises*, directing his efforts to eradicating all traces of his former dissolute life and inordinate attachments. The fine clothes of the nobleman and courtier were replaced by the rough garb of the pilgrim, and during the years of his pilgrim career he wore the most threadbare of garments. In the face of wintry winds and snow, he wore a thin and tattered cloak that provided little warmth and protection. In Barcelona his shoes often had no soles, even in the dead of winter. Instead of fine linen undergarments, he wore a hairshirt made of a heavy sack. Even during his days in Rome, the same fanatical ideal continued to hold sway in his mind, only gradually yielding to the demands of prudence and the need for moderation. Laynez recalled: "Ignatius is actually a despiser of the world. He told me that, if it depended on his own personal preference, he would be not in the least adverse to be considered insane as he would walk along with bare feet and with his deformed leg clearly in view or with horns on his head. But for the sake of souls he allowed none of this to become public knowledge" (FN I, 140).

His unrelenting insistence on poverty, both personally in the early years and institutionally in the Society, was driven by his consuming intention to follow in the footsteps of and imitate Christ poor and humble. His conscience subjected him to scrupulous torments over the meager sum he had collected for his trip to Jerusalem; he resolved the conflict by giving the money away. When he and his companions finally abandoned their projected journey to Jerusalem, the two hundred scudi they had collected for the trip was returned to their benefactors. They lived instead on alms begged from day to day. Even during his Roman period, when he was head of the Society of Jesus, his manner of life lost none of the simplicity and self-deprivation of the pilgrim. Dudon (1949) described the progression in his asceticism:

> In the beginning of his conversion he led a life of rugged penance, which left him broken in health for the rest of his days. At the time of his studies, his desire to carry the burden of intellectual labor without flinching led him to adopt a more moderate regimen. Later still, the pangs of illness and the sufferings of an early old age took the place of the fasts, the hair shirts, the bloody disciplines of Manresa. The flesh was conquered. The body had been reduced to impotence. Neither sleep nor food ever provided him with a temptation. He slept poorly, he ate little, and it made no difference what. (p. 372)

His quarters in the house of the Gesu was tiny, cramped even by contemporary standards, simple, with only the barest and simplest furniture. Dudon (1949) added, "From the day when he broke with his worldly life, this man had never been able to surround himself with any conveniences. The mere word "comfort" would have made him shudder" (p. 372). Thus his devotion to simplicity and poverty were persistent qualities of his personal style and were instilled into the *Constitutions* as normative for the style of life he required of his followers.

## Varieties of Asceticism

The life of persistent penance and abnegation that Ignatius exemplified in his own life and instilled into the spiritual doctrine and practice of his followers flies in the face of psychological hedonism and the simpleminded view of pleasure as a primary motivating force in human affairs — a view seemingly endorsed by Freud in his applications of the pleasure principle. In fact, the ascetical principle — that is, the foregoing of pleasure or the denial of pleasure in the interest of other goals or purposes — has a fundamental role in analytic thinking, both in terms of the yielding of the pleasure principle to the demands of the reality principle and in terms of the adaptation of wishes for satisfaction of one set of needs or drives in order to serve other needs or drives. The manner in which tendencies to seek pleasure and avoid pain can be modified by ascetical purposes have been classified by Flugel (1945). He offered the following categories:

*Utilitarian asceticism*: Any mental discipline or cultural achievement requires an ability to postpone immediate gratification and to endure a degree of delay and frustration for the sake of a greater accomplishment or gain. Denial of proximate pleasure for the sake of a higher or more remote satisfaction is almost a necessity for accomplishment of any kind — whether the basketball player who gives up time to relax or amuse himself to work on some fault in his game, or the student of the piano who devotes himself to long hours of practice to master the skills of the keyboard instead of amusing himself in some other manner, and so on. The point need not be belabored — it is merely common sense and common knowledge: he who wills the end wills the means.

There are cases, however, in which the goal is sufficiently remote or general and the period of renunciation or effort sufficiently prolonged to give it a distinctive character. This form of *disciplinary asceticism* can apply to the training of an athlete or soldier, or the prolonged course of study leading to advanced degrees or professions —

doctors, lawyers, doctoral candidates, etc. The distinction from utilitarian asceticism is largely a matter of degree.

In these forms of asceticism, the self-denial is valued insofar as it is a means to the end or goal, but in other forms of asceticism the pain achieves a value in itself, regardless of the attainment of the goal. In this sense, *epicurean asceticism* involves renunciaion or suffering that is essential to the ensuing satisfaction — Flugel uses the example of mountain climbing: to enjoy the accomplishment of reaching the top and enjoying the view, one has to climb the mountain. There are satisfactions in making the effort that are entirely lacking if you could get to the top by train or lift. Certain forms of artistic work may also fit under this category. The rewards of mastery, overcoming difficulties, meeting challenges are in these cases part of the process and are open to rich diversities of motivation and meaning.

*Masochistic asceticism* tends to enjoy the renunciation or pain for its own sake, not by reason of gaining an ulterior end or goal. This may involve the sexual perversion of masochism, or in the form of moral masochism would reflect the superego dynamic of unconscious guilt and the need for punishment. In this form of asceticism, the masochistic need tends to outweigh any moral considerations or the inflicting of self-punitive suffering for the purpose of gaining ulterior gratification.

The next category is *punitive asceticism,* in which guilt-motivated self-punishment outweighs any element of perverse masochistic pleasureful gratification. This category would include many forms of religiously motivated penances — fasting, self-inflicted pain, self-denial, etc. We have seen the saintly excess of such practices in Ignatius, and such penances are recommended, even prescribed, in more moderate form in his *Constitutions.* I would distinguish the specifically neurotic form from what we might designate as *penetential asceticism.* In the neurotic instance, the punitive element is usually not conscious and may be disguised as some other form of asceticism, usually disciplinary or utilitarian. In penetential forms, however, the self-punishment is conscious and purposeful, ordered to specific religious goals and functions, whether self-imposed or as part of institutionalized religious praxis. The degree of awareness can shade through degrees, and the mixture of masochistic and religious motivations is more the rule than the exception. The most reasonable judgment, in my view (Meissner 1993), of Ignatius' penitential practices is that a measure of masochistic motivation, in the form of moral masochism especially, cannot be excluded.

The final category, *aggressive asceticism*, is marked by the turning of aggression against the self, particularly destructive aggression. In its pure form, this form of asceticism takes place without much contribution from the perversion of pleasure in suffering nor from moral masochism. But aggressive asceticism rarely occurs in pure form — possibly in isolated acts of self-inflicted pain of short duration. The ascetical note, however, usually implies longer duration of effect. The turning of aggression against the self more often has a masochistic component that blends this asceticism with utilitarian, punitive or disciplinary variants. Moreover, the masochistic moment does not prevent a sadistic counterpart that finds expression in directing destructive aggression externally to others. The satisfaction of inflicting pain on one's enemies can reinforce the motivation for aggression toward the self — one's own suffering is placed in the service of making them suffer as well. Flugel cites the example of a hunger strike among political prisoners. A more mundane example would be a labor strike — whatever pain and suffering is incurred through the strike brings with it a degree of satisfaction from the injury brought against management and the owners against whom the workers have a grievance. The recently settled baseball strike, which interrupted one season and caused a delay in the opening of the next, serves as a pertinent case.

Thus, the ascetical phenomenon can be quite complex and can involve multiple layers and forms of motivation. In the religious context, ascetical mobilization of aggressive forces, of both a destructive and constructive mode, are put at the service of religiously motivated spiritual ideals that become internalized and personalized in the ego-ideal. However elevating and ennobling the ideal, the forces let loose in ascetical striving have a marked potential for destructive and self-diminishing outcomes. In concluding his discussion of asceticism, Flugel (1945) added a cautionary note that has relevant connotations for the religious sphere as for any other:

> Asceticism in its various forms and ramifications permeates our social life. It has indeed become to a large extent an integral part of our educational and religious systems, and it exercises a very considerable influence on our legal, political, and even medical and economic thinking. To some extent the renunciation of immediate satisfaction and the endurance of pain, effort, and distress are essential means to mental and social progress. But, under the influence of the various motives we have been considering, man would appear so far to have forgotten that this renunciation and endurance are from the biological standpoint no more than

> means, so far to have elevated deprivation and suffering into self-sufficient ends, that it would often seem that he might just as truthfully be called a pain-seeking as a pleasure-seeking animal. (pp. 93-94)

## Aggression

The preconversion Iñigo was a forceful personality, vigorous, testy, pugnacious. What happened to this aggression during his conversion and in the shaping of his postconversion personality? Despite the occasional breakthrough, the major outcome of his conversion experience was a turning away from his aggressive impulses — certainly from the bellicose model presented by in his father and brothers and from his interior identification with these phallic and aggressive objects.

His struggles to overcome evil inclinations of the past and to seek out a new and spiritual identity markedly expressed his underlying aggressive conflicts. The impulse to do in the poor Moor on the road to Montserrat was one example (Meissner 1992b). But in the cave at Manresa, this hostile force turned against himself both physically and mentally in the form of severe penances and deprivations, and more particularly took the form of superego severity. This turning of aggression against the self reached its high point in his suicidal ruminations. Had he taken the next step along that destructive path, we would never have come to know the saint and mystic who founded the Society of Jesus. I would venture to hypothesize that these same aggressive derivatives also played themselves out in the masochistic dynamics underlying his severe asceticism. It is also likely that the need to deny and defend against aggressive drives significantly contributed to his mystical experience.

## Superego Severity

The dominant role of aggression and its direction into external channels in the preconversion personality of Iñigo de Loyola was by a pattern of turning these hostile and destructive impulses inward. In the conversion experience, his self structure was transformed from being based on a model of phallic aggression to one of passive receptivity, to a defensive organization formed around reaction formation directed against persistent aggressive impulses. This intrapsychic conversion was put in the service of his emerging ego ideal, patterned after the model of the saintly lives in the *Flos Sanctorum*.

The regression, following on the dissolution of the pilgrim's psychic structure, most notably at Manresa, was accompanied by a more direct expression of these powerful instincts. In this more primitive state, aggressive drives became aggregated to the superego. Freud originally introduced the superego as the psychic agency whose function was to watch over the ego and compare it with an ideal standard — the ego ideal — and, in addition, to serve as the agency of repression of those instinctual impulses not in conformity with the standards of the ideal. Thus the superego came to be regarded as a sort of structural precipitate within the ego that comes into existence at the time of the resolution of the oedipal conflict. As a derivative of parental and other identifications, it represented the child's relation to parents and society and functioned as the vehicle of morality — primarily moral values assimilated from the parents. Freud also stressed that the superego was itself a channel for powerful drives, particularly aggressive drives that could readily be diverted by the superego against the self. Freud described this by saying, "The ego forms its superego out of the id." Thus, the greater the control or inhibition of aggressive impulses against external objects, the more tyrannical and hostile against the self the superego becomes. And this tyranny is manifested in a sense of guilt or worthlessness or in other self-punitive postures.

When external outlets are forestalled, as Freud (1923) had described, destructive aggression turned inward and was channeled through the superego, thus increasing the severity of superego aggression directed against the self. Despite his best intentions and efforts, Iñigo's capacity to manage and regulate his aggressive impulses during the early stages of his conversion was not very good — impulses to act out his aggression according to the dictates of his preconversion ideal were still much alive, although not without increasing conflict. The aggressive residues of the hidalgo, the impulse to fight, to defend the honor of his lady, and even to kill, were coiled and ready to leap into consciousness.

But, as the spiritual ideal became more firmly established, modifications in his superego increasingly took the form of extreme self-punitive penitential and ascetical practices. At a conscious level, the motivations involved guilt for past transgressions (as I have argued, there was probably plenty to feel guilty about!) and a lifelong shame for his failure to live up to his religious and moral ideals. Iñigo's conscience would have been formed in the intense Catholicism of the Iberian peninsula, a form of religious praxis that tended to absolutes and moral rigidity, and under the influence of Magdalena, whose piety and religious devotion were noteworthy. Guilt and shame would have provided motivating affects for his severe self-punishment. At the same time, these penitential practices would have fulfilled the important purpose of atoning for the past, and, in a more positive terms, would have expressed a more or less creative drive toward shaping a new identity congruent with his developing spiritual ego ideal. It is probably safe to say, therefore, that the pilgrim's extreme self-denial and penances were in large part motivated by the need to satisfy the demands of this newly formed narcissistically invested ego ideal. The superego was the instrument of execution of this intrapsychic drama, the motivating force behind his guilt, depression, scrupulosity, suicidal impulses, and masochism.[1]

In these terms, then, the pilgrim's systematic throttling of any expression of the pleasure principle contributed to the dissolution of the old ego ideal, which had served as a major mechanism for the fusion of libidinal and aggressive drives and thus provided the motivating power for the constructive demands of development and mature adaptation (Hartmann 1958). Destruction of the previous romantic-heroic ego ideal served to unleash these energies in their regressive, more or less primitive and deneutralized form, so that they suffused the pilgrim's psychic structure and had to be detoxified and diverted into other channels. An alternative means of expression was provided by the affinity of the superego to these basic energies. The pilgrim passed through a period of agonizing doubt, tormenting scruples, paroxysms of guilt, and feelings of worthlessness. His superego, feeding on its new-found aggression, not only tormented him with self-punitive impulses, but drove his floundering ego to seek relief from the inner punishment by severe physical penances and infliction of pain. This torrent of superego rage reached its apogee in the temptation to commit suicide — the ultimate masochistic gesture.

Another form of superego severity comes in the form of excessive narcissistic investment in the ego-ideal. In this case, the ideals can be set at such a height of idealized accomplishment that they exceed the capacity of the spiritual aspirant to attain. The disparity between these lofty ideals and the actual accomplishment of the self leave the door open to further superego onslaughts, usually taking the form of shame and guilt for the failure to achieve such spiritual ambitions. The individual is left vulnerable to diminished self-es-

[1] See my discussion of penance in chapter X above.

teem, depression, a sense of worthlessness, inadequacy, and failure. We have reason to think that Ignatius, more intensely during his conversion and pilgrim years but in some degree throughout his career, fell victim to this dynamic. We can also recall that if he was called to follow the path of spiritual excess in his own life and praxis, he had also to pay the price in physical and other human terms. Even so, he was forced to mitigate the intensity of his penances in later years as a matter of prudence and to permit his undertaking of the labors of his office; and he was clear in his recommendations on penance and ascetical praxis in the *Constitutions* that not everyone was called to this degree of heroic virtue and that his followers could not be expected to follow the same path. Penances and prayer were to be practiced in moderation and in a spirit of humility and obedience — this was the greater and more adaptive norm.

But such moderation is not easy to come by — we humans tend to err either on the side of laxity or excess, particularly when we are confronted with the heroic example of the great saints. We may have to accept the prospect that, with all good will and earnestness in seeking and following God's will, we may not be called to heroic sanctity but only to a humble acceptance of our role in life and the measure of grace that is our due. Monden (1965) has offered us a cogent comment on this score:

> The best spiritual authors always keep in mind the twofold meaning of the word holiness. But in ordinary preaching this was not always done, and the answer to the question, "Is everybody called to holiness?" frequently remained very ambiguous. It was often made to seem as if only our lack of generosity prevented all of us from becoming canonizable saints. At any rate, the outwardly perceptible result, to so-called *exercise of heroic virtue*, became as a matter of course the accepted criterion for the inner self-donation to God. . . . This abstract perfection, some kind of greatest common denominator of canonized sanctity, invited Christians to a purely material imitation — we might almost say, to an aping — of the lives of the saints. And in this imitation one's own ascetic endeavor obviously had to receive much more emphasis than grace, which was considered available as a matter of course. That grace, moreover, was seen in terms not so much of a personal dialog as of a force of propulsion, moving us towards the pre-ordained abstract ideal.
>
> Possibly the discovery of the considerable degree of determinism in man's activity has dealt the death blow to that *unconscious Pelagianism*. We are forced to distinguish again very carefully the several meanings of the word "holiness," and we can no

> longer take the very special vocation of the canonized saint as a norm of evaluation for the average Christian — not to mention equating holiness naturalistically with a superior, and perhaps fortuitous, human equilibrium. (pp. 69-70)

The pattern was articulated in Ignatius' own career in which the penitential imitation of heroic saintly virtue was the abiding norm in his early years and the shift from reliance on ascetical effort to acceptance and openness to grace came gradually to the fore. But perhaps we are faced here with a mystery of grace that extends beyond the reach of psychoanalytic reason. The analytic perspective would steer a course between the extremes that reflect the influence of neurotic underpinnings and distortions and would opt for moderation, prudence, and adaptive utility as behavioral norms. But this is not the option taken by the saints. They seem destined for excess, for the imprudence and extremes of penance and self-sacrifice, ordained to a transcendent mission to which they are called and impelled by grace. This is a range of spiritual experience in which psychoanalysis must lay down its arms in the face of the exstatic and ascetical discipline of transcendental spiritual life and the demands it places on the human organism. This does not mean, I would urge the point that remains central to this entire discussion, that such transcendent spirituality removes its self from the realm of human psychology. If the demands of mystical grace and the realm of human experience to which the mystic is called are driven by grace and reach beyond ordinary human comprehension and understanding, they remain nonetheless human and embrace in some meaningful sense a human psychology. Grace never replaces nature, but perfects it.

## MASOCHISM

We are beginning to encounter some complex issues related to the inherent pathology and purposefulness of penitential practices. The dimensions of the problem in grasping the meaning of such self-punitive behaviors from a psychoanalytic perspective are well exemplified in Ignatius and in his teaching on penance. The picture of the pilgrim in the cave of Manresa is that of a man buffeted by uncontrollable forces. He had unwittingly unleashed something that he could no longer control. His efforts began with more or less deliberate attempts at penitential self-punishment. The originating impulse was in some degree deliberate (coming from the ego), religiously motivated, but necessarily had some degree of superego involvement. The effort was penitential in intent, but its effect went beyond contrition. It unleashed destructive impulses that were much more readily enlisted in the service of the superego than of the ego. The superego came to dominate the conflict, and penance became to that extent masochistic. The rational was turned into the irrational. There is no surprise in this from a psychodynamic point of view. The inner life of Iñigo had always been, and was always to be, a process of dealing with powerful instinctual forces. The regression at Manresa merely allowed these forces their most unbridled display.

Mention of masochism raises a difficult question — to what extent can the the practice of penance as performed by the pilgrim and as recommended in the *Exercises* be regarded as masochistic? I am afraid I can only answer by provoking more questions rather than offering any closure. My opinion is that Iñigo's severe penances involved some form of masochistic perversion insofar as they reflected the degree of intrapsychic conflict he endured with respect to his instinctual life. These conflicts, which were recognizably libidinal, aggressive and narcissistic, took a more severe and extreme form in the early years of his pilgrimage, and it was only over time that his suffering gradually, and only partially, freed him from these conflicts. However, he was never able to completely free himself from the need for continued vigilance and strong repressive and other defensive countermeasures until the end of his life. His penances seemed to have been mitigated only in the face of severe and even life-threatening self-injury. But if we base our analysis exclusively on a masochistic dynamism, we will not have adequately understood or explained Ignatius' ascetical life.

Psychoanalytically speaking, masochism is a complex phenomenon (Berliner 1947). The sexual perversion of masochism is usually distinguished from moral masochism[2] in that the perversion involves sexual gratification derived from suffering. Freud regarded masochism as one form of the turning of aggression against the self. Masochism was linked to sadism, and the two served as opposite sides of the same coin. Often the sadomasochistic pattern takes place in an interpersonal context, in which one person takes the role of sadist and the other that of masochist. Many unhappily married couples fall into this pattern — and it is not at all unusual for the members of the pair to exchange places, the masochist acting out a sadistic role and the

[2] Masochism is a perversion that finds pleasure or gratification in humiliation or suffering. Moral masochism is a derivative form in which seeks victimization or the position of victim primarily out of an unconscious sense of guilt; sexual pleasure is not necessarily, or only indirectly, involved.

sadist becoming the suffering victim. In these cases, the masochist role usually serves as a defense against aggressive drives — it is better to suffer the aggression of another than to become the hostile and destructive agent oneself. In intrapsychic structural terms, this takes the form of a struggle between aggressive and victim configurations (introjects) that contribute part of the core of the individual's personality structure (Meissner 1978) and reflect underlying conflicts over aggression. In Iñigo's case, his need to seek the role of suffering victim in his penitential practices served as an effective defense against his severe aggressive conflicts. Ignatius' colloquy at the conclusion of the meditation on the Two Standards in the Second Week of the *Exercises* makes this clear:

> A colloquy should be addressed to our Lady, asking her to obtain for me from her Son and Lord the grace to be received under His standard, first in the highest spiritual poverty, and should the Divine Majesty be pleased thereby, and deign to choose and accept me, even in actual poverty; secondly, in bearing insults and wrongs, thereby to imitate Him better, provided only I can suffer these without sin on the part of another, and without offense of the Divine Majesty. (SE147)

This masochistic stand aims at countering the wish for wealth and pride — presumably desires that stirred in some form in the breast of the pilgrim and against which he had to exercise continuing vigilance. The self-denial has the purpose of seeking love and approval from a divine object rather than a human one.

In the sphere of the sacred, the masochistic stance is articulated with a religious ego ideal and often placed in the service of a spiritual set of values and objectives. We should not automatically assume that such religiously motivated masochism is pathological — this may or may not be the case. The masochism of the ascetic may elicit admiration or contempt; it may reflect psychic weakness or strength; it may be a vehicle for seeking or for expressing love. The masochistic surrender to God may serve as a way of avoiding reality, or the suffering and submission of the saint may serve as a vehicle for discovering increasingly meaningful levels of personal commitment and love of God. The mortification of the ascetic may reflect a profound love of God; it may perform an important adaptive function of alleviating guilt and expiating sin; it may be put to developmental uses — as, for example, growth in chastity and purity of mind and heart — or it may express a perversion that finds some degree of gratification in suffering pain (Charmé 1983).

It is probably reasonable to conclude that Ignatius suffered from a rather extreme degree of moral masochism, but that this masochistic bent was in many ways sublimated and adapted to a program of spiritual growth through the seeking of grace and an increasing love of God. Ignatius' penances were thus transformed into acts of love, driven more by seeking God's love and approval than by guilt or the need for punishment. If this be masochism, it is not simply the masochism of the neurotic or the moral masochist; it is masochism suffused with love and placed in the service of a highly narcissistically invested ego ideal, an ideal that is itself embued with the highest spiritual aims.

This consideration makes it apparent once again the extent to which Ignatius' ascetical practice and the role of ascetical and penitential praxis in his spirituality were highly determined by factors operating in his personality. The obvious inference is that this dimension of his spirituality can only be evaluated in this highly personal and derivative context, but that its ultimate value and its role in the spiritual journey of any soul seeking greater holiness and openness to grace may be changed or qualified by the inherent demands and needs of each individual's psychological structure. For this Ignatius' approach may provide a meaningful guide, but not necessarily a model.

## Obsessional Character Structure

One salient aspect of Ignatius' personality that intersects with other factors impinging on his asceticism is his obsessionality. Psychoanalysts would understand this aspect of his character as derived from the excessive severity of his superego — the need for obsessional control is based on the threat of breakthrough of instinctual impulses. Leakage of such impulses into consciousness is accompanied, in the classic freudian model, by guilt from both libidinal (incestuous) and aggressive wishes. In Ignatius' case I think we can add narcissistic impulses, which may result in shame more than guilt.

The obsessiveness is striking in his own spiritual practice and in his direction of the spiritual lives of his followers. His examination of his conscience, carried on almost hourly and with obsessive intensity, even to the point of compulsion, is notable. His spiritual teaching and direction, as evidenced in the *Spiritual Exercises*, for example, are highly structured and organized to the point that many have found them repellant and difficult to emulate. To the extent that this obsessional pattern reflects Ignatius' own spiritual experience, it offers us some insight into of his character as well as adding another dimension to our appreciation of his spirituality.

Particularly in his postconversion life, we get a sense of discipline, tenacity to the point of stubbornness or obstinacy, and a pattern of behavior impressive for its consistent degree of control — especially emotional control. We can find good evidence for defense mechanisms — isolation, intellectualization, and reaction formation, among others. We have also seen the breakthrough of obsessional doubts, frequently taking the form of intense scruples. That these scrupulous doubts plagued him, not only in the early years of his pilgrimage, but even into his advanced years as General of the Society in Rome, seems an established fact.

These behavioral reflections give us some hint of the conflictual struggles that permeated his inner life and powered the rigid self-discipline that characterized him in later years. One might argue as well that this need for inner control spilled over into his style of governing the Society, with his passion for establishing regulations (reflected in his obsessional immersion in the writing of the Constitutions) and his insistence on unquestioning blind obedience from his followers — no doubt related to his authoritarianism, conflicts and character. It is worth noting in this context that the one area of his experience that seemed exempt from this consuming obsessionality was his prayer life and mysticism.

## ASCETICAL THEOLOGY

These aspects of Ignatius' life of prayer and penance and self-discipline derived from and reflect his intense devotion, the elements of which revealed themselves in his intense love of God, his continuing familiarity with God, his incomparable capacity of finding God in everything, and his propensity for effective rather than affective love[3] that found expression in the service of God above all. These elements are summarized in the *Exercises* in the "Contemplation for

[3] Affective love is an emotional phenomenon — feelings of love, affection, and devotion — but confined to the realm of affective experience. Effective love shifts the emphasis away from the feeling state to the realm of action. Love is effective when it does that which is for the good of the loved one. Parents may experience an affection of love for their children, but unless their love is effective they can do their children great harm. Ignatius expresses this point with particularly poignancy in the contemplation for obtaining divine love, where he gives a classic statement about effective love [SE230-231].

Obtaining the Love of God" and are distilled into the famous prayer from that contemplation, the *Suscipe*:

> Take, Lord, and receive all my liberty, my memory, my understanding, and my entire will, all that I have and possess. Thou hast given all to me. To Thee, O Lord, I return it. Dispose of it wholly according to Thy will. Give me Thy love and Thy grace, for this is sufficient for me. [SE234]

The prayer expresses an ideal of self-abnegation for the love of God, which formed the essential core of the third degree of humility in the *Exercises* and later the eleventh and twelfth rules of the *Summary* of the Constitutions.

> Rule 11. They must attentively consider, and, in the presence of our Creator and Lord, hold it to be of the utmost importance as a help to progress in the spiritual life, to abhor completely and without exception all that the world loves and embraces, and to accept and desire with all their strength whatever Christ our Lord loved and embraced.
>
> For, as men of the world who follow the world love and very earnestly seek honors, distinctions, and the reputation of a great name among men, as the world teaches them; so they who are making progress in the spiritual life and are serious about following Christ our Lord love and warmly desire the very opposite — to be clothed, in fact, in the same garments and wear the same attire as their Lord, out of love and reverence for Him: and this to such an extent, that if it could be done without offense to His Divine Majesty, or sin on the part of their neighbor, they would wish to suffer abuse, injustice, false accusations, and to be considered and treated as fools (without, however, giving occasion for such treatment), their whole desire being to resemble, and in some way imitate our Creator and Lord Jesus Christ, by being clothed in His garments and raiment, since He first so clothed Himself for our greater spiritual benefit, and gave us an example to lead us to seek, as far as possible with God's grace, to imitate and follow Him, seeing He is the true Way which leads men to life.

> Rule 12. The better to reach so precious a degree of perfection in the spiritual life, each one should make it his first and foremost endeavor to seek in our Lord his greater abnegation and continuous mortification in all things possible.

# CHAPTER XXXIII

# SPIRITUAL DIRECTION

## The Role of Direction for Ignatius

Ignatius was not one to remain content with communicating his spiritual vision only in writing, be it in the little manual of the *Spiritual Exercises*, or in the magisterial *Constitutions* of the Society, or even in the endless stream of letters of consolation, advice, and exhortation that flowed from his pen. His bent was more toward doing and making himself an active instrument of God's work rather than a man of letters. He poured himself into apostolic activities at all points in his career, and even in the years of his generalate remained active in apostolic efforts, perhaps none more than the formation of novices and others in formation.

But one salient dimension of his apostolic involvement was his devotion to spiritual direction. His biography tells us how assiduously he sought such direction as an aid to his own spiritual progress — during the anguish of self-doubt, scrupulosity, depression and suicidal impulses that plagued him at Manresa, during his tormented conflictual episodes during his years of study, and when he went through the wrenching and conflicted decision to accept the role of general of the new Society thrust upon him by his founding companions. At each point of crisis, he instinctively turned to some source of spiritual guidance and direction for assistance — to the Dominican confessor at Manresa, to Father Theodore during his agonizing over the election as general, and so on. Spiritual direction played a significant role in his own spiritual journey.

## Ignatius as Director

Certainly one of the distinguishing features of the *Spiritual Exercises* is the place given to the director, the one giving the Exercises. As O'Malley (1993) notes: "If such guidance was helpful during the retreat, it might be helpful throughout one's life, either in confession or outside it. This kind of consultation of course antedates the *Exercises*, but, in great part because of Ignatius's book, "spiritual direction," or counseling, began to emerge with a new prominence in Catholicism as a formal and continuing relationship between the two persons involved" (p. 47). It was not until the twentieth century that the principle involved came to fuller realization in the pastoral counseling movement.

It should not surprise us, then, that spiritual direction should have been a salient component of his own spiritual ministry to souls in his constant effort to draw his fellowmen closer to God. Even in the early days at Manresa he was drawn to spiritual conversation, an attraction that would in time transform itself into spiritual direction. As Buckley (1976) noted, "Within the darkness of Manresa emerges a phrase, *ayudar algunas almas* which is to run like a leitmotif through the Autobiography, an apostolic care for the religious and interior needs of human beings which would grow in intensity and gather to a focus until it fathered forth the Society of Jesus" (p. 141). His active engagement in spiritual direction seems to have begun sometime after his return from Jerusalem, although any dating would be no more than conjectural. We hear nothing of it before that time.

But even at Barcelona, where his career as a student began, he began to engage others in spiritual conversation, even at Alcala beginning to gather a small group of followers. The basis for these conversations was the *Spiritual Exercises*. And although the numbers of people he contacted in this way was small, the influence he exerted on them was often profound — to the point that he began to attract attention and with it suspicion as to the nature of his doctrine. This was, in fact, the basis of the interest of the Inquisition in this activity at Alcala, at Salamanca, and even at Paris. Early in the Paris period, his influence on the three students, Pedro de Peralta, Juan Castro, and Amador de Elduayen, created a stir and aroused opposition to his efforts. Nor can we forget the good doctor of theology who lost the billiard game to our spiritual hustler and had to pay the price of making the Exercises (Meissner 1992b). Later, of course, it was his direction of his companions that sowed the seeds of their commitment to join together in God's service. The impact of the Spiritual Exercises and the charism of Ignatius on men like Peter Faber and Francis Xavier would turn them into saints.

Ignatius' practice became the model for the early Jesuits. Nadal wrote several dialogues providing exemplars of such conversations, and Peter Canisius wrote to the general Claudio Aquaviva commending devout conversation and holding out Faber as a model practitioner of the art. O'Malley (1993) summarizes Nadal's account of Ignatius' technique:

> He first required that one approach individuals with love and a desire for their well-being, while carefully observing each person's temperament and character. One began the conversation with subjects of interest to the other, so that with a merchant one spoke of trade, with a nobleman of government, and only gradually did one bring the discussion around to matters of the spirit. Ignatius often quoted the Spanish proverb that advised "going in by their door in order to come out by ours." If the Jesuit discovered that the individual consistently deflected the conversation from religious topics, he should then address them bluntly, turning from pleasant subjects to hell and divine judgment. The individual would either accept the turn and profit from it or walk away and not waste the Jesuit's time further. (pp. 111-112)

*Mutatis mutandis*, this description might have some relevance to a therapeutic encounter. We should not forget that its efficacy, coming from Ignatius as its source, had to be filtered through his extraordinary charisma and psychological intuition.

Throughout his trajectory, his apostolic passion was matched by a genius for the direction of souls, and even during his tenure in Rome he was widely consulted by the powerful and the humble. De Guibert (1964) listed among them Jacopo del Conte, who would paint the famous portrait of Ignatius after his death, the ambassador Mascarenhas and his wife Leonora, who was to play such a vital role in Ignatius' dealings with Spanish royalty (Rahner 1960; Meissner 1992b), and Juan de Vega, the viceroy of Sicily. There were others — Diego de Hocez in Venice, Gaspar de Doctis, the Spanish ambassador, Pedro Ortiz, the ambassador of Charles V who became instrumental in Ignatius establishing his Society, and probably also Cardinal Contarini in Rome. The data are fragmentary, but what we do know is that the work of spiritual direction utilizing the Spiritual Exercises was one of the main and most powerful instruments that Ignatius utilized in drawing influential souls to the support of his Society and to greater spiritual profit.

He knew how to console, how to encourage, how to read the hearts of those who came to him. People found him to be serious, attentive, kind, his words few but carefully chosen and penetrating — always the noble knight, the man of breeding and courtly manners, bearing himself with dignity and respect for his fellows, and great reserve (Wulf 1977). Despite this detachment, men and women were drawn to him irresistibly. As Ribadeneyra wrote, "Our father possessed to a high degree the art of winning the affection and trust of those who associated with him, and thus of leading them to God"

(Scripta I, 461). He had a gift for spiritual conversation that inspired and consoled others. Nadal's comments are typical:

> As he was inflamed with love for his neighbor and was outstanding in regard to the discernment of spirits and moral prudence, he so adapted himself to those with whom he conversed by the brevity and kindness of his words and caused them to be so well-disposed toward him that he evoked amazing movements of soul in them. He had such insight into them that he almost seemed to enter into their mind and heart. He spoke in such a manner that no one could withstand his words. Furthermore, a mysterious, divine power and light appeared to shine forth from his countenance, which much enkindled the love of spiritual things in those who looked upon him. (Epistolae Nadal IV, 662)[1]

## A Case in Point

Other evidence regarding his activity as a spiritual director comes from the series of letters to Sister Teresa Rejadella, a nun in the Convent of St. Clare in Barcelona. There were two letters from 1536, and again in 1547 and 1549. The latter letters are concerned mainly with Ignatius' refusal to accept the nuns of St. Clare under obedience to the Society, in spite of the pleas of Teresa, her prioress, and the support of Araoz and others. This stance was no doubt connected with Ignatius' intent to keep his men free to follow whatever mission the Holy See might direct them to, rather than to have them tied down to the spiritual care and direction of convents. This conviction would have been later reinforced by his somewhat traumatic dealings with Isabel Roser.[2] In the *Constitutions*, Ignatius made his attitude clear: "Likewise, because the members of this Society ought to be ready at any hour to go to some or other parts of the world where they may be sent by the sovereign pontiff or their own superiors, they ought not to take a curacy of souls, and still less ought they to take charge of religious women or any other women whatever to be their confessors regularly or to direct them" [CS588].

But in any case, Ignatius' earlier letters to Sister Teresa are treasures of spiritual wisdom that might give us some hint of the nature

[1] The radiance of Ignatius' face was commented on by others, including Philip Neri (Scripta II, 425-426, 428, 488, 491, 499, 559, 1010) and Isabel Roser (FN IV, 145). See Wulf (1977).

[2] For the Roser story and the difficulties surrounding her entrance into the Society and its painful resolution, see Rahner (1960) and Meissner (1992b).

of Ignatius' directive efforts. From the earliest days of his ascetic career, Ignatius devoted a great deal of effort to the reform of convents. He began in Barcelona, where a special target was the Benedictine convent of Santa Clara. One of the good sisters in this convent was Teresa Rejadella, daughter of a noble Catalan family. The regimen of the convent had grown lax, but a small group of nuns, led by Sister Teresa, was determined to bring about canonical and spiritual reform. Teresa met Iñigo and placed herself under his spiritual direction. Their efforts to reform the convent continued over the years until her death in 1552. Out of their correspondence comes one of the finest of Ignatius' spiritual letters — a kind of summary and commentary on the *Spiritual Exercises*. Teresa had written in June 1536 begging for his spiritual advice. His reply expressed his fatherly concern and presented a compendium of his basic spiritual ideas. The wiles and temptations of the enemy are described — first doubts, then vainglory, and finally false humility. The remedies are the familiar ones — detachment, indifference, and humility. Central to spiritual progress is the discernment of spirits by which the devout soul can make its precarious way between the temptations of the lax conscience to deny or minimize the seriousness of sin and the temptations of the delicate conscience to find sin and doubt where there is none, to distinguish the sorts of consolation and desolation that come from the evil spirit and those that come from the spirit of God.

The nun and the pilgrim would never meet again, but the conversation continued by way of letters between Rome and Barcelona. A recurring issue was the convent reform in which Teresa was so deeply embroiled. She would often complain when Ignatius failed to respond to one of her letters. Meanwhile, the canonical situation in the convent grew more complex and difficult. The little band of zealots was staging a revolt, insisting on frequent communion (at Ignatius' urging) to the dismay of the rest of the good sisters. In 1546 a new abbess was elected through the influence of her aristocratic relatives. Teresa and her cohorts refused in conscience to show her religious obedience. Father Araoz, the Jesuit provincial, was involved in consultations; he conveyed the details of the situation to Ignatius and suggested that one solution was to put Teresa's band under obedience to the Jesuits. Teresa was in collusion with Isabel Roser, and Isabel became the energetic advocate for Teresa's reform and the Jesuit connection to Ignatius.

All this placed Ignatius in a difficult and embarrassing position. Prince Philip of Spain and several bishops were pressuring him to address the serious problem of reform of Catalan nunneries generally. Ignatius set to work. Every influential connection was brought into play. He was firm about his apostolic commitment to the reform of the nunneries and equally clear that there could be no question of admitting nuns into the Society.

Teresa did not give up so easily; several more letters arrived in Rome imploring Ignatius to change his mind. The case of Santa Clara had become celebrated by this time. The abbess and the reformers were at war, and the religious life of the convent was a shambles. Efforts were made to reorganize the convent according to Franciscan rules since no help was forthcoming from the Jesuits. This plan failed too. Lawyers were called in and the case dragged on in royal and ecclesiastic courts for years. Finally an accommodation was made to continue the convent under Benedictine rule. Ignatius continued his spiritual support, but his view was that as long as the convent was under Benedictine jurisdiction, no real reform was possible without religious obedience — a familiar Ignatian theme. In the end all the planning and struggling came to naught; the convent remained unreformed until long after both Teresa and Ignatius had gone to their rewards.

In the midst of this turmoil and conflict, Ignatius wrote his classic letter of spiritual concern and direction to Sister Teresa on 18 June 1536:

> When I received your letter a few days ago, it gave me much joy in the Lord whom you serve and desire to serve better, to whom we ought to attribute all the good we find in creatures. As you said he would in your letter, Caceres has informed me at length about your affairs, and not only about them, but also about the suggestions or guidance he gave you for each particular case. On reading what he says to me, I find nothing else he need have written, although I should have preferred to have the information in a letter from you, for no one can describe sufferings so well as the one who actually experiences them.
>
> You ask me to take charge of you for the love of God our Lord. It is true that, for many years now, his divine Majesty has given me the desire, without any merit on my part, to do everything I possibly can for all men and women who walk in the path of his good will and pleasure, and, in addition, to serve those who work in his holy service. Since I do not doubt that you are one of these, I am pleased to find myself in the position of being able to put what I say into practice.
>
> You also beg me to write to you what the Lord says to me and that I should say freely what I think. What I feel in the Lord I will tell you frankly with a right good will and if I should appear to be

harsh in anything, I shall be more so against him who is trying to upset you than against you. The enemy is troubling you in two ways, but not so as to make you fall into the guilt of sin which would separate you from God's greater service and your own greater peace of soul. The first thing is that he sets before you and persuades you to cultivate a false humility; the second that he strives to instil into you an excessive fear of God with which you are too much taken up and occupied.

As to the first point the general course which the enemy follows with those who love and begin to serve God our Lord is to set hindrances and obstacles in their way. This is the first weapon with which he tries to wound them — by suggesting "How will you be able to live in such penance all your life without the enjoyment of parents, friends and possessions and in so solitary a life, without even some slight relief? In another way of life you could save yourself without such great dangers". He thus gives us to understand that we have to live a life which is longer, on account of the trials which he sets before us, than that of any man who ever lived, whereas he hides from us the many and great comforts and consolations which the Lord is wont to give to such souls, if the man who has newly embraced the Lord's service breaks through all these difficulties, choosing to want to suffer with his Creator and Lord.

Then the enemy tries his second weapon, namely, boasting or vainglory, giving the soul to understand that there is much goodness or holiness in it and setting it in a higher place than it deserves. If the servant of the Lord resists these darts with humility and lowers himself, not consenting to be what the enemy would persuade him to be, he brings out the third weapon which is that of false humility. That is, when he sees the servant of the Lord so good and humble that, when he does what the Lord commands, he thinks it all valueless and looks at his own shortcomings, not at any glory for himself, the enemy puts it into his mind that if he discovers any particular blessing given him by God our Lord, any good deed done, or good intention or desire, he is sinning by another kind of vainglory, because he speaks in his own favour. Thus the enemy strives that he should not speak of the blessings received from his Lord, so that there shall be no fruit either in others or in the person himself, for the recognition of what one has received is always a stimulus to greater things, although such speaking must be practised with restraint and motivated by the greater profit both of others and of the man himself, as opportunity provides and when others are likely to believe what we say and profit by it. When, however, we make ourselves humble, he tries to draw us into false humility, that is, into humility which is exaggerated and corrupt. Of this your words are clear evidence, for after you relate certain weaknesses and fears which are true of you, you say, "I am a poor nun, desirous, it seems to me, of serving Christ our Lord" — but you still do not dare to say: "I am desirous of serving Christ our Lord" or: "The Lord gives me desires to serve him", but you say: "I seem to be desirous." If you look closely, you will easily see that those desires of serving Christ our Lord do not come from you, but are given you by our Lord. Thus when you say: "The Lord has given me increased desires to serve him", you praise him, because you make his gift known and you glory in him, not in yourself, since you do not attribute that grace to yourself.

Thus we ought to be very circumspect and if the enemy lifts us up, humble ourselves, going over our sins and wretchedness. If he casts us down and dejects us, we ought to look upwards with true faith and hope in the Lord, going over the benefits we have received and considering with how much love and kindness he waits for us to be saved, whereas the enemy does not care whether he speaks the truth or lies, but only that he may overcome us. Ponder well how the martyrs, standing before their idolatrous judges, declared themselves Christ's servants. So you, standing before the enemy of the whole human race and tempted in this way by him, when he wants to deprive you of the strength the Lord gives you and wants to make you weak and full of fear with his snares and deceits, do not merely say that you are desirous of serving our Lord — rather you have to say and confess without fear that you are his servant and that you would rather die than separate yourself from his service. If he represents God's justice to me, I bring up his mercy; if he puts God's mercy before me, I reply with his justice. If we would avoid trouble, this is the way wherein we should walk, that the deceiver may in turn be deceived, applying to ourselves the teaching of Holy Scripture which says: "Beware that thou be not so humble that in excessive humility thou be led into folly" (cf. Eccles. 13:11).

Coming to the second point, as the enemy has placed in us a certain fear under the cloak of a humility which is false, and so suggests that we should not speak even of good, holy and profitable things, so he brings in its train another, much worse fear, namely whether we may not be separated and cut off from our Lord as outcasts — in great measure on account of our past lives. For just as through the first fear the enemy attained victory, so he finds it easy to tempt us with this other. To explain this in some measure, I will bring up another device the enemy has. If he finds a person with a lax conscience who passes over sins without adverting to them, he does his best to make venial sin seem nothing, mortal sin venial and very grave mortal sin of small account — so that he turns the defect he finds in us, that of too lax a conscience, to account. If he finds some other person with an overtender conscience — a tender conscience is no fault — and sees that such a person casts far from him mortal sin and as far as possible venial sin — for it is not in us to avoid all — and even tries to cast away from himself every semblance even of small sin, imperfection or defect, then the enemy tries to throw that good conscience into confusion, suggesting sin where there is no sin and defect where there is perfection, so that he may disturb and trouble us. In many instances where he cannot induce a soul to sin and has no hope of ever bringing that about, at least he tries to trouble it.

In order to explain more clearly how fear is caused, I shall speak, although briefly, of two lessons which the Lord usually gives or permits. The one he grants, the other he permits. That which he gives is interior consolation, which casts out all trouble and brings one to the full love of our Lord. To such souls as he enlightens with this consolation, he reveals many secrets, both at the time and later. In short, with this divine consolation, all trials are a pleasure and all weariness rest. In the case of him who walks in this fervour, warmth and interior consolation, there is no burden so great that it does not seem light to him, no penance or other trial so severe that it does not seem sweet. This shows and lays open to us the way we ought to follow, fleeing from the contrary. This consolation does not always remain with us — it follows its due seasons according to the divine ordinance. All this is to our profit, for when we are left without this divine consolation, then comes the other lesson, which is this — our old enemy now puts before us all possible obstacles to turn us aside from what we have begun, and he harasses us unceasingly, everything being the contrary of the first lesson. He often makes us sad, without our knowing why we are sad, nor can we pray with any devotion, contemplate or even speak of or listen to the things of God our Lord with relish or any interior delight. Not only this, but if he finds us to be weak and much dejected by these harmful thoughts, he suggests that we are entirely forgotten by God our Lord and we come to imagine that we are separated from God in everything and that however much we have done and however much we want to do, it is of no value whatsoever. Thus he strives to bring us into distrust of everything and we shall see that our great fear and weakness is caused in this way, for we then make too much of our miseries and are too passive in the face of his false arguments. It is necessary, therefore, that he who fights should look to what condition he is in. If it is consolation we should be humble and lowly and think that afterwards the test of temptation will come. If temptation, darkness or sadness comes, we must withstand it without any irritation and wait with patience for the Lord's consolation which will shatter all troubles and darkness coming from without.

> It now remains for me to say something of what we feel when we read about God our Lord, how we must understand what we read and, when it is understood, learn to profit by it. It often happens that our Lord moves and impels our soul to one particular course or another by laying it open — that is, speaking within it without the sound of any voice, raising it all to his divine love, without our being able to resist what he suggests, even if we wanted to do so. In accepting such suggestions, we must of necessity be in conformity with the Commandments, the precepts of the Church, obedient to our superiors and full of complete humility, for the same divine Spirit is in all. Where we can frequently deceive ourselves is that after this consolation or inspiration, while the soul remains in bliss, the enemy creeps in under cover of joy and an appearance that is good, to make us exaggerate what we have felt from God our Lord, so as to make us disturbed and upset in everything.
>
> At other times he makes us undervalue the lesson received, making us disturbed and ill at ease, because we cannot perfectly carry out all that has been shown to us. More prudence is necessary here than in any other matter. Many times we must restrain our great desire to speak of the things of God our Lord. At other times we must speak more than the desire or movement we have in us prompted — for in this it is necessary to think more of the good of others than of our own desires. When the enemy thus strives to increase or diminish the good impression received, we must go forward trying to help others, like someone crossing a ford. If he finds a good passage, that is, if he confidently hopes that some good will follow, he goes forward. If the ford is muddy, that is, if others would take scandal at his good words, then he always draws rein, seeking a more suitable time and hour to speak. (Epistolae I, 99-107 [Letter 7]; in Rahner (1960) pp. 331-5; also in Young (1959) pp. 18-23)

This letter stands on its own merits as a little classic of Ignatian spirituality. It is a minidigest of the essence of the *Spiritual Exercises*, enunciating the familiar themes of self-denial, the seeking for God's will, the focus on the wiles and deceits of the enemy of man's spiritual progress, the recourse to the discernment of spirits, and the emphasis on humility — all themes echoing the motifs of the *Exercises*.

And soon after, a second letter followed with words of spiritual support and advice:

> You say you find in yourself great ignorance and great cowardice, and so forth. To know this alone is to know much. But you go on to add that this condition is produced by the many and vague directions you have received. I agree with you that, when

one is indefinite, one does not understand, and helps less. But the Lord, who sees this need, will Himself come to your aid.

Every kind of meditation in which the understanding is engaged wearies the body. There are other kinds of meditation, orderly and restful, which are pleasant to the understanding and offer no difficulty to the interior faculties of the soul, and which can be made without interior or exterior expenditure of effort. These methods do not weary the body but rather help to rest it, except in the two following instances. The first is when you withdraw the natural nourishment and recreation which you should give to the body. By nourishment I mean when one is so taken up by such meditations that he forgets to give the body its proper nourishment at the proper hours. By recreation I mean to allow the understanding to roam at will, provided only that the subjects it deals with be good or indifferent, or at least not bad.

The second instance is this, and it is of frequent occurrence in those who are much given to prayer or contemplation., They find trouble getting to sleep because just before bedtime they exercise their minds on the matter of their meditation and keep thinking about it, and consequently find it difficult to fall asleep. It is the enemy who chooses this moment to present good thoughts to the mind. He has but one purpose, to make the body suffer by robbing it of its sleep. This must be avoided entirely. With a healthy body you will be able to do much. I don't know what you can do with one that is infirm. A healthy body is a great help either for good or evil: evil for those whose wills are depraved by evil habits, but good in those whose will is entirely given to God and trained to habits of virtue.

If, however, I do not know what meditations and exercises you make and the amount of time you give to them, I cannot say more than what I have written, unless Caceres has told you otherwise. And here once more I insist especially that you think of God as loving you, as I have no doubt He does, and that you correspond with this love and pay no attention whatever to the evil thoughts, even if they are obscene or sensual (when they are not deliberate), nor of your cowardice or tepidity. For even St. Peter and St. Paul did not succeed in escaping all or some of these thoughts. Even when we do not succeed fully, we gain much by paying no attention to them. I am not going to save myself by the good works of the good angels, and I am not going to be condemned because of the evil thoughts and the weaknesses which the bad angels, the flesh, and the world bring before my mind. God asks only one thing of me, that my soul seek to be conformed with His Divine Majesty. And the soul so conformed makes the body conformed, whether it wish it or not, to the divine will. In this is our greatest battle, and here the good pleasure of the eternal

> and sovereign Goodness. (Epistolae I, 107-109 [Letter 8]; in Young (1959) 24-25)

Once again, we can hear in these words echoes of the Two Standards from the *Spiritual Exercises.*

Another letter, dated over a decade later, responded to Teresa's continuing complaints. In her letters to Ignatius she undoubtedly returned with renewed emphasis to the question of the reform of her convent, and with renewed effort to engage Ignatius and his Jesuits in the cause of reform. In 1546 the saint attempted with fresh energy to undertake the reform of convents of nuns in Catalonia, and even to interest others in the effort, including the provincial, Father Anthony Araoz; the visitor, Father Miguel de Torres; Jaime Cazador, the bishop of Barcelona; Francis Borgia, the duke of Gandia and later of the Society; and Philip, heir to the throne of Spain and later king. Ignatius tried to exhort his correspondent to recognize her own defects and disown them, trusting that the reform, while difficult, will be successful.

> Rome, October 1547
>
> May the grace and love of Jesus Christ our God and Lord live always in our souls. Amen.
>
> Santa Cruz brought me your two letters in which, showing your dissatisfaction with the faults of the community and those of individuals, you give proof of the good desire God has given you that some means be found of correcting both the one and the other. May God in His infinite mercy hear your prayers, for it is written of Him, "The Lord hath heard the desire of the poor" (Ps 9: 17).
>
> Regarding the faults of individuals, it is certainly necessary that whoever knows himself should recognize the faults he has, for he will never be free of them in the state of our present misery until in the furnace of the everlasting love of God our Creator and Lord all our wickedness shall be entirely consumed, when our souls shall be completely penetrated and possessed by Him and our wills thus perfectly conformed to — or rather, transformed into — His will, which is essential rectitude and infinite goodness. But may He by His infinite mercy grant to all of us at least daily to regret and abhor all our faults and imperfections, and participate at last in the eternal light of His wisdom and lay hold of His infinite goodness and perfection, in the clear light of which even the least of our defects will appear to be insupportable. By thus attacking them we will weaken and lessen them with the help of the same God our Lord.

As to the defects of the community for which you ask a remedy from God's hand and hope that in His goodness He will provide one, this is not only my own desire but my hope also. We may take as a sign that God will condescend to effect this reformation the fact that the prince is also desirous to see a reform and that effective means are being sought to bring it about. That there are difficulties is nothing new, but rather to be expected in matters of any importance for God's service and glory. But the more difficult the work, the more pleasing it will be, besides being also the occasion for giving God our Lord more sincere and ceaseless thanks.

As to news about our Society, you will have some one closer at hand to keep you informed. Only, I beseech you for the love of Jesus Christ, our Society's head, even though He is also our common Lord and sovereign of all created things, to remember us earnestly in your prayers to His Divine Majesty, that He may deign daily to be better pleased and glorified by our Society.

My own health isn't much. Blessed be He who by His blood and death won eternal health for us by a share in His kingdom and glory. May He grant us the grace that, whether the condition of our health be good or bad, it and all else may always be employed in His greater service, praise and glory. Amen. (Epistolae I 627-28 [Letter 214]; in Young (1959) 153-154)

But Ignatius held firm to his principles and drew a firm line beyond which he was unwilling to go. His mind was firmly set against assuming spiritual responsibility for the direction of convents of nuns by his Society, just as he was firmly set against ecclesiastical preferment for his men.[3] Ignatius made his stand in a letter of consolation, but of gentle yet firm refusal, to two worthy religious of the convent of Santa Clara, Jeronyma Oluja and Teresa:

Rome, April 5, 1549

May the sovereign grace and everlasting love of Christ our Lord ever be our protection and support.

I have received letters from different persons in Barcelona, and from them I can see that our Lord has sent you trials, and thus given you no small occasion to practice the virtues which His Divine Goodness has bestowed on you and of proving their solidity, since it is in things that are hard that one can test one's spiritual progress. I have many an occasion to see this in His service. May it please Christ Jesus, who died and suffered so much for us all, to give us abundant grace to suffer with profit for His holy love what is given us to suffer, and thus apply a remedy to all that

[3] See chapter XXIV above.

> needs remedying in the way that will be most acceptable to His Divine Goodness. But this I hold for certain, that that remedy is not the one you have been indicating up to the present. For although the Society, in keeping with the many obligations for which in our Lord it has a special affection, has every wish to console and be of service to you in accordance with our profession, yet the authority of the vicar of Christ has closed the door against our taking part in the government or direction of religious women. The Society at the very beginning asked this, as it judged that it would be to the greater service of God our Lord to be as free as possible from these ties, so as to be able to hurry to any part of the world where obedience to the supreme pontiff and the needs of the neighbor should summon them. For this reason I do not think that the remedy you suggest would be at all pleasing to God our Lord, and I hope that in His infinite bounty another more fitting means will be found to attain your ends, which we all desire in our Lord, to your peace and special consolation.
>
> While I defer to what you, being on the spot, might think best, you will see from Master Polanco's letter how the matter presents itself to me. I will not therefore enter into details here. But I will say this, and I hope that you will believe me, that for the end we all have in view, which is the greater service of God our Lord, it would not do for us to accept the task in question. If we did have to undertake such a work for religious women, our services would be offered to you before all others.
>
> May it please the Divine Wisdom to grant that we may always know His most holy will and find our peace and happiness in ever fulfilling it. Your servant in our Lord . . . (Epistolae II, 374-375 [Letter 630]; in Young (1959) 187-188)

## THE *Spiritual Exercises*

The letters to Sister Teresa give us a clear sense of the centrality of the *Spiritual Exercises* in all of Ignatius' spirituality, but also the manner in which he brought them to bear in his spiritual direction. There were variations in the manner and degree to which he applied these principles to individual directees, but clearly, for individuals whose state of life was already fixed, whether laymen or ecclesiastics, Ignatius' principal tool was the making of the Spiritual Exercises. We have a letter written from Venice, on 16 November 1536, to Ignatius' former confessor at Alcala and Paris, Manuel Miona, inviting him to make the Exercises:

> Twice and thrice as many times as I can, I beg you for the service of God to do what I have already requested of you, in order that in

> the future His Divine Majesty may not be able to reproach me for not having asked you with all my strength, seeing that in this life I cannot think of, perceive, or understand anything that would be better, both for drawing some advantage for yourself and for helping many others to advance. If you feel no need because of the first motive, you will see that the Exercises will be useful for the second, far beyond anything you can imagine. (Epistolae I, 112-113 [Letter 10]; in Young (1959) 27-28; cited in De Guibert (1964), p. 106)

This letter offers us some sense of the importance Ignatius gave to the making of the Spiritual Exercises and the dominant role they played in all aspects of his spiritual apostolate —direction included. The same principles are put to work, whether among the members of his Society or with others. The service and glory of God is his constant and abiding goal. For all he urges the struggle to control and regulate inordinate attachments and passions by means of frequent examens and self-abnegation. But there are also differences. His advice to Sister Teresa, for example, is quite different than his directives to Jesuit scholastics regarding frequent communion. His letter to her of 15 November 1543 states:

> Even if there are not such greater interior signs or such wholesome inclinations of the soul, the good and sufficient testimony is the dictate of one's own conscience. What I mean is this. After all, the whole matter is lawful for you in the Lord if, apart from evident mortal sins or what you can judge to be such, you think that your soul derives more help and is inflamed more with love for our Creator and Lord; and if you receive Communion with this intention, finding from experience that this spiritual food sustains, soothes, and rests you, and by preserving you makes you better able for His greater service and glory, you may without doubt receive daily;in fact, it would be better for you to do so. (Epistolae I, 274-276 [Letter 73]; in Young (1959), p. 71; cited in de Guibert (1964), p. 107)

As de Guibert notes, the difference may have to do with the difficulties of Teresa's situation in which she lacked the kinds of support and safeguards available to Jesuit scholastics. His advice regarding mental prayer reflected similar breadth of outlook and adaptability. His letters to Teresa and those to Francis Borgia[4] give some hints as to his own experience of prayer of infused contemplation, from a time when

[4] See chapter XXXII above. The letter is cited in Doncoeur (1959).

he had yet to assimilate the lessons of experience that taught him the wisdom of greater reserve with respect to long hours of prayer.

De Guibert (1964) makes a summary evaluation of this aspect of Ignatius' spiritual teaching and practice that is worthy of quotation:

> Thus in all his activity as a molder and director of souls Ignatius appears above all as one faithful in transmitting the message he received from God in the graces of his mystical life — the message to promote a spirituality of service through love. But at the same time, he was very independent of his own interior ways while he directed each soul according to the ways marked out by God for it. Consequently he was very docile to the lessons of experience; he was penetrating and quick to discern and then to bring to accomplishment at any cost the chief desires of God with respect to each soul. He was constantly careful to know these souls ever better, and to take account of all the differences by which they were distinguished. He had very broad points of view so as never to look upon them as isolated individuals, but rather as persons within the whole ensemble of the Church's life. Very realistic, he never confused mere means with the true end, the accessory with the essential. Above all, he overflowed with charity, loving souls intensely because of his love of Christ their Redeemer, for whom he wished to win them. He forgot himself in everything, and in his spiritual direction as in all else he had but one thought: service — the better service, the greater glory of God his Sovereign Lord and his Master whom he ardently loved. (pp. 107-8)

# CHAPTER XXXIV

# THE *SPIRITUAL JOURNAL*

## The Book

Primary sources for study of Ignatius' mystical life are the *Exercises*, his *Autobiography*, and finally his *Spiritual Journal.* The *Exercises* reveal the methodology of his spirituality; it was apparently Ignatius' continual application of techniques discovered at Manresa and incorporated in this manual of spirituality that provided the core of his own ascetical practice as well as the model for spiritual formation of his followers. The autobiography provides accounts of some of the more meaningful and influential of his mystical experiences, particularly some of the more important visions and illuminations.

Most revealing of all with respect to the ecstatic and mystical dimension of his spiritual life are the pages of his *Spiritual Journal* that have survived. These fragments consist of two copybooks, each of only a dozen or so pages, written in Ignatius' hand. The first, covering the period from 2 February to 12 March 1544, is composed of rather extensive notes from Ignatius' long deliberation on poverty in the Society — lasting forty days. The second copybook, covering the period from 13 March 1544 to 27 February 1545, contains cryptic entrees with thoughts indicated by no more than abbreviations or algebraic signs.

There is little question not only that these notes were intended for Ignatius only and not for anyone else's eyes, but that he attached great importance to them and made considerable use of them in his own prayer life (de Guibert 1964; Haas 1977). He apparently transcribed certain sections from the *Journal* for his own more convenient use. They are probably only part of extensive notes Ignatius made but kept very much to himself. He refused to let even Gonzalves da Camara, to whom he communicated his autobiography, see any of them (Young 1958).[1] Toward the end of his life, he was careful to

[1] Da Camara was obviously interested in recording details of Ignatius' spiritual life, many of which are included in his *Memorial.* As minister in the professed house from September 1554 to October 1555, he had continual contact with

destroy most of these notes; the few remaining pages were discovered in his desk drawer after his death. As Haas (1977) commented: "In the *Diary*, . . . Ignatius lays completely bare the mystery of his intimacy with God. Consequently, no other document offers us a more penetrating insight into the magnificent world of faith that was the inner life of Ignatius" (p. 165). The importance he attached to these jottings is suggested by his framing of certain lines as being especially important, passages which he transcribed elsewhere. One use he made of these pages was to place them on the altar when he said mass to beg God for new illumination about his deliberations (Haas 1977).

## DEVOTIONAL LIFE

There are numerous testimonies from Ignatius' companions as to the intense spiritual life he led during his time as general when the *Journal* was composed. In addition to habitual recollection, keeping his mind focused on God and living in the presence of God, there were more intense experiences that seemed to overwhelmed him. Nadal remarked on his capacity to see the hand of God in all things and to live continuously in the presence of God; his recollection was such that he had to find ways to divert himself from it in order to follow any other pursuit. Ribadenyra made similar observations regarding the intensity of his spiritual consolations and the ease with which the saint could find recollection in the middle of a busy schedule of activity — echoing the theme of "*contemplativus in actione.*" The degree of this responsiveness was such that he would feel its effects as soon as he put himself to pray, with results so powerful that his body reacted in ways he could no longer control. Nadal commented, "At Mass he received great consolations and an extreme sensitivity to divine things. At times he was even obliged to omit saying Mass, for the disturbance was so strong that it weakened and damaged his bodily strength and his health" (SdeSI I, 472, 475; FN II, 123, 126; cited in de Guibert (1964) p. 45). The same problem arose in saying the divine office — the spiritual consolations, feelings and tears were so intense and so abundant that the office took too much time and his health suffered. Permission had to be obtained from Paul III to substitute shorter prayers. The *Journal* of 1544 reveals the extent to which these mystical graces and ecstatic experiences affected his daily mass.

Ignatius and kept a daily notebook of observations, sayings, and so on that provide additional information about Ignatius' spiritual experience for another decade after the *Journal*, up to the eve of his death (de Guibert 1964).

His effort to say mass daily had to yield to his diminishing strength, since the experience was wrenching and exhausting on every occasion. By 1555, he was celebrating only on Sundays and feast days, and he had to be content with hearing mass said by another. Manareo recalled, "His Mass lasted a little more than an hour, because he was hindered by frequent elevations of spirit and by his tears. This is why he celebrated somewhat rarely, especially in public. To this is added the great obstacle of his weakness; therefore for several months I have celebrated almost daily for him in his private chapel" (SdeSI I, 511; cited in de Guibert (1964) p. 46). Attendance at mass was usually followed by two hours of intense private prayer, a period during which no interruptions were allowed.

The *Journal* lends concrete expression to these details. He recorded the singular insights that came to him in prayer — on appropriation in prayer to the persons of the Trinity (Feb. 19), and on the same day illuminations regarding relations of the Trinity and processions of the persons, and further trinitarian insights on February 21st. Again on the 27th, he received "an experiencing, or more properly a seeing, beyond the natural powers, of the Most Holy Trinity and of Jesus, thus representing myself, or placing myself, or being in the midst of the Most Holy Trinity, in order that this intellectual vision might be communicated to me, and with this seeing and experiencing there was a flood of tears and of love."

Ignatius remarked repeatedly that the intensity of these experiences far exceeded his capacity to give them expression. He referred to "flashes of understanding too great to be written down" (Feb. 15), "experiencing and a seeing that cannot be explained" (Feb. 25), "respect and a wonderful depth of reverence which I find impossible to explain" (March 17), and "flashes of understanding so many and so exquisite that I have neither the memory nor the understanding to describe and explain them" (April 2). As de Guibert (1964) noted, these observations were not directed to others but solely to himself. He confessed to Laynez that he was able to find God supernaturally almost at will, but that any effort to limit or withdraw from this mystical invasion was beyond his control. About this effort to restrain his mystical immersion, he wrote: "Although I used force to prevent myself from raising on high the eyes of my mind, and to be content with everything, I asked God even that, if it were to His equal glory, He should not visit me with tears; nevertheless occasionally my mind escaped unexpectedly upwards, and I thought I saw something of the divine essence which at other times, in spite of my desires, it is not in my power to perceive" (March 8).

De Guibert (1964) recalled two accounts from Ignatius that help to put the material of the *Journal* in perspective. He was reported to have told Laynez, "After having read the lives of many saints, unless indeed there had been in their lives more than had been written, he would not readily consent to exchange with them what he himself had known and tasted of God — although he would not dare to prefer himself, or be rash enough to compare himself with the least one among them, he who was not a saint, but a poor sinner and a worthless man" (SdeSI I, 349; FN II, 339; cited in de Guibert (1964) p. 49). On another occasion he confided to Ribadenyra, when he naively suggested that if one didn't know Ignatius his observations might smack of vanity, that "there was no sin of which he had less fear; even more, that if he should ask himself whether there was question of the hundredth or the five-hundredth part [of God's gifts to him], he would conclude that he had not told even the thousandth part of God's gifts; for he thought that it was not proper for him to tell them, meaning to say that those who heard about those gifts would not understand them." To which Ribadenyra added: "He was accustomed to say that he was coming to believe that no other man could be found in whom God had so joined these two things together as in himself: on his part to have sinned so much, and on God's part to have granted so many graces. . . . When he sinned he desired to experience some suffering either sensible or spiritual, such as the privation of graces or of consolations and the like; and this experience never came to him, but it seemed that God visited him all the more" (SdeSI I, 395; FN II, 473-474; in de Guibert (1964) p. 49).

## THE DELIBERATION ON POVERTY

The first section of the *Journal* is given over to Ignatius' deliberation on poverty in the Society that extended over some forty days of intense prayer and meditation. Although he experienced profound mystical favors, his deliberations were also marked by doubts, false starts and stops, hesitations, and uncertainty. This deliberation reveals the manner in which he utilized the times of election to reach his decision.[2] The method seems to have made use of all three times in reaching a decision in matter that was highly complex and carried such a load of consequences for the future of the Society. The matter involved not merely what made good sense economically or financially, but what made sense for the spiritual wellbeing of the Society,

[2] See the discussion of the times of election in chapter XIII above.

for the safeguarding of the religious spirit in his men, and beyond all that, what God's will might have been with respect to these matters. In order to reach a more secure conclusion, he had to make use of any and all resources available to him, but in the Ignatian perspective, the strongest and most valuable resource was to be sought in prayer. Whatever methods might have been consistent with the third time for election, the more convincing and powerful input was sought in a prayerful seeking of divine inspiration after the model of the first time. That method seemingly carried greater conviction to the mind of Ignatius than any other.

Ignatius had accepted the commission of the companions to write constitutions for the new Society, and the issue of poverty was central to this endeavor. His discernments pointed in a single direction, along with a process of careful reasoning and thoughtful reflection (Feb. 6, 8-11, 16). But this conviction was no more than a consultative discernment that was to be submitted to the further judgment of the companions (Young 1958; Toner 1991). Whatever his determination of God's will, there was no guarantee that the companions might not reach a different conclusion. He had drawn up two series of reasons favoring complete poverty as ordered to the greater glory of God, when he recorded the following experience: ". . . the thought of Jesus occurring to me, I felt a movement to follow him, it seemed to me interiorly, since he was head of the Society, a greater argument to proceed in complete poverty than all the other human reasons, although I thought all the reasons for the past elections tended toward the same decision" (Young 1958, pp. 15-16). The influence of the third mode of humility and the principle of likeness to Christ seems to have played a confirming role (Toner 1991).

The "reasons" referred to here are not included in the *Journal*, but they are recorded in the "Deliberations on poverty" (Iparraguirre and Dalmases 1963). The norm of judgment is consistently the greater glory of God and greater likeness to Christ. The issue was, "whether our churches should have an income, and whether the Society could accept help from it" (Vita 100). The reasons included the fact that the ten companions had unanimously opted for complete poverty, without any source of income, to better follow Christ, who was himself without income and counseled his followers to follow his example when he sent them out to preach; that the proposal for this form of poverty had received papal confirmation; that complete poverty was closer to the evangelical norm and therefore more perfect; that the Society would gain greater spiritual profit by imitating our Lord in poverty, and it would have the effect of producing greater union and humility. The reasons are highly spiritual, following Ignatius' evangelical ideal, yet he still looked for some form of affective sign to gain greater assurance — a clear blending of third and second times of election.

The forty-day discernment is recorded in considerable detail, for the most part given over to seeking confirmation of the decision he had reached substantially by the eighth day. Toner (1991) describes the phases of this process. The first phase, from Feb. 2 to 11, reveals Ignatius' use of a combination of second and third time discernments to reach the conclusion that God willed perfect poverty for the Society. The final conclusion was reached by the evening of Feb. 9th. On the following days, he offered the decision to God in prayer and received great consolation and a sense of confirmation.

One might have thought that the decision was a done deal at that point, but he could not quite close the door. On the 12th, he began to experience temptations — doubts, hesitations, and a wish to allow some relaxation of perfect and complete poverty. He experienced distractions from prayer, and spent the 13th seeking pardon for this failing. The next few days, Feb. 14-16, brought consolations and a feeling of assurance that he was forgiven, and again a firm conviction of the rightness of his decision, concluding that any mitigation of complete poverty would have to be seen as a temptation. By the 17th, the matter was closed and no further confirmation seemed necessary. He determined to conclude the election with celebration of mass in honor of the Trinity. His sense of consolation and confirmation was at first strong and positive, but it did not persist as strongly, causing him to question the decision and brought on a fear of making a mistake. This was compounded with a feeling of impatience and frustration that the long and difficult discernment could not be brought to a close.

The third phase covered from Feb. 19 to March 11. He continued to experience many powerful mystical consolations, but seemingly not related to the election regarding poverty. But the final decision is still postponed — seemingly waiting for a final and decisive sign from God that would provide certain confirmation. Finally, the fourth and critical phase was reached on March 12th. The day began with great devotion, but was suddenly interrupted by a severe desolation, feeling estranged from the divine persons as though he had never had any experience of them and never would again. He experienced disturbingly negative thoughts about Jesus, feeling confused, and finding peace nowhere. He then realized that this desolation was the work of the tempter, and then he resolved to end his discernment and to seek no further proofs, arguing that this would be more pleasing to God. At the same time, he was conflicted about ending the election in a state of desolation rather than consolation. He declared the election finished, but not without further hesitations. But these, following his own principles of discernment of spirits, he brushed aside. As he put it, "A quarter of an hour after this, an awakening with understanding and clarity to how at the time that the tempter insinuated into me the thoughts against the divine persons and my mediators, he put or wished to put in me a doubt about the matter. On the contrary, when I experienced the visits and visions of the divine persons and my mediators, I was entirely steady and confirmed about the matter. I understood this with spiritual delight and with great security of soul, my eyes filled with tears" (March 12).

From a psychoanalytic perspective, none of this sounds unfamiliar. Given the conclusions previously drawn regarding the strain of obsessionality in Ignatius' personality (Meissner 1992b),[3] none of this is surprising. Granted that the decision regarding the status of poverty in the Society was weighty and fraught with implication, the obsessional vacillations described in the *Journal* account reflect a process of obsessional doubting and hesitating — reaching the decision, then undoing it with doubts and hesitations, then returning to a sense of confident assurance, only to have that again undone in a paroxysm of doubt, and the whole cycle seemingly endlessly repeated. But, nonetheless, it is interesting how he resolved the issue, utilizing his own rules for discernment and coming to a decisive resolution. Whatever dynamics of unresolved conflict were at work in him — and I would argue that residual conflicts over poverty, a deepseated ambivalence in his choice to follow Christ as his leader, and the tension between the difficult-to-maintain ideals of the evangelical spirit he had made part of his own ego ideal and the demands for institutional resources and an as yet unarticulated concept of corporate poverty were contributing factors — they did not prevent, but certainly prolonged his coming to a definitive conclusion.

The ultimate test for Ignatius, at least in the sense that it was the kind of confirmation he put the greatest stock in, was in the order of mystical illumination. That he was able to bring himself to a meaningful resolution of his ambivalent conflicts, on one hand, and to discern effectively the compromising aspects of his need for divine confirmation, speaks eloquently to his persistent ego capacities. Here

[3] See also the discussion of his obsessional traits and his scrupulosity in chapters IX, XVII and XXXII above.

again we find writ large the basic Ignatian paradox — he exerted every effort as though the outcome were dependent on the genuineness and strength of that effort, but prayed and sought the consolation of divine illumination as though everything depended on God. The criterion he established was strikingly subjective — a sense of security and a lack of any desire to seek any further confirmation. He spoke of "a certain feeling of security that it was a good election" (Feb. 10), "great tranquillity and security of soul, like an exhausted man who takes a good rest, neither seeking nor caring to seek any further, considering the matter finished except for giving thanks" (Feb. 11), and "confirmation with tears and with complete security about everything decided" (March 12). But this mystical inclination was interwoven with a more practical and down-to-earth mind-set that would not rest easy in this subjective certitude, but sought a broader base of security in data and reasons grounded in reality.

## MYSTICAL EXPERIENCES

That the *Spiritual Journal* reveals to us the heights of true mystical infused contemplation seems beyond question. De Guibert (1964) described the indications of Ignatius' authentic mystical experience, including:

> . . . an experience of God as being presence under a form of knowledge which is simultaneously general and obscure yet rich and satisfying; an experience of love penetrating and dominating the soul in its innermost depths, in a manner connected with passivity; the mystic's experiencing this passivity while he is under the all-powerful control of God; his complete impotence to awaken, prolong, or renew these experiences, or even to foresee their approach or their end; also, his inability to translate what he has experienced into forms of current language or, above all, to give an idea of them which is fairly clear to one who has never experienced anything similar. (pp. 44-45)

Ignatius' mystical favors were both intellectual and affective. His visions carried with them profound understandings, but at the same time were accompanied by the most intense affective experiences — he was often moved to the point of tears by sentiments of great love and devotion. Preparing for mass, he experienced "a deluge of tears and sobs, and a love so intense that it seemed to me to unite me with excessive closeness to the Trinity's own love — a love so luminous and sweet that I thought that this overpowering visit and love were outstanding and excellent among all other visits" (de Guibert 1964, p. 54). We would also want to remind ourselves that there is an intrinsic connection between the *Exercises* and the *Journal*. As de Guibert has written:

> While the *Exercises*, whatever may be the mystical horizons they open up and the adaptations of which they are capable, are in their very text first of all a book of supernatural asceticism, a method of personal effort to submit to the action of grace, the *Journal* places us from the beginning on the mystical level in the strictest sense of the word. The three principal features which theologians agree in considering the essential characteristics of infused prayer, here stand revealed on every page: simple and intuitive vision of divine things, without multiplicity of concepts or discourse; the presence and action of God experienced in the soul; complete passivity in infused knowledge and love, which are given and withdrawn by God with sovereign independence of all our efforts. (Cited in Young 1958, p. 200)

One form of this intellectual illumination would seem to be the interior and exterior *loquela* he spoke of in the *Journal*. For example, he wrote in the entry for 11 May 1544:

> Tears before Mass and during it an abundance of them, and continued, together with the interior *loquela* during the Mass. It seems to me that it was given miraculously, as I had asked for it that same day, because in the whole week, I sometimes found the external *loquela*, and sometimes I did not, and the interior less, although last Saturday I was a little more purified.
>
> In the same way, in all the Masses of the week, although I was not granted tears, I felt greater peace and contentment throughout Mass because of the relish of the *loquelas*, together with the devotion I felt, than at other times when I shed tears in parts of the Mass. Those of today seemed to be much, much different from those of former days, as they came more slowly, more interiorly, gently without noises or notable movements, coming apparently from within without my knowing how to explain them. In the interior and exterior *loquela* everything moved me to divine love and to the gift of the *loquela* divinely bestowed, with so much interior harmony in the interior *loquela* that I cannot explain it. (Cited in Young 1958, pp. 247-248)

Nowhere does Ignatius explain the meaning of these *loquelae*. Some further hints come from the entry of May 22:

> Many tears before Mass in my room and in the chapel. In the greater part of the Mass, no tears, but much *loquela*, but I fell into

> some doubt about the relish and sweetness of the *loquela* for fear it might be from the evil spirit, thus causing the ceasing of the spiritual consolation of tears. Going on a little further, I thought that I took too much delight in the tone of the *loquela*, attending to the sound, without paying so much attention to the meaning of the words and of the *loquela*; and with this many tears, thinking that I was being taught how to proceed, with the hope of always finding further instruction as time went on. (Cited in Young 1958, p. 249)

We are left in the dark as to the nature of these *loquelae*. Internal words are part of mystical experience, and this may be similar phenomenon. The speaking takes place internally and comes from God, a form of infused knowledge. But why exterior and interior *loquela*? Commentators have found these passages "obscure" and "strange" (de Guibert 1964; Ravier 1987). Egan (1976) connects them with the CSCP that carry the stamp of divine illumination:

> . . . The CSCP begins at the exercitant's deepest core and center, that point of the human spirit prior to its division into intellect and will. The interior *loquela* seem to be the CSCP, or that moment thereof, as the CSCP makes its way through the fine point of the soul and begins to affect the intellect as intellect and the will as will, but still in a non-conceptual way. (p. 52)

## Tears

One of the most striking of Ignatius' mystical gifts was the so-called gift of tears. Especially during periods of prayer, when reciting the breviary or saying mass, his devotion was so intense that his eyes would be bathed in tears. He often had to pause between phrases or words because his eyes were filled with tears and he could not see. Recitation of the office took an inordinate time, often the greater part of the day, as did saying mass. After a while the constant tears began to affect his eyes, so that his disciples sought a papal dispensation from the obligation of the office, substituting a certain number of Our Fathers and Hail Marys for recitation of the office. But even these prayers brought their burden of consolation.

Prudence dictated modifications in his prayer life in the interest of preserving his health (Dudon 1949; de Guibert 1964). In the *Spiritual Journal*, in the midst of intense and tearful devotion, he records: "Because of the violent pain that I felt in one eye as a result of the tears, this thought came to me: if I continue saying Mass I could lose this eye, whereas it is better to keep it." Reasonable discretion finds its way even into the mystical process. Late in his life he told Polanco: "Earlier I felt disconsolate if I could not weep three times during one Mass. But the doctor has forbidden me to weep, and I took that as a command of obedience. Since then, I experience much more consolation without tears." At times the physical ravages of his intense emotional reactions forced him to mitigate his ascetical and mystical practices: the tears and exacerbations of his "stomach" ailment were the primary problems. At times he did not celebrate Mass because of his fears of the visions and their aftermath. For a time he celebrated only on Sundays and feast days (H. Rahner 1977).

The experience of tears was usually accompanied by intense affects of sweetness, consolation, spiritual joy, and loving devotion. The experience of tears dominates the *Spiritual Journal*. For example, he wrote:

> Entering the chapel and overwhelmed with a great devotion to the Most Holy Trinity, with very increased love and intense tears, without seeing the Persons distinctly as in the last two days, but perceiving in one luminous clarity a single Essence, I was drawn entirely to its love, and later, while preparing the altar and vesting, great devotion and tears, grace always assisting with much satisfaction of soul. (March 3)

And again:

> Later, the thought occurring to me that tomorrow I should say the Mass of the Most Holy Trinity, to determine what was to be done, or to end it altogether, many movements came upon me and tears, and from moment to moment over some space of time, great movements, sobs and floods of tears, drawing me entirely to the love of the Most Holy Trinity, with many colloquies. (March 7)

Such experiences exemplify what he had in mind in his description of CSCP. He once told Laynez that he had such experiences six or seven times a day (Young 1958).

De Guibert (1964) commented that, although tears occur frequently in the accounts of other mystics, Ignatius has no rivals in the frequency and intensity of his tears. Yet he himself held them in suspicion. In a letter to Nicholas of Gouda, he wrote:

> The gift of tears should not be asked for in any absolute way. It is not necessary, and it is not good or profitable either absolutely or for all persons . . . . Some have the gift because their nature is such that in them the affections in the higher part of the soul have their reaction in the lower part, or because God sees that the gift would be profitable for them and grants it. But that does not cause them

> to have a greater charity, nor to do more good than others who do not have these tears, although their charity in the higher part of the soul is not less. . . . I tell Your Reverence that in the case of some persons, I would not grant this gift to them, even if it were in my power to give it, because these tears do not serve to increase charity in them, and are harmful to their body and head, and consequently impede many practices of charity. (Epistolae V, 713-715, cited in de Guibert 1964) p. 64)

De Guibert (1964) wondered, in the light of this mistrustful view of tears, why they continued to hold a dominant place in the *Spiritual Journal.* He answered that they were probably associated with infused graces that were so precious to him. Ignatius wrote to Borgia distinguishing three kinds of tears, those that arise at the thought of one's own or others' sins, those arising from contemplation of the life of Christ, and those flowing from the love of the divine persons (Epistolae II, 233-237 [Letter 466]; cited in de Guibert 1964, pp. 64-65; also in Young (1959) pp. 179-182). In the *Journal* he speaks of tears "terminating now at the Father, now at the Son, . . . now at the saints, but without any vision, except insofar as the devotion terminates now at one, now at another" (March 14).

We should also note that, if Ignatius was open to the most profound spiritual consolations, he was also beset by significant desolations. He recorded:

> Finishing Mass, and after wards in my room, I found myself alone and without help of any kind, without power to relish any of my mediators, or any of the Divine Persons, but so remote and separated, as if I had never felt anything of Them, or would never feel anything again. Rather, thoughts came to me sometimes against Jesus, sometimes against another, being so confused with such different thoughts . . . (March 12)

Even in the soul of one deeply united to God the sense of separation from God and spiritual desolation can enter the picture and cloud the mystical horizon. Such moments of desolation may represent a form of re-emergence of negative or resistive elements from the unconscious that could be rooted in an underlying and unresolved ambivalence. It is also possible that such periods of desolate withdrawal may reflect little more than the countercurrent of affective retreat from the exhaustion of the affective overload involved in mystical transports. The spirit, however willing, is constrained by the limits of the flesh and its own inherent potentiality. The retreat from peak experiences of mystical intensity may be experienced as desolation.

Both reactions are possible. The experience Ignatius described here came in the middle of a series of intense mystical consolations.

## THE TRINITY

Ignatius' mysticism is profoundly trinitarian and, as the *Journal* reveals, he often prayed directly to the "Most Holy Trinity" or the "Three Divine Persons." These designations appear frequently as the object of worship, love and reverence, along with abundant tears and interior movements, visions, and graces of ecstatic proportions. He spoke of the depth and intensity of the trinitarian illuminations he experienced in these states, encountering the three divine persons and experiencing a profound intellectual penetration of their essence. He even spoke of a mystical penetration into the heart of the mystery of trinitarian circuminsession (Feb. 21).

The Trinity is mentioned again and again in the *Journal.* Of the passages marked for special emphasis, a dozen deal with visions of the Trinity, and four others with Christ in his role as mediator to the Trinity. The trinitarian insights are diverse: on different occasions Ignatius sees one or other of the persons of the Trinity without the others, or he is plunged into the bosom of the Trinity without any distinction among the three persons, or again he sees the Son and Spirit within the Father. Again he experiences the divine essence in its unity "without seeing the distinct persons as on the preceding days, but perceiving the one essence as in a lucid clarity." Or, his prayer "terminates in the Most Holy Trinity, without his having understandings or distinct visions of the three persons, but merely a simple attention to the Most Holy Trinity or a representation of it." At times his vision depicts Jesus as guide and companion, but without losing the sense of being in the presence of the Trinity, and finds himself feeling even more united to the Trinity (de Guibert 1964; Stierli 1977). As Egan (1987) comments: "The Trinity bestowed upon him full participation in its life, especially through Ignatius' radical imitation of Christ's life, death, and resurrection. The triune God called Ignatius to the very depths of his spirit and beyond all narcissistic introversion to share fully in the divine life. Ignatius courageously risked everything and surrendered totally to the Trinity" (p. 20).

These accounts echo the themes of the *Spiritual Exercises,* in which the Trinity appears in some of the key mediations of the second week, with respect to the Incarnation [SE102, 106-9, 126] and through the Incarnation enters into the preparatory prayers and preludes of that and the third week [SE159-204]. The trinity pervades the background of both weeks — part of the "trinitarian horizon" of the *Exercises* (Egan 1976). The contextual frame for Ignatius' references to the "Divine Majesty" or "Divine Goodness" or "Divine Power" are trinitarian in both the *Journal* and the *Exercises.*

Along with the trinitarian emphasis, Ignatius' mysticism is also eucharistic, consistent with his long-standing devotion to Christ in the sacrifice of the Mass and his encouragement of daily communion. Much of his devotional life in later years centered around the celebration of the Mass, along with the preparations for it and its extensions into the rest of his day. He mentions graces received at Mass frequently in the *Journal.* De Guibert's (1964) summary judgment is that "the infused favors showered upon Ignatius were graces centered about Christ's Sacrifice of the Mass, and dominated by the Most Holy Trinity to whom this sacrifice gives us access" (p. 54).

## THE BLESSED MOTHER

We should not overlook the unmistakable role of the Blessed Mother in Ignatius' devotional life. She was there at the beginning in the convalescing soldier's sick room. When he left Loyola, he carried with him a book of the hours of Our Lady along with a picture of Our Lady of Sorrows. He lost no time in making his first nightly vigil at the shrine of Our Lady of Aranzazu on his way to Manresa. His second 'vigil of arms' was spent before the altar of Our Lady of Montserrat, having divested himself of his fine clothes. The sword and dagger that had been his pride for all of his young manhood were hung in her chapel as an *ex voto* as he left Montserrat; as a knight of God he had no need for worldly weapons. At Manresa, one of the great attractions for him was the plenitude of chapels to Our Lady in the area. One of his favorite places for prayer was the chapel of Our Lady of Villadordis. When he left Manresa the picture of Our Lady of Sorrows was still with him (Dudon 1964).

We can also note that important events were to take place on a feasts of Our Lady. The first vows of the companions in Paris were taken on the Assumption, August 15, and were renewed each year on that feast. Ignatius constantly turned to Our Lady to intercede for him with her Son and His Father. In the colloquies of the *Exercises,* she is regularly invoked as one of the mediators; the progression often goes from Mary to her Son and finally to the Father. The vision of La Storta followed on his prayer of petition to her to place him with her Son. In the *Journal* he records how he petitioned her to intercede for him with the Father and at Mass that day had a vision of Our Lady presenting his request to the Father:

> Later, on going out to say Mass, when beginning the prayer, I saw a likeness of our Lady, and realized how serious had been my fault of the other day, not without some interior movement and tears, thinking that the Blessed Virgin felt ashamed at asking for me so often after my many failings, so much so, that our Lady hid herself from me, and I found no devotion either in her or from on high. After this, as I did not find our Lady, I sought comfort on high, and there came upon me great movement of tears and sobbing with a certain assurance that the Heavenly Father was showing Himself favorable and kindly, so much so, that He gave a sign that it would be pleasing to Him to be asked through our Lady, whom I could not see.
>
> While preparing the altar, and after vesting, and during the Mass, very intense interior movements, and many and intense tears and sobbing, with frequent loss of speech, and also after the end of Mass, and for long periods during the Mass, preparing and afterwards, the clear view of our Lady, very propitious before the Father, to such an extent, that in the prayers to the Father, to the Son, and at the consecration, I could not help feeling and seeing her, as though she were a part, or the doorway, of all the grace I felt in my soul. At the consecration she showed that her flesh was in that of her Son, with such great light that I cannot write about it. (Young 1958, p. 211; de Guibert 1964, pp. 52-53)

There are other similar passages in which Mary served this mediating function. The same sentiment is often found in his letters; he wrote to Inéz Pascual, "May it please our Lady, to stand between us, poor sinners, and her Son and Lord. May she obtain for us the grace that in the midst of our sorrows and trials, she may make our cowardly and sad spirits strong and joyous to praise Him" (Epistolae I, 72; cited in Doncoeur 1959, p. 36).

Ignatius' devotion to Our Lady was by no means unique. Marian devotion had grown through the medieval period and had achieved great popular force. By the sixteenth century, her image had acquired almost divine attributes derived more from the Trinity than from goddesses of antiquity. The role of Mary in the economy of salvation was a point of controversy between Catholics and the Reformers. One view of the development of this devotion held that as the idea of God was progressively masculinized, the image of Mary as the feminine and maternal principle emerged with increasing emphasis. The quality of mercy and loving concern for poor sinners was entrusted to the figure of Mary, who could bring a mother's love and understanding to the inadequacies and failings of her children and plead their cause before the seat of divine judgment (Johnson 1989). She became in this sense the idealized image of maternal perfection, of loving forgiveness and maternal concern (Saunders 1981).

From an analytic perspective it does not escape us that these themes are redolent with oedipal derivatives, particularly focused around the interrelationship between the images of the Father and the Blessed Mother who serves as the mediatrix between Ignatius the son and the powerful image of the Father. We can hear in all this the echoes of longstanding and powerful transference derivatives stemming from early strata of the saint's years of development. We can wonder about the degree to which the unconscious fantasy images of God the Father might not echo residues of the unconscious representation of the powerful, often absent, remote and distant father of young Iñigo's boyhood. And in the same vein, might not the unconscious fantasies clustered around the image of the Blessed Mother not reflect something of the earlier attachments to the succession of mother-figures from the past — beginning with Iñigo's own biological mother whom he lost so prematurely, and including Maria de Garin, his substitute mother during the critical years of his boyhood, and finally his sister-in-law Magdalena who played such a vital part in his later childhood and adolescent experience. Without being able to advance this viewpoint in any greater specificity or detail, we can still appreciate the degree to which even the most elevated and spiritualized mystical experiences can still maintain their psychic roots in basic developmental dynamics, whether oedipal or even preoedipal.

## SUMMARY

De Guibert (1964) summarizes the distinctive traits of this mystical experience as they shine through the notes of Ignatius' *Spiritual Journal.* There was an experience of God as present under a form of knowledge simultaneously general and obscure, yet rich and satisfying; and experience of love penetrating the love and dominating it in its most profound depths; the experience of passivity under the control of God; an impotence to arouse, extend or renew these experiences; and finally, an inability to translate his experience into linguistic forms. His continual recollection was remarked by both Nadal, his secretary, and Ribadeneyra, his first biographer. This took the form of an habitual awareness of the presence of God in the midst of many activities, and in moments of prayer an almost consuming absorption in the reality of the divine presence.

The *Spiritual Exercises* served as a manual of spiritual development, leading to the highest levels of mystical experience — a reflection of Ignatius' own experience and the tortuous path of his spiritual journey. The movement of the Exercises, through the first week of sorrow and remorse for sinful ways, to the immersion in the life, death and resurrection of Christ, and on to the final consummation in the love of God, was compared to the stages of spiritual growth — purgative, illuminative, unitive — ascribed to Dionysius the Areopagite in the sixth century. The program of the *Exercises* was thus expanded into a design for a lifelong spiritual journey (O'Malley 1993).

The material in the present chapter pertains only to the mystical experiences described in the pages of the *Journal.* Descriptions of other mystical events are located in chapter XXXV below.

# CHAPTER XXXV

# MYSTICAL LIFE

## Mystical Phenomena[1]

While the *Spiritual Journal* offers us hints of Ignatius' mystical experience, it reflects the more mature level of his mystical career; we have to look to other sources for accounts of earlier levels, particularly the *Autobiography*. As we have noted with respect to other aspects of Ignatian spirituality, his mystical ecstasies are not divorced from the spiritual methodology contained in the *Exercises*. Not only were the *Exercises* conceived in the context of the Manresa experience, in which mystical experiences played such an important part, but the Exercises themselves, taken as a program of lifelong spiritual development, are meant to lead to increasing depths of spiritual immersion, including the achievement of mystical, even unitive, spiritual experience. In this chapter, I will focus on a more systematic description of Ignatius' mystical experience, and in the next chapter we can undertake an attempt at psychoanalytic understanding.

The basic qualities of mystical experience were described by William James in his classic work on *The Varieties of Religious Experience* (1902). James focused on four marks or qualities characterizing mystical states of consciousness: (1) *ineffability*, in that the subject cannot find words adequate to express the nature of the experience in a way that would enable others to understand it; it can only be experienced directly and personally and cannot be explained to any one else who has not had the experience himself; (2) *noetic quality*, emphasizing the cognitive aspects of mystical experience, despite its predominantly affective quality, insofar as it provides deep insight into truths beyond the grasp of discursive reasoning and logic; (3) *transiency*, suggesting that the mystical state lasts only minutes or at

[1] The material in the present chapter aims at presenting a descriptive assessment of Ignatius' mystical career. For a psychoanalytic reflection on this material directed to understanding mystical phenomena more generally, see chapter XXXVI below.

most hours; and finally, (4) *passivity*, meaning that, although mystical states may be induced by voluntary activity of the mystic, such as exercises of concentration, bodily postures, or — in Ignatian terms — spiritual exercises, when the mystical state takes hold, there is a sense of powerlessness, loss of control, and total passivity, as though the mystic were under the influence of another power against which he possessed no autonomous will of his own. While mystical states have parallels in other paranormal phenomena — prophetic speech, automatic writing, certain trance states found in certain mediums, or even to an extent in hypnosis — the mystic, in contrast, retains some memory of the experience along with a profound sense of the significance of the experience and its profound impact on his inner life. All these characteristics were present in Ignatius' mystical experience.

## Primary vs. Secondary Phenomena

Ignatius was one of the great mystics in the history of the Christian church, ranking with Francis of Assisi, John of the Cross, and Teresa of Avila. His mystical journey led to the heights of mystical experience that spiritual writers describe as infused contemplation. Theologians distinguish between acquired contemplation and infused contemplation, which requires extraordinary grace from God to achieve. As Egan comments:

> According to the mystical tradition, mystical prayer in the strict sense, or infused contemplation, cannot be attained through one's own efforts, even efforts aided by ordinary grace. This prayer requires God's special activity. God gives the person something new: the explicit awareness that God is present and that the person clings lovingly to Him. By actual experience the person becomes directly and immediately aware of God's loving, purifying, enlightening, and unifying presence. The person realizes that something *totally* new is occurring. (1987, p. 23-24)

Characteristics of this state include experience of God's presence in a form of knowing that is at once general and obscure yet rich and satisfying; the experience of love penetrates and dominates the soul as though the mystic is under the complete control of God — he is totally unable to arouse, elicit, prolong, or renew these experiences, or even predict their beginning or end; and finally he finds it impossible to express them in language or to convey to his fellowmen what they are like (de Guibert 1964).

As far as I can see, James' marks would qualify as primary dimensions of the mystical state and would be distinguished from secondary mystical phenomena. In this sense Ignatius was a mystic in the primary sense — certainly James thought so. This point has been elaborated by Egan (1988) who writes:

> The word "mysticism" is commonly associated with the unreal, the otherworldly, the vague, the parapsychological, the occult, the "spooky"" the poetic, or with altered states of consciousness brought about by meditation techniques or psychedelic means. Ignatius' mysticism has absolutely nothing in common with these.
>
> Some scholars contend that the essence of mysticism is found in visions, locutions, the stigmata, levitations, and isolated instances of irresistible raptures and ecstasies. To be sure, one does find many of these *secondary* mystical phenomena in Ignatius' mystical life. Secondary mystical phenomena, however, do not disclose what mysticism is in its primary and strict sense — in the full sense that makes Ignatius one of the greatest mystics in Christian history. (p. 21)

## SECONDARY MYSTICAL AND CHARISMATIC PHENOMENA

Ignatius' mystical experience was characterized by the following secondary phenomena.[2]

*Ecstasy and rapture*. Religious ecstatic experience involves a narrowing of the field of conscious awareness: the mystic becomes intensely focused on and absorbed in God as the sole object of contemplation and consequently his attention and awareness is withdrawn from everything else. All extraneous thoughts and feelings and all patterns of normal reasoning are eliminated until the unitive experience is reached; at that point the mystic's mind becomes empty, a blank screen. Through meditative techniques he concentrates his mind on one aspect of his belief system and induces a state of altered consciousness, in which he becomes aware of the supernatural while maintaining a sense of subjective distinctness and self-identity. In the contemplative state, the mystic is caught up in the transcendent reality of the numinous, the "wholly other." The immanence of divine presence is experienced as joyful, intimate, and transforming. In prayer the mystic strives for this state of total concentration on God, but in the ecstatic process the focus on the object cannot be resisted. Bodily processes — heart rate, respiratory rate, body temperature, and other metabolic functions — may be affected. Ecstasy is equivalently a trance state involving an experience of merger or psychic union in which all inner psychic processes are absorbed in an experi-

[2] I am following Egan's (1984) categorization of Ignatius' mystical experience.

ence of intimate and blissful merger with the object of sublime love. The mystic is transfixed, unable to move or speak, caught up in a state of inexpressible tranquillity and lucidity. The experience is intensely affective and at its pinnacle results in a state of mystical union.

Raptures present a somewhat different quality. They represent modifications of ecstatic states with sudden, involuntary, even violent onset. Unlike the usual prayerful ecstasy, which has a relatively tranquil and induced quality, the rapture is abrupt and uncontrollable, intruding on the subject's normal state of consciousness. The evidence suggests that Ignatius frequently experienced ecstatic states as a regular part of his prayer life and that some of these experiences seem to have had a rapturous quality as well.

*Visions.* Visions may take various forms: they may be sensible or corporeal, occurring as apparitions, in which the mystic sees an object or objects that others do not;[3] or they may be imaginative, involving dream-like images during sleep or ecstatic states. Usually apparitions represent some religiously significant figure — for example, the Blessed Mother appeared to Ignatius at Loyola, and other apparitions of Christ and our Lady, were repeated aspects of his prayer experience. Ignatius also experienced a variety of imaginative visions, such as the image of the Trinity in the form of three organ keys and other images of Christ in the eucharist. Visions can also have an intellectual component, exclusive of sensory or imaginative content. Many of the illuminations of the understanding of which Ignatius speaks quite frequently, would qualify as intellective visions. His experience by the Cardoner seems to have been such an experience, but obviously there were others, recorded in the autobiography and the *Journal.*

*Locutions.* Mystical words or auditions — Ignatius' *loquelae*[4] — may take an external, sensory form in which the mystic hears words as if spoken from outside — analogous to auditory hallucinations. Words may also be experienced as though coming from within or even as though taking place in the depths of the understanding without any sensory or imaginative component. For Ignatius both exterior and interior *loquelae* were like divine music accompanied by a sense of sweetness and a profound feeling of love of God. The affect was so overwhelming that he complained that he could not pay attention to the meaning of the words. Consequently, he was suspicious of this affective component.

[3] Psychiatrically these would qualify as visual hallucinations.

[4] See the discussion of *loquelae* in chapter XXXIV above.

*Revelations.* These are visions or *loquelae* with informational content pertaining usually to some aspect of the good of the church or the individual. These revelations are private and usually convey deeper awareness or understanding of revealed truths or mysteries. Such revelations, or illuminations, abound in Ignatius' accounts of his mystical experience, especially during the Manresa period, but continued ever more profoundly to the end of his life — profound insights into the Trinity, the Incarnation, and the presence of Christ in the eucharist. There are also suggestions that Ignatius might have had prophetic revelations permitting him to foretell certain events, astonishing his contemporaries. We should be aware of the hagiographic impulse in evaluating such stories.

*Touches, Tastes, and Smells.* The mystics frequently report experiences of divine touches, smells, and tastes analogous to actual sensory phenomena. There is a problem in disentangling metaphoric or poetic expressions from accounts of literal sensory experience. Ignatius urged the use of the senses as a technique for facilitating meditation — that is, seeing Our Lord, hearing his words, imagining the smells and sounds, and so on, the "application of the senses" of the *Exercises* [SE121-125] — using the imagination to make the meditative experience as vivid and real as possible. For Ignatius, application of senses was part of the process leading to mystical experience, not part of the mystical experience itself. He was in agreement with other authentic Christian mystics that sensory experiences in the mystical state itself are suspect. As Egan (1984) notes, most mystics hold such phenomena to be highly dubious, and, in fact, few authentic Christian mystics ever experienced them. There is no indication that Ignatius ever had such experiences.

## AUTHENTIC MYSTICAL EXPERIENCES

Contemporary witnesses attest to Ignatius' intense contemplative life. Nadal, who knew Ignatius intimately during the Roman years, reported that he was able "to see and contemplate in all things, actions, and conversations the presence of God and the love of spiritual things, to remain a contemplative even in the midst of action," and that he experienced "continual recollection, to the point that it was necessary for him to seek diversions and to apply himself to some other pursuit" (de Guibert 1964, p. 45). Ribadeneyra reported hearing Ignatius say that "as far as he could judge, it would not be possible for him to live without consolation, that is, without experiencing in himself something that was not and could not be a part of himself, but depended entirely on God." The catalogue of infused mystical gifts found in Ignatius' writings include tears, spiritual relish and peace, intense consolation, elevation of mind and divine illuminations, spiritual understandings and visitations, visions, interior and exterior locutions, intense feelings of love, touches, consolations without previous cause [CSCP], interior joy and attraction to heavenly things, quiet repose of the soul in his Creator and Lord, interior knowledge and divine inspirations (Young 1958).[5]

Laynez offered a description of his nightly prayer:

> At night he would go up on the roof of the house, with the sky there up above him. He would sit there quietly, absolutely quietly. He would take his hat off and look up for a long time at the sky. Then he would fall on his knees, bowing profoundly to God. Then he would sit on a little bench because the weakness of his body did not allow him to take any other position. He would stay there bareheaded and without moving. And the tears would begin to flow down his cheeks like a stream, but so quietly and so gently that you heard not a sob nor a sigh nor the least possible movement of his body. (FN IV, 746-749)

## MYSTICAL VISIONS

*Early visions.* Iñigo's mystical life was inaugurated by his vision of the Blessed Virgin and her divine son during his convalescence at Loyola. But it was the series of decisive events at Manresa that transformed him into a mystic in an authentic sense.[6] Rahner (1953) described the experience at Manresa as "God's mystical invasion into the soul of Iñigo, conquering all opposition, linking together all Iñigo's previous spiritual experiences, yet at the same time sovereignly transcending them with the object of making him, as he acknowledges in his autobiography, "a new soldier of Christ, a man of the Church" (p. 47). Ignatius himself recalled that the visions at Manresa "gave him such a great and lasting strengthening of faith that even if there were no Scripture to teach him these things of faith, he would be ready to die for the faith merely because of what he had seen at that time. . . . These illuminations were so great that all these things seemed new to

[5] Spiritual relish is a descriptive term referring to an affective state of savoring and delight in spiritual experiences. Interior and exterior locutions are discussed previously in this chapter.

[6] See chapter VI above for an account of the Manresa experience.

him, and he received such insights and was so enlightened that he felt himself almost a new man" (Vita 29; cited in Ravier 1987, p. 413).[7]

Many of these early visions had the quality of apparitions, like the image of the Virgin and Child at Loyola. Other experiences at Manresa are similar. Later experiences have more the stamp of imaginative visions. His visions of the Holy Trinity were especially compelling and meaningful (Rahner 1953). His account of one of these at Manresa bears repeating in this context:

> Now, one day, being about to recite the hours of our Lady on the steps of the Dominican monastery, his understanding began to be elevated. And it was as though he had seen the Holy Trinity under the form of three keys of an organ. And at this sight, he melted into tears until dinner. In the evening he spoke of nothing but the Holy Trinity. He could not keep from speaking of It; and he did so with an abundance of very different comparisons, his soul being filled all the while with joy and consolation. And from this experience dates the feeling of great devotion he has felt all his life when praying to the Holy Trinity. (Vita 23)

The truth of this observation is amply borne out by the regularity with which the Holy Trinity appears his *Spiritual Journal.*

The richness and frequency of these imaginative visions bear eloquent testimony to his inner spiritual life. They brought intense consolation and a deep sense of spiritual and intellectual enrichment which would last long after the vision had ended; Ignatius recalls how he would go through the day recalling the images of the Trinity to himself with great joy. The visions at Manresa were multiple and varied: visions of meat when he was fasting, images of the Trinity "in the image of three keys of the keyboard," visions of how God created the world, apparitions of Our Lord and Our Lady. Our Lord appears to him to help with his scruples, from which he is delivered. Or he sees clearly in a vision how Christ is present in the Blessed Sacra-

[7] As Silos (1964) observed, the *Autobiography* was not a simple straightforward narration, but rather a discerned account: "The author of the rules of discernment is at work sifting, interpreting, controlling, confirming the events, the thoughts, the motions in his soul from the fateful day when a cannon ball ended a career and initiated the pilgrimage which began at Pamplona and was to end in Rome. The Autobiography is not a simple narration of a life. It is the history of God's actions in a soul — discerned" (p. 7-8). Moreover, the mind set of the narrator is that every step along the way, every episode, every action and reaction, was dictated and guided by the hand of the Lord, drawing him along the predestined path of spiritual growth and glory. The uncritical acceptance of whatever appears in the autobiography as accurate and reliable has been scored as "Jesuit fundamentalism" (Endean 1987).

ment. Frequently he sees in his mind's eye the humanity of Christ without distinct physical form. Similar visions of Our Lady are recorded as well.

But there is much more to be learned from the rest of the pilgrim's account. He completes the story of Manresa and a recounting of his various visions in these words:

> At this time God treated him just as a schoolmaster treats a little boy when he teaches him. This perhaps was because of his rough and uncultivated understanding, or because of the firm will God Himself had given him in His service. But he clearly saw and always had seen that God dealt with him like this. Rather, he thought that any doubt about it would be an offense against His Divine Majesty. Something of this can be gathered from the five following points.
>
> *First.* He had a great devotion to the Most Holy Trinity, and thus daily prayed to the Three Persons distinctly. While he was also praying to the Most Holy Trinity, the objection occurred to him as to how he could say four prayers to the Trinity. But this thought gave him little or no trouble, as being something of only slight importance. One day while he was reciting the Hours of Our Lady on the steps of the same monastery, his understanding began to be elevated as though he saw the Holy Trinity under the figure of three keys. This was accompanied with so many tears and so much sobbing that he could not control himself. That morning he accompanied a procession which left the monastery and was not able to restrain his tears until dinner time. Nor afterwards could he stop talking about the Most Holy Trinity. He made use of many different comparisons and experienced great joy and consolation. The result was that all through his life this great impression has remained with him, to feel great devotion when he prays to the Most Holy Trinity.
>
> *Second.* Another time there was represented to his understanding with great spiritual delight the manner in which God had created the world. It had the appearance of something white out of which rays were coming, and it was out of this that God made light. But he did not know how to explain these things, nor did he remember well the spiritual illumination which at that time God impressed upon his soul.
>
> *Third.* At Manresa also, where he remained almost a year, after he began to feel God's consolations and saw the fruit produced in the souls with whom he dealt, he gave up those outward extremes he formerly adopted, and trimmed his nails and hair. One day, in this town, when he was hearing Mass in the church of the monastery already mentioned, during the elevation he saw with the inner eyes of the soul something like white rays that came from

above. Although he cannot explain this after so long a time, yet what he clearly saw with his understanding was how Jesus Christ our Lord is present in the most holy sacrament.

*Fourth.* When he was at prayer, he often and for a long time saw with the inner eyes the humanity of Christ. The shape which appeared to him was like a white body, not very large or very small, but he saw no distinction of members. He often saw this in Manresa. If he were to say twenty, or even forty times, he would not venture to say that it was an untruth. He saw it another time when he was in Jerusalem, and still another when he was on the road near Padua. He has also seen Our Lady in like form, without distinction of parts. These things which he saw gave him at the time great strength, and were always a striking confirmation of his faith, so much so that he has often thought to himself that if there were no Scriptures to teach us these matters of faith, he was determined to die for them, merely because of what he had seen.

*Fifth.* Once out of devotion he was going to a church which was about a mile distant from Manresa, and which I think was called St. Paul. The road ran along close to the river. Moving along intent on his devotion, he sat down for a moment with his face towards the river which there ran deep. As he sat, the eyes of his understanding began to open. He beheld no vision, but he saw and understood many things, spiritual as well as those concerning faith and learning. This took place with so great an illumination that these things appeared to be something altogether new. He cannot point out the particulars of what he then understood, although they were many, except that he received a great illumination in his understanding. This was so great that in the whole course of his past life right up to his sixty-second year, if he were to gather all the helps he had received from God, and everything he knew, and add them together, he does not think that they would equal all that he received at that one time.

After this had lasted for some time he went to kneel at a nearby cross to give thanks to God, where again appeared that vision which he had often seen and which he had never understood, that is, the object described above, which he thought very beautiful and which seemed to have many eyes. But he noticed that as it stood before the cross it did not have that beautiful color as heretofore, and he understood very clearly, with a strong assent of his will, that it was the evil one. Later it often appeared to him for a long time, but he drove it away with the pilgrim's staff he held in his hand and a gesture of contempt. (Vita 27-31)

The remarkable events recorded in this account suggest the intensity of the psychological effects being wrought in the pilgrim's soul. There were illuminations that deepened his understanding and conviction of the most profound spiritual realities. There were also striking apparitions, in part purified symbols, and in part images of brightness and light. The Trinity appears as three keys, the humanity of Jesus as a white body, images carrying with them overwhelming feelings of consolation, joy, and strength. He felt so enlightened by the vision of the Trinity that he even tried to write a treatise about it, according to Polanco (PolChron I, 22). These were all undoubtedly mystical experiences of the highest order.

There can be no doubt of the profound and meaningful character of these revelations and illuminations. The vision of the Holy Trinity under the image of the keys was so moving that, he tells us, "all through his life this great impression has remained with him, to feel great devotion when he prays to the most Holy Trinity" (Vita 28). Again, "These things which he saw gave him at the time great strength, and were always a striking confirmation of his faith, so much so that he has often thought to himself that if there were no Scriptures to teach us these matters of faith, he was determined to die for them, merely because of what he had seen" (Vita 29). And of the great illumination on the banks of the Cardoner, he observed: "This was so great that in the whole course of his past life right up to his sixty-second year, if he were to gather all the helps he had received from God, and everything he knew, and add them together, he does not think that they would equal all that he received at that one time" (Vita 30).

Iñigo's mystical life grew and developed as he made his way toward Rome. Even though there were periods in which he was forced to mitigate the intensity of his ascetical practices and prayer — for example while he was caught up in his studies in Paris — the current of infused graces seems to have continued unabated. His prayer may have been lessened, but it lost none of its intensity and sense of union with God. Once the work of intellectual preparation was behind him, divine grace once again inundated his soul. He wrote: "During his sojourn at Vincenza, it was the reverse of what had happened in Paris, the pilgrim had many spiritual visions, numerous and almost continuous consolations. During all these trips, and especially at Venice, when he got ready to receive priestly ordination and prepared himself to say Mass, he received great supernatural visits, similar to those which he had constantly had at Manresa" (Vita 95). The experiences of Manresa provided a foundation upon which the great cathedral of his mystical life was erected. His identity was being shaped and molded through years of pilgrimage and study, enabling him finally to scale the heights of sanctity and mystical experience (Rahner 1968).

*La Storta.* One of the nodal points in his mystical career came in the vision at La Storta, on his way to Rome to found the Society of Jesus. He and his companions had stopped to rest a few miles from the city walls at a little roadside chapel, where Ignatius took the opportunity to pray for God's blessing on the adventure that lie before them. Rather than a single event, this vision seems to have evolved in stages. He first prayed fervently to Our Lady to place him with her Son. At first, there was a *loquela*-like experience during the course of a mass celebrated previously in which Ignatius became aware of the inner words: "I will be favorable to you in Rome." Shortly thereafter the actual vision took place in the chapel at La Storta. He recalled, "It seemed to him that he saw Christ with his Cross on his shoulder and near him the Eternal Father who was saying, `I want you to serve us.' " In the *Autobiography* he recalled, "And one day when he found himself in the church saying prayers — it was a few miles before arriving in Rome — he felt such a change in his soul and he saw so clearly that God the Father was uniting him with Christ His Son, that he would never dare doubt that God the Father had united him with His Son" (Vita 96). Whatever else one can say about such an experience, it seems clear that it served an important wish-fulfilling function on the brink of significant and uncertain adventures in the Eternal City.

In this sublime mystical experience, Ignatius received the grace designated at the end of the meditation on the Two Standards in his *Spiritual Exercises* [SE147], the grace to be received under the standard of Christ as His companion in poverty and humiliations. A strong motif of Ignatian spirituality emerges in the further elaboration of the vision by Laynez to whom Ignatius had related the details of the vision. The Father said to Christ weighted down with his cross: "It is my will that you take this man for your servant." And Christ replied to Ignatius: "It is my will that you serve us." The notion of outstanding service to God was fundamental in Ignatius' interior life and belief, and it was this motif that he communicated to the Society he founded (de Guibert 1964).[8]

*Mature period.* The years of saintly maturity and increasing depths of mystical experience, and the full realization of that sense of spiritual identity which made him uniquely Ignatius of Loyola, came during the Roman period. He tells us in the closing pages of his Autobiography:

[8] The interpretations of the importance and impact of this vision on Ignatius and the founding of the Society have been varied. See Baumann (1958).

> His devotion always went on increasing, that is, the ease with which he found God, which was then greater than he had ever had in his life. Whenever he wished, at whatever hour, he could find God. He also said he still had many visions, especially that in which he saw Christ as a sun, as mentioned above. This often happened to him, especially when he was speaking of matters of importance, and came to confirm him in his decision. (Vita 99)

The years of his spiritual maturity were likewise years of continued growth and development. The same processes and mechanisms, first set in motion at Loyola and extended through the crisis of Manresa, continued the process of spiritual development that reached progressively higher levels of personal integration and mystical intensity. This growth in mystical experience was accompanied along the way by the continuance of intense asceticism. He had the practice of examining his conscience almost hourly, searching out faults that had previously escaped him. It was characteristic of him to bring to bear every human resource even where he was conscious of God's activity in him; this consciousness did not prevent careful attention to reasons for and against.[9]

## MYSTICAL ILLUMINATIONS

Other mystical manifestations had a more intellectual quality, taking the force of intellectual visions or illuminations. Ignatius described how in these experiences his understanding was deeply affected, but never without profound affect and emotion. De Guibert (1964) commented on the relative paucity of imaginative content of his visions and the profound intellectual insights and illuminations that retained powerful motivational impact on him years later. They seem to have been primarily spiritual illuminations of his mind — his understanding was elevated and his insights into the nature of the trinity, creation, the presence of Christ in the eucharist. One of the most significant of such illuminations was the famous episode on the banks of the Cardoner. Of this powerful illumination he said:

> . . . the eyes of his understanding began to open. He beheld no vision, but he saw and understood many things, spiritual as well as those concerning faith and learning. This took place with so great an illumination that these things appeared to be something

[9] This is reflected in the directions for the "third time" of making an election [SE178-188].

> altogether new. He cannot point out the particulars of what he then understood, although they were many, except that he received a great illumination in his understanding. (Vita 30)

Even thirty years after the event, Ignatius still attributed such importance to it. These were direct infusions of spiritual knowledge — Ignatius emphasized the elevation of his understanding and the breadth of his intellectual grasp. He was evidently experiencing the greatest mystical gifts even at Manresa (de Guibert 1964). As described by Laynez and Polanco, the Cardoner experience was a significant turning point in Ignatius' spiritual development. This mystical illumination seems to have been one of the most powerful and intense of Ignatius whole career. It is a prime example of CSCP in which a degree of understanding was produced that convinced Ignatius that the hand of God must be behind it. It represents the culmination of Ignatius' conversion experience that lent such profound insight and certitude that it put a definitive stamp on the rest of his spiritual journey.

## EXTRAORDINARY EXPERIENCES

As is the case for most saintly figures, Ignatius has been attributed a number of quite exceptional experiences — due, no doubt, to a pious and hagiographic impulse in his contemporaries and biographers.[10] Despite the investigation and authentication of such occurrences in the canonization process, it is difficult to know what to make of such accounts. Similar accounts and descriptions can be found in the lives of other mystics from many religions and cultures.[11] They should be taken with a 'grain of salt' as reflecting the hagiographic impulse in credulous and idealizing spectators. Such manifestations are the standard stuff of hagiographic enhancement of charismatic figures to transnatural levels; they were also hallmarks of sanctity in the popular mind of the intensely supernaturally oriented and religiously pious culture of sixteenth century Spain.

[10] See the account of some of these episodes in Dudon (1949) and Meissner (1992b).

[11] Similar accounts of such transnatural manifestations that seem to exceed the laws of nature can be found, for example, in the history of Sabbatai Sevi, the self-proclaimed messiah of seventeenth century Jewish kabbalistic mysticism. See Scholem (1973). For a more specifically psychological analysis of Sabbatai's messianic mission, see Falk (1982) and Meissner (1992c). There is good reason to think that Sabbatai was intermittently psychotic, probably manic-depressive.

Ignatius himself did not put much credence in such extraordinary manifestations or in secondary mystical phenomena generally. During a visit to the professed house in Rome, one Fray Reginaldo, a prominent Dominican, told a story about a nun in Bologna who was in constant ecstasy and bore the stigmata. Ignatius commented only that what was most commendable was the nun's obedience. When Ribadeneyra pursued the subject, Ignatius said, "It is for God alone to work in the interior of the soul; there the demon is powerless, but he has a way of deceiving through exterior phenomena that are plausible and false." When one of the fathers praised the prudence and holiness of the reknowned ecstatic Magdalena de la Cruz, Ignatius reprimanded him: "A man of the Society ought not to talk like that, nor show so much esteem for things that are, after all, only exterior" (Dudon 1949, p. 225-6). Ignatius knew that such extraordinary phenomena occurred, but he also knew that they were rich soil for illusion and deception. Delusion was the rule rather than the exception; and genuine mystical experience was the exception, never the rule (Rahner 1977).

He was often on his guard against illusion. He wrote to Adriaenssens, rector of the college in Louvain, that "to wait [before acting] for an interior movement to stir one, this does not seem to be proper, because [of the danger] of illusions and of tempting God." In 1554, advising the same religious superior about one of his tormented subjects, Ignatius wrote, "Don't be troubled, and don't get up because of these noises, or lose any sleep. The devil can do nothing without God's permission. If, however, some of these terrors are caused by a natural disposition inclined to melancholy, a doctor should be consulted" (Rahner 1977, p. 101). As De Guibert (1964) comments: "This reserve sprang also from the fear of possible illusions in this matter. It is certain that St. Ignatius, complete mystic as he was and precisely because he was such an eminent mystic, stood in great fear of the illusions of the life of prayer" (p. 563). We can add that his caution in this regard flowed out of his own experience and made the task of discernment even more central and weighty in his own prayer life and in his spiritual teaching of others.

In Rome, his mystical life was private, even secret for the most part. His effort was consistently directed to modulating the enthusiasm and indiscreet fervor of his subjects. When Rodriques wrote from Portugal about the "holy follies" of his overly zealous subjects, Ignatius urged moderation and discretion. He had to resist his own inner impulses to abandon himself completely to his mystical ecstasies and the folly of the Cross.[12] Discretion was never far from his mind.

## DISCERNMENT[13]

A constant problem plaguing the mystics and their commentators is that of discernment — that is, distinguishing the degree to which specific mystical experiences are authentic and come from the influence of God on the soul as opposed to influences that come from elsewhere and are therefore not authentic parts of the mystical state. In the late medieval context of Ignatius' life the devil was the leading alien influence.[14] From today's more psychoanalytic perspective, we are more likely to appeal to the individual's own psychic processes. It is precisely from this concern that Ignatius' rules for the discernment of spirits play such a central role in his spiritual outlook and constitute an essential aspect of his *Spiritual Exercises*. We also know that he applied these rules assiduously not only in his own spiritual life but in his efforts to help others discern God's will in their own lives and spiritual experience.

Most mystics and their commentators agree that intellectual influences of any kind, unlike sensory or other psychosomatic reverberations, are an authentic aspect of divine self-communication and an expression of infused contemplation. But there is question as to whether purely intellective infusions ever take place without some imaginative or sensory aftereffects. God's influence is assumed to affect the mystic's soul to such a degree and depth that his total organism must adjust to this radical and compelling input. Consequently, such secondary manifestations may represent an integral part of the overall experience, the core of which is intellective and spiritual. Thus, secondary and charismatic mystic phenomena may be signals of God's mystical presence that reveal a more intimate, and more meaningful infused contemplation. Egan (1984) expresses the tension between these more authentic expressions and other forces at work in the mystic's experience in the following terms:

[12] The "folly of the cross" refers to the internal contradiction of the subjection of the Son of God to the indignities and suffering of the crucifixion. The folly in ascetical terms was the excessive and unnecessary indulgence in penitential practices.

[13] See chapter XV and XVI for discussion of the role of discernment in Ignatian spirituality.

[14] See the discussion of the devil in chapter V above.

> Genuine secondary mystical and charismatic phenomena never occur alone. The mystic or charismatic normally experiences genuine, pathological, and diabolical phenomena during the course of his mystical ascent or charismatic life. These phenomena will reveal not only his God-induced psychosomatic integration, but also his brokenness and the presence of the demonic. Taken together, therefore, these phenomena manifest God's presence, the devil's presence, and the Christian's own healthy *and* pathological accommodations and resistances to both the divine and the demonic presence.
>
> Furthermore, it is not surprising that some of these phenomena reflect the Christian's infantile dreams, inordinate desires, immature projections, and pathological hallucinations. Others, however, counter directly the Christian's physically, psychologically, and morally pernicious tendencies. Conversion, renewed energy, strength, courage, authority, and peace accompany them. They bestow insight, knowledge, and wisdom, while deepening faith, hope, and love. (p. 330)

The flood of his mystical experiences thus created a problem for Ignatius: how could he know that these influences were from God? How could he be sure that they did not arise from some other source, even the evil one? How much was from God, how much from his own human nature? Ravier (1987) observes that the representational aspects of these imaginative visions were no more than psychological reactions to the deep emotion stirred in Ignatius by the intensity of his experience.

The rules for discernment, distinguishing between effects of God's action on the soul and effects of human psychological reactions, are intended to cast light on the sources of the visions. Intellectual light and infused love come from God, the imaginative components that may accompany these experiences are human reactions — human psychology responding in its own terms to the divine influence. The ability of the human organism to respond is limited in affective responsiveness, in imaginative representation, and in linguistic communication. Ignatius often tries to communicate the nature of his experiences in sensory terms — warmth, color, taste, sweetness, and so on. The images and language are inadequate to convey the richness and intensity of the experience.

But it is important to note the prevailing countercurrents in the Ignatian perspective on his mystical raptures. The first issue pervading his mystical life, as we have suggested, was discernment. Ignatius was a gifted introspective observer of the inner movements of his psychic experience, who retained his capacity for self-observation and reflection throughout, and who was also a sensitive observer of psychic phenomena in others. The second element was his gradual retrenchment from his excessive and fanatical ascetical practices, often as a matter of practicality, but always in the interest of furthering his mission of service to God's kingdom. Third, the distinctively Ignatian characteristic of drawing on the fruits of mystical contemplation to enrich his apostolic effectiveness. His earlier impulse was to scorn the world, to retreat into prayer and contemplation, to break utterly with the past and all attachments to human comfort. But as the years passed, he increasingly moved toward an integration of his ascetical life and mystical gifts with the demands of the life of service in the Society he founded and led. This transition is seen most clearly in the movement from the *Exercises* to the *Constitutions* — a transition from the more theoretic and inspirational to the specific and pragmatic.

## The Vision of the Serpent

The problem of discernment is dramatically displayed in the famous vision of the many-eyed serpent, which first appeared at Manresa.[15] This vision came hard on the heels of the extraordinary illumination at the Cardoner. Iñigo, ever the introspective psychologist, noticed that the apparition was accompanied not only a feeling of delight but also doubts about the arduous life of abnegation and following of Christ — how could he ever hope to continue for the full span of life? Applying his own rules of discernment, he finally concluded that the apparition was from the evil one and was a temptation.

The contrast between the affective quality of the preceding spiritual illumination and the prolonged struggle involved in the vision of the serpent is striking — the latter seems to have been connected with temptations against persevering in his spiritual path and led to agonizing scruples. Only by gradual discernment did Ignatius come to the conclusion that the serpent was from the devil. The great illumination, however, came in a flash with unerring conviction and acceptance — an example of CSCP as described in the rules for discernment. This can be seen as a development in Ignatius' capacity for discernment and an increasing understanding of the importance of such discernment in spiritual life. The experience at the Cardoner was a moment of realization in which the bitter and difficult lessons he had been learning were suddenly distilled into a principle that unified and gave meaning to the course of his experiences and confirmed him in the path he had chosen.

[15] The vision is recounted in chapter VI above.

This, then, in the theological perspective, is the touchstone for evaluating the authenticity of secondary mystical experiences. Influences from God are marked by a trail of increased faith, hope, love, humility, and peace. Influences that derive from internal drives, conflicts, or frustrated desires leave the subject feeling arid, empty, frustrated, anxious, and experiencing greater degrees of pride, narcissistic enhancement, shame, guilt, or bitterness. Genuine ecstasies, coming from God, bring a sense of humility, inner peace, and a greater readiness to embrace the cross as the means for mystical ascent. They are life-enhancing, whereas pathological states lead toward psychic disintegration and destruction. As Modell (1993) notes, echoing William James:

> James described a variety of religious conversions in which individuals felt themselves to be in the presence of a religious spirit described variously as God, the Son, the Holy Spirit, the Virgin Mary, and so forth. The experience might have been that of simply feeling the comfort of a protective presence; or the individual may have felt that his or her sense of self was given over to and swallowed up by the presence of the other. As a result of this merger with the holy presence, some experienced a sense of peace and harmony, whereas others reported that they had been cured of afflictions such as alcoholism and promiscuity. (p. 133)

Ignatius was suspicious of the sweetness of his experiences of *loquelae* because they distracted him from the meaning of the words that he thought came from God. This was analogous to his distrust of his ecstatic experiences in prayer, which distracted him from his studies; he saw the studies as God's will for him at the time, so that the spiritual rewards — however affectively consoling — had to be the work of the devil.

## Consolation Without Previous Cause (CSCP)

One of most characteristic aspects of Ignatian mysticism is focused in the concept of "consolation without previous cause."[16] Ignatius described this form of consolation in the *Exercises*: "It belongs to God alone to give consolation without previous cause, for it belongs to the Creator to enter into the soul, to leave it, and to act upon it, drawing it wholly to the love of His Divine Majesty. I say without previous cause, that is, without any previous perception or knowledge of any object from which such consolation might come

[16] See the discussion of CSCP in chapter XVI above.

to the soul through its own acts of intellect and will" [SE330]. The implication is that God alone can console in this way and that this is His way of consoling.[17] We can conclude, therefore, that CSCP includes the consolations and illuminations associated with mystical experiences. In fact, it would seem that the kind of spiritual illuminations and ecstatic experiences Ignatius described are prototypical expressions of CSCP.

The notion has been proposed as the high point of the movement of grace in the *Exercises* (Rahner 1976). It has been called the essence of the *Exercises* in that God holds sway over the soul and the soul responds with total surrender and self-depletion, thus realizing the profound unity between God and the soul in such consolation (Przywara 1938-9; cited in Egan 1976, p. 9-10). Fessard (1956) sees this consolation as the measure of every other experience, the "immutable center of the Ignatian perspective." It is a movement in which the temporal and the eternal become one because of the divine initiative drawing the soul into loving union with the Father and the Son.

For Rahner (1976) this consolation serves as a primary principle in the "supernatural logic" of Ignatius' mystical experience and the standard against which all other mystical experiences can be measured. In itself, it can neither deceive nor be measured, carrying within itself its own indubitable evidence. It touches the subject's deepest core and draws him beyond all created objects into the infinity of God's love; it is "radical freedom, spirit supernaturally present to itself, hence a mystical, creative self-presence which leads the person into his own mysterious depths and into the Father's love" (Egan 1976, p. 4). This basic form of consolation can be regarded as fundamental to the Ignatian method of discernment of spirits and as central to his entire perspective on the spiritual life. The question is whether the Ignatian formula is meant to exclude all created causes. Can there be such a profound and meaningful psychological experience without conscious or unconscious motivation? We shall return to this issue later.[18]

Other visionary experiences shed some light on the kind of affective certitude he attributed to CSCP and the importance he gave to it as a guide in spiritual matters. He told us in the *Autobiography* abut his vision of the meat:

[17] As Egan (1976) puts it, "The CSCP, therefore, is not simply one consolation among many, but *the* God-given consolation. Only God, and He alone, can and does console in this precise way" (p. 33).

[18] See also the discussion of unconscious causality in chapter XVI.

> While he was carrying out his abstinence from meat, without any thought of changing it, one morning as he got up, a dish of meat appeared before him, as though he actually saw it with his eyes. But he had no antecedent desire for it. At the same time he felt within himself a great movement of the will to eat it in the future. Although he remembered his former resolve, he could not hesitate to make up his mind that he ought to eat meat. Relating this to his confessor later, the confessor told him that he ought to find out whether this was a temptation. But he, examine it as he would, could never have any doubt about it. (Vita 27)

This carries reverberations of CSCP and the first time of election by which Ignatius attributed such conviction to the direct action of God. He went on to speak of "the firm will God Himself had given him . . . . [so that] he thought that any doubt about it would be an offense against His Divine Majesty" (Vita 27). The meat vision occurred without any previous desire of which he was conscious, reversing his previous resolution, and brought about a firm conviction and determination of his will. The phenomenology is clear, but its psychological meaning remains obscure. Without being able to probe more deeply into the unconscious significance of this vision, a psychoanalyst would have little difficulty in thinking that an unconscious and unacknowledged, even repressed or denied, desire to eat meat was at the root of it — but the repressed was allowed back into consciousness, not as his own desire, but as a divine inspiration which would give it legitimacy. Any further appeal to divine causality would then be superfluous — but could not be eliminated as a possible factor.

From a psychoanalytic perspective, therefore, the conflict between the wish to mortify himself and the wish to eat meat does not achieve complete resolution and so they continue to exercise their derivative influence. Supporting this view are the mystical experiences Iñigo described, including a variety of hallucinations along with ruminative states, which issued eventually into internal experiences of deep inner understanding and illumination. Some of these hallucinatory experiences he ascribed to the influence of the good spirit, some, like the dragon of the many eyes, finally to the evil spirit.

## THEOLOGICAL PERSPECTIVES

*Trinitarian.* Ignatius' mysticism carries the stamp of his individuality. It is a mysticism of service based on love rather than a mysticism of loving union. It emphasizes both the Trinity and Christ's sacrifice in the eucharist. The Trinity is mentioned again and again in the *Diary*; among the passages marked for special emphasis, a dozen deal with visions of the Trinity, and four others with Christ in his role as mediator to the Trinity. The trinitarian insights are diverse: on different occasions Ignatius sees one or other of the persons of the Trinity without the others, or he is plunged into the bosom of the Trinity without any distinction among the three persons, or again he sees the Son and Spirit within the Father. Again he experiences the divine essence in its unity "without seeing the distinct persons as on the preceding days, but perceiving the one essence as in a lucid clarity." Or, his prayer "terminates in the Most Holy Trinity, without his having understandings or distinct visions of the three persons, but merely a simple attention to the Most Holy Trinity or a representation of it." At times his vision depicts Jesus as guide and companion, but without losing the sense of being in the presence of the Trinity, and finds himself feeling even more united to the Trinity (De Guibert 1964; Stierli 1977). As Egan (1988) comments: "The Trinity bestowed upon him full participation in its life, especially through Ignatius' radical imitation of Christ's life, death, and resurrection. The triune God called Ignatius to the very depths of his spirit and beyond all narcissistic introversion to share fully in the divine life. Ignatius courageously risked everything and surrendered totally to the Trinity" (p. 20).

Ignatius' devotion was in the first instance trinitarian (De Guibert 1964; Egan 1976, 1984; Stierli 1977). He told da Camara about his devotion to the Trinity and his habit of prayer to the persons as well as to the Trinity as a whole. In his mystical transports, the Trinity is a dominating presence, while other figures, even Christ and the Blessed Mother, serve more as mediators to the Trinity than as direct objects of his prayer. The intense devotion to the trinity that began at Manresa continued during the rest of his life; he told da Camara, "Throughout his whole life he had kept this impression of his having a great devotion when praying to the Trinity" (Vita 28). Nadal confirms this:

> Father Ignatius received from God the singular grace to contemplate freely all of the Most Holy Trinity, and to repose in this mystery. For, at times he was seized by the grace of contemplating the whole Trinity, and impelled towards It. He united himself with It wholeheartedly, with great feelings of devotion and spiritual relish. Sometimes he contemplated the Father, sometimes the Son, and sometimes the Holy Spirit. He always received the grace of this contemplation very frequently, but in an exceptional way during the last years of his earthly pilgrimage. (Epistolae Nadal, IV, 651ff; in Young (1958) p. 201)

*Incarnational.* If Ignatius' devotion to his Lord and Master Jesus Christ takes second place to his devotion to the Trinity, the difference is difficult to discriminate. Christ is a central figure in the *Exercises* — he is the King who calls His followers to His service, the Leader to whom the exercitant seeks to devote himself in total self-denial and dedication and to follow faithfully and fully. It is Christ's life and example that form the substance of the second, third, and fourth weeks: in the second week Christ's hidden and public life, in the third His suffering and death, and in the fourth His resurrection and ascension to glory. The first companions were convinced that the essential parts of the *Exercises* derived from the vision at the Cardoner to which Ignatius himself ascribed such significance. In any case, there is little question that his theology and mysticism were centered on the figure of Christ (Rahner 1953). Service to God is translated into service to His Son, Who is God Incarnate. This service becomes a love of poverty and contempt with Christ poor and humiliated, the following of the spiritual standard taught by Christ rather than the riches, honors, and pride taught by the enemy.

Christ is above all the first and best of mediators (Egan 1976, 1984), who translates the love of the Trinity for man into human terms. In the colloquies of the *Exercises*, it is Christ as man who introduces the exercitant to the Trinity, who opens the way through his function as Son to the Father (Haas 1977). It is through the love, devotion, and following of Christ that the highest graces and mystical gifts are to be obtained. As de Guibert (1964) put it, "From this love will be born the insatiable desire to serve, to give oneself, and to sacrifice oneself for Him, as well as the tender and unwearied effort for the souls whom He loved and redeemed" (p. 590). Thus, Ignatius' spirituality has been called 'christocentric' in the fullest sense. In the vision at La Storta it was Christ, bearing his cross, who said to him, "It is my wish that you should serve us" (Rahner 1953). As Egan (1976) commented:

> The person of Jesus Christ became for Ignatius the very way in which and through which he grasped reality, his *a priori* stance, the very horizon against which and in which everything took its ultimate meaning. . . . When Ignatius says that the enlightened soul desires only Christ and Him Crucified, that Jesus Christ is the beginning, middle and end of all our good, that "all our wickedness shall be entirely consumed, when our souls shall be completely penetrated and possessed by Him," or that we should see all creatures as bathed in the blood of Christ, this is more than

> pious talk. It expresses Ignatius' emphatic Christocentrism, his appreciation of the christocentric dimension of all things. (p. 98)

*Eucharistic.* Ignatius' mysticism is also eucharistic, consistent with his long-standing devotion to Christ in the sacrifice of the mass and his encouragement of daily communion. Much of his devotional life in later years centered around the celebration of the mass, along with the preparations for it and its extensions into the rest of his day. He mentions graces received at mass frequently in the *Journal.* De Guibert's (1964) summary judgment is that "the infused favors showered upon Ignatius were graces centered about Christ's Sacrifice of the Mass, and dominated by the Most Holy Trinity to whom this sacrifice gives us access" (p. 54).

*Affectivity.* Ignatius' mystical favors were both intellectual and affective. His visions carried with them profound understandings, but at the same time were accompanied by the most intense affective experiences — he was often moved to the point of tears by sentiments of great love and devotion. Preparing for mass, he experienced "a deluge of tears and sobs, and a love so intense that it seemed to me to unite me with excessive closeness to the Trinity's own love — a love so luminous and sweet that I thought that this overpowering visit and love were outstanding and excellent among all other visits" (de Guibert 1964, p. 54).

De Guibert (1964) draws attention to the absence in Ignatius' mysticism of any nuptial images of the mystical union — a significant aspect of the writings of other great mystics. Ignatius does mention the Church as the bride of Christ, but never the individual soul in such a role.[19] His own sense of union with the Trinity or with Christ is expressed in the most loving and intimate of terms, but nowhere is it described as a spiritual marriage.[20] Ignatius will have none of the intense lyricism of John of the Cross, for example — "that burning aspiration toward an equality of love and toward a union consummated in the complete nudity of the spirit, that anticipation of the presence of the Well-beloved as one being approached through veils growing thinner and thinner, that advance toward clear vision" (de Guibert 1964, p. 56). His relation to the Trinity and to

[19] Buckley (1995) notes the exceptional use of the nuptial metaphor in regard to the church as spouse of Christ, and in addition the reference to the church as mother of all believers — both feminine images contrasting with counterbalancing more phallic and military metaphors.

[20] Ricard (1956) suggested that this may be related to the massive repression of sexuality during the conversion experience, reinforced by his vow of absolute chastity on the way to Montserrat. See Meissner (1992b) for details and chapter II above.

Christ is consistently that of the humble and loving servant. As he said in the *Journal, Dadme humilidad amorosa* — "Grant me a loving humility" — a sentiment that occupied the core of his spirituality (Rahner 1968). The thought of finding the grace to serve God, to seek and do His will, is uppermost in Ignatius' mind and prayer. Throughout his writings, even in his letters, the phrases recur with monotonous regularity: "the service and praise of His Divine Majesty," "the glory and service of God," "the service and praise of God."

*Kataphatic.* Ignatius' mysticism is more kataphatic than apophatic.[21] In the apophatic tradition, the mystic advances through the passive prayer of quiet toward ecstatic union and finally transcendental life within the mystical marriage. In the kataphatic tradition, the focus is on "a progressive simplification of prayer, which culminates in the highest levels of sacramental contemplation. The increasing transparency of the mysteries, images, and symbols of salvation history guides the mystic along the contemplative journey to mystical transformation and spiritual fecundity" (Egan 1984, p. 303). The *Exercises* would constitute a paradigm of an authentic kataphatic Christian mysticism.

[21] The kataphatic and apophatic are different forms of mystical experience and relate to different mystical traditions. The distinction is described by Egan (1984): "The apophatic tradition, the via negativa, emphasizes the radical difference between God and creatures. God is best reached, therefore, by negation, forgetting, and unknowing, in a darkness of mind without the support of concepts, images, and symbols. . . . Kataphatic mysticism, the via affirmativa, emphasizes the similarity that exists between God and creatures. Because God can be found in all things, the affirmative way recommends the use of concepts, images, and symbols as a way of contemplating God" (p. 31). Ignatius and Teresa of Avila would belong in the kataphatic tradition, John of the Cross to the apophatic.

# CHAPTER XXXVI

# MYSTICISM — A PSYCHOANALYTIC PERSPECTIVE

## Psychoanalytic Impressions

The present chapter is intended as a psychoanalytic reflection or meditation on the data of the mystical experience in the form it takes in Ignatian spirituality. Confronted with the extraordinary richness and variety of the mystical and ecstatic experiences of Ignatius of Loyola and the range of mystical expression implicit in his spirituality, what interpretive perspective can the psychoanalyst utilize to understand this exceptional range of human experience? In addition, Ignatius is only the leading exemplar of his spirituality and mystical achievement — there is a persistent question as to the extent to which his experience can be paradigmatic for others. Then psychoanalysis can deal with these phenomena from only a limited perspective, dictated by its own methodology and conceptual resources. We must deal with these experiences as phenomena somehow related to the natural capacities of the human organism. The question of ultimate cause, whether divine or otherwise, is beyond the reach of psychoanalytic understanding. The question of divine action exercising an extraordinary effect on the soul, whether of Ignatius or any exercitant or devotee of Ignatian spirituality, through grace does not fall within this purview — it is a matter for theological and faith-derived reflection.

From a psychoanalytic perspective, psychic processes and psychodynamic influences are active in both primary and secondary mystical states. Secondary manifestations are, in fact, frequently associated with states of mystical experience, and, if they are not essential to the mystical experience itself, they are found in the careers of all great mystics. Such secondary phenomena may help or hinder the mystic's spiritual progress. As Egan notes: "Ecstasies, raptures, visions, locutions, revelations, the stigmata, levitations, and other phenomena frequently occur with the primary phenomenon of *infused contemplation*, or God's experienced loving self-communication. If past studies tended to overemphasize these unusual phenomena at the expense of the essential mystical phenomenon, that is, infused contemplation, contemporary studies seem to dissociate them too sharply" (1984, p. 305). The general view in theological terms is that secondary phenomena are suspect, since they may not originate from divine influence — they may come from the devil or from the self. They should not be sought for themselves, and even if they seem to come from God they should not be valued at the expense of more central spiritual concerns. This was certainly the attitude of Ignatius in his skepticism regarding such extraordinary manifestations and his continued emphasis on self-abnegation and obedience.

These secondary phenomena manifest a degree of potential overlap with psychotic forms of experience. To varying degrees, the mystic detaches himself from the real world, either by attributing greater reality to his inner world and experience or by believing in a transcendent or supernatural world. Although this seems to resemble states of schizophrenic detachment, it differs in that detachment for the mystic is deliberate and to some degree under subjective control; for the schizophrenic it is not. Although the mystic devalues certain aspects of the real world, he may also attribute greater significance or value to other aspects. Moreover, the goal of mystical union is the highest reality, next to which all events of daily life pale in comparison. The mystic is driven by a supernatural love transcending all human love. The metaphors of mystical language are often sexual, but the relation between this consuming divine love and the more familiar object love and/or narcissism remains in question.

Taking the mystical and spiritual life of Ignatius of Loyola as paradigmatic, the phenomena defy simple explanation or reductive conceptualization. There is no question that many of the phenomena Ignatius experienced border on the pathological, but they cannot simply be reduced to the pathological. The ultimate question for the psychoanalyst is whether or not these experiences provide a template for mystical phenomena more generally that can be located within some intelligible framework allowing us to find psychological meaning and purpose in them. Whatever the nature and quality of the dynamic psychological forces unleashed in Ignatius' mystical transports, they took place in an otherwise well-functioning, capable, and effective human being. What psychiatric, psychological, and psychoanalytic insight can be brought to bear in understanding these phenomena? Or are we faced by an unbridgeable chasm between the supernatural and the natural, between the spiritual and the psychological, between the mystical and the psychic?

## THE MANY-EYED SERPENT

Let us go back to the vision of the colorful serpent to see what psychoanalytic hay can be made of it. The rigor of Iñigo's ascetic practices, particularly lack of nutrition and sleep, may well have induced states of altered consciousness in which regressive hallucinatory experiences would have been more likely. Such may have been the case in the vision of the many-eyed serpent.[1] The experience was disconcerting, and Iñigo finally decided that the apparition was due to the devil (Vita 31), but nonetheless it continued to appear occasionally for a period of fifteen years, until he went to Rome. In jungian archetypal terms, the serpent would represent unconscious libido, the symbolism expressing phallic erotic conflicts. "Snake dreams," Jung (1956) commented, "always indicate a discrepancy between the attitude of the conscious mind and instinct, the snake being a personification of the threatening aspect of that conflict" (p. 396); a freudian interpretation in terms of dream symbolism would reach a similar conclusion. This apparition would be taken as a symbolic representative of the libido, particularly in its phallic expression. In the earlier appearances, this vision appeared as beautiful and consoling. But in fact, the symbol was a thinly disguised representation of instinctual forces striving for expression. From the perspective of the elevated position of the pilgrim's ego after his illumination at the Cardoner, the vision no longer seemed beautiful. His intuition penetrated to the inner meaning of the symbol, and his ego came forth with renewed energy to slay what he now saw as a dragon. The experience of these visions thus reflects the dynamism of his deep psychic conflicts in the cave of Manresa, probably related to the climactic repression of libidinal impulses in the context of his conversion experience and the vision of our Lady holding the Christ Child during his convalescence at Loyola. To the extent that Iñigo's effort at repression succeeded, it would have excluded sexual impulses from his conscious mind, but not from the unconscious.

We can readily conjecture that the serpent that appeared to him in such curious fashion at Manresa reflected a resurgence of these

[1] See chapter VI above for his recounting of this vision, and the analysis of the role of discernment related to it in chapter XXXV.

same repressed elements from the depths of the unconscious — "the return of the repressed" (Freud 1915, p. 154). If so, it is interesting that this unconscious derivative presented itself in a symbolic form of such great beauty and that it elicited such consolation. We would argue that the pilgrim's ego could admit this threatening content to conscious awareness only in a highly symbolic and transformed manner. The symbol assimilates an unconscious content, thus reducing conflict between ego and id. The conscious ego perceives such a confluence as pleasurable because it results in reduction of inner tensions arising from the struggle to bring the impulses of the id into conformity with ego objectives and values. The struggle the pilgrim began in the cave reached into the depths of his unconscious and stirred the embers of libidinal desire. The regressive relaxation of his rigid repression permitted the resurgence of these unconscious elements. Relaxation of this persistent conflict was experienced as consolation. The question this assessment raises is whether the mechanism apparently at work in this vision can be taken as a prototype for secondary mystical phenomena and visions in general.

The evolution of such vivid symbolic imagery, therefore, would represent the resurgence of unconscious contents on one hand, and a form of regression of the ego, "regression in the service of the ego" (Kris 1952), on the other. The ego requires the capacity to tolerate a certain amount of regression in order to adapt adequately, specifically to achieve productivity and creativity in art and science. The artistic ego requires an ability to assimilate unconscious contents in such a way that these elements are permitted conscious expression in symbolic form. The symbol, therefore, functions as a mechanism for the translation of unconscious elements, which can be consciously expressed as a dream, a fantasy, an idea, a hunch, or a vision. In whatever form it appears, it makes itself felt as excitement, joy, consolation, or a sensation akin to intoxication. The assimilation to the ego of unconscious energies in this manner serves to vitalize and reinforce the ego.

## The Psychoanalytic Perspective

Whatever else can be said of Ignatius' mystical experiences, they took place within a human psyche and thus were subject to psychological influences and reflect the basic forces of human motivation. This fundamental fact gives the psychoanalyst license to examine the data and apply the resources of his scientific view to these otherwise transcendental experiences. His orientation is toward the latent as opposed to the manifest content of the experiences, toward the unconscious rather than conscious dimensions. As one distinguished commentator on Jewish kabbalistic mysticism has written:

> It is my conviction that psychological or psychoanalytic approaches to mystical texts must be employed with care, given the reductionist tendency inherent in their hermeneutical techniques. The chance of success in reconstructing the nature of a mystical experience from written texts is close to nil. As the components of this experience — the human psyche, the external and inner conditions, and the divine aspects that enter the experience — are either fluid or incomprehensible, or both, any reconstruction is mostly an approximation based more on the presuppositions and tendencies of the scholar than on recombination of the authentic components of the original experience. (Idel 1988, pp. 35-36.

Keeping this caution in mind, we can begin by accepting the idea that mysticism is a universal phenomenon, occurring in all religious systems, in all cultures. We can, therefore, take it to reflect a basic innate capacity in the human psyche for ecstatic experience and altered states of consciousness.

## MYSTICAL STATES AS REGRESSIVE

In assessing the nature of this affective and cognitive state in Ignatius' experience, we first of all note the intense affective quality of all his descriptions and the often diffuse, undifferentiated, obscure, and vague nature of the experiences. Psychoanalysts are usually attuned to the quality of any psychic experience resonating with infantile experience, in which sensory experience is relatively diffuse and disorganized and the distinction between affect and cognition is blurred, if not absent. The infant's experience is, to a much greater degree than the adult's, coenesthetic — reflecting a relatively unorganized mixture stimuli including proprioceptive,[2] thermal, equilibrial, tactile, vibratory, rhythmic, auditory, and others. The line between biological and psychological functioning is difficult to draw. As Ross (1975) put it, "The feeling *is* the thought, and the thought the feeling" (p. 86). Developmentally, this state probably extends to the point where self-awareness starts to emerge and enter into tension with the sense of fusion with the external world — that is, with the mother.

[2] Stimuli arising from muscles, tendons, and other organic tissues of the body.

This state of affective-cognitive diffusion is analogous to the "oceanic feeling" Freud described as the basic religious emotion. Romain Rolland, the French writer and mystic, proposed the oceanic feeling as a counterpoise to Freud's (1927) critique of religion, basing his claims on the occurrence of such a state in Oriental mystics, especially the Hindu prophets. For Rolland, the oceanic feeling was a sensation of the infinite, unbounded, limitless — a subjective experience that he believed to be the basis for religious belief and conviction. Freud (1930) did not challenge the occurrence of this feeling state, since he had experienced it himself. When he analyzed his own experience on the Acropolis, he reduced it to a piece of unresolved oedipal conflict (Freud 1936; Meissner 1984). He doubted, probably correctly, whether it could bear the weight of being the *fons et origo* of the whole religious impulse and ascribed it to a primary ego-feeling reflecting earlier infantile bonds between the ego and the surrounding world — a sense of "limitlessness and of a bond with the universe." Freud, in contrast, derived the source of religious needs, from the child's sense of helplessness and dependence on adult caretakers. For Freud, the oceanic feeling together with all religious sentiment and faith were regressive recourses to states of infantile dependence (Werman 1977). Thus, Freud put his definitive stamp on the psychoanalytic view of mystical phenomena as regressive and infantile.

Ross (1975) further argued that the mystical state represents a condition of intense affective arousal and heightened cognitive conviction together with feelings of passivity, loss of discursive reasoning, and a sense of merging with a pervasive object. He saw such states as regressions to a stage of symbiotic union with the mother, however as regressions essentially in the service of the ego and involving retention of a sense of identity. In this sense the mystical state was not a true symbiosis. The transient nature of the experience further reflected a defensive operation of the ego preventing further regression into a state of total disorganization.

In his ecstatic experience, the mystic enters an "altered state of consciousness" which has certain similarities to infantile states. The similarity to Mahler's (1975) concept of the symbiotic phase, with its intensification of narcissistic features, is striking. The ineffability of the experience may also reflect the extent of the regression to preverbal levels of infantile experience. The depth of regression carries its own perils, specifically the threat of uncontrolled regression into the depths of schizophrenic disorganization. Ross (1975) pointed to the frequent occurrence of mystical ecstasies as prologues to schizophrenic deterioration — possibly "a last desperate attempt to cling to the object world by restoring the ancient symbiotic union with the mother" (p. 91). The strength and intactness of the mystic's ego, however, could preserve him from such a fate.

These considerations raise the difficult question as to whether mystical states of consciousness are adequately interpreted as states of psychic regression or not.[3] Following Freud's lead, analysts have tended to persist in the view that mystical immersion reflects a symbiotic retreat to infantile states of self-absorption and regressive merger phenomena. I would like to depart from that perspective to suggest that ecstatic states of mind challenge our conventional categories and force us to entertain other possibilities than can be encompassed by the regression model. I will not go into detail on this subject which belongs more properly to an indepth study of mystical phenomena in its own right, but I would offer some points for future consideration and development.

The first consideration is that religious experience can be cast in terms of modes of religious experience reflecting developmental perspectives and attainments (Meissner 1984). The first and most primitive such mode reflects a variety of regressive features suggestive of integration on the level of primary narcissism. In developmental terms, this form of symbiosis precedes establishment of self-and-object differentiation. As I have written previously:

> The narcissistic experience is one of unconditioned omnipotence and absolute dependence. Faith cognition at this level is entirely undifferentiated, functioning in terms of a preconceptual and prelinguistic disposition to accept the conditions of life. This relates to the conditions of basic trust that characterize the symbiotic union of mother and child. The religious experience at this

[3] See the extended discussion of this point in Fauteux (1994). Fauteux argues that the regression to primitive psychic levels in mystical states carries an inherent potential for adaptive and redemptive resolution. This may be one possible way to formulate mystical experience, but, if so, we may have to deal with the question of whether such regression has anything to do with regression in clinical or psychiatric terms. It may be that the regressive model falls short of serving as an adequate base for understanding mystical phenomena. Adaptive reactivation of more basic, even infantile, psychic resources for mobilization to serve creative, adaptive, and transcendent psychic purposes may involve a very different process than is encompassed by the usual understanding of regression — even regression in the service of the ego. If the alternative model is ego (or self) expansion, what can we determine as to the processes and mechanisms involved? Is a psychological account of this spiritual expansion possible, or are we left with the metaphors drawn from the spiritual realm?

> level would presumably involve merging the boundaries between self-representation and God-representation. The sense of self is without cohesion, in a state of undifferentiated diffusion or severe fragmentation. This represents a state of extreme regression, which may take a psychotic form, issuing in delusions of total omnipotence and Godlike grandiosity. It may also express itself as profound and ecstatic mystical experiences involving loss of boundaries, diffusion of the sense of self, and absorption into the divine. While the mechanism and the level of organization may be similar, it seems reasonable to maintain a distinction between such mystical experiences and regressive psychosis. The vicissitudes of mystical absorption and its dynamics of self-cohesion remain to be clarified, but we cannot assume that they are equivalent to regressive psychotic states. . . . The problem can be stated in simplified form as follows: in terms of a developmental schema, are we to envision mystical states as embodiments of the highest, most differentiated, articulated, structuralized, and integrated attainments of an evolved religious capacity, or do they, on the contrary, represent regressive phenomena that reflect the most infantile levels of developmental fixation, if not aberration? (pp. 150-151)

In the Judaeo-Christian tradition, mystical states partake of the passivity, ineffability, submissive submersion in the experience of divine love, and sense of formless fusion with the divine object. Cast in regressive perspective, these phenomena represent reactivation of primitive states of oral symbiotic maternal fusion. But clearly the sense of mystical fusion differs considerably from states of regressive fusion to primary narcissistic union found in psychotic regressive states. Analytic interpretation runs into the difficulty of envisioning sustained self-cohesiveness and and a mature sense of identity in a context of mystical fusion. But, in contrast to regressive psychotic states, mystical experience has the capacity to not only not undermine or dissolve identity, but to stabilize, enrich, and elevate the sense of identity to new and spiritually more enhanced levels. I have referred to this dimension of spiritual development previously as spiritual identity.[4]

This set of considerations suggests that we require a new set of categories to describe such atypical forms of transcendental experience without being caught in the travails of the regressive model. There are suggestive examples — Kernberg's (1977) description of loving union with an other in terms of "crossing of boundaries" offers one possibility. He wrote:

[4] See the discussion of spiritual identity in chapter V above.

> In contrast to regressive merger phenomena, which blur self/non-self differentiation, concurrent with crossing the boundaries of the self is the persistent experience of a discrete self and, as well, a step in the direction of identification with structures beyond the self. In this process, there is a basic creation of meaning, of a subjective ordering of the world outside the self, which actualizes the potential structuring of human experience in terms of biological, interpersonal, and value systems. Crossing the boundaries of self, thus defined, is the basis for the subjective experience of transcendence. Psychotic identifications with their dissolution of self-object boundaries, interfere with the capacity for passion thus defined; in simple terms, madness is not in continuity with passion. (p. 95)

The application of this analysis of sexual passion to mystical states is analogous. Expansion of the capacity for object-relatedness opens the way to transcendence of self-boundaries, a crossing-over in a context of loving submission, resulting in submersion of the self in the object or conversely immersion in the loving presence of the object. As I (Meissner 1984) then noted, "Consequently, the capacity to reach beyond the boundaries of self, to empty out the self, as it were in the loving embrace of the object, is a transcendent capacity of the psyche to immerse itself in a loving object relationship. This need not in itself be regarded as regressive" (p. 152).

## Altered Consciousness

The mystical propensity, so widespread in humankind, may reflect a basic unfulfilled yearning of the self for union with and immersion in something outside itself. Diminishing self-consciousness while retaining a sense of identity is not altogether uncommon in states of trance-like absorption or intense concentration, for example in absorption in a book, or a piece of music, an idea, a poem, a scientific problem. During such concentration of attention, individuals sometimes lose all awareness of the passage of time and become relatively oblivious to their environment. There is often a subtle alteration of consciousness in such 'immersions,' without disturbing the sense of self or identity. There is, on the contrary, often a sense of enrichment or self-enhancement. In this sense, striving for a sense of wholeness, for transcendence of the ordinary human condition and its limits, for union with an omnipotent deity, may derive from forms of grandiose fantasy. As Bach (1977) remarked:

> Whether such fantasies are viewed as defensive regressions or as creative expressions depends not only on whether one consults a psychiatrist or a guru, but also on the meaning of this experience in the context of the person's life, a complicated issue which forms part of an as yet scarcely begun psychology of creative and mystical states. But perhaps we may assume that every narcissistic fantasy, omnipotent and transcendent as it may be, expresses in some distorted form an attainable human possibility as well as an unattainable divine one. (p. 287)

Psychoanalysts, following Freud's view of mystical states as regressive, have often emphasized the infantile and oral dimension of the mystical experience. The model for narcissistic union is the mother-child symbiosis (Bach 1977). Oral imagery often pervades accounts of mystical ecstasy, even appealing to images of maternal closeness and nursing at the breast — quite consistently with analytic interpretations in terms of symbiotic oral-incorporative narcissistic fusion. Ignatius' mystical ecstasies would certainly be congruent with these formulations. Again and again he returns to the theme of ecstatic union with God and the sweetness and joy of that experience. The psychoanalytic investigator is not interested simply in the manifest phenomenology of such experiences but seeks to discern the hidden elements that might reflect more basic infantile motivations. The important emphasis, it seems to me, is that, if such regressive connotations can be attached to mystical states of consciousness, they need not be reduced to that level of psychic implication — the relevance of such an account may be reductionistic rather than reductive.[5]

## INTERNALIZED MOTHER

Whatever interpretive perspective might bring us closest to a satisfactory understanding of mystical phenomena, the seemingly regressive aspects on which analytic reflection has concentrated, cannot be ignored. We might suspect that these dimensions of the motivational system that enter into mystical experience are not entirely devoid of tension and conflict. Moloney (1954) postulated a basic conflict with the internalized image of the mother as a contributory component of mystical phenomena. Infantile trauma and disturbances of the early mother-child relationship can result in the formation of

[5] See the discussion of this point in chapter V above.

introjects[6] that have the effect of internalizing the frustrating or denying image of the mother, thus creating an internal maternal demand system that the individual must constantly rebel against and struggle to escape. In this model, strivings for self-expression are in constant conflict with the maternal demands embedded in the superego. If this inner struggle is relaxed, if the armed neutrality between the self-system and the internalized mother-system diminishes, the result may be a theophany, a flash of inspiration that seems to resolve the internal conflicts. Self-strivings are surrendered, and the subject submits to the maternal authority he had previously struggled to defeat and destroy. The corrective forces within seek regression back to the developmental point when the disturbance between the self-system and the mother-system began, opening a potential path toward greater maturity and self-determination.

In the effort to gain domination of the self-system over the mother-system, there may be an appearance of pseudomaturity masking an ongoing rebellion against authoritarian domination. As Greenacre (1947) noted, "Mastery is attempted by . . . development of severely binding super-ego reaction-formations of goodness which are supplemented by or converted into lofty ideals" (p. 177). When the point of exhaustion is reached, a startling realignment of the tension between the self- and mother-systems may occur bringing about the sudden theophany or inspiration. The pseudomature elements of the self-system are drawn back regressively to the period of infantile dependence on the mother. There may be flashes of light, bright aureoles, even visual hallucinations. It would not strain credulity to envision this dynamic as part of Ignatius' mystical horizon. The conflict between the self-system of the phallic narcissistic hidalgo who dreamed of heroic exploits and libidinal triumphs, and the internalized prohibitive maternal system which would have been permeated by profound religious and moral values, may have set the stage for the inner struggle and transformation that characterized his conversion experience.[7] We can certainly entertain the hypothesis that Iñigo's phallic and narcissistic self-system had capitulated to the maternal-feminine superego and embraced the path of religious inspiration,

[6] A technical term indicating a form of internalization that is in some degree drive-determined and defensive so that what is internalized remains in the service of defense. Introjects tend to be poorly integrated and can remain vulnerable to regression and other defensive vicissitudes — among them projection. See Meissner (1981).

[7] See chapter II above for further details of the conversion experience and my previous (Meissner 1992b) analysis of the psychic underpinning of that experience.

rejecting the masculine and paternal values that had dominated his life to that point. His conversion, then, would reflect the binding of superego reaction formations in the construction of new and lofty ideals of religious perfection and the imitation of Christ.[8]

## AGGRESSION

What role does aggression play in the mystical resolution? Hartocollis (1976) argued "that those attracted to mystical movements are likely to be individuals who, sensitized by the violence around them, become preoccupied with their own potential for violence, which they find too threatening to express and are unable to neutralize within the available family and social context. Followers of mystical movements wish to cancel the aggression of the world in order to do away with their own" (p. 214). The peacefulness and sense of blissful union of the mystical state, whether induced by prayer and ascetical exercises, by psychedelic drugs, or by spontaneous conversion experiences, are identified as inspirational or transcendental and carry with them a sense of conviction analogous to delusional states, being in love, and vivid dreams. The experience requires no explanation but is taken as self-evident. As Bertrand Russell (1929) observed, "The mystic insight begins with the sense of a mystery unveiled, of a hidden wisdom now suddenly become certain beyond the possibility of a doubt. The sense of certainty and revelation comes earlier than any definite belief" (p. 9). The yearning for such enlightenment, along with the sense of undifferentiated unity, is usually regarded psychoanalytically as regression to preverbal levels that may be either objectless — a form of limitless narcissism connected with the oceanic feeling (Freud 1930) — or a fusion between the self and the maternal object, specifically the maternal breast (Lewin 1950).

The fantasy of such blissful and seamless fusion can correspond to the fantasy of escape from inner aggressive drives and their consequences in the form of anger, fear, anxiety, worry, and despair. The escape may be a reaction to the sense of one's own violent potential generally or more specifically to the sense of inner evil and destructiveness embedded in introjective configurations stemming from the aggressive and feared father on the oedipal level and at a deeper level from the frustrating or overexciting mother of infancy (Hartocollis 1976; Meissner 1978). The success or failure of the attempt at union

[8] Moloney (1954) even cited the case of Ignatius in support of his thesis.

is a function of the degree of aggressive contamination. Jacobson (1964) observed:

> Since normal experiences of ecstasy do not aim at destruction but are founded on a fantasy of libidinal union between self and object world, they result in a transitory sense of self-expression and the feeling that the self and the world are rich. Such experiences of merging, which may briefly retransform the images of the self and the object world into a fantasy unit vested with libidinal forces, permit an immediate reestablishment of the boundaries between them. By contrast, pathological regressive fusions caused by severe aggression may result in an irreparable breakdown of these boundaries and hence of the self and object representations. (p. 69)

In this formulation, when the libidinal charge is freed from all aggressive contamination, union can take the blissful and satisfying form that is the common experience of mystics. Hartocollis (1976) added:

> What, in turn, motivates the search for a mystical experience is the emergence into consciousness of one's own potential for violence and the fear that his hidden aggression may destroy the internalized "good" objects. . . . This emergent awareness of potential inner violence is the result of exposure to an environment where violence is prevalent but random, avoidable but non-negotiable; seen as a product of a "sinful," materialistic and exploitative civilization rather than as a means to an end, a necessary evil in the service of some personal or group ideology. (p. 224)

One of the pervasive motifs in the *Exercises*, cast in terms of the following of the humble and suffering Christ, is detachment from and overcoming of aggressive and destructive aspects of the self. Iñigo de Loyola was an aggressive, violent man — themes of aggressiveness and violence were clearly etched in his pre-conversion exploits, culminating in the disaster at Pamplona. The conversion was marked by revulsion at his former manner of life and his turning toward a life of total and uncompromising opposition to the past. Iñigo's conversion and subsequent ascetical life were in effect a turning of his powerful aggressive drives against himself in the form of self-conquest. The bliss of mystical ecstasy had to wait for resolution of these basic and powerful aggressive conflicts.

The identification with the image of Christ also resolved conflicts over aggression, since it was the suffering Christ that he followed and wished to imitate, the Christ who wandered the earth without a place to lay His head, who was poor and had to beg for his daily bread, the Christ who ultimately was rejected, humiliated, tortured, and crucified — the humble, suffering Christ, the model of victimization, the radical opposite of aggressive power and destructiveness. His struggle to follow in the footsteps of Christ can be seen as driven in part by his need to escape from and overcome the sense of inner violence, evil, and destructiveness, and demonic force buried in his inner world. Any occasion in which Ignatius had to suffer painful afflictions became a reason to glory in his infirmities and suffering, for through them he was walking in the path of the Savior. The identification with Christ, in other words, became the vehicle of masochistic fulfillment and gratification, all in the service of a narcissistic and religious ideal. The same identification enabled his psyche to consolidate the resolution of the libidinal conflicts that had so consumed and later tormented him and that were so strikingly resolved in his vision of the Blessed Mother at Loyola. The dramatic and massive repression that took place on that occasion could find powerful reinforcement by putting himself in the place of Christ, who was pure and chaste beyond any question or reproach. We can suggest that some of these same dynamic resolutions may be achieved in those who struggle to follow him in their ascent of the spiritual mountain.

But this model may not fully account for the transformation of aggression aimed at in the *Exercises* and embedded in the mystical resolution. Again and again, not only in the *Exercises*, but also in considerable detail in the *Constitutions*, and often in his letters, he calls on the capacity to mobilize resources and to take decisive and forceful action in the pursuits of spiritual goals and in the overcoming of obstacles to spiritual progress. Consequently, we would have to conclude that Ignatius' objective in following the path to spiritual achievement was to channel aggression from its destructive and spiritually impeding expression into more adaptive and growth enhancing potentialities for effective action and achievement. For psychoanalysts, this perspective on aggression and its spiritual vicissitudes may require a reconsideration and revision of the understanding of aggression and its role in the development of human personality and in adaptive and creative capacity.[9]

## NARCISSISM

Mystical immersion rests on a grandiose fantasy of union with an omnipotent and infinite love object that serves the function of

[9] For a revised theory of aggression in these terms, see Buie et al. (1983); Meissner (1986, 1991); Meissner et al. (1987); Rizzuto et al. (1993).

fulfilling basic narcissistic needs. The basically narcissistic substructure of Ignatius' personality, displayed so dramatically on the heroic stage of his courtly and military career, did not disappear when his hopes of becoming a heroic warrior were struck down, but were transformed into a determination to become a hero in the spiritual realm like the spiritual heroes — the saints, paragons of self-sacrifice and self-denial — to seek glory in the service of another and greater king. The meditations on the Kingdom and the Two Standards in the *Exercises* bear eloquent testimony to this aspect of his narcissism. We can also note that the narcissistic resolution falls far short of a psychotic identification with Christ, but rather takes the form of joining the fellowship of Christ's followers and imitators.

In this vein, his mystical experiences universally have the quality of wish-fulfillments — like dream experiences reflecting unconscious desires. His visions particularly seemed to offer gratification of narcissistically determined wishes. He wants to be favored by our Lady and so she appears to him in an apparition. He hopes to be chosen for the service of Christ, his Lord and Master; the wish is realized in the vision at La Storta. In these experiences he achieves the most complete fulfillment of his post-conversion ego ideal. As Chasseguet-Smirgel (1976) observes, "Mysticism follows the pattern of the fusion of the ego and its ideal. . . . It promises fusion with the primary object — even when on the conscious level it is identified with a God-Father, who in the end is equivalent to the mother before defusion" (p. 367). In terms of its narcissistic dynamics, mystical elevation is self-enhancing and contributes significantly to the mystic's self-esteem and self-integration. It serves to sustain not only a more integrated sense of self and identity in merely natural terms, but in spiritual perspective it results in consolidation and development of the mystic's spiritual identity and his capacity correspondingly to enter into the loving fusion with the self-communication coming from the divine. The mystical paradox reaches its apogee in this process — the more completely the mystic empties himself of all attachments to this world and to his own self — often referred to as "dying to self" — the more fully is that self restored to him enriched with profound spiritual consolations.

## VISUAL DIMENSION

Ignatius' accounts of his mystical experiences are quite remarkable for the frequency of visions and apparitions. This is not a universal or characteristic feature of mystical experience, but seems to reflect something about the Ignatian approach to the spiritual life. We should note first the largely visual character of Ignatius' mystical experience. Throughout his mystical journey, visual apparitions re-occur with striking regularity. His conversion was centered dramatically around the apparition of the Blessed Mother, his ecstasies at Manresa have a remarkably visual and symbolic quality — visions of the Trinity in the form of organ keys, the wonderful serpent. At Jerusalem the vision of Christ leading him on his way was prominent, and again at Vincenza he recounts his many visions. And the *Journal* indicates a rich tapestry of such visual phenomena.

To this catalogue we can add the frequent visual emphasis in the *Spiritual Exercises* — in his imaginative reconstructions of scenes in hell, in the many compositions of place that introduce the meditations, in the repeated directives to see the scene, to watch Our Lord acting in certain ways, and so on. Even in the preconversion framework, his imaginative representations of his deeds of daring and gallantry in the service of his lady have a largely visual quality. All of this adds up to an impression that his visual function had become endowed with special importance in his psychic life and that this played a vital role in of his mystical life.

The special investment in the visual function can reflect a form of focal symbiosis (Greenacre 1959) in which a particular bodily organ or area is selected to express the union between the special needs of the child and the projected pathology of the parent, usually the mother. Where the normal pattern of infantile mirroring is lacking, as it might be in the case of a narcissistic or absent mother, the result may be a heightened investment of the eyes, or indirectly through a cathexis from the mouth and/or genitals displaced to the eyes. The primacy of the visual function may be partially determined not only by early deprivation and frustration, but can be abetted by subsequent primal scene exposure, castration anxiety or even outright sexual abuse. The outcome in many patients may be a form of scopophilia[10] or hyperacuity with or without perversion. In Iñigo's case, there is evidence to support this speculation — the early maternal deprivation in conjunction with other possible factors that we can only imagine. Even the role of primal scene exposure is plausible, given a presumption of the living conditions in the peasant cottage in which young Iñigo was raised. In the tiny peasant cottage, the blacksmith and his wife probably slept in the same room as the children and the opportunities for primal scene exposure would have been ample.

[10] Scopophilia is a form of perversion in which sexual pleasure is derived from looking.

If we harken back to the many-eyed serpent, we can only guess at the determinants of the snake symbolism, but they undoubtedly reflect the influence of castration anxiety and phallic narcissistic drive derivatives. The unusual conjunction of phallic derivatives with the visual component (represented in the many eyes) points toward the interlocking of phallic themes with a degree of presumptive optical focal symbiosis.[11] Clinically the scopophilic emphasis often connects with ophidiophobia, the fear of snakes — but in Iñigo's case, with a fixation and fascination with the serpent imagery. Here speculation can run rampant. What experiences might have played a role that the veils of time and history conceal from our eyes? Could the infant, deprived of mother and the intimacy of maternal mirroring, been confronted with the potentially stimulating vision of adult copulation? of anxiety producing exposure to the phallic and genital endowment of the blacksmith? And with what effect? All of this raises questions that speak to the intersection of mystical experience with the given psychic substratum provided by the personality organization and structure of the individual mystic.

Mahony (1989) argues that in at least one of his patients, a snake phobia was derived from the negative oedipal complex along with elements of prior, essentially preoedipal, visual experiences and fantasies that had a primarily traumatic impact. Thus the core of the snake symptom was an accumulative symbol. He writes:

> A brief glance at other sources confirms this notion of accumulative symbol. Pandemic in mythology, religion, folklore, and dreams, the serpent symbolizes the phallus although it occasionally bears significance for the female genitalia. In the Gnostic biblical tradition, moreover, it underwent splitting so that Eve was impregnated by the bad serpent, and Mary by the good one (Hassal, 1919; Fortune, 1926). This notwithstanding, the pregenital meaning of a snake might better explain its worship as the most prevalent of all early religious practices. The snake's shape as a gut and a devouring mouth or as a *bolus fecalis* makes it eminently suitable to represent early aggressive impulses of the late oral and anal stages. Indeed, the phallic interpretation of the Fall of Man has obscured the pregenital meaning of the serpent's punishment, namely, to be deprived of its limbs and to crawl despisedly on its belly in the dirt. Seeing the serpent may stir up the uncanny feeling of the return of the repressed and the expelled hostile excrement as fully alive. (pp. 393-394)

[11] The focal symbiosis reflecting the conjunction of infantile needs and parental pathology is here centered in the visual function. See Greenacre (1959).

The vision of the many-eyed snake continued to plague Ignatius for about fifteen years — at least until he was situated in Rome (Tylenda 1985). I would speculate that the vision of the serpent was done in once and for all only after the dramatic and narcissistically enhancing vision of the Father and the Son at La Storta, on the threshold of Rome. That vision, in which Ignatius was placed under the special care and protection of God the Father and His Son, must have contributed powerfully to the resolution of the conflictual and ambiguous dynamic forces that found expression in the eerie serpentine apparition. Only when these conflictual elements and their attendant anxieties had found resolution in the promise of divine guidance — either from the powerful phallic and omnipotent father, or possibly also from the implicit promise of maternal presence — were the bases for the serpent vision finally disengaged.

I have pointed out the shifts in Ignatius' core identifications and the role they played in his mystical experience. To a large extent, the feminine aspects of his character are dominant in his mysticism, reflected in his yearning for love, his intense affectivity, his passivity and submissive yielding to the divine embrace, and the overwhelming experience of copious tears to the point of physical disability. I have suggested that at some level, his mystical absorption may have its psychic roots in the yearning of the abandoned child for its lost mother — the repeated floods of tears reflecting joy in reunion with the lost mother. I would not want to insist too emphatically on the hypothesis; nonetheless it does fit with the rest of the psychological portrait of the saint. While this configuration seems to provide a plausible substratum for Ignatius' mystical consciousness, I would also suggest that the paradigm may not be entirely alien for mystical engagement in general. In terms of the present endeavor, this question must remain open to further investigation in the experience of other mystics. We can suggest that, while the life circumstances and psychic endowments will differ from one to another, the configuration of internalizations may play a vital role in configuring the quality and character of individual mystical consciousness and experience.

## The God-Representation

The fact that these experiences took place in states of altered consciousness and in a realm removed from everyday human psychic experience brings into consideration the nature of the God-representation in these contexts and how we are to understand the peculiar nature of the mystical episode itself. The experience of God as an object in the psychic representational world of every human being is a product of a host of developmental factors that contribute to the distillation and integration of those experiences in the form of a special and unique mental representation (Rizzuto 1979).

The God-representation in the mind of Ignatius undoubtedly derived in large part from images of his father and mother — perhaps more from the mother, as the source of affective acceptance and love, than from his father, but certainly involving some balance of the influence of both. His God-representation became the restitutive substitute for the lost mother and fulfilled part of the deep unconscious longing left by her loss. Ignatius' resolution for conflicts of loss-and-restitution (Rochlin 1965) took the more sublimated form of a religiously tinged paternity and an Eriksonian generativity permeated by the nurturant and maternal qualities derived from his identification with the lost mother. The imagery was also cast in terms of majesty, infinite power, wisdom, and strength. The Divine Majesty of whom Ignatius speaks so constantly is a representation of the earthly majesties of Ignatius' experience, magnified to the immensity and transcendent glory of the divine. The images of the *Spiritual Exercises* in particular express the elements of this internal representation.

But the God-representation is not an object-representation[12] like any other. The most useful formulation I have found for thinking about transcendent experiences of this kind is the notion of transitional experience (Meissner 1978, 1984, 1990). The essential aspect of transitional experience is that it straddles subjective and objective realms of experience and thus partakes simultaneously of both. The model derives from Winnicott's notion of the transitional object (Winnicott 1953) — the doll or blanket or whatever other object that acts as the substitute for the mother, a sort of bridge between the infant's symbiotic attachment to the mother and the beginnings of investment in reality. In this view, the infant creates the mother that he requires in order to satisfy basic needs in the same context in which the real mother responds optimally to the child's expressed needs. The mother-object is thus created even as it is experienced. The experience itself is at one and the same time subjective and objective. Winnicott extends this analysis to transitional phenomena that constitute the realm of illusion. It is the basic human capacity for this kind of experience that lies at the root of all cultural experi-

[12] An object-representation is a mental representation of an external object — usually referring to persons as objects.

ence, including religion. Reading a poem, or immersing oneself in music or painting, for example, takes place in the intermediate realm of illusion, in which the esthetic experience is neither subjective nor objective but something of both.

The issue brought into focus by this analysis is the role of creativity in religious and especially mystical experience. The role of creativity in religious experience parallels or is at least analogous to that in artistic experience. As Oremland (1989) has recently written:

> Creative people seem to be developmentally those singular few individuals who maintain an extraordinary kinship to or maintain continuances of transitional phenomena. Pressing this developmental perspective, these perpetuators of transitional phenomena continue the ongoing capacity to explore the external and the internal anew and to invent, play with, and enact symbols akin to the initial discovering we all experienced as the differentiation of self from nonself progressed. . . . The emphasis on the transitional object closely parallels Emile Durkheim's (1915) description of the capacity to endow things with meaning as being the fundamental element of all religions, primitive and sophisticated alike. Pressing this developmental perspective, the transitional object links the art object and the religious object to the beginning of relatedness, a compelling parallel to the historical linkage between art and religion. Just as a historical commonality exists between the idolmaker and the artist, a developmental commonality seems to exist among the child playing, the primitive idolmaker, and the artist. (pp. 27-28)

For the artist as for the mystic, the creative urge is driven by an unconscious search for the primal object. Oremland (1989) continues: "creating is a reestablishing of primal union at a variety of levels with the primal object . . . . Like object relatedness, creativity seeks a version of the primal object out of which evolves the creation of a new object that is a version of the primal object. Creative individuals repeatedly "find" their mothers, themselves, and the world anew" (p. 29).

I would submit that, in periods of prayer and mystical ecstasy, Ignatius, like all his fellow mystics, enter such a realm of transitional experience — manifested by total absorption and intensity of emotional experience. Mystical experiences, then, are forms of illusion, in Winnicott's sense,[13] that express aspects of his inner subjective

[13] "Illusion" in this context has a specific meaning that requires careful exposition. See Meissner (1984). Briefly, Winnicott's notion of illusion stands in opposition to Freud's. For Freud, illusions were defined by their role as wish-fulfillments. If the illusion contradicted reality, it was for him a delusion. For Winnicott, the illusion is an intermediate form of experience in which wishes and fantasies can

psychic life, with its complex needs and determinants — infantile, narcissistic, libidinal, and otherwise — as they intersect with an external reality that can be described in theological terms as divine presence, grace, infused contemplation, and other transcendental manifestations. If one accepts the validity of such a conceptual device, it becomes possible, even within the limitations of a psychoanalytic understanding, to speak of the influence of drives, needs, psychic representations (the God-representation), and the whole range of dynamic and adaptational considerations impinging on the mystical experience, without passing judgment on the objective reality or unreality of the experience itself. That issue is not for psychoanalysis to decide. It can do no more that reach its own understanding, in terms that do no violence to the objective dimensions of our human efforts to fathom such transcendental experiences taking place at the limits, or the horizons, of human capacity.

## TRANSFORMATION AND TRANSVALUATION

As previously suggested,[14] the core transformative component of the Ignatian spiritual program is the spiritual value-orientation undergirding the entire system. The values are articulated most directly in the Principle and Foundation in the *Exercises* [SE23] and in the Contemplation on Obtaining Love [SE230-237]. To clarify, if one accepts, as men of religious conviction do, the existence of God and an order of spiritual realities, that order has an inherent structure and characteristic value dimension that distinguish it from other orders of reality. The existence of such an order of reality and its inherent values is a vital determinant in the lives of the saints from whom Ignatius drew his inspiration. The nature of this spiritual order is the burden of revelation, and the formulation and understanding of its implications and the values it implies are the work of systematic theology.

touch reality, in which the subjective and the objective can find common ground, and in which neither the reality of the objects of desire are denied nor the experience of wishes and fantasies ignored. A painting, for example, is an objective reality, but the experience of the painting involves not just the reality but the subjective complex of feelings and meanings brought to it by the viewer. In mystical raptures, there is an objective reality, the presence of God, but the experience of that presence is conditioned by a rich complex of subjective personality factors, some of which we have tried to illuminate.

[14] See the previous discussion of spiritual values and transvaluation in the Ignatian spiritual method in chapter V above.

In Iñigo's case, the values inherent in the lives of the saints were first assimilated to his old ego ideal. He saw the heroic deeds of the saints as projections of heroic chivalry to the level of the service of God rather than to the service of a human lord. He bears testimony to this assimilation when he tells that later, after his departure from Loyola, "He continued his way to Montserrat, thinking as usual of the great deeds he was going to do for the love of God. As his mind was filled with the adventures of Amadis of Gaul and such books, thoughts corresponding to these adventures came to his mind" (Vita 17). Plainly, then, the initial mechanism involved an ego-orientation and perception of an order of values, followed by assimilation of these perceived values to a pre-existent internalized value system. The impulses he felt stirring within him were still cast in the frame of his phallically narcissistic preconversion ego ideal and only through the transforming process of his continuing ascetical efforts and spiritual exercises centered on the imitation of Christ did the transcendent spiritual values shaping his spiritual vision find realization.

The transformation from Iñigo, the swaggering courtier, to Ignatius the saint, rather than involving the substitution of one value system for another, represented a transformation in which the old value system took on new significance and implication. Our interest here is in the psychic processes brought into play in achieving this transformation — integration of these value systems had to be the work of the ego in its synthetic function. In his spiritual naivete, the pilgrim tried to reconcile these divergent value systems by assimilating the newly perceived spiritual values to the older and more evidently narcissistic system. But as his understanding of the dimensions of the new value system deepened, he was gradually compelled to face the impossibility of reconciliation — a realization that precipitated the crisis of Manresa. The shift somehow implied that the order of spiritual realities, which his religion had taught him, gradually entered into a new relation in which there was borne in on him the actuality of its existence and its pertinence to himself. This realization and the process by which it became operative in him were fundamentally an activity of the ego, accepting and internalizing this segment of reality. This implied a new awareness and a deepened understanding. It implied also an initial and possibly hesitant commitment of himself to the values that slowly became apparent to him. His experiences in the course of this wrenching and spiritualizing transformation were distilled into the *Spiritual Exercises* and by extension into the more evolved spiritual vision of his mature years.

Values must be perceived, recognized, however implicitly, considered, and accepted. Cognitive functions of the ego play an essential role. The reality, maturity, and viability of such values depend in great measure on the ego's capacity for reality-testing and orientation. The ego's basic capacity to relate to the real can be distorted by influences stemming from id or from superego. The value structures themselves are permeated by ideals necessarily involving superego derivatives — with specific reference to the ego ideal and an "ideal self." By the same token, values can be eroded by deneutralized instinctual influences which flood the ego with aggressive or libidinal impulses, or distorted more subtly by the defensive or drive-dependent demands of the superego.

The distortion of values by superego influences is the more likely prospect in general because the superego has a role in the formation of values. The integration of values into the psychic structure demands a compromise with the unconscious demands of the superego. Anna Freud (1936) observed that the division of functions between ego and superego is apparent only when they are in conflict; when they are functioning normally without conflict, superego and ego act as one. The fluctuating alignment and division of these psychic agencies make it all the more difficult to draw a clear line of demarcation between them. Values are assimilated and internalized primarily by the ego, but only under the influence of and in concert with the superego.

The ego ideal in this context can be viewed as that part of the superego which sets up standards by which the ego maintains its sense of narcissistic equilibrium. If the ego fails to live up to the ego ideal, the superego punishes the ego. Conformity to the ego ideal is accompanied by ego-enhancement; deviance by ego-deflation, guilt or shame. Ego deviation from the demands of ego ideal and superego gives rise to conflict between ego and superego. However, the agency of change and modification is the ego, for it is the ego that keeps at least one face open to the world and reality and is subject to the modifying influences of that reality.

Internalization of values and the corresponding modification of the ego ideal must be engineered by the ego, but they cannot be accomplished without superego compliance. Carrying as it does the unconscious residues of infantile experience, particularly those derived from parental identifications, the superego along with its expression in the ego ideal is not easy to change. Consequently the ego can meet tremendous superego resistance. One cannot think of the process in any mechanical sense. As a rule, the complex apprehension of the ego initiates a process which issues into value formation only in so far as the functioning of ego and superego are conjoined in it. The ego does not assimilate a set of values and then present them to the superego. Rather, the complex apprehension of the ego initiates a process that issues into value formation only in so far as the functioning of ego and superego are conjoined in it. Values are not internalized without superego compliance and conjoined activity. The ego ideal lies at the interface of ego and superego and is profoundly affected by both sets of functions. For values to be incorporated into it requires the activity of ego as well as the permissive endorsement of superego. To this extent, superego itself is modified. The unremitting exercise of penance and mortification were part of the mystic's continuing effort to preserve and deepen the sense of internalization and realization of the spiritual values he had made his own. Only in the reaffirmation of these values and in the renewed effort to live and act in accord with their standards can greater degrees of psychic integration be achieved, greater mastery of instinctual forces guaranteed, and through the progressive fusion of instincts richer resources of neutralized energy made available for constructive ego efforts.

In Iñigo's case, one of the central determining aspects of this process of transvaluation had to be his deep-seated and strongly motivated identification with Christ, his Lord and Master — a theme that assumes central importance in the *Exercises*. This core identificatory process, operating at an unconscious level, provided the essence of his postconversion ego ideal, and drew to itself all of the narcissistic libido unleashed in his conversion crisis and regression. If there had been messianic strains in his preconversion self, these narcissistically determined elements could come to rich fruition and focus around the Christ-identification. It answered to his narcissistic needs most effectively — to be like Christ would be to fulfill his most ardent wishes to be singled out as one of God's heroes, one of God's chosen saints — like the heroic and self-sacrificing images of Francis and Dominic and Onofrius that had so stirred his imagination on the sickbed of Loyola.

Identification with Christ, then, in an Ignatian perspective, is overdetermined[15] and serves multiple functions in the psychic economy of the believer. The pattern traced by Ignatius can be taken as prototypical. In the beginning, the emphasis fell fervently and sim-

[15] Overdetermination refers to the fact that psychic formation (symptoms, dreams, character traits, and so on) can be influenced by multiple determining factors — either in the sense that it is the resultant of multiple causes, or in the sense that is open to different levels of meaning and interpretation.

plistically on imitating the behavior and manner of life of Christ. Only gradually did it evolve into a more spiritually meaningful and mature internalization of the spiritual values inherent in the Christian ideal. In particular it integrated the derivatives of his powerful narcissism, his stifled and conflicted aggression, and his repressed but rebellious sexual and libidinal drives in a way that was consistent with his ego ideal and formed the basis for the articulation of his saintly psychic and spiritual identity. The integration took place on several levels. If the identification with Christ could serve these multiple functions in helping to resolve conflictual and drive-related compromises in the integration of Ignatius' personality structure, it also encompassed the internalization of spiritual values that were embedded in the figure and teaching of Christ. These values were gradually internalized and consolidated to become a central component of Ignatius' ego ideal, and the centerpiece of his revitalized and transformed spiritual identity.

The substantive effect of this process was internal growth within the ego itself. Looked at solely from the point of view of the psychology of the ego, that growth is achieved through increasing integration within the ego and between ego and superego and by the progressive integration of instincts and the resultant availability of psychic potential to the ego for its conflict-free synthetic and integrative functions. The correlate of this growth is an enrichment and deepening of the self-structure and the related sense of identity. Identity is linked to the internalization of a value system and its integration in a cohesive self-structure. To speak of one is to imply the other. What the pilgrim experienced, then, *pari passu*, was a growth in his own sense of identity — more fully realized as he grew in internal realization of a fuller, more realistic, and more spiritual system of values. It is this same path of spiritual development that Ignatius proposed to exercitants following the program of the *Spiritual Exercises* and laid down as the spiritual ideal and path to spiritual maturity for his subjects and followers in the Society he founded.

# REFERENCES

Abse, D.W., and Ulman, R.B. (1977) Charismatic political leadership and collective regression. In Robins, R.S. (ed.) *Psychopathology and Political Leadership*. (Tulane Studies in Political Science, Vol. XVI) New Orleans: Tulane University Press.

Adorno, T.W., Frenkel-Brunswik, E., Levinson, D.J., and Sanford, R.N. (1950) *The Authoritarian Personality*. New York: Harper.

Alemany, C., and Garcia-Monge, J.A. (1991) Prologo. In Alemany, C., and Garcia-Monge, J.A. (eds.) *Psicologia y Ejercicios Ignacianos*. 2 vols. Bilbao-Santander: Mensajero-Sal Terrae, vol. I, 13-15.

Allport, G.W. (1955) *Becoming*. New Haven, CT: Yale University Press.

Bach, S. (1977) On narcissistic fantasies. *International Review of Psychoanalysis*, 4: 281-293.

Barnes, D.F. (1978) Charisma and religious leadership: an historical analysis. *Journal for the Scientific Study of Religion*, 17: 1-18.

Becher, S.J., H. (1977) Ignatius as seen by his contemporaries. In Wulf, S.J., F. (ed.) *Ignatius of Loyola: His Personality and Spiritual Heritage, 1556-1956*. St. Louis, MO: Institute of Jesuit Sources, 69-96.

Begg, E. (1985) *The Cult of the Black Virgin*. London: Arkana.

Beirnaert, S.J., L. (1964) *Expérience Chrétienne et Psychologie*. Paris: Epi.

Berliner, B. (1947) On some psychodynamics of masochism. *Psychoanalytic Quarterly*, 16: 459-471.

Bertrand, S.J., D. (1985) *La Politique de S. Ignace de Loyola*. Paris: Les Editions du Cerf.

Birtchnell, J. (1969) The possible consequences of early parental death. *British Journal of Medical Psychology*, 42: 1-12.

Birtchnell, J., Wilson, I.C., Bratfos, O., et al. (1973) *Effects of Early Parent Death*. New York: MSS Information Corp.

Blet, S.J., P. (1956) Les fondements de l'obéissance Ignatienne. *Archivum Historicum Societatis Jesu*, 25: 514-538.

Boyer, J.C. (1956) La puissance de la grace selon saint Ignace. *Nouvelle Revue Theologique*, 37: 355-365.

Boyle, M.O. (1983) Angels black and white: Loyola's spiritual discernment in historical perspective. *Theological Studies*, 44: 241-257.

Bradley, S.J. (1979) The relationship of early maternal separation to borderline personality in children and adolescents: a pilot study. *American Journal of Psychiatry*, 136: 424-426.

Breier, A., Kelsoe, Jr., J.R., Kirwin, P.D., Beller, S.A., Wolkowitz, O.M., and Pickar, D. (1988) Early parental loss and development of adult psychopathology. *Archives of General Psychiatry*, 45: 987-993.

Brodrick, S.J., J. (1940) *The Origin of the Jesuits.* New York: Longmans Green.

Brodrick, S.J., J. (1956) *St. Ignatius Loyola: The Pilgrim Years.* London: Burns and Oates.

Buckley, M.J. (1973) The structure of the rules for discernment of spirits. *The Way*, 20 (Suppl.): 19-37.

Buckley, S.J., M.J. (1976) Jesuit priesthood: its meaning and commitments. *Studies in the Spirituality of the Jesuits*, 8/5.

Buckley, S.J., M.J. (1979) Mission in companionship: of Jesuit community and communion. *Studies in the Spirituality of the Jesuits*, 11/4.

Buckley, S.J., M.J. (1984) Freedom, election, and self-transcendence: some reflections upon the Ignatian development of a life of ministry. In Schner, G.P. (ed.) *Ignatian Spirituality in a Secular Age*, Waterloo, Ont.: Wilfred Laurier University Press, 65-90.

Buckley, S.J., M.J. (1993) Ecclesial mysticism in the *Spiritual Exercises*: two notes on Ignatius, the church, and the life in the spirit. Unpublished MSS.

Buckley, P. (1981) Mystical experience and schizophrenia. *Schizophrenia Bulletin*, 7: 516-521.

Buie, D.H., Rizzuto, A.M., Sashin, J.I., and Meissner, S.J., W.W., (1983) Aggression in the psychoanalytic situation. *International Review of Psychoanalysis*, 10: 159-170.

Buonaiuti, E. (1968) Symbols and rites in the religious life of certain monastic orders. In Campbell, J. (ed.) *The Mystic Vision: Papers from the Eranos Yearbooks*. Princeton: Princeton University Press, 168-209.

Calveras, S.J., J. (1948) Los "confesionales" y los ejercicios de San Ignacio. *Archivum Historicum Societatis Jesu*, 17: 51-101.

Calveras, S.J., J. (1958) *Ejercicios espirituales: Directorio y documentos.* Barcelona.

Charmé, S.L. (1983) Religion and the theory of masochism. *Journal of Religion and Health*, 22: 221-233.

Chasseguet-Smirgel, J. (1975) *The Ego Ideal.* New York: Norton, 1985.

Chasseguet-Smirgel, J. (1976) Some thoughts on the ego ideal: a contribution to the study of the 'illness of ideality.' *Psychoanalytic Quarterly*, 45: 345-373.

Christensen, C.W. (1963) Religious conversion. *Archives of General Psychiatry*, 9: 207-216.

Clancy, S.J., T.H. (1976) *An Introduction to Jesuit Life: The Constitutions and History Through 435 Years.* St. Louis, MO: The Institute of Jesuit Sources.

Clemence, J. (1951-1952) Le discernement des espirits dans les Exercises spirituelles de saint Ignace de Loyola. *Revue d'Ascetique et de Mystique*, 27: 347-375; 28: 64-81.

Clemence, J. (1956) La meditation du Regne. *Revue d'Ascetique et de Mystique*, 32: 152-172.

Coathelem, S.J., H. (1971) *Ignatian Insights: A Guide to the Complete Spiritual Exercises.* 2nd edit. Taichung, Taiwan: Kuangchi Press.

Codina, S.J., A. (1926) *Los Origenes de los Ejercicios Espirituales de San Ignacio de Loyola.* Barcelona: Balmes. Pp. 5-72.

Coemans, S.J., A. (1932) Quandonam S. Ignatius decrevit leges scriptas dare Societati: utrum iam ab initio an solum post aliquot annos? *Archivum Historicum Societatis Jesu*, 1: 304-306.

Conn, W. (1986) *Christian Conversion: A Developmental Interpretation of Autonomy and Surrender.* New York: Paulist Press.

Cusson, S.J., G. (1988) *Biblical Theology and the Spiritual Exercises.* St. Louis, MO: The Institute of Jesuit Sources.

Dalmases, S.J., C. de. (1985) *Ignatius of Loyola: Founder of the Jesuits.* St. Louis: The Institute of Jesuit Sources.

de Grandmaison, L. (1920) L'interpretation des Exercises. *Recherches de Science Religieuse*, 11: 398-408.

de Aldama, S.J., A.M. (1973) La composición de las Constituciones de la Comañpia de Jesús. *Archivum Historicum Societatis Jesu*, 42: 201-245.

de Aldama, S.J., A.M. (1989) *An Introductory Commentary on the Constitutions.* Saint Louis, MO: Institute of Jesuit Sources.

de Cervantes, M. (1980) *Don Quixote*. Edited by M. de Riquer. Barcelona: Planeta.

de Guibert, S.J., J. (1964) *The Jesuits: Their Spiritual Doctrine and Practice*. Chicago: Institute of Jesuit Studies, Loyola University Press.

Deikman, A. (1966) De-automatization and the mystical experience. *Psychiatry*, 29: 329-343.

de Tonquedec, J. (1953) De la certitude dans les etats mystiques: a propos d'une regle ignatienne du discernement des esprits. *Nouvelle Revue Theologique*, 75: 399-404.

Deutsch, H. (1937) The absence of grief. In *Neuroses and Character Types*. New York: International Universities Press, pp. 226-236.

de Vries, S.J., P.P. (1971) Protestants and other spirituals: Ignatius' vision and why he took this position. *Archivum Historicum Societatis Jesu*, 40: 463-483.

Divarkar, P. (1991) La transformacion del yo y la experiencia espiritual: el enfoque ignaciano a la luz de otros modelos antropologicos. In Alemany, C., and Garcia-Monge, J.A. (eds.) *Psicologia y Ejercicios Ignacianos*. 2 vols. Bilbao-Santander: Mensajero-Sal Terrae, vol. I, 23-34.

Doncoeur, S.J., P. (1959) *The Heart of Ignatius*. Baltimore, MD: Helicon Press.

Dudon, S.J., P. (1949) *St. Ignatius of Loyola*. Milwaukee: Bruce.

Durkheim, E. (1915) *The Elementary Forms of the Religious Life*. New York: The Free Press, 1965.

Earle, A.M., and Earle, B.V. (1961) Early maternal deprivation and later psychiatric illness. *American Journal of Orthopsychiatry*, 31: 181-186.

Egan, S.J., H.D. (1976) *The Spiritual Exercises and the Ignatian Mystical Horizon*. St. Louis, MO: The Institute of Jesuit Sources.

Egan, S.J., H.D. (1984) *Christian Mysticism: The Future of a Tradition*. New York: Pueblo.

Egan, S.J., H.D. (1987) *Ignatius Loyola the Mystic*. Wilmington, DL: Michael Glazier.

Emonet, P. (1990) The Constitutions: context for discernment and confirmation in the exercise of government. Reflections of a provincial. *Centrum Ignatianum Spiritualitatis*, 20: 110-119.

Endean, S.J., P.E. (1987) Who do you say Ignatius is? Jesuit fundamentalism and beyond. *Studies in the Spirituality of Jesuits*, 19/5.

*Epistolae et Instructiones Sancti Ignatii (Monumenta Ignatiana)*. MHSJ, MI Series I. 12 vols. Madrid: 1903-1911. [Epistolae]

Epstein, M. (1990) Beyond the oceanic feeling: psychoanalytic study of Buddhist meditation. *International Review of Psychoanalysis*, 17: 159-166.

Erikson, E.H. (1950) *Childhood and Society*. New York: Norton.

Erikson, E.H. (1959) *Identity and the Life Cycle*. New York: International Universities Press. [Psychological Monographs 1]

Erikson, E.H. (1963) *Childhood and Society*. 2nd ed. New York: Norton.

Erikson, E.H. (1964) *Insight and Responsibility*. New York: Norton.

Erikson, E.H. (1966) Ontogeny of ritualization. In Loewenstein, R.M., Newman, L.M., Schur, M., and Solnit, A.J. (eds.) *Psychoanalysis — A General Psychology: Essays in Honor of Heinz Hartmann*. New York: International Universities Press, 601-621.

Erikson, E.H. (1968) *Identity: Youth and Crisis*. New York: Norton.

Falk, A. (1982) The messiah and the qelippoth: on the mental illness of Sabbatai Sevi. *Journal of Psychology and Judaism*, 7: 5-29.

Fauteux, K. (1994) *The Recovery of Self: Regression and Redemption in Religious Experience*. New York: Paulist Press.

Fessard, S.J., G. (1956, 1966) *La Dialectique des Exercises Spirituelles*. 2 vols. Paris: Aubier.

Festugiere, A.J. (1949) A propos des aretalogies d'Isis. *Harvard Theological Review*, 42: 209-234.

Fisher, A. (1966) Freud and the image of man. In Meissner, S.J., W.W. *Foundations for a Psychology of Grace*. Glen Rock, NJ: Paulist Press, 124-145.

Fleming, S.J., D.L. (1978) *The Spiritual Exercises of St. Ignatius: A Literal Translation and a Contemporary Reading*. St. Louis: The Institute of Jesuit Sources.

Fleming, J., and Altschul, S. (1963) Activation of mourning and growth by psychoanalysis. *International Journal of Psychoanalysis*, 44: 419-432.

Fontes Narrativi. MHSJ, MI Series IV. 4 vols. Revised edition. Rome, 1943-1960. [FN]

Fortune, R. (1926) The symbolism of the serpent. *International Journal of Psychoanalysis*, 7: 237-243.

Freud, A. (1936) *The Ego and the Mechanisms of Defense*. New York: International Universities Press, 1946.

Freud, S. (1900) The interpretation of dreams. *Standard Edition*, 4 and 5.

Freud, S. (1905) Three essays on the theory of sexuality. *Standard Edition*, 7: 123-245.

Freud, S. (1913) The disposition to obsessional neurosis. *Standard Edition*, 12: 311-326.

Freud, S. (1914) On narcissism. *Standard Edition*, 14: 67-102.

Freud, S. (1915) Instincts and their vicissitudes. *Standard Edition*, 14: 109-140.

Freud, S. (1916-1917) Introductory lectures on psychoanalysis. *Standard Edition*, 15 and 16.

Freud, S. (1917) Mourning and melancholia. *Standard Edition*, 14: 237-260.

Freud, S. (1923) The ego and the id. *Standard Edition*, 19: 1-66.

Freud, S. (1925a) An autobiographical study. *Standard Edition*, 20: 1-74.

Freud, S. (1925b) Some additional notes on dream interpretation as a whole. *Standard Edition*, 19: 127-138.

Freud, S. (1927) The future of an illusion. *Standard Edition*, 21: 1-56.

Freud, S. (1930) Civilization and its discontents. *Standard Edition*, 21: 57-145.

Freud, S. (1931) Libidinal types. *Standard Edition*, 21: 215-220.

Freud, S. (1936) A disturbance of memory on the Acropolis. *Standard Edition*, 22: 237-248.

Fromm, E. (1941) *The Escape from Freedom*. New York: Avon Library, 1965.

Fromm, E. (1947) *Man for Himself; An Inquiry into the Psychology of Ethics*. Greenwich, CT: Fawcett Publs., 1970.

Fromm, E. (1955) *The Sane Society*. New York: Rinehart.

Fromm, E. (1956) *The Art of Loving*. New York: Harper and Bros.

Furman, R. (1964) Death and the young child: some preliminary considerations. *Psychoanalytic Study of the Child*, 19: 321-333.

Furman, R. (1968) Additional remarks on mourning and the young child. *Bulletin of the Philadelphia Association for Psychoanalysis*, 18: 51-64.

Furman, E., and Furman, R. (1974) *The Child's Parent Dies*. New Haven: Yale University Press.

Futrell, S.J., J.C. (1970) *Making an Apostolic Community of Love*. St. Louis, MO: The Institute of Jesuit Sources.

Gadamer, H.-G. (1989) *Truth and Method*. 2nd rev. ed. New York: Crossroad.

Galatzer-Levy, R.M., and Cohler, B.J. (1993) *The Essential Other: A Developmental Psychology of the Self*. New York: Basic Books.

Ganss, S.J., G.E. (ed.) (1970) *The Constitutions of the Society of Jesus*. St. Louis, MO: The Institute of Jesuit Sources. [MHSJ, MI Series III, 4 vols. Rome, 1934-1948] [Constitutions]

Gies, F., and Gies, J. (1987) *Marriage and the Family in the Middle Ages*. New York: Harper and Row.

Gil, S.J., D. (1971) *La Consolacion sin Causa Precedente*. Rome: Centrum Ignatianum Spiritualitatis.

Gilmore, M.M., and Gilmore, D.D. (1979) "Machismo": a psychodynamic approach. *Journal of Psychoanalytic Anthropology*, 2: 281-299.

Greenacre, P. (1947) Vision, headache and the halo. *Psychoanalytic Quarterly*, 16: 177-194.

Greenacre, P. (1959) On focal symbiosis. In *Emotional Growth*. vol. I. New York: International Universities Press, 145-161.

Greenacre, P. (1965) On the development and function of tears. In *Emotional Growth*, vol. 1. New York: International Universities Press, 249-259.

Gregory, I. (1985) Studies of parental deprivation in psychiatric patients. *American Journal of Psychiatry*, 115: 432-442.

Haas, S.J., A. (1977) The mysticism of St. Ignatius according to his *Spiritual Diary*. In Wulf, S.J., F. (ed.) *Ignatius of Loyola: His Personality and Spiritual Heritage, 1556-1956*. St. Louis: Institute of Jesuit Sources, pp. 164-199.

Harris, T., Brown, G.W., and Bifulco, A. (1986) Loss of parent in childhood and adult psychiatric disorder: the role of lack of adequate parental care. *Psychological Medicine*, 16: 641-659.

Hartmann, H. (1958) *Ego Psychology and the Problem of Adaptation*. New York: International Universities Press.

Hartmann, H. (1960) *Psychoanalysis and Moral Values*. New York: International Universities Press.

Hartmann, H. (1964) *Essays on Ego Psychology.* New York: International Universities Press.

Hartmann, H., and Loewenstein, R.M. (1962) Notes on the superego. *Psychoanalytic Study of the Child,* 17: 42-81.

Hartocollis, P. (1976) Aggression and mysticism. *Contemporary Psychoanalysis,* 12: 214-226.

Hassal, J. (1919) The serpent as a symbol. *Psychoanalytic Review,* 6: 295-305.

Holt, R.R. (1965) Ego autonomy re-evaluated. *International Journal of Psychoanalysis,* 46: 151-167.

Huonder, S.J., A. (1932) *Ignatius von Loyola. Beiträge zu seinem Charakterbild.* Köln: Katholische Tat-Verlag.

Idel, M. (1988) *Kabbalah: New Perspectives.* New Haven: Yale University Press.

Ignatius. (1956) *St. Ignatius' Own Story.* Chicago: Regnery. [Vita]

Imoda, F. (1991) Ejercicios espirituales y cambio de la personalidad. Significado de un limite. In Alemany, C., and Garcia-Monge, J. (eds.) *Psicologia y Ejercicios Ignacianos.* 2 vols. Bilbao-Santander: Mensajero-Sal Terrae, vol. II, 271-286.

Imoda, F. (1992) The *Spiritual Exercises* and psychology. *Centrum Ignatianum Spiritualitatis,* 23: 11-67.

Iparraguirre, S.J., I. (ed.) (1955) *Directoria Exercitorum Spiritualium (1540-1599).* Rome: Historical Insitute of the Society of Jesus. [MI, vol 2; MHSJ, vol. 76]

Iparraguirre, S.J., I. (1959) *A Key to the Study of the Spiritual Exercises.* Bombay: St Paul Publications.

Iparraguirre, S.J., I. (1965) *Orientaciones Bibliograficas sobre san Ignacio de Loyola.* Rome: Achivum Historicum Societatis Jesu.

Iparraguirre, S.J., I., and Dalmases, S.J., C. de (eds.) (1963) *Obras Completas de San Ignacio de Loyola.* Madrid: Biblioteca de Autores Cristianos.

Jacobson, E. (1964) *The Self and the Object World.* New York: International Universities Press.

James, W. (1902) *The Varieties of Religious Experience.* New York: Collier Books, 1961.

Johnson, C.S.J., E.A. (1989) Mary and the female face of God. *Theological Studies,* 50: 500-526.

Jones, E. (1913) The God complex. In *Essays in Applied Psychoanalysis II.* London: Hogarth Press, 1951.

Jones, E. (1923) The nature of auto-suggestion. In *Papers on Psychoanalysis.* Boston: Beacon Press, 1948.

Jung, G.G. (1956) *Symbols of Transformation.* New York: Harper and Bros.

Kelly, H.A. (1968) *The Devil, Demonology and Witchcraft.* Garden City, NY: Doubleday.

Kernberg, O.F. (1979) Regression in organizational leadership. *Psychiatry,* 42: 29-39.

Kets de Vries, M.F.R., and Miller, D. (1985) Narcissism and leadership: an object relations perspective. *Human Relations,* 38: 583-601.

Knapp, P.H. (1967) Some riddles of riddance. *Archives of General Psychiatry,* 16: 586-602.

Koch, S.J., L. (1934) *Jesuiten-Lexikon. Die Gesellschaft Jesu einst und jetzt.* Paderborn.

Kohut, H. (1966) Forms and transformations of narcissism. *Journal of the American Psychoanalytic Association,* 14: 243-272.

Kohut, H. (1971) *The Analysis of the Self.* New York: International Universities Press.

Kolvenbach, P.-H. (1992) The letters of St. Ignatius: their conclusion. *Centrum Ignatianum Spiritualitatis,* 23: 71-85.

Krejci, J. (1969) A new model of scientific atheism. *Concurrence,* 1: 82-96.

Kris, E. (1952) *Psychoanalytic Explorations in Art.* New York: International Universities Press.

Krueger, D.W. (1983) Childhood parent loss: developmental impact and adult psychopathology. *American Journal of Psychotherapy,* 37: 582-592.

Lacey, J.H. (1982) Anorexia nervosa and a bearded female saint. *British Medical Journal,* 285: 1816-1817.

Larrañaga, S.J., V. (1956) La revisión total de los ejercicios por San Ignacio: en París, o en Roma? *Archivum Historicum Societatis Jesu,* 25: 396-415.

Lawlor, F.X. (1943) The doctrine of grace in the Spiritual Exercises. *Theological Studies,* 3: 513-532.

Leavy, S.A. (1993) Self and sign in free association. *Psychoanalytic Quarterly,* 62: 400-421.

Leturia, S.J., P. (1933) A propósito del "Ignatius von Loyola" del P. Huonder. *Archivum Historicum Societatis Jesu*, 2: 310-316.

Leturia, S.J., P. (1941) Genesis de los Ejercicios de S. Ignacio y su influjo en la fundación de la Compañía de Jesús (1521-1540). *Archivum Historicum Societatis Jesu*, 10: 16-59.

Leturia, S.J., P. (1948) Libros de horas, anima Christi y ejercicios espirituales de S. Ignacio. *Archivum Historicum Societatis Jesu*, 17: 3-50.

Leturia, S.J., P. de. (1949) *Iñigo de Loyola*. Syracuse: Le Moyne College Press.

Lewin, B.D. (1950) *The Psychoanalysis of Elation*. New York: Norton.

Lichtenberg, J.D. (1983) The influence of values and value judgments on the psychoanalytic encounter. *Psychoanalytic Inquiry*, 3: 547-664.

Liebert, R.S. (1983) *Michelangelo*. New Haven: Yale University Press.

Lifton, R.J. (1961) *Thought Reform and the Psychology of Totalism: A Study of "Brainwashing" in China*. New York: Norton.

Loevinger, J. (1966) The meaning and measurement of ego development. *American Psychologist*, 21: 195-206.

Lofy, C.A. (1963) *The Action of the Holy Spirit in the Autobiography of St. Ignatius of Loyola*. Unpublished dissertation. Rome: Gregorian University.

Longhurst, J.E. (1957) Saint Ignatius at Alcala. *Archivum Historicum Societatis Jesu*, 26: 252-256.

Loyola, I. (1956) *St. Ignatius' Own Story*. Chicago, IL: Henry Regnery, 1956 [Vita].

Lukacs, S.J., L. (1968) De graduum diversitate inter sacerdotes in Societate Jesu. *Archivum Historicum Societatis Jesu*, 37: 237-316.

Mahler, M.S., Pine, F., and Bergman, A. (1975) *The Psychological Birth of a Human Infant*. New York: Basic Books.

Mahony, P.J. (1989) Aspects on nonperverse scopophilia within an analysis. *Journal of the American Psychoanalytic Association*, 37: 365-399.

Marcel, G. (1952) *Man Against Mass Society*. Chicago: Regnery.

Maslow, A.H. (1971) *The Farther Reaches of Human Nature*. New York: Viking Press.

Meissner, S.J., W.W. (1964) Prolegomena to a psychology of grace. *Journal of Religion and Health*, 3: 209-240.

Meissner, S.J., W.W. (1965) *Group Dynamics in the Religious Life*. South Bend, IN: University of Notre Dame Press.

Meissner, S.J., W.W. (1966) *Foundations for a Psychology of Grace*. New York: Paulist Press.

Meissner, S.J., W.W. (1971a) *The Assault on Authority — Dialogue or Dilemma?* New York: Orbis Books.

Meissner, S.J., W.W. (1971b) Freedom of conscience from a psychiatric viewpoint. In: Bier, W.C. (ed.) *Conscience: Its Freedom and Limitations*. New York: Fordham University Press, pp. 125-142.

Meissner, S.J., W.W. (1973) Notes on the psychology of hope. *Journal of Religion and Health*, 12: 7-29, 120-139.

Meissner, S.J., W.W. (1978a) *The Paranoid Process*. New York: Aronson.

Meissner, S.J., W.W. (1981) *Internalization in Psychoanalysis*. New York: International Universities Press. (Psychological Issues, Monograph 50)

Meissner, S.J., W.W. (1984) *Psychoanalysis and Religious Experience*. New Haven: Yale University Press.

Meissner, S.J., W.W. (1985) Psychoanalysis: the dilemma of science and humanism. *Psychoanalytic Inquiry*, 5: 471-498.

Meissner, S.J., W.W. (1986a) Aggression and theology. *Thought*, March (240): 90-104.

Meissner, S.J., W.W. (1986b) Can psychoanalysis find its self? *Journal of the American Psychoanalytic Association*, 34(2): 379-400.

Meissner, S.J., W.W. (1987) *Life and Faith: Perspectives on Religious Experience*. Washington, DC: Georgetown University Press.

Meissner, S.J., W.W. (1990) The role of transitional conceptualization in religious thought. In Smith, J.H., and Handelman, S.A. (eds.) *Psychoanalysis and Religion*. (Psychiatry and the Humanities, vol. 11) Baltimore: Johns Hopkins University Press, pp. 95-116.

Meissner, S.J., W.W. (1991) Aggression in phobic states. *Psychoanalytic Inquiry*, 11: 261-283.

Meissner, S.J., W.W. (1992a) The concept of the therapeutic alliance. *Journal of the American Psychoanalytic Association*, 40: 1059-1087.

Meissner, S.J., W.W. (1992b) *Ignatius of Loyola: The Psychology of a Saint*. New Haven, CT: Yale University Press.

Meissner, S.J., W.W. (1992c) Medieval messianism and sabbatianism. *Psychoanalytic Study of Society*, 17: 289-325.

Meissner, S.J., W.W. (1993) Self-as-agent in psychoanalysis. *Psychoanalysis and Contemporary Thought*, 16(4): 459-495.

Meissner, S.J., W.W. (1995) *The Therapeutic Alliance.* New Haven, CT: Yale University Press, 1996.

Meissner, S.J., W.W., Rizzuto, A.M., Sashin, J.I., and Buie, D.H. (1987) A view of aggression in phobic states. *Psychoanalytic Quarterly*, 56: 452-476.

Miller, J.B.M. (1971) Children's reactions to the death of a parent: a review of the psychoanalytic literature. *Journal of the American Psychoanalytic Association*, 19:697-719.

Mintz, I. (1971) The anniversary reaction: a response to the unconscious sense of time. *Journal of the American Psychoanalytic Association*, 19: 720-735.

Modell, A.H. (1973) Affects and psychoanalytic knowledge. *Annual of Psychoanalysis*, 1: 117-124.

Modell, A.H. (1984) *Psychoanalysis in a New Context.* New York: International Universities Press.

Modell, A.H. (1993) *The Private Self.* Cambridge, MA: Harvard University Press.

Moloney, J.C. (1954) Mother, god and superego. *Journal of the American Psychoanalytic Association*, 2: 120-151.

Monden, S.J., L. (1965) *Sin, Liberty and Law.* Kansas City, KS: Sheed and Ward.

*Monumenta Ignatiana* (MI). The Spiritual Exercises are found in MI, Series II, Vol. I. Madrid, 1919.

Mouroux, J. (1954) *The Christian Experience.* New York: Sheed and Ward.

Murray, S.J., J.C. (1966) Freedom, authority, community. *America*, 115 (December 3), p. 734.

Murray, S.J., J.C. (1967) The danger of the vows. *Woodstock Letters*, 96: 421-427.

Newman, J.W. (1985) *Transference and Spiritual Exercises.* Ann Arbor, MI: University Microfilms International. [Columbia University Ph.D. Dissertation]

Nicolau, S.J., M. (1957) Fisonomía de San Ignacio según sus primeros compañeros. *Archivum Historicum Societatis Jesu*, 26: 257-269.

Niebuhr, R. (1941) *The Nature and Destiny of Man: A Christian Interpretation. Vol. I. Human Nature.* New York: Scribner's.

Niebuhr, R. (1949) *Faith and History*. New York: Scribner's.

Niebuhr, R. (1953) *Christian Realism and Political Problems.* New York: Scribner's.

Nussbaum, M. (1988) Love's knowledge. In Mclaughlin, B.P., and Rorty, A.O. (eds.) *Perspectives on Self-Deception*. Berkeley, CA: University of California Press, 487-514.

O'Leary, S.J., B. (1979) The discernment of spirits in the Memoriale of Blessed Peter Favre. *The Way*, 35 (Suppl.): ? .

O'Malley, S.J., J.W. (1982) The Jesuits, St. Ignatius, and the Counter Reformation: some recent studies and their implications for today. *Studies in the Spirituality of Jesuits*, 14/1.

O'Malley, S.J., J.W. (1993) *The First Jesuits.* Cambridge, MA: Harvard University Press.

Orlandis, R. (1936) De la sobrenaturalidad de la vida en los Ejercicios. *Manresa*, 12: 195-223.

Oremland, J.D. (1978) Michelangelo's *Pietas. Psychoanalytic Study of the Child*, 33: 563-591.

Oremland, J.D. (1980) Mourning and its effect on Michelangelo's art. *Annual of Psychoanalysis*, 8: 317-351.

Oremland, J.D. (1989) *Michelangelo's Sistine Ceiling: A Psychoanalytic Study of Creativity*. Madison, CT: International Universities Press.

O'Sullivan, S.J., M.J. (1990) Trust your feelings, but use your head: discernment and the psychology of decision making. *Studies in the Spirituality of Jesuits*, 22/4.

Padberg, S.J., J.W. (1993) Ignatius, the popes, and realistic reverence. *Studies in the Spirituality of Jesuits*, 25/3.

Parry-Jones, W.L. (1985) Archival exploration of anorexia nervosa. In Szmukler, G.I., Slade, P.D., Harris, P., Benton, D., and Russell, G.F.M. (eds.) *Anorexia Nervosa and Bulimic Disorders: Current Perspectives.* Oxford: Pergamon Press, 95-100. (*Journal of Psychiatric Research* 19 (2/3).

Peeters, L. (1931) Vers l'union divine par les Exercises de saint Ignace. Louvain: Museum Lessianum.

Pinard de la Boullaye, S.J., H. (1950) *Les Etapes de Rédaction des Exercises de S. Ignace*. 7th edit. rev. Paris: Beauchesne.

Pollock, G.H. (1970) Anniversary reactions, trauma, and mourning. *Psychoanalytic Quarterly*, 34: 347-371.

Pollock, G.H. (1989) *The Mourning-Liberation Process*. 2 vols. Madison, CT: International Universities Press.

Post, J.M. (1986) Narcissism and the charismatic leader-follower relationship. *Political Psychology*, 7: 675-688.

Pousset, S.J., E. (1971) *Life in Faith and Freedom*. St. Louis, MO: The Institute of Jesuit Sources, 1980.

Przywara, E. (1938-1939) *Deus Semper Maior: Theologie der Exerzitien*. 3 vols. Freiburg-im-Breisgau

Pruyser, P.W. (1968) *A Dynamic Psychology of Religion*. New York: Harper and Row.

Przywara, E. (1938-9) *Deus Semper Maior.* 3 vols. Freiburg i. B.

Quay, S.J., P.M. (1981) Angels and demons: the teaching of IV Lateran. *Theological Studies*, 42: 20-45.

Rahner, S.J., H. (1953) *The Spirituality of St. Ignatius Loyola*. Westminster, MD: Newman Press.

Rahner, S.J., H. (1956) Notes on the Spiritual Exercises. *Woodstock Letters*, 85: 281-336.

Rahner, S.J., H. (1960) *St. Ignatius Loyola: Letters to Women*. New York: Herder and Herder.

Rahner, S.J., H. (1968) *Ignatius the Theologian*. New York: Herder and Herder.

Rahner, S.J., H. (1977) "Be prudent money-changers": toward the history of Ignatius' teaching on the discernment of spirits. In Wulf, S.J., F. (ed.) *Ignatius of Loyola: His Personality and Spiritual Heritage — 1156-1956*. St. Louis, MO: The Institute of Jesuit Sources, 272-279.

Rahner, S.J., K. (1964) *The Dynamic Element in the Church*. New York: Herder and Herder.

Rahner, S.J., K. (1967) *Spiritual Exercises*. London: Sheed and Ward.

Rahner, S.J., K. (1968a) Angels. In Rahner, S.J., K. et al. (eds.) *Sacramentum Mundi: An Encyclopedia of Theology*. Vol. I, New York: Herder and Herder, pp. 27-35.

Rahner, S.J., K. (1968b) Devil. In Rahner, S.J., K. et al. (eds.) *Sacramentum Mundi: An Encyclopedia of Theology*. Vol. II, New York: Herder and Herder, 73-75.

Rahner, S.J., K. (1969) Towards a theology of hope. *Concurrence*, 1: 23-33.

Rahner, S.J., K. (1976) Foreword. In Egan, S.J., H.D. *The Spiritual Exercises and the Ignatian Mystical Horizon*. St. Louis, MO: The Institute of Jesuit Sources, xiii-xvii.

Rahner, S.J., K. (1977) The Ignatian process for discovering the will of God in an existential situation: some theological problems in the rules for election and discernment of spirits in St. Ignatius' *Spiritual Exercises*. In Wulf, S.J., F. (ed.) *Ignatius of Loyola: His Personality and Spiritual Heritage — 1156-1956*. St. Louis, MO: The Institute of Jesuit Sources, 280-289.

Rampling, D. (1985) Ascetic ideals and anorexia nervosa. In In Szmukler, G.I., Slade, P.D., Harris, P., Benton, D., and Russell, G.F.M. (eds.) *Anorexia Nervosa and Bulimic Disorders: Current Perspectives*. Oxford: Pergamon Press, 89-94. (*Journal of Psychiatric Research* 19 (2/3).

Ramsey, P. (1962) *Nine Modern Moralists*. New York: New American Library.

Rangell, L. (1989) Action theory within the structural view. *International Journal of Psychoanalysis*, 70: 189-203.

Ravier, S.J., A. (1987) *Ignatius of Loyola and the Founding of the Society of Jesus*. San Francisco: Ignatius Press.

Ravier, A. (1992) The life of Iñigo de Loyola and his first companions at the University of Paris (October 1525 - December 1536). *Centrum Ignatianum Spiritualitatis*, 23: 86-102.

Reich, W. (1949) *Character Analysis*. 3rd ed. New York: Farrar, Straus and Giroux.

Ricard, R. (1956) Deux traits de l'expérience mystique de Saint Ignace. *Archivum Historicum Societatis Jesu*, 25: 431-436.

Rickaby, S.J., J. (1923) *The Spiritual Exercises of St. Ignatius Loyola*. London: Burns, Oates and Washbourne.

Ricoeur, P. (1970) *Freud and Philosophy*. New Haven, CT: Yale University Press.

Rizzuto, A.-M. (1979) *The Birth of the Living God: A Psychoanalytic Study*. Chicago: University of Chicago Press.

Rizzuto, A.M., Sashin, J.I., Buie, D.H., and Meissner, S.J., W.W. (1993) A revised theory of aggression. *Psychoanalytic Review*, 80: 29-54.

Rochlin, G. (1965) *Griefs and Discontents: The Forces of Change.* Boston, MA: Little, Brown.

Rochlin, G. (1973) *Man's Aggression.* Boston, MA: Gambit Press.

Ross, N. (1975) Affect as cognition: with observations on the meanings of mystical states. *International Review of Psychoanalysis,* 2: 79-93.

Russell, B. (1929) *Mysticism and Logic.* London: Allen and Unwin.

Sacks, H.L. (1979) The effect of spiritual exercises on the integration of the self-system. *Journal for the Scientific Study of Religion,* 18: 46-50.

Saunders, G.R. (1981) Men and women in southern Europe: a review of some aspects of cultural complexity. *Journal of Psychoanalytic Anthropology,* 4: 435-466.

Schafer, R. (1976) *A New Language for Psychoanalysis.* New Haven, CT: Yale University Press.

Scholem, G. (1973) *Sabbatai Sevi: The Mystical Messiah.* Princeton: Princeton University Press.

Sievernich, M. (1991) Dificultades para la vivencia del pecado en el contexto de los Ejercicios y de la cultura actual. In Alemany, C., and Garcia-Monge, J.A. (eds.) *Psicologia y Ejercicios Ignacianos.* 2 vols. Bilbao-Santander: Mensajero-Sal Terrae, vol. I, 44-57.

Silos, S.J., L. (1964) Cardoner in the life of Saint Ignatius of Loyola. *Archivum Historicum Societatis Jesu,* 33: 3-43.

Stanley, S.J., D.M. (1968) Contemplation of the gospels, Ignatius Loyola, and the contemporary Christian. *Theological Studies,* 29: 417-443.

Staudenmaier, S.J., J.M. (1994) To fall in love with the world: individualism and self-transcendence in American life. *Studies in the Spirituality of the Jesuits,* 26/3.

Steger, A. (1949) Grace in the spirituality of St. Ignatius. *Woodstock Letters,* 78: 205-224.

Steiner, J. (1990) The retreat from truth to omnipotence in Sophocles' *Oedipus at Colonus. International Review of Psychoanalysis,* 17: 227-237.

Stern, D. (1985) *The Interpersonal World of the Infant.* New York: Basic Books.

Stierli, S.J., J. (1977) Ignatian prayer: seeking God in all things. In Wulf, S.J., F. (ed.) *Ignatius of Loyola: His Personality and Spiritual Heritage, 1556-1956.* St. Louis: Institute of Jesuit Sources, pp. 135-163.

Strachey, J. (1934) The nature of the therapeutic action of psychoanalysis. *International Journal of Psychoanalysis*, 15: 127-159.

Tartakoff, H.H. (1966) The normal personality in our culture and the Nobel Prize complex. In Loewenstein, R.M., Newman, L.M., Schur, M., and Solnit, A.J. (eds.) *Psychoanalysis — A General Psychology: Essays in Honor of Heinz Hartmann*. New York: International Universities Press, pp. 222-252.

Tetlow, S.J., J.A. (1989) The fundamentum: creation in the principle and foundation. *Studies in the Spirituality of the Jesuits* 21/4.

Theissen, G. (1978) *Sociology of Early Palestinian Christianity*. Philadelphia: Fortress Press.

Toner, S.J., J.J. (1974) The deliberation that started the Jesuits. *Studies in the Spirituality of the Jesuits*, 6/4.

Toner, S.J., J.J. (1982) *A Commentary on Saint Ignatius' Rules for the Discernment of Spirits: A Guide to Principles and Practice*. St. Louis, MO: The Institute of Jesuit Sources.

Toner, S.J., J. (1991) *Discerning God's Will: Ignatius of Loyola's Teaching on Christian Decision Making*. St. Louis, MO: Institute of Jesuit Sources.

Tornos, A. (1991) Identidad, culpabilidad, autoestima. In Alemany, C., and Garcia-Monge, J.A. (eds.) *Psicologia y Ejercicios Ignacianos*. 2 vols. Madrid: Mensajero-Sal Terrae, vol. I, 35-43.

Tylenda, S.J., J.N. (1985) *A Pilgrim's Journey: The Autobiography of Ignatius of Loyola*. Wilmington, DL: Michael Glazier.

Veale, S.J., J. (1996) Saint Ignatius speaks about "Ignatian prayer." *Studies in the Spirituality of Jesuits*, 28/2.

von Matt, L., and Rahner, S.J., H. (1956) *Saint Ignatius Loyola: A Pictorial Biography*. Chicago: Regnery.

Volkan, V.D. (1988) *The Need to Have Enemies and Allies*. Northvale, NJ: Jason Aronson.

Waelder, R. (1936) The problem of freedom in psychoanalysis and the problem of reality testing. *International Journal of Psychoanalysis*, 17: 89-108.

Wallace, E.R. (1985) *Historiography and Causation in Psychoanalysis*. Hillsdale, NJ: Analytic Press.

Wallwork, E. (1992) *Psychoanalysis and Ethics*. New Haven, CT: Yale University Press.

Webber, R.A. (1970) Perceptions of interactions between superiors and subordinates. *Human Relations*, 23: 235-248.

Weber, M. (1947) *The Theory of Social and Economic Organizations.* New York: Oxford University Press.

Werman, D.S. (1977) Sigmund Freud and Romain Rolland. *International Review of Psychoanalysis*, 4: 225-242.

Wickham, John F. (1954) The worldly ideal of Iñigo Loyola. *Thought*, 29: 209-236.

Wilkens, G. (1978) *Compagnons de Jesus: La Genese de l'Orde des Jesuites.* Roma: Centrum Ignatianum Spiritualitatis.

Wilner, A.R. (1984) *The Spellbinders.* New Haven: Yale University Press.

Winnicott, D.W. (1953) Transitional objects and transitional phenomena. In *Playing and Reality*. New York: Basic Books, 1971.

Wolfenstein, M. (1966) How is mourning possible? *Psychoanalytic Study of the Child*, 21: 93-123.

Wolfenstein, M. (1969) Loss, rage and repetition. *Psychoanalytic Study of the Child*, 24: 432-460.

Wulf, S.J., F. (ed.) (1977) *Ignatius of Loyola: His Personality and Spiritual Heritage — 1156-1956.* St. Louis, MO: The Institute of Jesuit Sources.

Young, S.J., W.J. (1958) Spiritual journal of Ignatius Loyola. *Woodstock Letters*, 87: 195-267. [Original in MHSJ, MI Series IV, Vol. I. Rome, 1934.]

Young, S.J., W.J. (ed.) (1959) *Letters of St. Ignatius of Loyola.* Chicago, IL: Loyola University Press.

Zetzel, E.R. (1965) On the incapacity to bear depression. In *The Capacity for Emotional Growth.* New York: International Universities Press, 1970, 82-114.

Zetzel, E.R. (1970) *The Capacity for Emotional Growth.* New York: International Universities Press, 1970.

# SUBJECT INDEX

## A

## D

## F



## G

## H

## I

## J



## K



## L

M



N



O

## R

## S

## T

## Z

# INDEX OF NAMES

## D

## E



## F



## G

H



I



J



K



L